THE COLONIAL WORLD

THE COLONIAL WORLD

A HISTORY OF EUROPEAN EMPIRES, 1780S TO THE PRESENT

Robert Aldrich and Andreas Stucki

BLOOMSBURY ACADEMIC

LONDON • NEW YORK • OXFORD • NEW DELHI • SYDNEY

BLOOMSBURY ACADEMIC
Bloomsbury Publishing Plc
50 Bedford Square, London, WC1B 3DP, UK
1385 Broadway, New York, NY 10018, USA
29 Earlsfort Terrace, Dublin 2, Ireland

BLOOMSBURY, BLOOMSBURY ACADEMIC and the Diana logo are trademarks of
Bloomsbury Publishing Plc

First published in Great Britain 2023

Cover image: Mr Sternberg and his bullock cart, Sri Lanka, 1903.
© (Photo by F. Sternberg/Royal Geographical Society via Getty Images)

A catalogue record for this book is available from the British Library.

A catalog record for this book is available from the Library of Congress.

ISBN: PB: 978-1-3500-9240-2
HB: 978-1-3500-9241-9
ePDF: 978-1-3500-9242-6
eBook: 978-1-3500-9243-3

Typeset by Deanta Global Publishing Services, Chennai, India
Printed and bound in Great Britain

To find out more about our authors and books visit www.bloomsbury.com
and sign up for our newsletters.

CONTENTS

Contents

ILLUSTRATIONS

Figures

Illustrations

Maps

PREFACE

Writing a history of European colonialism presents a formidable and indeed forbidding task, as the subject covers hundreds of years and encircles the globe. No single volume can hope to provide a comprehensive account of the myriad experiences and countless themes that are part of Europe's often violent encounters with the wider world. Choices must be made, and this book picks up the story in the 1780s, although European colonialism has a much longer history. The volume covers colonialism around the world, though to different degrees. There is a dedicated chapter on the British Dominions of Australia, Canada, New Zealand and South Africa and references to these countries elsewhere, but as they represent a particular case of settler colonialism, they receive somewhat limited attention. The continental empires within Europe, such as those of Napoleon and the Habsburgs, and the contiguous European and Asian empire of Russia, are excluded except as directly linked to overseas colonialism; Britain's nearby 'colony' of Ireland is present only in the margins. The book, as the subtitle indicates, similarly excludes the history of non-European empires, whether continental or maritime, such as those of Japan, China and the United States, though these play a part in the international history of colonialism and appear in several chapters.

Following a historiographical essay, the book is divided, as readers will discover, into three parts. These provide varying perspectives by time period, theme and place, and they illustrate different levels of detail. Part I offers a chronological overview, necessarily a broad-brush depiction of colonialism. The second treats a selected number of broad themes – such as 'Colonialism and the Body' or 'The People of Empire' – with examples drawn from multiple colonies and time periods. In Part III, chapters centre on a particular location and pivot around a chosen year. In some cases, these are 'snapshots' of colonial situations at a certain moment; in other cases, they move further before and beyond the date indicated. While the chronological overview furnishes the necessary background, the thematic part is a reflection of the cultural turn in empire history over the last few decades. The case studies in Part III allow for a more detailed discussion of particular areas and time periods; an epilogue emphasizes the long-lasting impact of European colonialism to this day.

Our organization of this volume draws inspiration from Fernand Braudel's *The Mediterranean and the Mediterranean World in the Age of Philip II*. Originally published in French in 1949 and translated into English in the early 1970s, the long study is considered a masterpiece of modern historical research and writing. Braudel (1902–85) did not call himself a colonial historian, yet his work encompassed many of the themes and geographical areas now central to colonial history. Braudel's life spanned the period from the extension of European empires at the beginning of the twentieth century through independence of most of the colonies after the Second World War. With almost a decade of teaching at the University of Algiers, in the then French colonial North African territory of Algeria, from 1923 to 1932, and time spent in the mid-1930s in Brazil – a Portuguese colony until the 1820s – aiding in the setting up of the University of São Paulo, Braudel was personally acquainted with colonialism and its heritage. Having spent the Second World War as a German prisoner of war after being captured during service in the French army in 1940, he was undoubtedly sensitized to issues of warfare, occupation and incarceration. Braudel's *The Mediterranean* presented a number of key arguments. One was about basic commonalities around the Mediterranean region, from southern Europe to northern Africa and further east, in geography, climate and natural resources, and in the lifestyles they produced. The sea, not surprisingly, was central to life in coastal areas and further into the interior, and also provided the conduit for European ventures into the wider world. Braudel argued that the Mediterranean retained its central importance in international commerce, politics and culture well into the sixteenth century and later, a position that revised received wisdom that it was in the near aftermath of Columbus's voyages to the Americas in the 1490s, and the establishment of the European empires in the 'new world' (including that of Spain's Philip II) that the centre of gravity for Europeans was displaced from the Mediterranean to the Atlantic.

Methodologically, Braudel's most original concept was a division of history into three strata. At base, there was the 'long duration' (*longue durée*), a deep current of transformations, particularly visible in the natural environment, that occurred over centuries and millennia. At another level, he identified 'conjunctures' (*conjonctures*), shorter periods with clusters of connected economic, social and cultural change. Finally, the 'waves' on the ocean (a metaphor Braudel employed) were political events, what he labelled 'event history' (*histoire événementielle*) – though vitally important in their own time, and the core subject for most earlier historians, such events sometimes disguised more significant, longer-term changes both in history and in traditional scholars' narratives of history. With these ideas and his work on the Mediterranean world, on capitalism and material life, and on the construction of French identity, Braudel became one of the leaders of the *Annales* school of historians (named after their journal). A highly influential, though disparate, group, they pioneered 'new social history' in the mid-twentieth century, often seen as 'history from the bottom up' because of focus on common people, on processes rather than simple causality, on daily life, on *mentalité* (collective ideas, identities and perceptions of the world) and on developments that unfolded over long stretches of time.

The Colonial World does not adopt Braudel's exact divisions or organizational plan. Whereas he placed the *longue durée* first, the *conjonctures* second and the *histoire événementielle* third in his text, here we begin with a section on chronologies that underlines the event-making politics (in a broad sense) of colonization and decolonization, then move on to some of the deep-seated and long-lasting transformations (in such areas as migration, daily life and culture) wrought by colonialism in the second section, and conclude with a series of case studies that examine conjunctures in particular colonies over relatively short period in the third section. We do not limit the 'long duration' so strictly to environmental changes (though they receive a chapter) as did Braudel. Here, as in Braudel's pioneering study, the three levels of history, it should be underscored, are tightly intertwined and exercise mutual influence on each other. Just as Braudel emphasized the impact on Europe of changes in the wider world, so we stress that colonialism had a great impact on Europe as well on the places colonized by Europeans.

Readers are unlikely to read this book in chapter order, from start to finish. Indeed, it is designed so that they can go straight to whichever period, theme or place attracts interest, and move back and forth among the sections. Each chapter thus can be read independently from the other, though in the first chronological section there is more of a continuous narrative. Because of this, there is some degree of inevitable and intentional repetition from chapter to chapter so that readers coming to a chapter afresh are not left adrift without basic contexts, points of reference and crucial names and dates. We have kept end notes to a minimum in order not to encumber the text with a surfeit of references. In fact, in Part I of the book, we have avoided end notes altogether, as subsequent chapters provide leads to the more specialized literature. At the end of the volume, a limited set of books published in English provides a guide to further reading; their bibliographies will lead readers to yet more works, especially to monographic studies. Maps guide readers to the baffling assortment of colonial places, and give clues to how colonizers moved from one place to another in search of geostrategic advantage. The images reproduced here are meant not just as illustrations but as documentation: drawings, paintings and photographs, which reflected and created perceptions, are an important part of the colonial archive.

Colonial history of the nineteenth and twentieth centuries often concentrates on the two largest overseas empires, the British and the French, but we have made a special effort to incorporate material from the history of other European empires and lesser known colonies. This focus becomes especially apparent in Part III. Several chapters serve as a reminder that small places such as islands and enclaves can tell big stories about lived experiences in colonial settings and about European colonialism in general.

This volume does not seek to provide an overarching theory about colonialism or authoritative interpretations – even if such were possible – but to survey the overall history of modern colonialism and examine representative cases. It is hoped that the text will provide material for discussion and debate, further reading and exploration of diverse sources and methodological and theoretical approaches. Readers will consider different interpretations from their wider reading, and draw their own conclusions about the subjects that make colonialism such an important, fascinating and wide-ranging field. We trust, too, that they will see the legacies that tie the colonial past to the present.

ACKNOWLEDGEMENTS

This book builds on the work of many scholars of colonialism who have informed our views and approaches, including historians whose works we have read, scholars with whom we have worked, and those whom we have taught. It is impossible to reference fully the countless studies and individuals to which we are indebted, yet we would like to thank friends and colleagues around the globe, and librarians from Sydney to Bern, for their support during our research. We are particularly indebted to all those who read and commented on earlier drafts of one or several chapters. Thanks go in particular to Elisabeth Bäschlin, Tanja Bührer, John Connell, Josep M. Fradera, Albert Garcia Balañà, Matthias Häussler, Harshan Kumarasingham, Kirsten Mackenzie, Jim Masselos, A. Dirk Moses, Hinnerk Onken, Susie Protschky and Rea Vogt. Robert Aldrich would also like to thank Cindy McCreery, Mark Seymour and other Sydney colleagues for invaluable insights.

CHAPTER 1
WRITING (AND READING) COLONIAL HISTORY

Writing the history of European empires was, from the start, an imperial project in itself, as colonialists were eager to record their discoveries and conquests, place their achievements within national narratives and analyse the documentation they amassed. Official centres of documentation – archives, libraries, museums – overflow with records of the colonial past. There are many private collections as well, including letters and mementos still forgotten in attics and cellars. Historians draw on a wealth of other material, too, pioneering novel ways of understanding traditional evidence and identifying new sources that allow varied perspectives on colonial situations. Once thought of as a rather hoary area of historical writing in the wake of the eclipse of modern empires, cultural and global approaches developed since the late twentieth century have helped turn the history of colonialism and decolonization into one of the most vibrant contemporary fields of historical study. Courses on colonial history form mainstays in university curricula, and works on colonialism attract readers from the general public as well as those who watch broadcast documentaries. Present-day issues – on such questions as the legacy of slavery, international migration, multiculturalism, the memory of the colonial past and the restitution of art and artefacts taken by colonizers – have galvanized interest, provoked debates about colonial legacies and underlined the political significance of studying the colonial past.[1]

Inventing a glorious imperial past

Colonial history-writing is as old as colonialism. In the ancient world, chroniclers wrote accounts of Greek settlements around the Aegean, the Roman conquest of an empire that reached from Scotland to North Africa and the wars that pitted one power against another in the struggle for land, natural resources and spheres of influence. Some of those accounts became classics in Western literature, such as the record of Caesar's campaigns in Gaul famous for his imperial boast of 'I came, I saw, I conquered'. Furthermore, memoirs and history-writing from Antiquity offered templates and rhetoric for later Western expansion, and indeed Western conquerors and their emulators consulted those writings as manuals on colonial expansion and rule. History was thus tied to the modern initiatives of expansion, creating a genealogy of conquest from ancient times to the eighteenth and nineteenth centuries. The classical antecedent offered a legitimation for later conquest, since Greece and Rome were considered foundational periods in Western civilization. History could provide a mandate for imperialism.

One of the signal historical works of the Enlightenment period was Edward Gibbon's six-volume *The History of the Decline and Fall of the Roman Empire*. The first volume was published in 1776, the year in which thirteen American colonies declared their independence from the UK, a date that conveniently marks the start of the undoing of the European empires established in the Americas from the end of the 1400s. Gibbon's final volumes were printed in 1788 and 1789, years that again were full of historic moments in Europe and beyond. In 1788, the British established a penal colony on the eastern shores of Australia, part of the extension of the British Empire in what is now called the Indo-Pacific after the loss of some of its North American possessions. The following year, the eruption of a revolution in France brought forward new ideas about 'liberty, equality and fraternity'. Slogans did not bring about the end of France's empire, and the revolutionaries and their successors devised rationales to excuse colonialism and remodel the institutions of rule. Yet such precepts eventually provided ideological tools for nationalists and anti-colonialists to attack the very intellectual and political bases on which subjection of non-European peoples were erected. As Gibbon's title intimates, he was preoccupied with the question of why the great Roman Empire had 'fallen', and the historian and his readers were worried in their time about the eventual decline of the British Empire, and eager to forestall its ruin. Old empires therefore were meant to provide cautionary lessons for new and remodelled ones.

When read today, Gibbon's work, though still a masterpiece of historical literature, seems rambling, pedantic and moralistic, but in fact Gibbon was innovative in his use of evidence, citation of sources and interest in historical causality. History was no longer, as it had often been in earlier ages, a canon of myths, the simple lineages of rulers and prophets, or the unfolding of God's plan for the world. In the nineteenth century, writers increasingly used history to promote rising nationalism and underpin state-building. The idea of empire remained important in Romantic historical narratives as a font of national pride and component of national identity, while evocation of the landscapes and cultures of foreign places contributed to European fascination for the exotic. By the late 1800s, history as an academic endeavour claimed to be a science, with demands that arguments be substantiated, based on close and critical study of primary sources, and credentialized with archival references. It nevertheless remained intimately linked to the political priorities of the age, the construction of unified and independent European nations, the search for profit in the midst of the industrial revolution and internationalization of commerce, and commitment to spreading European religion and culture. Not surprisingly, contemporary accounts of empire-building (as had earlier ones) were generally cast in heroic mode, emphasizing the bravery of intrepid explorers, the indomitable spirit of pioneers pushing back frontiers, the self-sacrificing nobility of missionaries, the acumen of planters and traders. All, in a real sense, were 'making history': the writing of new chapters in national and international history by both the actors in colonial expansion and the historians who recorded their deeds.

Colonial history-writing functioned in many ways. The idea of 'Greater Britain' set the British Isles into a worldwide empire, and portrayed Victorian Britain as the culmination of a trajectory of economic development, global expansion and the triumph of science and technology linked to British seafaring and industrial prowess, entrepreneurial initiative, parliamentary democracy and allegiance to the Crown. In France, the history of colonialism tied together the old and new regimes, evidenced French 'genius' and followed the dissemination of the French Revolution's ideals, in principle, though often not in practice: the achievement of a 'Greater France'. For Italians, the Roman Empire provided inspiration for the Risorgimento and restoration of Italian greatness. Similarly in Germany, colonial extension became a prolongation of the campaign of national unification and, for its promoters, a necessary effort to give the new Reich a seat at the table of the great powers in the 1880s. The Netherlands' vast and old domains in the East Indies, and small holdings elsewhere, provided both a historical legacy of the 1600s and an assurance of a continuing international role. The kingdom of Denmark boasted a patrimony, dating back to the Middle Ages, that extended over the seas to the North Atlantic and to other points on the globe. Colonial history offered a memory of the age of Lusitanian glory during the sixteenth-century 'age of the explorers' for the small country of Portugal, with the remaining colonies incarnating at least a vestige of earlier power. In Spain, colonial history was a story of empires lost in the nineteenth century, but an imperative for the Spaniards to reconstruct society and economy on the 'peninsula'. The history of empires, therefore, was politically and morally inflected, the study of colonialism as much about contemporary challenges as past glories.

This version of colonial history, of course, was current in countries that had created empires (even if they had lost some holdings over time), much of it written by men – the majority of academic historians – who promoted the maintenance and expansion of empires. European settlers overseas largely shared these visions. Indigenous peoples, however, held different perspectives, though Europeans were apt to denigrate the oral and written recording of history in other parts of the world, which they charged did not conform to the new 'scientific' rigour of European research. Thinking of history in terms of written records, and considering 'primitive' cultures unchanged for centuries, they sometimes went so far as to say, for instance, that Africa had no 'history' before the arrival of the Europeans. But Africans, Asians and other indigenous peoples, it should be remembered, possessed their own forms of keeping, interpreting and presenting history, with their own narratives of glorious pasts, great leaders, powerful states and brilliant cultures. They celebrated the grandeur of their empires – those of the Aztecs or Incas, the Chinese and Mongols, the Mughals, the Abbasid caliphate and the Majapahit Empire, the historic African realms – frequently in the same culture-bound ways as the Europeans lauded their own empires. Indigenous historians – a word not limited to the writers of history books – kept the record and memory of experiences of European conquest but also resistance against invasion and occupation. Encounters, benign or belligerent, episodic or long-lasting, were seen from different perspectives, though it would take time for the (former) colonizers to listen to, read or look at indigenous records with due regard, take seriously their traditions of keeping history and acknowledge their interpretations of the past.

From economics and empire to geopolitics

Much of history-writing as a Western discipline in the nineteenth century concentrated on politics, government, wars and treaties, and the colonial world provided countless episodes for these accounts: conquests of new territory, wars between European and indigenous armies and between rival European ones, and the evolving structures of administration provided staples themes. Research and writing also focused on 'great men' (the gendered word is apposite), and the great men of empire – explorers, military heroes, governors – occupied pre-eminent positions in the pantheon. From the early years of the twentieth century, economic history emerged as a discipline in European universities, and empire and imperialism again provided key subjects with investigation of the location and use of natural resources, the building of infrastructure, the creation of networks of trade, finance and investment, the growth of large and small colonial companies. In fact, 'economics and empire' moved into central position in works on colonialism, as scholars tallied up imports and exports, calculated the cargoes of steamships, measured the kilometres crossed by rail lines and praised or damned the quest for profit.

Two big questions dominated. One that obsessed many historians was whether economics provided the major motivation of empire, if in the words of a leading British commentator, J. A. Hobson, writing in 1902, economics provided the 'taproot of imperialism'. Hobson, a professional journalist basing his work on personal observations during the recently concluded South African War (1899–1902), argued that it was; once many of the avowed political and cultural interests in proclaimed justification for colonies were stripped away (though Hobson conceded that these were crucially important), then profit was the principle.[2] That conclusion did not necessarily rankle colonialists, though they continued to clamour about the civilizational and humanitarian benefits of colonialism, for they made no secret about hopes for monetary gains from empire; indeed, having possessions was primarily worth the effort when they turned a profit or promised to do so. Others of Hobson's points sat less well with empire-promoters. Hobson suggested that contrary to colonialists' arguments that overseas expansion provided benefits for the whole body politic, it actually favoured wealthy financiers and industrialists, a small elite who lorded it over not only the indigenous communities of the colonies but the working class back at home. Empire, in other words, provided a way for a certain elite to enrich itself at the expense of workers at home and abroad. Furthermore, Hobson charged that colonial rule – arbitrary and authoritarian, depriving subject peoples of rights to political participation and legal status – represented a betrayal of the very values held so dear by Victorian Britons.

Inspired in part by Hobson's work, but applying Karl Marx's theories of historical materialism and the stages in human history, alongside rousing political calls for a revolutionary and proletarian overthrow of the capitalist order, Vladimir Lenin during the First World War offered an even more non-compromising indictment.[3] For Lenin, imperialism represented 'the highest stage of capitalism', in which a system in its death throes – in particular, because of declining profits in Europe during the late nineteenth-century economic depression – had been forced to seek cheaper raw materials, new markets and compensating profits overseas, in large part through an aggressive conquest of foreign countries. (Lenin, like Hobson, was taking evidence from and writing primarily about European colonialism in sub-Saharan Africa in the last decades of the 1800s.) Perfervid competition among the capitalist and colonialist powers rebounded in Europe, as the Great War was at base, Lenin argued, a war among imperialist powers.[4]

Neither Hobson nor Lenin was a trained historian, but their theories had enormous influence and a long and provocative life as economists, historians and other commentators argued about whether colonialism was or was not profitable and for whom it made a profit. It was not necessary to be either a raging Marxist or a gung-ho capitalist to focus on the economics of empire. In the 1950s, one of the most potent new contributions to the understanding of colonialism came from the mainstream British historians Ronald Robinson and John Gallagher. They suggested that there existed an 'imperialism of free trade' as well as imperialism of conquest and colonialism, in which countries such as Britain had at times sought profits (of various sorts) not by imperial acquisition but by the imposition of international free trade. This was a trade in which Britain, because of its financial and industrial clout in the nineteenth century, became a prime beneficiary.[5] Economics also provided a theme for writers from the colonies. In Australia, historians emphasized the role of economics in history; gold-mining and sheep-raising provided persuasive evidence about the key role of economics in British colonial rule, and for some outright exploitation, of the continent. Indian commentators meanwhile charged that British manufacturing had ruined indigenous Indian textile-making and that the British had effectively robbed the Indians by expropriating their resources and labour and exporting the profits.

For promoters as well as for defenders of colonialism, and for historians observing from the sidelines, economics often continued to hold centre stage. In the 1980s, Peter J. Cain and Anthony Hopkins suggested that London finance, rather than the industry for which Victorian Britain was so renowned, was the main driver of and profiteer from empire.[6] Across the Channel, Jacques Marseille, with a finely grained analysis of French business, argued that the empire held only marginal economic importance to France in terms of the volume of imports and exports, and the general contribution of imperial trade in the French balance sheet, though it remained vital in some niche areas.[7] Others similarly disaggregated the statistics to investigate business strategies, the development of particular markets and types of manufacturing, and the specific economic profile of each colony.

Emphasis on business as the core of empire did not produce unanimity among scholars. Some had always insisted that geopolitical advantage had served as prime mover of expansion. For instance, Henri Brunschwig, in France, wrote in the 1950s and 1960s about the ways in which Britain and France, as the two leading European and colonial powers, and occasional enemies during much of the nineteenth century, had been locked in a battle that was not so much about profit as power, in Europe and abroad.[8] Annexing colonial territory, garrisoning armies, sending out fleets, gaining sway over still independent countries, forging alliances: all proved keys to political status in Europe and the wider arena. The rise of a unified and modernizing Germany that had humiliated France in war in 1870–1 and that, in some industrial sectors, was outstripping Britain in production and growth by the end of the nineteenth century introduced a new great player into the political game. As Germany and other states began to contract the alliances that finally divided Europe into two armed and hostile camps in the early years of the twentieth century, colonies provided status, leverage and resources. Other colonial powers were also emerging – the king of Belgium, a country that gained independence only in 1830, had a vast colony in Africa by the 1880s, and Italy, unified in 1861, had joined the colonizers by the end of the century. Elsewhere, Russia had consolidated what was a massive colonial empire stretching from central Asia to Siberia, the United States took over colonies in the eastern and western Pacific, Asia and the Caribbean from the 1860s through the 1890s, and Japan acquired overseas territories in the 1890s and after the turn of the century. Historians, at the time and later, stressed the ways in which colonies served as geopolitical chips in international military and diplomatic games.

For British historians, not surprisingly, imperial history was particularly about the British Empire, and how and why Britain had created the world's largest and most diverse colonial empire. For the French, the story was often about the ways in which France had challenged British might, managed to secure the world's second largest empire and developed its own modes of colonial rule. While a considerable amount of attention in Britain centred on India and on the British settler colonies, French historians looked particularly at the French outposts of northern and sub-Saharan Africa. Historians in other countries found their own case studies for historical research and periods of specialization: for the Portuguese, the age of Vasco Da Gama, Magellan and Portuguese conquests from South America to the South China Sea in the 1500s, for the Dutch, the East Indies in the 'golden age' of the seventeenth century. Spanish historiography in large part focused on the late sixteenth century, the time of King Philip II, who coined the phrase (later applied to the British) that he reigned over an empire over which the sun never set. Conservative historiography during the years of Francisco Franco's dictatorship (1939–75) virtually ignored the 'decadent' nineteenth century when the past glories were lost; only in recent years have Spanish historians rediscovered the significance of colonies such as Cuba for Spain's modern nation-building at home. Germany and Italy ruled overseas colonies for only a few decades in the late 1800s and early 1900s and, after their loss following the First and Second World Wars, respectively, scholars showed relatively little interest in their colonial history. The myth of Italians as *brava gente*, that is, as upstanding and largely benevolent colonizers, long endured. For German historians the country's colonial history became a major subject only when connected with the study of the roots and causes of Nazism.

From the critics of empire to decolonizing colonial history

The comments made in the previous paragraphs only sketch some of the currents of historical scholarship, which produced an uncountable number of general and specialized works, many now superseded, others still authoritative. Some historians placed themselves enthusiastically in the service of the colonial cause, and the power of academic institutions affiliated with and indeed often dependent on the state favoured those with largely supportive views of a nation's colonial undertakings. Not all 'colonial historians', however, espoused the necessity of colonialism. Opposition to colonialism, and to the Western economic and political systems on which it was built, had always been present in Europe, including in the scholarly world. The anti-slavery movement in Europe in the late 1700s and early 1800s owed much to historical and contemporary documentation of the evils of slavery. Historical work critical of colonialism gained ground in particular among those influenced by Marxism (in both its orthodox and reformist varieties), in response to stronger currents of anti-colonialism from the 1920s onwards, and in the context of the political events within Europe in the early twentieth century. By the 1950s, many scholars of colonial history had become professedly anti-colonial. In the case of France, for example, a number of distinguished scholars, though not all the historians of colonialism, expressed strong opposition to the Franco-Indochinese War of 1946–54 and especially to the Franco-Algerian War of 1954–62. Some historians in Britain similarly opposed the lack of decolonization of the remaining possessions in sub-Saharan Africa and elsewhere, and they became increasingly pointed in critiques or condemnation of Britain's overall colonial record. They had peers in other European countries, though political pressure muted criticism of empire and censorship hampered the discipline of history in Spain and Portugal until the 1970s. Historians and other scholars took on board ideas of the 'New Left' in the 1960s, with its indictment of capitalism as exercised by the old colonial powers, and some leant sympathetically towards new forms of anti-colonial Marxism developed in Mao's China and Castro's Cuba. The popular notion of the 'Third World', formulated by a French journalist in the mid-1950s, identified commonalities among former colonies during the Cold War that divided supporters of the 'Free World' (centred on the United States) and the Communist 'bloc'. The idea of 'neocolonialism', popularized in the writings of Kwame Nkrumah, the first president of independent Ghana, gained much currency. The actions of the United States, especially the long war in Vietnam but also American interventions in South America, seemed to some observers colonialism under a different name (as did, for others, Soviet, Chinese and Cuban interventions in overseas 'wars of liberation').[9] Such perspectives, once again, drew lines between developments in the colonial past to the political stakes of the present.

In anti-colonialist perspectives, verities dear to colonialists were upended. Scholars re-evaluated and valorized the indigenous histories of colonized countries and called on cognate disciplines such as social anthropology to understand the dynamics of non-European societies. The shortcomings of colonial efforts in such areas as education and healthcare, rather than their achievements, were assessed. The violence of the colonial order became a prominent theme. Moreover, there was a vogue for regional studies and histories of each newly independent country, with 'regional studies' put forward as an alternative to an increasingly discredited older version of 'colonial history' that centred on the metropoles and European issues.

Historians increasingly searched for, and found, strong traditions of 'resistance' to colonial rule, from armed uprisings to efforts to preserve language and customs. Whereas for colonialists (and some colonial historians), indigenous people who had 'collaborated' with Europeans were seen in a positive light, now the 'resisters' were championed. Old colonial 'heroes' were toppled from their pedestals, replaced with new ones – those who resisted, leaders of independence movements who had dared to fight against the colonial order and the 'martyrs' fallen in the struggle. That narrative, somewhat ironically, largely replicated a 'great man' view of history (especially since men were more prominent in the accounts than women) and a focus on the achievements of the shakers and movers of history: for pro-colonial historians, there had been Stanley and Livingstone, for anti-colonial specialists, they were Gandhi and Ho Chi Minh. While colonialism had been a process of imperial state-building vaunted by historians of the colonial age, now anti-colonial nationalism, contestatory movements and the process of nationalist state-building in the moves towards independence gained pride of place, with, in both cases, a trajectory charted as linear and teleological. In one version, the formation of empires was the end-point; in the other, the emergence of independent states. Anti-colonial history nevertheless provided a valuable corrective to older works, especially those of the late nineteenth and early twentieth centuries complicit in the colonial project, and with scholarship that continued to present colonialism almost entirely from the standpoint of what the West had done in the rest of the world.

Increasingly, history-writing in a Western scholarly mode was also being produced by non-European historians, though in some newly emancipated countries, the infrastructure for research, including libraries and archives, funding and freedom from state control were sadly lacking. Yet historians from Africa and Asia, including diasporic intellectuals in Europe and North America, were more and more frequently writing about the past of their own countries, often in innovative fashion. The 'subaltern studies' historians who emerged in the early 1980s provided a notable example.[10] The key exponents were specialists of modern India, many of them diasporic Indians in universities in the United States and the United Kingdom. Subaltern scholars pioneered the study of groups that had attracted little attention from colonial historians, including anti-colonialists, who concentrated on political, cultural and economic elites and the leading cohorts of independence movements. For these specialists, 'subalterns' constituted the vast mass of people on the Indian subcontinent, those whose lives had been less directly touched by colonialism than were urban populations. Their focus was particularly on the peasant farmers who formed the majority of South Asians and whose daily lives took place in a world different from that of either the architects of British rule or those of Indian independence. Scholars elsewhere initiated a 'Pacific school of history' that promoted an 'island-centred' study of Oceania, examining the islands not so much from the standpoint of colonizers as from the experiences and perspectives of the islanders. Like colleagues in subaltern studies, they were eager to incorporate ethnohistory, a field that drew on social anthropology and oral history, and to use 'microhistories' of particular situations to move beyond Western-centred and globalizing portrayals. Meanwhile, there occurred a great outpouring of scholarship in the United States (and also in Britain and France) on the history of slavery and its legacies, much of it written by African Americans and Black scholars in Europe: investigations of the practices of slavery, the daily life of the enslaved, the struggle for emancipation, the racism that continued to infect Western societies and the discrimination from which descendants of the enslaved suffered.

Gendering colonial history, post-colonial studies and the 'new' imperial histories

Several general intellectual trends were beginning, by the 1970s, to produce a profound impact on colonial history-writing. The 'new social movements' of the 1960s and 1970s – the 'civil rights' movement in the United States, the women's movement, the 'gay liberation' movement – had brought marginalized communities and their demands to the fore. The feminist movement, in particular, not only demanded attention to the 'forgotten' figures of women in history. It also called attention to wider notions of gender and the ways that political, religious and social attitudes towards gender inflected all of life and all of history, though that fact had frequently simply been ignored, intentionally or not, by historians whose conceptions of the world remained masculinist and patriarchal.[11] Another impulse came from the writings of the French philosopher Michel Foucault, whose works began to be translated into English in the 1970s and who attained cult status for his techniques of excavating the 'archaeology of knowledge' by reading texts in new ways and reflecting on the very articulation and categorization of learning, for his notion of 'power' as a force immanent in the world exerting its influence in multiple directions, and for his investigations of such topics as 'biopower' and sexuality. Foucault's wide-ranging work was decisive in the emergence of 'postmodernism' as an academic speciality, in which historians were commanded to interrogate their sources more critically and to read both primary sources and colonial-era works 'against the grain', look at 'representations' (such as pictorial images) as a key to understanding historical attitudes and circumstances, and to place race, class and gender as privileged axes of analysis.

This approach, which achieved great prominence in Western academia in the 1980s, linked with the 'postcolonialism' inspired by the work of Edward Said. A Palestinian by background, and a professor of literature at New York's Columbia University, Said's *Orientalism*, published in 1978, remains a landmark study.[12] Said dissected Western views of the 'Orient', that is, the Arabic and Islamic Middle East and North Africa, in the early modern and colonial periods, identifying deeply entrenched assumptions about their peoples and cultures. For Said, the stereotypes omnipresent in Western representations – the 'Orient' as backward and exotic, yet perversely fascinating, the land of fanatical clerics, authoritarian potentates and erotic harems – had served as grounding for Western imperialism in the region. These ideas had motivated and legitimized Western incursions in the Middle East from the Crusades onwards and culminated with nineteenth- and twentieth-century interventions. Said was writing in the context of a renewed Arab–Israeli conflict in the Middle East, including the wars of 1967 and 1973, the American-backed Israeli occupation of Palestinian territories and the oil shock of 1973, when the older, colonial-era tropes were still instrumentalized for political objectives.

Said's later works, including the wide-ranging *Culture and Imperialism* of 1993, reflected more broadly on the often occluded presence of the colonial, and the colonial 'other', in Western life.[13] He pointed to ways in which colonialism had formed a vital theme for such canonical English-language novelists as Joseph Conrad and E. M. Forster, but also how colonialism had appeared, sometimes only in the deep background, even in the novels of writers like Jane Austen. Said further demonstrated how other discourses and cultural representations, such as Western opera and artwork, revelled in preconceptions about the 'exotic' East and buttressed imperialist and neocolonialist ideas and policies. Said's works stimulated a large cohort of scholars, even those who did not agree with all of his conclusions (and, indeed, Said later modified some of his initial arguments), and 'Orientalism' became a generic term to refer to Western images of most any other part of the world and the policies they engendered. Scholars such as the historian John Mackenzie, however, took issue with what they felt was Said's essentializing of the West, in the same way as he had accused Westerners of essentializing the Orient, and they pointed to many images and texts about the 'Orient' that counterbalanced the negative depictions that provided evidence for Said's arguments.[14]

Discussion about literary texts and visual images of colonialism fit into, and inspired, the 'cultural turn' in history in the 1980s, a trend that remains a potent current. 'Culture and empire' replaced 'economics and empire' – and even 'politics and empire' – as a basic analytical framework, with stress now laid on the intellectual 'taproots' of colonialism: notions about race, gender, religion and ethics, and the hierarchies of knowledge. Whereas an earlier generation had pored over the account books of businesses and the papers of parliamentarians, now historians (sometimes borrowing techniques from literary studies and discourse analysis) eagerly studied newspapers and advertising, exhibitions and museum collections, film, printed and archival works by non-canonical novelists and poets, 'interrogating' and 'deconstructing' the 'discourses' and 'representations' of colonialism and 'alterity'. The new vocabulary became a strength or a weakness of the approach, depending on readers' training and viewpoint. Scholars such as Homi K. Bhabha and Gayatri Chakravorty Spivak gained renown as literary theorists of the new approaches.

Historians drawing on the new currents of thought and auxiliary disciplines but also centring their work on more traditional historical methods – critical use of primary sources, close attention to the specificities of place and time, concern with causality and process, and with politics and economics – helped to mould what by the 1990s was called in the English-speaking countries the 'new imperial history'. Perhaps the term, however, was newer than the burgeoning field, as historians had for a number of years explored various types of colonial experience, as seen in the monumental (and continuing) series of books initiated under the general editorship of John Mackenzie, a historian who had pioneered study of such subjects as imperial propaganda and colonial culture. The 'new imperial history' was not a single 'school', it had no leader, institution or masthead publication, and it lacked a defined set of methods and themes. In fact, the approach encouraged the use of multiple sources, varied approaches and diverse interpretations. Those who have been closely associated with the 'new imperial history' (though they do not always use the phrase to describe themselves), such as Antoinette Burton, Tony Ballantyne, Ann Laura Stoler and Frederick Cooper, among many others, have been notable for methodological innovation and new interpretations, and to them belongs considerable credit for the revitalization of the study of colonialism.

First, the 'new imperial historians' have tried to move past, or jettison, simple binaries of seeing the colonized world in black and white: the colonizers and the colonized, Europe and the world outside Europe, Europeans and 'natives', indigenous 'collaborators' versus 'resisters'. They have disaggregated both the 'colonizers' and 'colonized' into diverse, complex groups that were transformed in varying fashion in different times, places and circumstances. They have examined ways in which individuals and groups accommodated colonial rule (by choice, coercion or necessity), and how they manoeuvred within colonial situations, including strategizing to achieve emancipation. Second, they foreground rather than background indigenous populations, looking closely at the myriad ways in which disparate peoples experienced colonial rule and reacted to it. Similarly, they have given greater attention to once often overlooked diasporic populations – such as free and bonded migrants from one non-European colony to another, including Indians and Chinese – and to people of mixed heritage (*métis, mestizos, mestiços*), such as Eurasians. Third, women, both colonizing and colonized, have provided a subject for greater investigation than ever before, with gender becoming a central pivot for understanding and theorizing colonialism. Fourth, 'new imperial historians' have emphasized the lived experiences of colonialism, whether those of well-known people or, more often, 'common' people – peasants, artisans and labourers, urban and rural masses – some previously obscure or utterly absent in traditional narratives. They include criminals, adventurers, soldiers-of-fortune and fraudsters who lived on the margins of society or beyond the pale of the law. The very ordinariness and sometimes near anonymity of many affected by colonialism provide unique insights into the dynamics of conquest, rule and responses to it. Fifth, and very significantly, instead of examining the impact of Europe on the rest of the world as a unidirectional movement, practitioners of the 'new imperial history' have looked at the multifarious effects of colonialism in Europe itself, discovering the widespread and often previously un-noted ways in which colonialism permeated European life: in systems of knowledge, consumer goods, food and clothing, entertainment, daily habits, careers, art and culture. Rather than thinking of 'Europe' and 'the colonies' as separate, they have brought them into the same field of analysis. Finally, they have identified and studied the connections – of migration, trade, the passage of ideas – that linked colonies to one another rather than remaining in a simple bilateral relationship with their respective metropoles. They have found how different empires interconnected and interacted, investigating the comparative history of empires over time and space. The 'new imperial historians' have written about often widely strung but dense 'networks' that joined individuals and groups, and about the 'transnational' aspects of colonial situations that crossed national boundaries. In this regard, the 'new imperial history' is closely connected with a 'geographical turn' in history at the end of the twentieth century and with a renewal of world history and global history. In fact, some colonial historians and their writings of the 1970s and 1980s can arguably be labelled as global historians *avant la lettre*, and in certain universities 'colonial history' has merged into 'global history'.[15] Yet 'new imperial history', 'global history' and 'world history' have sometimes served as a catch-all term, while scholarly categories, fields and specialities are more porous and entangled than ever before.

The 'new imperial historians' and other recent historians of European expansion have built on earlier trends in colonial history, including the economic, political, social and cultural history of colonialism. And it should be repeated that exceptional and innovative research on colonial history was published by scholars in many countries throughout the 1960s, 1970s and 1980s, long before the 'new imperial history' or 'post-colonial theory' gained prominence, though it would be ill-advised to enumerate what would be a long, but necessarily selective, list in this overview. Scholars in different decades, and pursuing different research strategies, have all contributed to the reframing of the history of European empires.

The expansion of research is remarkable, including the introduction of topics that had earlier only received sporadic coverage, and ones previously considered unfit for serious historical study. One example is the history of sexuality in colonialism, including prostitution, concubinage, homosexuality and venereal diseases, and the regulation of sex by colonial authorities – sexuality, once a near taboo subject, is now seen as a major dynamic of colonialism. Not only have art, literature and other elements of 'high' culture received renewed attention, but so too have advertising, 'romantic' novels and crime novels, popular music, fashion, food, even beauty pageants. The study of 'biopolitics' (the way that the body and mind were diagnosed, treated, regulated and trained), linked to the history of medicine and psychiatry, has become a burgeoning area of colonial studies.[16] Greater stress on the way legal codes and the enforcement of law structured colonial life has led to new work on colonial legal history. Contemporary historians have revitalized the study of colonial warfare, the economic history of colonies, the study of religions in colonial contexts, the scientific, environmental and ecological history of colonialism.[17]

Writers and readers of colonial history now explore every aspect of life, discovering new areas, crossing borders – and research on colonial situations has enriched every branch of historical study. Series such as Manchester University Press's *Studies in Imperialism* and Oxford University Press's multivolume *The Oxford History of the British Empire*,[18] as well as many other academic volumes and publication series, are witness to the breadth of research. So, too, do veteran and newer journals: *Outre-Mers* (a French-language journal founded in 1913, whose long history is especially revealing of the changes in colonialism and colonial history-writing), *The Journal of Imperial and Commonwealth History* in Britain (established in 1972) and the Dutch-published

Itinerario (since 1976), as well as newer journals such as the *Journal of Colonialism and Colonial History* (established in 2000), and regionally specific publications like the *Journal of African History* and *Journal of Pacific History* provide forums for monographic articles, book reviews and debates. Any reader of more general historical journals will be aware of the great place now held in their pages by studies of colonialism.

Colonial history-writing has also been stimulated, and on occasion, dragged into debate, by present-day issues, such as migration to Europe from former colonies, questions surrounding cultural practices like the wearing of headscarves by Islamic women in Western countries, and attempts to define communitarian or national identities. Research on colonial history has become more acutely sensitive to concerns about the legacies of colonialism – most notably, the long-lasting heritage of slavery – and demands by former colonies for restitution of looted artefacts and documents. Exposés of colonial violence, including torture, have forced a reconsideration of narratives about colonial benevolence. The 'Black Lives Matter' movement has raised issues about wrongs past and present, and the toppling or defacement of the statues of figures once thought colonial heroes has raised questions about how the past is remembered and forgotten.

Decolonizing colonial history – yet again?

All of these developments have led to demands to 'decolonize' history and knowledge: history-writing and history teaching, museum collections and exhibitions, historical monuments and historical commemorations, even the very words used to describe people, events or situations. Proponents of the 'decolonial' movement identify ways in which racialist or racist colonial-era stereotypes endure, how public institutions such as museums can perpetuate, explicitly or implicitly, a favourable impression of colonialism, and how public spaces are filled with anachronistic and often offensive markers of colonialism in statues, plaques and street names.[19] 'Decoloniality' as a campaign provides a reminder that the study of colonialism, now as in the past, remains closely linked to the social contexts and political imperatives of the day, and that the colonial record has always been a battleground for competing interpretations, perspectives and political objectives.

As they continue to investigate various aspects of colonial history, scholars differ – sometimes dramatically, even furiously – about colonialism and its legacy. Many outside of academia take part in the debate, including descendants of those whose families were connected with colonialism in some direct way. Thematic blogs and social media, among other platforms, have provided new channels that reach beyond academic books and scholarly articles. For those whose forebears were colonial subjects, and especially for the descendants of the enslaved, issues relating to colonialism hold visceral significance. Colonialism and its legacy have been, and are likely to remain, a hot topic, one where scars remain raw, sentiments inflamed and memories conflicting. Debates about the colonial past hold great pertinence, for they touch on issues of international relations, discrimination and disenfranchisement, the control of resources. They relate closely to notions of identity and narratives of history, and arguments about which groups are fully a part of a nation. They pose questions about who determines history and to what use history is put.

Colonialism is a phenomenon that, just in its modern iteration, spanned almost 500 years from the late 1400s through the late 1900s. It encompassed all the continents and oceans of the world, and no society or culture (including those in Europe or the rare non-Western countries that managed to retain their independence) remained untouched. It involved all the great powers of Europe, and several of the smaller ones, and people in countries that claimed no colonies. Colonial conquest was not a monopoly of Europeans, though no others had the means and the will to make it so extensive and long-lasting as did Europeans from the end of the fifteenth to the middle of the twentieth century. Colonialism provided an umbrella under which sheltered individuals and groups with many often competing motives and objectives, from the most idealistic to the most base. Colonialism metamorphosed from decade to decade, and from one site to another. Experiences of colonialism were varied, positions ambiguous and viewpoints frequently ambivalent.

Searching for simple overarching explanations that easily explain such a long-term and wide-ranging phenomenon runs the danger of vague generalizations that avoid specificities of time and place. Disaggregating the history of colonialism provides scope for more fine-grained analysis: thinking about particular moments and places allows a 'zooming in' to where details stand out in higher relief, while 'big pictures' remain vaguer in definition. The goal of this book is to walk the fine line between a necessary overview and closer examination. Any study must be selective and even eclectic – every country and group touched by colonialism, in Europe or overseas, has its own history, and each individual touched by colonialism has his or her own experience and narrative. Any history of colonialism remains but a work in progress and, one hopes, a stimulus for further study.

PART I
CHRONOLOGIES

The empires of Antiquity provided material, rhetorical and conceptual templates for much later conquests – the deployment of legions of soldiers, resettlement of indigenous populations and settlement of new ones, the building of roads and aqueducts, the rhetoric of civilization and the imposition of codes of law proved no less important to the colonialists of the modern period than to ancient Romans. Yet colonialism altered dramatically over time. New technologies, from sleek caravels to steamships, made accessible to modern Europeans countries of which their forebears only dreamed. New forms of weaponry contributed to the subjugation of foreign peoples, though co-option of local elites and the promises of benefits in return for cooperation remained a staple of empire. Growing markets and novel forms of production demanded commodities from afar. Ideas evolved, ideologues and colonial promoters devising new justifications for extending European suzerainty and the European brand of civilization. Even in the last decades and years of colonialism ideas and practices were recast to provide more updated rationales for keeping empires, while nevertheless recapitulating old arguments about the need for land and its resources, labour, modernization and 'progress'.

This first part of *The Colonial World* divides the history of modern colonialism into four periods, though there exist many links from one to the next. The story begins in Chapter 2, somewhat arbitrarily, in the late 1400s, in European history traditionally labelled the era of the 'explorers'. Such a dating and mapping, of course, is based on European history and perspectives, not those of people in other places and cultures, and it is important to remember that such ideas as 'exploration' and 'discovery', and indeed the periodization of history and cartography commonly used in the West, have a colonial-era and European provenance. This chapter discusses the rise (and sometimes eclipse) of the Spanish, Portuguese, Dutch, British and French overseas empires down until the end of the 1700s, and the emergence of new webs of trade, migration and culture that tied together Europe with the Americas, Africa and Asia.

Chapter 3 covers the making of new European empires in the nineteenth century and the dividing up of the Asian and African continents, Australasia and Oceania among the colonizers, both veteran ones and new powers, including Germany, Italy and Belgium. It examines arguments behind the new bouts of imperialism, the processes of colonial takeover and the colonial structures created, and the early decades of resistance to European incursions.

The First World War, a global cataclysm with great repercussions in the colonies, introduces Chapter 4. The war and the post-war settlement led to a redrawing of the colonial map, and saw the introduction of some revised policies of colonial governance.

The interwar period also witnessed the accelerating growth of anti-colonialism – while European countries celebrated colonialism and its 'achievements' in grandiose expositions, anti-colonialism in the colonies grew ineluctably stronger and more manifest.

Finally, Chapter 5 traces the 'unmaking' of empires, though the disintegration of the colonial world had already begun before the Second World War. That conflict threw the colonial order into great turbulence once again, with Japanese occupation of European colonies in Asia, divided loyalties and the cutting off of colonies from Europe. At the end of the war, European governments' commitment to colonialism remained strong, but they struggled to reimpose dominion by military and political means, repression and new development plans. Soon many Asian colonies moved towards independence. Over the next decades, bloody wars of decolonization were fought between nationalists and colonizers in Asia and Africa, yet with smoother paths to independence in some regions. The 'wind of change' buffeted the colonies, ultimately sweeping away colonial regimes. That outcome was neither assured nor foretold in the mid-1940s, colonizing countries long resisted the emancipation of their 'possessions' and various options for political evolution were essayed.

This centuries-long chronological overview shows the expansion and contraction of empires, and the various forms of adaptation and metamorphosis of the infinitely malleable theory and practice of colonialism. While identifying certain patterns, the chapters underscore variations in experiences in both colonizing and colonized countries over a period of 500 years and around the globe. They reject notions of a clear and straightforward path from the establishment of colonial overlordship to the acquisition of national independence. They point to the complexities in the processes of both colonialization and decolonization, the need to see the big picture but also to be mindful of smaller details (even if space does not allow the closer examination that the history of each colony merits). These survey chapters underscore the worldwide extent of European expansion and highlight the development of a globalization closely linked to colonialism.

CHAPTER 2
EARLY MODERN EUROPEAN COLONIALISM, 1490s–1815

The period from the 1400s until the late 1700s in the Western world covers 'early modern history', though the term has more limited applicability elsewhere. It encompasses the time from the Italian Renaissance of the mid-fifteenth century and the voyages of 'discovery' at the end of that century down to the French Revolution of 1789. This era saw a new relationship between Europe and the rest of the world – the exploration by Europeans of oceans, continents and islands previously little known or completely unknown to them, the establishment of settler societies in the Americas and trading outposts in Asia and Africa, and the emergence of a global network of commerce, free and forced migration, and cultural exchange. The Caribbean islands, North, Central and South America were brought in large part under European dominion. Europeans took possession of islands in the Indian Ocean and established bases, ranging from coastal enclaves to extensive territorial holdings (mainly in India), along the coasts of Africa and Asia. The building of stronger European dynastic states and mercantilist economies, especially along the Atlantic – Spain, Portugal, France, Britain, the United Provinces (the Netherlands) – in part came from power and wealth derived from overseas, though with the later decline of some states in the face of successful competition from imperial rivals.

Colonial expansion during this period laid out pathways for later imperial endeavours, yet with marked differences between the early modern enterprise and that of the nineteenth and early twentieth centuries. American continental colonies claimed by the British, Portuguese and Spanish largely gained independence from the late 1700s to the early 1800s, though those in the Caribbean (excepting Haiti) remained under European control. The United States took on the role of conquest and colonization west of the thirteen original colonies comprising the new nation. In Asia and Africa, the early European coastal outposts served as beachheads for expansion inland; the Australian continent became a huge new domain for British colonization. Early modern trade routes remained key conduits for the movement of commodities, people and ideas. The enslavement of Africans and others continued well into the nineteenth century, replaced by new forms of indentured and coerced labour. Ideas and policies from the early modern age persisted beyond the 'imperial meridian' (as Christopher Bayly memorably labelled these years) of the decades from 1780 to 1830, which saw, in particular, a turn eastwards in British imperial interests.

This chapter will survey the genesis and evolution of overseas empires in early modern history through connections to several cultural, political and economic trends in Europe – and it is important to underline how the colonial world contributed to those very transformations. Some of the themes introduced here will be examined in greater detail elsewhere in this volume. One of these themes is colonial violence. The conquest of colonies in the first imperial age, as later, entailed a continuing series of violent encounters and wars between European invaders and indigenous populations (and wars provoked between indigenous peoples and between rival European powers). Indeed, warfare and violence were a constant in colonial history. As in all armed conflicts, colonial wars inflicted enormous physical and mental suffering on individuals and communities, and the loss of homes, property, resources and livelihoods. Fighting on the home territory of indigenous people widened the deleterious effects on communities. Given the destructive power of European weaponry and the extremely derogatory European attitudes towards 'natives', the indigenous population bore the brunt of the exactions, including sheer brutality, torture, sexual abuse and pillage. The level of indigenous deaths almost always considerably exceeded that of Europeans. The number of victims is difficult to calculate with accuracy, with any accounting provoking considerable debate. Some historians speak of 'extermination', 'genocide' and 'massacre' around the world, concepts that remain contested in certain cases, more widely recognized in others. That being said, the violence committed by colonialists, often intentional and systematic, remains one of the most heinous aspects of the colonial record.

Science and expansion

The Renaissance is associated with new currents of art and architecture, and the works of the 'old masters' in Florence, Venice, Rome, other Italian cities and those of northern Europe. Their work formed part of a larger cultural 'awakening' marked by new interest in Greco-Roman Antiquity, a spirit of individualism that challenged the corporatism of the Middle Ages and privileged human achievements, and the Scientific Revolution with its emphasis on experimentation, discovery and rational understanding of the 'laws of nature'. That new spirit was eminently visible in the European long-distance voyages.

In the early fifteenth century, the Portuguese and Spanish took advantage of their propitious geographical location to inch down the western African coast and outwards into the Atlantic Ocean. Encouragement from royal patrons, notably Prince Henry the Navigator in Portugal, and new types of ships, such as faster caravels outfitted with lateen sails (which could sail further from the coast) and better techniques of navigation, propelled voyages onwards. In the first half of the 1400s, Iberians settled what are now the Portuguese provinces of the Azores and Madeira and the independent Cape Verde islands, and the Spanish colonized the Canary Islands. Some were unoccupied, and others had a sparse population eliminated in the process of conquest. On the African continent, the Spanish and Portuguese set up posts for trade in gold, ivory and other coveted goods, and soon trade in slaves. In 1488 the Portuguese Bartolomeu Dias rounded the southern coast of Africa, and his compatriot Vasco Da Gama pioneered the first European sea route to India on a voyage from 1497 to 1499 – a major feat of navigation and seamanship that took the Europeans towards the fabled 'Indies' and 'Far East'. By 1522 ships commanded by another Portuguese, Ferdinand Magellan, had circumnavigated the globe, though Magellan died en route. Meanwhile, Christopher Columbus, a Genoese sailing under the flag of Spain, had set off for the 'Indies', in Asia, but the winds took his ships westwards across the Atlantic. In 1492 he landed on a Caribbean island in what became the 'West Indies', and was long credited with having 'discovered' America. The Portuguese Pedro Álvares Cabral followed with the 'discovery' of Brazil in 1500. When they landed, the men grandly planted flags to claim territories for the kings and queens who had dispatched them and whose dominions now reached over the seas.

Europeans created maps and ocean charts, studied and collected new species of flora and fauna, came into contact with foreign cultures, and prospected for resources and markets. The voyages helped perfect the use of such equipment as astrolabes and profoundly enriched European knowledge in almost every field. It is not surprising that 'cabinets of curiosity' overflowed with strange and wondrous treasures that travellers brought home: preserved plants, animals and human remains, minerals and handicrafts, as well as such oddities as bezoar stones and supposed unicorn horns. Living specimens were brought back to Europe as well – the hippopotamus or elephant, plants set out in botanical gardens and, on occasion, living human 'specimens'. Some of the Africans were employed in service (or forced into servitude) in royal palaces and the mansions of the wealthy; their images can be glimpsed in the background of Renaissance paintings or occasionally featured in portraits. Others worked on ships, in dockyards and in other sorts of urban labour.

The Europeans marvelled at their 'discoveries', but of course, the landscapes and nature, and the art and objects of daily life were well known to the Native Americans, Africans and Asians who lived in those countries, and to those with whom they already engaged in commercial or cultural exchange. Movement of people, goods and ideas around the non-European world long predated the arrival of Europeans. Navigators and scholars from outside Europe had for centuries travelled around, compiling information about their own 'discoveries'. For instance, the Muslim, North African-born Ibn Khaldoun, a prolific scholar of history and what are now called the social sciences, journeyed around the Mediterranean and wrote influential texts in the late 1300s. The Chinese admiral Zheng He from 1405 to 1433 explored south-eastern Asia and the Indian Ocean, and sailed as far as eastern Africa. Notwithstanding his 'discoveries', the Chinese decided, unlike the Europeans, not to claim territory, establish trading outposts, or implant settler societies. The coasts of Africa and India were well known to traders from the Persian Gulf, and Indian scholars and rulers, as well as merchants, were familiar with countries extending from North Africa to Southeast Asia. Religions such as Buddhism and Islam had spread far beyond the countries where they originated, in northern India and the Arabian Peninsula, respectively. Asians and Africans possessed considerable knowledge about Europe, even if that knowledge (just as European knowledge of Africa, Asia and the Americas) was often vague or partial, and ideas about such places fantastical.

The Colonial World

The word 'discovery' correctly indicates the first European encounters with sites, people and things unknown to them, but the word is erroneous in suggesting that these were unknown to others. 'Discovery' and 'exploration' are terms that, despite the genuine scientific curiosity and accomplishments they connote, also mask the religious hostilities, racism, rapacity and violence of many early encounters. Furthermore, the words, used in a casual or politically inflected sense, wrongly centre the acquisition of knowledge and the charting of the world outside Europe on the actions of Europeans. The context for the 'discoveries' is far more complex than the simple sighting of new lands or finding of new plants or animals. The exploits of Vasco Da Gama, Columbus and others must thus be considered from a more critical and less ethnocentric and hagiographical perspective.

These voyages, and the fields of knowledge they expanded, nevertheless made an enormous contribution to the Scientific Revolution in the 1600s and the Enlightenment in the 1700s. By the eighteenth century, European cities boasted new botanical gardens, natural history collections and menageries of exotic creatures. Learned societies of scientists and amateurs avidly pursued botany, zoology, astronomy and other disciplines, including the nascent fields of ethnology and anthropology. Science, therefore, had been both a major instigator and a key beneficiary of European expeditions, the objectives of the scientists intertwining with the aims of other actors. As the Portuguese poet and seafarer Luís Vaz de Camões proudly put it in his 1572 epic of Portuguese exploration, *The Lusiads*, Portugal had given 'new worlds' to the world. Those 'new worlds' in West and East would forever exercise an irresistible pull on Europeans of diverse vocations.

Religion: Catholics and Protestants

Despite challenges to the doctrines of Christianity and the power of the church from the Renaissance through the Enlightenment, early modern Europe remained thoroughly invested in religion. The church was a major landowner, employer and provider of education and medical care, and considered itself the possessor of 'gospel truth' and guardian of morals. Until the early 1500s, the Catholic Church, under the papacy, held a monopoly over Christianity in Western Europe. In 1517, however, Martin Luther's proclamations signalled a fracturing of Christianity. Protestant Lutherans, Calvinists, Anglicans, Anabaptists and others in 'reformed' churches rejected the authority of the papacy and many Catholic doctrines and rites. The Catholic Reformation (or Counter-Reformation) in the mid-1500s provided a riposte with reaffirmation of the supremacy of the papacy, and traditional beliefs and devotions, alongside establishment of the Inquisition, charged with the judgement and punishment of heretics. The Counter-Reformation also saw the founding of new religious orders, notable among them, in 1540, the Society of Jesus (the Jesuits), with a mission to spread Catholic Christianity beyond Europe. The Jesuits became a major force in both America and Asia, proselytizing and occupying central functions in colonial administration; indeed, the order grew so strong that, in an effort to regain control, in the mid-1700s, the Spanish and Portuguese governments temporarily expelled the Jesuits from Spain and Portugal and their empires.

The pope declared conversion of heathen a sacred duty and sanctioned the work of missionaries and the persecution of heretics, and the Inquisition operated in colonial South America and Asia just as in Europe. The early Spanish, Portuguese and later French colonizers carried Catholic Christianity with them, the erection of a cross and celebration of mass among the first acts performed when they landed on foreign shores. Moved by the biblical injunction to spread the 'true faith' of Catholicism – a directive that also served as a pretext for land grabs – they evangelized native peoples, yet with varying degrees of success. In Latin America, missionaries attempted to convert Amerindians with compulsion by rounding them up into 'reductions', church-controlled settlements. They destroyed Inca, Aztec and other indigenous 'idols', replacing them with statues and paintings of saints housed in grandiose Christian churches often erected on the ruins of indigenous temples. However, old pre-Christian beliefs lived on, syncretically mixed in with Christianity.

The Spanish, sailing from Mexico to eastern Asia, took Catholicism to the Philippines. The Portuguese in the 1500s, via the Indian Ocean, took Catholicism to Goa in India, Ceylon and Japan, converting a goodly number of people, though most stayed true to ancestral Hinduism, Buddhism or Islam. The Spanish-born St Francis Xavier, a Jesuit, preached in Portuguese India, Borneo and the Maluku Islands of the East Indies, and was the first Christian missionary in Japan. Dying from illness in China in 1552, buried in Goa and canonized in 1622, he became a model for many later missionaries. Missionaries and converts killed in persecutions of Christians, as in Nagasaki, Japan, in 1597, won veneration as martyrs.

The Iberians and their Catholic faith became firmly rooted in South America, the Philippines and smaller enclaves elsewhere in Asia, and French Catholics in 'New France' (especially in what is now part of eastern Canada). Protestants meanwhile hoped to win their share of souls. Though the Dutch seemed less interested in evangelization than trade, British Protestants took their various denominations to North America in the 1600s and 1700s. The persecution of 'Dissidents' from the established Anglican Church presented a motive for the setting up of colonies by Puritans in Massachusetts, Quakers (the Society of Friends) in Pennsylvania, and Methodists in Georgia. The British sent Protestant missionaries to India in the 1600s (though indigenous Christian churches already existed there), and by the end of the 1700s, to Tahiti in the South Pacific. In the Caribbean, Catholics and Protestant groups vied for the souls of the few surviving indigenous people and the more numerous enslaved Africans, with Catholicism gaining the most converts in the Spanish and French islands, Protestantism widely represented in the British and Dutch ones. Missionaries similarly established congregations along the coast of Africa, whose supposedly 'primitive' people they considered direly in need of conversion and where Christians hoped to limit the spread of Islam.

Religion played a major role in legitimizing the conquest of early modern empires and in the profound cultural changes within indigenous societies that ensued. The Americas became largely Christianized by the 1700s and even much earlier in some places, as was the Philippines (except in the southern, largely Muslim, region). So were the Pacific islands by the late 1800s, by which time Christian missions spread around the globe, with China offering a promising new mission field. Christianity, whether Catholic or Protestant, provided a mandate for political takeover of territory, indoctrination of local peoples and attempts to dismantle indigenous cultural practices. Conversion led to the emergence of new Christian elites, and Christianity also took hold among some subaltern populations, such as 'untouchables' marginalized by Hindu practices. Europeans who ventured to foreign parts included numerous priests, pastors and members of religious orders. Institutions associated with the church such as schools, hospitals and charitable bodies became firmly established. However, some countries and communities sought to repulse Christianity by keeping missionaries out and through episodic persecution of clerics and converts. Religion remained a key aspect of colonialism, and a point of encounter and conflict, for centuries to come.

Commerce and colonialism

Science and religion motivated early modern expansion, and so too did commerce. An initial objective for Iberian navigators had been to find a maritime route to the Indies in order to access goods that had previously arrived via overland routes through Asia, then were shipped from the Middle East across the Mediterranean. With the Ottoman conquest of Constantinople, the capital of the Byzantine Empire, in 1453, routes from western Asia to Europe were endangered. For early modern Europeans, the Indies first and foremost meant spices – a portmanteau term that designated pepper, cinnamon, ginger, nutmeg and the leaves, bark and fruit of many other plants used for cooking, medicine and manufacturing. Pepper, quite literally, was worth more than gold by weight in the Renaissance, a precious commodity obtained from faraway places like India and the 'spice islands' of the East Indies (now in Indonesia). Many other exports from the East whetted European appetites: gemstones from Ceylon and continental South Asia, silks and porcelain from China, the tea quickly becoming a beverage of choice – though these long remained luxury goods enjoyed only by the happy few. The demand for such commodities is hard to overestimate, especially as they became more affordable, and the profits from their procurement and sale were massive, despite the perils of long ocean voyages.

The American colonies offered their treasures as well. Plantations set up by Europeans produced vast quantities of cane sugar; used to flavour tea and coffee, pastry and confectionery, sugar was already becoming an addiction in the early modern period. Native American foodstuffs such as potatoes, tomatoes, maize, chillies and cocoa were introduced into European diets (and taken to Asia), and tobacco from the 'New World' became another addiction. Indigo and rice provided further plantation crops in the Caribbean, the southern colonies of North America and the huge Portuguese colony of Brazil. Cotton developed growing markets with the beginnings of the industrial revolution in the mid-1700s, and America, India and later Egypt provided supplies. Of particular interest to Europeans in South America were precious metals. Intriguing rumours had circulated in Europe about a huge golden American city or golden king,

El Dorado; though the dream proved just that, Europeans found considerable deposits of gold, for instance, in Portuguese Brazil, and silver in the mines of Spanish Peru and today's Bolivia. Gold and silver held extraordinary value, turned into coinage, jewellery, tableware and decorative objects: then as now, they glittered as status symbols. Silver also crossed the Pacific on ships ploughing the 'galleon route' from Veracruz in Mexico to Manila in the Philippines, where it was traded for Asian exports: a global Spanish trade route extending from eastern Asia to the Americas across the Atlantic to Europe and on to Africa.

Most colonies provided something of monetary value for Europeans, and the search for or creation of marketable products represented a core imperative of the colonial project. The colonies of what is now eastern Canada, for instance, exported the furs of seals, beavers (and castoreum from beavers used for medicines and flavouring) and other animals much appreciated in cold European winters, Caribbean islands produced tasty rum as well as sugar, fishing fleets in the northern Atlantic caught the cod that fed slaves and became a staple foodstuff in Portugal, ivory from the tusks of elephants offered a treasure from Africa and Asia. Other decorative items, such as seashells and the feathers and eggs of exotic birds, beguiled consumers. Cotton textiles woven in India – 'madras' and 'calico' cloth Europeans named after Indian cities – found a ready market in Europe and served as trade goods in Africa. Sugar and tobacco, chocolate and tea, silk fabrics and imported china became ever more available and less costly because of expansion of trade and the orienting of production in the Americas and parts of Asia and Africa to export. This brought colonial goods into more and more European lives by the 1800s, a veritable consumer revolution dependent on the colonial world.

New transcontinental trading networks consequently arose, one of the most important and notorious the 'triangular trade' in which manufactured goods were shipped from Europe to Africa to buy slaves, who were transported to the Americas, the ships then filled with sugar and other tropical products for the journey home. Europeans also entered into extant and more localized commercial networks, competing with Asian merchants, for instance, in coastal trade around Indian ports and between Southeast Asia and eastern Asia. They and the companies for which they worked earned handsome profits, with earnings for the most successful invested into country estates and elegant townhouses, and used to underwrite lives of luxury. Profits from colonialism provided capital for the new factories that, in Britain, would revolutionize the economy in the late eighteenth century. Royal rulers and their exchequers pocketed substantial sums through taxation, commissions and the issuing of trading licences, though few profits trickled down to the 'common people'.

Much of the business between metropoles and colonies was in the hands of 'chartered companies' established by royal charter and given a monopoly over trade in designated, yet often extensive, regions. The most famous was the English (and later British) East India Company founded in London in 1600 – from the mid-1700s to the early 1800s, it accounted for roughly half of the world's long-distance trade. Down to the mid-1800s, the 'Honourable Company', as it was called, operated several hundred trading posts, some of limited duration and activity, from the Persian Gulf to the South

China Seas. The company enjoyed not only rights to trade but, remarkably, rights to acquire territory, make treaties with local rulers, levy taxes from the residents of lands it controlled and raise armies and fight wars. In this way, it amassed large territorial holdings on the Indian subcontinent through conquest or by cession of land negotiated with indigenous rulers (in return for payment or much desired weaponry and other commodities). Britain's early colonization of India was, in effect, subcontracted by the Crown to a private company of exceptional power, wealth and geographical reach. The profits made by some company employees, the 'nabobs' (the word taken from India; see Figure 2.1), amidst challenges of widespread corruption, led to scandals, parliamentary investigations and trials in London in the late 1700s, but the East India Company managed to maintain its primacy, even as other merchants entered the market. It was eventually brought down, in large part by insurrection in India, only in the mid-1800s. The governors of the three 'presidencies' of Bombay, Madras and Calcutta presided over

Figure 2.1 An official of the East India Company, perhaps William Fullerton (a surgeon and mayor of Calcutta), smoking a water-pipe, attended by servants. Dip Chand, *c.* 1760–64. Collection of the Victoria and Albert Museum, London. © Wikimedia Commons (public domain).

the administration of huge territories and multiple ventures. The East India Company provided employment for large numbers of 'writers' (clerks) and soldiers, and in 1806 even set up a school in Hertfordshire to train its employees. The company's headquarters in Leadenhall Street was one of London's most impressive buildings, and visitors could see a display of Asian *objets d'art*. In India and elsewhere, the company constructed imposing administration buildings, warehouses, port facilities and residences, and it commissioned paintings, furniture and textiles from local artisans. Among company employees were ruthless profiteers but also men who became serious scholars of Asian cultures, proficient linguists, prolific writers and avid collectors.

An energetic competitor with the English East India Company was the Dutch United East India Company, the Vereenigde Oost Indische Compagnie (VOC), chartered in 1602. It also set up 'factories' (as trading posts were named) around the Indian Ocean, but focused on the Spice Islands and other islands such as Java, Sumatra and Bali in what became the Netherlands East Indies. Controlled by a committee, the 'Gentlemen Seventeen', and with offices, warehouses and facilities in several cities of the Low Countries (today's Netherlands and Belgium), it was one of the largest companies of the day and the spearhead for the Netherlands' major colony. As with the British company, the VOC's activities extended to politics, diplomacy, building of infrastructure and scholarship. Other countries, not to be outdone by the British and Dutch, established their East India Companies – the Danish from 1616, the French in 1664, the Swedish in 1731– and charters went, as well, to West India Companies for trade in the Caribbean and the American continent. The model of chartered companies was later used for European expansion in sub-Saharan Africa.

Geopolitical rivalries

Commercial competition was part and parcel of geopolitical rivalries, as old and new powers strove for military advantage, profit, cultural influence and the glory of their monarchs. These jousts between Europeans remained integral in overseas expansion. Spain and Portugal, the pioneers, were pitted against each other for control of the 'unknown' world until, with the Treaty of Tordesillas of 1494, the pope – resolving the conflict as mediator between Catholic sovereigns – divided unclaimed lands at a meridian of longitude in the Atlantic Ocean, those territories to the west going to Spain, those to the east to Portugal. The fact that the meridian passed through the eastern part of the South American continent meant Portuguese rule over what became Brazil, while most of the rest of South and Central America came under the Spanish, an early example of the arbitrariness of colonial boundaries (Map 2.1). By the early 1500s, however, the French king François I remarked that the sun shone on him just as on other sovereigns, and argued that nothing in the biblical Adam's will divided the world between the two Iberian countries. The British, Dutch and Danish certainly agreed.

The Portuguese amassed a collection of outposts in the 1500s along the western and eastern coasts of Africa (Angola and Mozambique, respectively, as well as several island

Map 2.1 Colonial Latin America. © Adapted from map by cartographer Peter Palm.

groups), on the Persian Gulf, in India and Ceylon (though they controlled only a very small part of India and not all of Ceylon), Malacca (now Melaka) in the Malay Straits and Macau on the South China Sea. They erected fortifications, built churches, imposed law codes, converted a substantial number of indigenous people and became clients for local products and vendors of European goods. However, aspiring to challenge Portugal in Asia was a rising European power, the United Provinces – the country most familiar as Holland from the name of one of the provinces. The VOC acquired territory not taken by the Portuguese, such as Batavia (now Jakarta) on Java, and its armies progressively wrested away colonies from the Portuguese – in 1640, the Dutch took the Portuguese outpost in Ceylon, and the following year they seized Malacca. In 1652, the Dutch established a settler colony at the Cape of Good Hope, on the southern tip of Africa, a homeland for migrants who eventually became known as Afrikaners (and who still speak Afrikaans, a language derived from Dutch). Cape Town provided a vital node on international trading networks for ships heading from Europe to the Indian Ocean.

The English king, rivalling the Dutch, had sent an initial trading mission to the court of the Mughal Emperor in India in 1612; the East India Company followed by setting up 'factories' at Surat in 1619, Madras (Chennai) in 1639, Bombay (Mumbai) in 1668 and Calcutta (Kolkata) in 1690, and then established outposts further east, such as Canton (Guangzhou) in China in 1713. (Bombay, an old Portuguese outpost, had come into the possession of the British Crown as part of the dowry of the Portuguese princess Catherine of Braganza when she married King Charles II – a dynastic way that colonies could pass from one monarch to another.) 'Company rule' meant that European states were turning themselves into military and political powers in Asia as well as increasingly important trading partners and economic actors, ever seeking to increase holdings at the expense of European rivals as well as indigenous rulers. Thus, the British, through the East India Company, in the 1700s conquered Dutch holdings in Ceylon and, at the end of the century, the Cape Colony and Malacca. That Malay city, therefore, had fallen successively under the control of the Portuguese, the Dutch and the British, as one colonizer displaced another.

On a more limited scale, other countries acquired territories. In the early 1600s, the Danish re-established a medieval claim over Greenland, yet it did not implement effective control until a century later, and the Danish monarch also ruled over Iceland and the Faroe Islands in the North Atlantic. The Danish East India Company and the Danish West India-Guinea Company propelled that small country's colonialism further afield. The Danes held outposts on the west African coast and at Tranquebar (Tharangambadi) and Serampore in India before selling these territories to the British in 1846. In the West Indian islands, the Danes took over St Thomas in 1672 and St John in 1718, and bought St Croix from the French in 1733; the islands remained under Danish administration until sold to the United States in 1917. Sweden too acquired a West Indian island, Saint-Barthélemy, ceded by the French in 1784 in return for trading rights in Gothenburg (though it was returned to the French in 1877).

The West Indian and Atlantic islands – both those uninhabited and ones with indigenous populations dramatically reduced in number and marginalized after European occupation – were divided among the colonizers (Map 2.2). The North Atlantic island of Bermuda, settled from 1609, is Britain's oldest colony; Britain claimed Barbados in 1625, after it was abandoned by the Portuguese, and conquered Jamaica from the Spanish in 1655, eventually adding many other islands. The British portfolio extended

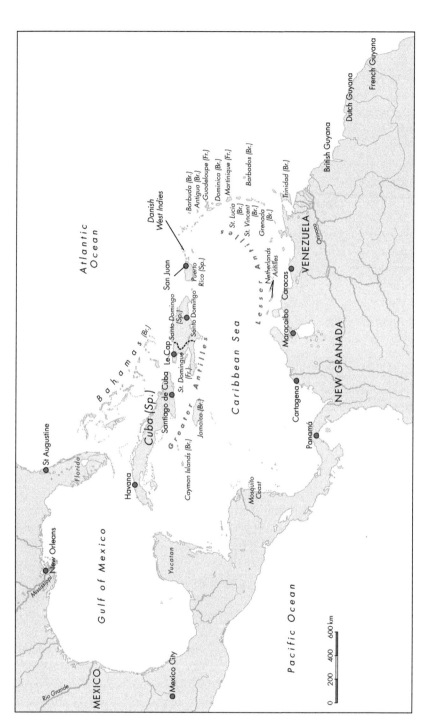

Map 2.2 The Caribbean in the 1780s. © Adapted from map by cartographer Peter Palm.

to the South Atlantic with St Helena (1659), Tristan da Cunha (1777) and Ascension (1815), minuscule islands 'discovered' by the Portuguese, and the Falkland and South Georgia Islands. The Spanish claimed Cuba, the largest island in the Caribbean, as well as what is now the Dominican Republic (on the eastern side of the island of Hispaniola) and Puerto Rico. The French acquired the western part of Hispaniola – Saint-Domingue (now Haiti) became its most valuable possession by the 1700s – as well as Martinique, Guadeloupe and a handful of other islands. For the Dutch, there was Aruba, Bonaire and Curaçao in the southern Caribbean, and Saba, Sint-Eustatius and Sint-Maarten in the east. (The Europeans divided up part of the Caribbean coast of South America with British, French and Dutch Guyana side by side.) With the French and Dutch both coveting the tiny island of St Martin, the two countries agreed, in gentlemanly fashion, to share it, reputedly by having two soldiers stand back to back and then march to the other side of the island to determine the demarcation line between the two territories (which remain, respectively, under French and Dutch administration).

Europeans also invaded, divided and occupied the American continents. In North America, the British consolidated holdings in what is now Canada. The British established thirteen colonies further south, from Massachusetts, founded in the 1620s, to Georgia, settled in the 1730s. The Spanish claimed territories from California on the Pacific through lands along the Mexican border to Florida on the Atlantic. The French ruled 'New France', an enormous swathe of territory reaching from Quebec in the north down the Mississippi River to New Orleans on the Gulf of Mexico. The Russians had colonized Alaska. In Latin America the Spanish had founded four viceroyalties, with New Spain (established in 1535) and the Viceroyalty of Peru (in 1543) the largest and most important. The Portuguese lay claim on Brazil, a colony that covered almost half of South America. The western hemisphere, in short, was at least on paper completely brought under European rule in various stages from the 1500s to the 1700s.

The extent of actual European control of colonies, and the boundaries between them, both sometimes fairly nominal, frequently altered as the powers fought wars and won territorial spoils. Mauritius, in the Indian Ocean, for example, was in succession a Portuguese, Dutch, French and British colony. Strategies for acquiring colonies were multiple: claiming uninhabited lands, overpowering an indigenous population, wresting a colony from a European rival, occupying a colony abandoned by earlier claimants, buying a possession from its previous 'owner', receiving territory ceded by a local ruler, exchanging colonies, even obtaining one through royal marriage. A famous exchange concerned the island of New Amsterdam on the eastern seaboard of North America. As the British and Dutch battled each other in Europe and overseas, the British acquired the island and renamed it New York. In return, the peace settlement in 1667 gave the Dutch the island of Run, in the Banda archipelago of the East Indies; with nutmeg and mace from the spice island, the Dutch considered that they got the better part of the deal.

One of the most sustained European military conflicts occurred late in the early modern period, with North America a distant theatre in the European Seven Years' War of 1756–63. The 'French and Indian War', as termed in US historiography, ranged the British and the French (and their Amerindian allies) against each other. The British came out ahead in the struggle, consolidating control over what is now eastern Canada by taking Quebec (after earlier taking Acadia). While fighting in North America, the British and French were similarly battling against each other in South Asia (on which more presently).

In the background of these moves were state-building, the unification and expansion of dynastic and national territory, alongside attempts to administer and tax lands more effectively through a modernized bureaucracy. The economic theory of mercantilism, or state capitalism, as it is also called, emphasized the role of international trade in the creation of national wealth, the need for intense competition and identification of trade opportunities to capture commerce from competitors, the role of the state as the manager of business either directly or through chartered companies, and the protection of trade monopolies over colonies. Another vital ideology in domestic and international affairs was absolutism, that is, government by an absolute monarch with a God-given right to rule, and who served as military commander, head of the administration and judiciary, commissioner of public works, and patron of the arts. Though royal absolutism was defied by parliamentarianism in Britain (and challenged by familial rivalries, warfare and conquest, coups d'état, rebellion or assassination elsewhere, and occasionally in Britain), in many places the king or queen reigned as supreme lord. Colonies constituted part of the sovereign's domain, and the greater the dominions over which a monarch reigned, the greater the glory. Thus, in the late 1500s, Philip II, who was king of Spain and Portugal, and ruled over southern Italy and the Low Countries, was also the monarch of Spain's American empire (which then included a quarter of North America) and African outposts. The British monarchs were sovereigns over British America, the British islands of the West Indies and the East India Company's Asian territories already at the start of the 1600s, and Louis XIV king over French colonies scattered from New France to Pondichéry in India in the late seventeenth century. Dynastic rule, state religion, thriving business and control of territory at home and abroad factored into the equation of power and status. (Given distance from metropolitan capitals, the difficulties of communication and uncertain policies, however, viceroys, governors and other officials wielded more day-to-day power than the sovereign and ministers.) Overseas possessions added lustre to crowns, and revenues they produced stockpiled royal treasuries. For the monarch's European subjects, being Spanish, Portuguese, English (or British after the Act of Union of 1707), French, Dutch or Danish meant belonging to a realm of political, trade and cultural influence that extended far beyond European homelands.

By the 1700s, Europeans were firmly ensconced around the globe – globalism at an early stage, in large part the result of colonialism. Relatively small cohorts of planters, traders and officials exploited territories in Asia and Africa, with growing settler populations in the Americas. Europeans had not yet penetrated Africa far from the coastline, but the Americas and parts of Asia were no longer the unknown territories of two centuries earlier. What remained almost completely unknown to Europeans down to the mid-1700s was the southern Pacific Ocean. Since Antiquity, Europeans had theorized and fantasized about a great *terra incognita* whose existence was supposedly necessary to balance the northern continents. However, not until the 1500s did Portuguese seafarers perhaps sail past the western shores of Australia; the Dutch undoubtedly did so in the 1600s. Neither group claimed land or set up colonies in what looked unpromising terrain, and map-makers could not even draw in the contours of the continent until very late in the following century. The Pacific islands remained largely unfamiliar, though Spanish and Portuguese captains had sighted and given names to some. Only gradually from the 1760s, with the voyages of such men as Captain James Cook, did the map of the island Pacific begin to take shape, and did islands like Tahiti begin to work such seductive magic on the European imaginary. Blank spots remained in the European cartography of the world, but by the end of the eighteenth century the age of maritime 'discoveries' begun at the end of the fifteenth century was largely complete. Europeans had laid effective or nominal claim to much land in the wider world. For a century and a half more, established powers jousted for yet unclaimed territory, stretched occupation from coasts to hinterlands, strove to preserve their colonies, captured possessions from rivals – and competed with new entrants in colonial scrambles.

Indigenous peoples and the Europeans in the early modern period

Few of the places where Europeans established themselves overseas, except for some islands in the Atlantic and Indian Ocean, had no indigenous populations. Parts of the American continents were sparsely populated to be sure, but Native Americans, or Amerindians, as well as Inuit in the north, had lived there for millennia. These peoples had developed a variety of cultures and political institutions, including the grand empires of the Mayans and Aztecs in Central America and the Incas in South America. Asia and Africa were home to countless different indigenous cultures and ethnic groups (1,300 in what is now Indonesia), some regions densely populated and others, such as the Sahara desert, the territory of rare nomadic groups. Asia contained the largest concentration of people on the globe.

In the early modern period, Europeans had already developed deeply ingrained stereotypes about indigenous populations, views dating back to the medieval Crusades, the voyages of Marco Polo in the late thirteenth century and other early encounters, or simply the product of fancy, fear or fantasy. These were paralleled, *mutatis mutandis*, by emerging Amerindian, African and Asian stereotypes about Europeans, who were themselves 'discovered' by indigenous peoples as they moved around the world. On first meeting, each no doubt looked strange to the other – conquistadors dressed in heavy metal armour, priests vested in cassocks and merchants sporting doubloons, embroidered waistcoats, wool coats and hats face to face with peoples in tropical countries scantily clad in sarongs, Indian saris and 'pyjamas' (the word and clothing style originated in India), or other unfamiliar apparel. Even body types – stature, hirsuteness, colour of hair, skin and eyes – created surprise and uncertainty about the origins, or even humanity, of strange creatures from afar. Initial encounters inspired curiosity, bafflement and suspicion, yet impressions dangerously hardened into diehard certainties – for Europeans, the idea that the peoples of America, Africa and Oceania were 'primitive', and that the Asians, though perhaps heirs to the glorious civilizations to which their architectural monuments testified, had fallen into 'decadence'.

Despite Europeans' politics of absolutism and practice of libertinage, they held that non-Western countries suffered under cruel, unbridled despots, and that foreigners were lascivious and addicted to vice. Not all stereotypes were negative – a genuine admiration for the arts and crafts of Asia translated into yearning for such luxuries of the East as silks, ceramics and lacquerware; indeed the aesthetic quality of these products, as much as their market value, captivated Europeans. For some European commentators, distant places might even appear superior to their own societies. As travellers told tales of Tahiti in the late 1700s, Jean-Jacques Rousseau mused that what he called the *bons sauvages* ('good savages') of the South Seas seemed to live happily without the shackles of Western civilization, kings and churches, industry and puritanical morals. Images of luxuriant scenery, nubile women and statuesque men – and rumours of their easy morals – beckoned. So, too, did depictions of grand maharajas' palaces and Levantine casbahs, the snow-capped Himalayas and the oases of the Sahara.

The number of Europeans in the wider world, especially in Africa and Asia, long remained very small, initially only dozens of sailors on a ship moored in a foreign port, then a few traders or missionaries. They constituted fragile bands, weakened by long voyages, disoriented by new environments, fearful of attack, beseeching local people for supplies of food and water, and trying to barter for goods. In the Americas, Europeans moved quickly to assert dominance, aided by superior firepower, scattered populations (particularly in North America), disaggregation of local societies and rivalries among local leaders. Some of them entered into alliances with the foreigners. Thus a coalition defeated rulers such as the Aztec emperor Montezuma in 1520. In the Caribbean, dominance often came through the massacre of native peoples.

The first encounters in Asia were generally asymmetrically balanced in favour of indigenous people and powerful local dynasties. In the 1500s and for a considerable time afterwards, Europeans remained junior partners in developing relationships. Commercial advantages lay with the sellers of Asian wares so much in demand among Europeans. With large populations, absolutist dynasties, strong armies and well-organized bureaucracies, as well as control of landscapes and waterways unknown to Europeans, rulers could hold foreigners at bay and deftly bargain with them. They adroitly offered trading privileges, concessions of territory and permission for evangelization in return for trade goods and weaponry, and especially support against rivals or rebels. Furthermore, Asian monarchs could play off one European contingent against another.

Siam (Thailand) in the late 1600s provides one example. Ayutthaya, capital of King Narai, was a grand city of canals, palaces and Buddhist temples. A major commercial and diplomatic crossroad, it sent and received trade ships throughout Southeast Asia, China and Japan. The king allowed the first Europeans to arrive, the Portuguese in the 1500s, to trade and set up missions. When they became overbearing, Narai welcomed the Dutch as a counter-force, then the British and the French. King Narai – whose senior counsellor, a Greek named Constantine Phaulkon, was one of the itinerant Europeans who found positions in indigenous courts – sent an ambassadorial delegation to the court of King Louis XIV. The French monarch in return dispatched an embassy to Ayutthaya. The Siamese thus treated on a par with the Europeans, and Narai wrote to Louis XIV with self-assurance as a fellow sovereign of power and majesty. The different Europeans continued to vie for influence in Ayutthaya, and used it as a way-station to other countries. Domestic opposition to the outward-looking Siamese policy nevertheless led to a palace revolt, the execution of Phaulkon and the end of the ailing Narai's reign.

Other countries set limits on European incursions. The Chinese Empire for long remained closed, as the Chinese saw little advantage to international trade or expansion beyond the neighbouring 'tributary states' which it kept in a vassal relationship. The Chinese regarded Europeans as inferior and uncivilized. Eager as Westerners were to gain entrée to China, regarded as a treasure-trove of precious goods, the Chinese allowed trade only in very few ports, notably Macau (over which the Portuguese acquired a permanent lease in 1557) and Canton. The authorities entrusted commerce with foreigners, a depreciated occupation in the eyes of Confucian mandarins, to a *cohong*, a set of merchants who bargained to Chinese advantage. The foreigners searched desperately for a sales item that would spark interest among the Chinese; by the nineteenth century, they settled on opium. Japan came to show even greater resistance to European incursions. The Portuguese had traded and evangelized after they first landed in Japan in 1542, but the Tokugawa shoguns who came to power in the early 1600s and unified the archipelago closed Japan to foreign trade and cultural influence. Until the mid-1800s, they allowed only the Dutch among the Europeans to trade, and just from the minuscule island of Deshima – 75 x 120 metres in size – in the harbour of Nagasaki. The shoguns' officials determined the terms of trade and any other interactions, with the Dutch allowed off the island only on rare occasions. Deshima nevertheless provided a small window for intercultural exchange: the genesis of European fascination for Japan and its culture, and Japanese curiosity about Europe and what they referred to as 'Dutch knowledge'. Not until the 1850s, and the foreigners' resorting to 'gunboat diplomacy', did Japan open itself to wider exchange with the West.

Some groups outside Europe nevertheless welcomed foreigners bringing new commodities and ideas, purchasing their products, offering military alliances and armaments, even serving in their armies. Their rulers nevertheless could rebuff foreign influence; the hope of French priests for conversion of King Narai came to nought, and at various times Japan and Vietnam drove out Christian missionaries. Indigenous states, religions and cultures continued to flourish, even more so away from the trading ports where Europeans congregated. Coastal areas provided a meeting place of the local and global, and lives and cultures intermingled. Sexual relations between men (generally Europeans) and locals (usually women) – ranging from rare marriages to more frequent concubinage and sometimes rape – led to an increasing number of mixed-race children. In Asia in the 1600s and 1700s, many Europeans learned local languages, occasionally adopted 'native' dress and customs, and enjoyed local cuisines. The East India Companies found limited fraternization necessary and beneficial, yet later colonial officials frowned upon those who pursued too intimate contacts or 'went native'. Clashes, however, were common, especially apparent in the New World. Many Amerindians died from warfare or the more destructive imported pathogens and diseases. Indigenous empires and kingdoms crumbled, though societies such as those of isolated Amazonians and the North American 'tribes' fell apart less rapidly than did the states of South America.

Throughout the colonial world, violence was a constant, just as in Europe in this period, whether warfare, criminal acts, torture, corporal and capital punishment, or the use of fists or arms to settle personal disputes or to abuse enemies, rivals or marginalized people. In contemporary perspectives, victorious warfare won praise for soldiers, with the killing of defeated enemies their just due. Warfare over territory, people and resources punctuated life, fought by professional, mercenary and conscripted soldiers, with much looting, pillage and rape. The arrival of Europeans overseas had added a new dimension as conflicts frequently took on the character of Westerners versus 'natives', Christians versus practitioners of other faiths, whites versus non-whites, powerful European guns against swords and spears (though increasingly against guns imported from Europe as well). Indigenous people bore the brunt of warfare, the colonizers' exactions and imported diseases, with their death rates much higher than those of the Europeans. The colonizers, certain of their civilizational superiority over 'savages', seldom held back in slaughtering indigenous opponents. Since fighting took place entirely on local soil, destruction of housing, crops and natural resources, often intentionally carried out by European soldiers, was great and its effects long-lasting. The number of victims of warfare is often highly disputed to this day. Historians refer to 'extermination' or 'genocide', particularly when trying to grasp the destruction in the early modern Americas. The violence committed by colonizers and their indigenous allies stands out as an atrocious aspect of the colonial record.

Strategic alliances between indigenous rulers and Europeans meant, however, that battle lines were seldom neatly or permanently drawn, and few were innocent of perpetrating some violence. Colonizers' defeat of indigenous forces, and continuing brutal efforts to 'pacify' opposition, triggered further resistance. Intense warfare alternated with negotiation, peace, collusion or accommodation. Diplomacy and armed force, concluded agreements and rejected initiatives, public shows of amity and backroom plotting, cultural interest and more avaricious motives characterized manoeuvres in extremely complex relationships between Europeans and local people – relationships, however, where the use or threat of violence was never absent.

Slavery: The trade in humans

One particularly infamous feature of early modern European empires was slavery and slave trading, now recognized as a 'crime against humanity' by some countries. This is a complex and wide-ranging theme that can only be discussed in brief here. Slavery was not new in the West, as it had existed in Europe in classical times. The practice was not limited to European enslavement of other peoples, as slavery was widely practised within parts of Africa, the Arab world, Asia and Latin America before and after the arrival of Europeans, and other varieties of bonded labour existed around the world (including the serfdom in Russia that lasted until the 1860s). Africans were not the only people to be enslaved by Europeans; the Dutch, for instance, kept slaves in the East Indies. However, the phenomenon of slavery that burgeoned from the 1600s to the early 1800s was different for several reasons. One was its sheer magnitude. Although it can never be known exactly how many Africans were enslaved to Europeans, estimates range from seven to twenty million, with relative consensus on twelve million. Moreover, the transcontinental nature of the slave trade was dramatic, for most slaves were transported across the Atlantic. There they became the overwhelming majority of the population in many Caribbean islands and a very large proportion of the population in Brazil and in the southern colonies of British North America. The crucial importance of enslaved Africans as a source of labour in the Caribbean and the rest of the Americas (and to a lesser extent in the Indian Ocean) was another defining aspect.

The first European incursions into the Americas led to a decline in indigenous populations, as mentioned, because of warfare, diseases brought by Europeans to which local people possessed no natural immunity, and the poor conditions of surviving Amerindians forced to work for colonizers. The need for labour was primordial, especially as Europeans took possession of land, developed plantations, exploited mineral resources and built cities. Many considered fellow Europeans physically unfit to work in tropical climates, and European migrants in any case were not numerous enough to supply the large demand. Africa provided an alternative source. Europeans had speculated about whether Africans had the same ancestry as Europeans. Most were not Christian, which removed them, in early modern views, from the regard reserved for believers in the 'true' faith (or even the faithful of other major religions). Furthermore, they were characterized as 'primitive', bereft of what Europeans considered civilization, and stalled at an early stage of human development. Increasingly, Europeans saw 'backwardness' in terms of race, genetically and physiologically determined. Religious and secular officials agreed that slavery as an institution found justification in the Bible through the opportunities it presented to spread Christianity to 'heathen' – and by the desperate need for colonial labour. Slave traders, an influential group of businessmen linked to the thriving intercontinental commerce, saw enormous profits to be made from transporting slaves. African rulers and other indigenous elites often proved willing to sell fellow Africans to the Europeans – those defeated in warfare, people from the interior captured and brought to the coast, those from different and rival ethnic groups. In many cases, European slavers simply raided African communities and kidnapped those they would sell. Slavery, thus, was a business legitimized by personal ambition, cultural and religious views with a racial cast, and quest for profit.

An enormous amount has been written on slavery and the horrors of captivity, the 'Middle Passage' of slaves across the Atlantic in fetid and overcrowded ships in which as many as a third of the captives died, the ignominious sale of men and women on wharves, the miserable conditions in which they worked on plantations and in mines, the physical and sexual abuse and corporal punishments they suffered, the poverty to which they were condemned, the perpetuation of slavery from one generation to the next. Only a small number managed to gain freedom through manumission, that is, paying for emancipation or, rarely, being granted liberty by their masters for services rendered. Others, known as 'maroons', escaped into the jungles of South America and the Caribbean islands or, in North America, fled from southern plantation to slave-free northern cities, yet facing severe penalties if apprehended. Not all Black men and women in the Americas and Indian Ocean islands were slaves. In fact, even in the 1700s, there were Black merchants, artisans and free settlers who earned relatively good incomes and gained respect from neighbours, though not political rights. Most of the Africans in the diaspora, however, were enslaved, with the indignities and hardships such a condition imposed.

The success of sugar plantations in the Caribbean and Brazil, cotton plantations in the south of the United States and other productive activities throughout the Americas depended on slavery, as did household economies reliant on servants. It is no exaggeration to say that Europeans in parts of the western hemisphere earned much of their fortune on the backs of enslaved Africans. They, and those in Europe who similarly profited from slavery and slave trading, were stoutly opposed to giving up the benefits. But not all Europeans approved of slavery and, particularly from the mid-1700s, opposition to slavery mounted, especially in humanitarian and religious circles; in Britain, in particular, key members of the Society of Friends, Anglicans such as Bishop William Wilberforce and active anti-slavery societies raised loud voices in condemnation of the inhumanity. Enlightenment philosophers who championed equality and political rights began to question the subjection of humans to slavery, though they did not unanimously call for its cessation. Defenders of slavery countered that slavery was necessary for the prosperity of the colonies. Slaves themselves revolted with regularity and surprising force; Europeans in general wielded the power to repress insurrection with ruthless measures.

Denmark was the first European country to ban the slave trade, in 1792. The radical post-revolutionary National Convention in France abolished slavery in the French colonies two years later, though it was reinstated by Napoleon in 1802. Britain banned the slave trade in 1807, and the United States followed suit the following year. However, slave trading continued illegally despite patrols by the powerful British Navy off the African coast and its seizure of slave-carrying ships – indeed fully a quarter of those enslaved in Africa were transported across the Atlantic after 1807. Formal abolition of the trade did not mean the abolition of the institution or the emancipation of the enslaved. Abolition of slavery occurred in the British Empire in 1834, definitively ended in France in 1848, and continued until the 1880s in the Spanish and Portuguese Empires (including the former colony of Brazil). When freed, slaves were left without land, money or other wherewithal, while slave-owners frequently received compensation. Provisions for emancipation often required ex-slaves to work as 'apprentices' for former owners, for meagre wages, over as long a period as ten years. Slave-like conditions of labour and daily life persisted, with impoverishment the lot of most. Opportunities for education and social advancement remained slight. Racism, discrimination and violence against Black people continued, making the intellectual and social success that some achieved all the more remarkable. The legacies of slavery proved long-lived, and the record and heritage of slavery today animate political debate in countries where descendants of the enslaved live and in countries from which they were taken.

Colonial metamorphosis

The last decades of the eighteenth century and the first years of the nineteenth redrew the colonial map of the world. British colonists in thirteen colonies of North America railed at 'taxation without representation' – they lacked representation in the British parliament but paid increasing taxes for such items as tea and the stamps required for official documents – and at the arbitrariness of vice-regal rule. The European population of these thirteen colonies in British America was now mostly locally born, and more confident, prosperous and assertive in claims to 'inalienable rights' and self-government. Enlightenment ideas spread with cosmopolitan figures such as Benjamin Franklin and Thomas Jefferson, and the rights to 'life, liberty and the pursuit of happiness' proclaimed in a Declaration of Independence signed in 1776. The proclamation represented a call to war against the British, even if a fifth of the people of European heritage in what became the United States remained loyal to the British (many seeking refuge in Canada or other British colonies). It took the rebels seven years of fighting to secure London's recognition of independence, their military campaigns buttressed by aid from the French – motivated by geopolitical rivalry with the British rather than deep-seated empathy with the Americans. Another military clash between the United States and Britain followed in the War of 1812, but by that time the United States had firmly established itself as an independent country. The United States was also laying the groundwork for its own colonial expansion. In the Monroe Doctrine of 1823, Washington demanded that Europeans not interfere with affairs in the Americas, an affirmation of the USA's self-appointed hegemony. Furthermore, policymakers proclaimed a 'manifest destiny' said to give Americans a right to expand from the original colonies along the Atlantic across the continent to the Pacific, expelling Native Americans or confining them to reservations as they pushed into the 'Far West', and taking territory still claimed by the British and Spanish.

The ideas of revolution and emancipation circulated in other European colonies as well as North America. Leaders of the French Revolution that began in 1789 did not renounce colonialism. Indeed they held on tightly to France's overseas outposts, while allowing the election of colonial delegates to the Paris parliament. Noteworthy among them was Jean-Baptiste Belley, a Black man from Saint-Domingue, France's largest Caribbean colony. Yet a large slave revolt erupted in Saint-Domingue in 1791, and slaves proclaimed their own emancipation. Despite French military and political opposition, the Black population of the island finally achieved the independence of Haiti, as Saint-Domingue was renamed, in 1804. François-Dominique Toussaint Louverture gained fame as leader of the Haitian revolution; though at certain moments he had allied with them, the French ultimately arrested and deported Toussaint Louverture to France, where he died in detention. Elsewhere in the Caribbean, slave revolts similarly broke out, but

Europeans largely managed to restore control. In the French island of Guadeloupe, Louis Delgrès and followers resisting the re-imposition of slavery blew up their gunpowder stores, committing suicide, rather than surrender – Toussaint and Delgrès count among those honoured by emancipationists and nationalists, and worldwide descendants of Africans, for their struggle and martyrdom.

Great changes in colonialism took place in many parts of the world at the time of the French revolutionary and Napoleonic Wars that raged from the 1790s until 1815 – wars that might well be considered a 'world war', that is, a global conflict that saw land and sea battles in the Caribbean, Indian Ocean, Africa, Asia and Europe. The French revolutionaries proclaimed the universality of their principles, and tried to export their ideologies and institutions around Europe, prompting reactions against French intervention, invasion and overlordship. Napoleon's armies succeeded for a time in conquering much of the European continent, turned back by the Russian army and the Russian winter. This 'colonization' of the continent by the French saw the placing of Napoleon's family members and generals on the thrones of occupied states such as Spain and Holland, forced adoption of French law codes, collection of taxes for French coffers and the ravaging of resources and populations by Napoleon's troops. Napoleon's megalomaniac vision extended past Europe. In 1799, as an ambitious young general in the revolutionary armies, he had invaded Egypt with hopes of using it as a base to dislodge the British from India, though the British soon ousted the French from the land of the pharaohs.

India had been a terrain for British and French imperial manoeuvres for many decades, with especially intense fighting between them on the subcontinent in the 1750s and 1760s. Another bout of warfare erupted in the 1790s, with the British facing off the ruler of Mysore, Tipu Sultan, who was backed by the French. The British proved victorious at the battle of Seringapatam in 1799, with Tipu killed, putting paid to French hopes for carving out a large empire on the Indian subcontinent or ejecting the British. France was left with only five small enclaves – the *comptoirs* (trading posts) of Pondichéry, Mahé, Karikal, Yanaon and Chandernagor – scattered along the coasts, while the British entrenched themselves even deeper in their expanding territories. By the time Napoleon met his Waterloo and was sent off to exile on St Helena, the French overseas empire had been greatly reduced: Napoleon had sold France's vast territories in continental North America to the United States for fifteen million dollars in the 'Louisiana Purchase' of 1803, Britain had taken some of France's Caribbean islands as well as the Seychelles islands and the Ile de France (today's Mauritius) in the Indian Ocean, and Haiti had gained independence. France was left with only the tiny islands of Saint-Pierre and Miquelon off the coast of Newfoundland, Martinique and Guadeloupe and several smaller islands in the West Indies, French Guiana in South America, trading posts on the west African coast, La Réunion in the Indian Ocean and the Indian enclaves.

The revolutionary French invasion of the United Provinces in the 1790s had meant nominal French rule over the Dutch colonies. Such an intolerable situation provided the opportunity for the British in the 1790s to take over the thriving Dutch Cape Colony in South Africa, to oust the Dutch from strategically and commercially valuable Ceylon and to move into the Dutch East Indies. The occupations were meant to be temporary;

the British eventually withdrew from the East Indies, but remained in the Cape Colony and Ceylon. The Dutch thus retained their East Indies colonial empire. The British soon gained a prize in Southeast Asia, in 1819, with Singapore, a small island destined to become an invaluable base in the 'East'.

The British had already begun looking towards eastern Asia when, in 1786, they acquired the island of Penang, off the western coast of today's Malaysia, ceded by a sultan in return for military aid. Two years later, they found a much larger outpost when they occupied what became New South Wales and then took over the island of Tasmania, the beginnings of expansion over the entire continent of Australia and further into the South Pacific. In 1788, the British were particularly interested in establishing a penal colony far from home, the 'transport' of prisoners promoted as a way to rid the country of malefactors and, in principle, redeem criminals through yeoman labour and populate a settler society. The British would discover a wealth of agricultural and mineral resources in Australia, to the profit of British settlers and largely to the detriment of Indigenous Australians. The takeover of the Australian continent, from 1788 to the 1820s, compensated for the loss of America and reinforced developing British involvement in what is now called the 'Asia-Pacific'.

At the end of the Napoleonic Wars, Britain had significantly strengthened its colonial position. The East India Company controlled an ever larger part of India, as well as Ceylon, Penang and soon Singapore in Asia, the former French colonies of Mauritius and the Seychelles in the Indian Ocean, the nascent colonies in Australia and Norfolk Island in the South Pacific, the Cape Colony in southern Africa, Canada, a large collection of islands in the West Indies, and outposts in Central and South America, as well as in Africa. France, as mentioned, had a residue of outposts stretching from the Atlantic to the Indian Ocean. The Dutch had kept their place in Southeast Asia, and Spain held on to the Philippines. However, Spain's South American colonies were in turmoil. Ideas of independence had spread among the American-born Spanish elite (*criollos*), and the wartime occupation of Madrid by French troops spurred a call to action, with armed conflict between colonial republicans and royalists in 1807 and full-blown nationalist wars in the following years. By the 1820s, most of Spain's American colonies were on the road to independence or had already gained it. Portugal, for its part, had kept Brazil for the moment, as well as its African and Asian territories. In one of the more curious repercussions of the Napoleonic Wars, with the French invasion of Portugal in 1807, the Portuguese royal family and court decamped to Rio de Janeiro; until their return to Lisbon in 1821, Portugal and its empire was ruled from the South American colony. (The following year, Brazil gained independence – with a son of the Portuguese king as its new emperor). In the first decade of the nineteenth century, the old colonial powers – an endangered Spain and Portugal, a triumphant Britain, the resilient Netherlands and a weakened France – thus remained the major European actors in the Americas, Africa and the Asia-Pacific, even with a partially redrawn colonial map.

International commerce resumed after the wars and grew stronger, stimulated by the industrial revolution in Britain and the principle of free trade articulated by Adam Smith in his 'gospel' of capitalism, *The Wealth of Nations*, published in 1776. The century after

The Colonial World

1815 would see new justifications for colonialism, the further expansion of the British Empire, the rebuilding of a French overseas empire, a shift of the Iberian empires from the Americas to Africa, and the entry of new European powers into 'scrambles' for colonies. Slaves achieved freedom, but they and other colonial 'subjects' would largely be denied citizenship and political rights, and remained victims of economic exploitation and racism. European empires grew markedly through the 1800s, but many of the ideas and institutions of colonial rule were an enduring inheritance of early modern colonialism of the old regime: stereotypes about non-Western peoples and cultures, strategies of rule and 'pacification', trade routes and international commerce based on exchange of colonial primary products for European manufactured goods, thriving European settlements overseas and geopolitical rivalries among imperial powers.

CHAPTER 3
THE MAKING OF OVERSEAS EMPIRES IN THE LONG NINETEENTH CENTURY, 1815–1914

By the late 1700s, the American continents and the islands of the Caribbean had been effectively colonized by Europeans, or at least brought under nominal European rule, for several centuries, but tumultuous political changes in the last, 'revolutionary' decades of the 1700s and early 1800s brought major changes. Thirteen colonies claimed by Britain in North America declared independence as the United States in 1776, and France lost almost all of its North American Empire by 1815. Most of Spain's colonies in Latin America and Portugal's huge colony of Brazil gained independence by the early 1820s. There remained Danish-controlled Greenland, the extensive British settler colonies in North America that became Canada, several European colonies in Central and South America (such as the British, French and Dutch Guyanas), and the Spanish, British, French, Dutch, Danish and Swedish islands of the West Indies (yet Haiti was now independent). These mostly remained under European administration through the nineteenth century and even later, though with self-government and federation in the Canadian colonies by the 1860s. Meanwhile, the United States pushed westwards from the Atlantic to the Pacific, conquering what became the forty-eight continental states, then purchasing Alaska from Russia, and at the end of the century annexing Hawaii and Puerto Rico, occupying Cuba and taking over the Philippines.

During the 1800s, the focus of European colonialism shifted away from the Americas to Africa, Asia and Oceania, regions that would be largely brought under European suzerainty. By 1914, only Thailand remained independent in Southeast Asia, only Ethiopia and Liberia, the latter founded for freed African slaves, in Africa. Japan kept its independence and became a colonial power by acquiring Taiwan in the 1890s and Korea a few years later, as did China. However, foreigners acquired 'concessions' of territory along the Chinese coast and substantially undermined its government. Colonizers had divided up even the smallest island groups of the Pacific Ocean.

As the case of the British in India and Australia had foreshadowed, colonial lobbies by the late 1800s were no longer content with coastal trading posts and island bases but pushed further into the interior of continents. Surging political, economic and cultural forces in Europe – industrialization, nationalism and missionary evangelism, among others – motivated a 'scramble' for greater expansion. The invention of new technologies, from steamships and more powerful weaponry to medications used to combat tropical disease, made feasible ventures near impossible in earlier times. The players in the colonial 'game' altered, as veteran colonizing nations were joined by the new entrants of Belgium, Italy, Germany and Russia, as well as Japan and the United States. The purported 'white man's burden' of colonialism became a mission shared by many nations, a cause championed (though wrongly) as providing almost unlimited benefits for Europeans and those subjected to European rule. Yet domestic debates about colonialism remained intense, imperial rivalries at times threatened war between the great powers, 'pacification' of conquered areas was never assured and colonized peoples suffering dispossession, disenfranchisement and exploitation continued to mount anti-colonial resistance and trial new strategies and ideologies for their struggles. This chapter provides an overview of the 'long nineteenth century', focusing more on the big-power dynamics of European expansion rather than on the dynamics within particular colonies, during the period that saw the unprecedented 'triumph' of global colonialism in theory and practice.

Europe and its colonies in 1815

France in 1815, defeated in the Napoleonic Wars, was a diminished colonial power. Britain, by contrast, had gained much colonial territory during the generation before 1815, despite the secession of thirteen American colonies: the East India Company continuously spread its dominion over India, Britain found a toehold in Southeast Asia with Penang island in the Strait of Malacca in 1786 and two years later established a settler colony on the eastern coast of Australia. The British took the Cape Colony from the Dutch in southern Africa (though the Dutch recovered the East Indies) and, in the Indian Ocean, captured Ceylon from the Dutch and Mauritius from the French. With a string of outposts from St Helena to southern Africa, across to the Indian subcontinent, and on to Southeast Asia and the South Pacific, Britain commanded an extraordinary maritime route and land-based empire.

For the other old powers, the revolutionary epoch had produced fewer gains; for Spain and Portugal there would soon be dramatic losses. Locally born settler elites, the *criollos*, including families established in Spanish America for generations, increasingly baulked at rule from Madrid and at interference in local affairs by the *peninsulares* recently arrived from Spain. Enlightenment ideas, and the examples of the American War of Independence and French Revolution, inspired nationalists, and *criollos* also sought to guarantee the continuity of their privileges. The white elite's vision for their emerging new nations thus overwhelmingly built on the social stratifications of the old Spanish Empire – to the detriment of indigenous populations and *mestizos*, those of mixed indigenous and Spanish descent. Indeed, it took them at least another century to acknowledge the indigenous past as a feature of Latin American identities.

One by one in the early 1800s, South American and Central American colonies declared independence and set up republican governments – Chile, Colombia and Mexico in 1810, Paraguay and Venezuela in 1811, Argentina in 1816, Costa Rica, El Salvador, Guatemala, Honduras and Peru in 1821, Bolivia and Uruguay in 1825. Spain held on to its Caribbean colony of Santo Domingo, today the Dominican Republic, until 1844; after occupation by Haiti, it briefly again became a Spanish colony until 1865. Madrid also kept Cuba and Puerto Rico, as well as the Philippines and several Micronesian islands in the western Pacific, until they were seized by the United States in 1898. Spain thus remained a colonial power, in the Caribbean and Asia, and through its small African possessions, throughout the nineteenth century. Even if Spain's massive 300-year-old continental empire in the Americas was no more, the legacies of colonialism remained strong: the Spanish language and the Catholic religion, political and economic domination by descendants of Spanish settlers over indigenous populations and exploitation of natural resources for their own profit, and governments that were often far from democratic. Spaniards continued to migrate in large numbers to South America and the Caribbean, Madrid nurtured relations with its ex-colonies, and the cultural concept of an international Spanish world, *Hispanidad*, replaced the old colonial empire in the Spanish mind even after 1898.

Brazil, Portugal's South American colony – a territory larger than the continental United States – followed a different pathway to independence than the Spanish outposts. With the Napoleonic occupation of Portugal in 1807, the king and royal family, accompanied by thousands of officials and courtiers, set sail for Rio de Janeiro. In 1821, King João VI returned home after a liberal revolution in Lisbon, leaving his son Pedro as regent. Facing increasing resistance among the population, Pedro declared the independence of Brazil in 1822 and was proclaimed its emperor. In 1831, he abdicated in favour of his son, Pedro II, and headed back to Portugal amidst a dynastic struggle for its throne. Pedro II continued to rule until a republican revolution in 1889. The dominant position of descendants of European settlers, in a country where 'whites' constituted less than half of the population among a majority of former African slaves and *mestiços*, as well as indigenous peoples, endured long afterwards. Spain and Portugal would fall back on their African and Asian possessions (and, in the Spanish case, on Cuba), just as Britain and France began looking towards Africa and Asia for further conquests.

The emancipation of slaves and the introduction of indentured labour

Plantation economies producing sugar and other tropical agricultural products, and mines in countries such as Brazil, relied on the labour of enslaved Africans. By the late eighteenth century, as discussed in the previous chapter, there was rising opposition to slavery, in particular to the slave trade, as well as more militant movements among the enslaved populations, marked by escape from plantations, refusal to work, attacks on Europeans and full-scale revolts. Efforts to safeguard ancestral traditions, and to craft new ones outside European norms, represented cultural resistance to slavery. Indeed, while older literature has focused on 'enlightened' intellectuals and European action for the end of the slave trade, recent scholarship underlines slaves' and former slaves' agency in ending the trade and eventually securing emancipation.

However, the slave trade, formally ended by the British in 1807, continued to be carried out clandestinely by many Europeans. Slavery as an institution was not abolished until 1834 in the British Empire, 1848 in the French colonies, and much later in the Portuguese colonies, the United States and Brazil. Abolition, however, did not mean dramatic amelioration of the lives of the formerly enslaved, as they often faced an obligation to work as wage-labourers for former masters for some years and continued to suffer poverty, lack of opportunity and racist discrimination. Moreover, the end of slavery also did not mean the end of revolts by former slaves, the most dramatic the Morant Bay Rebellion in Jamaica in 1865. Slavery had been abolished in the Caribbean sugar-producing colony three decades earlier, and free men of colour had won election to the local assembly, but miserable conditions persisted. The rebellion began as a protest march led by a pastor following the arrest of a Black man for trespassing on a disused plantation. There ensued confrontations with a volunteer white militia, the burning of a courthouse and a number of deaths, followed by a colony-wide uprising: a general protest about colonial violence, injustice, poverty and British rule. The governor responded with violent repression that caused the death of around 400 rebels and the arrest of several hundred more (and the subsequent execution of a number of them). The severity of the governor's action provoked much criticism in Britain and led to his replacement. The leaders of the rebellion, Paul Bogle and George William Gordon, now have the status of Jamaican National Heroes.

Since former slaves tried to escape plantation labour associated with slavery, emancipation created a demand for replacement workers. The British and French continued to hire some Africans under contract, but increasingly turned towards India as a source of cheap labour (as is discussed in further detail in chapter 8 of this volume). With poverty and lack of opportunities in parts of the Indian subcontinent, and often armed with false promises and specious contracts, recruiters found it easy to engage labourers for service overseas. They encountered long hours of hard labour and paltry earnings sometimes paid only on the expiry of a contract and charged against debts run up at 'company stores'. Some historians thus label indentured labour as 'contract slavery'. The after-effects of slavery and the situation of bonded and coerced labour would traverse colonial history throughout the nineteenth century and beyond.

Nineteenth-century expansion: Why and where?

It was sometimes assumed that a hiatus separated European expansion between the end of the Napoleonic Wars in 1815 and a so-called new imperialism after 1870. However, this is not really correct. With the invasion of Algeria in 1830, France began to rebuild its overseas empire, and during the middle decades carved out colonies in Africa, the Indian Ocean and Oceania. The Netherlands entrenched its rule in the East Indies, especially on the large island of Java, and the Spanish and Portuguese continued to rule their remaining possessions with (unrealized) hopes of expansion. Britain substantially increased its imperial portfolio, adding Singapore in 1819 and coastal areas of Burma in the 1820s (with more territory added after a second war against the Burmese in the 1850s and the remainder of the country after a third war in the 1880s). The British formally claimed the western part of the continent of Australia in 1827, and took over New Zealand in 1840, Hong Kong in 1842 and Natal (in southern Africa) in 1843. The East India Company, under the auspices of the Crown, meanwhile conquered further territory on the Indian subcontinent, one of the biggest prizes the Punjab, in the 1840s. A major insurrection in 1857 – called a 'mutiny' by the British but the 'first Indian war of independence' by later Indian nationalists – was harshly repressed. The following year, the Crown formally took over control of the territories of the East India Company, which was soon disbanded. Three-fifths of the Indian subcontinent now came under direct rule by Britain, the remainder (except for the Portuguese and French enclaves) indirectly ruled by the British through the intermediary of maharajas and other Indian princes. For Britain, with its overlordship consolidated, India constituted the most precious part of the empire, the so-called jewel in the Crown, confirmed in 1876 with the proclamation of Queen Victoria as Empress of India (Map 3.1).

In addition to military action in India and Burma, during the half-century after 1815, Britain, France and other European powers became embroiled in several foreign wars, notably the so-called Opium Wars in the 1830s–40s and 1850s. Among their objectives were acquisition of widened spheres of influence and the opening of more ports for trade in China. War by the British and French against Russia in the Crimea in the 1850s sought to curb tsarist designs in the Black Sea and towards the Mediterranean, as well as on the borders of Britain's Indian empire. In acts of belligerency elsewhere, the British (and white settlers) waged wars against indigenous people in the settler colonies: the New Zealand Wars against the Maori, 'frontier wars' against Aborigines in Australia and the later Zulu Wars (and other wars) in southern Africa. The French meanwhile pursued warfare against indigenous Algerians from the 1830s to the 1870s, and, like the British, battled rulers in sub-Saharan Africa as they gradually occupied more territory.

Imperialism also presented other faces than military conquest in the mid-1800s, including what Ronald Robinson and John Gallagher in the 1950s termed the 'imperialism of free trade'. Economic theorists and policymakers championed removal of international trade barriers, and in particular, tariff walls, but free trade did not necessarily imply equitable trade. The industrial revolution was giving European countries, foremost among them Britain, manufactured goods to market, capital to invest and a growing need for primary products, as well as the technology of transport and communication to facilitate commerce. Free trade encouraged British and French business to establish stronger and advantageous positions in the economies of independent countries such as the Ottoman Empire and Persia, and indeed in less developed Russia, the Iberian countries and South America. This led to their greater dominance of international trade for which they could set the terms. There was, moreover, 'soft' imperialism – the export of European consumer goods (encompassing luxury items beloved by upper classes overseas), the teaching of European languages, the courting of foreign elites, missionary work and the general dissemination of European culture. This served to bolster European influence in such places as Japan and China, as well as countries that would eventually

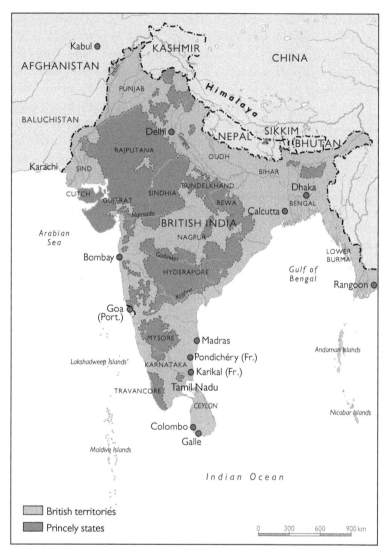

Map 3.1 British Empire and South Asia, 1880s: India including Burma and Ceylon. © Adapted from map by cartographer Peter Palm.

become colonies or protectorates, for example, Morocco and Egypt. When Britain and France launched an accelerated push to acquire new territories in the last decades of the nineteenth century, the initiative built on advance actions taken over the previous fifty years.

In the middle decades of the 1800s, despite their already considerable holdings in Africa and Asia, European powers scouting for new colonies still prospected for coastal enclaves or islands that offered deepwater ports for sailing ships, provisions of fresh water and foodstuffs, and a capacity to be easily defended. Having a locally produced tradable commodity was an advantage, though not a necessity. Colonizers sought to outscore rivals by acquiring strategic sites, especially on the sea lanes of international commerce and geopolitical interest. Neither Singapore nor Hong Kong was a resource-rich, populous island when Britain acquired them – in 1819 and 1842, respectively, it may be remembered – but each (like Penang, annexed earlier) afforded good seaports and a strategic location. Singapore became the leading international port in Southeast Asia, and Hong Kong, Britain's entry point for the China trade. The two archetypal colonial port cities – filled with imposing buildings of government, financial institutions and trading companies, busy docks and warehouses, the mansions of wealthy merchants, the 'shop-houses' of more modest local traders, the poor quarters of migrant labourers, and the low life of the harbours – became Britain's most important outposts in eastern Asia. From Singapore and Penang, Britain expanded through the Malay states, and near Hong Kong island, it leased mainland territory from China. Such ports as Penang, Singapore and Hong Kong linked the Indian Ocean to the Pacific, British India to colonies further east and coastal regions to continental hinterlands.

The island Pacific presented a particularly significant theatre for colonial campaigns. Though many islands were small, dispersed over an enormous geographical area and with limited known commercial resources, they provided nodes across the ocean linking the Americas to Asia and Australia (Map 3.2). Already in the mid-1800s, especially during gold rushes in the United States and Australia and with feverish interest in China and Japan (newly 'opened' by foreign incursions), commentators predicted that the centre of the world's political and economic gravity would soon shift from the Atlantic to the Pacific. Talk about the opening of a canal through the Central American isthmus further stimulated great and aspiring powers to mark out territory across Oceania.

In the South Pacific, the British and the French – colonial rivals and still potential enemies – played tit-for-tat in island hunting. The British took prime position in Australia. In 1840, as a private French company sailed towards New Zealand to found a settlement, the British pipped them to the post and signed an accord with Maori chiefs, the Waitangi Treaty, by which Britain claimed sovereignty over the country. Among the various foreigners in Tahiti and the Society Islands, the British established a dominant missionary and consular presence, but in 1842, the French sent in warships to proclaim a protectorate over the most fabled of Polynesian islands. In 1853, they occupied New Caledonia and the Loyalty Islands to obtain a port for their mercantile and military fleet in the southwest Pacific and (following the British precedent in Australia) a place to send convicts. Then in 1874 Britain annexed Fiji, and so it went until by the end of the century, the islands of Oceania had been divided between the British and the French, as well as, from the 1880s, such new 'proprietors' as Germany and the United States (which divided the islands of Samoa). The Dutch reaffirmed claims to the western half of the island of New Guinea, while the Germans and the British divided the eastern part. In the wake of colonial officials and sometimes well before their arrival came missionaries, traders, planters and miners, imposing the whole infrastructure of the colonial system.

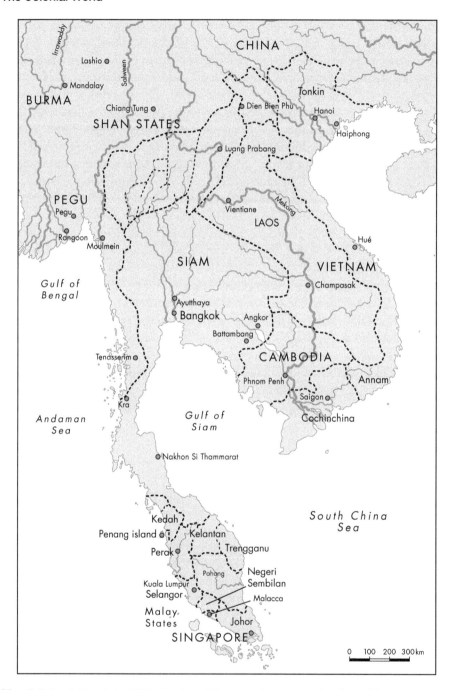

Map 3.2 South East Asia, 1890s. © Adapted from map by cartographer Peter Palm.

The acceleration of colonial expansion in the late 1800s

From the 1850s, a gearing up in European international interventions and colonial expansion was noticeable, first in Asia, and then with greater intensity, in Africa from around the 1870s or 1880s. Historians disagree about the weight of various imperatives, and much ink has been spilled trying to identify the key causes. Some argue for the primacy of economic motives, others for the crucial importance of political rivalries and geopolitical strategies, and yet others privilege cultural incentives and legitimations in the division of the world. In fact, all of these issues entered into play, in variable fashion depending on location, time and circumstances, with different justifications for expansion favoured by particular theorists, government officials and colonial lobbyists in European capitals or invoked by those in the field. The motives can be analytically disaggregated, but it is important to remember that they reinforced each other and intertwined. All of those who promoted expansion hoped for profit – personal and collective, economic and political, material and cultural – from the conquest of new territories, even if only the vague potential of eventual return on the investment of men, money and political will glimmered like a mirage on the horizon. Potential profit encompassed income earned, careers built, souls 'saved', adventure pursued, convicts rehabilitated, military bases secured and 'civilization' spread, notwithstanding great debits in lives lost, funds wasted, conflicts provoked and dreams turned into nightmares. Not always was there a positive sum at the bottom of the balance sheet, and seldom so when viewed from an indigenous vantage point. The world nevertheless presented a ledger on which Europeans of many backgrounds, intentions and vocations attempted to write their designs, realize their ambitions and reap the rewards.

Politically, the nineteenth century saw a determined effort at nation- and state-building in Europe, and colonialism formed an integral part of nationalism for established and up-and-coming powers. 'Great' powers should have colonial outposts, as Spain, Portugal, Britain and France had shown over the past centuries. Small countries such as the Netherlands, Portugal, Belgium and Denmark could make up for lack of size and population by the takeover of lands overseas. Colonies not only provided resources, proven or hoped for. They offered ballast in big-power diplomacy. They could serve as bargaining chips in negotiations, with one colony traded for another to resolve conflicts and contour spheres of influence. Colonies offered prestige, places to raise and wave the flag. They provided ports for warships, bases for troop garrisons and reservoirs for recruiting soldiers. They were heralded as lands of settlement, terrains for military and civilian talent to exercise itself, places of unbounded opportunities for agricultural, mining and business initiative, outlets for national aspirations and proving-grounds for national mettle. Promoters laboured hard, through publications, exhibitions, the setting up of booster committees and societies, and the lobbying of parliamentarians and voters, to instil belief in the legitimacy of expansion and to convince compatriots of the merits of far-flung colonies.

Not all proved receptive to the propaganda. Many Europeans remained well outside the orbit of colonialist circles, more preoccupied with the problems of daily life, the cycles of sowing and harvesting on farms, the routines of artisan labour, or drudgery in the new factories. They faced epidemics such as the cholera that periodically infected Europe, lack of land, the hardships of industrial ghettos, periodic famines, political ructions, and racial and religious persecution. The colonies beckoned, even if more often eyes turned towards the Americas (and, in the case of Britain, the settler colonies) as a 'promised land' for migrants rather than Africa or Asia. Yet migration also posed the fear of distance, unknown countries and possibly hostile environments, and for many, permanent separation from kith and kin. Politicians of both left and right expressed caution, and for some, outright opposition to colonial expansion and the expenditures of men and money that wars and administration entailed. They argued that problems closer to home, rather than foreign ventures, ought to be priorities. Voting reform, the status of Ireland and the effects of the industrial revolution preoccupied the British, and the French were caught up at the barricades during revolutions in 1830, 1848 and 1871. After a humiliating defeat by Prussia in 1870, nationalists clamoured that French efforts ought to concentrate on recovery of the provinces of Alsace and Lorraine that Paris had been forced to cede. National unification, not colonial ventures, loomed as the immediate objective for Germans and Italians. Otto von Bismarck, Prussian chancellor and architect of German unification, only reluctantly engaged Germany in conquests in Africa and Oceania. Social reformers everywhere campaigned for amelioration of the lives of the masses – working conditions, education, housing, political rights; this campaign, they argued, was far more urgent than colonialism. For socialists, what was needed was not an overseas empire that would further enrich the owners of capital, but a revolution that would transfer power from the bourgeoisie to the proletariat. Humanitarians expressed reservations about the strategies of conquest and rule, shocked by warfare, blatant violence and abuse, and by reports of corruption and scandal. And entrepreneurs found many opportunities for business within Europe or through profitable international dealings that did not depend on the acquisition of colonies. Even for those who cheered on or silently acquiesced to colonial conquests, the real level of commitment to empire remains difficult to ascertain.

Despite disinterest or reluctance, arguments in favour of colonialism proved persuasive, thanks to the efforts of energetic promoters, the vested interests of certain business, military and religious groups, and the general climate of nationalism combined with growing militarism. Humanitarians might also be swayed by avowed campaigns to eliminate slavery and misrule and to share European civilization with those less fortunate. Migrants could be attracted by offers of land and employment, priests and pastors by the biblical command to convert the heathen, scientists by the expansion of knowledge, businessmen by hopes for markets and raw material, adventurers by dreams of fame and fortune (or perhaps flight from chequered personal situations). Even radicals who rallied to colonialism could convince themselves that expansion offered a chance to spread the ideas of reform and socialism, and an opportunity to better the life of comrades overseas. Words and images, reflecting reasoned arguments and visceral feelings, cannot be underestimated for their role in drumming up support for colonialism. Sensationalistic reports about incidents in which Europeans were injured or killed, suffered injustices in law or trade, were persecuted for Christian proselytism, and faced slights to national honour (or were alleged to have faced such treatment): all stirred basic and base sentiments and demands for revenge, especially when said to have been committed at the hands of bloodthirsty tyrants, religious fanatics, rampaging hordes or savages. Such language, stock-in-trade of colonialist discourse, stimulated the emotions, and was frequently deployed during such events as the Indian 'Mutiny' of 1857, especially potent with the depictions of British women whose virtue and lives were threatened by rebels. European battlefield victories and accounts of the 'achievements' of 'pioneers' stoked nationalistic pride, as fears and hopes coalesced into a kind of collective colonialist hysteria. Once colonies were conquered, national honour then made it shameful to abandon them, and any menace – by insurgents inside, enemies outside, or anti-colonialists at home or abroad – simply contributed to that state of mind. This emotional, intangible side of colonialism, in addition to the material benefits and costs, should not be discounted in explaining the phenomenon.

Colonialism, however, meant different things for different countries. Britain was inseparable, and indeed unimaginable, in the nineteenth century apart from its empire, and the colonialism of past centuries provided a birthright for the Victorians. After all, Britain's North American Empire dated back to the beginning of the 1600s; parts of India had been under British control for more than 200 years by the time Queen Victoria ascended the throne in 1837. Britain took pride in sea power, intimately connected with the Royal Navy and its global reach. Factories demanded raw materials from overseas, such as cotton and wool, and the finished products they churned out needed markets. 'New Englands' – a term used for regions of both the United States and Australia – provided lands for colonists at a time of unprecedented population growth (and, in the 1840s, famine in Ireland), and the British boasted about the success of settler colonies and the allegiance of settlers to the 'mother country'. Empire, in short, was stitched into the very fabric of British life.

The French situation appeared somewhat different. France's military might came primarily from armies, not navies, and French policy initiatives more often turned towards the Continent, or across the Mediterranean, than towards more distant shores. A lower rate of population growth than in Britain, the greater access to land that peasants enjoyed (thanks to legal changes during the Revolution) and slower industrialization meant fewer potential migrants. France, moreover, felt obliged to rebuild an empire to compensate for earlier loss of colonies, to reverse course, as it were, while Britain was steaming ahead. The rulers of France during the Restoration (1815–30) and July Monarchy (1830–48) were far from devoid of colonial ambitions, most notably in the 1830 invasion of Algeria, the acquisition of such territories as Mayotte in the Indian Ocean and Tahiti in the Pacific, and preservation of the remaining plantation colonies. But Napoleon III (nephew of Napoleon I), elected as president in 1848 and then promoted to emperor after a coup in 1851, harboured more ambitious dynastic and colonial plans. He pressed on with French subjugation and occupation of Algeria and wrangled increased territory in western Africa, joined Britain in the Crimean War of 1853–6, sent troops to China in the 'Second Opium War' (or Arrow War) in the late 1850s. The French took over New Caledonia in 1853, and French forces also invaded Korea in 1866 (and spirited away a large collection of antique books and manuscripts when they withdrew). Napoleon III sponsored a short-lived and ill-fated empire in Mexico under a Habsburg archduke proclaimed emperor of that country in the 1860s. Napoleon III's forces acquired a French foothold in southern Vietnam and Cambodia in Southeast Asia. Rivalry with Britain, efforts to affirm France's status as a great power, and the 'Napoleonic' character of the French ruler thus inflected Paris's policies at mid-century, and made the emperor's reign a period of French colonialist revival. After 1870, in the wake of the French defeat, Napoleon III's ouster and the establishment of the Third Republic, colonialists faced the challenge of re-presenting their cause to the French with renewed arguments about the value, indeed necessity, of expansion for France's commercial, political and cultural standing. France had played second fiddle to the British, but it was now playing to catch up. Even though opposition to colonialism was stronger than across the Channel, by the end of the century France had amassed the world's second largest overseas empire.

Prussia was a rising power in nineteenth-century Europe, using persuasion, coercion and warfare in the formation of a newly unified Germany. Bismarck, the 'Iron Chancellor' of Prussia and, from 1871, the German Reich, as mentioned, at first opposed colonial expansion. However, by the 1880s, Germany's leaders had decided that Berlin must find its place on the colonial map. Building on earlier scientific and economic involvement overseas, they began Germany's quest for outposts in eastern and south-western Africa, Polynesia and Melanesia, and China. Another newly unified country was Italy, which also sought colonies to affirm its 'big power' status; by the 1890s, the Italians were making colonizing forays into the Horn of Africa and they later turned their attention to North Africa. The most ambitious or megalomaniacal of the European sovereigns was King Leopold II of Belgium, who commissioned explorers to reconnoitre lands in central Africa. In 1885, he founded the Congo Free State, a territory over seventy times the size of Belgium. Leopold ruled the African colony as his private realm; only in 1908, after loud criticism of the abuse of African labourers, did the monarch cede his nominally independent state to Belgium.

Spain, Portugal and the Netherlands were not new colonial powers, but some of the oldest ones, and they acquired no new colonies. Spain lost its remaining territories in the Americas and Asia by the end of the 1890s, but placed new hopes in its residual African holdings. Portugal was stymied in the hope to expand its empire in Africa but maintained its existing colonies there (and smaller possessions in India, Timor and Macau). The Netherlands, implanted in the East Indies for over 200 years by the mid-1800s, consolidated its effective control through warfare, administration and policy, but except for extending its claim to New Guinea, did not move further; its limited colonies in the Western hemisphere remained a legacy of the first overseas empire. In sum, the British expanded on an already large empire, the French rebuilt theirs, the Belgians, Germans and Italians conquered one and the Dutch, Portuguese and Spanish tried to hold on to what they had (though the Iberian powers largely failed).

Europe's pro-colonialist elite praised the hardiness of explorers, the bravery of soldiers, the tenacity of settlers and the acumen of traders. All, they constantly repeated, were adding to the glory of the nation. Countries needed to buttress themselves within Europe, and prepare for possible war. Colouring ever greater areas of global maps in the appropriate colours was, they affirmed, proof of the prowess of their citizens and the greatness of their nations. There was talk of 'Greater Britain' and of *la plus grande France* encompassing widening empires, and for all the colonizing countries, the very fact of having colonies made them 'greater', or at least so trumpeted the propaganda. As well, they proclaimed that they were participating in a noble crusade to 'civilize the savages', bring the Gospel to the 'heathen', eradicate slavery – after having early practised slavery and then freed slaves, they had the faith of converts – and 'develop' the world's resources. At home, empire could be used to satisfy the demands of interest groups, rouse the masses and advance leaders' ambitions, though in fact not always successfully in any of these areas.

When conflicts threatened in Africa or Asia, European governments rattled swords and dispatched troops to defend their patches against other colonizers, indigenous rulers and rebels. For the military, protecting extant colonies and winning new ones provided an arena for valour and, for soldiers and sailors, an avenue to quick promotion and proof of the vital role of armies and navies in national life. A slight by an indigenous ruler, a move by an imperial rival or a real or trumped up argument about the need to protect compatriots provided ample legitimation for a lightning foray or for one of the 'little wars of empire' (some of which were not so little). Increased militarization in the last decades of the nineteenth century encompassed conscription in some countries, development of modernized weaponry such as rapid-fire guns and armoured ships, and heroization of soldiers as exemplars of national pluck. In the absence of any international court or peace-keeping organization, and with the rules of warfare set by the Europeans, conquest was a free-for-all, a case of 'first come, first serve' in new territories and of *prises de possession* by commanders in the field even without a directive from metropolitan superiors.

There existed no preordained, coherent or remote-controlled grand plans for amassing empires, and much acquisition of territory was contingent and dependent on opportune circumstances. However, a certain number of patterns can be discerned in thinking about where colonial powers went. An established colonial power wanted to protect the borderlands of existing territories and routes of access to its colonies. Thus, the British pushed northwards from India towards Afghanistan and the Himalayas in the 'Great Game' played against an expanding Russia on the other side, and moved into Burma to protect the eastern reaches of its Indian Empire. London had a keen interest in the eastern Mediterranean, Egypt and Aden (on the tip of the Arabian Peninsula), especially after the opening of the Suez Canal in 1869, so as to safeguard the maritime lifeline to India and colonies in Asia and Australasia. It was not surprising that, after France took Algiers in the mid-1800s, it moved south into the Sahara desert, and from the Algerian coast east into Tunisia in 1881 and west to Morocco in 1911. New acquisitions created new frontiers, and often provoked new bouts of resistance, thus instigating yet further expansion in a snowball effect of conquest (however inappropriate that metaphor may be for tropical or desert regions).

Europeans also wanted to connect their colonies, though they did not always realize these ambitions. The French failed to join up their holdings in western and central Africa with Djibouti on the eastern coast. In 1890, the British vetoed Portuguese plans for linking up Angola and Mozambique on the opposite shores of Africa. The British dreamed of creating a great corridor tying Cairo to Cape Town, but only for a short period were they able to boast of having done so. Yet another guiding objective was to obtain a base in different parts of the world, especially if a competitor was already present there. Britain had done this with great aplomb in Australasia, and (as noted previously) the French were intent on procuring possessions in the South Pacific to contest the British. Although King Leopold's empire was confined to central Africa, the Belgian king dreamed of establishing outposts in Asia, mooting sites from Cambodia to the Philippines. The Germans did better; fellow latecomers to colonialism, they managed to obtain colonies on both coasts of Africa, the eastern and western South Pacific, and a major 'concession' in China. The French had set their sights on Djibouti because of the British across the water in Aden, and nearby Somalia provided a site for neighbouring British, French and Italian colonies. France had been desperate for a base in Southeast Asia, and tried to gain land in the southern Philippines before finally carving out a colony in southern Vietnam. All of the colonizing countries wanted a piece of China. Finally, there was also a preclusive colonialism, with countries taking over unclaimed regions, even tiny sub-Antarctic islands, simply to forestall annexation by others. And big powers lay claims to parts of Antarctica itself.

In the last decades of the nineteenth century, colonizers' attention, indeed preoccupations, turned increasingly to sub-Saharan Africa. The interior of the 'dark continent', as Europeans called it, was one of the last frontiers, relatively little known to Europeans, and still largely untouched by colonizers despite the existence of colonial outposts on the littoral dating back centuries. Long-standing fantasies about its riches now turned into promises of the wealth that could be gained from agriculture, mining and trade. This was especially the case as businessmen looked for new sources of profit during the economic depression that affected Europe from the mid-1870s to the mid-1890s and as the 'second industrial revolution' of those decades created a demand for new raw materials that could come from sub-Saharan Africa: vegetable oils, especially palm oil and also peanut oil, used for lubrication of machinery and manufacture of soap, and rubber for tyres. Europeans, said colonial promoters, sometimes presciently, could develop and exploit new plantations of cacao, coffee, tea, groundnuts, bananas, coconuts and other tropical fruit, and there were cloves in Zanzibar, fish in the Great Lakes and rivers, and tropical hardwoods in equatorial Africa. Kenya seemed ideal for the raising of livestock and the planting of coffee and tea. The Congo offered rubber and a horde of minerals, there was copper in what is now Zambia, phosphate in Senegal and many other minerals already known or soon to be discovered and mined, including the gold and diamonds that made fame and fortune for prospectors in South Africa. Some countries presented few obvious trade products, but that did not discourage ardent colonialists from proclaiming the potential they represented. Africa seemed a place where Europeans could pursue their most grandiose (or deluded) development projects, building railways and ports, creating new cities, modernizing production. Furthermore, in 1900, there were 100 million Africans, all potential labourers and consumers. Sub-Saharan Africa presented massive hazards of landscape, disease (as 'the white man's graveyard') and warfare, but it promised unbounded benefits – at least, in the propaganda of booster committees and publicists. Not surprisingly, the key image that many people still retain of colonialism is a simplistic depiction of the scramble for Africa, with pith-helmeted adventurers, gun-wielding conquerors and hardy traders in remote outstations.

From coastal beachheads, Europeans made their way into hinterlands, arduously moving up the Congo, Niger, Zambezi and other rivers and across dense jungles, savannahs and deserts to raise flags, set up trading posts and scout for resources. To make a long story short: the French assembled vast domains that they organized into two colonial federations, French West Africa and French Equatorial Africa. The British claimed colonies large and small nearby, in particular Nigeria (across from French Niger), the large and resource-rich colonies of Uganda and Kenya in the east, South Africa and the neighbouring areas (now Botswana, Zambia, Zimbabwe and Malawi) of southern Africa. Portugal (primarily in Angola and Mozambique) and Germany (in what became Namibia and Tanganyika) both had large holdings on the western and eastern coasts, Italy an outpost on the Horn of Africa.

As colonial division of the world was drawing to a close, European colonizers 'mopped up' the map, taking whatever territories remained. In 1911, for instance, Italy snatched from the Ottoman Empire the territories of Cyrenaica and Tripolitania (combined as Italian Libya), the only territory not claimed by Europeans in North Africa. Once they acquired colonies, countries proved reluctant to relinquish them, although trade-offs occurred: Britain ceded Heligoland, an island in the North Sea, to Germany in return for Zanzibar, off the east coast of Africa, in 1890, and in the early 1900s, France and Britain negotiated outstanding claims ranging from Newfoundland to the New Hebrides. On rare occasions, a country relinquished colonies entirely, as Denmark did in Africa and India, and eventually in the Caribbean, and Russia did in Alaska.

From time to time, arbitration resolved a dispute, as when France and Mexico in 1931 asked the king of Italy to decide which country held a rightful claim to the uninhabited island of Clipperton off the west coast of Mexico; the monarch decided in favour of the French. Other disputes, however, remained and remain unresolved, as those between Britain and Spain over Gibraltar, or between Britain and Argentina over the Falkland Islands. Imperial division resulted in arbitrary borders: straight lines drawn between colonies in parts of Africa with no consideration for local populations and resources, the separation of South Pacific archipelagos between rival powers. The island of Borneo was cleaved by the British, the Dutch and the 'white rajah' of Sarawak – Charles Brooke, an English adventurer who, with his descendants, ruled Sarawak for a century. The Gambia formed a thin British colony running on either side of a river in the middle of French Senegal. There were enclaves and exclaves, such as the Cabinda territory, separated from the rest of Portuguese Angola by the Belgian Congo. Even with European powers apportioning territory on the ground and at conferences in Berlin in the 1870s and 1880s, and cartographers carefully shading in the matching colours, colonial maps were never logical or neat, and borders seldom unchanging or secure. Colonial maps in the early years of the twentieth century, sometimes decorated with fanciful emblems of the outposts, showed the results of decades, and indeed centuries, of colonial conquest, and the global reach, in particular, of the British and French empires (Map 3.3 and 3.4).

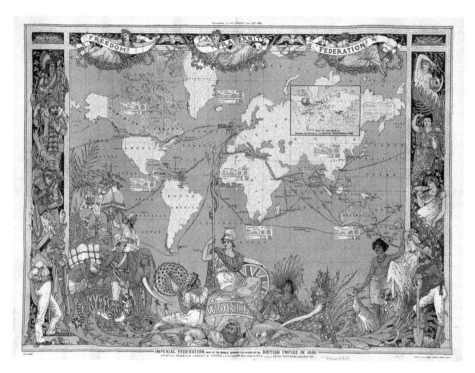

Map 3.3 Map of the British Empire, 1886, by Walter Crane. © Wikimedia Commons (public domain).

Map 3.4 French colonial empire, 1938. © Alamy Stock Photo.

Maps show the extent of empires, the baffling array of different colonies, the way they linked together (or did not), and disparities among them. Some colonies were massive: the Sudan, ruled by the British in colonial times, covers 1.9 million square kilometres (while the British Isles amount to only 315,000), the single island of Sumatra in the Dutch East Indies was more than ten times the size of the Netherlands and the island of Madagascar slightly bigger than France. However, overseas empires also encompassed tiny and sometimes uninhabited islands lost in oceans, places of little real value and largely immune to development. Colonies gave European countries territory and subject populations far greater than in the homeland: Portugal covered around 92,0000 square kilometres in Europe, but its two largest colonies, Angola and Mozambique, totalled over 2 million square kilometres. In 1900, the Netherlands counted a population of five million, but the Dutch queen reigned over forty-three million subjects in the East Indies. The acquisition of so much territory and sovereignty over so many people was remarkable. The hubris of Europeans claiming to rule so many places was staggering. And the real challenges faced in governing and, in colonial parlance, pacifying, developing and modernizing their domains was formidable indeed.

Strategies and limits of conquest

The question remains of how Europeans were able to conquer so many colonies around the world. The answer is complex, as it involves a mix of new technologies, coercion, cooperation and power brokering, often as a drive for expansion by colonial officers on the spot. One simple answer is that military means and the force of arms, either used in practice or threatened, made conquest possible. By the mid- to late nineteenth century, European military technology was more advanced than that in countries colonizers invaded, which explains why non-Western rulers proved so keen to acquire sophisticated industrial weaponry. Europeans could blast their way into a country, bombarding forts from their ships and marching contingents of soldiers with modern firearms against indigenous troops with older, less powerful weapons, or simply enforce submission by brandishing arms and massing soldiers as commanders made demands that could not be refused at risk of great destruction. However, landing troops did not automatically mean taking over territory. Military campaigns included advances and retreats, and lands needed to be occupied effectively by troops moving like a spreading puddle of oil (in the metaphor of one French officer). Dramatic reverses could occur, as when the Italians suffered defeat in trying to conquer Ethiopia in the 1890s.

Europeans frequently conquered new colonies with troops recruited from old ones. For instance, in India, the bulk of 'British' forces were the sepoys, local soldiers hired by the East India Company and deployed from one region to the other. Certain groups that the British considered 'martial races', such as the Sikhs, proved particularly valuable. After first fighting against the Gurkhas in the early 1800s, but impressed by their bravery, the British recruited these Nepalese for their army (as they still do).

In expanding through sub-Saharan Africa, the French used soldiers recruited in their older colonies, such as Senegal, though the generic term *tirailleurs sénégalais* (Senegalese sharp-shooters) came to refer to Black soldiers from throughout French West Africa deployed in warfare from Algeria to Indochina. The French also established a Foreign Legion in 1830, composed of soldiers from outside France – with the legend that the legion attracted former criminals and ne'er-do-wells – who were posted around the empire. The Dutch recruited a considerable number of soldiers from the Maluku islands for service throughout the East Indies. The Italians later used *askaris* from Somalia and Eritrea in their campaign in Ethiopia in the 1930s.

Wages and other benefits provided for military service appealed to indigenous soldiers. Soldiering was often considered an honourable profession and a good career within Asian and African societies, though forced recruitment occurred throughout the colonial world. In British India or French sub-Saharan Africa, fighting in a European army against a 'native' ruler or military was not necessarily viewed as a betrayal of indigenous peoples since power politics had often revolved around armed competitions between local leaders and populations for territory and influence. Serving on the European side followed a tradition of strategic alliances. That does not mean, however, that non-Europeans in colonial forces always supported European colonialism, and their mistreatment provoked open rebellion, as happened most famously in India in the 1850s. Indigenous men in large numbers later joined the ranks of pro-independence fighting forces. Those who continued to serve the Europeans sometimes suffered reprisals or were forced into exile when the Europeans were ousted, as happened with those who fought for the Spanish in Cuba in the 1860s and for the Dutch and the French during wars of independence after the Second World War.

European conquest frequently took advantage of the disaggregation of pre-colonial states and regional enmities. Historians long ago pointed out how the weaknesses of local rulers, and domestic conflicts between factions, dynasties or ethnic groups, compromised the capacity of rulers, and their states and armies, to resist incursion. In India, the mighty Mughal Empire had reached its apogee in the 1600s, but subsequently faced debilitating challenges from other Indian states, as well as Europeans; by the mid-1800s, the Mughal emperor, whose predecessors had ruled much of the subcontinent, reigned over a realm that barely reached outside the city of Delhi. European colonizers often wore down local states in wars of attrition lasting many years; the British conquered Burma over a period of sixty years. In Vietnam, the French, after sending in gunboats at the end of the 1850s, forced the emperor of Annam to cede several provinces on the Mekong delta; they moved into Cambodia in the 1860s, Annam, or central Vietnam, in the 1870s, northern Vietnam, or Tonkin, in the 1880s, and Laos in the 1890s, taking more than thirty years to amalgamate the lands contained in 'French Indochina'. The neat colonial maps of early twentieth-century Africa revealed the outcome of chaotic spasms of expansion in the 1880s and 1890s as Britain, France, Germany and Italy hurried to mark out their territories, fighting wars, coercing agreements from local rulers, occupying land, negotiating boundaries back in European capitals. There were cases of successful lightning strikes and quick takeovers, to be sure, but conquest generally involved prolonged engagement and gradual establishment of European authority. Indeed, the usual handy dates cited for European takeover of particular colonies can mislead, as they mask the long years and complex tactics of offensives, negotiations and alliances needed to gain control.

European takeovers almost always involved insidious manoeuvres as well as sheer military might. Europeans might convince a leader to cede a parcel of territory in return for some benefits. Or a European state might offer 'protection' to a ruler, a seemingly benign overture for a country endangered by a neighbouring indigenous ruler. A treaty would be duly negotiated, with responsibilities and rights outlined. However, the terms of such treaties – written by the Europeans, based on European concepts of sovereignty and statehood – might hold little meaning to those with completely different notions of rulership and independence. Moreover, the Europeans carefully worded such treaties so that failure by a local ruler to adhere to obligations would provide an excuse for further European incursions – and such failures were easy to find or to manufacture. 'Protectorates' were a vague but internationally recognized legal status in which a ruler (generally a hereditary emperor, king, sultan or rajah) retained nominal independence, and was in theory 'protected' by the European state against aggression or subversion. But when convenient, Europeans could cite any activity unacceptable to them, such as opposition to their very role as 'protectors', as grounds for abrogation of the treaty, deposition of the ruler, abolition of the dynasty or annexation of the country. In yet another sleight-of-hand, the British in the early 1800s had declared that they possessed the right to annex any Indian princely state whose throne fell empty in the absence of an appropriate heir, with the British solely able to decide on the suitability of candidates. Coercion, subterfuge and hypocrisy marked the progression of European control over most conquered areas.

Europeans, at the time of conquest and throughout their *imperium*, relied on the cooperation, or at least acquiescence, of individuals and groups within the local population. These included some traditional rulers eager to retain their privileges as 'protected' vassals and protect themselves against rivals, such as the sultans of the East Indies or many of the Indian princes. Particular ethnic or religious groups, especially those whose minority numbers caused tension with compatriots, such as Christians in largely Islamic societies, the Parsis in India or 'tribal peoples', might also cast their lot with the Europeans (though some joined the nationalists). Diasporic migrants similarly might feel ill at ease living in the midst of large indigenous populations, and see Europeans as guarantors of their welfare. Some local people simply saw advantages to be gained – education, employment and new occupations, profits from entrepreneurship, release from ancestral or communal constraints, what they considered a more 'modern' outlook and way of life – from willing accommodation of the colonizers.

Europeans constituted a small minority of the population in almost every outpost outside the British settler dominions. In the mid-nineteenth century, there were about 20,000 British officials and troops in India among a total population of 300 million. In 1930, those with Dutch legal status accounted for less than 0.5 per cent of the population of the East Indies, 240,000 people (three-quarters of them Eurasians) out of almost 61 million. A decade later, only about 39,000 French men and women lived in Vietnam, 0.2 per cent of the population. The Europeans, in fact, could not have run their empires without some measure of collaboration from indigenous administrators, intellectuals, soldiers and labourers. This by no means implies that someone belonging to a particular class, ethnic group or religion, or someone who was eager to embrace Westernization, would happily serve the Europeans or oppose indigenous nationalism. It does mean that, given the limited options available under European control, acquiescence to the colonial order – sometimes only temporarily and strategically – was one option, whether in fear, with resignation or with some degree of genuine belief and support.

Finally, it should be emphasized that many colonies were never fully 'pacified'. Resistance continued from the first efforts to repel European invasion through continuing warfare, often dismissed by Europeans as isolated 'revolts', 'insurrections', 'mutinies' or 'banditry'. Surveillance and efforts at control by the military, police and judiciary, censorship of publications, arrest of dissidents and prison or exile for opponents continued to be necessary for Europeans to maintain control. Almost every colony at some point experienced armed action or other militant and violent protest against the colonizers, even if only carried out by a fringe group, as well as the growing current of anti-colonialism channelled through voluntary organization, publications, demonstrations and political campaigns. Moreover, towards the borders of many colonies, European control remained weak or nominal, for instance, among the 'hill tribes' of Southeast Asia and the nomadic populations of the Sahel in Africa. Groups in particularly isolated regions had only episodic contact with rare Europeans, even if formally subject to European-imposed law codes and taxation regimes.

Europeans took over much of the world by all means fair and foul, obtaining territory by cession, treaties of 'protection' and outright conquest. Violence was generally involved, either enacted or threatened, and the process was longer and more complex than might first be appreciated from a simple list of colonies and dates of conquest. Resistance continued, no matter what assurances Europeans preached about having mastered subjects, defeated opponents and suppressed dissidents. When they seemed to have done so, custom and tradition remained resilient, old sources of authority commanded respect, new ideas circulated and rebellion was latent; European hegemony had its limits. Even many of those considered thoroughly Westernized and loyal turned into anti-colonialists and led national struggles for independence.

CHAPTER 4
COLONIAL RULE AND MISRULE, 1914−40

On the eve of the First World War, the maps of European continental and colonial empires appeared relatively fixed and stable (except in the Balkans). The old Habsburg, Russian and diminished Ottoman Empires lived on, as did the newer German Empire. Overseas, Britain's North American, Australian and South African settler colonies had united to form Canada, the Commonwealth of Australia and the Union of South Africa, self-governing but still part of the empire, and the British flag waved over a truly global empire. King Leopold II, in the face of international outrage at labour conditions in the Congo Free State, had ceded his private colony to Belgian state administration. The last decades of the nineteenth century had seen the further extension of several European empires, though with Portugal stymied in its hopes for expansion, and Spain had lost the Philippines and its remaining Caribbean possessions. By 1914, Britain and France, by contrast, had consolidated and augmented their territories in sub-Saharan Africa and Southeast Asia, the Dutch had waged wars in Sumatra and Bali to solidify their control of the East Indies, Italy had occupied Libya and France had declared a protectorate over Morocco. France's interest in Morocco aggravated tensions with Germany, the 'Moroccan crisis' of 1911, but war was averted. That would not be the case three years later, when the assassination of Archduke Franz Ferdinand in Sarajevo, Bosnia – a territory whose incorporation into the Austro-Hungarian Empire in 1908 (along with Herzegovina) showed several parallels with colonial expansion – led to the outbreak of the 'Great War'.

The colonies and the First World War

The First World War was one of the great cataclysms of history in terms of lives lost, economies and infrastructures ravaged, daily life transformed, and national and international politics remoulded. Whereas fighting on the Western Front soon became static trench warfare, combat in the east was dynamic and extended to the Ottoman Empire (allied with Germany and Austria-Hungary) and the Black Sea. Battles also took place in the European colonies of Africa, including Anglo-French campaigns against the German possessions of Togo, Cameroon and German Southwest and East Africa, and Portuguese defence of its continental territories faced with invasion by troops from the German outposts. Even in faraway Oceania, a German warship bombarded Tahiti, and New Zealand occupied German Samoa; action similarly took place in New Guinea, where Australian troops occupied the German colony on the north-eastern quadrant of the island. The First World War thus was a global conflict in terms of the 'theatres of war', the people involved in fighting and the way that colonies were politically and commercially drawn into the fray.

European states summoned support from their overseas possessions in the form of military forces, industrial workers, agricultural provisions and financial contributions. The very fact of colonialism meant that much of Africa, Asia, Oceania and the Caribbean was involved directly and indirectly in a 'total war', mobilizing the home front as well as the battle front and almost the entire resources of belligerent nations. European countries needed workers to staff the industries vital for production of ammunition and other military matériel, and men from the colonies (and independent countries, especially China) were targeted. Some 49,000 workers were brought into France from Indochina, for instance.

An astonishing number of troops from the European empires served in the First World War, though Germany and Belgium did not generally use colonial troops in Europe, and the Netherlands stayed out of the fighting as a neutral power. In Australia, 416,809 men enlisted from a population of fewer than five million; more than 60,000 were killed, and 156,000 wounded, gassed or taken prisoner. New Zealand had a population of just over a million, but 100,000 Kiwi soldiers and nurses served overseas; the 16,697 killed and 41,317 wounded represented a casualty rate of 58 per cent. Around 620,000 Canadians enlisted, with 60,600 killed. Descendants of settlers bound by the 'crimson thread' of kinship to their ancestral homeland were not the only men to rally to Britain. Over a thousand Indigenous men from Australia and 2,200 Maoris (and more than 450 Pacific islanders) served with imperial forces, and the 250,000 volunteers in South Africa included 146,000 whites, 83,000 Blacks and 2,500 'coloureds' and Indians. Around 1.3 million soldiers from the Indian subcontinent served in Allied forces, and more than 74,000 died. There were, as well, 15,000 soldiers from the relatively small British Caribbean islands. French colonies provided between 550,000 and 600,000 recruits, about 450,000 of whom served in Europe; 270,000 men were mobilized from North Africa and 180,000 from French sub-Saharan Africa. Seventy thousand died for France. Indigenous troops (including in the German and Italian Empires) were deployed within the colonies and elsewhere in Africa.

Though the military brass were reassured that colonial soldiers would be a boon to their armies – the valuable *force noire* (Black force) that one French officer had heralded before the war started – the recruitment of men in the colonies did not occur without opposition. British Dominion soldiers often joyfully set off to fight for 'king and empire', but Boers with memories of the recent South African War proved less enthusiastic; heated debates took place in Australia about conscription. Recruiters of indigenous soldiers resorted to strong-arm tactics, sometimes compelling enlistment. Combined with increased taxation and shortages in provisions, this sparked anti-colonial resentment. A rebellion in the French South Pacific colony of New Caledonia in 1917 was in part triggered by recruitment drives. In French Dahomey and Upper Volta, revolts provoked by recruitment dragged on for almost a year – and there and in New Caledonia were put down with severity.

Historians do not agree about whether colonial soldiers were used as 'cannon fodder' intentionally to spare European lives. What is clear, though, is that colonial troops were sent in large numbers to the frontlines in 1917 and 1918. Warfare proved as hellish for them as for others. Military strictures were harsh, European customs sometimes baffling, 'home leave' impossible. Men from tropical countries found the cold of European winters particularly punishing. Many non-European colonial soldiers endured racism, abuse and occasional physical attacks. Individuals and voluntary associations nevertheless made efforts to provide assistance to the African, Asian and other troops.

Letters home from Indian soldiers – letters that, however, were subject to censorship – spoke of such discrimination, but equally of pride in fighting for the king-emperor, a sense of solidarity and camaraderie with each other and European troops, admiration for the bravery of fellow soldiers, and interest in the society and culture of the Europeans among whom they found themselves (see Figure 4.1). They told of privations, suffering and grief at the loss of friends and of acts of kindness they received. Soldiers worried about kith and kin in India, and offered advice on family life and the management of farms or businesses. The letters give proof of courage and resilience. For African and Asian colonial soldiers, tours of duty in Europe often brought realization that the attitudes of people there were not always what they were in the colonies, and that wartime conditions sometimes attenuated the usual racial divides. As one west African corporal in the French army put it: 'I was ranked . . . among the "white" men. I was even giving orders to some "white" men'. Being enlisted 'in the same army' and fighting (or dying) together for France sometimes led to the conclusion that 'we were all equal; we were all the same', another *tirailleur* emphasized. The war forced the British and French themselves to reconsider their views of Africans and Asians in light of the large number who served and the presence of as many as 600,000 African and Asian soldiers in Europe at one time. The image of the African in French advertising, for example, metamorphosed from the dangerous or comical 'savage' towards a brave and faithful soldier. Prejudice nevertheless persisted during the war and afterwards, and Asian and African soldiers never fully, and only tardily, received the rewards and recognition accorded to white soldiers.

Colonial soldiers who survived the war returned home with varying perspectives. Wartime experience had given some a greater awareness of disparities between human rights and participatory political life enjoyed by Europeans and their lack for indigenous and diasporic people in the colonies. Aboriginal soldiers, for instance, found that though they shared trenches with white mates on the battlefront, they could not share a drink with them in pubs back in Australia from which 'natives' were barred. Some soldiers were actively politicized. They encountered anti-colonial perspectives, reformist political movements and the ideologies of socialism and Communism while in Europe, and the intermingling of soldiers from different regions and countries helped to spark feelings of national and international solidarity. At home, continuing inequities perhaps became more evident. Returned soldiers collected pensions, though payments were lower than for European veterans. The incapacitated and those who suffered from what is now called post-traumatic stress faced great difficulties in re-adaptation. The lauded heroism and sacrifices did not guarantee old soldiers the rights of citizens, such as the

5. - NANTES. — GUERRE EUROPEENNE 1914
Nos alliés : Soldats Anglais et Hindous

Figure 4.1 French First World War postcard: 'Nantes - European War 1914 - Our allies: English and Hindu soldiers'. © Alamy Stock Photo.

vote. They soon discovered that the 'self-determination' so championed by peacemakers for Europeans was not to be extended to colonized peoples.

Changes in the political map

In 1916, in the midst of the war, the leader of the Russian Communists, Vladimir Lenin, then in exile in Zurich, wrote an essay entitled 'Imperialism, the Highest Stage of Capitalism'. It argued that the First World War was a war to the death involving the capitalist and imperialist countries that had divided the non-European world for plunder. Lenin arrived back in Russia in 1917 after a revolution had overthrown the tsar, and Lenin's Bolsheviks then initiated a new revolution aiming to establish a Communist society by rejecting capitalism, expropriating the old elites, murdering the tsar and his family, and establishing a 'dictatorship of the proletariat'. Lenin also withdrew Russian forces from the war and signed a peace treaty with Germany. In 1919, he set up the Third Communist International (or Comintern), which proclaimed the goal of fomenting a Marxist-inspired, Communist-led and proletarian-based socialist revolution in Europe and the rest of the world, including the colonies. The organization, and its ideas, would attract enormous attention over the following years, and a number of nationalists from the colonies journeyed to Moscow for training and the building of networks. Communism, though the degree of support it received among the colonized varied significantly, provided one new rallying point for opposition to European rule.

The victory of the Allied powers in 1918 – after the exit of Russia from the war, but with the crucial entry of the United States – saw the dissolution of the Austro-Hungarian, German and Ottoman Empires. Austria-Hungary had no overseas colonies for victors to divide up, but they soon set about parcelling out the possessions of the other vanquished states. Germany was forced to cede its colonies in Africa and the South Pacific. Britain picked up German Southwest Africa (Namibia) and East Africa (Tanganyika), France acquired Togo, Britain and France divided Cameroon, Australia took German New Guinea and Nauru, New Zealand formally took possession of German Samoa and Japan was given Germany's islands in Micronesia. In theory, these were to be ruled as 'mandated territories' under the new League of Nations with the expectation that at some time, perhaps in the distant future, they would become self-governing. In practice, they became colonies, and the overseas portfolios of Britain and France expanded to their maximum in the wake of the war (Map 4.1).

The Ottoman Empire had been the theatre for intense fighting, most famously the battles on the Gallipoli peninsula (where ANZAC troops from Australia and New Zealand fought alongside Indian and French soldiers), and in Palestine and Arabia, with the 'Arab Revolt' against the Turks supported by the Allies. After the war, the British and French split up the spoils from the carcass of the Ottoman Empire – Britain took Palestine and Transjordan (today's Jordan), as well as Iraq, while France moved into Syria and Lebanon. They administered these territories, technically also 'mandates' under the League of Nations, until the 1940s. The arrangement made the European powers more significant players in the politics of the Middle East than in the past, and provoked growing disputes between Jews, Christians and Muslims in Palestine and among fractious religious groups in Syria and Lebanon. Turkey, the heartland of the old Ottoman Empire, escaped colonial takeover, and emerged as an independent nation; under the modernizing and secularist Kemal Atatürk, it became a beacon for many aspiring nationalists in the colonies.

The 'Fourteen Points' proclaimed by the American president Woodrow Wilson as an agenda for peace negotiations in 1918 set out the principle of self-determination: the right and opportunity for peoples freely to decide upon their own national status and form of government. One of Wilson's points stipulated that adjustment of colonial claims must be 'based upon a strict observance of the principle that in determining all such questions

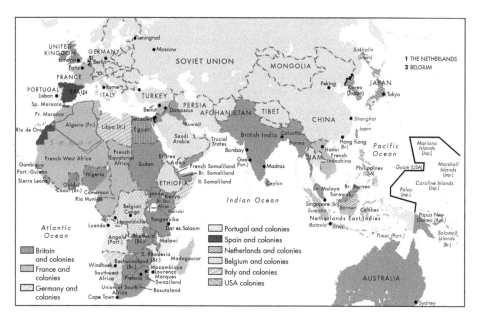

Map 4.1 The Colonial World (general), 1920s. © Adapted from map by cartographer Peter Palm.

of sovereignty the interests of the populations concerned must have equal weight with the equitable claims of the government whose title is to be determined'. The League of Nations set up in the aftermath of the war – but which the United States refused to join, and the Soviet Union entered only in 1934, and from which defeated Germany and Austria were initially excluded – was meant to resolve disputes between states peacefully, an ambitious, if improbable, aim of conflict resolution after the 'war to end all wars'.

The League, from its headquarters in Geneva, regularly discussed colonial issues, and its expert bodies articulated plans for economic and social development. Neither Wilson nor the League called for the end of empires, and the prominent role played in the organization by such colonial powers as Britain and France made such a stance unthinkable. Anti-colonial nationalists nevertheless took heart from Wilson's position, approached the League to seek amelioration of the situation of the colonized, and on occasion (notably when Italy invaded Ethiopia in 1935) implored the League to condemn aggression. The colonies that had come under its aegis after the end of the war were divided into three categories of mandates, the highest destined for independence in the relatively near future because of their stage of maturity; by contrast, the 'C' class mandates were fated to an indeterminate period of foreign rule because of perceived backwardness. The view that immediate sovereignty was not on offer won general consensus. Indigenous leaders nevertheless hoped for a better 'deal' within imperial states, perhaps self-government, as had been promised, or at least implied, for instance, in British statements made to stimulate wartime support in India. Requests for reform were put forward by representatives of the overseas territories, such as the Indian delegate at the post-war Paris Peace Conference, the Maharaja of Bikaner. (India, as well as the British Dominions of Australia, Canada, Newfoundland, New Zealand and South Africa, was separately represented from Britain, though no British colonies or those of other states were.) Delegates at a Pan-African Conference meeting in 1919 hoped to petition the Allies on colonial matters, but to no avail. The more radical Ho Chi Minh, a leftist Vietnamese nationalist then going under the name of Nguyen Ai Quoc, tried to present an anti-colonial message to the peace conference, but the door was shut in his face. Reform from those inside might be considered, but proposals for more substantial change put forward by those outside were not.

Transformations: Colonialism in the interwar period

The image that many people have of nineteenth-century colonialism is one of pith-hatted explorers hacking their way through near impenetrable jungles, or battle-hardened soldiers fighting to bring new territory under their nation's flag. Such images hardly present a full or nuanced view of colonial situations in the 1800s, but by the early 1900s, they had become anachronistic in many European colonies. For sure, there was still reconnaissance of places where 'no white man' had gone, and Europeans remained preoccupied with consolidating rule over peripheral regions. Settlers continued to talk about 'opening' new lands to agriculture, pastoralism, mining and trade. Old-style planters, isolated missionaries and lonely 'district agents' working 'up-country' had not disappeared.

Nevertheless, by the 1920s and 1930s, particularly in urban areas, the colonial world was a very different place than a generation or two earlier. Already in the late 1800s, a dense network of rail lines connected large cities and provided conduits for the movement of ever-increasing volumes of goods and numbers of people. Intercontinental steamships joined together ports and economies in worldwide exchange and travel. There was also now air travel, though it remained unusual, costly and time-consuming – an experimental London to Sydney mail flight on Imperial Airways in 1931 took twenty-six days to reach its destination, with over thirty stops along the way, and the next year, the first passenger flight between London and Cape Town took ten days. Colonial business, exemplified by such companies as P&O lines, Lever Brothers, Royal Dutch Shell, the Banque de l'Indochine and the Michelin rubber and tyre company, had become very big businesses indeed, adopting innovations such as managerialism and Taylorism. Companies producing petroleum represented an especially promising new concern. The Batavian Oil Company (part of Shell), founded in 1907, and the Anglo-Persian Oil Company (later British Petroleum), set up in 1909 as a subsidiary of the Burmah Oil Company, were exploiting what would become the world's leading fossil fuel and one of the major items of trade and profit. Meanwhile, the telegraph had long provided rapid communication, and the radio, which came into its own after the First World War, beamed news, propaganda and entertainment around the colonies and across the world. Telephone communication was similarly becoming more common.

The cinema, including the 'talkies' that premiered at the end of the 1920s, already provided a popular leisure activity for the middle and upper classes in colonial cities, and films included newsreels and documentaries – another vehicle for colonialist propaganda. Typewriters had changed office life, as well as the types of records created and archived. Sewing machines, in particular those of the famous Singer Company, found a place in colonial European homes and in those of up-and-coming indigenous people, offering a possibility for women, in particular, not only to make clothing for their families but also to find sources of income. Colonial department stores marketed the latest fashions, to Europeans and the elite of the colonized who could afford luxury. Motorcars were becoming increasingly common and desirable, and some colonial cities inaugurated tram and bus networks. Colonial capitals constituted growing and bustling metropolises (though mostly segregated into separate areas for 'whites' and others) with universities, art galleries, concert halls, grand hotels and other amenities. Indeed, some colonial cities were more modern than European ones – Batavia, in the Dutch East Indies, installed electric lighting before most cities in the Netherlands. However, new-fangled styles of life in the islands of modernity represented by cities seldom yet penetrated provincial and remote areas, where agriculture remained the mainstay, the majority of people lived in villages, and such devices as lifts, telephones and motorcars were seldom seen.

In colonial government departments, bureaucrats busied themselves devising plans for 'development', 'modernization' and what they saw as 'progress' through science, technology, investment and Europeanization, coupled with social initiatives and what they lauded as more enlightened approaches than in the past to 'native affairs'. In 1901, the Dutch queen had announced a new 'ethical policy' (*ethische politiek*) for the Netherlands' colonies, stating that improvement in the welfare of local populations should be the priority. This new perspective, and acknowledgement of moral responsibility for indigenous peoples, was closely connected to social questions in the Netherlands itself. In the colonies the 'ethical policy' could lead to consolidation of control, greater levels of economic exploitation and increasing distancing of colonial subjects from their ancestral cultures, though it did also bring benefits in education and healthcare to a select few. For the French Empire, Albert Sarraut, a seasoned governor general of Indochina and senior official in Paris, in the 1920s proclaimed a policy of *mise en valeur* that became a leitmotiv of French politics and propaganda; the word means 'valorization', and the idea encompassed wholesale improvement in the commercial and social infrastructure of the colonies and the better activation of their resources, including human resources, though colonizers unsurprisingly became prime beneficiaries. The ideas of 'valorization' of colonial potential and a more 'ethical' approach to rule, with similar views in Britain to those in France and the Netherlands, became principles driving government initiatives and limited reform during the interwar years. In the Spanish and Portuguese cases, objectives and realizations fell short even of those set by other colonial powers, in part due to authoritarian governments, less vibrant economies and more limited means in the Iberian countries.

The 1920s brought a boom to the world's economy, with a great increase in trade and a surfeit of capital. In French Vietnam, British Malaya and Sumatra in the Dutch East Indies, among other colonies, production of rubber – especially important with the growing automotive industry – expanded rapidly in the interwar years. A buoyant international economy created heightened demand for exports from colonial farms and mines: foodstuffs for swelling urban populations, raw material for factories, minerals used in new technologies. There was greater industrialization in the colonies, including both export and import-substitution industries – Bombay, with a huge textile industry, for instance, had become a major manufacturing centre. Most colonial cities had food-processing industries, breweries, factories making clothing and similar types of products, though heavy industry was less common. Tourism was becoming an increasingly important economic activity thanks to ocean liners, travel agencies, advertising and the popularity of faraway destinations. The British travel agency Thomas Cook, dating back to the 1840s, organized tourism on an international scale. The French Michelin company owned rubber plantations in Vietnam, made automobile tyres and spruiked tourism in the guidebooks it published.

There was wealth to be had, with many fortunes indeed made by businesspeople in the colonies or those in the metropole who invested in colonial business. The British settler societies, particularly Australia and Canada, counted among the most prosperous countries in the world and enjoyed some of the highest standards of living. The elite in European colonies lived better than many of their compatriots in the 'mother country' thanks to good salaries, spacious houses, imported luxuries and bevvies of servants. However, not all enjoyed the riches by any means. First Nations people in Australia and Canada, Africans in South Africa and Arabs in Algeria, and most of the other colonized peoples, lived a life of poverty, hard labour and limited opportunities far removed from the comforts of the privileged. Except for a small traditional and newer elite – often fabulously wealthy maharajas, the prosperous owners of factories and trading houses, more senior bureaucrats, professional people such as doctors and lawyers – the lot of most Indians, for example, was penury, exhausting work and drudgery; access to education, medical care and effective sanitation (such as sewage disposal and clean water) was severely limited or for a large number impossible. That was the lot, as well, of the indigenous people of other colonies. The materially impoverished – often excruciatingly poor by European standards – formed the majority, some reduced to begging or scrounging for a living or throwing themselves on the mercy of charitable institutions. (There were some poor European settlers and their descendants eking out a modest living in the colonies, of course, but they at least could fall back on claims of racial superiority.) There were nonetheless important emerging indigenous, diasporic and *métis* groups in many colonies, albeit limited in size, that encompassed office clerks, small businesspeople, employees in transportation (such as the railways), clerics, teachers, journalists and others: an indigenous middle and lower-middle class. Though they, and the indigenous lawyers, doctors and other university-trained professionals, were numerically few, they occupied key positions – they were the *évolués* (the 'evolved' ones, as the French pointedly referred to this cohort, with similar labels in other languages). They formed an intermediary stratum between the Europeans, on the one hand, and the indigenous and diasporic masses, on the other. They proved able to manipulate European business practices, law, knowledge and social conventions to their advantage, though still disparaged by white masters and usually denied political rights.

Colonial economies and societies thus had become increasingly complex structures during the early decades of the twentieth century, still marked as in the past by great disparities of wealth and political rights based particularly on race. 'Race' remained the great denominator of status and rights. European descent constituted the ultimate privilege, catapulting even poor and uneducated whites upwards in social hierarchies, at least in legal terms; for non-Europeans, social ascent meant overcoming racial barriers put in place by colonizers. It is important to remember, however, that despite the primacy of race, there existed many fault lines, and often antipathies, within both indigenous and settler societies between religious, ethnic and regional communities, and the presence of peoples who moved from one colony to another further textured social relations.

Race determined inclusion or exclusion in many domains, painfully in evidence in institutions such as European social clubs that forbade the entry of 'natives' (except as servants); even educated and prosperous indigenous people could not easily cross such a race line. Nineteenth-century theories of 'race', put forward as scientific, and based on the supposed inherent gradations of physical and mental capacities between 'Black', 'brown', 'yellow' and 'redskin' people (and those of 'mixed-race' origin), retained common currency. Relatively few even in the early twentieth century questioned belief in the real existence of different 'races' with particular traits – and those on the political far right in the 1930s hardened their views and became more public about plans for discrimination against or even elimination of inferior 'races', in Europe and elsewhere. The word 'race' remained a widely accepted term in scientific literature and popular parlance – its use ranging from casual, daily speech to hate-filled invective about savagery, primitivism and the incapacity of certain 'races' for education, self-rule or civilization. Europeans not surprisingly placed themselves at the apex of racial hierarchies. 'Race' had justified conquest and slavery in European eyes, and it continued to legitimate denial of political rights, economic exploitation, disparagement of local cultures and discrimination. The notion of 'race' remained firmly and dangerously embedded in the mindset of colonials and in the institutions they established, even in the supposedly more modern and enlightened interwar years. Racialized and racist perspectives suggested and accorded with ideas about the need for economic and social 'modernization' and 'development', assumptions that the European (implicitly, white) was new and modern, the indigenous old and backward. Economics, politics and cultural perspectives remained as intertwined, and potently so, as they ever had been in colonial situations.

Colonialism between confidence and crisis

Ever since the Crystal Palace exhibition in London in 1851, the colonies had gone on show at the national and international expositions and fairs that became regular occurrences. These continued, in increasingly grand style, in the interwar years, with the British Empire Exhibition at Wembley (in London) in 1924–5, the Ibero-American Exposition of 1929 in Seville, the International Colonial Exposition in Paris in 1931 and the Portuguese World Exhibition in Lisbon in 1940. The exhibitions presented the products of the colonies, showed off European accomplishments in law and order, technology, and schooling and medical care, and they displayed indigenous art and artefacts, and often included groups of indigenous people brought from the colonies to perform 'traditional' music, dances and artisan skills as entertainment. The fairgrounds were impressive, in Paris, centring on a huge reconstruction of the Cambodian Angkor Wat temple dramatically illuminated in the evening, and handsomely and appropriately decorated pavilions dedicated to each of the colonies. The French Colonial Ministry, colonial associations and businesses mounted their displays, and there was a purpose-built Catholic Church (with a curious mélange of European, Indochinese and Arabic-inspired architecture) to testify to evangelization. Visitors enjoyed military processions, viewed collections of colonialist painting, savoured 'typical' foods and drinks in cafés and restaurants, and of course bought souvenirs. The great and good put in appearances; the guest of honour at the Paris fair was the emperor of Vietnam, considered by anti-colonialists a puppet of the French, and over five months, eight million visitors came from near and far. The scenario was similar at the other fairs.

Such exhibitions, planned to be educational and enjoyable, were intentionally also designed as propaganda that it was hoped would stimulate support for colonialism and inspire colonial vocations. The interwar fairs represented colonialism in its most triumphant phase and most successful guise, at least from the standpoint of the Europeans, but they also revealed enduring stereotypes about picturesque and exotic cultures, and about perceived contrasts between the 'traditional' (indeed 'primitive') and 'modern'. They brought the empire home in a very visible way, to the pleasure of some and the consternation of others. In 1931, the French Communist Party sponsored a small but pointed 'Anti-Colonial Exposition' in Paris; its displays showcased images of atrocities, poverty, exploitation and forced labour, taboo at the celebratory fair across the city, and activists passed out leaflets beseeching Parisians to boycott the official exhibition.

Colonial fairs took on particular importance in the context of the unsettled situation in Europe in the wake of the Great War and during the troubled 1920s and 1930s, decades marked by economic booms and busts, the rise of new extremist movements of left and right, and growing anti-colonialism. The Wembley exhibition (Figure 4.2) underlined the role of the empire in Britain's post-war recovery, the ties of kinship that bound the British to settlers overseas and the extent and might of an empire without parallel. The Seville fair affirmed Spain's continuing ties with and influence over former colonies across the Atlantic. As Communism gained ground in France, the siting of the fair in the working-class eastern neighbourhood of Paris was intended to buttress liberalism, nationalism and colonialism as more acceptable creeds. Ideology was similarly manifest in Lisbon in 1940. As a poor European country, Portugal was eager to claim that its colonies brought wealth and international status. Such an impression held special value for the dictatorial government, in power in Lisbon since 1926, which wanted to shore

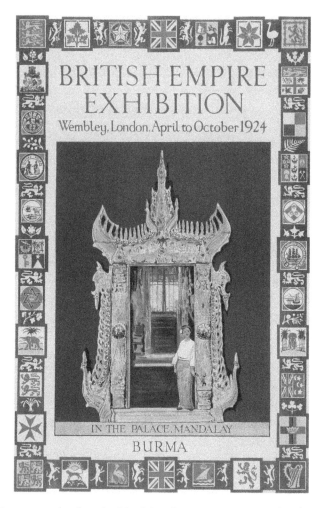

Figure 4.2 Former royal palace in Mandalay, Burma, on a poster for the British Empire Exhibition, London, 1924. © Getty Images.

up its anti-democratic authority, establish global *bona fides* and promote Portugal's neutrality as the Second World War began. By including Brazil in the fair, Portugal, like Spain in its earlier exhibition, insisted that cultural, social and political ties lived on beyond the formal end of colonial rule.

Despite the fanfare, the 1930s proved a time of great difficulty for the colonies, and for the vision of colonialism proffered by Europeans. Triggered by the New York Stock Exchange crash in 1929 and its spreading international repercussions, the Depression caused a dramatic plunge in the price of the primary products that composed the bulk of colonial exports, such as coffee and tea, rubber and minerals. This wrought predictable effects on owners of plantations, mining companies and merchants, but even more so on their employees, most of them indigenous or diasporic people. Many factories involved in the processing of colonial goods closed for lack of capital and markets, leading to greater unemployment. The crash of stock markets destroyed companies and investor portfolios that relied on colonial business, and thus the wages that had become the livelihood of a growing number of the colonized.

In the case of the Belgian Congo, which provides an example, the value of shares in colonial companies on the Brussels Stock Exchange in 1931 reached only about 15 per cent of the 1928 quotations. In 1930, the value of copper exports, the colony's main commodity, stood at 737 million Congolese francs; in 1932, it had dropped to 102 million. In the Katanga province, where mining centred, three-quarters of the European workers lost their jobs; the number of African workers fell from 73,000 in 1930 to 27,000 three years later. Prices for cotton and palm oil declined dramatically as well. The story was much the same elsewhere (including in independent countries of Latin America, whose economies were similarly based on export of primary products), the rapid fall in prices explained by the world's economic situation and overproduction in the boom years of the 1920s. The price of Kenyan coffee dropped from 86 shillings per 100 pounds in 1929 to 23 shillings in 1938; that of cocoa, the Ivory Coast's major export, fell by 86 per cent during the Depression. Many indigenous workers had to return to their villages and subsistence farming, though production and exports eventually rebounded.

Policymakers were faced with solving the economic problems at home and in the empire – unemployment, a fall in export volumes and prices, and a decline in tax revenue. Despite the depression in their overseas possessions, they hoped that the colonies would substantially aid recovery. The British established preferential tariffs for trade between the UK and its dominions and colonies, and other countries relied more heavily than before on colonial markets and raw materials. Some in France claimed that salvation from the country's economic woes, in fact, would come from the colonies. To many budding nationalists in the colonies, however, the 1930s Depression revealed the structural weakness of the capitalist economic system and belied the prosperity that colonial powers had promised. Images of workers in London and Paris dole queues hardly strengthened the colonizers' reputation, and civil strife in Europe showed the deepening fractures in politics and society in the metropoles.

Anti-colonial nationalism

In different ways, colonized people had long resisted occupation of their countries by Europeans and others. They waged war against conquest, and rose in insurrection against foreign rule. Some sought to undermine the Europeans by sabotage and subterfuge. Many worked to preserve traditions and inherited social structures against impositions from overseas. Indigenous people looked to ancestral institutions and old dynasties as bulwarks against the colonizers. Nineteenth-century 'native' rulers such as Sultan Dipenegoro in Dutch Java, Béhanzin in French West Africa and Gungunhana in Portuguese Mozambique had led campaigns against colonization, even if ultimately defeated, exiled or killed. The Indian rebels of 1857 chose the Mughal emperor, Bahadur Shah Zafar, as nominal leader of their struggle. In the mid-1880s, the Cao Vuong

('Restore the Emperor') movement in Vietnam promoted revival of a monarchy that had been turned into a vassal institution of the French. Elsewhere, pretenders to abolished thrones emerged to try to instigate opposition, as occurred in the Saya San movement in Burma in the 1930s. Millenarian spiritual groups in various countries backed prophets who promised liberation.

However, anti-colonialists, especially those of a younger generation, by the early twentieth century and especially after the First World War and the disappointments that failure of promised reform and hoped for self-determination produced, increasingly took on Western precepts as well. Ideas about 'liberty, equality and fraternity' spread, as did belief in constitutionalism and parliamentarianism, freedom of the press and freedom of assembly – and the potential for wholesale and militant revolution. In the eyes of this generation, rights championed by Europeans for Europeans should equally apply to colonized peoples, and for some, Marxism or anarchism could be adopted as an ideology and strategy of anti-colonial resistance. By the interwar years and well before in some colonies, an articulate cohort of figures, often with Western-style education, had emerged to marshal European ideas as well as the religious, political and social principles of their own cultures to fight colonialism.

Regular interchange among these figures and the associations they founded connected them across colonial boundaries as well as with peers in Europe and the Americas. Already in the late 1800s, for instance, the Filipino political theorist and novelist José Rizal (1861–96) maintained links with critics of colonialism in Spain and in Cuba, an intellectual and political network that traversed the Hispanophone world of Asia, the Caribbean and Iberia, and even stretched into Germany. An early twentieth-century developing literary and political movement among African Americans, and Anglophone and Francophone Africans in Europe and the colonies, represented swelling opposition by colonized and diasporic Black people to racism and discrimination. W. E. B. Du Bois (1868–1963), an African American, was arguably the most internationally famous Black writer and activist of the early twentieth century. He had curated a display of photographs ('An Exhibit of American Negroes') for the Paris world's fair of 1900, and compiled an anthology of Black writings. Du Bois played a large role in eight Pan-African Congresses convened in London in 1900, in Paris in 1919, and episodically on to 1945, and attended by many emerging leaders of African independence movements. Other figures of resistance acquired an international reputation as well. Critics of colonialism looked towards independent non-European countries to find support and as models for self-government and national regeneration. Japan provided a key focus for nationalists in Southeast Asia, since Japan had maintained its independence, successfully modernized and industrialized, and become a colonial power (though colonized Taiwanese and particularly Koreans demurred from admiration of the 'land of the rising sun'). Reformers in imperial China, such as Liang Qichao (1873–1929), exercised widespread influence, and the overthrow of the Qing dynasty in 1912 and setting up of a republic under Sun Yat-sen (1868–1925) provided an example of successful regime change and forward-looking reform. Independent Siam, which had repulsed the British and French, provided another beacon for nationalists in Asia. In the Arabic and Islamic world, an important nineteenth-century anti-imperialist figure was the writer Jamal al-Din al-Afghani (1838–97); born in Afghanistan or possibly Iran, he travelled in India and central Asia, then to Egypt, published an Arabic newspaper in Paris, lived for a time in London and died in Turkey, exemplary of the mobility of anti-colonialists in his own time and afterwards and of the role of writing and the press in mobilizing activists. Post-Ottoman Turkey under Atatürk, from the 1920s, as previously mentioned, offered a further case of a strengthening country, as did Egypt as it partially emancipated itself from the British in that decade.

The internationalism of anti-colonialism, building on nineteenth-century antecedents, is one of the hallmarks of the early twentieth century, aided by the greater facility of travel and communication. Political figures, books and newspapers, and ideas circulated widely around the world with remarkable speed and impact. Despite strenuous efforts by colonial authorities to control 'subversive' thought, open and clandestine anti-colonial networks flourished. The peregrinations of anti-colonial activists and the transmission of their ideas across countries and continents are indeed remarkable given the legal, judicial and police power of colonial governments. These activities illustrate, too, how anti-colonialism as well as colonialism functioned as an international and transnational phenomenon. As colonialists celebrated empire in European jamborees, so anti-colonialists, through secret contacts and personal networks, promoted opposition to European rule, even at the heart of empire.

Vietnamese nationalists, Ho Chi Minh (1890–1969) notable among them, gathered in Paris, where they came into contact with new ideas, met nationalists from other colonies, found support from the Communist Party (and some other political groups) and published articles in its anti-colonial newspaper, *Le Paria*. But there was also a Paris Indian Society, presided over by a Parsi woman, Bhikaji Rustom Cama (1861–1936), that provided support for the nationalist movement in the British Raj. London became a centre for protesters against British rule in India – around 1908, around 100 politically aware Indian students in Britain congregated at 'India House' (considered a dangerous hotbed of agitation by the British) under the inspiration of Vinayak Savarkar (1883–1966), noteworthy for having written about the 'Mutiny' of 1857 as *The Indian War of Independence*. London brought together reformers and revolutionaries from the subcontinent, Africa and the Caribbean, as well as conferences of intellectuals and writers such as the First University Races Congress, convened to discuss and combat racism in 1911. The story was repeated elsewhere: the first African newspaper published in Lisbon, for instance, the work of writers from several Portuguese colonies, was established in 1911, the embryo of protest against Portuguese colonial rule. European capitals thus were capitals of colonialism but also of anti-colonialism.

The ideas, strategies and objectives of nascent movements differed. Some of the early groups, such as the Indian National Congress, established in 1885, and the African National Congress, founded in 1912 as the South African Native National Congress, aimed at reform rather than revolution. Certain colonial nationalists either for strategic reasons or from conviction stopped short of demanding independence. They called rather for a widening of the suffrage (since most non-Europeans remained ineligible to vote), greater political representation for indigenous peoples in local consultative or legislative councils dominated by whites, better working conditions and equitable salaries, easier entry for local peoples into the higher ranks of the civil service and military, abrogation of discriminatory law codes and taxation regimes, greater recognition of local cultures and expanded access to education and health care. Some Europeans supported these objectives (and a few spoke in favour of outright independence for the colonies), though vested interests generally staunched major change in the colonial order.

As colonial authorities resisted nationalist demands, even moderates became more and more convinced that only self-government and, for a growing number, sovereignty could satisfy their grievances. The persistent failure of the British to deliver on promises of eventual self-government in India mooted during the First World War, the very limited success of colonial reform under the leftist Popular Front government in France in the 1930s and of the 'ethical policy' in the Dutch colonies, and the refusal of the Belgians and Portuguese to recast the administrative, political and economic system in their colonies pushed nationalists to more uncompromising positions as the years passed.

Anti-colonial violence made episodic appearances in these movements, though roundly rejected by activists such as Gandhi, who continued to champion nonviolent tactics of resistance. Violence was loudly condemned by most Europeans, the perpetrators branded terrorists. Europeans were sometimes victims in the colonies, with attacks carried out even in Europe, as when one senior colonial official was assassinated in London. Uprisings, assassinations and what the colonial authorities euphemistically labelled 'disturbances' punctuated twentieth-century colonial history with increasing frequency. It was, however, nationalists contended, the obduracy of the colonialists that forced them into such strategies.

Culture and resistance

In all of the movements, moderate as well as radical, culture provided a foundation for nationalist sentiment. Not surprisingly, religion offered a sense of heritage and communitarian bonding, and often political structure, as well as a spirituality. Islam remained the central point of identification for Muslims looking to the Prophet Muhammad, the Quran, pilgrimage to Mecca, the solidarity of the Islamic community (the *umma*) and for some, *shari'a* law and holy war (*jihad*) as rallying points, locally, nationally and internationally. The mosque and the Muslim school (*madrasa*) became focal points for dissemination of the faith in the face of widening Europeanization, with the *hajj* (pilgrimage) providing ample opportunities for activists to get in touch with and promote transnational Islamic and anti-colonial identities and networks. Elsewhere, Buddhism and Hinduism, and other non-European spiritualities provided reference points for colonized people. So did Christianity, whose indigenous and European clergy and parishioners could be critics as well as supporters of colonialism – many future leaders of independence movements received an education in Christian schools, and Protestant leaders, in particular, were increasingly willing to contest colonialist administrations and settler elites.

Europeans had habitually denigrated African history and culture, though progressive anthropologists and connoisseurs of 'primitive' art held more nuanced views and relativistic perspectives on 'civilization'. In the 1920s and 1930s, an important movement emerged that sought to valorize African heritage. Diasporic Africans and Black West Indians in Europe and the United States took the lead in the *négritude* movement. Paris provided a centre, though Africanist movements were active in Britain, in the American 'Harlem Renaissance' and elsewhere. The French capital attracted budding African and West Indian intellectuals because of its universities, publishing houses and tradition of avant-garde culture. *L'Étudiant noir*, published in 1935, as its name indicates, by Black students, counted among several important, if short-lived, journals of the young intellectuals. One noteworthy leader among the ones in interwar Paris was Paulette Nardal (1896–1985). Born into a prosperous Black family on the Caribbean island of Martinique, she went to Paris to study at the Sorbonne and became a teacher, journalist and writer. With two of her six sisters, she presided over a literary salon frequented by many young cultural figures of the diaspora, and in 1931, the sisters, along with a Haitian, an African American and a metropolitan Frenchman, founded the *Revue du monde noir*, a pioneering journal. A promoter of women's rights, in 1944 Nardal set up a feminist organization in Martinique, and the next year, in Paris, she began publishing a journal entitled *La Femme dans la cité*; she later served on the United Nations' Commission on the Status of Women. The Nardal sisters joined a number of Black women intellectuals and activists from the French colonies – including Suzanne Césaire, Eugénie Éboué-Tall, Jane Vialle and Andrée Blouin – who contributed new perspectives on African culture, feminism, colonialism and contemporary events.

A key male leader of the *négritude* movement was Léopold Sedar Senghor (1906–2001), a Christian from Senegal who journeyed to Paris to study in 1928. He became a renowned poet and eventually a member of the Académie Française. Senghor's itinerary spans long decades from involvement with the Africanist movement in Paris in the 1930s to the end of the century. In the complex history of decolonization, Senghor was first considered by the French as a model for the success for the *mission civilisatrice*, the holder of university degrees, a new literary voice and a moderate political reformer (with socialist affiliations). In the 1950s, Senghor served as a minister in the French government, though he also led the Senegalese independence movement; he became the first president of independent Senegal in 1960, serving in the position for twenty years and honoured as an elder African statesman and literary figure.

Aimé Césaire (1913–2008), the husband of Suzanne Césaire, was another important figure. Like Nardal, he arrived in Paris from Martinique to pursue university studies. Similarly to Senghor, Césaire became a major poet and playwright, and his *Cahier d'un retour au pays natal* (literally, Notebook of a Return to the Native Land), published in 1939, was heralded for Surrealist-inspired use of language and exposition of the sentiments of a Black man who felt profoundly dispossessed both in Paris and back home in Martinique. Though Césaire joined the Communist Party (resigning in 1956), in 1945 he promoted the full integration of the 'old' colonies of Martinique, Guadeloupe, Guyane and La Réunion into the French Republic – a measure, he hoped, that would give Blacks and *métis* full equality with whites. He later expressed some support for Martinique's independence. Césaire served as a long-time mayor of Martinique's major city, Fort-de-France, and a member of the French parliament. Yet another outstanding figure was the Guyane-born poet Léon-Gontran Damas (1912–78). The geographical background of these individuals varied, but common African ancestry, participation in Parisian intellectual life and experience of discrimination as Black men and women provided common links. They came from the 'old' Caribbean colonies and, in Senghor's case, from one of the five towns in Senegal where residents were full-fledged French citizens, but their work, both literary and political, resonated with other Africans, and they inspired a wider re-evaluation of African culture and heritage among Europeans.

Africa, these writers affirmed, contrary to the stereotypes of colonialists, could take pride in a rich history, with lineages, institutions and civilizations that stood comparison with any in the world. Despite regional and ethnic differences, Africans shared a common culture, an international one transported far beyond Africa. They also shared the painful legacy of enslavement, colonization and exploitation with each other and with other colonized peoples. As Césaire wrote in his *Discourse on Colonialism* (1950), colonial rule had not only materially dispossessed Africans and other colonized peoples, it had suppressed their cultures and denigrated their heritage. Africans, those in the diaspora and non-Africans as well, needed to recognize and respect African-derived cultures (and not just through vogues for folklore, jazz and entertainment). For some in the *négritude* movement, that implied full emancipation from colonial rule.

Another major cultural and political movement, indeed the most famous, was associated with the Indian Mohandas Karamchand ('Mahatma') Gandhi (1869–1948). Born into a Hindu merchant family and trained as a lawyer in London, Gandhi went to South Africa in 1893. There he became famous, and controversial, for legal and political defence of the migrant Indian population against poor conditions, discrimination and violence. Gandhi returned to India during the First World War and joined the Indian National Congress, which he led from 1921. Gandhi was a philosopher and activist, his actions motivated by a deep commitment to non-violence and the idea that spiritual regeneration and purification were necessary for individuals to combat colonialism and construct a new society. *Satyagraha* was a brand of active non-violence – Gandhi never considered his efforts as just 'passive resistance' – both spiritual and political, individual and collective. Faced with lack of political reform in India, Gandhi called for non-cooperation with the British. He asked Indians to boycott British imports, especially the cheap manufactured textiles competing with Indian production. Gandhi himself ceased wearing European coats and ties, preferring the simple loincloth (*dhoti*) of a peasant. The image of Gandhi sitting cross-legged on his mat spinning cotton became one of the most powerful icons of the late colonial period, an emblem of Indian self-reliance and rejection of industrial production and foreign rule.

In 1930, in another of his undertakings, Gandhi led a Salt March, a 400-kilometre journey to the sea, to protest the tax on salt that Indians were obliged to pay. Gandhi's other strategies, including general strikes (the *hartal*), hunger strikes and civil disobedience, led to his arrest on numerous occasions. Undaunted, he continued the campaign to get Britain to 'Quit India', and the number of his followers burgeoned. Gandhi, still clad in his Indian peasant's clothing, took part in Round Table Conferences held in London from 1930 to 1932, at which British and Indian politicians, including the nationalists, discussed constitutional reform, though the British still failed to satisfy Indian demands.

Gandhi was undoubtedly the most recognizable leader of the Indian nationalist movement, but the man who became the first prime minister of independent India in 1947 was Jawaharlal Nehru (1889–1964). An Eton- and Cambridge-educated lawyer whose talents lay particularly in organization, negotiation and the devising of plans for a future independent India, Nehru aspired to a sovereign India with national unity, a parliamentary democracy and a socialist economy. Both Gandhi and Nehru, like the majority of Indians, were Hindus, and Muslims were concerned about what fate would be reserved for them in an independent India. Muhammad Ali Jinnah (1876–1948), the most prominent voice of the subcontinent's Muslim population and also a highly respected lawyer, led efforts to secure an independent Muslim-dominated state on the subcontinent. In 1947, India and Pakistan became separately independent with 'Partition', though hasty and badly planned division of the subcontinent came at great human cost with estimates of deaths ranging from hundreds of thousands to several million, and the displacement of between ten and twenty million, as Muslims fled north and Hindus fled south. The carnage, however, was not the fault of Jinnah or his programme, and he served as the founder and first governor general of Pakistan. Gandhi, Nehru and Jinnah represented only the internationally most celebrated of a large number of nationalists who brought about decolonization of the subcontinent.

Other nationalists, including some in India, were attracted by more radical creeds than the conservative and spiritually oriented nationalism of Gandhi or the parliamentarianism of Nehru and Jinnah. Marxism exercised a strong pull on anti-colonialists. Though Marx's theory had been articulated with the immediate objective of a socialist revolution in industrialized society, its tenets of the overturning of a bourgeois order that exploited an underclass of peasants and proletarians offered a powerful message to the colonized. Tactics such as organization of trade unions, general strikes, public demonstrations and the setting up of clandestine cells and networks provided a battery of strategies in countries where most of the indigenous and diasporic non-European populations were denied the franchise. Marx's idea of international solidarity among the working class suggested common causes and collaboration among colonized people around the globe.

By the early twentieth century, various currents of Marxist-influenced politics competed for support. The reformist strands of the socialist movement in Europe in the 1800s had largely come to favour the taking of power through parliamentary processes rather than revolution. Though many had initially opposed colonial expansion, the socialist parties by and large came to accept the fact of empire, hoped to use their base to improve the lot of the colonized, and promoted changes that might eventually, though not always in the immediate future, lead to independence. The Communist movement, which split off from the mainstream socialists after the Bolshevik revolution, generally promoted more direct action to subvert the bourgeois and capitalist colonial order. The Moscow-based Comintern promoted the Soviet brand of Marxism throughout the colonized world. By the 1930s, in the aftermath of Fascism coming to power in Italy (in 1922), authoritarianism in Portugal (from 1926), Nazism in Germany (with Hitler appointed chancellor in 1933) and the Francoist movement in Spain (which defeated republicans in a civil war by 1939), as well as extreme right-wing movements in Britain and France, Communism to many, not just in the colonies, appeared a persuasive ideology with which to combat dictatorship, despite the unknown or ignored atrocities of the Stalinist regime in Russia. The Depression and indecisive government action against unemployment and poverty further popularized its appeal as an alternative to bankrupt liberal politics and neo-orthodox economic policy.

Ho Chi Minh was arguably the most celebrated Marxist anti-colonialist, the man who took Vietnamese nationalists to victory over the French in 1954. Born the son of a Confucian scholar and magistrate who was demoted for abuse of power, Ho seems to have been politicized during a 1908 tax revolt in Vietnam. He went overseas three years later, working in odd jobs in Europe and the United States and making contact with fellow Vietnamese dissidents. The end of the First World War found Ho in Europe, and in 1920, he joined the new French Communist Party and wrote articles for its newspaper. By 1923 he was in Moscow studying at a Comintern training school; then he went to China, where he organized political education classes for expatriate Vietnamese in Canton. After moving around Asia, in 1930 Ho presided in Hong Kong over the foundation of a unified Vietnamese Communist Party, which led to his arrest by the British. After release, he continued to live in exile until returning to Vietnam in 1941, during the Second World War. Ho's anti-colonial theory rested on an adaptation of Marxist principles for an Asian society, where peasants, rather than factory proletarians, would make the revolution. He promoted close cooperation with other Communist forces (taking the Soviet Union as mentor) and the mobilization of the masses for an uprising against the French. He resorted to a form of guerrilla warfare against which the French found it difficult to contend. Ho's objective was outright independence with the organization of a new society based on Marxist precepts. Yet at the same time, he remained an ardent nationalist, his campaigns deeply rooted in Vietnamese culture (as seen in his poetry), though he rejected the pre-colonial Vietnamese order as feudal and anachronistic. Ho's influence spread far beyond Vietnam, and outlasted the end of French rule.

Between reform and revolution

There were many other figures associated with anti-colonialist movements in the interwar years and after, with varying goals, philosophies and strategies. Faced with the strength and resistance of the colonial powers, none proved successful in securing independence in this period, and in many cases factional fighting, ideological disputes and difficulties in mobilizing support provided handicaps. The colonial regimes agreed to make only limited and gradual reforms, ones that preserved the rights of colonial states and settler communities, conceding limited political participation by non-Europeans in local assemblies. Such moves, to some degree, comforted reformists and assuaged colonialists, but came nowhere close to satisfying those who demanded independence.

Peaceful protests and, less frequently, armed nationalist actions punctuated the interwar years and were brutally suppressed by the colonial military and police forces. One of the most notorious and bloody responses to demonstrations came in the Indian city of Amritsar in 1919. On 13 April, a crowd of between 10,000 and 20,000 gathered at the Jallianwala Bagh square, a former garden used as a recreational area near the most sacred Sikh site, the Golden Temple, to celebrate a festival and protest the arrest of two independence leaders and general British policies. Some of those present, however, were simply passing through as they returned home from worship or a visit to a livestock fair. The British had banned the gathering, and posted fifty soldiers to the bagh. The crowd remained peaceful as the brigadier in charge of operations instructed them to disperse, but the officer then blocked the exit from the square (enclosed on three sides by buildings) and ordered his men to open fire and continue shooting. At least 379 people were killed, with some placing the toll much higher, and over a thousand were injured. The Jallianwala Bagh massacre (also called the Amritsar massacre) stunned Indians and shocked even some British leaders – 'one of the worst, most dreadful, outrages in the whole of our history', according to a former British prime minister. The incident inspired the non-cooperation movement in the early 1920s, and, in the long term, strengthened the resolve of nationalists.

The British continued to suppress protests in later years, while attempting to avoid a repeat of the massacre at Amritsar. Other colonizers faced and defeated rebellions that developed into full-scale war, as occurred with French and Spanish actions against a movement led by Abd el-Krim (1882–1963) in the 'Rif war' of 1921–6 in Morocco. The French also suppressed the 'Druze rebellion' of 1925 in Lebanon, part of the longer-lasting and more widely spread 'Great Syrian Revolt' of the mid-1920s, as well as an uprising at Yen Bay in Vietnam in 1931. Similar incidents of greater or lesser magnitude erupted in other colonies.

Colonial authorities tried to maintain their stronghold by methods extending to war and massacres. In a more regular and continuous strategy, they censored 'subversive' literature and closed down critical periodicals, outlawed nationalist organizations, banned demonstrations, spied on suspected rebels and meetings, arrested, imprisoned and sometimes executed anti-colonial leaders (with extra-judicial killings as well). Along with the 'stick' went the 'carrot', with efforts to win the hearts and minds of the colonized through propaganda, modest reforms, development projects, support for leaders considered loyal and overtures to more moderate nationalists. All the while, imperial rulers continued to celebrate empire egregiously in expositions, publications and broadcasts, claiming that they had 'pacified' colonies and were advancing progress and modernization for the good of their subjects. By the late 1930s, however, with persistent economic dislocation, successful or rising extremist ideologies, growing anti-colonialism, cultural resistance movements and new and more militant anti-colonial political organizations, as well as the looming probability of another 'great war', the empires – and, in fact, the democratic European states – looked increasingly fragile.

CHAPTER 5
THE UNMAKING OF OVERSEAS EMPIRES, 1940–75

The Second World War proved a seminal event in the history of colonialism, particularly in Asia; indeed, some argue that it began with the Japanese invasion of China in 1937. Hitler's invasion of Poland in 1939 touched off a European war, and the conflict that developed encompassed much of the globe. The British Dominions and colonies declared their allegiance to the empire and mobilized forces, and the administrators of Italy's colonies ranged themselves behind Mussolini. Portugal and Spain remained formally neutral, which largely exempted their colonies from fighting, but France, Belgium, the Netherlands and Denmark suffered invasion and occupation by the German army, thus placing their colonies in a parlous position.

The situation was especially complex in the case of France. The German army within only a month of fighting defeated France in June 1940. An aged First World War hero, Marshal Philippe Pétain (1856–1951), signed an armistice with the Germans, who occupied the north of the country, leaving him in control under the Vichy regime (headquartered in the spa town of that name) confined to central and southern France. However, a young general who had escaped to London, Charles de Gaulle (1890–1970), on 18 June made a radio appeal for the French to resist the Germans and the Vichy government. France seemed divided into two camps, 'collaborators' versus *Résistants* (who continued to oppose the Germans and Pétain at home) alongside the 'Free French' forces led by de Gaulle from abroad – though, for the metropolitan French, as for settlers and colonized people, the binary terms of 'collaboration' and 'resistance' enclosed a broad spectrum of stances and actions.

The French colonies were thus faced with a choice between two governments, each claiming legitimacy. Henri Sautot (1885–1963), senior French administrator in the New Hebrides islands, was one of the first to proclaim support for the Free French, and soon New Caledonia 'rallied' to de Gaulle. In Africa, Félix Éboué (1884–1944), a Black man born in Guiana who served as governor of Chad, also joined de Gaulle's camp. Elsewhere, governors general and governors initially recognized the Vichy regime because of uncertainty about de Gaulle's ability to lead a campaign, feelings that Vichy's modus vivendi with the Germans provided the best arrangement obtainable as Hitler's forces swept the European continent, or from sympathy with Pétain's programme. Establishing an authoritarian 'French State' (État Français), Pétain's government undertook a conservative 'national revolution', symbolized by replacement of the revolutionary slogan of 'liberty, equality, fraternity' with the corporatist 'family, work, fatherland'.

Vichy's ideals of order, hierarchy and the primacy of the white race sat well with the bulk of Europeans in the colonies. Its policies and laws, applied somewhat erratically through the empire, extended to virulent anti-Semitic legislation, especially significant in North Africa with its large population of Jews and an enduring current of anti-Semitism that dated back to the Dreyfus affair. Over the next years, however, most of the colonies would one by one join de Gaulle, though Indochina, and several others, remained under Vichy-aligned governments until the end of the war. After the liberation of North Africa by Allied forces, Algiers became headquarters for the Free French-sponsored provisional government of France in 1943.

The war, to varying degrees, cut off colonies from European metropoles, restricting trade and the movement of people, limiting communication and creating scarcities of basic provisions. Relative isolation triggered regional commerce and a search for new markets, and European outposts in the Caribbean, Indian Ocean and Africa managed as best they could. Colonial soldiers were recruited to fight in Europe, North Africa and the Middle East. India provided the largest contingent, with about 2.5 million men, many of whom fought in North Africa. Indigenous troops from Africa proved crucial to the liberation of southern France, a contribution to the war effort that until recently received scant recognition; a pertinent quotation from the poet Léopold Sedar Senghor inscribed on a monument to the Black soldiers in Fréjus reads: 'Passer-by, remember: they fell in fraternal unity so that you could remain French.'

Around 4,000 French Africans soldiers died or were taken prisoner. In total, more than a million African soldiers served in Allied armies during the Second World War. Among a million Canadians in the armed forces during the war, 250,000 were stationed overseas in 1943, and 42,000 were killed. Canada also provided an important base for the training of 130,000 Allied pilots and other support services. Around 500,000 Australians served overseas in the Second World War, of whom 39,000 died and 30,000 were taken prisoner (two-thirds captured by the Japanese in Southeast Asia). The British Dominions and the colonies, in short, made a vital contribution in military personnel, medical and nursing services – 3,500 women worked as Australian Army nurses at home or overseas – and back-up support.

The Mediterranean became a particularly important theatre of war because of German aggression in North Africa, the presence of the Italians in Libya and Mussolini's invasion of Albania, expansion in the eastern Aegean and designs on Tunisia. The British scuttled the French fleet in Mers-el-Kébir, Algeria, in July 1940, afraid that it would fall into the hands of the Germans, and intense fighting took place throughout North Africa, the Middle East and southern Europe. The Mediterranean had long been a central axis for British international policy. Gibraltar, on the southern tip of the Iberian peninsula overlooking the western entry to the Mediterranean, had provided an important British naval base since the early 1700s and remained so during the war, though most of the population – a cosmopolitan community with Italian, Spanish, British and other ancestries – were evacuated. Malta, strategically located between Sicily and Tunisia, had been British since 1813 and hosted the headquarters of the British Navy's Mediterranean fleet (until its move to Alexandria, Egypt, in 1937). German and

Italian forces bombarded Malta, and the British used the islands for air attacks on the Axis and intelligence-gathering. Further east, the British administered Cyprus, leased from the Ottoman Empire in 1878 and fully taken over in 1914. Thirty thousand men of Greek, Turkish and other backgrounds enlisted in the Cyprus Regiment formed in 1940 and fought in France, Italy, Greece, Palestine and Ethiopia. Egypt and Palestine, also under British control, became embroiled in war as well, with fighting, spying, the movement of refugees and efforts to maintain British influence and supply chains.

Colonies in the Atlantic similarly felt the effects of war, but they escaped fighting. After the German occupation of Denmark in 1940, American forces occupied Greenland, strategically placed in the North Atlantic, and installed military bases and surveillance facilities. Bermuda served as a censorship centre for the British; 1,200 employees monitored letters, telegrams and telephone calls passing between Europe, North America and other destinations. Despite Portugal's neutrality, Lisbon allowed the British and Americans to use bases in the Azores islands. The United States even built Wideawake airfield (named for a species of tern) on the minuscule British territory of Ascension Island.

The Second World War in Asia and beyond

Asia and the Pacific islands became major battlegrounds during the war. Japan was already in colonial control of Taiwan (from 1890), Korea (from 1905) and several Micronesian island groups (after the First World War). Citing the need for resources and land for settlers, and profiting from political chaos in China, Japanese armies moved into Manchuria, in north-eastern China, in 1931 and set up the puppet state of Manchukuo. A full-scale invasion of China in 1937 instituted brutal militaristic rule over conquered areas, notoriously so in the Nanking (Nanjing) massacre. In 1940, Japan formally joined Germany and Italy in the Axis pact, and in December 1941, it attacked an American base at Pearl Harbour, in the US colony of Hawai'i. Japanese armies then pushed southwards in continental Asia, and, in February 1942, conquered the supposedly invincible British colony of Singapore. This represented an ignominious defeat for the British, who were unable to deploy troops from Europe to defend the island. The Japanese soon took control of all of the British colonies in Southeast Asia – the Malay states and Burma as well as Singapore – and even mounted a few small-scale attacks on Australia. They occupied the Dutch East Indies as the colonial army there surrendered. The Japanese refrained from occupying French Indochina, though they forced the compliant Vichy-aligned authorities to allow them to station troops on French colonial territory and provide resources and funds. For all practical purposes, much of Southeast Asia and eastern Asia, therefore, had fallen under Japanese control, with great fears among the Allies about potential Japanese moves into South Asia.

The Japanese attack in Hawai'i had brought the United States into the war, and the Americans garrisoned large numbers of troops in the French colonies in the South Pacific (as well as in Australia and New Zealand). They used these bases for attacks on the Japanese elsewhere in the Pacific. The presence of Americans, with seemingly endless supplies of men and matériel, for some settlers and indigenous people in New Caledonia, French Polynesia and Wallis raised questions about the benefits and permanency of French rule. Battles took place in and around several island colonies of the Pacific, and the Guadalcanal campaign, launched by Americans on the Japanese-occupied British colony of the Solomon Islands (1942–3), proved a major turning point in the Pacific war.

Japan ruled areas it occupied as colonies, expropriating natural resources and labour. The Japanese army treated defeated prisoners of war ruthlessly, the sufferings in the Changi prison camp in Singapore and on the 'death railway' built in Thailand and Burma infamous. Europeans in the colonies were sometimes imprisoned or had their houses requisitioned for Japanese officials, and local people were subjected to forced labour. Large numbers of women in occupied areas (and in Korea) were forced to work as 'comfort women' – prostitutes – for the Japanese army. The Japanese suppressed opposition, whether from Europeans or indigenous people. Tokyo nevertheless proclaimed that as an Asian power Japan was liberating the colonies from European overlordship and announced the creation of a 'Greater East Asia Co-Prosperity Sphere'. This, they promised, would promote economic and social development by harnessing the 'freed' territories to a powerful and modern Japan.

Certain anti-colonialists, in fact, did see Japanese occupation as a means to throw off the European yoke. Important figures in later independence movements, such as General Aung San (1915–47) in Burma and Sukarno (1901–70) in Indonesia, showed sympathies with the Japanese, though the former later swung behind the British. Gandhi and others in his movement reluctantly supported the British in the war while continuing a 'Quit India' campaign initiated in 1942, but Subhas Chandra Bose (1897–1945), with Japanese backing, tried to organize anti-British forces to seize control of India. Bose managed to gather an 'Indian Army' of more than 40,000 men. Eight thousand fought against the British Empire troops at Imphal, where Japan tried but failed to invade the Raj on its eastern frontier in 1944. The battle pitted Indian troops battling for and against the British, adding both a civil war–like aspect and an anti-colonial feature to warfare on the subcontinent. Aligned with the Japanese during the war, Bose's movement, which failed militarily, continued to press for an independent India after 1945; Bose himself died of illness in that year.

In March 1945, only months before the end of the war, the Japanese finally occupied French Indochina, and the emperor of Vietnam and rulers of Cambodia and Laos, under some duress, proclaimed the independence of their countries. Such nominal independence proved only temporary. In other parts of the colonial world, as well, the Axis powers had tried to marshal support from colonized people. Nazi Germany sponsored radio broadcasts in Arabic, proclaiming respect for Islam and desire to bring about the end of European colonialism in North Africa and the Middle East, though only a minority of listeners were convinced. The Italians attempted to persuade a Tunisian nationalist leader, Habib Bourguiba, to throw his support behind the Axis when he was released from French detention, but Bourguiba refused; the sultan of Morocco meanwhile cast his lot with de Gaulle's Free French. The defeat of the Axis powers put paid to any hopes, however unlikely they may have been, that Germany, Italy or Japan would have truly emancipated colonized peoples from foreign rule.

Efforts to restore empires and to gain independence

The end of the Second World War, like that of the First World War, saw a transformation of the global map of empire. Defeated Japan lost its colonies and the areas occupied in the 1930s and 1940s, as did Italy, though none immediately gained independence. The British Southeast Asian possessions returned to their old colonial overlords, even if the French and the Dutch, as will be seen, faced the task of reasserting control. The peace settlements and the United Nations, created in 1945, effectively mandated a continuation of colonial regimes.

Events on 'Victory in Europe Day' in Algeria make for a good example of the different meanings represented by the war's conclusion for Europeans and colonized people. In Sétif, French security forces opened fire against the celebrating masses on 8 May 1945 when those who had raised the green and white flag of the Algerian independence movement refused to take it down. In reaction, and in an expression of long-standing grievances and a hunger crisis, Algerians killed several Frenchmen over the following days. This incurred a dramatic reprisal by French authorities and settlers' militias. French retaliation cost the lives of more than 10,000 Muslims (and Algeria officially cites a toll more than four times as high). The liberation of France from German occupation in 1944 did not imply emancipation of the French colonies. The Sétif uprising foreshadowed a war of independence that erupted in Algeria nine years later.

More immediately, France was embroiled in a war against nationalist Vietnamese that began in 1946 and dragged on until 1954 and was involved in suppressing an uprising in Madagascar from 1947 to 1949. The Dutch fought a losing battle from 1945 to 1949 to restore colonial authority in the East Indies. The British were moving ineluctably, if reluctantly and chaotically, towards the independence of India and Pakistan, which occurred in 1947, and Burma and Ceylon the following year. Europeans sought to maintain control of colonies throughout Africa, where wartime and post-war conditions had contributed to the strengthening of anti-colonialism. It was clear to most that some degree of administration needed to be devolved to colonies. The French, for instance, in 1946 created a Commonwealth-style Union Française with its territories, sounding promises of greater political participation (though self-government was ruled out) and economic and social development. The British gradually transferred some powers to elected legislative councils in its colonies. But from London and Paris to The Hague and Brussels, governments hoped the situation would return in large measure to the status quo ante bellum. Commitment to colonialism was shared in Lisbon and Madrid. (Indeed, as Franco threw support behind Hitler in the 1940s, he dreamed of expansion of Spain's small African empire, but Hitler refused to countenance any initiative.) Neither Spain nor Portugal, both under authoritarian regimes and not formally belligerent powers, envisaged far reaching changes to colonial rule in the early post-war period. Few in Europe expected that within a decade after 1945, most of the Asian colonies would become independent and that in ten more years, almost all of the African colonies would follow.

Decolonization, in retrospect, may seem a straightforward and inevitable process of the liberation of conquered domains from foreign control, but in fact it was complex, uncertain and often haphazard. Moreover, decolonization did not just involve the lowering of one flag and the raising of another; it must be understood as much more than the transfer of sovereignty. Decolonization represented a long-range process, in some ways going back to the nineteenth century when resistance and anti-colonial movements emerged. They metamorphosed as national, rather than regional or ethnic, allegiances began to crystallize; men and women from new elites entered the political scene, new strategies were essayed, new ideologies proposed. In the background lay profound transformations – urbanization, wider access to European-style culture, greater facilities for travel and transnational contacts among nationalists, the spread of print and broadcast technology – that altered the parameters of activism.

Furthermore, though an 'Independence Day' might mark a particular moment in a nation's history, one of exultation for the colonized if melancholy or resentment for the colonizers, 'decolonization' as a historical phenomenon extended well into the period after independence if taken to encompass transitions that subsequently took place or were attempted. The fact that nationalist groups often talked about 'revolution' rather than simply 'independence' intimated that they did not aspire to return to a pre-colonial age – many lambasted the 'feudalism' associated with pre-colonial regimes – but to bring about profound political, social and economic change. For such militants, decolonization involved not just the founding of new states but the restructuring of society along radically different lines from either the pre-colonial or the colonial age. Others, no less nationalist or anti-colonial, foreshadowed less dramatic transformation, with the building of new states in line with Western models.

For still others, including some indigenous people and many diasporic and settler populations, security and prosperity depended on the retention or even strengthening of formal ties with metropoles. In 1946, four of France's four oldest colonies were fully incorporated into the French Republic, largely at the instigation of Black politicians who argued that assimilation would ensure equality between Blacks and whites, and between the overseas territories and the metropole. A number of political leaders in the French African colonies initially gave support to continued, if significantly altered, French sovereignty under the Union Française. In 1954, 80 per cent of the Maltese electorate voted for representation in the Westminster parliament and virtual integration into the UK, yet London refused.

Not all people, beyond the settlers and their descendants who opposed independence, were enthusiastic about the end of modified 'colonial' rule. Some feared dominance by majority ethnic groups, as was the case among those of African ancestry in Mauritius and indigenous islanders in Fiji, where Indians formed a majority. Religious minorities, including Christians and Jews in predominantly Muslim colonies, worried about their fate without strict safeguards for community rights. Certain old elites, like most of the maharajas of India and sultans of the Dutch East Indies, had accommodated colonial states that recognized their hereditary rights and privileges, which they felt threatened by the rule of the 'masses' and republican government. Those in peripheral geographical regions of emerging states, such as the Shan and Karen in Burma, who had enjoyed some autonomy in colonial situations, worried about heavy-handed rule from the centre with independence. African colonies, as well as Asian ones, were home to multiple and discordant ethnic, linguistic and religious groups held together in arbitrarily demarcated colonies by foreign domination, and ethnic and regional loyalties often remained stronger than proto-national ones. What sort of power-sharing would be obtained in independent states caused concern. Even some nationalists who supported eventual independence felt the time not yet right, and hoped that continued 'colonial' ties with metropolitan states would secure economic and social investment not otherwise on offer. Such reservations, and arguments against independence, ironically had long been sounded by Europeans to postpone self-determination to a distant day.

Europeans in the colonies included significant populations descended from settlers established in South Africa for centuries, and in French Algeria and New Caledonia, British Kenya and Southern Rhodesia for many decades, as well as smaller communities elsewhere. 'White' populations in Portuguese Angola and Mozambique, and the Belgian Congo, indeed grew with new currents of migration after the Second World War. Recently arrived or long-established Europeans believed, and had been taught to believe, that they dwelled secure in what they considered their homelands overseas; moreover, they placed trust in the rights shared with compatriots in the metropole. Most strongly favoured some type of possibly reformed or rebranded colonialism, defended imperial paramountcy, campaigned to preserve their privileges and refused to accept the legitimacy of a majority rule that would spell the end of their favoured position. They had often resented the strong-armed powers exercised by metropolitan governments, to be sure, promoting creation of local assemblies, tax concessions and other advantages. But they dreaded independence and potential social revolution in newly independent countries that would make them unwelcome or render their privileges untenable. After decades or longer of misguided certainty about white superiority and imperial rule, the spectre of an overturning of the established colonial order was haunting. Some resolved to resist independence, and what they would consider abandonment by politicians in the metropoles, by force if necessary.

The stakes of independence

Despite government pronouncements about commitment to the colonies, opinion polls in Europe in the late 1940s showed growing public ambivalence about overseas empires as attention turned towards reconstruction and renewal of the war-battered continent. As enthusiasm for empire – never unanimous and, it might be argued, more superficial and sustained by propaganda than deep-seated – began to weaken, political and economic elites persisted in championing the real or potential resources or geopolitical advantage colonies offered. Colonies, they insisted, still made countries like Belgium, the Netherlands, Spain and Portugal greater powers than they could otherwise be, and a French politician memorably remarked that without its colonies, France would only be a European country, not a global one. Empire remained an integral part of national heritage and identity.

Time-worn mantras for empire were reiterated, and new arguments formulated. Migrants might find land, jobs and comfortable lives under their national flags in the colonies (and British Dominions). Service in the colonial military, administration and private enterprise afforded an outlet for youthful vigour and ambition. The *mission civilisatrice* was repackaged, as were stereotypes about 'primitivism' and 'native' incapacities for self-government, with renewed promises of modernization and development. New natural resources could be located and greater profit extracted from already established agriculture, industry and mining – proven or suspected deposits of petroleum and such minerals as uranium became particularly important in the mid-twentieth century. Asia and Africa offered ample and inexpensive labour in situ, and for a Europe experiencing a long economic boom from the 1940s, migrants from the empire would provide much-needed labour on farms and in construction, factories and the public service (especially health and postal systems). The tense international situation – Communist takeovers of eastern European states in the late 1940s and mainland China in 1949, the Cold War, the Korean War in the early 1950s, and other actual or threatened conflicts – called for foreign bases. Whether most Europeans believed such arguments was not guaranteed, but colonialism remained an umbrella under which disparate political, commercial, military, social and cultural ambitions and interests gathered.

The question arose of whether Europeans were willing to commit the substantial resources necessary to perpetuate colonial rule, and whether they were willing to fight to hold on to the colonies if necessary. In some cases, the answer seemed to be yes, at least from the political elite, as the French and Dutch fought in Southeast Asia, and the British and others battled 'insurgency' there and in Africa. There were renewed plans for costly colonial development – the French allotted more funding to their sub-Saharan African colonies in the fifteen years after 1945 than in all the previous decades of French rule combined. Business continued to invest in the colonies. The number of soldiers stationed overseas grew, and dramatically so in some places. Yet increasingly vocal and persuasive critics pointed to human rights abuses, condemned exploitation, asked if colonialism was not anachronistic and simply wondered whether the 'gold and the blood' (in the nineteenth-century phrase) required to maintain empire was worth the cost.

The big question about keeping colonies implied specific questions about how to do so or how to relinquish them. Should governance continue as in the past or in a recast form? Might some colonies (which ones?) be let go so as to hold on to others? What were the appropriate objectives for development programmes? Should administration (and how much?) be devolved to local governments (and to governments that whites might no longer control)? Should some or all indigenous and other non-European residents be fully enfranchised? What sort of half-way houses might exist between colonial and independent status? Would denial of self-government weaken moderate nationalists and dangerously embolden the more radical? Was it possible to defeat 'subversives', 'rebels' and 'terrorists' and what were the ways to do so? These and other questions provided perennial topics for debate.

The pathway along which moves to independence proceeded was often tortuous, a more or less amicable separation in a few cases but an especially bloody and protracted confrontation in others, notably in the East Indies, Vietnam and Algeria. Moves towards independence involved violence by both nationalists, often through guerrilla tactics, and colonizers, who deployed the army, police and (settler) militias; violence provoked further violence, and hardened the positions of pro- and anti-colonial factions. Physical attacks on Europeans and their property shattered victims and outraged authorities. The colonial state, seeking to reimpose authority, resorted to forced resettlement of indigenous populations, arbitrary arrests and torture, assassinations and summary executions, and collective punishment of entire villages said to harbour rebels. Efforts to hide or deny brutalities compromised Europeans at home and in the international community. The use of torture, traumatically experienced at the hands of Nazis during the Second World War, but supposedly disavowed by 'civilized' countries, was especially at issue: beatings, deprivation of food and water, solitary confinement, waterboarding, use of electric shocks with electrodes applied to the most sensitive parts of the body and mutilation. Revelations at the time shocked newspaper-readers, and much more was later exposed, especially about Algeria. Though torture was not employed everywhere, or always in a systematic fashion, it is impossible to exculpate colonial governments and their agents of such inhuman violence. Colonial authorities nevertheless contended that extreme tactics were necessary to preserve law and order, protect settlers and loyal supporters, identify and undo terrorist plots, and safeguard sovereignty.

For nationalists other than strict Gandhians and other firm proponents of non-violence, violence (including in some instances torture) similarly provided a tool, used unwillingly or in extremis in some cases, at other times embraced. In their view, it formed an unavoidable component of the struggle for freedom given the overwhelming power and obduracy of colonial states. It represented a response to repression, a measure forced upon them by intransigent rejection of demands for emancipation. Violence in the quest for independence, freedom fighters insisted, was a reaction against the initial violence inflicted by Europeans during the takeover of their homelands and continued arbitrary rule. Violence committed, some theorists postulated, might provide psychological catharsis for violence endured. Military installations and government offices, and civilian and military agents of the state, provided legitimate targets. Violence directed at European civilians might cause more qualms, but desperate circumstances, some independence fighters pleaded, justified direct action against those who profited from exploitation, refused to recognize the rights of indigenous peoples and participated in or condoned state-sponsored violence.

There was also fratricidal violence in both Africa and Asia. Wars of independence took on the character of civil wars as indigenous people sided with or against the nationalists – and carried out exactions against the other side. Some groups coerced financial contributions, service in independence armies or other aid from compatriots. Those who supported Europeans, labelled collaborators and traitors by nationalists, became targets for revenge before and after independence. Violence between independence movements or factions was not uncommon, as groups espousing different ideologies, loyal to a particular leader, representing different regional or ethnic interests, or backed by opposing international patrons jousted for primacy. Intense rivalries continued, often with further tolls in the dead, wounded, exiled or gaoled, in many newly independent states.

Violence remained a continuing issue of debate for colonial and anti-colonial factions, and in the general public. The institutions and policies of future governments and the degree of power-sharing among multiple interests and groups, before or instead of independence (and afterwards), became another ongoing preoccupation. For the colonizing and the colonized, the boundaries of states presented yet another issue. Conquest and administrative organization left ethnicities jumbled together within colonial boundaries or separated between different colonies (and, on occasion, different empires). There was debate in France and French Africa in the 1950s about whether the two large federations of colonies, French West Africa and French Equatorial Africa, should remain united after independence or, as occurred, be broken up into separate states. British attempts to create federations of former colonies, notably in an East Africa Federation and a West Indies Federation, ultimately floundered because of disputes between people and regions (or islands). Non-Burman ethnic groups only reluctantly accepted incorporation into the new state of Burma by provisions for regional autonomy and recognition of traditional rulers. The British colony of North Borneo (now Sabah) and the protectorate of Sarawak (ruled by the Brooke dynasty of 'white rajas'), also on the island of Borneo, were brought into independent Muslim-dominated Malaya (now Malaysia). Yet the island colony of Singapore, with its large Chinese population, seceded from that state several years after its independence. As newly independent countries were born, regional groups attempted to break away, notably in the Moluccas (Maluku) islands in the Dutch East Indies and Katanga in the Belgian Congo. National boundaries, often illogical enough in Europe, remained an imposition in overseas areas where forms of government historically did not accord with the nation-state model. Paradoxically, the emergence of Western-style nation states around the globe, even at the behest of indigenous nationalists, was itself a product of colonialism.

Achieving independence: Contexts, ideas and strategies

Three general impulses led to independence for the colonies in the decades after the Second World War. The first was the international context (despite the argument, mentioned earlier, that colonies remained strategically necessary in the context of the developing Cold War). The Second World War proved the catalyst for independence of Indonesia; indirectly accelerated independence in India, Pakistan and Burma; and brought Vietnamese nationalists to the centre of manoeuvres concerning the future of French Indochina. At the end of the war, the United States and the Soviet Union, the world's new superpowers, proclaimed opposition to colonialism, even if both practised imperialist policies in their spheres of influence and, according to critics, the Soviet

Union established a 'colonial' system in eastern Europe. The United States, for its part, supported initiatives by Britain, France and the Netherlands to reinstate control in Asia and worked against independence movements that were Communist-led, Marxist-inspired or linked to the Soviet Union or, from the 1960s, Castro's Cuba. The Maoist revolution in China in 1949 had made Beijing another force for anti-colonialism, and provided a further template for revolution, despite the government's dictatorial rule, the suppression of regional minorities, military action in Tibet and a death toll of up to forty-five million during Mao's 'Great Leap Forward' of the late 1950s and early 1960s.

Meanwhile, in 1955 delegates from thirty countries – accounting for over half of the world's population – met at a conference convened by Indonesia, India, Ceylon and Pakistan (see Figure 5.1). Representatives at the Afro-Asian Conference (or Bandung Conference) sought what they intended as a third option in international relations in a world increasingly polarized between a 'Western bloc' linked to the United States and Western Europe, and an 'Eastern bloc' attached to the Soviet Union and Communist states. They cautioned about the dangers of emerging states allying with and subsuming their interests to either of the blocs, while strongly backing independence for remaining colonies. The conference marked a significant step towards formation of the Non-Aligned Movement and provided a platform for transnational anti-colonial support. A so-called Tricontinental Conference in Havana in 1966 prolonged the anti-imperialist 'spirit of Bandung' (to use an optimistic contemporary expression), bringing Latin America into the movement, 'in an effort to expand the Third World project'. Indeed, the very phrase 'Third World', coined by a French journalist in the mid-1950s, symbolized the sense of

Figure 5.1 Delegates at the Afro-Asian Conference, Bandung, Indonesia, April 1955. © Alamy Stock Photo.

commonality among the former and remaining colonies, and the gaps that separated them from the two dominant blocs.

The United Nations had initially accommodated colonialism under pressure from the colonial powers that counted among its founders. However, the Universal Declaration of Human Rights, adopted in 1948, contained principles hardly compatible with 'classical' colonialism. Support for still active independence movements grew stronger as newly independent nations joined the forum, and through backing from the Soviet Union and its allies. In a 1960 resolution, though relatively late in the period of decolonization, the UN General Assembly stated that all countries, no matter their geographical or demographic size or level of development, possessed the right to self-determination. That must be achieved, according to the United Nations, as an act of free choice, and it might result in independence, full and equitable integration of a former colony into a nation-state, or some other agreed upon relationship; in practice, independence became the usual option.

A second impulse propelling independence from 1945 to the 1960s, if later for the Iberian colonies, lay in Europe itself. The horrors of Hitler's ideology and policies forced a rethinking among Europeans about the racial ideas on which colonial rule was based. Although some theorists, especially in places where apartheid or segregation remained the norm, still defended older notions of racial hierarchies and white superiority, their views became increasingly discredited in academic and political circles. Scientists and social scientists developed new views about human differences and put forward statements on 'the race question', especially from the 1950s, that indeed questioned race as a concept. Racial stereotypes endured, and racism remained – still officially sanctioned, systematic and institutionalized – even if authorities tried to temper or obfuscate it with euphemisms or talk of humanitarianism, reform, development and progress under their guidance. However, it was no longer possible to proclaim European racial supremacy in the way that such belief had underpinned the 'classical' colonial system.

Furthermore, European countries whose resources had been drained by the Second World War found it difficult, or electorally compromising, to dedicate the wherewithal to sustain military opposition to armed independence movements, though the Netherlands and France tried. Certainly, they outlaid vast expenditures on the colonies that reform and development demanded, but reconstruction and rapid economic growth at home in the late 1940s and early 1950s paradoxically provided alternative opportunities for businesses. The sort of 'imperial preference' promoted during the Depression of the 1930s no longer carried conviction. Some policymakers suggested (rightly, as it happened) that even if colonies went free, metropoles could negotiate access to natural resources, labour and military bases, and obtain them without the responsibilities and costs of administration and social 'uplift' of local populations. Though defenders of colonies talked up the strategic benefits colonies supplied, the new security alliance of the North Atlantic Treaty Organization (NATO) provided reassurance, as did development of new military hardware including nuclear weapons in the United States, Britain and France. The French transferred their nuclear testing programme from the Algerian Sahara to French Polynesia, and Western powers worked out arrangements to base troops in various former colonies.

Suggestions were advanced that some colonies could be shed in order to keep others. If the British lost South Asia in the late 1940s, reassuringly, they still had the African colonies, as well as the Malay outposts, Hong Kong and islands in the Caribbean and elsewhere. The journalist Raymond Cartier proposed in the early 1950s that France's Asian colonies might be given up voluntarily to concentrate French efforts in Africa. Meanwhile, the French Communist Party, which garnered as much as a fifth of the votes in the 1950s, became an ever more vocal critic of colonialism, and liberal voices there and in other countries – yet to a lesser degree in Portugal and Spain, where they were silenced – spoke more openly in favour of independence for at least some of the colonies. Adamant opposition to decolonization, to be sure, existed in Britain, the Netherlands and especially France (above all, concerning Algeria), but a persuasive argument gained ground: the best policy would be to sponsor a smooth transition of power to seemingly moderate nationalists, a process that would avoid power being wrested from colonizers by radicals unfriendly to the Western powers. This would be what some leaders claimed to have done, as when the French president, Charles de Gaulle, grandly proclaimed that he had decolonized the French African empire because it was in France's interest to do so. By the 1970s, the British and Dutch, though less so the French, and the Portuguese after the 'carnation revolution' in 1974, indeed seemed eager to divest themselves of remaining colonies that now seemed to hold questionable value or even be burdens or embarrassments.

The final dynamic of decolonization lay in the independence movements in the colonies; decolonization is often understood as the victory of these movements. They were extremely diverse in ideology, strategy and objectives, but they drew inspiration from similar sources. The first was indigenous culture (in the widest sense of that word) and the sentiment that it had been trampled upon by colonizers, sometimes for centuries of foreign rule. As already occurred in the 1930s, and before, anti-colonialists stressed local languages, traditions, religions and lineages as part of what it meant to be a people and a nation, and the ways that these had been denigrated or effaced by colonialism. They evoked the achievements of ancient dynasties, pointed to great works of literature, art and architecture, and emphasized spiritual heritages. From Mauritania to Indonesia, Islam became a central platform in nationalism among Muslim populations. In India, Hinduism and Islam both inspired nationalists, albeit religious divides led to partition of the subcontinent in 1947. Islam and Christianity competed for followers in much of sub-Saharan Africa, with each mobilizing anti-colonialists while creating religious and regional fractures within emerging states. Christianity, despite colonial roots, came to occupy a large place in autonomy and independence movements as indigenous clerics spoke of biblical precepts of brotherhood and equality, and used international religious networks, forums and publications to galvanize support for change (although conservatives were often unresponsive). Catholics tried to convince the Vatican of the continuing mission the church could fulfil in independent countries.

A second source of nationalism came from European political philosophy. Primary among the principles was the very doctrine of nationalism itself: the idea of an internationally recognized, sovereign and independent nation-state encompassing a population bound together by shared territory, institutions and aspirations (even though the criterion of shared culture key to most European nationalist movements applied even less easily to the disparate populations of most colonies than in Europe). Nationalists argued that independence for colonies represented a continuation of a world-historical process so evident in nineteenth-century Europe. Other European ideas similarly offered inspiration: the Enlightenment notions of inalienable human rights and equality of peoples, Wilsonian principles of self-determination (given renewed prominence in the 1948 UN declaration), traditions of majority rule, free elections, universal suffrage and parliamentary process. Activists cited, too, a current of anti-colonialism that had always existed in Europe: anti-colonialism was itself part of a European endowment.

Many Asian and African nationalists, including some of the most radical, were well versed in European political philosophy, and they deftly used hallowed principles of Western democracy in their campaigns, damning the double standard that denied those principles for colonized non-Westerners. For some, the presidential or parliamentary system of European countries provided suitable models for governance once independence arrived, the market economy (though perhaps reshaped) would lead to prosperity unavailable when colonizers exploited labour and resources and siphoned off profits, and friendly but more equitable ties could be maintained with the former colonial powers.

However, anti-colonial architects such as Kwame Nkrumah and Julius Nyerere espoused larger objectives, reaching beyond political self-determination. They spoke of the need to build different sorts of societies. They promoted cooperation with neighbouring countries sharing their heritage – a central tenet of the Pan-African movement – and of collaboration in international groups, as represented by the Non-Aligned Movement. Aware of the fragility of newly independent nations in a world system dominated by former imperial powers, they sought what was later termed a 'new international economic order'. Nkrumah, in Ghana, railed against what he famously termed 'neo-colonialism', a reincarnation of Western exploitation. Nyerere, in Tanzania, developed the concept of Ujamaa, which emphasized the community rather than the individual in society; for Nyerere, communitarianism would serve as a basis for an indigenous 'African socialism' different from that propounded in orthodox models, an alternative model of development to that offered by the colonizers.

Such terms as 'African socialism' spoke of the important influence of socialist and Marxist theories – a third source of nationalist inspiration, and one that, of course, originated in nineteenth-century Europe. From the 1940s through the 1970s, Marxism remained a potent body of theory throughout the world, though interpretations of theory and practice differed. The path to power followed by Marxist groups in the Soviet Union and China offered nationalists strategies for combating the colonialists. The Marxist view about political revolution necessarily coupled with economic and social revolution accorded with visions for new societies. While most conservative, moderate and even socialist parties defended colonialism, Marxist parties stood out for their proclaimed anti-colonialism in the years after the Second World War (as before). The Soviet Union, the independent Marxist states in eastern Europe, the People's Republic of China and Castro's Cuba appeared different models to those of Western liberal democracies and capitalist economies, and those states offered financial assistance, training and political backing – and sometimes military advisers, soldiers and weaponry – to independence movements that aligned with them.

Often, however, both liberal and Marxist ideals, ideological stances and rhetoric brushed over local conflicts and long-standing social and political divisions in the colonies, and only a close examination of local histories and politics can provide a deeper understanding of the platforms, allegiances and strategies of independence campaigns and indeed anti-independence ones. Moreover, the ways in which different local, national and international dynamics intertwined and the ways that indigenous, Western liberal and Marxist-derived components combined in struggles for independence varied greatly from one colony to another. Marxism provided a guiding force for independence in Vietnam, but anti-Communism prevailed in the Philippines. Marxist ideas gained no traction in the South Pacific islands and relatively little in the Caribbean outside Cuba. Christianity was invoked by many nationalist figures in Africa, Oceania and the Caribbean (as well as the Philippines), though not, of course, in the Muslim world. Muslim supporters of independence ranged from secularists to promoters of *shari'a* law and theocratic organization of the state. Similar variety characterized independence movements and coalitions elsewhere. Moreover, as circumstances changed, factions competed for prominence and new cohorts of leaders came to the fore, with focuses and emphases altered.

Independence in regional perspective: The Middle East

Independence in the Middle East was bound up with the League of Nations mandates by which Britain administered Palestine and Iraq, and France administered Syria and Lebanon, and then with the events of the Second World War. In Iraq, the British had set up a monarchy under the Hashemite dynasty, in 1921; independence formally arrived and the mandate ended in 1932. Yet from the late 1930s, Iraq suffered a series of coups; when a pro-Nazi government came to power in 1941, British troops invaded to overturn it, but left Iraq independent. The French in 1936 negotiated, but never ratified, an agreement for eventual independence of Syria and Lebanon, and French authorities remained overlords of the local administrations. In 1940, Syria fell into the hands of a Vichy representative, prompting the British and Free French to move in to gain control. Independence was proclaimed in 1941 but, with renewed procrastination, not recognized by the French until 1944. Even then, French troops remained in Syria, sparking protests to which the French in 1945 responded by occupying the parliament building and cutting off supplies. Four hundred Syrians died in the disturbances. British troops arrived, Syria finally achieved independence in 1946, and the French fully withdrew the following year. Lebanon was briefly occupied by the British in 1941; when the Free French landed, they announced that the country would move towards independence, but it was a new Lebanese government that unilaterally declared independence two years later. The French briefly put government officials under arrest, but soon recognized Lebanon's independence, yet with no resolution of conflicts between Muslims, the Druze and Christians that would later plunge Lebanon into civil war. The British and French acts, and postponement of independence, showed the priority mandate powers placed, especially in wartime, on keeping the upper hand in a strategically important region.

In 1946, Britain recognized the independence of the kingdom of Transjordan (now Jordan) and it achieved noteworthy stability, but neighbouring Palestine was more complicated because of the mixture of Jews, Muslims and Christians in the 'Holy Land'. (See a more detailed treatment in Part III of this volume.) In the late 1800s, European Zionists had campaigned to establish a homeland for the Jews, and during the First World War, the British had agreed to facilitate establishment of such a state. Migration of persecuted European Jews – but also British restrictions on migration – in the 1930s and 1940s created additional issues, while the Holocaust and the murder of six million European Jews cast the issue of a Jewish homeland in a new light. Zionists continued to pressure the British, sometimes with violence, and finally, with the approval of the United Nations, the state of Israel was established in 1948. That provoked an immediate war with neighbouring Arab countries, the forced migration of dispossessed Palestinians (both Muslims and Christians) to neighbouring countries, and a situation unresolved three-quarters of a century later.

Decolonization of the coastal areas of the Arabian Peninsula, societies under the rule of sultans, emirs and sheiks, was also a complex affair. The strategic port of Aden (which the British took over in 1839), and its hinterland, what is now Yemen, became a British crown colony. In 1959, Britain created a South Arabian Federation of Emirates for neighbouring groups with which it also maintained treaty relations, and Aden acceded to the federation in 1963. However, a National Liberation Front had been mounting attacks on the British garrison, leading to the 'Aden Emergency', to which London responded with troop deployments. In 1965, both the British and the Front came under attack from a rival Front for the Liberation of Occupied Southern Yemen. Britain left the colony two years later, part of a general policy to withdraw from 'east of Suez'. The Trucial States (including Dubai, Abu Dhabi and Oman), as well as Bahrain and Kuwait, remained British protectorates in all but name until the early 1970s through treaty arrangements that allowed for prospection and exploitation of petroleum resources. Several united as the fully independent United Arab Emirates in 1971; Oman, Bahrain and Kuwait remained separate.

South and Southeast Asia

In the years immediately after the independence of India and Pakistan in 1947, the British colonies of Ceylon and Burma followed. In Ceylon, where the push for independence had been far less militant than in India, the British handed over power to an elite steeped in British traditions. In Burma, the leader of the independence movement, General Aung San, after he cast support behind the allies in the Second World War, looked to be a leader also moulded in the Western tradition and able to unify diverse ethnic groups.

His assassination in 1947 deprived Burma of a strong figure, though a handicapped democratic government struggled on until overthrown by a military coup in 1962.

The independence of the South Asian colonies left Britain with the Malay states, where, during the 'Malayan Emergency', a guerrilla army founded by Communists fought against the British from 1948, and continued fighting the government of independent Malaya, established in 1957, for three more years. Malaya (now Malaysia) nevertheless emerged in 1957 to become a stable and prosperous state, despite the later withdrawal of Singapore. The year 1957 also saw the independence of the Maldives, an archipelago off the southwest coast of India. Not until 1984 did Brunei, a small but oil-rich sultanate on Borneo, gain independence, and the British sovereign presence in Asia ended only with cession of Hong Kong to the People's Republic of China in 1997.

Two days after the Japanese surrender in the Pacific war in 1945 and in the power vacuum left behind, the veteran nationalist leader Sukarno proclaimed independence for the Netherlands East Indies under the name of Indonesia, and was chosen president of the republic. The government faced great disunity among the nation's hundreds of ethnic groups in a population of sixty-eight million spread across thousands of islands – an archipelago only forged into a single entity through Dutch colonial authority. The major immediate issue, however, was the determination of the Europeans to re-establish control. In 1945, British imperial forces occupied the East Indies at the end of the war and oversaw the repatriation of 300,000 Japanese soldiers, with numerous clashes involving the remaining Japanese, British, Dutch and Indonesian nationalists. Dutch authorities and the military soon largely replaced the British despite the parlous position of the Netherlands, recovering from occupation by the Germans. In the Linggarjati Agreement of 1946, the Dutch agreed to de facto recognition of the Indonesian republic over some regions, and in principle eventual establishment of a federal state linked to the Netherlands under the Dutch queen. However, this failed to satisfy either the nationalists or the intractable colonialists. With a major offensive in 1947, the Dutch began a military campaign (labelled 'police action' against the rebels by the Dutch) essentially to reconquer their old colony, ultimately deploying 220,000 troops, mostly East Indians serving in the colonial army.

As republican and colonial forces alternately advanced and retreated, bitter fighting saw atrocities on both sides, especially and more systematically, according to recent research, in the Dutch campaign. Dutch efforts to gain international support scored scant success, especially from newly independent countries such as India. In 1948, the UN brokered a ceasefire, but the Dutch initiated a new military offensive, which provoked further international criticism and unsettled conditions (including the declaration of an 'Indonesian Soviet Republic' in one region of Java, and an 'Islamic Republic' in another). Finally, worn down by the war and the expenditures it demanded, facing defeat on the ground, waning enthusiasm for empire at home and international opprobrium, the Dutch agreed to negotiations with the nationalists. In 1949, the Netherlands finally recognized the independence of the Indonesian republic (though keeping western New Guinea as a colony until the early 1960s). The death toll of the war was high: 2,300 Dutch soldiers, 45,000–100,000 nationalist soldiers, tens of thousands of Indonesian civilians, including

Eurasians and Chinese who often were targets of Indonesian Muslim attacks. Estimates of the displaced rise into the millions. Most of the Dutch, many of the Eurasians and a number of those who had fought for the Dutch fled the newly independent country. Indonesia, under Sukarno, emerged as an influential actor in international affairs as the government pursued a revolution based on *pancasila*, the five principles of belief in God, international humanism, Indonesian nationalism and unity, a 'guided democracy' and social well-being.

The record of prolonged warfare between nationalists and colonial armies was repeated in French Indochina over the same period as the Indonesian conflict, though it lasted years longer. In Indochina (today's Vietnam, Laos and Cambodia), France aimed to restore colonial authority in the wake of almost five years of Vichy rule and Japanese occupation. At the end of the war, Chinese troops occupied much of the north of Vietnam, and British troops the south, while Ho Chi Minh, in Hanoi, proclaimed independence and Emperor Bao Dai abdicated. The next ten years saw immensely complex manoeuvring by Ho and French authorities. France reluctantly agreed to a union of the three regions of Vietnam (Tonkin, Annam and Cochinchina), a unification stoutly rejected until then, and recognition of Vietnam as an 'associated state' of the Union Française, but still under French sovereignty.

After first supporting Ho, the French turned against him, and in 1949, they repatriated Bao Dai from voluntary exile to become head of state of Vietnam, in hopes of the former emperor serving as a bulwark against the Communists. By that time, fighting raged: in 1946 all-out war had broken out between the Communist-led nationalists and the French. Ho's forces steadily gained ground against the French, who struggled to counter the nationalists' guerrilla tactics. Despite pouring men and money into Vietnam, and gaining American backing, the French steadily retreated. In 1954 they made a last stand at Dien Bien Phu, their remaining active forces taking refuge in a site they thought safe from the nationalists' army. Encircled by the Vietnamese, the surprised French suffered a humiliating defeat, their soldiers led away to captivity. The collapse of the French represented more than a lost battle. It meant French withdrawal from Southeast Asia as a colonial power, a symbol for the crumbling of European colonialism in and beyond the region.

An international conference convened in Geneva to discuss Vietnam mandated the division of the country (meant as a temporary measure) into two states: the Democratic Republic of Vietnam, in the north, controlled by Ho and the Communist nationalists, and a Republic of Vietnam in the south, supported by the French and Americans. Within a few years, a new war began, this time between the northern and southern governments, and between the Vietnamese aligned with Ho, including the Viet Cong in southern Vietnam, and their international allies, versus the Americans and their allies. The United States proved as incapable as the French of winning a war against Ho's forces, and the war stimulated great dissent within the United States, forcing the Americans to withdraw in 1973. In 1975, six years after Ho's death, the Communists took the south, and the following year unified Vietnam.

France's two other Southeast Asian possessions pursued a different trajectory. In Cambodia, King Sihanouk, chosen and crowned in 1941 as 'protected' monarch by the French – who hoped the nineteen-year-old would make a loyal ally – came to lead the nationalists. He deftly negotiated with the French and achieved independence for Cambodia, without the warfare that had engulfed Vietnam, in 1953. Laos had remained a collection of loosely linked polities under the French, and at the end of the Second World War, they promoted the ruler of Luang Prabang to the position of King of Laos. Royalist, republican and Communist factions contested leadership of the nationalist movement until the fragile nation gained independence under the monarchy in 1953. In both countries, lack of political unity persisted, leading to decades of struggle, violence and regime change.

Several small areas in Asia remained to be decolonized. Independent India was strongly committed to incorporating the old French and Portuguese enclaves. There was much support for joining India in the small French territories, albeit only in 1954, not coincidentally the year of French defeat in Vietnam, were four residual *comptoirs* effectively transferred to India. The Portuguese government adamantly refused to hand over Goa and its two other enclaves to India, and only military action by the Indian army, in 1961, succeeded in wresting them away. That left Portugal with two colonies in Asia. East Timor was half of a small island in the East Indies that Portugal had claimed since 1702. After the democratic revolution in Lisbon in 1974, Portugal withdrew, and the Timorese declared independence. The Indonesians soon invaded and occupied the island until, after a bloody conflict, it became independent in 2002. By that time, Portugal had relinquished its colony of Macau to China, in 1999, over 442 years after formally establishing a base on the east Asian mainland. That move finally wound up the European colonial presence on the continent.

North Africa

The North African countries achieved independence in the 1950s and 1960s. With defeat in the Second World War, Italy ended its rule over Libya, with independence proclaimed in 1951. In Italy's other major colony, Ethiopia, Emperor Haile Selassie, dethroned and exiled after Italian invasion in 1935, returned during the war as Allied armies defeated the Italians, and Ethiopia regained full independence (and incorporated the former Italian colony of Eritrea).

Egypt came under virtual control by London after British forces bombarded the coast in 1882. From 1914 to 1922 Egypt was a British protectorate, and the British, especially because of interests in the Suez Canal, continued to retain a dominant political and commercial presence after formal independence in that year. In 1952, a revolution led by military officers led to the overthrow of the Egyptian monarchy. Gamal Abdel Nasser (1918–70) emerged as strongman, served as Egyptian president until his death and became a major personality in the history of decolonization. Nasser's regime set itself up as a model of a strong and modernizing government that attempted to limit Western influence. A leader of the pan-Arab movement, he lent moral and material support to independence movements in French North Africa and was a fervent opponent of the state of Israel (with which Egypt fought a war in 1948–9 and subsequently).

From the end of the 1800s, the Sudan, one of Africa's largest countries, had been administered as an Anglo-Egyptian condominium, though effectively as a British colony, imperial control assured by garrisons of soldiers and agents of the Sudan Political Service. As elsewhere, nationalist groups emerged, gained support and in the 1930s held inconclusive negotiations with the British. President Nasser, in a manifestation of his increasing power, opposed maintenance of the status quo, and Sudan gained independence without great conflict, but with few clear arrangements for the new state, on the first day of 1956.

Nasser's policies and Egypt's growing links with the Soviet Union appeared to the West as a menace. The answer to Nasser's nationalization of the Suez Canal in July 1956 was invasion of Egypt by Britain, France and Israel, though the United States declined to join in. The Suez war seemed to many as a reprise of nineteenth-century imperial gunboat diplomacy, a last hurrah for Western colonialists. Nasser's troops and pressure by the United States halted the intervention, further strengthened Nasser and stimulated pride in Arabic countries. The year 1956 also witnessed the independence of Morocco and Tunisia, French protectorates (although Spain had a sphere of influence in Morocco, and Tangiers was an 'international city'). The French had been faced with steady growth of nationalist movements since the Second World War. Demands for independence were not assuaged with either gradual reforms or repression, including the exile in 1953 of the sultan of Morocco, who had shown sympathies for the independence movement. Indeed, reaction to his banishment proved so strong that the French had to permit Mohammed V (1909–61) to return to Morocco, to a jubilant reception, two years later. The sultan forced the French to concede independence and took the title of king. The Spanish zone of northern Morocco and Tangiers were incorporated into the new kingdom, though not Spain's residual Mediterranean enclaves of Ceuta and Melilla, and its territories on Morocco's Atlantic coast. Tunisia similarly gained independence, under the leadership of Habib Bourguiba (1903–2000), who served as its president for more than thirty years. The French had been unable to resist decolonization of the two protectorates – but it nurtured hope for continuing close diplomatic and profitable commercial links with them – because of the groundswell of nationalism, and the fact that the crisis in Algeria commanded their attention.

By the mid-1950s, the French had become mired in a war in Algeria, the theme of a detailed chapter in Part III of this volume. In brief, the French government adamantly resisted the independence demanded by indigenous Muslim nationalists, largely because of the presence of a million descendants of European settlers, the *pieds-noirs*. Outright war began in 1954 and dragged on for eight years, one of the most dramatic and bloody of all the wars of decolonization. Any chance of compromise disappeared in the wake of guerrilla actions by nationalists and violent repression by the state, but the outcome was what the French and *pieds-noirs* had once said would never happen: independence of Algeria under majority rule.

Decolonization in sub-Saharan Africa

Sub-Saharan Africa remained the largest preserve of colonialism by the mid-1950s. Despite large cities, growing economies and European-educated elites in Africa, colonial policymakers, still imbued with racist stereotypes of primitivism, predicted that it would take decades of development before colonies there might be 'mature' enough for independence. In any case, the French, British, Belgians, Portuguese and Spanish found arguments to hang on to African possessions as long as possible. With the independence of Asian colonies, African ones assumed greater real or potential value. Governments announced grand development plans and made overtures to political leaders considered moderate, while fiercely repressing insurrection and dissent.

Nationalist militancy was nevertheless particularly evident in Kenya, a large colony with a substantial European population. In 1952, in the 'Mau Mau rebellion', ethnic Kikuyu initiated a war of independence against the British, a conflict exacerbated by clashes between ethnic groups (in part because of the colonial policy of 'divide and rule'). British repression of the Mau Mau, including large-scale incarceration of rebels and use of torture, prompted later accusations of a British 'gulag' in Kenya. The official death toll, the victims almost all African, was 11,000, with the actual figure more than twice that number. Independence was postponed for a decade. Violence also permeated French colonies in conflicts over decolonization, notably in prolonged guerrilla actions in French Cameroon, with a predictable response of repression and counter-violence (including assassinations of several pro-independence leaders). Though British and French colonies escaped the full-scale wars that occurred in Indonesia, Vietnam, Algeria or, later in the Portuguese colonies, such cases show that any contention that decolonization of Black Africa was thoroughly peaceful and amicable is erroneous.

Through negotiation, parliamentary and extra-parliamentary action, and occasional bouts of violence, African nationalists in the British and French colonies pressed on with their campaigns through the 1950s. In 1957 the Gold Coast, renamed Ghana under Kwame Nkrumah, led the way to independence for the British colonies in sub-Saharan Africa, followed the next year by the French colony of Guinea, under Sékou Touré (1922–84) – both leaders viewed with suspicion in the colonizing countries, but lauded as fathers of independent states by African compatriots. In 1960, in a speech in Cape Town, the British prime minister Harold Macmillan famously spoke of a 'wind of change' gusting through Africa, 'growing African national consciousness', that is, the wind of independence. In that year, most of France's African colonies, Britain's Nigeria and Somaliland (from 1950 to 1960 a United Nations trusteeship under Italian administration), and the Belgian Congo gained independence, with others, including a dozen more British African colonies, following suit later in the decade (Map 5.1).

The British and French congratulated themselves for having successfully brought about decolonization in Africa, a process they had long resisted and sometimes fought against. Yet the strength of nationalism, declining European resolve to keep control combined with hopes of retaining commercial and political benefits from independent countries, and the changing international situation (as well as, for France, the morass of

Map 5.1 Africa at independence (including country names and dates of independence). © Adapted from map by cartographer Peter Palm.

the Algerian war) reversed years of opposition to the granting of independence, decades of formal rule since the late nineteenth-century 'scramble for Africa' and centuries of European imperialist interventions.

By the late 1960s, no more European colonies existed in Africa except the Portuguese and the Spanish colonies, and French Djibouti and the Comoros Islands. South Africa, however, remained under the apartheid regime of the white minority (also controlling Namibia until 1990), and the white government of Southern Rhodesia (now Zimbabwe) in 1965 issued a 'unilateral declaration of independence' to forestall independence under an African majority (and majority rule did not eventuate until 1980). Spanish Guinea (Equatorial Guinea) attained independence in 1968. The Portuguese colonies only achieved independence between 1974 and 1975 thanks to the 'carnation revolution' in Lisbon that brought democracy to Portugal and after decades of anti-colonialist activity and, in several colonies, warfare between African nationalist movements and the Portuguese army. Though assassinated by a nationalist rival before independence, Amílcar Cabral (1924–73), a Portuguese Guinean agricultural engineer, poet and writer, was internationally celebrated, like Nkrumah and Touré, for his role in ending colonialism. (Further details appear in the chapters on the Portuguese colonies and on Spanish Sahara in Part III.) In 1974, the French held a referendum in the Comoros islands; three of the islands voted in favour, while one, Mayotte, voted against and it remains a French overseas outpost. Three years later, Djibouti, France's remaining African outpost, gained independence. Formal decolonization thus proved as messy and often as chaotic a process as had been the acquisition of European colonies in Africa.

Decolonization in the islands

Islands in the Caribbean and Indian Oceans counted among the oldest European overseas territories. They were also among the last places to be decolonized, yet the process began earlier close to European shores. In the eastern Mediterranean, the ethnically Greek majority population of Cyprus overwhelmingly supported the campaign for *enosis*, union of the island with Greece, led by the Greek Orthodox archbishop Makarios III (1913–77) in the 1950s. Turkish Cypriots, a quarter of the population, strongly opposed the union and favoured division of the island, a proposal Greek Cypriots rejected. The British were unwilling to countenance either alternative. After a more militant Greek nationalist movement, EOKA, began violent attacks on the British in the mid-1950s, London declared a state of emergency and exiled Makarios to the Seychelles (though later allowing him to return). The Cypriot situation assumed international dimensions because of support from Greece and Turkey for their respective ethnic communities and with concern in NATO (of which both were members) and the United Nations. The UN proved unable to broker a solution, and conflict in the Middle East and the Suez crisis of 1956 further complicated matters. In 1959, negotiators worked out a plan for independence, but with *enosis* and division of the island off the table. A power-sharing arrangement was devised: the president would be Greek Cypriot (with Makarios elected to the post), and a Turkish Cypriot vice-president. As independence followed the next year, conflict continued, and a Turkish invasion in 1974 led to de facto division of the island and the creation of a Turkish Republic of Northern Cyprus (recognized only by Turkey). Meanwhile, Britain retains two military bases as 'sovereign territory' in Cyprus. Local issues thus had linked to ethnicity, religion and nationalist aspirations, as well as international involvement and the desire of the colonial power to effect an orderly transition but maintain its influence: factors common in many other colonies. Elsewhere in the Mediterranean, Malta's independence in 1964 occurred with none of the violence and far less of the discord that marked Cyprus.

By the mid-1960s, several island colonies outside Europe had gained independence, led by (Western) Samoa – from New Zealand, which had taken over the archipelago from Germany after the First World War – in 1962 (while neighbouring American Samoa remains under US administration) in the Pacific, as well as Jamaica, and Trinidad and

The Colonial World

Tobago, in the Caribbean in 1966. Others followed, albeit with reservations by colonial officials, and some in the islands, who felt that small islands or archipelagos would not be able economically and demographically to sustain independence. Many islands saw a relatively limited militant push for sovereignty, and almost none of the violence, so evident in Asia or Africa. While colonial powers reaped limited benefits from many of them, others provided valuable agricultural products, minerals, strategic locations (or, for the French in Polynesia, sites for nuclear testing), and 'windows on the world'. The British nevertheless moved more rapidly to decolonization of its islands in the 1970s, though Britain, like France and the Netherlands, has retained island groups in various parts of the globe.

Denmark had sold its Virgin Islands colony to the United States in 1917, while Iceland gained full independence in 1944. Like Iceland, the Faroe islands in the North Atlantic was populated by people of Scandinavian background, and it remains essentially an autonomous offshore Danish province. Conditions of a sparse population and the absence of a strong independence movement similar to that in many other island colonies were also present in Denmark's geographically large colony of Greenland, where indigenous Inuit experienced similar disadvantages to 'native' peoples elsewhere in the colonial world. Greenland moved towards greater autonomy in the 1960s and attained 'Home Rule', self-government, but still as part of the kingdom of Denmark, in 1979.

The eclipse of empires

Each colony has its own inevitably complex history of decolonization, just as its own experience of colonialism, one that merits greater consideration than can be accorded here. The independence of the European colonies represented a tectonic historical change, a remarkable turnaround over just three decades from the end of the Second World War. This contrasted with a time when much of Asia, Africa, Oceania and the Caribbean had been under the suzerainty of colonial powers, masters who confidently expected to retain dominion. The change proved triumphalist claims about empire and incessant declarations about the indefectible attachment of colonies to metropolitan states to be false.

The transformation of metropolitan, colonial and international contexts meant it was no longer possible for European powers to keep overseas colonies, except for a handful of residual outposts. As wars in Indonesia, Vietnam, Algeria and the Portuguese African colonies dramatically illustrated, they were indeed impotent or at least unwilling to do so. Strong-arm efforts, from the silencing of anti-colonialists and suppression of nationalists to grandiose designs for development and modernization, alongside gradual enfranchisement and limited transfer of administrative powers to win 'hearts and minds', failed in the long run to secure the survival of empires. Some in Europe, as well as white colonial elites, fiercely opposed withdrawal, and showed themselves willing to fight to the bitter end, a determination matched by nationalists committed to struggle through to the final negotiations or the last battles.

For Europeans, decolonization meant loss of territory, though not by any means the closure of access to overseas resources or the end of close diplomatic, commercial and cultural links with many former colonies that critical commentators branded 'neo-colonial'. The old colonial powers, however, would need to recast their sense of nationhood, to become nations without empires. Diehard and nostalgic colonialists, and settlers' descendants and others who took flight from newly independent countries, lamented loss of empire, but most others did not bemoan the passing of an age. In the colonies, independence was widely greeted with joy, relief and hope, mixed with concern and uncertainty about the future. It was celebrated as the culmination of decades or centuries of resistance, the restoration to full rights of nations, peoples and cultures subjected and abused by foreign control, an opportunity for the formation of new governments and social orders. Prime Minister Jawaharlal Nehru's speech to the Indian parliament as midnight – the moment of independence – approached on 14 August 1947 eloquently brought together a vision of India's past and future and resonated with later speakers marking similar transitions:

> Long years ago . . . we made a tryst with destiny, and now the time comes when we shall redeem our pledge. . . . At the stroke of the midnight hour, when the world sleeps, India will awake to life and freedom. A moment comes, which comes but rarely in history, when we step out from the old to the new, when an age ends, and when the soul of a nation, long suppressed, finds utterance.

Implicit in those words was acknowledgement of the challenges the new nation would face and of the scars and legacies colonialism left behind.

PART II
THEMES

Introduction

For people living in a 'colonial situation', empire directly or indirectly produced a great impact on all areas of life. The beliefs of the colonizers challenged indigenous knowledge; an increasingly globalized economy geared to the empires' demands restructured labour and production; taxation, law and military recruitment placed new burdens on populations, colonial violence sought to enforce obedience. For some, however, colonialism provided new opportunities, new points of view and alternative social trajectories. Colonial subjects accommodated, resisted, adopted and negotiated with foreign overlordship in various ways.

Most historians concur that colonialism had great repercussions for the populations of the colonizing countries, though in a far less coercive fashion than for the colonized. Products from the tropics or other distant climes increasingly became commonplace and more affordable in Europe. Colonial promoters persuaded most of their compatriots of the merits, and indeed necessity, of overseas expansion, and they showed off the spoils of conquest at colonial exhibitions. Many genuinely believed that colonialism meant development, emancipation of foreign peoples from tyrants, introduction of the 'true gospel' of Christianity and the beneficent establishment of European-style legal and political systems. Some were called to colonial vocations: as soldiers and sailors, evangelists, traders, settlers and academics. A 'colonial culture' of art and literature captivated Europeans fascinated by exoticism, though some painters and writers presented contrary perspectives on colonialism.

This second part of *The Colonial World* looks at the ways that colonialism affected the people and countries claimed by Europeans and at reflections and echoes of colonialism in the European metropoles. The first chapter is about the natural environment which, no less than the people who lived in it, underwent a process of colonization: mapping and charting, the introduction of new species of flora and fauna and the extinction of others, the modification of the very landscape through the building of new cities according to European design, the laying of railway lines and construction of ports, and purportedly more modern, efficient and productive projects for agriculture, industry and commerce.

Three chapters then look at the people involved in empire. Colonialism is about grand projects and overarching ideas, but it is also about the lived experiences in the colonial world. Experiences and relationships were diverse, amicable or inimical, brief or enduring, but often they were stories of crossed destinies. Europeans and non-Europeans did not generally meet on equal terms given the power structures that colonialism imposed, but there were margins of manoeuvre. The binaries of 'collaboration' and 'resistance' for the colonized, once favoured by scholars as an organizing concept, have proven to be reductive. Case studies of individuals (and groups) – only a sample of whom can be examined in a brief chapter – show ways in which colonialism affected daily lives, underlining the manifold, but varying, experiences of colonialism. The next chapter focuses on enslaved Africans and another particular cohort of migrants – spurred by compulsion, need and sometimes opportunity – that came to the fore from the time of the abolition of slavery in the mid-1800s: indentured labourers and free migrants from the Indian subcontinent who went to Southeast Asia, the Caribbean, the Pacific islands and parts of Africa. They were neither indigenous, in the sense of having an immediate hereditary attachment to the lands where they migrated, nor were they colonizers in the sense of possessing the economic and political power, and the claimed cultural superiority, of the colonizing masters – though, in various ways, they came to be considered, by some, as both. Another experience is covered in a chapter on the history of settler colonialism in the British 'Dominions' of Australia, Canada, New Zealand and South Africa; this represented a particular type of settler colonization though the parallels with other settler societies (and, in fact, with some non-settler ones) are patent. As in the Americas at an earlier age, colonialism in the Dominions involved the permanent rooting of a substantial European population in foreign lands, and led to a different path of decolonization than in Africa or Asia, while creating and perpetuating a colonialist-style rule over indigenous people.

'Body, mind and soul' are traditional divisions of human nature, no matter how blurred such a categorization may be, and the next three chapters take those terms as reference points. Given the comprehensive nature of colonialism, discussion must be selective: a chapter on 'colonialism and the body' highlights the topics of sexuality and medicine, one on 'colonialism and the mind' focuses on European science and scholarship, and that on 'colonialism and the soul' devotes greater attention to Christianity and Buddhism than to other creeds. Fortunately, there is now a burgeoning literature for further reading, much of it under the rubric of the 'new' imperial history and enriched by post-modern and post-colonial theory. Such works explore the ways that colonial domination reached every corner of life, private and public.

'Representations' is a term that came to the forefront of scholarship in the late twentieth century and retains value for understanding how one society portrayed another. Studies of representations are concerned with relating written texts and images, as well as objects of material culture and the built environment, to colonialism and with how the wider world was depicted and reflected, realistically or fantastically. Colonial-age authors and creators of art, sculpture and photography produced many masterworks, now critically scrutinized because of the suppositions that they conveyed about indigenous peoples and foreign countries and the manner in which they directly or indirectly underpinned the colonial project. Colonial culture was disseminated throughout Europe, in periodicals and museum displays, in vogues for particular forms of music or fashion. However, people in the colonial world – and their successors in independent countries – have also represented Europe and the European colonizers who ruled over them, often in a critical gaze, a kind of 'anti-colonial', and now post-colonial, culture. Representations were always a two-way mirror, reflecting back on their creators as well as providing views of others.

In this part of the book, we move towards a more panoramic vision of empire than in the chronologies of the first section. With the amplitude of the phenomenon of colonialism, this must necessarily be a bird's-eye view, but occasionally one from closer up. The examples are a reminder to consider the diversity of experiences – of Europeans and other peoples – and of the need to look at the particular as well as the general, to think about what it was actually like to be involved in colonialism, as ruler or subject, to consider what options were available to people on a personal level and on a day-to-day basis.

One theme highlighted in this section is that of connection. The use of that term does not imply that all connections between individuals and cultures were peaceful, reciprocal, voluntary or just – indeed, many were the opposite, marked by coercion and violence. However, connections and exchanges of various sorts occurred as people, commodities and ideas circulated around the world and exercised influence on each other. To different degrees all societies incorporated and remoulded populations, goods and cultures from afar. Colonialism, with its effects, often in long-term fashion, joined together environments, people, practices of daily life and modes of representation, and this remains an ongoing process in the post-colonial, globalized world.

CHAPTER 6
LAND AND SEA
COLONIALISM AND THE ENVIRONMENT

'Few countries in the world are so unknown and so rarely visited as the Philippines, and yet none is more pleasant to travel in than the lavishly endowed island kingdom; hardly anywhere will the naturalist find a greater abundance of unexploited treasures.' With this trope of the 'unknown', a German adventurer and researcher, Fedor Jagor, concluded the preface to his travelogue of a journey to the Southeast Asian archipelago in 1859 and 1860.[1] In the preface, he did not give his readers further details about the unexploited treasures, yet the context suggests Jagor referred to the land and the sea, to nature. Indeed, he was an avid observer during his travels and wrote about diverse subjects ranging from the rich fishing grounds around the islands to plantations of coffee and cacao. He was fascinated by unpredictable and majestic volcanoes, such as Mount Mayon with an elevation of close to 2,500 metres, located on Luzón, 330 kilometres southeast of the capital and shown in the background of Figure 6.1. Manila itself, with roughly 200,000 inhabitants, reminded him of a Spanish provincial city. For certain, almost any European description of faraway lands, and their flora and fauna, highlights the novelty of the 'discoveries' made in the name of science, paving the way for future colonial takeover.

For the Philippines, which Spain had claimed as a colony 300 years before Jagor's visit, in the late 1500s, however, Jagor's assertions about the 'unknown' might come as a surprise. Yet Europeans' knowledge of such topics as the geology of the Southeast Asian archipelago remained limited in the mid- and late nineteenth century; 'the peripheral islands' of the colony, in particular, had long 'been all but ignored by the Spanish authorities', who concentrated their attention on Manila and the main island of Luzón. Only in the 1860s did an intensification of surveying for mining and forestry attract greater notice to remote regions of the Spanish outposts in Asia, the Caribbean and Africa.[2]

Yet in the 1880s and beyond, Spanish colonial governors still pointed to the meagre documentation and limited dominion even on Luzón; there was a 'vast independent territory' lying outside of Spanish control on the northern island. The Spanish grip on Mindanao, the second largest island, further south, continued to be weak as well in the 1890s. After fighting a formidable Filipino independence movement led by Andrés Bonifacio and Emilio Aguinaldo during that decade, Spain lost the Philippines in a war against the United States in 1898. Filipino resistance against the new foreigners nevertheless persisted; the country achieved independence only in 1946.

Figure 6.1 Ruins of the sixteenth-century Spanish Cagsawa church with Mount Mayon volcano in the background, Albay, Philippines, undated. © Getty Images.

With sketchy knowledge about the land and the sea, that is, the colonial environment in the Philippines, the Spanish were no isolated case. The Dutch in neighbouring Indonesia were somewhat embarrassed when it was non-Dutch explorers who mapped the highlands of the island of Celebes (Sulawesi), south of Mindanao, at the turn of the twentieth century.[3] Hence it comes as little surprise that Jagor's account of the Philippines was swiftly translated from German into Spanish, richly illustrated with sketches and photographs depicting people, cultures and nature. Other European travellers in Southeast Asia in the late nineteenth century, like Henri Mouhot, venturing among islands, navigating the Mekong, and moving into dense jungles and hinterlands distant from the better-known coasts, similarly produced works that enchanted readers and provided much-needed information for colonial officials and promoters of European expansion. These publications contributed to the construction of both an exotic paradise and a virtual hell in the European vision of the 'East'.[4] Here was a terrestrial heaven, perhaps with vast reserves of gold and precious gems along with tropical luxuriance, and an inferno with devastating monsoons, destructive earthquakes, ferocious animals and murderous diseases. Yet decades and centuries of European colonialism, encompassing wars, the introduction of new species of crops and animals (as well as germs), migration and remodelling of the environment through land clearance, vast building programmes and urbanization, combined with periodic natural catastrophes, including climatic phenomena such as El Niño, transformed the land and the sea of the colonial world in unprecedented and lasting fashion.[5]

In a very basic way, the land and the sea provided the foundations of European expansion: the sea as the conduit for exploration, conquest and trade as well as a trove of marine resources, and foreign lands as the terrain for settlement and city-building, plantations and mines, and the coveted commodities they offered. Particularly significant was the boundary between land and water: the seashores where landfalls were made and first encounters between Europeans and indigenous peoples often occurred, the places goods were loaded onto and off of ships, the sites for fortresses, trading houses and port facilities, the beachheads for expansion inland and the launching of further campaigns of conquest. The great colonial cities grew up along the shores of oceans and rivers, and cosmopolitan populations of Europeans and other migrants, rich and poor, congregated in their largest numbers on the banks of waterways.

A variety of landscapes awaited Europeans overseas, from the tropical islands of the Caribbean to the snow-covered peaks of the Himalayas, from the equatorial jungles of Africa to polar ice, from the fertile river plains of India to the Sahara desert. Europeans yearned to discover and explore, measure and map, affix their own names to geographical features, collect specimens of flora and fauna. These activities constituted an integral part of conquest and rule, though they were not confined to places Europeans brought into their formal empires. The travelogues, atlases and encyclopaedic works they produced constitute an invaluable archive of colonial knowledge, one marked by a European perspective on the wider world. Trekking through seemingly impenetrable forests or summiting an unscaled mountain peak can also be understood as symbolic appropriations of territory and claims of possession. Explorations had a significant impact in their home countries, too, with members of expeditions heroically cast as exemplars of curiosity and valour, geographical societies disseminating their findings to eager audiences, and museums enriched by objects they brought back. 'Conquering' mountains, rivers and deserts in the name of exploration and science became inextricably linked to the ideas and policies of colonialism.

The first certified ascent of Mount Everest, by the New Zealander Sir Edmund Hillary and the Nepalese Tenzing Norgay, took place in 1953 and was proclaimed the greatest feat of the age. Those who reached the top of the world's highest mountain were applauded in Europe and elsewhere as worthy successors to generations of explorers harking back to the seafarers of the 1400s who had given new continents to the world, as a Portuguese epic described their work. Advertising the 'discoveries' glossed over the fact that these places, home to countless people, were thus primarily introduced to the 'European' world. Interesting enough, even those from European countries that claimed no colonial possessions took on the competition to conquer new ground. In the 1950s, an age of decolonization, Swiss climbers in the Himalayas tried to reconcile the asymmetries of power inherent in relationships with Nepali porters through a brotherly attitude as fellow mountaineers. However, they still reproduced colonial stereotypes of backward natives whose main duty was to carry the loads.[6]

The relationship between colonizers and the environment, and the changes colonialism brought to the countries occupied, form a major theme in colonial history,

115

what Alfred Crosby labelled 'ecological imperialism' and one aspect of which Richard H. Grove termed 'green imperialism'.[7] There has been much subsequent scholarship on colonialism and ecology, in part sparked by increasing environmental consciousness over recent decades. This chapter can only provide an overview of two key themes: the transformation of the natural environment by European intervention and the creation of a new built environment by the colonizers. Taken together, they encompass some of the longest-living impacts of colonial rule on the wider world.

Europeans and the natural world

Colonizers, to borrow a famous phrase from Julius Caesar referring to the Roman takeover of Gaul, 'came, saw and conquered', and that conquest was, in part, ecological. Plants and animals moved around the world along with humans, new species were introduced while others became extinct, physical environments changed dramatically. In the 'Columbian Exchange' of the early modern period, such indigenous American plant species as chillies, cacao, maize, tomatoes and potatoes were introduced into Europe and transported to Asia, becoming staples in cuisines around the world. At the same time, the conquerors brought plants and livestock, as well as pathogens, to the 'new world'. Among the farm animals the Spanish and Portuguese imported to the Americas was the pig, with profound long-term effects on diet but also, given the destruction that roaming pigs could cause, on the environment. Moreover, empire-building in the Americas contributed to wider circulation of local crops throughout continents and islands within the Western hemisphere, 'making the intra-American exchange nearly as important as the Columbian Exchange'.[8]

Exchanges took place everywhere travellers went. Australia provides a good example. Before the arrival of Europeans, marsupials were almost the only mammals on the continent other than bats. Imported sheep brought by the British became the mainstay of the colonial rural economy, and cattle, horses, dogs and other introduced species became common – and camels were introduced as beasts of burden in the desert. Meanwhile, Europeans marvelled at picturesque and unknown creatures, kangaroos and koalas, emus and kookaburras. Especially curious was the platypus, and European scientists, looking at drawings or dissecting preserved specimens or the rare live platypus that survived the voyage from the antipodes, long puzzled about how to classify an animal with a furry body, duck-like snout and webbed feet.[9]

Contacts between countries inevitably alter ecosystems, intentionally or by accident. Rats and fleas counted among stowaway passengers travelling aboard any colonial ship, as did cats carried to keep rats under control and dogs for companionship. A menagerie of animals, as well as plants, bacteria and other organisms, thus found passage from one place to another. Europeans introduced plants and animals considered vital or beneficial to their survival – familiar foodstuffs, for instance – and to the commercial development of the lands over which they had established authority: wheat to Australia, tea to Ceylon, tobacco and rubber to parts of Southeast Asia. There were benefits for both indigenous people and settlers, but new species could prey on native ones, become pests (as were rabbits in Australia) and denude land through grazing.

Colonization, moreover, brought about the extinction of certain species. The archetypal example is the dodo, a large and ungainly flightless bird that flourished with no natural predators on the Indian Ocean island now called Mauritius. European visitors first mentioned the dodo in accounts at the end of the 1500s, but the bird seems to have become extinct only sixty years later. Europeans found the dodo unpalatable to eat, but shooting the birds provided an easy, if not very challenging, sport; meanwhile, land clearance diminished the bird's habitat, and European dogs feasted on its eggs. 'Dead as a dodo' provided a rather cavalier epitaph, though the dodo memorably made a later resurrection in Lewis Carroll's *Alice in Wonderland*. It remains a sad symbol of the way that colonialism could kill off a species, but the dodo is by far not the only victim. Another was the shy, striped dog-like thylacine, the Tasmanian tiger. Before the arrival of the Europeans, it had become extinct on the Australian mainland but survived on the island of Tasmania. By the 1920s, the Tasmanian tiger was a rare beast indeed. The last one to be killed in the wild perished in 1930, while several survived in zoos for a few more years, remembered in photos and film.

Plants, animals and sub-soil resources were, of course, crucial to European survival in the colonies and for their plans for profitable development of conquered lands. Supplies of fresh water and food provided justification for the takeover of islands along long ocean routes. A basic question surrounding where to establish a colony was whether it provided fertile land, though negative evaluation of sites did not prevent acquisition of deserts and Arctic regions with scarce resources. Survival was not assured for early colonists in the Americas and Australia, in particular, as the supplies they brought ran short, crops failed and in unaccustomed environments they lacked indigenous knowledge of how to find food and water. Animals, both local and especially introduced ones, were major auxiliaries in European colonization. Horses provided necessary transport, powered agriculture, carried the cavalry, offered recreation through races and gave a sense of 'home' to European settlers.[10] Cattle gave milk, meat and leather; sheep produced wool, milk and meat. The fur from beavers and similar animals provided the major export from Canada in the early 1800s. Whaling was a major activity in the Atlantic, Pacific and Southern Oceans in the nineteenth century, producing oil for lamps and the 'whalebone' used as stays in corsets. Fish and other seafood from oceans, rivers and lakes gave nourishment to settlers, and dried fish such as cod became an important foodstuff taken around the colonial world. The development of refrigeration and canning in the late 1800s made frozen and tinned meat and fish, as well as such 'exotic' fruits as bananas and pineapples, accessible to those living far away.

A vogue for 'exotic' animals endured in nineteenth-century Europe, as evidenced by the story of Zarafa, a Nubian giraffe given by the ruler of Egypt to the king of France in 1826, one of three sent to European monarchs; Zarafa's stately progress along the roads from the Mediterranean to the botanical garden in Paris, where she lived for eighteen years, made her a celebrity and created a fashion trend for giraffe-printed accessories and decorations.[11] Birds provided feathers for European high fashion, and collectors bought pretty seashells for their display cases. Parrots, particularly budgerigars, and other colourful birds became popular house pets. Many animals were captured for zoos, while preserved specimens filled shelves of laboratories and museums – the natural world, alive or dead, brought home. Countless animals in the colonies were also slaughtered for 'sport', with big game-hunting buttressing notions of masculinity in the colonies (and providing recreation for some women as well).[12]

Many animals were seen, sometimes with good reason, as a threat to Europeans. Poisonous snakes such as cobras regularly killed Europeans and indigenous people, and the bites of some spiders were also lethal.[13] Sharks were viewed with terror, and other venomous creatures haunted the waters. Mosquitoes carried malaria, yellow fever and other deadly viruses. Animals, great and small, ravaged crops. Lions and tigers were objects of particular awe and fear for Europeans, noble beasts admired for strength and beauty, but also 'man-eaters' (though more in myth than actuality); shooting them was occasionally necessary for safety, but more often as proof of 'sporting' prowess and vainglory.[14]

Elephants held a particular place in the colonial imaginary and colonial life. They were wantonly killed for the ivory of their tusks, much in demand on the international market for carving and decoration, and shot with horrifying frequency as trophies. Elephants were also beasts of burden, for instance in logging, particularly in Southeast Asia, as they could shift the huge trunks of hardwood trees. Europeans did not adopt a pre-colonial Asian practice of using elephants for warfare, but they did play a great ceremonial role bearing maharajas, European officials and tourists, and taking part in processions.[15] Camels provided transport in caravans across the Arabian Peninsula and deserts from the Sahara to the Gobi. Colonizers thus often simply adopted local ways of employing animals in utilitarian ways, just as they followed indigenous practice in festooning themselves with fur and feathers.

The polar lands provide an extreme example of colonial-era encounters with nature. Though the Arctic and Antarctic appeared barren and inhospitable to outsiders, the urge to explore and chart icy continents and waterways was no less keen than to cross deserts or traverse continents. The American Robert Peary's claimed 'conquest' of the North Pole in 1909 and the Norwegian Roald Amundsen's expedition to the South Pole, where his team beat a rival British expedition in 1911, added to the ongoing saga of exploration and heroic feats. The survival – or death – of men crossing polar ice symbolized the challenges of nature and the desire to master it, with the fur coats, ice-sleds and other paraphernalia of expeditions testimony to technological ingenuity, human grit and international competition. The polar regions, moreover, presented resources such as fish and other maritime animals, and held out the promise of new oceanic routes – notably, in the long, if fruitless, nineteenth-century search for a 'Northwest Passage' that would connect the Atlantic to the Pacific. They provided lands over which to lay claim, and indigenous peoples, notably the Inuit, with whom to engage and over whom to rule. The British imperium over the territory reaching from the settlements in southern Canada towards the North Pole, Danish control of Greenland, the annexation of unoccupied sub-Antarctic islands by the British and French, and the staking out of territory on the Antarctic continent – albeit a 1959 treaty eventually forbade claims of sovereignty there – showed how lands and seas at the ends of the earth represented new, mythified experiences of nature and areas of imperial manoeuvre.

Reshaping the land

Europeans, in a literal sense, reshaped the sea and the land.[16] The construction of dams, bridges and artificial lakes, the rerouting of rivers, reclamation of land from the sea, draining of marshland and construction of irrigation systems, urban sewers and sanitation networks channelled water in line with European notions of hygiene, convenience and economic utility. The Suez Canal, built by an international workforce under French design and management, opened in 1869, and the Panama Canal, completed under US direction in 1914, stood as dramatic interventions in the natural world at the height of imperialism.[17] New sorts of sailing vessels followed by larger and faster steam-powered and eventually petroleum-fuelled ships plied the oceans and rivers. Wastes from mines, artificial fertilizers, industry and migrant populations increased maritime and riverine pollution. Yet Europeans also enjoyed new types of recreation on the seashore, such as the ocean-bathing that gained in popularity from the mid-1800s, then surfing (adopted from Polynesia) and other aquatic and nautical sports. Humans have always turned rivers, seas and lakes to their own use, but the scale of intervention – and the capital and technology available to do so – in the colonial era was far greater than in the past, as depicted in paintings of colonial harbours where great steamships dwarfed traditional outrigger canoes, dhows or praus.

Changes to the land appear even more visible and dramatic than those at sea, particularly manifest in the building of bridges and opening of mountain tunnels for the passage of railway lines. 'Land clearance' became a priority for settlers who felled forests to provide space for houses, farms and livestock pastures, and to obtain wood for fuel and building. Indeed, colonials considered land clearance as a key sign of progress, carving out a place for themselves in the 'wilderness' and replacing indigenous vegetation perceived as unproductive with crops for sustenance and sale. Levelling, ploughing and planting land, often with new crops and new techniques, was heralded as an achievement of pioneers. Nineteenth-century images of settler colonies proudly portray homesteads surrounded by verdant lawns, neat flower gardens and vegetable patches, proof of the domestication of the natural environment to European use and European taste. Europeans saw themselves 'battling' – an often used word – jungles and deserts, monsoons and tsunamis, flooding and droughts. Nature might be generous, but it was fearsome. Brought under control, it became valuable and homey.

Europeans dug into the earth, or with the invention of dynamite blasted it open, to quarry minerals for which the industrial revolution created an insatiable market – copper in central Africa, nickel in New Caledonia, iron and coal in many places, silver and gemstones such as the sapphires of Ceylon and the rubies of Burma, and many other sub-soil resources, including sandstone, granite and other building materials. The search for gold and diamonds, in particular, became an obsession, and proved successful from Australia to South Africa in the 1800s. The environment, and local or migrant populations employed in mines, paid a price for the fortunes made by successful mine owners and merchants. Large-scale open-pit mining left huge holes in the ground and desolate landscapes, the tailings polluting water supplies or rendering land infertile, while underground mining created honeycombs of subterranean chambers. The small island of Nauru in the South Pacific offers a prime example of colonial mining, left as a near wasteland because of the mining of phosphate, an essential ingredient in new chemical fertilizers and other industrial products invented in the nineteenth century.

On cleared land, Europeans in the 1800s introduced new crops, just as they had planted sugar in the tropical islands of the Caribbean and Indian Ocean in the first imperial age. In Vietnam, the Malay peninsula, Java and Sumatra, they cleared land for plantations of profitable coffee, tea, vanilla, tobacco and indigo, altering the distribution and extent of native plant species and the habitat for local animals. Rubber plantations covered large expanses in Southeast Asia, the sap sold for making tyres, insulation and other industrial uses; 'coolie' labour provided employment, with back-breaking work and exploitative conditions, for local and diasporic people. Large-scale planting of groundnuts and palm trees (primarily for oil) in western Africa and of coconuts (with oil for soap and margarine) in the Pacific islands affected the diversity of vegetation, and altered proprietorship with dispossession of indigenous populations, the imposition of European land titles and new forms of wage labour.[18] The cutting of tropical timber – teak, ebony, mahogany – became a major business in Southeast Asia and Africa, a trade that satisfied European furniture-makers and consumers, but deforested land and, with new planting, reduced areas covered in species with less commercial value.

'Acclimatization' of plants aimed at developing their commercial value through agronomy and horticultural efforts to maximize production and the expansion of farming. Europeans thus transplanted coffee and tea from one colony to another. Eucalyptus trees indigenous to Australia spread to North America and Southern Europe, and were introduced by French colonists into Algeria in the 1860s. In Australia, the purple jacarandas that came from South America in the mid-1800s, and the bright red and yellow proteas introduced from southern Africa, are now common sights, alongside the native gums and European deciduous trees and flowers. The extensive Australian vineyards of today had their origin in vines brought from France and Germany in the early 1800s.

European colonizers were by no means the first to alter the land – human land clearance, for instance, goes back to the dawn of history – but the extent and rapidity of the changes were remarkable. Not all transformations were catastrophic or wholly detrimental, but they did add up to a remoulding of landscapes, redistribution of species around the globe, and change in uses to which land and waterways were put. The restructuring revealed European attitudes towards the natural environment, and the use of land and sea often clashed markedly with the perceptions of indigenous people, in particular the ways in which some groups endowed land with profound spiritual significance rather than primarily with use value, or regarded themselves as custodians of land rather than its owners. The effects of colonial intervention on land were therefore cultural and social, as well as environmental and economic.

Despite colonial ecological depredations, the years from the late 1700s to the early 1800s, as Grove points out, marked the beginnings of environmentalism in European thought, drawing considerable inspiration from Indian and Chinese ideas, techniques and philosophies. Interest in the natural world prompted study, experimentation and the beginning of conservation. An important step was taken with the establishment of botanical gardens, both in Europe – the one at Kew, outside London, especially notable – and in the colonies, for example, botanical gardens set up by the Dutch on Java and in South Africa, the French on Mauritius and the British in Australia. Specifically 'colonial botanical gardens', filled with 'exotic' species, had existed in Lisbon from the 1760s, with one created in Paris at the end of the nineteenth century.[19] Botanical gardens offered aesthetic pleasure, leisure and recreation, but they were working gardens with herbaria of specimens, and laboratories and greenhouses for scientists, agronomists and horticulturists. The specialists catalogued and studied plants, worked at acclimatizing useful species for Europe or other colonies, and sought ways to improve yields.

'Zoological gardens' paralleled the botanical gardens, though 'wild' animals were often kept in appalling conditions in tiny cages with little to recall their native habitats. Gawping at cute or ferocious beasts from afar was recreation that fed into colonial fantasies, but the increased knowledge about animals and plants convinced some of the need to protect wild creatures and their environments, for example, with programmes of reafforestation and conservation. By the early twentieth century, colonial officials in many places had set up parks and reserves, even as land clearance, introduction of non-native species and near unregulated hunting for 'sport' continued apace. Modern environmentalism owes much to early efforts to regulate destruction of species and habitats as well as, paradoxically, to the evidence of the deleterious impact of colonialism.

Meanwhile, new medical research underlined the importance of hygiene and sanitation in public health, and systems of drainage, sewerage and refuse collection were gradually developed in the colonies. The areas inhabited by Europeans were invariably the first to receive attention, and travellers continued to describe quarters around ports and the crowded neighbourhoods in which the poor lived as foul and insalubrious. Promotion of public health, seen in Europe and beyond as a sign of progress, was also an important tool of empire. Epidemic diseases such as malaria and cholera were a fact of life in parts of the non-European world, affecting local people and colonizers alike, while yellow fever was relatively mild for locals but often deadly for recently arrived foreigners. For instance, in the war for Cuban independence against Spain, between 1895 and 1898, more than 40,000 Spanish soldiers – 22 per cent of the Spanish army on the island – succumbed to disease, mostly to tropical fevers. Not in vain did anti-colonial fighters refer to the annual months of rampant yellow fever as the Cuban nationalist army's most prolific generals. When Cuban and US scientists identified the *aedes aegypti* mosquito as the vector of yellow fever towards the end of the nineteenth century, an accessory as simple as a mosquito net aided the smooth US occupation.[20] Whereas the older historiography has seen disease control as a benevolent side of imperialism, recent studies highlight its necessity for guaranteeing further domination.²¹ It represented another form of intervention in the natural environment of the colonized world, though in the long term with substantial benefits for global health – an illustration of the complex legacy of colonialism, and perhaps varying views from different perspectives and periods.

Building cities

City-building formed one of the great colonial projects.²² In the early modern age, several cities in Asia were much larger than London or Paris, and urban cities of greater or lesser size existed in many parts of the globe. However, in the nineteenth century, industrialized Europe itself became far more urban, and the trend spread and accelerated. Colonialism, given the demand for ports and commercial centres, the migration of people from hinterlands and overseas, the clustering of settlers along seashores and the desire to create European-style public spaces, created cities where none had existed (as in Australasia, the Pacific islands and parts of Africa) and the massive expansion of those that did. Urban growth and the design of new cities became further signifiers of modernization and progress, and affirmations of European control over the environment. Colonial cities served as transport hubs, government centres, sites of industry and commerce, places of cultural and recreational activity. Some examples show the dynamics of colonial urbanism.

'Marvelous Melbourne', as Victorians called one of Australia's leading cities, was founded in 1835, but grew populous and prosperous after the nearby gold rushes in the following decades. An imposing parliament building for the colony of Victoria rose over the course of several decades from the 1850s, and a state library was established in 1854. Along the neat grid of streets bordering the Yarra River, a town hall was first built in 1854, succeeded by a far more grandiose one in 1870. The domed Royal Exhibition Building, raised in 1880, provided a venue for colonists to display their achievements. A Gothic Revival Anglican cathedral was finished in 1891 (with spires added later), and a Catholic cathedral consecrated six years afterwards. Cable-drawn trams began operation in 1885 and soon the service was electrified; the striking Flinders Street railway station was erected in the first years of the twentieth century. Arcades in the central city connected streets and housed shops; banks and trading companies commissioned buildings reflecting their wealth, and Victoria Market presented an emporium of foodstuffs. All of those facilities still function in Melbourne, a legacy of colonialism and the nineteenth-century architectural styles adopted throughout Queen Victoria's empire. Such buildings, however, can nevertheless be seen as markers of the dispossession of Australian Aborigines and their lands.²³

In the early nineteenth century, Hanoi, located on the Red River in northern Vietnam and the future capital of French Indochina, was dominated by a citadel designed by French engineers under contract to the Vietnamese emperor; ironically, it was largely destroyed by the French when they conquered Tonkin in the 1880s. The French left in

78. - HANOI - Le Pont Doumer

Figure 6.2 Pont Doumer, now the Long Biên Bridge, Hanoi, Vietnam, undated photograph on French postcard. © Alamy Stock Photo.

place the artisanal quarters of Hanoi on the north side of Lake Hoan Kiem, which stands near the centre of the city; groups of tradesmen, from goldsmiths to woodworkers, concentrated their workshops in one of the neighbourhood's '36 Streets'. East and southeast of the lake, the French laid out a new, Europeanized city, with shops lining a Parisian-style boulevard leading to a municipal theatre, commonly known as the 'opera house', built over the decade after 1901. Taking pride of place in Hanoi was the Pont Paul Doumer (Figure 6.2), a bridge spanning the Red River and linking the urban centre to the agricultural hinterland, a structure designed and largely built in France and named after a colonial governor. Hanoi boasted a majestic palace for the governor general of Indochina, another for the resident-general (in effect, governor) of Tonkin, expansive offices for the powerful Banque de l'Indochine and other big businesses, a covered marketplace, a university founded as a medical college in 1902, a large railway station, a fine arts museum and the other public buildings and amenities, including the luxurious Metropole Hotel. With its avenues, shops and cafés, in European eyes Hanoi was the 'Paris of the East' (other cities also vied for that title), though most of the Vietnamese population lived in far from glamorous lodgings, their crowded slums the breeding ground for anti-French nationalism.[24]

The architecture in Hanoi mirrors the evolution of French urban design. The late nineteenth-century Gothic Revival St Joseph's cathedral appears as if it were parachuted from a medieval French provincial town, and the opera house would not have looked out of place in nineteenth-century Paris. Indeed, the French were intent on re-creating a city that made them feel 'at home' in Indochina. Around the turn of the twentieth century, however, an urban planner named Ernest Hébrard began to introduce Asian motifs, yet not always specifically Vietnamese ones, into the buildings he designed, such as the National Museum of Vietnamese History (as it is now called). This hybridized architecture implied that the French were now more securely established in Vietnam, more willing to take on board local styles and allow a *métissage* of cultures; in fact, though the buildings might look vaguely Asian on the outside, the interior layout and many features remained markedly European. In the 1920s and 1930s, a new style, Art Deco, arrived in Vietnam, with houses, shops and – with particular pertinence for the age – cinemas constructed with stripped-back ornamentation, curved façades, porthole-like windows and modernist furnishings. This was, in Hanoi and elsewhere, architectural modernism brought to the colonies, an embrace of the new and the up-to-date by the colonizers and some in the local elite.

Yet another example of urbanization is Asmara, a small town on the Horn of Africa occupied by the Italians in 1890 which became the capital of Eritrea and, by the late 1930s, a city of almost 100,000 people (half of them Italian). The Italians built a cathedral and municipal theatre in traditional European style, but a modernist Cinema Impero and Cinema Roma. Sleek bars made for what the Italians hoped was the ambiance of a *piccola Roma*. Asmara retains a remarkable collection of Art Deco and Futurist buildings, notably the Fiat Tagliero service station, depicted in Figure 6.3 with lettering in Italian and Amharic, a concrete building in the shape of an airplane with a tall central tower and 30-metre spreading wings. A villa with dramatic elliptical design, balconies

Figure 6.3 Fiat's Tagliero service-station in Asmara, Eritrea, built in 1938. © Getty Images.

and terraces now houses the World Bank office. The architecture reflected the design influences popular in Mussolini's Italy, but also the rejection of the Eritrean vernacular traditions. Asmara remains testimony both to a particular period in the history of the African country under colonialism and of the evolution of international architecture.[25]

In the colonial world, European neighbourhoods (*villes blanches*, 'white cities', as the French termed them) grew up alongside pre-existing cities, their geometric grid of streets, boulevards, parks, bungalows and shops – including fashionable department stores, a mid-nineteenth-century innovation soon imported to the colonies – consciously contrasting with indigenous quarters. This was the case, for instance, in North Africa, in such cities as Algiers and Marrakesh, where the tidy, efficient and airy European neighbourhoods were juxtaposed, in the imaginary as well as in reality, with the twisting, rambling and (in European eyes) mysterious and forbidding labyrinths of the casbah, the old Muslim centre. The towers of Christian churches competed in the skyline with the minarets of mosques; colonizers had intentionally razed some Islamic places of worship in Algiers. Wide streets accommodated trams and motorcars in the European sections while narrow alleys provided pathways for donkeys or human porters in 'native' areas. People crossed boundaries, of course, including the domestic workers who serviced the European houses, and the Europeans who dived into 'native' quarters for local colour or a *louche* escape from respectable society. And increasingly members of the Arab elite, having gained a European-style education, holding jobs in offices of commerce or government, and fluent in European languages, moved between both zones, and both cultural worlds. Meanwhile, other populations – Italians, Jews, Greeks, Armenians, especially apparent in a city such as Alexandria under the British overlordship of Egypt – carved out niches in the cityscape and colonial society.

Certain establishments held particular significance in colonial metropolises. Hotels provided a place where disparate groups crossed paths, though not on the same terms. The Galle Face Hotel in Colombo, capital of Ceylon (Sri Lanka), occupies a prime position along the shores of the Indian Ocean. Its spacious rooms accommodated visiting royals and celebrities, and the wealthy tea planters and merchants, who savoured curries under swirling fans in ornate dining rooms or sipped sundowners on the lawn. In Southeast Asia, similar establishments remain famous, including hotels built by the Armenian Sarkies brothers – the famed Raffles in Singapore (with its equally famous 'Singapore sling' cocktail), the Eastern and Oriental in Penang, Malaysia, and the Strand in Rangoon (Yangon). Here was colonial 'society' at its height, the European colonial upper class at leisure, rubbing shoulders with a few from the upper echelons of indigenous or diasporic populations and increasingly numerous foreign tourists looking for a blend of exoticism and modern comforts.[26]

Arguably even more exclusive were the 'clubs', gathering places for European settlers from which indigenous peoples were generally barred (similar clubs were pointedly set up by those denied admission to European establishments). The ambiance in the British clubs was, it was hoped, reminiscent of London clubs with dining rooms, billiard rooms, reading rooms and the all-important bar – drinking provided a consuming activity for Europeans in the colonies, the peg of whiskey or the gin and tonic (the latter, at least, considered a prophylactic against malaria because of the quinine in the tonic water) an essential of colonial life. Gossip was exchanged, friendships made and broken, plots concocted and unravelled, and what was, for many, the simple boredom and loneliness of colonial life combatted. Some of the clubs, such as the Pegu Club in Rangoon, became legendary, and club life provided a scenario caricatured and critiqued by writers such as Somerset Maugham.[27]

Among other important buildings were post offices, railway stations and ship terminals, from which communication and transportation spread out through colonies, overseas and back to the metropoles.[28] Sending and receiving mail and telegrams provided a vital form of contact, and post offices like the vast Italian Renaissance–inspired General Post Office in Sydney, completed in the early 1890s, mirrored architectural fashion and the importance of the services provided. Also impressive in Sydney with its Italianate clock tower was the Central Railway Station; one in Kuala Lumpur was designed in fanciful neo-Moorish or Indo-Saracenic style. Perhaps the grandest was the Victoria Terminus (now Chhatrapati Shivaji) in Bombay, completed in 1887. With a soaring central dome, broad staircases and florid High Victorian design, the station remains a marvel of late nineteenth-century architecture and a centre of one of the world's largest and busiest railway networks – the city's suburban train network now carries 7.5 million commuters a day. Government houses, rail stations, bank buildings, museums and grand hotels, in the colonies as in Europe, bespoke local and metropolitan pride, prosperity and confidence in the future of imperial rule.

Christian cathedrals and churches, Catholic and Protestant, counted among the prominent colonial buildings, representations of faiths brought from Europe and the desire to evangelize the 'heathen'; visually and symbolically, by size, central location and often neo-Gothic architecture, Christian places of worship competed with Buddhist and Hindu temples and Muslim mosques. Edifices such as the Catholic cathedral in Dakar, built between 1910 and 1936, showed the links between religious congregations, settler groups, local converts and the colonial state, and the Senegalese cathedral also commemorated African soldiers who died fighting for France in the First World War.[29] Larger cities in the British Empire boasted both an Anglican and a Catholic cathedral as well as churches of other denominations – in 1835, an Armenian church, for instance, opened in Singapore, an example of the way migrant communities carried their religion with them; many Indian cities have places for worship for Hindus, Muslims, Parsis, Jains, Sikhs, Christians and Jews. Synagogues for indigenous Jewish communities existed in North Africa long before imperial conquest, and were introduced elsewhere in response to Jewish migration, such as the Great Synagogue of Sydney in the 1870s. Even remote locations, as in the Australian outback, had churches looking as if they were lifted from English country towns. The building of churches was a priority for missionary societies, providing places for worship and work. Norwegian missionaries in 1913 even consecrated a church in the (British) South Georgia Islands, and the French built a chapel in sub-Antarctic Kerguelen island in the 1950s, though neither territory hosts a permanent population.

Despite a fondness for neo-classical, neo-Gothic or Renaissance style, or of hybrid local and imported design, in public buildings, Europeans wanted to enshrine local culture, in particular through museums. Most colonial cities were graced with a museum, just as every self-respecting European city boasted a museum, as well as library and concert hall, in the 1800s. Cape Town's South Africa Museum, founded in 1825, is one of the older ones in the British Empire. The Prince of Wales Museum in Bombay (now the Chhatrapati Shivaji Museum), whose foundation stone was laid by the visiting heir to the British throne in 1905, offers an especially fine example, representing the culmination of colonial Orientalism – in the sense of the work of archaeologists, philologists, ethnographers and other scholars delving into the Indian past. Public collections had existed in the Dutch East Indies since the late 1700s, and in 1868 an expansive new museum was opened in Batavia (now Jakarta). The Portuguese opened a museum in Lourenço Marques (now Maputo), Mozambique, in 1911, and installed it in a typically Manueline-style building in 1933. Such museums served as repositories for the preservation, conservation and viewing of artefacts and art objects, and signalled the role of colonial administrations as self-appointed guardians of local cultures collected, categorized and encased in displays.

Not to be overlooked in colonial cities were public parks and sports grounds. Cricket was the 'imperial game' of the British, pitches springing up around the colonies, with a plethora of fields for rugby (often joined to British-style schools). Football (soccer) was a British export that spread even further than the British Empire, the game frequently played in informal spaces as well as stadiums. Horse-racing and the betting that accompanied it enjoyed popularity in the colonies, necessitating the building of racecourses and stables. Sports and the venues where competitions were held attracted large numbers of indigenous spectators and participants, though they were often organized in separate teams from the 'whites' and spectators segregated in the stands.

Away from sites of culture and recreation, colonial cities contained utilitarian warehouses, docks, factories and covered marketplaces where the wheels of commerce turned, and the barracks, police headquarters, courthouses and prisons where colonial order was enforced. The Maison Centrale gaol in Hanoi, known as the 'colonial Bastille', housed as many as 2,000 prisoners, including many nationalists, by the end of French rule in the 1950s. Around the edges of most colonial cities grew up shantytowns, where indigenous people and poor migrants lived in makeshift housing and unsanitary conditions, slums where disease proliferated, public services were largely absent and petty crime was rife. Colonial cities all also had their lowlife neighbourhoods of bars and brothels, standing side by side with gambling dens and, especially in eastern Asia, opium dens, establishments tolerated if officially lambasted by colonial authorities and moralists. The symbiosis between the built environment and populations – indigenous, settler and diasporic peoples, a Europeanized elite and an urban proletariat – was a constant, illustrating the complicated warp and weft that textured colonial society and urban space.

Much scholarly work has been published on colonial cities and urbanism – on Bombay and Calcutta, Algiers and Dakar, among many others.[30] Each city has a biography, with details encompassing design and architecture, the arteries of roadways and railways, grandiose public buildings, comfortable bungalows, grimy industrial zones and grim slum-dwellings. The story of colonial cities is also the economic, social and cultural history of the people who lived there, encounters between different ones drawn to the city, how they mixed and mingled, the way that they made urban life and how urban life remade them. Cities in former colonies provide a visual record of colonialism and its influences; in Malacca (Melaka), as a case in point, visitors can see the pre-colonial Malay sultan's palace, a large Chinese quarter, the vestiges of a Portuguese fort, the former Dutch town hall, and buildings of the British age – as well as post-independence shopping centres. In George Town, on the island of Penang, in very close proximity stand Anglican and Catholic Churches, a mosque, a Chinese temple and Chinese clan houses, an ornate Victorian town hall and the remains of a fort; nearby are shop-houses, port facilities and nowadays tourist shops and cafés. They testify to the emergence of a socially cosmopolitan and architecturally composite colonial and post-colonial city.[31]

Transformative encounters

The natural and built environments of Africa, Asia, Australasia and other regions bear the distinct imprint of European colonialism in many guises, from the monumental to the mundane: colonialism is written on the landscape. The changes were not restricted just to the large ports or growing metropolises, for even remote places – isolated mines, farms and pastoral properties, outstations, country towns – were refashioned through colonial projects. Metamorphoses in the physical and built environment could bespeak progress or dispossession, depending on perspective. The European myth of local people not yet ready for the competitive globalizing world or for self-government often went hand in hand with the romanticized image of 'primitive' or 'traditional' indigenous communities living in harmony with a picturesque nature in conditions that, as journalists incessantly repeated, had not changed for hundreds of years. That was a misperception of the evolution of the environment by constant human intervention everywhere in the world. However, in spite of the deep connection of indigenous people with the land and the sea, they 'still deforested, hunted beasts to extinction, and carved the face of the landscape to meet their material and cosmological needs', according to a statement made about Latin America that is applicable elsewhere, including Europe itself.[32] Triumphalist European claims of modernization of rural and urban areas also represented something of a misapprehension, as evidenced by the social and environmental costs entailed. The history of the former colonies since they gained independence has produced ecological changes and transformations to the built environment as great, or even greater, than did the colonial period. Yet even in the smallest and remotest colonies, the flora and fauna, the rural and urban landscape, and the sea and rivers bear witness to the deep impact, for better or worse, that colonialism wrought on the earth.

CHAPTER 7
CROSSED DESTINIES
THE PEOPLE OF EMPIRE

'I have never forgotten the first time I tried to run away. That time I failed and spent a number of years enslaved by the fear they would put the shackles on me again. But I had the spirit of a *cimarrón*,' a runaway slave, the Cuban-born Esteban Montejo remembered about the time of his youth as a slave in the central sugar province of Las Villas in the Spanish colony of Cuba in the 1870s and 1880s. Other enslaved people told him that 'if some slaves escaped, they would be caught anyway'. Yet Montejo did not care. 'I had always had the fantasy that I would enjoy being in the forest', the *monte*, that is, the tropical hills, and living a solitary life there. 'And I knew that working in the [cane] fields was like a living hell. You couldn't do anything on your own. Everything depended on the master's orders.'[1] As a runaway, Montejo constantly feared betrayal. Therefore he preferred life in solitude and did not join other escapees in a *palenque*, a clandestine community of former slaves.

At over 100 years in age, the Afro-Cuban former slave Montejo held long conversations with the young Cuban social anthropologist Miguel Barnet in the early 1960s. On the basis of many hours of recordings and notes, Barnet wrote down Montejo's life story as a first-person account. Barnet referred to this fusion of narrated autobiography and biographical writing as 'The Documentary Novel'.[2] At the time, Montejo provided a unique insight into the cultural and social life in the slave barracks, which was moulded by the cultural patterns of African-born elders and therefore different from the better-known experiences of domestic slaves. The result of the exchanges between Montejo and Barnet remains a unique portrait of a man whom Barnet called 'a legitimate actor in Cuba's historical process'.[3]

Indeed, throughout his long life, Montejo was both witness and actor in war and revolution on the tropical island. He had endured the hardships of slavery, which was abolished only in the 1880s, and experienced the struggles for survival as a runaway. He fought in the ranks of the Ejército Libertador Cubano (Cuban Liberation Army), against the Spanish in the 1890s; experienced American occupation of the island and more than sixty years later, welcomed the revolution of the Castro brothers and the Movimiento 26 de Julio that overthrew the dictatorship of Fulgencio Batista in 1959. Montejo had lived through significant upheavals in nineteenth- and twentieth-century colonial and post-independence Cuban history, and his biography is worth scrutinizing as a reminder of how individual experiences contribute to a better understanding of colonial history from 'below'.

Life stories: Between testimony and political exploitation

In the historical context of the 1960s, Montejo's testimony could be read in Cuba as living proof of Fidel Castro's claim that his revolution was the continuation as well as the happy ending of a cycle of (frustrated) revolutions that spanned more than a century from Cuba's Ten Years' War against Spain in 1868 to the war in 1895, thwarted by US intervention three years later, to redemption in 1959. Montejo's story seemed to strengthen the claim that Castro was picking up the legacy of the late nineteenth-century revolutionaries, particularly the poet and independence fighter José Martí (1853–1895), who had died on the battlefield. In this vein, the mid-twentieth-century heirs of earlier rebellions claimed to be *cimarrones* as well. It comes as little surprise that Barnet ended Montejo's account at the turn of the twentieth century with the Spanish withdrawal from the island and subsequent US occupation.[4]

It is rare to read an (almost) first-hand account of everyday life and attitudes in the Cuban slave quarters from the late nineteenth century. Montejo's eventual relief when learning that slavery had formally ended in the 1880s turned to despair when he realized that several aspects of slavery remained in place. Although the barracks were no longer under guard, living conditions remained unchanged, as were long days working in the cane fields. As Montejo recalled, on the plantations and the sugar estates, 'the same horrors' continued beyond abolition.[5] Montejo's experiences paralleled those of other enslaved Africans in the Caribbean, Indian Ocean islands and Latin America before and after the British abolished slavery in 1834, the French in 1848, the Dutch in 1863. In Brazil slavery continued well beyond independence until 1888.

Field slaves and runaways, along with many other marginalized people, have left fewer traces in the archives than the elite. In the 1960s, Montejo's lived experiences, as recorded by Barnet, 'produce[d] counter narratives – that is, unofficial histories about the lives of individuals who are also representative of larger groups or communities and whose perspectives often clashed with written accounts detailing the same events'. As Montejo's and Barnet's collaboration illustrates, life stories may even work as 'a corrective to the "archival" records'.[6]

Having said this, individual life stories and particular experiences, whether of the rich or the poor, the powerful or the powerless, are not necessarily representative of the people of empire as a whole. The cast of characters involved in empire totals a countless number of those in the colonized and colonizing countries. Indeed, it could be argued that in some way, if to varying degrees, all of the people of Europe and the colonized world were involved as actors in the dramas of colonial expansion and decolonization. Often those people are divided into two camps – Europeans and 'natives', or at least non-Europeans – and these are seen to represent the two sides of colonialism and anti-colonialism. However, such a division is a historical falsehood, for the backgrounds of individuals, their identities and actions, and the parts they played are far more complex. The numerous interconnections do not allow for simple dichotomies.

Beyond resistance and collaboration: An official in French service

The complex relations between indigenous people and European colonialists, and the ambivalent opinions indigenous subjects held about their conquerors, can be discerned in a number of writings. One unparalleled source is *The History of Kham Thong Luang* by Upahat Ba Phoi, which its translator, Peter Koret, characterizes as the first Lao autobiography and the most extensive piece of first-hand writing by a Lao about the French takeover and first decades of colonial rule of the country in the late nineteenth century.[7] The history of the work is itself extraordinary. Composed between 1884 and 1920 as a poem in the Lao language, written on 786 palm leaves (totalling 1,500 pages when transcribed into a typed work), it was found only in 2006 by researchers from the École Française d'Extrême-Orient, a French research institution. The manuscript had been stored in the house of the author's great-granddaughter, who was not literate and thus unable to read it. Her ancestor, Ba Phoi, was born in 1863 in a remote region in what is now the Salavan province of Laos. Although of elite status as the descendant of the ruler of the *meaung* – a word meaning village, community and small political unit – his family had suffered poverty before his grandmother married a nobleman. Ba Phoi, however, was born out of wedlock and orphaned as a child; he then, for a time, became a Buddhist monk. Later he married the daughter of the *meaung* leader, which provided opportunities for social advancement. Eventually, under the French he became the second highest official, the *upahat*, in the *meaung*.

Ba Phoi sets the history of the Kham Thong Luang of his day within Buddhist and traditional Lao beliefs. Developments are credited or blamed on lack of devotion to the Buddha and the making of merit, and to accumulated good or bad karma. He invokes 'celestial deities' to guide his writing. This makes his history a religious as well as an historical and autobiographical composition, a reminder that indigenous people often saw colonialism within their ancestral and spiritual world view not through a Western lens. European notions, for instance, of collaboration or resistance, 'nationalism' and 'independence' may or may not have accorded closely with such perspectives. Ba Phoi, moreover, saw current events as part of the longer history of his region, which he evokes in the opening pages as he paints a picture of the land, sometimes with lyrical descriptions of the flowers that he loved, and the tigers, elephants and snakes that he feared when touring villages on official business. He writes of pleasure in good food and drink, and reveals his keen eye for attractive women, though he sorely missed his wife and daughter when he was absent from home.

Kham Thong Luang, with a population of Lao and other ethnic groups, particularly the Kha (or Akha), had been under the 'colonial' control of the Siamese before they were displaced by the French – Ba Phoi wrote a fine account of the visit of the Siamese king in a great procession of elephants and soldiers. Kham Thong Luang lay on the eastern bank of the Mekong River, and the French in the 1890s were attempting to secure control over the territory on that side of the waterway. '[The French] are not fearful of any land. They can overpower every land underneath the sky' (line 2085), he said, with a reference, as well, to rivalries between the British and French in Asia: 'The English defeated India militarily and made its people their subjects' (1437), while 'the French will rule over the land of the Lao', just as they had earlier taken over Vietnam and Cambodia. The French impressed Ba Phoi with their capacities: 'No one was able to hold up against the intellect [of the French]', which 'was sharp in every different field. Many people exclaim with great commotion: "the French have so many kinds of food". There are various types of alcohol that they drink together with food at all time'. French technology proved similarly impressive: 'How amazing the boats in the river,' he exclaimed about the French arrival; they 'moved with great speed as if people riding galloping horses in the early evening' with the steam-driven motors. Other French practices surprised and amused Ba Phoi; for instance, 'The Lao are even given money to collect the shit once [the French] have emptied their bowels' (2098). He noted that the French, and the Vietnamese who accompanied them into Laos, had sex with Lao 'women who are whores in the market place', but he disapproved of the way the women degraded themselves. He commented on the French abolition of indigenous slavery: 'Now Lao [Laos] was in a saddened state, having lost all of its former slaves,' he commented with the perspective of an aristocrat (and belief that slavery represented the just dues of bad karma). He added that 'the slaves praised' the French for abolition, but he lamented the nobles' loss of status.

Ba Phoi described the deleterious effects of the French presence, including poverty, scarcities of food and the excessive use of conscripted labour: 'How sad the state of Lao in the present' (2043). But he also took Buddhist monks to task for not being true to their vocation and occasionally branded the Lao 'stupid'. He manifestly disliked the menacing presence of the Vietnamese soldiers deployed by the French. He criticized French prohibition of the previously flourishing trade between the Lao with Siamese and Chinese in Ubon Ratchathani on the other side of the Mekong and the obstacles colonizers placed to movement back and forth across the river. Yet Ba Phoi's personal links with the French were cordial, and he remarked with empathy that the French faced great personal hardships in Southeast Asia: 'this is known as having wound up in a foreign land, far from one's own zodiac signs' (2633).

The French programme of public works provided a regular subject for the author: land clearance, the building of roads, the erection of new buildings, the setting up of telegraph lines. He mentioned the railway and recounted his first excited sight of an airplane. He wrote about his duties under the French, taking a census and collecting taxes – he did not object to the taxes as such, only to their very onerous levels. The French required each village to build a stretch of road; indeed, Ba Phoi found the French obsessed with these projects: 'the French . . . do nothing but order [the Lao] to build roads' (2131). They demanded the construction of public buildings and rice granaries, too, and Ba Phoi recorded with shock that the French on occasion tore down temples to build their camps. A few local people converted to Christianity, though Ba Phoi sternly remarked that 'whoever believes in the religion of Jesus abandons the dharma of the Buddha' and would suffer in the lowest reaches of hell. A long section was devoted to the French suppression of a rebellion against labour conscription in the early years of the twentieth century by the Kha people – whom Ba Phoi conceded were traditionally exploited and marginalized by the ethnic Lao. The 'Holy Man's Rebellion' was led by Ong

Kaew, a Buddhist who harnessed magical practices to his struggle but was killed by the French in 1910.

Much more can be learned from Ba Phoi's long work, but these comments suffice to illustrate local people's curiosity and wonder at the foreigners, and chart the way the French replaced another outside power, how they drew boundaries around countries, imposed foreign systems of administration, law and taxation, introduced new technologies, conscripted labour and undertook public works. Many Lao suffered, though Ba Phoi accommodated the French and worked in their employ. His sadness at the conquest of his country is manifest, but his work does not express commitment to strong resistance or a campaign for independence. He was clearly a patriot, and a defender of Buddhism and the pre-colonial elite, though he nevertheless saw advantages in Western technology and benefits from the colonial administration he served. Ba Phoi emerges in his extraordinary work as an alert observer of the monumental changes through which he lived, a thoughtful and personable man, and a gifted poet, a proud though modest and long forgotten Lao who made his way as best as possible under the French colonizers.

Paradoxes of colonialism: Nationalist leaders in British colonial Africa

The paradoxes of colonial destinies can be seen in the lives of five nationalists from British colonies in sub-Saharan Africa. Figures with varying backgrounds and political views, they challenged colonial authority, then led independence movements, and each served as the founding president of his country. The oldest were Jomo Kenyatta (1897–1978) from Kenya and Hastings Banda (c. 1898–1997) from Nyasaland (Malawi); the younger men were Seretse Khama (1921–80) from Bechuanaland (Botswana), Julius Nyerere (1922–99) from Tanganyika (united with Zanzibar in 1964 as Tanzania) and Kenneth Kaunda (1924–2021) from Northern Rhodesia (Zambia).[8] Khama was a great-grandson of the king who had accepted a British protectorate in 1885, and son of the paramount chief, of the Bamangwato people, and Nyerere the son of a Zanaki chief, Kenyatta and Banda were the sons of farmers, and Kaunda was born on a mission station where his father was a Church of Scotland pastor and his mother the first Black teacher in a British school in the colony. All the men had the sort of secondary and tertiary education, four in international institutions, that was seldom accessible to their compatriots. Kaunda trained as a teacher in Northern Rhodesia. Kenyatta in the 1930s studied at a university in Moscow and attended occasional classes at University College London and the London School of Economics; Khama went to the then Fort Hare University College in South Africa, spent a year at Balliol College, Oxford, and qualified as a barrister in London. Nyerere undertook his tertiary education at Makerere College (now University) in Uganda and the University of Edinburgh. Banda had a particularly international educational itinerary; with aid from patrons in the Church of Scotland, of which he was a member, in 1925 he went to the United States and studied at historically Black Central State University in Ohio, then at the University of Chicago, earned a degree in medicine in Tennessee, and received his British medical qualifications from the University of Edinburgh. He then practised medicine in Newcastle and London, and lived outside of Africa for a total of four decades. Education remained important in all of their lives, and in their visions for independent Africa. Kenyatta was, for a time, a school principal in Kenya (and published an account of Kikuyu society and culture in 1938), Nyerere and Kaunda were also teachers, and Kaunda a headmaster. Khama held a position in the colonial administration as a 'tribal secretary' in the early 1960s (Figure 7.1).

Study, travel and knowledge of international and colonial affairs politicized the four young Africans from their student days. Anti-colonialism, the independence movement in India and the early twentieth-century pan-African movement all proved formative. Kaunda credited his political awakening to the writings of Gandhi, and Nyerere also was much influenced by Gandhi and by European democratic socialism. Kenyatta's influence came, in particular, from other activists from the African diaspora he met in Europe, along with whom he participated in a Pan-African Congress in Manchester in 1945. Back in Africa, they played leading roles in political movements – Kaunda in the Northern Rhodesian African National Congress from 1949, then the breakaway Zambian African National Congress in 1958, Kenyatta as head of the Kenya African Union in 1947, Nyerere as a founding member of the Tanganyika African National

Figure 7.1 Sir Seretse Khama, independence leader and future president of Botswana, with his wife and children. Undated. © Getty Images.

Union in 1954, Khama in the Bechuanaland Democratic Party set up in 1961, Banda in what became the Malawi Congress Party. (The names indicate the example provided by the Indian Congress Party and the South African–based African National Congress.)

Despite the generally moderate nature of their ideologies and strategies (and Banda's and Kenyatta's strong anti-Communism), they ran afoul of British authorities. Kenyatta, who spent most of the years 1929 to 1946 overseas, representing and promoting the Kikuyu Central Association, back at home was arrested and convicted in 1952, wrongly charged with participation in the Mau Mau nationalist movement, and was not released from prison until 1961. Kaunda was imprisoned for two months in 1955 for subversion, and Banda was arrested in Nyasaland in 1959 and spent a year in prison. Colonial-era restrictions also affected their personal lives, especially evident in the case of Khama. Khama's 1948 marriage to an Englishwoman provoked great opposition from the British (and also from some of his family members), he was banned from South Africa (where intermarriage was prohibited) and the British government banned him from his native Bechuanaland from 1949 to 1956.

By the mid-1960s, however, the political parties of the five leaders were winning elections for colonial legislative assemblies and negotiating with the British as independence for the colonies seemed ineluctable. They were appointed formal or de facto prime ministers in late colonial governments, and then elected presidents when independence arrived: Banda served as president of Malawi from 1966 to 1994, Khama in Botswana from 1966 until his death in 1980, Nyerere in Tanganyika, and then Tanzania, from 1962 to 1985, Kenyatta in Kenya from 1964 to 1978, and Kaunda in Zambia from 1964 to 1991. Sometimes controversial overseas for their policies, Kenyatta, Nyerere and Khama are regarded as national heroes in their homelands – though the dictatorial and kleptocratic Banda was forced out of power and placed under house arrest by his successor, accused of ordering the murder of several rivals and other human rights abuses – and defining figures in modern African history.

The careers of Khama and Kenyatta show how men from pre-colonial African elites entered into new European-educated and anti-colonialist elites, and the case of two others, the sons of farmers, and Kaunda illustrate how European missionary schools provided one avenue for 'self-made' men. All were nominal or practising Christians. Though tertiary education was a luxury available for only a select few Africans, it exposed them to foreign metropolises – Cape Town, London, Chicago, Moscow – and to the welter of new reformist, radical and internationalist ideas circulating around the world in the interwar years, as well as to rising movements of anti-colonialism in Asia and Africa. The education and employment – as a lawyer, doctor, teacher and administrator – that colonizers hoped would instil imperial loyalty in Africans, in fact, propelled them into challenging the colonial order.

The men's relationship with Britain remained complex. Khama, so severely harassed by the British, was knighted on the eve of Botswana's independence. Nyerere translated Shakespeare's 'Julius Caesar' and 'The Merchant of Venice' into Swahili. None gained the firebrand reputation of their peer Kwame Nkrumah, the nationalist leader of the British colony of the Gold Coast (Ghana). These leaders of former British colonies were long-term acquaintances, and often mutual admirers, of each other, key members of the international current of African liberation. Their political movements successfully employed the parliamentary strategies that became available with the establishment of colonial legislative councils, but also mobilized support through extra-parliamentary means, which on occasion extended to violent acts, even at great personal risk to activists. Personal charisma, oratorical talents and skills at negotiation with the British, and the dedicated building of nationalist organizations, served them well, despite British repression. Their long tenure in presidential office, not unusual for early African post-independence rulers, sparked some opposition, and the countries under their control witnessed variable levels of democracy and material prosperity. The legacies of anti-colonialist Africans reared in colonial situations are visible in multiple ways, including in the political dynasties they founded – Jomo Kenyatta's son Uhuru was elected president of Kenya in 2013, and Seretse Khama's son Ian served as his country's president from 2008 to 2018. The death of Kaunda only at the beginning of the third decade of the twenty-first century is a reminder not only of his own longevity but of the long shadow cast by these men and their work.

Was it a man's world?

Colonialism and, sometimes, decolonization were often considered men's work, whether for administrators, soldiers and sailors, explorers hardy enough to withstand jungles and deserts, and traders braving frontier posts. Chartered colonial companies hired men; the English East India Company indeed engaged only single men during much of its existence. Colonial bureaucracies were literally 'manned' by governors, residents and agents, and even the majority of clerks and other employees were male until near the end of empire. European women, of course, were involved in various ways in the colonies as wives of administrators, merchants and planters, and also – in ways not always recognized – as teachers, nurses, missionaries and clerical workers.[9]

In a similar vein, colonialism has long been seen as a chronicle of the heroic deeds of white men. Explorers – such figures as David Livingstone and Pierre Savorgnan de Brazza, just to cite two in nineteenth-century Africa – counted among the most lionized figures associated with colonialism, pushing back the frontiers of land and sea, reconnoitring distant parts, taking possession of countries in the name of European sovereigns and states. However, explorers provoked criticism even during the colonial age for their often derogatory views of indigenous peoples and the methods they employed, in particular the use of human porters as beasts of burden and the violence meted out to those who worked for them or whom they encountered. Exploration displayed personal and national hubris, as revealed in the very language of 'discoveries' of the 'unknown' and purportedly 'unoccupied' places, the attaching of European names to sites that already had indigenous ones, and 'claims' to 'possession'.

Explorers, of course, constituted only one group – and indeed a small, if well-publicized, cohort – of the Europeans who personally participated in colonialism. In the early years of conquest, military figures, traders and a handful of civilian government officials predominated, but by the mid- to late nineteenth century, and certainly in the twentieth, the 'white' communities in colonies encompassed a great diversity of people with varied occupations and lives, and different mindsets and political views. Larger colonial cities were demographically and socially complex. Nearly every profession was represented by a migrant from Europe or the descendant of a settler, as shown by colonial business directories and newspaper advertisements for doctors and accountants, seamstresses and music teachers, electricians and plumbers, hairdressers and undertakers. The empire, for Europeans who ended up in the colonies, was variously an adventure, a vocation, an escape or an assignment in the context of employment in business, service in the military or membership of a missionary congregation; for some Europeans, transportation as prisoners was involuntary. For those whose families lived in the settler societies such as the British Dominions or Algeria, or in India or the Dutch East Indies, and some of the other colonies, for several generations over decades or even centuries, colonial life was an inheritance and a birthright. Motives for going to the colonies or staying there were mixed, and almost always there was hope for a better and more enriching life, or at least a more satisfying one away from Europe, sometimes with hopes for emancipation from the familial, economic or social constraints under which individuals laboured at home. Ambition overlapped with wanderlust, careerism, rapacity, humanitarian sentiments, desperation and many other emotions in combinations and to degrees unique for each individual. Europeans overseas ran the gamut from wealthy and powerful nabobs, through more ordinary public servants and office employees, to struggling small farmers and artisans. There was a white working class in some colonies, and Europeans who lived in destitution as well. Colonial situations meant that Europeans could nevertheless frequently enjoy privileges many lacked at home – the work of domestic servants one of the most obvious benefits – and racial attitudes, wealth and administrative regulations meant that they could lord it over indigenous people; even a 'poor white' in the colonies was still white. Some Europeans developed close relationships with local people – seen, for instance, in mixed marriages, despite the disapproval that such unions encountered – while others abused the indigenous populations or simply tried to keep their distance. Yet contacts of one sort or another between the Europeans and local people were omnipresent and quotidian, even if limited in extreme circumstances largely to houseboys, cooks, maids, nannies and drivers.

The glorification of European explorers, and a tradition of vaunting the exploits of the white colonizers in the history-writing of the imperial age and beyond, have often obscured the fact that colonialism and colonizers were always dependent on local knowledge and local people. This is true for the early days of conquest in the Americas in the 1500s, and still for Europeans in Asia, Africa and Australasia in the twentieth century. Europeans relied not only on the manual labour of the 'natives' but also their familiarity with geography, climate and resources, and their skills and knowledge as trackers and interpreters. A number of Europeans, including military men, administrators and settlers, developed an abiding interest in local cultures, and they, too, depended on local interlocutors to teach them about languages, history, religion and daily life. Colonialist, nationalist and even anti-colonial writing does not give the full measure of these complicated relationships when they separate groups into 'collaborators' and 'resisters'. Where, for instance, could one easily place an African or Asian who converted to Christianity and perhaps became a priest or nun? Or a peasant who sought employment from the Europeans, or joined a European colonial army, to seek a better life? Or someone like Ba Phoi? In recent years, simplistic views on cleavages within colonial societies, and the experience of colonialism by colonized and colonizing groups have been convincingly challenged.[10]

The same is true for the trope of the male enterprise of colonization. Officials of empires long considered that European women were unsuited for much of colonial life in Africa and Asia (or the Arctic regions) because of danger, climate, disease, risks surrounding childbirth, and what they saw as threatening moral environments – as well as the physical and mental inferiority that many men continued to ascribe to women. With prevailing European attitudes about the 'weaker sex', yet the need for women in the colonies as wives and mothers of Europeans, authorities were faced with dilemmas. Only women, after all, could assure the future of settler societies through natural reproduction. Moreover, officials hoped that women would refine expatriate life, smoothing the edges of the rough-and-ready European men in port cities, mining camps and the frontier, curbing their excesses and helping to 'make the empire respectable'.[11] The colonies might also serve as a place of redemption and rehabilitation for women prisoners and 'fallen' women. Missionary orders saw women as valuable evangelists, able to gain contacts with other women, and entrée to women's quarters off-limits to men, as well as to perform the caring duties in education and health that they associated with the female sex. However, it was only by the early twentieth century that women were becoming more common as salaried employees in the tropical colonies, though they remained relatively moderate in number even in the settler colonies (and were paid lower wages than men).

Women remained second-class citizens – women could not vote until 1918 in Germany and not on the same basis as men in Britain until 1928, and Portugal (with some restrictions) until 1931; female suffrage arrived in France and its territories, and in the Dutch East Indies, only in 1945. By contrast, several settler societies instituted female suffrage before European countries, led by New Zealand in 1893 and Australia in 1902. Women in Ceylon, in 1931, were among the first in Asia to gain the vote. Until well into the twentieth century, however, women were not admitted to certain liberal professions, and husbands often possessed legal rights over their wives' property; divorce was frequently either legally difficult or considered a taboo. Any perceived misbehaviour, especially of a sexual nature, severely compromised women's reputations, a standard to which men were not held.

Given women's status at home and in the colonies, it is not much of a surprise that the education and inclusion of local women in the colonial system (beyond subaltern and household work, and sex work) figured low on the colonizers' list of priorities. A change in the colonizers' mindset was needed. It was often the wives of colonial administrators on the spot who in the early twentieth century felt the urge to provide paths towards

Western education for a few indigenous girls and young women. 'At a tender age' they were meant to gain familiarity with European concepts of hygiene, cleanliness, decency and morals, as a Portuguese educational project 'exclusively destined for indigenous girls' in Angola put it around 1912.[12] A profounder change in the colonizers' mindset only came about with the re-evaluation of women's roles in society promoted in international organizations such as the UN and its agencies in the 1950s (to which the efforts of second-wave feminism contributed in a major way from the 1960s) – by which time many colonies had gained independence. Male-dominated administrations held fast to stereotypical attitudes: indigenous women were meant to contribute to the stabilization of colonial societies in times of rapid socio-economic and political change and to bring metropolitan culture to the remotest corners of the empire. Particularly for the late colonial period, there is still little research about the integration of local women into the colonial institutions of the healthcare sector, education, the administration and business.[13]

However, the record of those women who did so is remarkable, as a few examples of women doctors show. In 1919, Lee Choo Neo, the daughter of a merchant, graduated from the Singapore medical school – an unusual achievement for a woman in the British colony. She first worked in a hospital, then set up a private practice, founded the Chinese Ladies (later Women's) Association and campaigned against polygamy. Marie Thomas was the only woman among 200 students when she enrolled at the School of Training of Native Physicians in the East Indies in 1922; she became the first Indonesian woman obstetrician and gynaecologist, and an early advocate of birth control. In Vietnam, Henriette Bui Quang Chieu, who was born in 1906 and completed her medical studies in France in 1934, was the first fully qualified doctor of European medicine in her home country. Though there were similarly few European-trained women physicians in the African colonies, the Nigerian Agnes Yewande Savage (whose father was a Nigerian doctor and whose mother was Scottish) graduated in medicine from the University of Edinburgh in 1929; nine years later another Nigerian woman, Elizabeth Abimbola Awoliyi, qualified as a doctor in Dublin. She later became head of the Lagos Red Cross, president of the Business and Professional Women's Association in Nigeria and chair of the Holy Cross Cathedral Parish Women's Council. In Tunisia, Tewhida Ben Sheikh received her medical degree in 1936 and became noteworthy as an advocate of family planning. Similar 'firsts' could be listed for indigenous women lawyers, engineers, architects and other professionals.

The 'bargains' of cooperation: A view from the margins

In the 1960s, late colonial powers such as Spain and Portugal deployed their official youth and women's organizations through the remnants of their empires. They followed the paths of the British and the French, who had promoted women's education in their colonies at least since the interwar period. From Macau to Angola, Mozambique and Guinea-Bissau, the Mocidade Portuguesa Feminina (Portuguese

Female Youth) organized choirs and Portuguese folk dances, among other activities. Its Spanish counterpart, the Sección Femenina (Women's Section, or SF), also began to include indigenous women in its programme in the small African colonies of Spanish Guinea and the Spanish Sahara in the 1960s, after the colonies had been declared 'provinces' of the Spanish nation.[14] Almost irrelevant at home, the Spanish 'Señoritas in Blue'[15] faced a difficult task overseas. Superficial knowledge about local societies stemming from episodic fact-finding missions did not do the job. The Spanish Women's Section's archival record from the African colonies regularly hints at SF envoys' surprise when African women did not correspond to the stereotype of the allegedly 'passive' Black woman.[16]

This was the case when the Spanish SF-delegate María Ángeles Mallada González organized one of the first 'cultural summer trips' for girls and young women from Spanish Guinea to Spain in the mid-1960s. Trinidad Morgades, a local Black teacher, challenged the SF's selection process and particularly the fact that the Spanish were about to exclude young women who did not meet the Catholic moral standards the SF aimed to impose. Morgades made sure that students with 'records of abortion' – prohibited by the Catholic Church and the Spanish state – were allowed to travel. What might seem a minor issue is a reminder that daily conflicts in a colonial situation could yield rather unexpected outcomes.

The colonial power matrix depended on several factors, with race one of the most powerful markers. Yet in this specific context, Mallada González's 'whiteness' (and even accusations of Black racism) did not trump Morgades's indigeneity: education, age and local political connections tipped the balance in the latter's favour. Born in Santa Isabel, on the island of Fernando Po (today's Malabo), in 1931, Morgades came from an influential and well-connected family. She was the first Spanish Guinean woman to graduate from a Spanish university, earning a bachelor's degree in English in 1958.[17] These attributes, along with her age, provided the ingredients for a strong intervention on behalf of the students who were about to be excluded from the SF's summer tour. Not even Mallada González's complaints at the Women's Section's main offices in Madrid turned the table. Morgades knew how to navigate the clientelist colonial system and employ it to her own and her kin's benefit.

For example, Morgades mobilized her contacts within the colonial administration as well as within the Women's Section to have her ten-year-old niece admitted to a summer camp near Madrid. Morgades' standing and assertiveness were further strengthened with the autonomy regime installed in Guinea in 1964. The new autonomous government, although still under Spanish tutelage, beefed up Spanish Guinean politicians' and Morgades' power in the bargain. 'We are interested in fulfilling the petitioner's [request] in the best possible way,' a Madrid-based SF representative added to Morgades' request to place her niece in a camp near the Spanish capital when handing it over to the colleague responsible for the organization's summer activities. And yet, a note saying that the girl was the 'daughter of one of [Trinidad Morgades'] brothers . . . and of a white' woman indicates how race remained a key denominator shortly before the colony achieved independence in 1968.[18]

Morgades continued to thrive after her country's independence, when she was appointed first secretary of the embassy of Equatorial Guinea (as the country was now called) in Nigeria. Her diplomatic career later took her to Ethiopia, before she moved into academia, teaching literature in Tetouan, Morocco; in 1975, she took up a lectureship in English literature in Málaga, in southern Spain. In the mid-1980s Morgades headed back to Equatorial Guinea to become general secretary at the Malabo branch of Spain's National University of Distance Education. Throughout the years Morgades earned a reputation as a gifted writer and poet, as well as a specialist of the Spanish spoken in Equatorial Guinea. In 1991 she completed an African version of the ancient Greek drama *Antigone*, and in 2009 she was elected a corresponding member of the Real Academia Española (Royal Spanish Academy). She died in Malabo in 2019 after a life spanning thirty-seven years of colonial rule and a half-century in the public life of her independent homeland.[19]

Morgades' life points to the crossed destinies within colonial societies, highlighting her combined Afro-Iberian cultural heritage.[20] Morgades' biography is no easy fit for the common categories of the oppressed and the oppressor. While she was effectively subverting the late colonial order, Morgades was closely connected to Spain through language, culture and employment. To put it in more general terms and in her own words, her vocation was to 'try to bridge (*coordinar*) the two worlds: the African and the Western world'.[21] The years after independence continued to show her resilience and skills at social and political organizing in the face of the kleptocratic and autocratic family regime of the young African republic. Morgades' literary works bear witness to the continuous 'failure of the democratic efforts in her nation', the tragedy of Equatorial Guinea.[22]

From the particular to the whole

Each individual involved in colonialism has a particular story to tell, and increasing numbers of them have become available through autobiographies and biographies, interviews and recordings. Reading these accounts provides insight into personal perspectives and experiences, though they need to be situated within wider contexts and treated with the due care that must be taken with all life-writing. They allow readers to follow and reflect on the life and times of a teacher in French Africa, nationalists in colonized Vietnam, Indian maharajas and maharanis, and many more.[23]

This chapter has focused on a rather neglected cast of characters in the empire – a Cuban descendant of Africans abducted and shipped as slaves to the Americas, a Lao administrator in France's service, nationalist leaders in British colonial Africa, indigenous European-trained women doctors and a Guinean woman whose life connected Africa and Europe. Empires were mosaics of different peoples, languages and cultures, metamorphosing over many centuries, and both in Europe and in the colonies individuals and groups had very different experiences of colonialism. Encounters could be amicable and belligerent. Blood was shed on both sides in many initial meetings and long afterwards. Europeans might be welcomed as suppliers of beneficial trade goods or knowledge, viewed with curiosity and suspicion, or repelled as invaders.

Experiences of colonial life, from first encounters to decolonization and beyond, differed enormously even between groups – indigenous people, diasporic migrants, the enslaved, indentured labourers, those of mixed heritage and Europeans. It is a mistake to assume that personal and collective experiences were much of a muchness, or to essentialize reactions to European rule. The overall majority of local people suffered under colonialism, a select few profited in various ways, still others – including some in high mountains or on remote islands – were relatively lightly touched by the incursions of foreigners. Local people were able, as the case of Ba Phoi shows, to situate colonialism within their own cultural narratives and spiritual beliefs as well as in European perspectives. However, there exists a central aspect to relations between Europeans and others, the issue of 'race' and all that the concept implied in colonial times, a key marker clearly revealed in Trinidad Morgades' life. Although having to combat discrimination in the colonies as in Europe, some remarkable non-Western men and women managed to enter the world that had largely been reserved to 'whites', and women similarly proved able to enter that considered the preserve of men. The lived experiences of individual women and men hint at their adaptation to and sometimes subversion of European colonialism throughout the centuries.

CHAPTER 8
SLAVERY, INDENTURED MIGRATION AND EMPIRE

Kunti, an indentured Indian woman, was clearing a banana field on a plantation in the Rewa province of the largest island of Fiji, a British colony in the South Pacific. On Thursday afternoon, 10 April 1913, Kunti was working alone on the secluded field – working in solitude was meant as a punishment for causing the overseer 'a great deal of trouble', as the official files put it. On this occasion, she was sexually harassed by the overseer, though she resisted the attack and fled. In her despair, Kunti jumped into a nearby river, whose current carried her quickly downstream. A boy pulled Kunti out of the water and saved her. Young women like Kunti, away from home, were often sexual objects and victims of plantation owners, just as enslaved women had been.

This is how Kunti's story was retold in India by several newspapers, and 'Kunti's Cry' came to embody the struggle to end the infamous bonded labour system that replaced slavery in many parts of the world in the mid-nineteenth century. 'Even though of lowly cobbler caste, Kunti was eulogised by the still caste-conscious Indian press for her "bravery, patience and strength of mind", and her name joined the "list of honourable and brave ladies" in Indian history,' in the words of Brij V. Lal, a distinguished historian of Indian indentured labour in Fiji. Lal thus highlights the repercussions on the subcontinent of sexual aggression on island plantations. The Indian indenture system in Fiji was finally phased out in 1916.[1]

Under the indenture system, men and women were given contracts for a certain number of years – typically three or five – of often poorly paid and hard labour in designated activities in a particular colony. The migrants' passage to the colony where they would work was usually paid by the employer, but not always their repatriation, even though it was expected that they would return home on the expiration of the initial or renewed contracts. In the early days of indentured labour from India, only men (like the anonymous 'Indian laborer' depicted in Figure 8.1) were recruited for the plantations throughout the British Empire and beyond. Yet fears of miscegenation and homosexual activity among male migrants led to recruitment of women as well. In the 1870s, 'Indian women became an unavoidable adjunct to Indian male labour,' as Karen A. Ray explains.[2] Indian women did domestic work, and looked after children, but also the heavy work on plantations. In Fiji's planter society, however, indentured women were regularly viewed as causing problems, such as 'suicide, murder, [high] infant mortality and the general moral degradation of the Fiji Indian community', and not as victims of an abusive forced labour system. Yet Indian free and indentured men did not hold back

Figure 8.1 Indentured Indian labourer in Fiji gathering latex from a rubber tree, *c.* 1930s. From 'Tour of the World', Keystone View Company, Meadville, PA, © Getty Images.

from certain prejudices, making Indian women carry 'the double backpack of racism and sexism'.[3]

It comes as little surprise that British administrators tried to defuse the upheaval around Kunti in the press, arguing that her 'whole statement' (along with that of several witnesses) was 'a fabrication'. The refutation continued: 'It is absolutely untrue that female indentured immigrants are violated or receive hurts [*sic*] or cruel treatments at the hands of their overseers.'[4] Nevertheless, 'Kunti's Cry' contributed to launching 'an independent enquiry', with its report issued in early 1916. The preface stated that 'attempts to show, on the one hand, the serious nature of the evils which exist under the indenture system' lay at the heart of the investigation. 'On the other hand, it endeavours to explain what painstaking efforts are now being made by the Fiji government to deal justly by the Indian settlers' – contract work, if duly restructured, was still considered an appropriate source of labour.[5]

Given the circumstances of how women were recruited in India, the report highlighted, indentured labour 'cannot be called a fair contract'. Women were 'not told' that they 'will be compelled, under penal clauses to work incessantly, day in, day out, with no time to cook' for their families, nor 'to look after [their] own children'. Women were 'never told anything . . . of the condition of the coolie "lines" [that is, huts] in which [they] will be compelled to live, without any privacy or even decency, for five years, with no possibility of change'.[6] The report's findings put the overall conditions of work and life of Indian migrants in a nutshell. Although the individual circumstances of the indentured and their situations varied, Kunti's case is illustrative of the fate faced by many bonded migrants across the colonial world.

Focusing on the example of indentured Indian labour in the nineteenth and twentieth centuries, this chapter shows that the theme of migration provides a key to understanding colonialism as a type of circulation of people, commodities and cultures. While the railways and steamship lines of the industrial age provided new arteries and veins for movement around a globalized system, the transfusion of migrants, goods and ideas – to continue with the organic metaphor – variously revitalized and weakened parts of the world and left it profoundly transformed. With a focus on the truly global extent of migration in the age of empire, the following sections point to inter-imperial connections. Migration, a phenomenon as old as humankind, also brings questions about indigeneity to the fore.

Forced migration: From slavery to indentured labour?

Colonialism moved people around the world: the enslaved, indentured labourers, convicts, poor and sometimes wealthy free migrants, as well as the administrators and military figures who represented imperial authority.[7] Some were transients, returning to their homelands after tours of duty had ended, contracts had expired, fortunes had been made or lost, or great expectations dashed, but settlers and their descendants made the social structures of American, Asian, African and island countries even more variegated than they had been before. Migration, forced and free, in some places reduced indigenous populations to a minority, and everywhere made demographic and social structures more complex. It introduced populations of entirely different backgrounds, creating new hierarchies and fault lines. To different degrees, cultures adapted, blended and metamorphosed. Questions of inclusion or exclusion, entitlement, political rights and the sense of identity and belonging became more pertinent.

Particularly dramatic, and shocking, in forced population movements was the slave trade. For around three and a half centuries, Europeans engaged in the slave trade, though they were not the only ones or the last ones to do so. Colonialism did not produce slavery, as societies around the world have practised slavery in various forms since ancient times; slavery had indeed been practised by indigenous people (particularly with defeated enemies reduced to servitude) and Arabs in many parts of pre-colonial Africa. What was different was the magnitude of the phenomenon in early modern European colonialism, the focus on Africa as a source for slaves (even if men and women were enslaved elsewhere, for instance, by the Dutch in the East Indies), the racist arguments underpinning the trade, the rapacity of the traders and the way that slavery became such a vital component in the formation of new empires of settlement and trade. The fact that so many descendants of the enslaved now live in a large number of countries, such as the United States, Brazil and the Caribbean islands, as well as in Europe – and often continue to suffer discrimination and marginalization – ties the past to the present in a particularly manifest connection and burdensome legacy.

Although the European powers, in principle, agreed to ban the slave trade in the early years of the nineteenth century, slavery persisted in the British Empire until around 1834, in the French colonies until 1848 and in the Portuguese and Spanish possessions until the 1860s and 1880s, respectively, and certain types of forced labour continued in the Portuguese colonies in Africa until the 1960s. Only after long and sustained campaigns by abolitionists, as well as revolts by slaves, and despite the persistent objections of slave-owners, did formal slavery come to an end in the European empires, and in the United States, it only did so after a civil war in the 1860s. When enslaved men and women gained freedom, however, most of them and their immediate descendants remained in the colonies to which they had been taken by force. Ideas about the inferiority of Black people changed little in the late 1800s and early 1900s, and descendants of slaves remained objects of exploitation for their labour and had to endure racism and violence in daily life.[8]

During the transition from slave to free labour in the nineteenth century, Europeans sought new sources of labour for agriculture, mining, the building of infrastructure and growing urban economies in the colonies. They continued to recruit workers, now paid a minimal salary, from Africa, and looked to Mexico, the Pacific islands, India and China to recruit further workers. For the British Empire, and for the declining colonial power of Spain and independent Latin American countries, India and China with their huge populations and widespread poverty provided a reservoir of potential migrant workers.[9] The destination of the largest numbers of indentured labourers from India, not surprisingly, was the British colonies, though the French and Portuguese also recruited contract workers (and promoted free migration) from their enclaves on the subcontinent. Routes of indenture built on previous and continuing currents of free migration from the Indian subcontinent around the Indian Ocean, Southeast Asia and eastern Africa, all of which had communities of long-established Indian merchants, artisans and seafarers.

According to UNESCO data, the diaspora of indentured Indians to the colonies from the 1830s to the 1940s totalled at least around 1.2 million people. The largest numbers, other than to Ceylon, went to Mauritius in the Indian Ocean (453,000), Malaya in Southeast Asia (400,000), (British) Guyana in South America (239,000), Natal (now part of South Africa) (152,000) and Trinidad in the Caribbean (144,000), as depicted in Figure 8.2. Indians became the majority in Mauritius by the 1850s or 1860s; the Indian population similarly surpassed that of indigenous islanders in Fiji in 1945. Indians similarly went to Hong Kong, East Africa (especially Uganda) and British colonies in the Caribbean in addition to Trinidad. There were 34,000 Indian migrants to Dutch Guyana (now Suriname), and some to the French colonies in Indochina as well.[10] Despite eventual legislation that discriminated against 'non-whites', there was an Indian presence in the Australian colonies and Canada.[11] Some examples of the displacement will evidence the

Figure 8.2 Newly arrived Indian indentured labourers in Trinidad, *c*. 1897. Photographer and details unknown. © Wikimedia Commons (public domain).

amplitude of colonial-era migrations, the role that diasporic non-Europeans played in the colonies and the life experiences of those who moved.

Fiji, located in the central South Pacific and with an indigenous culture that bears both Polynesian and Melanesian traits, was a prime site of indentured migration with the arrival of 60,965 workers from South Asia between 1879 and 1916. Sir Arthur Gordon, who became governor of Fiji after serving in Mauritius and becoming a supporter of indenture there, invited an Australian company, the Colonial Sugar Refining Company, to Fiji in 1882; this created a burgeoning demand for plantation labour. India, in particular the population of the north-western provinces and Oudh (Awadh), burdened by taxes, the commercialization of agriculture, the decline of artisanship and episodic famines, provided the main source of *girimitias* (so named for the contract to which they agreed). Brij Lal characterizes indentured labour as a 'traumatic ordeal', especially during the 1880s and 1890s, beginning with the long ocean voyage and landing in the unfamiliar environment of the islands. 'Overtasking' meant that the migrants were assigned larger amounts of work than most could manage, and employers frequently got away with not paying the statutory minimum wage. The Indians needed permission to marry and faced other restrictions in daily life. Nine-tenths of the indentured labourers were convicted for some breach of often trivial ordinances during their contract, with lost pay, fines or an extension of the indenture period as penalties. Beatings and other corporal punishments were not uncommon. There were 230 cases of murder (mostly of women) among the Indians from 1885 to 1920, and 200 suicides. The labourers were at the mercy of employers and the *sirdars*,

147

the Indian foremen, and abuses could be hidden during occasional visits by Inspectors of Immigration.

Scholars disagree when it comes to classifying indentured labour. Authors such as Hugh Tinker have seen in the contracts 'a new system of slavery', picking up on the perception among Indian politicians around 1915 – 'moderate and extreme [politicians] alike, . . . do not hesitate to call [indentured labour] by the name of slavery', the government of India informed the British Secretary of State for India. Lal argues that indeed 'indenture was a harsh experience', yet he is hesitant to qualify contract labour as slavery. For its part, the British 'Report on indentured labour in Fiji' highlighted that 'recruiting . . . in India, [was] frequently unscrupulous and that the indenture itself [was] neither a free nor an intelligent contract'. What was more, indentured men told inspectors in 1915 that 'they were no better off in their cost of living in Fiji' than in India. Still, for some contract labourers, indenture provided an income that was higher than the wages to which they were accustomed, and offered release from caste and other social constraints at home. Many of the indentured remained in Fiji after the expiration of contracts. There they lived alongside a growing number of free Indian migrants, and eventually became a prosperous community in business and the professions.[12]

Cultural circulation: South Asian diasporas

Migration took Indians around the Bay of Bengal, the shores of which (except for Thailand) had come under British rule by the late 1800s. Sunil S. Amrith has underlined the diasporic and cultural links across the region, and notes that Tamil migration to the Straits Settlements began almost as soon as Francis Light established a British outpost at George Town on Penang Island in 1786 and lasted until the 1930s. Colonizers had a great demand for labour in the ports of Penang and Singapore, and on the sugar and coffee plantations of the Malay peninsula. Around the turn of the twentieth century, the expansion of rubber plantations on the peninsula increased that demand dramatically. The number of South Indians on Penang island grew from 2,700 in 1848 to 6,000 in the 1860s, 22,000 by the 1880s and over 100,000 in 1911. By 1931, around 600,000 Indians lived in the Straits Settlements of Penang, Singapore and Malacca and the remainder of the mainland of Malaya. Many migrants from India, primarily Tamils of lower caste or *Dalit* background, were technically not indentured but 'assisted' or 'statute' migrants, yet the conditions of employment varied little from those of bonded workers, including physical abuse, malnutrition, overwork and indebtedness.

From the late 1800s, plantation owners recruited workers through the intermediaries of largely Tamil foremen under the *kangany* system. Plantation foremen returned to their home regions in India to recruit labourers; the migrants then worked off the money advanced to their families. The Tamils carried their culture with them, particularly the practice of South Indian forms of Hinduism and Islam (though some converted to Christianity). However, living among Malays and large numbers of Chinese migrants, as well as the British, led to transformations in Tamil culture and life, and to the development of what Amrith terms an 'oceanic consciousness' with which they kept links to India: 'A central feature of Tamil cultural circulation around the Bay of Bengal is the sense of continuity it evokes between the two coasts of the Bay of Bengal. The streets of the Straits Settlements formed part of a continuous realm with the Tamil country. The sea was a means of connection as much as separation.' The migrants developed a sense of settlement and belonging, while indigenous Malays would sometimes contest that allegiance. Furthermore, 'being part of a diaspora was, by the 1930s, an essential part of what it was to be modern.'[13] Already in the late 1800s, Tamils in the Malay colonies set up associations, published newspapers and petitioned colonial officials for redress of grievances. Yet commentators in India expressed concern about the fate of the Tamils and other Indians overseas, and complained that the 'coolie trade' impugned the reputation of India by projecting it as a source for cheap manual labour.[14]

Ceylon provided another important destination for Indians. A total of eight million Indians, free and indentured, migrated to the island between 1840 and 1940, with an average of 173,500 new arrivals each year between 1914 and 1938 (though there was a strong outmigration too). Many were the Tamils who became the labour force on the tea plantations that developed rapidly, and produced the island's main export, after the 1860s – Tamil 'tea-pickers', especially women, became the chief labour force in the fields of tea. Tamils joined a substantial Indian community already resident in Ceylon, including families established there for centuries. This older Tamil population and the new migrants (once released from contracts) were attracted into other areas of employment such as business, and the British regularly hired Tamils for the colonial administration; among the most prominent intellectuals and professionals in the colony were many of Indian ancestry. Northern Ceylon, and its main city of Jaffna, hosted a particular concentration of Hindu Tamils, as did the capital of Colombo, and Muslim Indian shopkeepers were present in most smaller towns around the island. As elsewhere, ethnic disputes occurred, with anti-Indian riots in the early 1900s. Ceylon gained independence in 1948, but festering ethnic disputes erupted into a prolonged civil war in the last decades of the twentieth century.[15]

Burma, with an indigenous Indian minority of both Hindus and Muslims, also attracted increasing migrants since living conditions in the Southeast Asian colony were considered slightly better than in many parts of neighbouring India. The population of Indians in Burma grew from 421,000 in 1891 to just over one million in 1931 (40 per cent of whom, by the end of the decade, were Burmese-born). Over half of the population of Rangoon, the capital of British Burma, had Indian background, and the capital appeared to many observers as more of an Indian than a Burmese city. Indians occupied positions at all levels of the Burmese economy, from street-sweepers and scavengers, manual workers and artisans, up to a prosperous elite; 83 per cent of bankers and moneylenders, 58 per cent of merchants and 55 per cent of importers and exporters were of Indian background. Similarly, in small and medium-sized towns, over half of the shopkeepers were Indians.

The prominence of Indians in business provoked some hostility. Anti-Hindu and anti-Indian riots erupted in Burma in the 1930s. The legacies of ethnic tensions between the ethnically Burmese (and largely Buddhist) majority and the Indians (especially Muslims) who descend from colonial-era migrants endure today; the government of Myanmar (as the country now calls itself) refuses to recognize the citizenship of many residents of Indian background, and persecution of Muslim Rohingyas in Rakhine state, on the shores of the Bay of Bengal, has led to the flight of several hundreds of thousands to Bangladesh in the early twenty-first century. The terrible fate of descendants of migrants from colonial times, and their exclusion from citizenship until today, raise questions about the current understanding of rights linked to indigeneity, in Burma and elsewhere. Who can and cannot claim legitimacy when looking back on many decades or even centuries of sometimes involuntary displacement? How many years or generations must a people reside in a country to feel that it belongs and to enjoy full rights, entitlements and recognition? Some of today's religious and ethnic conflicts, and not just in the case of diasporic Indians, are in part enduring repercussions of European colonialism.

Globalization from the 'Global South': Indians in Africa

Indians, particularly traders of ivory and agricultural products, had regularly moved between the subcontinent and eastern Africa long before Europeans arrived in the Indian Ocean. The circulation of people across the western Indian Ocean can indeed be traced back to ancient times; archaeological data point to cultural contacts millennia before the Common Era. Given the economic interconnections and the sociocultural (particularly religious) cross-fertilization in the 'interregional space' of the Indian Ocean, the historian Sugata Bose has called for 'a radically new perspective on the history of globalization' from the nineteenth to the late twentieth centuries – a perspective from the Global South, challenging the notion of a European- or a Western-dominated narrative.[16]

The intensification of European colonialism in the western Indian Ocean in the 1800s and early 1900s left deep social and economic imprints. In particular, the establishment of British colonies – Uganda, Kenya, Tanganyika and Zanzibar – broadened conduits of Indian migration to East Africa. Along with the stationing of Indian troops serving in the British imperial army to Africa, especially important was the recruitment of 37,000 indentured labourers and other employees, largely from the Punjab, for the building from 1895 to 1901 of the so-called Uganda Railway, which linked the port of Mombasa to the interior of Kenya, Uganda and Lake Victoria. Most of the indentured workers returned to India, but some remained and other Indians followed. In 1962, around the time of independence, there were 175,000 residents of Indian background in Kenya, 77,500 in Uganda, 92,000 in Tanganyika and 20,000 in Zanzibar, many of them post–Second World War migrants who held managerial positions in commerce and government. Their situation provoked rising hostility from Africans. About half of the Indians left Kenya and Tanzania (the name of the unified country of Tanganyika and Zanzibar) under duress after independence, and the dictatorial government of Idi Amin expelled 70,000 from Uganda in 1972.

Although men and women of lower castes statistically predominated in Indian migration, there were diasporic migrants from every level of Indian society, including Hindus of all castes, Muslims, Parsis, Jains and those of other faiths. A particularly significant group was the Sikhs, a people with a distinct language and religion who came primarily from the Punjab region conquered by the British in the 1840s – one of the most famous Sikh 'migrants' was Maharaja Duleeep Singh, the defeated and deposed Punjabi ruler exiled to Britain. In Hong Kong, where the first Sikhs arrived in 1867, they became known for service in the police; by 1901, migrants were numerous enough to build a Sikh temple, and by the end of the colonial period, they numbered around 10,000. Between 30,000 and 50,000 Sikhs went to the Malay states, as many as 10,000 to Canada and several thousand to British East Africa.

In Portuguese Africa, particularly in Mozambique, Hindu and Muslim traders were already part of the population in the seventeenth century. Given the racial prejudice and restrictive immigration legislation Indians faced in the British colonies in Africa after the 1930s, Mozambique became an alternative for many Indian business families. By the mid-twentieth century, traders from India and of Indian descent were important players in the colonial economy, especially in Mozambique's credit and banking sector. When India achieved independence from Britain in 1947, the Portuguese still clung to the enclaves of Goa, Diu and Daman that it had ruled since the 1500s, keeping migration channels open. When the Republic of India in 1961 forcibly incorporated the Portuguese outposts, taking captive 3,000 Portuguese soldiers and civilians, Portuguese vengeance targeted Indian minorities throughout Lisbon's remaining empire.

In the aftermath of this so-called Goa crisis, Portugal dispossessed and expelled some Indian nationals and people of Indian descent from its colonies. Purportedly as a humanitarian measure in order to protect them and their assets, resident men, women, and children of Indian background endured administrative internment – over 2,000 people were sent to camps in Mozambique between 1961 and 1971. Properties and assets of Indian businesses were seized. However, deportation and dispossession affected mostly poorer Indian families. For the wealthy traders vital for Mozambique's import and export economy, the colonial government opened up pathways to citizenship. Others with the financial wherewithal and connections beyond the Portuguese colonies shifted their transnational business networks to other African countries or Latin America. Although treated as 'second-class' citizens or at least as a 'subaltern elite', prosperous Indians in Mozambique remained agents of globalization within and beyond the Portuguese Empire until decolonization in 1975.[17]

From colonial to global history

The arrival of migrants from all parts of the world irrevocably changed the population structures and the cultures of colonized countries. Anyone visiting a city such as Singapore – with its indigenous Malay quarter, large Chinatown and Little India – is immediately struck with how colonialism moved people around the world, voluntarily or involuntarily. People on the move occasionally became a new majority or occupied essential sectors of the economy or professions, often finding positions in those areas because migrants lacked the lands ancestrally possessed by indigenous residents. Anti-colonialism and nationalism saw a pushback against such immigration and attacks on diasporic groups erupted. In the post-imperial world, some fled or were expelled, and new constitutions in places such as Malaysia gave political preference to *bumiputra*, those politicians considered indigenous peoples (Malay on the peninsula and other indigenous groups on Borneo), giving a particular meaning to indigeneity. However, a more recent surge of migration has brought an increasing number of Indians to such countries as Canada and Australia, former British settler societies that at the beginning of the 1900s sought to limit or stop migration by 'non-whites'. Large numbers of migrants from the Indian subcontinent, particularly from the 1950s, also arrived in Britain, where around 1.5 million people of Indian subcontinental heritage now live. It was not only in the colonies that migration, free and unfree in the age of empire, and continued movement along imperial pathways, lastingly altered the demography and social structures, and greatly enriched the cultures of countries around the globe.

CHAPTER 9
SETTLER COLONIALISM
THE BRITISH DOMINIONS

On 19 August 1914, as the First World War began, the prime minister of Canada, Sir Wilfred Laurier, summoned his compatriots to support the 'just war': 'That union of hearts which exists in the United Kingdom exists also in Canada, in Australia, in New Zealand, yea, even in South Africa – South Africa rent by war less than twenty years ago, but now united under the blessing of British institutions with all, British and Dutch together, standing ready to shed their blood for the common cause.' He hoped 'that from this painful war the British Empire may emerge with a new bond of union, the pride of all its citizens'.[1] The stentorian words championed patriotism, solidarity and commitment in Britain's settler colonies, yet the allusion to the South African War (or Boer War, as the British long called it) pointed both to the way that colonial conquest had brought different settler groups together and to the antipathies it engendered. They remained manifest in Laurier's country as well, with disputes between the Anglophile, Protestant majority and Laurier's own Francophone, Catholic community. While many indigenous peoples in the countries he mentioned rallied to defence of the empire in wartime, others then and later demurred from wholehearted endorsement of the 'blessing of British institutions'. The Canadian statesman's language nevertheless provides a summation of the public ideals of empire loyalists in the 'Dominions'.

Settler colonialism in the Dominions and elsewhere represents a sui generis form of colonialism.[2] Though large-scale settler colonialism was not unique to the British – as shown by the history of the Spanish and Portuguese in Latin America, the French in Canada, Algeria and New Caledonia, the Portuguese in their larger African territories – the British case, because of its expanse and specific evolution, constitutes a particular form of European expansion to countries with generally temperate climates considered congenial to 'white' settlement. More particularly British was the early devolution of administration to settler elites with the institution of 'responsible government' under elected assemblies and ministers. The word 'Dominion' came into usage in the British Empire in the late 1800s, and more officially from 1907. It was applied in 1867 to the new 'confederation' of Canadian provinces and to the Commonwealth of Australia created in 1901. It was first used for New Zealand and Newfoundland in 1907, and the Union of South Africa, established in 1910. The designation was then applied to the Irish Free State (from 1922 to 1949) and, after the Second World War, briefly to India and Pakistan, and for a longer term to Ceylon.

'Dominion', a word now no longer common, more usually evokes a certain era in the history of Australia, Canada, New Zealand and South Africa when their white leaders affirmed and nurtured ties with Britain, fellow Dominions and the wider empire, all the while claiming and practising self-government and championing particularistic identities.

The countless volumes published about these four countries evidence how the recording and interpreting of history has formed a critical ingredient in empire-building and nation-making, and also in the contesting of received opinion and policies.[3] Even in the nineteenth century, heroic narratives about brave pioneers pushing back frontiers and rooting British civilization in foreign soil were challenged by indigenous resistance, settler demands for greater autonomy and articulations of new national cultures in each Dominion. A tussle between indigenous and settler perspectives, and among local, national and imperial ones in historical analysis and politics, continued through the twentieth century. The radicalism of the 1960s and 1970s – and, in regard to South Africa, mounting opposition to the apartheid regime – produced more militant criticism of oppression of 'First Nations' and historical British exploitation. Indigenous history has since become a central axis of research. In the wider public opinion, the language and the perspectives implied about British 'invasion', 'frontier violence' and 'genocide' remain controversial, and some argue that conflicts about resources such as land link settler colonialism with 'the elimination of the native'.[4] That idea, however, needs to be nuanced, especially in the case of South Africa – with a far larger indigenous population than in the Dominions of Canada,, Australia and New Zealand – where settlers relied heavily on local labour for mining and agriculture.

Australia's past was especially debated in the 1980s and 1990s.[5] Polemical exchanges referred to 'black armband' versus 'white blindfold' versions of history, and 'history wars' became a common phrase. More recently, historians, in Australia and elsewhere, have found novel ways to wind together the strands of the history of indigenous, settler and diasporic groups, and to show the complicated web of enmity and amity, confrontation, cohabitation and cooperation that existed.[6] This rich historiography, in which previously ignored groups, occluded events and the lived experiences of individuals have featured, merits far more detailed exploration than is possible in the present volume.

In this chapter, with a particular focus on Australia, several specific topics provide a bare outline of the history of the Dominions, with the caveat that while grouping them together corresponds to the way that they were often seen from the imperial metropole and the settler colonies themselves, it risks flattening the high relief of their histories. The subjects selected are the marginalization of indigenous people and their efforts to obtain recognition and justice; the demographic, economic and cultural bases for the growth of small settler societies into nation states; the moves towards self-government and unification; and the place of the Dominions in the British Empire and the world. First, however, a reminder about the general shape of British colonization of the expanses of the globe covered by the Dominions.

From settler outposts to Dominions

When Britain put its empire on show at London's Crystal Palace exhibition in 1851, the settler colonies were well represented, though their displays of agricultural, pastoral and forest products and mineral resources could not quite outshine the glitter of India's diamonds and the sheen of its textiles.[7] At that time, the colonies of 'British North America', the future Canada, included some of Britain's oldest overseas outposts: Britain formally took possession of Newfoundland, its first North American colony, in 1583. By contrast, New Zealand, annexed by Britain only in 1840, was one of the newest of Queen Victoria's possessions. The British had taken over New South Wales, its first colony on the Australian mainland, in 1788, and wrested the Cape Colony in southern Africa from the Dutch in 1795. Although it would take decades, indeed centuries in the case of Canada, for Britain to extend its rule from coastal bases over great hinterlands, the initial takeover of embryonic colonies thus marked rather distinct periods in British expansion. The move into Canada was part of the 'discovery' and colonization of the 'new world' of the Caribbean and Americas by the European Atlantic powers in the early modern age. Eastern Australia provided compensation for the loss of the United States in the 1780s, and offered a site for penal colonies as lawmakers were increasingly concerned about crime in a Britain greatly unsettled by industrialization and urbanization. As the 'imperial meridian' was shifting eastwards, new outposts in eastern Australia gave Britain a further base for expansion into the 'Far East' and South Pacific. The *prises de possession* of New South Wales and especially of the Cape Colony, were bound up with long rivalry and episodic belligerence between Britain and France – the wars of the 1790s in the case of the African colony – and the takeover of New Zealand several decades later precluded French colonization there and extended Britain's reach into Oceania.

At the time of the Crystal Palace show, the later pastoral and mining booms of the Dominions lay largely in the future, as did the spread of the British from Sydney and Cape Town, and indeed from Toronto and Montreal, through the American and Australian continents and large reaches of southern Africa. The Canadian, Australian and South African possessions nevertheless already constituted flourishing colonies, and the newly acquired one, New Zealand, held great promise. Furthermore, the exhibition-goers were confidently told, they provided true homes for settlers carrying Britain's flag and European civilization to North America, Africa and the Asia-Pacific. Even if in 1851, Britain was still transporting unwilling convicts to Western Australia (yet no longer to the eastern colonies of the continent), it was hoped that redemption would turn malefactors into productive and loyal subjects, and that alongside free migrants, they would develop prosperous societies linked by kinship, allegiance to the Crown, trade networks and British traditions to the 'motherland' of the UK. Indeed, Australia's 'respectable' population by the early 1800s included many who had first arrived as convicts – men such as Francis Greenway, convicted of forgery in London, but the leading architect in colonial Sydney – though many families long tried to hide their chequered past.

The British settler societies were disparate and complex places. Geographically, they stretched from the polar extremes of northern Canada to the southernmost point of Africa, the Cape of Good Hope. The British banner waved over Arctic ice, and the deserts and tropical zones of the antipodes. Resources and economic development differed as well: in Canada alone, spanning the old fishing, fur-trapping and trading posts of Newfoundland and Nova Scotia in the Maritime provinces to the cereal-growing Prairie provinces of Manitoba, Saskatchewan and Alberta, and on to the Yukon, which gained fame for a mid-nineteenth-century gold rush, and British Columbia, a window onto the Pacific. By Queen Victoria's time, cities such as Melbourne and Sydney were busy metropolises, but there also existed extremely isolated European settlements, as well as indigenous communities, in the seemingly endless Australian outback. Demographically, not all of the Australian colonies – South Australia was an exception – had been recipients of transported prisoners, nor was New Zealand. When the 'First Fleet' landed in Botany Bay in 1788, no other Europeans lived on the Australian continent, though in South Africa the new British overlords and settlers had to accommodate a population of European descent who traced their origins back to the setting up of an outpost by the Dutch East India Company in 1652. In Canada, battle victories over the French in the late 1700s brought the *Acadiens* (in the Maritime Provinces), *Québécois* and other French-speakers under British rule. Over the course of time, many non-Britons, including migrants from outside Europe, would swell the populations and broaden the cultures of the Dominions. In fact, many French Huguenot refugees had migrated to Dutch South Africa in the 1600s; the first British settlement of 1,500 men and women in Australia in 1788 included Americans, Frenchmen and Africans among passengers from thirty countries. Migrants from the 'Celtic fringe' of the British Isles figured largely in the growing 'pioneer' populations. Numerous Irish Catholic migrants in Australia harboured long-standing grievances against the English, who in their view treated Ireland as little less than a colony. The Scots, proudly preserving a culture different from that of the English, established a particularly firm presence in eastern Canada and New Zealand. Even in their early days, the Dominions were multicultural.

Places of worship testify to the variegated nature of nineteenth-century Australian society. In 1878 a Grand Synagogue was inaugurated in central Sydney, and a Greek Orthodox church in 1899; the first mosque in Australia, serving 'Afghan' camel-drivers from the Indian subcontinent, was built in South Australia around 1882. There were Chinese temples, called 'joss houses', in places such as Bendigo, a centre of mid-century gold rushes. Members of these communities played an important role in the formation of Australian society, though they often suffered discrimination. One prominent example of a Chinese migrant who did well is Quong Tart. Born in Canton (Guangzhou), he moved to New South Wales as a poor nine-year-old in 1859. By the time he was twenty-one, he had grown wealthy on the goldfields, and through import business, tea and silk shops and restaurants. Much appreciated in Australia for his philanthropy, Quong Tart was also made a mandarin by the Chinese imperial government in 1888. His autobiography, posthumously published in 1911, bore the telling title of *How a Foreigner Succeeded in a British Community*.

The history of Australia is filled with characters who illustrate different backgrounds and trajectories. Yet despite burgeoning migration from Britain, continental Europe and well beyond, total populations in the Dominions long remained small: in 1900, Canada, with 5.5 million people, counted a population similar in size to that of Greater London. Australia had fewer than four million, and New Zealand only 816,000. South Africa had a population of five million people, but only a fifth were classified as 'white' and thus enjoyed the supposedly sacred rights of 'free-born Englishmen'.

The Indigenous peoples and British conquest

Europeans, from lack of knowledge or wilful intent, indulged in many fantasies and falsehoods about the lands and people they claimed to rule. In the case of Australia, the British proposed that the continent was legally a terra nullius, under the jurisdiction of no one before Europeans arrived and settled (or, as some historians put it, invaded and conquered), a manifest inaccuracy connected with both arcane philosophical doctrines about natural rights and outright racism. There are more than 500 indigenous nations in Australia – the word 'nations' is now used by indigenous groups and more widely – to whom the generic word 'Aboriginal' was applied; in addition, there are the indigenous people, closer in culture to Melanesians than to those on the mainland and Tasmania, of the Torres Straits Islands off the northern coast. The native people of Canada in colonial times were called Indians and Eskimos, though Canada now recognizes three general indigenous categories: the First Nations, Métis (those with both First Nations' and European ancestry) and Inuit. 'First Nations', a term used from 1980, covers dozens of groups, among the best known to outsiders the Chippewa of the northern woodlands, the Algonquin of the Great Lakes and the Kwakiutl of the Pacific coast. There are nine distinct divisions of Maori in New Zealand, subdivided into a larger number of *iwi* (often translated as 'tribes'), as well as the Moriori of the Chatham Islands and the Polynesians of the New Zealand dependent territories in the South Pacific. In South Africa, the indigenous people are the hunter-gather San people (called 'Bushmen' by the colonizers) and the cattle-herding Khoi ('Hottentots') of the Cape, and five Bantu-speaking groups – the Nguni (including the Zulu, Swazi and Xhosa), Shanganu-Tsonga, Sotho-Tswana and Vihavenda.[8]

It is important to remember that the original peoples within the Dominions had their own multiple languages, systems of beliefs, histories and ways of living. While the Maori arrived in New Zealand only from the ninth century of the Common Era and had not fully settled what they called Aotearoa ('the land of the long white cloud') until around the year 1000, the Aboriginal presence in Australia has been dated back to as far as 80,000 years ago, and South Africa was first peopled soon after the dawn of human history, with subsequent waves of migration from other parts of Africa over the centuries. Indigenous cultures changed over time, novel sorts of practices and ideas emerged, and contacts with other groups, including Europeans, provided new influences and, frequently, produced dislocation.

What united the indigenous peoples of the future Dominions, however, was that they were considered by the colonialists, in varying degrees, to be primitive. Even when they were painted in a more positive light, as was the case with North American 'Indian braves' and Maori, Zulu and Aboriginal chiefs and warriors, the representation by foreigners was generally stereotypical, folkloric and racialized (and frequently straightforwardly racist). In European definitions of civilization and commonly accepted stadial theories of human development (from 'primitive' to 'advanced'), such peoples occupied an inferior rank on the ladder of development, an assertion that Europeans claimed gave Westerners the right to annex countries, dispossess indigenous people of their lands and culture, appropriate their resources and impose new laws and government. That is precisely what happened, though the strategy and process differed around the world. In southern Africa, the British signed treaties with some indigenous groups and indeed provided formal recognition to the Zulu king and several other indigenous rulers. The British nevertheless fought wars with the Zulus, the signal British defeat at Isandlwana and the subsequent defence of Rorke's Drift in 1879 becoming legendary in imperial military history. In New Zealand, the British in 1840 signed a formal accord, the Waitangi Treaty, with over 500 Maori leaders, who in the British view ceded the country in return for the retention of certain rights. These rights, however, were in part honoured in the breach, and warfare ensued, as the British took over more and more Maori land and undertook a policy of Anglicization of the indigenous people. In Canada, there were seventy-odd treaties (by the British and Canadian governments) with First Nations groups between 1701 and 1923, yet many were obtained through coercion and with limited knowledge among First Americans about what the agreements entailed. Later policy was paternalistic at best. In Australia, there was no treaty with any of the Aboriginal nations, a situation that today motivates calls for a treaty between the Australian government and traditional owners of the land, and the formal recognition in the Australian constitution of indigenous people as first occupants and custodians of the land.

The British expanded colonial control of the Dominions through war, battles between the British and French and their 'Indian' allies in North America, the 'frontier wars' throughout Australia, the 'Maori Wars' in New Zealand from 1845 to 1872 and wars against Xhosa, Zulu and other peoples in South Africa. The colonizers displaced local populations, with Native Americans, for instance, moved into reserves, and 400-odd surviving Palawa, the Aboriginal Tasmanians, confined to Flinders Island in 1835. Indigenous peoples everywhere were driven from property seized and declared Crown land, sold or given to settlers or private companies, or simply 'squatted' by European migrants. Like most native inhabitants under colonial rule, indigenous people in the Dominions were generally denied a political voice in elected or appointed consultative or legislative councils. In New Zealand, however, four seats were set aside in 1867 as Maori constituencies in Parliament, and a Maori was appointed a minister in the government in 1923. (Maori delegations were also regularly greeted in public acts as depicted in Figure 9.1.) Although in the British Cape Colony, no formal racial restrictions on the franchise existed, property qualifications, dramatically raised in 1892, effectively disenfranchised most non-white men (and women did not then enjoy the suffrage

Figure 9.1 Edward, Prince of Wales (the future King Edward VIII), greeting Maori women during a tour of New Zealand, 1920. © Getty Images.

anywhere in the British Empire); the franchise was denied to Africans most everywhere else. In Australia, few indigenous people had the right to vote, and Aboriginal people were not even counted in the census until 1967. Generations of indigenous infants and children in Australia, as well as in Canada, were removed from their families – the 'stolen generations' – and placed in so-called orphanages, residential schools or other institutions set up with the idea of training them in European ways. Christian missionaries, inspired by religious beliefs but complicit in colonialism, tried to spread the Gospel throughout the Dominions (see Figure 9.2) to combat what they regarded as heathenism and immorality, with consequent damage to ancestral cultures, sacred sites and social structures. The exact degree of impact nevertheless differed among the various Dominions and First Nations peoples.

No matter the low regard in which they were held, indigenous people offered essential knowledge to the colonizers, particularly about geography and natural resources; the work of Aboriginal trackers proved indispensable for European explorers. Indigenous people provided essential labour, even if under compulsion. Aboriginal people worked on sheep stations and other pastoral properties, in construction and in domestic service, often in poor conditions and badly paid; scarcity of labour nevertheless meant the bringing in of workers from overseas, including from Asia and the South Pacific islands. In South Africa, Africans provided the bulk of the labour force for gold and diamond mining, but the demand was so great that mining companies resorted to

Figure 9.2 Wesleyan Church missionary the Reverend Thomas Crosby with an unidentified First Nations man in Canada, *c.* 1860s. © Getty Images.

labourers from Portuguese Mozambique. Africans and First Nations people worked on settler properties in rural areas and found subaltern urban employment. In general, conditions for indigenous workers were onerous, wages low, employment episodic and chances for professional advancement seriously limited. Indigenous people were also incorporated into the armed forces, and many distinguished themselves in battle during the First World War and other wars, though in some cases with only tardy recognition of returned soldiers.

Indigenous populations dropped dramatically in number in Australia, Canada and Australia with colonization, the toll of epidemic diseases such as smallpox, warfare, forced labour, substandard living conditions, and outright slaughter and massacres by Europeans. The Australian Frontier Massacres Map, compiled by the University of Newcastle, lists hundreds of unlawful killings for the years between 1780 and 1930. Among the most notorious were the Cape Grim Massacre in Tasmania in 1827 and

Myall Creek Massacre in New South Wales in 1838 (the latter unusual because of the prosecution of the white perpetrators), down to the Coniston Massacre in the Northern Territory in 1928.[9] From an estimated 300,000 to one million indigenous Australians before 1788, the population plunged to 50,000 in 1930; Europeans considered Aboriginal people a dying race, fated to extinction, but the population eventually recovered and numbers around 800,000 today. There were an estimated 150,000 Maori in New Zealand in the 1760s, but the number dropped to 45,000 by 1896, then revived to 82,000 by 1936 and 137,000 twenty years later. In 2021, self-identified indigenous people made up 4.9 per cent of the population of Canada and 3.3 per cent in Australia, but 16.5 per cent in New Zealand. Africans now form the overwhelming majority in the Republic of South Africa, with 76.4 per cent, compared with – using the apartheid-era classification scheme – 9.1 per cent white, 8.9 per cent coloured and 2.5 per cent South Asian people.

Several associations were established in Britain and throughout the empire to address the plight of indigenous peoples, notably the Aborigines' Protection Society set up in London in 1837 and active in Australia, New Zealand, Canada and South Africa as well as other colonies. Under the slogan of 'Of One Blood', it promoted measures to ameliorate the health and education of 'uncivilized tribes' – that phrase revealing contemporary attitudes notwithstanding the humanitarian efforts – though it 'came close to becoming a champion of imperialism'.[10] Legislative measures such as the Indian Act in Canada in 1876 and Native Land Settlement Act in New Zealand in 1929 sought to address the situation of indigenous people within the context of regulation and paternalism, and with little, if any, questioning of the supremacy of European settlers and their institutions and values. Indigenous people themselves mounted efforts to secure redress of their grievances: warfare and other acts of resistance, petitions to the British monarch, lobbying of settler leaders and the formation of such associations as the South African Native National Congress (now the African National Congress) in South Africa in 1912. Indigenous cultures, in fact, proved remarkably resilient, despite the odds, preserving and adapting themselves, and finding new outlets of creativity. First Nations people, through the colonial period, under successor governments to British imperial rule, and today campaign for the full rights of citizens, attention to the inequities that glaringly exist between them and their compatriots, and acknowledgement of colonial misdeeds.

Creating settler societies in the Dominions

Although southern Africa and Canada had experienced the effects of colonialism for several centuries before 1800, parts of Australia felt a dramatic and immediate impact after 1788, and increasingly frequent encounters between Maori and outsiders indeed occurred already in the early 1800s, the nineteenth century brought more remarkable change to the Dominions. Three of these changes, which are discussed here, were the related phenomena of a great growth in the settler population; economic booms founded on agriculture, pastoralism and mining; and moves towards self-government and (in the case of Australia, Canada and South Africa) federation of separate colonies.

'Settlerism', to use a concept popularized by James Belich, was closely connected to the British Dominions, and to the spread of non-native populations over the Midwest and West of the United States – the formation of an 'Anglo-World', what others have called the Anglosphere or, within the confines of the British Empire, the 'British world'. Belich does not hesitate to label the demographic surge, and the social and political repercussions it produced, as a 'settler revolution'.[11] Particularly important were the schemes devised by Edward Gibbon Wakefield, which foresaw large-scale free white settlement, assisted or free passage for migrants to their new homes, concessions of land to migrants and hopes for a kind of yeoman paradise overseas, a vision that reflected an idealized image of rural life, an attempt both to address the problems of industrial Britain and to promote imperial geopolitical objectives. Migration to settler societies (including the independent countries of the Americas) in the 1800s constituted one of the largest currents of human movement in history, with dreams of land, political freedom and possibilities for advancement (and possibly fortune), though for some migration was involuntary.

One of the most dramatic stories in the history of modern migration was the transportation to several of the Australian colonies (as well as Norfolk Island) of 160,000 convicts over the eighty years from 1788 to 1868. Many were convicted for what would now be considered minor offenses such as petty theft, fraud and debt, but transportation was considered a way to rid Britain of undesirables, rehabilitate wrongdoers and populate the Australian continent. Much has been written about the supposed hell of a convict life marked by corporal punishment, draconian sentences for repeat offenders, back-breaking labour, confinement and abuse, though historians have shown that convicts in Australia statistically lived a better life, measured in terms of health and nutrition, than their social peers in Britain, and many acquired land, employment and eventual respectability. Convictism did stain Australia in the eyes of increasingly numerous free settlers and British reformers, with the penal colonies castigated as pits of vice, corruption and immorality. By the middle of the 1800s, most new arrivals were free settlers, especially with the gold boom and the continent's flourishing pastoral economy.

Migrants to New Zealand, Canada and South Africa were primarily free settlers, yet poverty, lack of land, the conditions of factory labour in Europe and other constraints provided a powerful impetus to move overseas, as did the famine in Ireland in the 1840s and difficult economic conditions for crofters in the Scottish highlands. Most migrants from the British Isles settled along the coastlines of Australia, South Africa and New Zealand, or along the southern and maritime borders of Canada. Despite enduring myths of the frontier and the outback, the Dominions of Australia, Canada and New Zealand were some of the most urbanized countries in the world during the nineteenth century. Conditions were tough, multiple skills necessary for survival, prosperity not assured; the 'tyranny of distance', to use a famous phrase of the Australian historian Geoffrey Blainey to mean both the domestic distances within a country such as Australia and with 'home' in Britain, would be a long-lasting fact of life even with railways, steamships and the telegraph. Migrants of all sorts and conditions making their way to the Dominions, particularly in the last decades of the 1800s, were taking part in flight from Britain and Continental Europe. They included younger sons of nobles left landless by primogeniture, 'remittance men' who survived on handouts from their British families, aspiring bourgeois, landless peasants and artisans, urban proletarians, and not a few adventurers and those who hoped to re-invent themselves in the colonies.[12]

The tide came not just from the British Isles, though they accounted for most of those who ended up in the Dominions. People from around the world tried their luck on the colonial gold-mining fields, including Chinese miners and shopkeepers. The Chinese provided a vital labour force in the construction of the transcontinental railways in Canada and Australia, and there was a steady migration of Indians (mostly Sikhs) to Canada until racial restrictions were put in place. Indentured Melanesians, primarily from the Solomon Islands and the New Hebrides, worked on the sugarcane fields of Queensland from 1864, and over five decades, 200,000 indentured Indians worked on the sugar plantations of Natal in southern Africa. There were German winegrowers in Australia, as well as French migrants ranging from wool-buyers to music teachers – enough for a French-language weekly newspaper to be published in Sydney at the end of the 1800s.[13] Migrants to Canada came primarily from the British Isles, but during the US war of independence (1776– 83), they included 4,000 refugees who remained loyal to the British Crown. Slaves and others displaced by the US Civil War (1861–5) later drifted northwards across the border. Migrants from the Russian Empire, Ukrainians prominent among them, streamed into the Prairie provinces of late nineteenth-century Canada.

Migrants from outside Britain and Ireland were not always welcomed in the Dominions, especially if they were not 'white'. Asians, in particular, were blamed for social ills, from gambling and drug-taking to prostitution and the plague that infected Sydney in the 1890s. Episodic legislation sought to restrict Asian migration in various colonies, and the Immigrant Restriction Act adopted by the new Commonwealth of Australia's parliament in 1901 enshrined exclusionary measures. The 'White Australia' policy effectively closed the doors for decades to most non-European migrants, and Canada applied similar restrictions. While the Dominions proclaimed themselves proudly British, historians have recovered the history of many non-'Anglo' migrants who did settle, and have shown the crucial contribution that they made. It must be conceded, however, that the Anglo-Celts thoroughly dominated the Dominions, though not numerically in South Africa, and held near monopolies over business and government until the mid-twentieth century, and in South Africa (alongside Afrikaners) until the 1990s.

Despite capitalist cycles of boom and bust, the Dominion economies thrived in the nineteenth century, especially as suppliers of primary products. Australia became one of the world's leading producers of wool, a vital raw material for Europe's textile factories, and also exported beef, grain, timber, tobacco and other rural products. The Australian colonies inserted themselves into a global network of trade through the British Empire – rum came to Australia from the Caribbean, for instance – and beyond. Already in the early 1800s, New South Wales traded regularly with China for tea and porcelain, and with India, from which it received textiles and furniture and to which it exported horses, among other goods. New Zealand was similarly a prosperous producer of wool and other agricultural and pastoral products, especially with the invention of refrigerated cargo ships that made possible the export, from the 1890s, of frozen meat to world markets. Canada's midwestern area was a breadbasket, a huge source of cereal crops, and there was timber and fish from Canada as well.

An extraordinary new development in all of the Dominions at mid-century was the minerals boom, especially the mining of the gold that was all-important in backing up currency in the era of the gold standard. In 1851, gold was mined at Bathurst in New South Wales, then near Melbourne at Bendigo and Ballarat, and within only several years 40 per cent of the world's gold was extracted just in the Australian colony of Victoria. The goldfields lured miners from near and far, personal fortunes were made (and sometimes lost), and the profits from mining provided the capital for the monumental growth of 'marvellous Melbourne' and the gold-mining towns whose grandiose public buildings bespeak the wealth and confidence of settler society during the mining boom. In the 1860s, gold was also discovered in Queensland, and in 1892 in Western Australia, where the remote centres of Coolgardie and Kalgoorlie became synonymous with febrile mining and rough living. In New Zealand, prospectors discovered gold near Dunedin in 1861, and it made the fortune of the Otago region of the South Island. There was gold in Canada as well: gold was found in Quebec in 1864, though the rush there was overshadowed by the larger if relatively short-lived Klondike gold rush in the Yukon from 1896 to around 1907. In southern Africa, the gold rush began in 1886 in the Witwatersrand, in the Transvaal – an independent territory ruled by Dutch-descended Afrikaners and not yet a British colony. *Uitlanders*, those not of Dutch descent and coming from elsewhere in southern Africa and overseas, poured into the 'Rand', and the gold rush did much to advance British annexationist designs on the Transvaal and the Orange Free State – in 1914, South Africa produced 40 per cent of the world's gold.

Some of the capital for South African gold-mining came from the diamond mining that had developed in the North Cape from around 1870. (Indigenous miner-workers are shown in Figure 9.3.) It was led by the De Beer brothers at Kimberley, whose mine would produce the world's largest uncut diamond, suitably presented to King Edward VII. One of the founders of the De Beers Mining Company was Cecil Rhodes, who bought up his competitors' businesses and established a monopoly on the sale of diamonds. In 1887, Rhodes set up Consolidated Goldfields, which soon became one of the leading gold-mining companies in the Transvaal. Rhodes, born in 1853 the son of a vicar in Hertfordshire, had arrived in southern Africa in 1870 to work on a cotton farm, but soon began to acquire diamond mines in the Kimberley area. From business, his interests extended to politics, and he served as prime minister of the Cape Colony between 1890 and 1896. Hero for some and villain for others, Rhodes was synonymous with unbounded imperialism, and the prime mover for British expansion in eastern Africa and in the area north of the Limpopo River that was named in his honour, the colonies of Southern Rhodesia (now Zimbabwe), Northern Rhodesia (Zambia) and beyond. Diamonds and gold, and a wealth of other sub-soil resources, contributed greatly to the prosperity of the South African colonies and their elites, and to both a sense of incipient nationalism and,

Figure 9.3 Zulu workers at De Beers diamond mines, Kimberley, South Africa, *c.* 1885. © Getty Images.

somewhat paradoxically, empire allegiance among British settlers. Success also impelled expansionism more widely in Africa.

From the early decades of the nineteenth century, settlers yearned for a greater share in the governing of the 'Anglo' colonies. Historians differ about the arbitrary nature of British imperial rule under appointed governors – opinion varies from considering them enlightened in terms of public works and development to charging them with authoritarianism and outright despotism. As settler societies matured and financial resources strengthened, there emerged a conviction that settlers and their descendants had a right to some degree of self-government. Initially, members nominated from the social elite served on legislative councils. With the adoption of limited manhood suffrage in several colonies by the mid-1800s, legislative assemblies included some elected members in a form of 'representative government'. There followed moves towards 'responsible government' in which assemblies were elected on the basis of wide, if not universal (male) suffrage (whether indigenous men could cast a vote remained contentious), and a premier led a cabinet. Britain's imperial authorities, however, retained control of defence and foreign affairs among other key areas, the British Parliament could override legislation enacted by Dominion assemblies and a governor or governor general represented the Crown and exercised extensive reserve powers. Responsible government came to the provinces of British North America largely between 1848 and 1860, to New Zealand in the mid-1850s, and to the Cape Colony in 1872 and Natal in 1893; New South

Wales, Victoria and Tasmania led the way among the Australian colonies in gaining responsible government at mid-century. The establishment of responsible governments inspired a lively political life in the Dominions, though one from which women and indigenous people were largely excluded.

There was also, perhaps most apparent in Australia, a growing sense of cultural commonality among neighbouring colonies, especially from the 1880s: a fuller appreciation of the Australian landscape and the symbolism of such figures as the swagman, jackeroo, digger and squatter, promoted by the popular writings of Henry Lawson and 'Banjo' Paterson in the nationalist *Bulletin* magazine. White men and women living on the continent (at least those of British stock), they argued, were bound together by a history and destiny that made them different from kinsfolk in the British Isles. As the centenary of the first British colony in Australia arrived, identification with an Australian homeland that transcended colonial boundaries became more apparent.

Paralleling such developing cultural consciousness came the move towards political union of colonies in Australia, Canada and South Africa. The separate colonies of New South Wales, Van Diemen's Land (Tasmania) and Victoria had been the early administrative divisions on the eastern side of the Australian continent, though settlement of Moreton Bay led to the separation of Queensland from New South Wales, and new colonies were set up: the Swan River Colony (Western Australia) in 1829 and South Australia (which at the time incorporated the Northern Territory) five years later. Meanwhile, in British North America, New Brunswick had separated from Nova Scotia in 1784, while Upper Canada (largely, what is now Ontario) and Lower Canada (Quebec) were united under a single administration in 1840. There were British settlements further west, all the way to Fraser River, in the future British Columbia, as the British gained land through treaties with First Nations people or by simple proclamation. In southern Africa, Britain had taken over the Cape Colony in the 1790s and annexed Natal in the far southeast in 1843. In these three cases, British settlement and administration encompassed legally separate territories. New Zealand was not divided, and even its provincial councils were abolished by 1876.

The nineteenth century saw many conflicts involving indigenous people, settlers and British authorities throughout the Dominions. The wars between the British and the Xhosa and Zulus in southern Africa, the 'Maori Wars' (as they were called at the time) in New Zealand and the frontier wars in Australia, which have been mentioned, were the most sustained. Revolts by settlers against their imperial masters also occurred. Armed rebellions, involving both Anglophones and Francophones, broke out in the late 1830s in Upper and Lower Canada (and involved an effort to seize Toronto), but were suppressed within less than a year; over fifty French-speakers were exiled to Tasmania. Then in 1869, Louis Riel, a Métis, led a rebellion in the Red River area, part of today's Manitoba. The British soon re-established control over a short-lived republic, but an amnesty allowed Riel to win election to parliament, though he never sat. Riel later fled to the United States, then returned to Canada to lead another insurrection in 1885, for which he was hanged. In the Australian colony of Victoria, in 1854, gold-diggers rose in opposition to corruption in the issuing of prospecting and mining licenses, burned a hotel and barricaded themselves at the Eureka Stockade in Ballarat. The insurrection ended in a skirmish that left thirty rebels and five soldiers dead, but the Eureka Stockade and its flag lived on as powerful symbols of working-class and republican militancy.

There were other ways to protest against political and social conditions. In South Africa, 15,000 Boers, descendants of Dutch migrants unhappy with British rule in the Cape Colony and the abolition of slavery, moved in the Great Trek (giving them the name of Vortrekkers) into the interior of southern Africa in the 1830s and set up the Transvaal and the Orange Free State. In New Zealand, the Kingitanga movement promoted the installation of a Maori king in 1858; though the move did not receive official approbation, the king and his successors gradually gained some recognition and hold an honoured customary position today. Other contestatory movements grouped around Maori spiritual leaders, and the Young Maori Party grew out of a student group. Throughout the Dominions, trade unions regularly mounted actions against the domination of the elite.

In the midst of these ructions, the various colonies, and regions within the colonies, were coming together during the nineteenth century, despite substantial differences – in Australia, for instance, between those defending free trade and those favouring economic protectionism. Technology, commerce and culture, among other drivers, were integrating the colonies. Telegraph lines and railway tracks, in particular, tied them together in a literal sense, as seen with the great Canadian-Pacific railway that traversed North America from 1886; shipping lines similarly connected colonial ports. The colonies traded with each other, despite tariff barriers (and even different railway gauges in Australia), and commodities, capital and people moved relatively freely from one to another, although with persisting restrictions on the movement of indigenous people. There were the shared institutions of Britishness: the cult of the monarchy, the notion of the rights of 'free-born Englishmen' and parliamentary process, the Anglican Church (though many colonists were 'Dissenters' or Catholics), the educational institutions, such as the universities established in 1821 in Montreal, 1829 in Cape Town (initially as the South African College), 1850 in Sydney (see Figure 9.4) and 1869 in Dunedin, New Zealand. Not to mention sport, notably cricket, which in Australia also featured some First Nation teams, though it never really caught on in Canada. There was, too, the 'crimson thread' of kinship that joined settlers in the colonies, and linked them to relatives in the British Isles. This manifested as 'race pride', the feeling of belonging to a superior British 'race' spread around the globe, in tandem with a 'colour line' that separated whites from those of other, non-white 'races'. There was, too, sentimentality about Britain as 'home', and security in sheltering under the umbrella of the world's premier industrial and military power.

Economic development, denser inter-colonial connections and the evolution of settler society and culture, combined with the effective marginalization of indigenous populations: all provided impetus to the federation of colonies in Canada, Australia and South Africa. Another force was international affairs. Canadians had long been concerned about not always subtle calls for expansion northwards voiced in the United States, especially as US nationals aggressively pressed further into the 'Wild West'. Fears about US irredentism were stoked with Washington's war against Mexico in the 1840s

Figure 9.4 Engraving of the University of Sydney, *c*. 1880. © Alamy Stock Photo.

and victory over the secessionist Southern states in the 1860s. Australians looked warily at developments in Asia, with xenophobic and racial fears of the demographic mass of China and the rising might of Japan from the 1860s – the 'yellow peril'. There was continuing concern with the French colonial presence in the South Pacific, from the 1840s, and with the establishment of German colonies in Oceania in the 1880s. Whites in southern Africa wanted to consolidate their strongholds and eliminate the Afrikaner states that stood between the Cape Colony and Natal, and they were further concerned about rivals to Britain in the 'scramble for Africa' as Berlin's colonizers established German Southwest Africa (now Namibia) in 1884, the Portuguese made an overture to unite their colonies of Angola and Mozambique (though a British 'ultimatum' put paid to the plan in 1890), and the territories and resources of Bechuanaland (now Botswana) and Nyasaland (Malawi) beckoned. Unification of disparate colonies in North America, southern Africa and Australasia appealed as a response to outside threats and a strategy to exploit land, labour and other resources more effectively.

The upshot was the 'confederation' of 'Canada' (the union of the former Upper and Northern Canada, which became, roughly, the provinces of Ontario and Quebec), along with Nova Scotia and New Brunswick, in 1867, under a constitution approved by the British Parliament. In 1870, Manitoba and the Northwest Territories were incorporated, followed by British Columbia in 1871, Prince Edward Island, the Yukon (separated from the Northwest Territories) in 1898, and Saskatchewan and Alberta in 1905, although Newfoundland in the east did not join Canada until 1949 – the formal construction of Canada within its present-day borders thus took over eighty years. The 'Commonwealth of Australia' was born on 1 January 1901 with due festivities; the new constitution made a provision for New Zealand to join the Commonwealth, though with little support on either side of the Tasman Sea for that eventuality. The Union of South Africa emerged in 1910, but only after the lengthy turn-of-the-century war between the British and the Boers had resulted in the defeat of the Afrikaners in the Transvaal and the Orange Free State. In a novel arrangement, South Africa ended up with three centres of government – Parliament meets in Cape Town, the offices of the central administration are in Pretoria and the appellate law court sits in Bloemfontein. The union might have included neighbouring British colonies, but South Rhodesia voted in 1922 not to join, and Northern Rhodesia, Nyasaland and Bechuanaland continued as separate colonies, while Swaziland (now Eswatini) and Lesotho, landlocked within South Africa, remained British protectorates under their indigenous monarchs.

These developments brought together huge territories – the new Union of South Africa roughly the size of the British Isles, and Australia as large as the continental United States. Unification promoted a sense of nationhood and gave the Dominions an enhanced international presence. However, the nascent unified countries willingly remained obeisant to the British Crown and the imperatives of British policy, and most residents thought of themselves as loyal subjects of the distant monarch. It was decades before they carried Australian, Canadian, New Zealand or South African passports, and they long continued to enjoy rights of abode in the UK. Decades were to pass as well before the Dominions secured full control of their military forces or established fully accredited embassies in foreign countries.

The Dominions were thus not completely independent, and indeed did not wish to be so, for many of their people cherished being part of an empire that advertised the *pax Britannica*. Loyalty to Britain and the empire was manifest in the sending of Australian soldiers to fight for the British in the New Zealand wars, then of New South Wales deploying a small contingent with the British in the Sudan in the 1880s. In the South African War, which lasted from 1899 to 1902, Canada contributed 7,000 troops, Australia 16,000 and New Zealand 6,500 to the imperial forces battling Boers. Around 22,000 British and imperial soldiers, 34,000 Boer civilians and soldiers, and considerably more Africans died in the conflict. In the First World War, even more troops from the Dominions – including indigenous men – fought shoulder-to-shoulder with the British, soldiers from elsewhere in the empire (and other allied forces) on the Western Front, at Gallipoli and in further theatres, apparent proof of the 'union of hearts' lauded by Prime Minister Laurier.

The First World War marked a rite of passage in warfare and international affairs for the Dominions. For Australians, defeat by the Turks at Gallipoli became a key national myth; sacrifice and ultimate victory in the war, according to some, finally washed away the convict taint that had blotted Australian history. The Dominions' leaders played a role in the war councils in London, and in the peace negotiations at Versailles, to which they (as well as India) sent delegates. As the world changed, the Dominions assumed a more autonomous relationship with the UK. In 1926, the Balfour Declaration adopted by an Imperial Conference in London stated that the United Kingdom and the Dominions were all 'autonomous Communities within the British Empire, equal in status, in no way subordinate one to another in any aspect of their domestic or external affairs, though united by a common allegiance to the Crown and freely associated as members of the British Commonwealth of Nations'. Five years later, the Statute of Westminster further institutionalized the autonomy and equality of the Dominions with Britain. It was not ratified by Australia until 1942 and New Zealand until 1947. Given the assumption of self-government and confederation, but with continuation of institutional links with Britain, historians struggle to find a specific date of independence for any of the Dominions.

The Dominions in the empire and the world

The Dominions from the mid-1800s to the early 1900s had become self-governing, unified, economically modern and militarily proven countries – with the indigenous populations paying a price for what colonialists and the white elite trumpeted as progress, economic development and near independence. Canada, South Africa, Australia and New Zealand were no longer colonies, in the sense of being governed by foreigners (and indeed most of those in local elites had for long been locally born and reared), subject to laws and regulations for the most part enacted at the imperial centre, and exploited largely for the profits of metropolitan business. With democratic political systems, prosperous economies and vibrant societies, for many observers, especially those who turned a blind eye to the situation of indigenous people, the Dominions were great success stories.

The Dominions in several respects indeed offered models of progressive policies. New Zealand instituted universal manhood suffrage with no property qualifications from 1879, and in that country, in 1893, women first achieved the right to vote but not yet the right to stand for election. Australian women gained suffrage on an equal basis with men in 1902, something British women did not achieve until 1928. Australia was heralded in a 1901 book by a French commentator, Albert Métin, as a country of 'socialism without doctrine', where the power of labour unions and a system of arbitration for industrial disputes seemed exemplary. Philippa Mein Smith, a present-day New Zealand historian, has identified a distinctive brand of Australasian government in which the state played a strong role in economic activity, promoted harmony between capital and labour (despite episodic industrial action), and set up wide-ranging social welfare systems. Both Australia and New Zealand were perceived, though rather naively, as paradises for workers in the late 1800s and early 1900s. Despite frictions, the cohabitation of Anglophones and Francophones in Canada, and of Afrikaners and the British in South Africa after the Anglo-Boer War, seemed far removed from the fractious ethnic disputes, and the violence of revolutionary and anarchist movements, that plagued other countries. Alongside India, the Dominions stood as pillars of the British Empire.

The Dominions were assuming a larger role in world affairs. Australia had begun exercising a 'sub-imperialism' in the South Pacific in the late 1800s, sending out missionaries and traders to the islands. In the 1880s, Australian interests persuaded the British to annex the south-eastern quadrant of the large island of New Guinea just north of Australia (where the Netherlands controlled the western part and Germany claimed the northeast); after the First World War, Australia took over the colonial administration of Papua New Guinea, including the former German colony in the northeast of the island, until its independence in 1975. New Zealand, too, was expanding into the Pacific, with the small islands of Tokelau and Niue (which remain New Zealand dependencies), the Cook Islands and Western Samoa, the last acquired from Germany after the First World War. As Germany was ousted from Southwest Africa as well, South Africa moved into that territory, which it administered until 1990, and South African influences in neighbouring British colonies remained powerful.

The mid-twentieth century saw the loosening of ties between Britain and Australia, and to a lesser extent between Britain and New Zealand. The Japanese defeat of Britain in Southeast Asia in 1942, and the manifest impossibility of Britain to defend the Australasian Dominions if they should be attacked, led to a pivoting towards defence agreements with the United States, though prime ministers through the 1950s and 1960s steadfastly proclaimed loyalty to Britain and the Commonwealth of Nations. Gough Whitlam's Labor government, in power in Australia from 1972 to 1975, adopted 'Queen of Australia' as title for the monarch and a new national anthem – symbolic of distancing between Australia and Britain; the dismissal of that government by the queen's representative, the governor general, in 1975, seemed to point up the anachronism of residual imperial times. Meanwhile, in 1973, Britain distanced itself from the 'old' Commonwealth when it joined the then European Economic Community, and Margaret Thatcher's government in the 1980s ended the right of abode for Commonwealth citizens in the 'metropole'. Canada had arguably already moved away from Britain, adopting a flag on which the British Union Flag did not figure, in 1965; in 1982 the Canadian constitution was 'repatriated', ending the prerogative of the British Parliament to amend the country's foundational charter. The monarchy, a Westminster-style government, a social welfare system and an independent trajectory in foreign policy nevertheless helped distinguish Canada from its overbearing southern neighbour, though Ottawa faced a secessionist movement in Quebec. Large-scale migration, and the removal of bars to 'non-white' migrants, changed the demography of Canada and Australia, in particular. A policy of 'multiculturalism' from the 1970s replaced preservation of Britishness in national life. New Zealand seemed less eager to distend traditional links with the UK. Australia increasingly began to situate itself as a country of the Asia-Pacific, and New Zealand reaffirmed its positioning in the South Pacific.

The most serious development in the Dominions concerned South Africa. As anti-colonial nationalism gained force throughout the British, French and Belgian colonies in Africa during the first half of the twentieth century, white South Africans felt increasingly threatened, and latent tensions between those of British and Dutch heritage re-emerged. In 1948, the conservative and Afrikaner-dominated National Party gained power and soon formally established a regime of racial segregation, or apartheid. Strict racial categories (Whites, Coloureds, Africans and Asians), prohibition on mixed marriages and sexual liaisons, requirements that Blacks carry passes and reside only in certain areas, among other measures, marked a racist regime. The white elite determined to maintain its hold over government and the economy, even in the face of growing condemnation from the outside world, the move to independence of other colonies in Black Africa and rejection of apartheid by some whites within South Africa. Strengthening opposition in Britain to apartheid led to a referendum in South Africa in 1960 that turned the country into a republic, severing its connections with the Crown, and South Africa withdrew from the Commonwealth of Nations. The African National Congress was subsequently banned, the government undertook violent repression of dissent in the Black townships, imprisoned such leaders as Nelson Mandela (1918-2013), stood firm in the face of international sanctions and obdurately continued to practice apartheid. By the 1980s, however, the system began to break down, and finally Mandela – the most revered political activist in the non-Western world since Gandhi – was freed in 1990; he became the first president of South Africa after the formal abolition of apartheid.

If British colonialism seemed, in reality, a thing of the past, a heritage to be assumed but one of declining centrality in national life, and 'Dominions' fell out of usage, for the indigenous populations, many unresolved questions remained. These involved recognition of their status as first occupants of their countries, land rights, acknowledgement and redress of wrongs suffered, official acceptance of traditional customs and institutions, and efforts to reduce the gaping inequalities that persist between them and other Australians, Canadians, New Zealanders and South Africans.

Steps, though only gradually, have been taken to addressing grievances. In 1975, New Zealand set up a permanent Waitangi Tribunal to consider claims of breaches in the Crown's responsibilities according to the 1840 treaty with Maori. In 1992 the Australian High Court, in the *Mabo* decision, effectively voided the claim of terra nullius and ruled that Aborigines' land rights had not been extinguished by British colonization, and the Australian prime minister in 2008 made a formal apology in parliament to the 'stolen generations' of indigenous people taken from their families. From 1996 to 2003, in an effort at restorative justice, a Truth and Reconciliation Commission heard heart-rending testimony about the injustices of apartheid rule in South Africa. The Canadian parliament in 1999 created the autonomous Nunavut territory, a huge expanse of the northwest where more than three-quarters of the population are Inuit. Canadian governments have issued several apologies about treatment of First Nations people and have agreed to pay compensation to 'stolen children' confined to institutions. Efforts at reconciliation continue in all of these countries, but in the eyes of many, the deleterious imprint of colonialism has nowhere fully disappeared.

CHAPTER 10
COLONIALISM AND THE BODY

In sickness and in health, from birth to death, the bodies of the colonizing and the colonized served as key sites on which colonial encounters left their mark. As Elizabeth M. Collingham states, and her argument is not just valid for the British or only for India: 'The British experience of India was intensely physical. . . . [T]he body was central to the colonial experience.'[1] In the overseas empires, Europeans and those they ruled came into contact with different physiognomies, perspectives on the body and social codes that surrounded bodily functions and malfunctions. Evolving notions of race informed attitudes, behaviours and policy. The 'native' body was an object of wonderment, lust, suspicion and abuse for Europeans, who tried to regulate the bodily activities of subject peoples through law, medicine, morals and violence: what is now termed the 'biopolitics' of colonialism. Concern with their own health preoccupied colonizers confronted with the pleasures and pains of unfamiliar geographical and social situations. Disease and its treatment were major issues in the colonies, from the need to protect the lives of the colonizers to a self-appointed duty to spread European medical and social practices to indigenous and diasporic peoples.

In the background of colonial medical intervention lay revolutionary changes in biopolitics in Europe in the nineteenth and twentieth centuries. The 'Pasteurian revolution' introduced new theories about the spread of disease by pathogenic microbes and the prophylactic benefits of vaccination; great campaigns sought to wipe out diseases such as smallpox, rabies, tuberculosis, anthrax and plague (see Figure 10.1).[2] Medical theory increasingly stressed the importance of hygiene in controlling diseases like cholera, which regularly devastated Europe. New drugs, notable among them, penicillin, were developed, X-rays improved medical diagnosis and anaesthetics reduced the horrors of surgery. Gradually, too, new ideas about psychology made treatment of those with mental illnesses more humane, though their lot remained grim. National and municipal authorities built systems to provide clean water and take away sewage and waste, and to construct hospitals, clinics and 'lunatic' asylums. Public and medical authorities by the end of the nineteenth century were placing increased stress on physical fitness, mirrored in the growing popularity of sport. Educationists promoted the idea of a 'healthy mind in a healthy body'.

Other attitudes about the body were changing. Some reformers advocated for vegetarianism, yet meat-eating remained dominant. Clothing continued to constrict and hide bodies with corsets and long skirts, heavy suits and stiff collars, yet there were increasing demands for healthier and more comfortable types of apparel. Critics bemoaned the poor and crowded state of workers' housing, and the disease, crime

Figure 10.1 Inoculations at the Plague Hospital, Bombay (Mumbai), India, 1922. © Alamy Stock Photo.

and vice said to fester there, prompting calls for slum clearance, 'social housing' and moral regeneration. Debate raged about sexuality, including prostitution, 'deviance', masturbation and homosexuality, revealing how medicine, religion, law, politics and social mores intertwined.

Medical knowledge and practice were becoming standardized and institutionalized in an increasingly professionalized corps of doctors, nurses, researchers and technicians. However, they faced challenges from methodologies later dismissed as pseudo-science or charlatanism – such as phrenology, which held that mental traits and behaviour could be diagnosed by bumps on the head, or mesmerism, whose practitioners believed in invisible magnetic currents and their use in healing, as well as the widespread sale of patent medicines. Eugenicists argued that humans could be genetically improved, with disease, handicaps and mental incapacity reduced, by selective human breeding – an approach that could dangerously legitimize racism, cruel medical experiments and even genocide. Social reformers, less frighteningly, talked up programmes to improve the bodies, minds and souls of compatriots. The state, more perhaps than ever before, intervened in private life to pursue these objectives.

European concerns and perspectives were transported to the colonies, and indeed appeared in high relief in situations where European norms came face to face with those of different natural environments and cultures. The study of biopolitics, colonial medicine, attitudes towards and regulation of the body and mind, and sex and sexuality now constitutes a major body of work in colonial history-writing. Only several areas can be examined in this chapter, though food and cuisine, sport, hygiene and many other topics are worth consideration and have provided topics for recent scholarship. Not least among them are themes such as boredom and empathy in the colonies, examples of the rich, but still little explored, emotional history of colonialism.[3]

The body, clothed and unclothed

Europeans for centuries had remarked on, and been fascinated by, differences in bodies around the world: the colour of skin and eyes, type of hair, stature and other physical features. The observation and measurement of human bodies became a near obsession for colonizers, mirroring scientific interest and evolving notions of racial superiority and inferiority. Calibrations of height, weight, the shape and size of noses and other parts of the body (including the genitals) were accepted strategies for researchers equipped with instruments ranging from calipers to cameras, no matter how invasive physical examinations might be for those subjected to them. On the basis of their findings and speculations, Europeans categorized populations by race and 'type', and inferred their physical, intellectual and emotional capacities. As late as the 1960s, Spanish doctors still conducted 'urogenital' examinations on girls and teenagers in Spanish Guinea (Equatorial Guinea) and assessed their mental health to determine whether to approve their travel to Spain.

Unfamiliar bodily practices provoked voyeuristic interest and widespread disapprobation, sometimes imitation. Tattooing was widely practised in Polynesia and Japan, and many Europeans, particularly sailors and soldiers, had tattoos applied even if designs lacked the cultural signification they held for peoples of the South Pacific or Asia. Ritualistic scarification, practised in parts of sub-Saharan Africa, and the tradition of knocking out a tooth during rites of initiation, common among some Aboriginal groups in Australia, were viewed with thorough disapproval. The painting of the body (which, of course, Europeans practised with make-up) provoked less negative views but much curiosity. Female circumcision in Africa and elsewhere – today combatted as genital mutilation – appeared a savage practice, yet European authorities generally did not try to control it. 'Child marriage', the arranged betrothal and marriage of partners even before adolescence, though such unions were consummated only much later, provided further grounds for European offense. The binding of the feet of Chinese women evoked a mixture of titillated description and shock, its abandonment promoted as a by-product of modernization. Practices around birthing were regarded with consternation by Europeans who branded them medically invalid or 'primitive', and found that maternity wards allowed for safer conditions and closer oversight of indigenous populations. The body itself was thus not only a screen on which non-Western cultures revealed their specificities but also one on which Europeans projected their fears, fantasies and notions of governance.

Europeans compared their bodies with those of other peoples (and the gaze was reciprocal): height and girth, musculature, genital endowment. Bodies that conformed to European ideals, such as those of young Polynesians frequently described in terms of Greco-Roman statuary, won praise, while those that did not provoked scorn – aesthetic

175

appreciation or the lack of it influenced racial and racist categorization more than may be acknowledged. Men with slighter builds than northern Europeans, as was generally the case in south-eastern and eastern Asia, were thought weak and effeminate, while those of sturdier build were considered martial or menacing. Long hair, so alluring on women, was similarly criticized as effeminate on men, while short hair on women was 'mannish'. In South Asia, Europeanized Bengalis, the *babus* who worked for the British in the administration, were contrasted with warrior 'races' such as the Punjabi and with 'manly' Englishmen.[4]

Clothes, as the cliché has it, maketh the man, and so they made the colonial and the colonized man and woman. By the nineteenth century, the unclothed body was seen primarily through an erotic lens by Europeans, who covered their own bodies from head to toe; even recreational swimming, which gained popularity from the mid-1800s, required bathing costumes that hid most of the body. Especially for respectable women, at least until the early twentieth century, modesty meant full-length skirts, hats and gloves, though décolletage was permitted in formal evening wear. Codes of clothing differed greatly around the non-Western world. Muslim women often covered themselves even more fully than did Westerners, while in parts of Africa, Southeast Asia and Oceania, women (especially those of lower social status) were customarily bare-chested; men, clad in sarongs or loincloths (or, in some Pacific islands, only penis sheaths) went around immodestly naked in Western eyes. Missionaries, in particular, promoted demure clothing, above all for women, popularizing and even imposing long, loose-fitting dresses with flower patterns and lace decoration: *robes mission* (missionary dresses), as the French called them. Europeans nevertheless marvelled at non-Western fabric and clothing, particularly the fine textiles of Asia made into saris, kimonos and other apparel. Silk fabrics, in particular, had long been highly desirable imports into Europe for clothing and furnishings. There were episodic vogues for what would now be termed 'ethnic' clothing, and regular borrowings from non-Western styles, in European fashion: Madras prints, cashmere shawls, silk gowns in Japanese or Chinese style.

Clothing in the 1800s and early 1900s, even more obviously than today, denoted status and role: among men, the uniforms of soldiers and sailors, the vestments of clerics, the frock coats and top-hats of prosperous businessmen and professionals, the ragged apparel of poor migrants. Gold braid, military medals and official decorations denoted achievement and commanded deference, and proper dress bespoke respectability. Expatriates, in principle, adhered to European dress codes even in the tropics despite the inappropriateness of European outfits in such climates, with dinner jackets and evening dresses mandatory for elite gentlemen and ladies at formal occasions almost to the end of the colonial age. In daily life and particularly in outstations, clothing conventions were necessarily loosened to facilitate work, but 'going native' in clothing, at least in public, suggested a disavowal of European standards.

No item of clothing was more stereotypical of the modern colonial age than the pith helmet, also called a 'solar topee' (from *topi*, Hindi for 'hat') or, in French, *casque colonial* (colonial helmet). As one missionary wrote: 'The *topi* was a fetish; it was a tribal symbol [for the Europeans]. If you did not wear a *topi* you were not merely silly, you were a cad.

. . . You had gone native.' Developed in colonial India in the 1820s or 1830s, the wide-brimmed cork hat, covered in tough khaki or white fabric, was considered essential to protect Europeans from the tropical sun and sunstroke, though its real value may have been as much psychological. Yet for some, pith helmets provided an object of mockery. The Brazilian intellectual Gilberto Freyre saw in the pith helmet the shortcomings and lack of adaptation of Europeans: 'Pure Occidental civilization does not adapt itself to the tropics', where Europeans 'are inflexibly European'.[5] Those en route to the 'East' donned the pith helmet when passing through the Suez Canal, and sometimes ceremoniously threw it into the water when they crossed the canal on their return. Paired with shorts and boots for men, it remained a common form of workwear until at least the 1930s, while exact styles altered, and more elegant pith helmets matched with suits and ties, military uniforms or even women's day wear. Pith helmets feature in almost every depiction of colonial life, and production of the iconic headgear represented a niche industry. Indigenous people also adopted the pith helmet – a variant is still worn, yet increasingly less so, by workers in Vietnam and policemen in several former Caribbean colonies.[6]

European bodies, it was believed, had to be protected in other ways as well. Flannel underclothes were recommended in the 1800s as being good to ward off chills and soak up perspiration, with broad woollen cummerbunds to protect the internal organs. Punkah-wallahs in India spent hours pulling huge fans hanging from the ceiling to provide a breeze, and window shades were wetted to cool the temperature. A mosquito net was de rigueur for sleeping. Beds were raised high off the floor to ward off 'miasmas', and insect and rodent pests, and good ventilation was considered vital; loose pyjamas (another Indian word that made its way into English) became common nightwear. Regular bathing – an irregular practice in Europe – became more common in the colonies because of the heat, often by shower rather than immersion in a tub; shampoo (yet another word from Hindi) was used for washing the hair, an infrequent practice for nineteenth-century Europeans. Changing clothes several times a day became customary, made easier by the multitude of servants who looked after the Europeans.

Colonials were keen followers of fashion. The bright silk and satin outfits worn by men in the eighteenth century gave way to sober black broadcloth suits in the early decades of the following century. White linen suits, complete with waistcoats, became as common as the pith helmet for day wear. Women in the colonies long resisted concessions to European conventions, so donned the corsets, petticoats and frocks considered ladylike in Victorian times, while some dared to wear trousers. By the mid-1800s, neither men nor women so frequently put on indigenous apparel as they had earlier, part of what Collingham calls a 'ban on the East' in terms of expatriate British sahibs' and memsahibs' refusal or reticence to adopt Indian styles of life. Tailors and seamstresses in the colonies, as well as speciality shops in European capitals, vied to outfit colonizers in the latest styles: fashion, politics, medical opinion and commerce joined together.[7]

Shoes are another item of clothing that say much about colonialism, symbolized by the contrast between the standard leather European shoes and boots, and the footwear most common in different cultures – sandals, fabric slippers, shoes made from wood or fur – as well as the practice of going barefoot, which was unusual in Europe except among the very poor or destitute. In Algeria, where sandals were the ordinary footwear, European settlers became known as *pieds-noirs* or black feet probably because of their black leather shoes, though there is some disagreement about the origin of the term. In Asia and Africa, people removed footwear before entering houses, places of worship or official buildings. Yet European officials on occasion ostentatiously refused to shed their shoes when they went into royal or sacred buildings, a calculated expression of disdain for local custom. Europeans in some colonies nevertheless banned servants from wearing shoes, and required male servants to wear shorts, reinforcing differences and suggesting the child-like station of indigenous servants.

The 'veil' served as a marked denominator of status and a particularly delicate issue under colonial regimes in Islamic societies. Although the Quran does not require Muslim women to cover their heads or faces, many do so with a scarf over only part of the head and hair, a veil over most of the face, or a body-enclosing garment that leaves only a narrow opening for the eyes. Such clothing can be brightly coloured or severely black, depending on the culture. Associated by Muslims with modesty and piety, for Europeans these face- and body-coverings were part of the mystery they saw in the Arab world (and their fantasies about the harem), but were also considered emblematic of the perceived subjection of women. Some Europeans and some Islamic women called for women to cast off their 'veils' as a gesture of emancipation and modernization. During the Franco-Algerian War of the 1950s and early 1960s, French authorities charged that women could transport weaponry and messages or even hide bombs under their ample dresses and move about unidentified under veils, allowing them more easily to support anti-colonial movements and commit terrorist acts; some women were unveiled by force.[8] In recent years, the wearing of head coverings by Muslim women in Europe, and particularly face coverings and the burqa, has provoked much debate, with several countries, on the grounds of commitment to secularism, restricting or banning them in public. Attitudes towards apparel continue to provide a way of charting encounters between different cultures, the adoption or adaptation of different styles, and the social and political connotation of the clothing or unclothing of the body.

For indigenous people, and non-Western migrants in the colonies, ascension up the social ladder often meant putting on European dress, at least for certain activities. In general, indigenous men were more apt to dress in a European manner than were women, corresponding with their more public role in colonial society and the supposed vocation of women as guardians of tradition. Some preferred to retain traditional clothing that was closely tied to status, religion or ethnic identity (for instance, Sikh turbans) or that was simply more comfortable and less costly (flowing robes in the Arabian desert, sarong-type cloths in the tropics). Garments could be combined in hybrid styles, as when someone wore a European hat with a sarong, sported shirt and trousers while barefoot, or donned European items in unconventional ways – sartorial mixtures greeted with amusement and derision by Europeans.

Choice of clothing showed changing policies and ways of representation of the self and others. For instance, the Spanish had imposed *polleras* (multi-coloured skirts) on women in the Andes; such clothing then became subject for mockery as the dress of rural people, but now these skirts are a proud symbol of indigeneity. Early sketches of Queen Pomaré of Tahiti, over which France established a protectorate in 1842, show a nubile scantily clad young Polynesian woman; in an oil portrait and photographs made several decades later, she looks like a Victorian matron in a modest and simple black dress, though still with flowers in her hair. In the 1880s, the French presented another 'protected' queen, Madagascar's Ranavalona III, with elegant Parisian gowns, perfumes and jewellery in an attempt to gain her allegiance; even after she was dethroned and exiled, newspapers described her dresses in detail when she visited France. Wealthy Indian princes and their consorts amassed large wardrobes of clothing designed by European *couturiers* as well as their own tailors, and they changed styles of clothing to perform different roles. Complementary sets of portraits of the very fashionable and very wealthy maharajah and maharani of Indore, celebrity figures in the 1930s, show the couple in both traditional Indian dress and European evening wear. A rare hereditary woman ruler in India, Jahan, the Muslim Begum of Bhopal, sometimes wore a burqa, at other times only a crown-like hat; some wives and daughters of Muslim princes abandoned veils, while others did not.

The Malay sultan Abu Bakar of Johor, an ardent Anglophile, dressed in Saville row suits, and he (like the king of Tonga) had a European crown crafted so that he would appear a 'proper' monarch in European eyes. A British missionary society had such a crown created for the monarch of Tahiti. European clothing styles caught on for particular activities, such as 'cricket whites' and 'tennis whites' for sport, suits for public servants and livery for domestic servants at vice-regal palaces and elite residences. In some late colonial societies, trendy and colourful Western clothing announced the urban, modern lifestyle of youth, for instance, in the flamboyant and dandified jazz-loving youth culture of the Congo. Different styles were alternated and juxtaposed – from 'traditional' wear to standard Western attire to more creative creations – as a way for individuals to position themselves in society, though some options were available only to the more affluent or bold.[9]

Meanwhile, the making of textiles and clothing, for local and export markets, provided a major economic activity, the types of fabric and design associated with particular regions, from the kente cloth of western Africa to the batik of Southeast Asia. Many indigenous women, like their European peers, sewed clothing for their families, and the import of the Singer sewing machine into the colonies – one of the most omnipresent of all European machines – transformed sewing and provided a new source of income for women, and men as well, who could work at home or in small workshops.[10] Tailors were familiar figures in bazaars and souks at a time when few clothes were bought off the rack. Major producers of raw materials and owners of textile factories, both European and indigenous, amassed fortunes. The department stores established in colonial cities purveyed styles from Europe. Traders sold items such as feathers, fur, mother-of-pearl, ivory and tortoiseshell for sartorial purposes, and the mining of gold and gemstones for jewellery was big business in places such as South Africa, Ceylon and Burma.

The political nature of clothing was dramatically on show at the 1911 Delhi Durbar, at which King George V and Queen Mary were proclaimed emperor and empress of India. New imperial crowns of gold and precious stones were created as symbols of imperial paramountcy. The regimental uniforms worn by soldiers in the Indian army (often decorated more elaborately than typical British uniforms) and the woollen suits of those in the administration contrasted with the silks and jewels of the princes who approached the durbar throne to pay homage to the king-emperor, with further variety in the *saris* or *salwar kameez* of women (with styles differing according to the region, religion or ethnic group from which wearers came), and the *dhotis* of 'ordinary' Indian men on the sidelines of the spectacle. Clothing became a way of expressing opposition to British rule. In his early life in India and South Africa, Mahatma Gandhi dressed as the successful London-trained lawyer that he was, but as a nationalist Gandhi famously later exchanged suits for the simple white loincloth of the peasant, even daring to wear his *dhoti* in chilly London to meet the prime minister for negotiations about Indian independence. Gandhi pleaded with his compatriots to reject the textiles produced by British factories, imports that had destroyed much of Indian manufacturing. Some of the best-known photographs of the Mahatma show Gandhi sitting at his spinning wheel. The homespun *kadi* cloth made of locally grown cotton became an emblem of Indian self-sufficiency and anti-colonialism (and today must be used for official Indian flags).

Jawaharlal Nehru, another nationalist and the first prime minister of India, differed from Gandhi in dress. He generally wore a natty *sherwani*, a tunic in the style of a frock-coat, and Indian-style trousers tight in the legs; a short coat with stand-up collar became known as the 'Nehru jacket', though Nehru did not in fact wear the short version. Nehru also wore a white cloth cap, as did Gandhi (hence the name 'Gandhi cap'). Muhammad Ali Jinnah, the Muslim leader, usually dressed in a Western suit and a peaked astrakhan hat ('Jinnah cap') associated with the northern subcontinent, the future Pakistan. Clothing has everywhere served as a marker of ethnicity, taste, income, social status and political position, in colonial times and subsequently.

The sexualized body

The extension and consolidation of empires in the nineteenth century occurred at the time of profound European changes in attitudes to sexuality and gender. New medical and psychological interpretations of gender and sexual behaviour circulated during the 1800s and early 1900s, including the psychoanalytical theories of Sigmund Freud. 'Homosexuality' was coined as a term in the 1870s, a homosexual emancipation movement began in Germany in the 1890s, and the Oscar Wilde scandal in Britain brought same-sex orientation into public view. There were demands for reform of legislation regarding divorce, greater discussion of family planning and increasing attention to the life-phase of adolescence. The seductive *femme fatale* symbolized a freer female sexuality, and promoters of the 'new woman' called for sexual as well as political and social emancipation. Traditional moralists, however, thundered against vice and long upheld notions of women as physically and intellectually incapable of being educated in the same way as men, doing 'man's work' or voting. Meanwhile, widespread concern about prostitution revealed further moralizing perspectives and the social conditions that led to sex work, and raised medical concerns about venereal diseases. All of these issues played out, as well, in the colonies.[11]

Sex was for long ignored as a topic in colonial history, but questions of sexuality and gender now occupy a central position, and a large number of studies have appeared, many informed by feminist theory, queer theory and post-colonial approaches. Colonies, as Ronald Hyam suggested in a pioneering work, provided terrains of sexual discovery and opportunity for the men who formed the bulk of Europeans in the empires, especially until the early twentieth century.[12] Later research has examined questions surrounding gendered aspects of colonialism, masculinity and femininity, sexual behaviour and the emergence of new sexual cultures in the colonies.[13]

In plantation colonies, European men preyed on the enslaved African women who were their property, and sexual abuse and rape were not uncommon elsewhere. It was the practice for young and not so young unmarried European men to take concubines in the colonies, women who became cooks, housekeepers and bed mates, but who otherwise remained excluded from white society. Such easy arrangements – where behaviour and emotions ranged from violence and coercion through affection and respect, and indeed love – for many seemed part of the rewards, or consolation, for life in the tropics. Liaisons endured until interest waned or the European moved on to a different posting or returned home. After he departed, a concubine might switch to another European or re-join her own people, though often bearing the stigma of such unions, sometimes the scars of abuse or disease, and frequently with children fathered by a European. Sex was available for money throughout the colonial world, and most everywhere else as well, and the boundaries between prostitution, concubinage and other sexual arrangements, for both the colonized and their subjects, were porous.

The poverty of many of the colonized and the relative wealth of Europeans facilitated commercial sexual encounters and European domination of their partners. The physiques of Africans, Asians and other non-Europeans provided a special attraction for some Europeans, blending in with fantasies and stereotypes about sexual talents and proclivities. Even if Spanish travellers complained that 'rugged, rugged is Africa, and so are its women', for settlers, businessmen and visitors, Spanish Guinea was the country of the three Cs: *coñac, coño y, coña*, which referred to sex and alcohol.[14] Works from outright pornography to treatises that claimed to be scientific displayed and discussed the purported sexual capacities, attributes and allure of the colonized. In short, sex permeated colonial culture, from legally sanctioned and socially respectable marital unions between European settlers (and, on occasion, between Europeans and indigenous or diasporic partners) to a variety of arrangements and contacts that, though widely engaged in, were officially considered taboo.

Not all Europeans sought sexual and romantic satisfaction with those of a different gender. Some famous colonials, such as Henry Morton Stanley, Cecil Rhodes and France's Marshal Hubert Lyautey, preferred the intimate companionship of men to that of women, yet it is uncertain whether homosociality and affection in their cases extended to physical relations. The masculine ethos of military barracks, penal colonies and outback stations could prove congenial to homosexual men, as well as to those open to 'situational' homosexual behaviour. Many non-European cultures did not prohibit same-sex activity or consider it – as did most in Europe – as a sin, illness or, in countries such as Britain and Germany, a crime. In fact, colonies beckoned to men who saw possibilities of gaining sexual satisfaction overseas in ways made illegal or dangerous by laws at home. However, homosexual relations did provoke scandals in various colonies, and in German Southwest Africa (today's Namibia), same-sex acts with minors could lead to expulsion.[15]

In some areas outside Europe, there also existed traditions – from the *hajiris* of India to the *fa'afafine* and *maheu* of the Polynesian islands – of transgender identity. Though Christian moralizers looked askance at such sexual variation, for theorists of homosexual emancipation in late nineteenth- and early twentieth-century Europe, such as Edward Carpenter and Magnus Hirschfeld, the social acceptance of same-sex behaviour (and of diverse sexualities) elsewhere in the world provided a powerful argument that it was a natural orientation, not an unnatural act.[16] Lesbian acts were less often criminalized in Europe than sex between men, and there was greater acceptance of intimate female friendship. Such companionships and partnerships between women similarly developed in the colonies; there is as yet limited research on the subject.

Official attitudes towards sexual activity between Europeans and non-Europeans changed over time. In the 1700s and even through much of the 1800s, it created little real concern, so long as liaisons involved prostitution or concubinage. Marriage was less condoned, though legal unions between European men and other women were not unknown, even in the upper echelons of society, and some indigenous spouses returned to Europe with their husbands. Many East India Company 'factors' and government officials had sustained relationships with women in the 'East', authorities feeling that this improved the morale of the Europeans and introduced them to 'native' life. With the dawn of 'Victorian' moral strictures, inter-ethnic unions aroused greater disapprobation, and by 1909 a directive sent by the British Secretary of State for the Colonies, the Crewe circular, warned men in the colonial service not to enter into relations of concubinage with local women, and threatened penalties for those who did so.

Sexual activity, colonial authorities conceded, was normal and necessary, especially for young men such as soldiers and sailors, and if they could not gain access to women, they might turn to other sorts of 'vice'. Regulation was nevertheless required. Officials demarcated specific districts of cities where prostitution was permitted, what the French termed *quartiers réservés*. The military set up 'camp brothels' for soldiers on campaign. Authorities instituted programmes for the registration and medical testing of prostitutes for syphilis or gonorrhoea, with detention of infected women in 'lock hospitals'.[17] They adopted law codes that, in principle, regulated the age of consent for sexual intercourse and marriage, and often prohibited homosexual acts. British laws criminalizing homosexual acts, often introduced at the onset of British colonial rule and strengthened in the late 1800s, remain on the statute books of many former British colonies today or have only recently been repealed – one of the longer-lasting legacies of colonial jurisprudence.

Sexual politics nevertheless varied in the colonial world. While the British outlawed homosexual acts, the French (among others) did not since they had been decriminalized with the Revolution of 1789. The Portuguese – wrongly – considered themselves lacking in racial discrimination and accepting of informal sexual unions and marriage between European men and indigenous women, and indeed large mixed-raced populations emerged in Brazil and the African colonies, notably Cape Verde. Even in the British world, the very preoccupation of authorities with prostitution, 'sodomy' and other non-approved sexual activities suggested that many colonials did not adhere to the moral codes loudly proclaimed from pulpits and parliaments.

One way of trying to normalize sexual behaviour was through recruitment of women colonists. The huge imbalance in the ratio between European men and women in the early decades of colonialism, and even later in more remote locations, was thought to be an incentive to relationships with 'natives'. European women would provide prospective partners for regular marriages, and the traits ascribed to women would further 'decency' and respectability; in giving birth, women would increase the European population, an especially important objective in settler communities. Migration societies and government offices sought out volunteer women migrants, including widows and prisoners (despite the dubious reputation of imprisoned women), and they sometimes sent orphan girls (as well as boys) to the settler colonies, giving them no choice about such forced migration but with reassurance about a better life awaiting them overseas. The population of European women in the colonies increased over the years, but the degree to which their presence greatly changed sexual and social cultures is debated by historians.[18]

The regulation of sexual activity, of course, had a great impact on indigenous and diasporic peoples. Christian clerics preached the sanctity of pre-marital chastity, legal marriage and monogamy, and new laws concerning sexual behaviour were enforced, if somewhat randomly, among local and diasporic people as well as Europeans. A major objective, attained with decidedly mixed success, was to 'reform morals' and instil norms of sexual behaviour considered acceptable to Europeans. In India, the British tried to raise the legal level of consent to limit 'child' marriages, and they sought to combat *sati*, the practice of women immolating themselves on the funeral pyres of deceased spouses. Europeans nevertheless generally did not challenge the polygamy allowed in Muslim law (and in other traditions), though marriage to multiple partners might disqualify a person from particular rights, including European citizenship. Europeans generally turned a blind eye to sexual life that did not overly impinge on or involve Europeans. Only rarely did they act against the human trafficking that supplied prostitutes to brothels or try to address the economic situations that forced women into sex work. Sexual abuse and contraventions of European law codes were punished primarily when cases became egregious and public, in response to pressure from morals campaigners and journalists, or when the police and judiciary intended to make a point about European norms.

Figure 10.2 Tunisian man with two women, *c.* 1900. © Alamy Stock Photo.

The colonies continued to represent, in myth and to a degree in reality, places where the strictures of European sexual conventions were relaxed (see Figure 10.2). That could offer liberation or toleration for individuals' pursuits, but the situation often involved inequitable relationships between Europeans and local partners, instances of abuse, a louche urban low life where commercial sex, alcohol and drugs were interlaced, and the frequent refusal of European men to recognize or support the children they sired with local women – all masked by façades of integrity and European superiority, and images of happy European families living lives of domestic contentment overseas. Sexual realities in the colonies challenged Christian ideals, while the imposition of European law codes and mores similarly challenged indigenous attitudes and behaviours. Debates on sexual respectability and disreputableness, 'natural' and 'unnatural' sex, modesty and eroticism, as well as the appropriate level of public intervention into private lives, would continue to animate debates long after Europeans left the colonies.

The body in sickness and in health

Health and illness were pressing issues in colonial governance, and in the experience of colonialism by both Europeans and subject peoples. Growing academic interest in the area has led to many works on disease, medical research and the institutions of public health in the colonial world. This research tends to question earlier accounts that simply celebrated colonial medical achievements by scrutinizing the objectives of the state, pointing to the limited access to medical care provided to local people and looking at the confrontation between Western and non-Western medical practice.[19]

Colonial conditions, especially in the tropics, were considered deleterious to 'white' men and women, with evidence drawn from European death rates and in line with early European theories linking climate and disease (as seen in the belief, persistent until the late 1800s, that malaria was caused by 'bad air'). Europeans had to protect themselves with prevention, medication and, when possible, trips away from the tropics – visits to spas in the cooler highlands, and the practice of therapeutic bathing and hydrotherapy treatments, which gained popularity in the 1800s, were prescribed as one way to keep Europeans healthy. Hill stations such as Dalat in Vietnam and Buitenzorg (Bogor) in the Dutch East Indies proved popular for tourism, recreation and socializing, and occasionally the whole colonial government decamped during the most torrid months – as occurred when the British administration in India moved from Calcutta (and later New Delhi) to Simla in the Himalayan foothills.[20]

Prevention, diagnosis and cure of disease were requirements of colonialism from the very outset of expansion and trade; medical doctors accompanied European ships to the Americas and Asia in the 1500s. Colonialism became closely tied to research and the development of public health policies at home and abroad.[21] The priorities lay, not surprisingly, in treatment of Europeans overseas, and in keeping contagious foreign diseases from spreading to Europe – thus, the rigour of quarantine measures for those arriving. There was special concern about soldiers and sailors, particularly since death from disease often far exceeded deaths on the battlefield in campaigns of conquest and 'pacification'.[22] Colonial rule necessitated fit and healthy military personnel, but they were constantly endangered, physically and mentally, by disease and 'vice'.[23] The colonies indeed threatened exposure to a catalogue of life-threatening maladies: various forms of malaria, yellow fever, sleeping-sickness, dengue fever and other 'tropical fevers'. Cholera, well known for its endemic ravages in Europe, was common elsewhere in the world.

Tropical conditions were not the only ones that posed risks of disease and accident, as there was potentially fatal frostbite in the polar regions and high mountains, dehydration in the desert and numerous illnesses at sea (though Europeans learned that fresh fruit and vegetables could prevent the scurvy that had traditionally disabled seamen). Many diseases prevalent in the colonies remained unknown or for long little known to Europeans, and efficacious prophylaxis, diagnosis and treatment took time to develop. For women, it was widely thought that supposedly fragile constitutions increased the dangers; while that contention was dubious, it is true that pregnancy and childbirth held extra risks in locations with scant access to specialists such as obstetricians and gynaecologists.

Explorers and later Europeans going abroad travelled with substantial kits of medicines – phials of drugs (including antiseptics, common remedies and opiates to relieve pain), bandages and dressings; surgeons carried their instruments, yet submitting to the knife was a desperate prospect for patients. Professional physicians and surgeons, in the first instance, were usually officers serving in the navy or army; the speciality of 'tropical medicine' was near coterminous with 'military medicine' in the nineteenth and early twentieth century. Missionaries played a very important role in providing medical care as well, particularly for non-Europeans. Members of Catholic religious orders and Protestant clerics and their spouses, with greater or lesser degrees of training, maintained and staffed clinics, and the churches considered medical care one of their primary duties. The role of women – including nuns and Protestant women missionaries, nurses, a growing number of female doctors and researchers – should be underscored, as they were 'front-line' practitioners and had greater access to female patients and children.[24]

The establishment of clinics, dispensaries and hospitals was urgent for colonial authorities, particularly in settler colonies, and grand hospital buildings became features in colonial cities and larger towns. In isolated locations, medical installations remained more rudimentary, and European or European-trained local doctors and nurses were rarer. Colonial officials, such as district agents, and private individuals with only elementary training (if that) dispensed medications and provided basic treatment in such outposts. The need was great, with illness common, accidents frequent, mortality rates high and specialist care distant. Few Europeans abroad did not contract some nasty disease – malaria was particularly widespread – or suffer a serious accident.

The mental state of Europeans in the colonies provoked further concern. Among the most prevalent maladies was 'tropical neurasthenia'; almost any symptom – ennui, listlessness, fatigue, bowel problems, insomnia, hypochondria, poor eyesight or hearing, loss of appetite, violence, excessive consumption of alcohol – could be blamed on the effects of tropical life, in particular in a 'primitive' environment. From the Gold Coast, as a case in point, nearly as many colonial officials repatriated on medical grounds suffered from tropical neurasthenia as from malaria. The vague disease category corresponded to the general perception that tropical environments were debilitating for Europeans, though it corresponded to a similar variety of neurasthenia identified in European cities; the illness reflected, as well, late nineteenth-century fears of degeneration. In the colonies, however, it was allegedly the 'isolation from modernity' that 'drove whites crazy'.[25] Yet it has been suggested that tropical neurasthenia also provided a means for officials to manage colonial personnel, keeping them in post, allowing them a holiday or sending them home. Taking up a hobby, settling down with a (European) spouse, pursuing 'civilized' leisure activities such as attending concerts or reading, resting at a cool hillside retreat or simply returning to Europe were common prescriptions for neurasthenia. Both European and tropical neurasthenia largely disappeared from the diagnostic inventory after the mid-twentieth century, perhaps not coincidentally at the time of decolonization.[26]

Colonial authorities, and those recruiting colonists, military personnel and administrators, judged that only those healthy in mind and body were fit to serve or settle, though scrupulous selection procedures did not extend to transported convicts (and, in practice, many other migrants). Interviewers for intending British colonial officials rejected candidates who appeared unmanly or weak, and those whose families showed evidence of mental illness or disease. Counsel to avoid immoderate drinking and an overly active sex life, as well as drugs, particularly opium, were intended to preserve the capacities of Europeans, even if recommendations were commonly ignored. A life of energy and action was promoted as the colonial ideal – 'caution, care, patience and decision' was the catchphrase at the time.[27] Sport was good to strengthen the body, and promote manliness and esprit de corps. Colonial promoters praised settlers' physical prowess in places like Australasia and Algeria, men and women hardened by a life of work, fresh air and the challenges of 'pioneer' society. They compared settlers favourably to what they saw as the flaccid and dissipated inhabitants of Europe weakened by urban and industrial conditions. From Portuguese Africa, administrators nevertheless complained in the late colonial period about lack of rigour when selecting settlers, portrayed after their arrival as filthy and badly educated troublemakers rather than shining examples for Africans, as the Portuguese regime's propaganda proclaimed.

Colonizers' concerns for the health of indigenous and diasporic people were in the first place motivated by self-interest, but also by genuine humanitarian sympathies, religious and social convictions, and the undeniable dedication of doctors and nurses. Healthy 'natives' were better workers, with less labour time lost to illness. Better health among local people reduced the spread of diseases that could infect Europeans. The advancement of medicine provided a point of honour in the imperial record, and acceptance of Western medical treatment, as well as training of local medical personnel, was seen to reveal the success of the colonial order and subject people's acknowledgement of the superiority of European medical models.

Yet the European presence often had detrimental effects on local health. European diseases spread in new environments, especially with migration induced by labour markets and transportation systems. Corporal punishments liberally meted out by colonizers (including, in some cases, to fellow Europeans) – quotidian brutality, floggings, deprivation of food and water, incarceration, various forms of torture, as well as sexual abuse – could cause permanent physical and mental damage. The scars of whips and marks of the branding of captured maroon slaves preserved the evidence, as did the wounds of indigenous men serving in imperial armies. Notoriously, in the Congo Free State, hands of workers were occasionally amputated for failure to produce quotas of rubber. Famines were common in the colonies, the most terrible with hundreds of thousands or more deaths, with colonial authorities sometimes unable or unwilling to undertake actions to control them and often accused of making matters worse by stockpiling food and restricting distribution.

Overwork on European plantations, in mines and in urban labour took its toll, workplace accidents were common and mortality rates of indentured labourers and others in subaltern employment were high. Sanitary conditions in the growing urban 'native quarters' to which migrants flocked and places such as mining camps remained especially poor, facilitating the propagation of disease. The much trumpeted medical care proffered by Europeans proved accessible only to those who lived in proximity to doctors and nurses and, for many services, had the ability to pay, as well as willingness to commit themselves to unfamiliar techniques and medications. Europeans might lament injury, disease and death among local people, but accepted these as seemingly unavoidable facts of life (as they often were for many Europeans), even when suffering was directly or indirectly attributable to conditions imposed by Europeans.

Medical services, for both Europeans and local people, represented an important part of the colonial bureaucracy.[28] In India, the British established the Madras General Hospital as early as 1679, and over 200 physicians and surgeons worked in hospitals in Madras, Calcutta and Bombay by the 1780s. A Public Health Commissioner was appointed for the Government of India in 1869, and a reformed and united Indian Medical Service set up in 1896. Europeans established colonial medical schools, one of the earliest in Asia the Calcutta Medical College opened in 1835; the Dutch opened a medical school in the East Indies (known by the acronym STOVIA) in 1898, and the French started one in Hanoi in 1902. Medical education focused particularly on the training of 'native doctors', taught a shorter curriculum and given lesser qualifications than full-fledged physicians; they became vital agents in the dispensation of medical care. Indigenous students could gain full qualifications in the colonies and in the metropoles, yet admissions criteria, cost and distance set obstacles in their path; the University of Edinburgh, for instance, attracted a number of medical students from throughout the British Empire.

A career in medicine offered an inviting prospect for young indigenous and diasporic people, as doctors occupied respected positions in colonial society; most were men, but by the early twentieth century, indigenous women doctors also worked in a few colonies. Though they were trained in European systems, a career in medicine did not guarantee allegiance to the Europeans; indeed, in STOVIA in the Dutch East Indies and in other colonies, medical schools educated some of the leading nationalists as exposure to Western ideas, and the discrimination that even highly educated indigenous people experienced, contributed to anti-colonialism.[29]

Medical encounters

In the colonies, Western medicine encountered varied corpuses of medical theory and practice, including Ayurvedic medicine in South Asia and 'Chinese' medicine in East Asia. Non-Western medicine had different approaches to diagnosis and treatment to those common in the West, with those practices generally disparaged by European scientists and doctors. This was especially the case when local healers saw physical or mental illness as caused by evil spirits and treated patients with incantations and other ceremonies along with 'folk' remedies. Colonial thought held that Western medicine and treatment were scientific and effective, and others largely spurious. Only a few doctors – as well as ethnologists and naturalists – displayed serious interest in indigenous medicine during the colonial period, and few were willing to incorporate local practices into their treatments.[30]

Many non-Western systems of knowledge ascribed mental problems or aberrant behaviour to spirit possession (or the all-encompassing 'vice'). Europeans were particularly fascinated, in scientific terms as well as fantasy, by the phenomenon in Malay culture of people 'running amok', engaging in a bout of frenzy, fury and often violence directed at an individual or group, or turned on the afflicted person himself or herself. Blamed by Malays on possession by a tiger spirit, 'running amok' represented a case of psychopathology for Western practitioners. As European psychology and psychiatry were introduced to the colonies, Western concepts were employed to diagnose mental problems, and 'lunatic asylums' were set up – institutions with similarly lamentable conditions, if not worse ones, than those prevailing in Europe.[31]

Cambodia provides a good example to bring together some of the issues surrounding colonial medicine and reactions to it. Sokhieng Au's study shows that the Khmers, long after the arrival of the French in the 1860s, continued to see health and illness within the spiritual parameters of Buddhism and ancestral beliefs. Women, in particular, would consult European doctors only as a last resort, and Cambodians regarded physicians largely as the purveyors of medications (generally then taken in rather dilatory fashion). Prophylactic recommendations, such as advice to use mosquito nets, were seldom heeded outside the elite. Resistance to hospitalization, examination of women by male practitioners and delays in burial of corpses (for instance, when post-mortems were ordered or when bodies of plague victims were kept in morgues to avoid contagion) was strong. While the French opened hospitals, most births and deaths continued to take place at home, presided over by community practitioners or family members. The French, however, attempted to universalize European medical practices through programmes of vaccination, general medical care, the building of hospitals, training of doctors and promotion of hygiene. They created a Colonial Health Service in Cambodia in 1890, followed by a Native Medical Aid bureau in 1907. A Pasteur Institute, similar to ones set up elsewhere, became the central medical research centre.[32]

The French widely administered vaccinations against rabies, smallpox and the plague. Though occasional deaths from vaccines dissuaded Khmers – the French ascribed reticence to be vaccinated to peasant fatalism – many indeed received them, the roving vaccinator often the only European with whom Cambodians in remote areas had contact. A cholera vaccine introduced after the First World War initially proved less attractive to Khmers than the generally accepted smallpox vaccine. Attempts to train local physicians and nurses did not score great success, in part because of the long years of study necessary, including study in France for those seeking full medical qualifications; there were no indigenous Cambodian doctors even in the 1930s, yet a few Vietnamese physicians worked in the country.[33]

In Cambodia, women attracted particular medical attention. Regulation of venereal diseases was a preoccupation, as in other colonies, because of the frequent infection of soldiers, and by 1912 a medical treatment centre for prostitutes was attached to the hospital in Phnom Penh, the capital. Maternity was another priority in a colony where many children died in infancy, though prenatal care remained limited. A maternity hospital opened in Phnom Penh in 1907, but most women gave birth with the aid of local midwives or family members; only one in 1,500 births occurred in a maternity ward. By the 1930s, the French stepped up efforts to promote the health of mothers and infants through medical and social initiatives. These included establishment of a school for midwives (most of whose students came from mixed ethnic or Vietnamese backgrounds), the setting up of a 'rural birth attendant programme' and even the holding of baby contests with awards for those who best met French standards of infant care.[34]

The medical history of overseas empires varies greatly because of different sorts of diseases, cultures and policies around the world. There were, nevertheless, common problems between Cambodia and other countries, foremost the need and desire to control contagious diseases such as smallpox, tuberculosis, leprosy and the plague, and the use of strategies of vaccination, confinement and quarantine.[35] Sexually transmitted disease was an omnipresent preoccupation; like opium addiction, it was blamed on 'vice'.[36] Efforts to treat local people and Europeans for disease were hampered by lack of sufficient funds and medical personnel, especially in rural areas. Public health initiatives, praiseworthy though they were, fell short of the claims to beneficence championed by colonizers, and great disparities existed in access to care between the prosperous and the impoverished, and between urban and rural populations. Medical care was bound up with racialized Western preconceptions about foreigners, whose perceived lack of attention to sanitation, hesitation to accept Western treatments and enduring belief in spirit possession and 'traditional' cures were propounded as causes for continuing poor conditions of health.

'The most intimate colony'

'The body is in many ways the most intimate colony, as well as the most unruly, to be subject to colonial disciplines', as Tony Ballantyne and Antoinette Burton put it.[37] The body, and the mind as a part of the body, proved a very real site of fears and fantasies, regulation and intervention by the colonizers. For Europeans, healthy bodies and healthy minds were ideal prerequisites for colonial success, yet overseas conditions showed the physical and mental fragility of Westerners prey to a forbidding inventory of physical and mental health dangers. However, different norms from those at home, for instance in the realm of sexuality, at the same time brought into question European verities. For indigenous people, foreign medicine and practices surrounding health and sickness – as well as such daily aspects of life as clothing – posed challenges to received behaviour and perceptions, and introduced new paradigms of science and social life that were sometimes welcomed, at other times rejected. Colonial education and medicine, evangelization, labour and the colonial state provided agents through which bodily actions were censured, regulated and, to varying degrees, transformed.

CHAPTER 11
COLONIALISM AND THE MIND

In 1783, following his return to Britain after eight years of service with the East India Company, William Marsden published *The History of Sumatra: Containing an Account of the Government, Laws, Customs, and Manners of the Native Inhabitants, with a Description of the Natural Productions, and a Relation of the Ancient Political State of That Island*. The capacious title was typical of eighteenth-century works, and Marsden was following a custom for travellers to write up their impressions for the benefit of European readers. (The frontispiece and title page are depicted in Figure 11.1.) Marsden proved a gifted observer, and the book became an enduring reference on the Southeast Asian island. Marsden, a graduate of Trinity College in his native Dublin, had learned Malay and later published a *Grammar and Dictionary of the Malay Language* as well as various scholarly papers. In London, he pursued a career in the British Admiralty and served as a vice-president of the Royal Society, the most prestigious scientific academy in the country. He donated his collection of Asian coins to the British Library and his manuscripts to King's College London before his death in 1836.

In twenty-three chapters, *The History of Sumatra* surveyed the large island – one-and-a-half times the size of the British Isles – in encyclopaedic fashion. The first chapter covered geography and climate, monsoons, volcanoes, surfs and tides, with the second devoted to the inhabitants, including 'persons and complexions' and 'clothing and ornaments'. Flora and fauna, village life, agriculture, social customs such as the chewing of betel, gift-giving, circumcision and funerals, commerce, arts and manufactures, languages, marriage, political structures and a history of the kingdom of Aceh and other states offered subjects for subsequent chapters. Nothing escaped Marsden's attention, with sections on beeswax, arithmetic, 'titles of the sultan', cock-fighting, food, 'theft, murder, and compensation for it' and 'use and effects of opium'. Twenty aquatints illustrated the volume: images of a pepper-plant, the mangosteen and rambutan, weaponry, a village house and 'A Malay Boy, a Native of Bencoolen'. Marsden celebrated the island, where the East India Company had operated a trading outpost for a hundred years, though the Dutch eventually incorporated it into the Netherlands East Indies: 'In point of situation and extent, [Sumatra] holds a conspicuous rank on the terraqueous globe, and is surpassed by few in the bountiful indulgences of nature.' The writer summarized his objective:

> I have been the more scrupulously exact . . . because my view was not, ultimately, to write an entertaining book to which the marvellous might be thought not a little to contribute, but sincerely and conscientiously to add the small portion in my

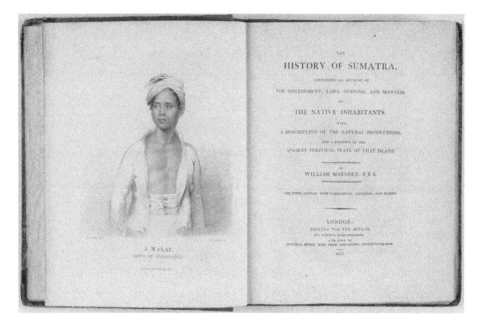

Figure 11.1 Frontispiece and title page of William Marsden's *History of Sumatra* (first published in 1783). © Out of Copyright.

power to the general knowledge of the age; to throw some glimmering light on the path of the naturalist; and more especially to furnish those philosophers whose labours have been directed to the investigation of the history of Man with facts to serve as data in their reasonings, which are too often rendered nugatory, and not seldom ridiculous, by assuming as truths the misconceptions or wilful impositions of travellers. The study of their own species is doubtless the most interesting and important that can claim the attention of mankind. . . . A regular series of authenticated facts is what alone can enable us to rise towards a perfect knowledge of it.[1]

Those comments marked Marsden out as a man of the Enlightenment, with a strong commitment to the pursuit of knowledge and an equally strong belief in scientific truth. Read today, Marsden's account not only contains lacunas and inaccuracies but also betrays the condescendingly ethnocentric ideas about foreign cultures that he shared with peers. Like his compatriots, Marsden was interested in the commercial benefits the British could derive from trade in Sumatra and worried about the position of the Dutch; he was an unapologetic colonialist. Yet his work remains a fine example of a long-lived and unbounded European curiosity about different places and cultures, efforts to study them and the hope of compiling accurate, thorough and interpretative presentations of findings about the natural world and human societies around the 'terraqueous globe'.

Many similar works to that of Marsden's appeared in the late 1700s and through the 1800s and afterwards – and indeed had been published in the 1600s, often by authors who were employees of the national East India Companies and other chartered companies. An outstanding early example is the German-born Georg Rumphius (1627–1702), a merchant in the Dutch East India Company. Despite going blind, losing his wife and daughter in an earthquake, and losing his library in a fire, Rumphius compiled a six-volume compendium covering over a thousand species of plants on Ambon. His work, however, saw publication only in 1741 because of the Company's concern about the commercially sensitive nature of information about the valuable plants of the Spice Islands.

Although professional scientists accompanied voyages of 'discovery', such as those sent to Oceania in the late 1700s, or gained commissions from governments or learned societies for dedicated scientific expeditions, the boundaries between amateur and professional long remained porous. The disciplines of natural history such as botany and zoology were well established, but from the late 1700s other fields developed, notably anthropology and ethnography. In fact, the European encounter with overseas societies played a major role in the emergence of the social sciences. A discursive, even rambling, style of writing, punctuated with moral judgements and anecdotes, frequently characterized publications at the time, and academic conventions that later became mandatory (such as references to sources) were not common. The work done, despite its scientific, political and moral limitations from a present-day perspective, remains remarkable.

Colonial scholarship

Colonialism created a vast body of scholarship, and it is hard to overestimate the place of exploration, conquest and colonial rule in opening up new territories and subjects to European academic interest and research. Expansion took scholars to places unknown to Europeans; colonial governments sponsored and funded learned societies, libraries, museums and archives; and European institutions collected manuscripts, artworks and artefacts brought home from the colonies. Encounters with the wider world enriched almost all fields of knowledge. The acquisition of knowledge, of course, must be placed in context. Like all scholars, those of the age of empire carried with them the intellectual baggage of their time. Accounts of foreign places were individualistic and impressionistic. Authors made errors, and misunderstood customs and traditions. They seldom acknowledged what they had learned from local people and frequently disparaged indigenous knowledge. Few questioned the objectives and methods of colonialism. All of that, however, does not negate the efforts by scholars such as Marsden to understand a world that was, to them, new and fascinating.

It is impossible here to survey all the branches of knowledge with which colonialism had a link and on which it had an impact, and several, including natural history and comparative religion, are covered in other chapters. In this chapter, two topics – the establishment of European-style cultural institutions and archaeological work – illustrate how the quest for knowledge represented both a cause and a product of

European expansion. It should be remembered that while the Europeans expanded their knowledge, they deployed that system of knowledge and imposed it on the colonized people. They assumed that Western science and scholarship, notably in such areas as the 'hard' sciences and medicine, were superior and that only the 'scientific method' provided a valid methodology. They held that European strategies of research, categories of learning and institutions of teaching inherently possessed more legitimacy than local ones, whence the frequent depreciation of indigenous guardians of knowledge, including those branded as 'shamans' and 'witch-doctors', and of their wisdom and beliefs, often dismissed as 'superstition' or folklore. Europeans counterposed the 'traditional' knowledge of indigenous societies – the word 'traditional' in some senses denoting outdated, ineffective or erroneous – against the 'modern' and 'scientific' knowledge they brought or developed through observation and experiment. However, the ways in which indigenous people appropriated European knowledge for their benefit also forms part of the history of colonialism. They did so by adopting new techniques of agriculture and manufacturing, using materials previously unknown or unfamiliar, seeking out Western-style medical care and education, writing in Western languages and genres, producing theses and treatises that closely followed European academic practice. For both Europeans and, arguably to a greater extent for non-Europeans, research and knowledge became hybridized, though introduced techniques and approaches did not necessarily negate old beliefs. That is a very large story, and the current chapter, by choice, focuses on the European acquisition of knowledge.

Institutions of colonial knowledge

Throughout their colonies, and also at home, Europeans set up institutions to promote study of the wider world. These included learned societies – voluntary organizations of scientists, scholars and amateurs that flourished in the Enlightenment and subsequently – as well as libraries, museums, universities and colonial institutes. The earliest were created in the western hemisphere – with the first officially established universities chartered by the Spanish king in Peru and New Spain (Mexico) in 1551 – but they eventually emerged in many places where Europeans established bases.[2]

In 1778, a naturalist in the Dutch East Indies initiated the Royal Batavian Society of Arts and Sciences. Six years later, in Calcutta, Sir William Jones founded the Asiatic Society (or 'Asiatick', as it was then spelled) 'to inquire within the bounds of Asia about Man and Nature; whatever is performed by the one, or produced by the other'. The society accepted only European members until 1829, but elected its first ethnically Indian president in 1885. It amassed a monumental collection of manuscripts, books and maps, opened a museum and published a journal. In 1824, it affiliated with the Royal Asiatic Society of Great Britain and Ireland, headquartered in London, which set up branches in other Indian cities, Ceylon (1845), Malaysia (1877), Japan (1877) and Korea (1900); all remain active to this day. The Literary Society of Bombay (founded in 1804), the Bombay Geographical Society and the Anthropological Society of Bombay merged into the Asiatic Society, as did the Madras Literary Society (organized in 1812). Others groups in India included the Scientific Society (1864), established by a Muslim college principal; the Indian Association for the Cultivation of Science (1876), spearheaded by an Indian physician, the Indian Institute of Science (1909), the Indian Science Congress Association (1914) and the Indian Academy of Sciences (1934), all welcoming both European and Indian members – evidence of shared interests and sustained intellectual cooperation in the colonial world.

The breadth of the societies' interests can be gauged from the illustrated 375-page first issue of the *Journal of the Royal Asiatic Society of Great Britain and Ireland* in 1834. It offered work on indigenous coastal vessels of India and Ceylon, the Hindu school system, the Indus river, Nepalese law, ancient Chinese vases, Ceylonese religious processions, 'a remarkable Hospital for Animals at Surat', the Circassians, a 'Political and Statistical History of the Province of Gujarat' and far more. There were biographical sketches of Deccan poets, the Mughal emperor Jehangir, the Prince Royal of Persia, a late British surveyor-general of India and a Hungarian traveller in Asia. There were notices on new publications, including a book on Hindu architecture written by a 'Native Judge and Magistrate at Bangalore'. The journal editors and authors were mostly British men, ranging from civilian and military employees of the East India Company to a 'master shipwright of His Majesty's Naval Yard at Trincomali [Trincomalee, Ceylon]' and clerics, though with several Indian writers, including the 'Head Translator and Pundit in the Literary and Antiquarian Department, Calcutta'.[3]

Many parallel organizations and publications existed, including the Royal Africa Society, which was established in London in 1901. In Paris, a Société d'Histoire des Colonies was set up in 1913, and an Académie Coloniale, meant to bring together scholars with eminent political and commercial figures, opened in 1922. The pre-eminent French research institution for Asia (which called itself a 'school' though it did not have students), the École Française d'Extrême-Orient, dates from 1900, with headquarters in Paris and branches around Asia.[4] These institutions, some with changed names, are still active today, though not others such as Les Amis du Vieux Hué, which from 1914 to the 1940s published a journal of Indochinese studies. Similar institutions existed elsewhere in Europe, often playing a major role in promotion of colonialism: in Belgium, a Société d'Études Coloniales (1894) and Institut Royal Colonial Belge (1928), in Spain, the Sociedad Geográfica de Madrid (1876) and much later the Instituto de Estudios Africanos (1945).[5]

Museums constitute another important category of learned institutions. India was again one of the first sites for European-style museums, set up in Calcutta (1814), Madras (1851) and Bombay (1872), and culminating in the grand Prince of Wales Museum opened in Bombay in 1905. Elite Indians shared enthusiasm for museums. The City Palace Museum, opened in Jaipur in 1880, represented a joint project by the Maharaja of Jaipur and the British chief engineer and chief surgeon of the princely state, and in the 1890s, the Maharaja of Baroda set up a museum in his capital. In Singapore, the Raffles Library and Museum opened in 1849, and in Colombo, Ceylon, a museum opened in 1877. A large museum built by the Dutch in Batavia (Jakarta) in 1868 consolidated and expanded collections dating back almost a century. The French opened an equally impressive museum in Phnom Penh in 1920. The first director was George Groslier (1887–1945), an outstanding archaeologist, and coincidentally the first Frenchman born in Cambodia. Elsewhere in Southeast Asia, the French constructed museums in Hanoi, Saigon (now Ho Chi Minh City), Hué, and Tourane (Da Nang) in Vietnam, and in Vientiane, Laos.[6]

European colonial governments built around a hundred museums in sub-Saharan Africa.[7] Early ones in the British colonies were located in Salisbury, Rhodesia (now Harare, Zimbabwe) (1903) and Kampala, Uganda (1908). The French opened a museum in Senegal in 1863, though it lasted for only a few years; the longer-lived Institut Français d'Afrique Noire, established in 1936 in Senegal's new capital of Dakar, maintained its own museum and sponsored ones in other French west African colonies. The 1930s saw a spate of museum building: by the Portuguese in Dundo (1936) and Luanda (1938) in Angola, the British in Khartoum, Sudan (1932), Livingstone, Northern Rhodesia (now Zambia) (1934) and then Dar es-Salaam, Tanganyika (now Tanzania) (1940). The Belgians in the same decade built a museum in Léopoldville (Kinshasa) in the Congo, as did the Italians in Somalia. Indeed, Spanish Guinea remained the only African colony without a museum by the end of the colonial period.

The earliest museum collections in sub-Saharan Africa centred on natural history, and gradually extended to ethnography. In the colonies, as in Europe, preserved plants and taxidermied specimens of animals, arranged in vitrines or in dioramas representing natural environments, were popular. Collections of rocks, minerals and gemstones highlighted sub-soil resources with commercial interest for Europeans. Indigenous weaponry – spears, arrows and other arms neatly arranged in panoplies pointedly called 'trophies' – regularly featured. Museum-goers could see craftwork, such as finely woven textiles and intricate jewellery. Curators, like ethnographers, paid particular attention to 'traditional' and ordinary objects of everyday life, especially those considered representative of particular regional or cultural groups, though they showed less interest in modern or urban *objets d'art*. This selection tended to 'freeze' African and other colonized societies in a pre-modern and rural context and to privilege 'authenticity'. Only tardily were historical sections added to museums, in line with persistent European notions that Africa had no real history before the arrival of the Europeans. Displays frequently stressed perceived European achievements in colonization, as with military museums opened in Kumasi, Ghana and Lourenço Marques (now Maputo), Mozambique, in the 1930s to boast of British and Portuguese conquests. In the settler colony of Southern Rhodesia, the focus was on white 'pioneers' (and indigenous people were admitted to the museum, in limited numbers, on only one day a week).

The objectives of museums were subsumed to European science, scholarship and collecting, and, importantly, to colonizers' political intentions. These were explicitly avowed, for example, in a speech by the director of education in Senegal at the opening of Dakar's museum in 1936: 'Science is the auxiliary of colonisation. Science is necessary for Africa . . . in order for France to know Africa not for its [geographical] accidents and incidents (*accidents et incidents*)' – by which he simply meant the varied landscapes and historical developments – 'but for its resources and its human reality. This is necessary so that Africa can reveal itself to itself, so that the educated natives [can] acquire a greater knowledge of their countries, [and] the love of their lands, which will make them ever more our collaborators and our associates.'[8] The text, with the intimation that science is European, that Europeans needed to teach Africans about their own cultures and that trained Africans would be of use to the French, is blatant. That being said, colonial museum directors and curators, such as Groslier in Phnom Penh and Théodore Monod (1902–2000), director of the Institut Français d'Afrique Noire and a renowned naturalist and anthropologist, did much, along with their local associates, for the conservation of heritage items and study of indigenous culture. The fact that colonial museums founded by Europeans and learned academies such as the Asiatic Society branches still operate in now independent countries remains part of the European legacy.

Museums in Europe reflected rising interest in the colonial world, and such places as Japan and China, with burgeoning collections from overseas. In recent years, many questions have been raised about the provenance of objects – a considerable number taken as war booty, stolen, purchased for derisory sums or obtained through dubious intermediaries, though others were acquired in good faith and through fair transactions.[9] Private donors often included military officers, administrators and settlers directly implicated in colonial expansion and rule. There are increasingly louder demands for restitution of objects to the societies that created them, demands met with mixed responses by museum boards and governments. Since countless European museums possess objects from former colonies (including in those countries that claimed no colonies), the issue is an especially complex one involving art history, museography, law, politics and moral considerations. Certain it is that objects from former colonies are legion in institutions such as the British Museum,[10] and especially in ones intentionally set up as repositories and displays of objects in a colonialist perspective: the Imperial Institute in London (whose collections have been integrated into the Victoria and Albert Museum), the Tropenmuseum (as it is currently called) in Amsterdam and the former Colonial Museum in Paris (whose collection is largely now in the Musée du Quai Branly), as well as many smaller public and private museums. In colonial-era establishments, a quest for knowledge and a quest for political and economic advantage were not mutually exclusive, as has been shown in Alice Conklin's study of the evolution of ethnographic collections (and the way in which they were displayed) in Paris in the Musée d'Ethnographie du Trocadéro opened in 1878, and its successor, the Musée de l'Homme, in 1937 – the forebears of today's Musée du Quai Branly, which dates from 2006.

Archaeology and European fascination for 'ruins'

Many colonial and European museums housed sculptures and other artefacts from the ancient civilizations of Africa, Asia and Latin America. Europeans, especially from the eighteenth century onwards, had a near obsession with the ruins of ancient cultures.

Study of classical Greek and Latin provided the foundation of elite education, and visits to sites in Italy and other parts of the Mediterranean were a 'must' for grand tours by young gentlemen and ladies. The 'pleasure of ruins' provided a link with generations past, a picturesque scenario for literary and philosophical musings, and a cautionary reminder about the passage of time and the 'rise and fall' of empires – a view encapsulated in Percy Bysshe Shelley's poem 'Ozymandias'. As poets were lyricizing, archaeologists were digging.

European expansion into northern Africa and to the north-western borders of India brought new traces of Western Antiquity into their purview: vestiges of Alexander the Great's Hellenistic empire in Afghanistan and those of the Roman Empire (and other early cultures, like that of the Phoenicians) in North Africa. The French excavated in Algeria and the Italians carried out work at Leptis Magna in Libya, one of the best preserved of all Carthaginian and Roman sites. In fact, archaeologists, and those searching for classical works to souvenir and sell, long preceded Italian colonizers in Libya. With authorization from the previous Ottoman rulers, a Frenchman had taken away 600 classical columns from 1686 to 1708, some used intact or cut into slabs and incorporated into Louis XIV's palace in Versailles. A British expedition removed more works in 1817, in part for an imaginary classical 'ruin' near Windsor Castle, although the Englishmen were dismayed to see that Libyans had sawed other columns into pieces to use as millstones.

An estimated twenty-eight 'free-lance' archaeological expeditions took Europeans and Americans to Cyrenaica, part of what is today Libya, between 1706 and 1911. After the 1911 invasion of Libya, Italians, proud of their Roman heritage, justified the conquest as restoration of European rule over North Africa. As Nancy C. Wilkie points out, they facilely credited grand ancient constructions to Europeans when, in fact, they represented the work of Romanized North Africans, such as Septimus Severus, the Libyan-born Roman emperor. Looking for building stones for roads, soldiers discovered impressive ancient mosaics, and statues such as the beautiful Aphrodite Rising from the Bath installed in a Roman museum and exhibited in the Paris Colonial Exposition of 1931. In addition to furthering research and propaganda, the Italians also explicitly wanted to use archaeological sites to bring tourists to their new colony.[11]

The Italians were similarly intrigued by the ancient Axum civilization in Ethiopia, which became an Italian colony in 1936. Mussolini's troops carried away a 24-metre tall obelisk, which dated to the fourth century CE. It was pointedly re-erected outside the Italian Ministry for Africa in Rome – a manifest way of appropriating African heritage and boasting of Italian imperial achievement. Despite many pleas for the Italians to honour a promise to return the Axum Column, it was not sent back to Ethiopia, which had regained independence in the mid-1940s, until 2005.

As they roamed around the world, Europeans came across archaeological vestiges of many ancient civilizations.[12] Perhaps the main outcome of Napoleon's brief occupation of Egypt was the birth of Egyptology as a field of enquiry in Europe and 'Egyptomania', a long-lived fascination with pharaohs, mummies and pyramids renewed by the opening of King Tutankhamun's tomb by a British archaeologist in 1922. The sites of ancient Egypt drew scholars and tourists, their passage facilitated by Britain's domination of the modern Egyptian state from the 1880s until the 1920s, and overweening Western influence there until the mid-1950s. Sub-Saharan Africa and Asia presented other marvels for exploration, study and fantasy – and ones with political value as well. Europeans, although responsible for much depredation of antique ruins and more modern cultural sites, nevertheless became concerned with their preservation. The French in Indochina, for example, in 1900 passed a law mandating certain types of conservation, and officials compiled an inventory of historic sites the following year.[13] Lord Curzon, the Oxford-educated viceroy of India, was so shocked on a visit to Rangoon by the destruction and desecration of sites in Burma that he ordered the preservation of monuments in that colony.[14]

Southeast Asia provides a good example of colonial interest in and conservation of ruins, though the word 'ruins' is not entirely appropriate given that sites from the past represented religions and cultures still thriving in Asia (unlike the Greco-Roman vestiges in North Africa). Britain ruled Java only from 1811 to 1815, having taken control of the large East Indian island after the French occupied the Netherlands during the Napoleonic Wars, but its culture riveted Sir Stamford Raffles. The lieutenant governor during the period before the East Indies were returned to the Netherlands, now better known as founder of the British colony of Singapore, Raffles was a major scholar and collector, the author of a *History of Java* that long remained authoritative, and donor of a collection of artefacts to the British Museum (an even larger collection was lost in a shipwreck). For Raffles and other visitors and scholars, the most important built features of the Javanese landscape were the *candi*, ancient temples with ornate carvings depicting Hindu and Buddhist cosmology that ranged from small shrines to the grand edifices of Prambanan and Borobudur, two of the most splendid temples in Southeast Asia. After the conversion of the Javanese to Islam, older religious buildings fell into disrepair and were overgrown with vegetation; stones were repurposed for building projects.

Descriptions and aquatint illustrations of the *candi* circulated widely in Britain, as in Raffles's book, though European designers often reworked on-site drawings by British officials and soldiers to enhance the evocative, romantic image. They offered a vision of once great civilizations fallen into decay, but the printed images, according to Sarah Tiffin, also suggested an indolent society with 'natives' lolling around while British surveyors and archaeologists busily measured and catalogued relics. Furthermore, accounts contrasted British archaeological work with the alleged neglect shown by the Dutch, who stood accused of concern only for money-making and not for the cultures and sites under their dominion. Not surprisingly, some Europeans viewed the *candi* as evidence of the 'heathenism' of early Javanese, even if they admired the technical skills and aesthetics of the creators.[15]

The Dutch did become increasingly interested in the archaeological sites of the East Indies, in particular Borobudur, a ninth-century temple of nine platforms with a central dome, and multiple stairways and corridors depicted in Figure 11.2. A monumental representation of Mount Meru, the sacred mountain at the centre of the universe, Borobudur is covered in 2,762 carved relief panels with scenes from Hindu and Buddhist

Figure 11.2 The temple at Borobudur, central Java, Indonesia, *c.* 1900-1950. © Getty Images.

cosmology, and 72 statues of the Buddha placed around the platforms. Raffles sent a Dutch engineer to cut down trees that had overgrown the site and to dig away the earth that obscured its lower levels. After the return of the Dutch to Java, the temple was completely revealed in 1835, the first photographs taken in 1872 and the first full-scale study published in 1873.

The major structural problem facing Borobudur was that the temple was unstable and in danger of collapse, seriously weakened by a thousand years of history, the incursion of the jungle and lack of care. From 1900, the Dutch initiated efforts to preserve the building and safeguard the site, beginning by cataloguing the monument's features and searching for stones and carvings scattered around the environs. The leader of the project, Theodoor Van Erp (1874–1958), developed innovative methods to stabilize the temple, later adopted at sites around the world, called anastylosis. Among other techniques, this involved the full disassembly of several levels of the temple, insertion of supports where necessary and the use of concrete to prevent cracking of the carving, then reassembly using the original building blocks and recovered ones. This necessitated lengthy and painstaking work, and restoration of Borobudur, now a World Heritage site and leading tourist destination in Indonesia, was completed long after the departure of the Dutch.

Outshining even Borobudur in the Western imaginary was Angkor Wat and neighbouring temples and other buildings in northwestern Cambodia. Angkor Wat, dating from the twelfth century, is the largest religious edifice in the world. Originally a Hindu temple, it became a Buddhist place of worship and, like Borobudur, is a figuration of the sacred mountain at the centre of the universe. It, too, is covered in extraordinary bas-relief carvings; over the temple rises a quincunx of towers. The building stands within an outer wall of 3.6 kilometres in length and a moat, part of a very complex network of water reservoirs constructed under the Khmer kings. This extraordinary system, testifying to the engineering skills of Khmer architects and engineers, provided fresh water and irrigation for the fields of between 700,000 and 900,000 people. Dozens of other temples dot a large area around the town of Siem Reap.[16]

The local Khmer people, of course, were intimately familiar with the Angkorian sites, though the region had been gradually depopulated and partially abandoned because of economic and possibly climate change. The Portuguese were perhaps the first Europeans to come upon the Angkorian sites in the late 1500s. However, the French adventurer Henri Mouhot (1826–61) claimed to have rediscovered Angkor in 1860, and his accounts popularized the temple and its precincts in Europe. Several years after his expedition, the French established a protectorate over much of Cambodia and began archaeological investigations, though not until 1907, when the French forced Siam to cede the province in which Angkor was located, did the complex come under colonial administration. In the late 1890s, the French had begun a systematic programme of study and restoration, later adopting the techniques of anastylosis; as with Borobudur, restoration was a long-lasting (and still ongoing) operation. Angkor became a key focus for the École Française d'Extrême-Orient, which also shipped Khmer sculptures to France (many now in the Musée Guimet in Paris) and institutions elsewhere. The practice of moving, and sometimes selling objects, provoked criticism. A future French minister of culture, the writer André Malraux, was briefly put under arrest in the 1930s for trying to spirit away Angkorian sculptures.

The Angkorian sites remained a centrepiece in French colonial archaeology and loomed large in their view of Asia. Pierre Loti (1850–1923), one of France's most popular writers, and an officer in the French Navy, published an account of his brief visit, *Pilgrimage to Angkor*, in 1901, one of many accounts that evoked the temples and conveyed a sense of the mystery of giant sculpted heads of King Jayavarman, intricate reliefs recounting the creation of the world and the 'churning of the ocean of milk', and the beautiful carvings of *apsaras*, heavenly female spirits. As Penny Edwards has shown, the Angkorian sites provided a 'French' archaeological patrimony that rivalled the sites in Britain's India.[17] Performances by the young female Khmer court dancers who accompanied the Cambodian king to Paris in 1906 further contributed to a 'cult' of Angkor, which was capitalized on as a tourist destination. A replica of the central temple of Angkor Wat was the highlight of the Colonial Exposition in Paris in 1931. The sites remain central to the Cambodian national narrative, and Angkor Wat features on the Cambodian flag.

In sub-Saharan Africa, archaeological interest focused on palaeontology and prehistory. Archaeology, especially in southern Africa, was also directly connected to prospecting and the search for gold and diamonds; in Angola, the leading archaeological work in prehistory took place under the auspices of a diamond-mining company. One quest of particular significance was the search for early human remains, especially with an emerging view that the 'cradle of humanity' lay in Africa. Attracting much international attention was the work of Louis Leakey (1903–72), his wife Mary (1913–96) and other members of their family at Olduvai Gorge, in eastern Africa in the British colony of Tanganyika, beginning in the 1930s (though the site had been explored by predecessors as far back as 1913). If a hunt for 'treasure' and collection of 'primitive' artefacts dominated some early African expeditions, by the 1930s, archaeological and anthropological theories were changing and research becoming more systematic and regulated, even if still inflected by colonial situations and perspectives.[18]

One African example comes from the site of Great Zimbabwe (the Shona word, meaning 'houses of stone', gave the new name for the former British colony of Southern Rhodesia). A city of as many as 20,000 residents at its height, Great Zimbabwe thrived as a centre for trade in gold, ivory and other commodities from 1200 to 1500, the extent of its contacts evidenced by the Syrian glass, and Chinese and Persian dishes found there. The site is renowned for its fortress towers, structures such as the Great Enclosure constructed of one million blocks but whose function remains unclear, and for soapstone carvings. The city, explored by a German in 1871, excited European fantasies about Ophir, the reputed source of the biblical King Solomon's hordes of gold. A procession of explorers, looters and archaeologists followed, the lines between those categories on occasion vague. The British government dispatched an official archaeologist, James Theodore Bent (1852–97), in 1891, though his muddled digs destroyed some evidence of the old Zimbabwe culture.

Four years later, the newly formed Rhodesia Ancient Ruins Company received exclusive rights, from Cecil Rhodes, to 'explore and work for treasure'. The company's pillaging of sites led the Legislative Council of Southern Rhodesia in 1902 to adopt a preservation ordinance for archaeological sites. Believing that Black Africans could not have been able to accomplish such impressive constructions, researchers hypothesized that Phoenicians or Arabs were responsible for Great Zimbabwe; some simply ignored local knowledge of the constructions and Shona history. David Randal-MacIver (1873–1945) in the first decade of the twentieth century, however, confirmed that the site did not date back to the days of King Solomon and was indeed the work of Africans, and proof of indigenous construction found confirmation with the digs of Gertrude Caton Thompson (1888–1985) in the late 1920s. Many European settlers in Rhodesia continued to contest the evidence, and the white-led and apartheid government of the later self-proclaimed independent state of Rhodesia censored publications on Great Zimbabwe from 1965 until majority rule was won in 1980. Great Zimbabwe then gained recognition as a World Heritage site.[19]

Archaeological excavations reflected scientific curiosity and enduring popular curiosity about 'lost civilizations'. Colonialism provided new terrains for exploration, and authorization and funding from colonial states, inciting competition by nations and adventurous archaeologists for 'discovery' and unveiling of sites, development of restoration techniques and heritage policies, and the use of ruins for colonial propaganda and tourist promotion. However, one must be wary about a view that stigmatizes archaeology – or any branch of knowledge – as simply subservient to the political objectives of colonialists or that judges its practitioners incapable of distancing themselves from the presuppositions underlying colonialism. Examining French archaeological work in Tunisia, for example, Clémentine Gutron explains that French interest in the North African country's sites began in 1837, more than forty years before the establishment of a French protectorate, with the formation of a society for exploration of the ancient city of Carthage. The French set up a Service des Antiquités in Tunisia in 1885, only four years after their takeover of the country, though it focused on European ruins and did not include a department of Muslim archaeology (or of Punic or prehistoric archaeology) until 1948. Colonial apologists such as the novelist Louis Bertrand (1866–1941) certainly popularized the notion of a Latin North Africa reclaimed by Europeans, but Gutron argues that European interests in ancient Roman and Punic settlements appeared perfectly understandable to many Tunisians. French settlers who wanted to expand farmland meanwhile found government prohibitions on destruction of sites galling, and unscrupulous ones were not above vandalizing and selling antiquities to tourists and dealers, but French archaeologists worked diligently to protect ancient sites. Gutron points out that archaeological research could influence politics to the benefit of local people, as when one scholar's work on agriculture convinced the French government in the 1930s to rescind a regulation aimed at sedentarization of local populations.[20] Such comments suggest that though science served as an auxiliary to colonization, it was not always a docile handmaid.

Colonial knowledge in retrospect

Archaeology provides one example of a discipline inserted into and deriving benefits from colonial rule, and there were many others. Volcanologists, for instance, learned much from studies of colonial volcanoes and eruptions, from the 1883 eruption of Krakatoa in the Sunda Strait of the Dutch East Indies to that of Mont Pelée, which destroyed the city of Saint-Pierre, killing 30,000 people on the French island of Martinique in 1902. Specialists in maritime sciences studied ocean currents, coral reefs and sea life. Meteorologists studied climates and monitored weather from colonial observatories. Lexicographers compiled dictionaries of non-European languages, allowing further reading of non-Western manuscripts and providing documentation for comparative linguistics. Jurists and specialists in administrative law learned about indigenous law codes and bureaucracies, such as the mandarin system in China and chieftainships in Africa and Oceania. Urbanists examined Asian cities older and larger than many in Europe, and specialists in agriculture chronicled different farming techniques. The examples could be multiplied, and in each case the role of local scholars, 'native informers' and guides, and written and oral documentation produced by those whose countries had been colonized proved crucial, if not always formally acknowledged, to developing European understanding.

The work of European archaeologists, anthropologists and other social scientists operating under colonial regimes, paradoxically, also provoked questioning of notions of European superiority by revealing the existence of ancient and modern cultures with complex administrative systems, trading networks and social structures. They showed the technical skills of indigenous people, so evident in buildings as ornate and sometimes grander than ones in Europe at comparable periods, the terracing of hillsides for efficient rice cultivation, and sophisticated water catchment and irrigation works. The social scientists developed greater understanding of indigenous systems of knowledge, spiritual beliefs and social organization, raising questions about arrogant and ethnocentric European views of 'native' politics, religion and morals. They pointed towards more relativistic notions of human accomplishment and valorization in Western eyes of the arts of Africa, Asia and Oceania. Evolving colonial knowledge, in short, contributed to undermining the intellectual substructure of colonialism itself.

The canon of knowledge accumulated during the colonial era, as exemplified in the studies of Marsden and Raffles, the descriptions of sites like the *candi* of Java and Great Zimbabwe, the Angkorian 'discoveries' of men such as Mouhot and the protean work of scholars associated with the Asiatic Society and the École Française d'Extrême-Orient, not surprisingly bears the marks of its time. It reveals the 'mindset' of individuals and institutions, and the state of research of a particular age: scientific techniques, the theories that held credence, and the political imperatives under which scholars worked, either voluntarily or involuntarily. Post-colonial scholarship has rightly interrogated and critiqued ethnocentric bias, racialized suppositions and lingering assumptions about the superiority of European science and learning. New methods and disciplines have discredited fields once accepted as genuine science – craniometry and phrenology, for instance, as well as simplistic stadial theories of human social development. Over the last generation indigenous knowledge has been re-evaluated and indigenous guardians of knowledge and scholars have become more widely recognized, consulted and honoured. No doubt in future, scholarship will further contextualize and question colonial-era perspectives, and those of the post-colonial world of today as well.

CHAPTER 12
COLONIALISM AND THE SOUL

Colonial encounters touched the bodies and minds of the Europeans and the people who fell under their influence and rule, but it also, intentionally, was an encounter of 'souls'. There was a growing number of free-thinkers, agnostics and atheists in Europe and elsewhere from the 1700s onwards, and especially from the late 1800s when science and new philosophies had brought into question the precepts of traditional religions. However, most of those involved in colonialism, both as colonizers and as colonized, probably held nominal or deeply felt religious or spiritual beliefs and had some formal affiliation with religious institutions. Disseminating Christianity – 'propagating the faith' or 'spreading the Gospel', as believers said – was an avowed mission of many who promoted and took part in Western expansion. Non-Western religions counted among the 'discoveries' of European expansion, and the emergence of hybrid systems of belief forms part of the colonial-era mixing and mingling of cultures. Religion, moreover, became a key plank in the platform of anti-colonialist and nationalist movements seeking independence and the revival or preservation of Hinduism, Islam and other faiths undermined or disparaged by rulers in the colonial period.

The missionary position

For Christians, evangelization of the 'heathen' was a biblical injunction, as the Christian scriptures hold that their god is the only true god, their faith is universal and their deity mandates conversion of those who have not yet 'seen the light' represented by Jesus Christ. A proclaimed mission of Spanish and Portuguese conquistadors in the Americas was to introduce Catholicism, action roundly endorsed by the pope, and a cross and a flag were literally planted on foreign soil together when Iberians landed on shores unknown to them.

In the Americas and elsewhere, religious doctrines, symbols and practices appeared mysterious to those of different creeds. Christians railed against local 'idols' and 'idolatry', but their crucifixes, chalices, holy medals and saints' relics objectively differed little from the paraphernalia of religions that the missionaries damned. Christians condemned blood sacrifices, but many held that the Eucharistic rite transformed bread and water into the flesh and blood of a god for consumption by the faithful. Christianity, like other religions, had its clerics with special powers, sacred scriptures and places of worship, as well as taboos and prohibitions.

Christians pursued evangelization in both peaceful and coercive ways, extending to forced conversions and the rounding up of the converted into 'reductions' in South

American settlement areas under the control of priests. The Inquisition, exported to America and Asia, authorized persecution, torture and execution of 'heretics'. New religious orders established during the Catholic Counter-Reformation, notably the Society of Jesus (the Jesuits), founded in 1540, spearheaded efforts at proselytism.[1] The Protestant Reformation had meanwhile created a cleavage in the Western church, and multiple denominations of Protestants came into being.

Each group was interested in proselytizing, with rivalry and mutual persecution by Protestants and Catholics (and between Protestant groups). The 'great awakening' in Britain in the mid-1700s, an evangelical revivalist movement among Protestants, led to the foundation of the London Missionary Society by a Welsh Congregationalist minister in 1795. It became the leading British missionary group, noteworthy for its implantation in relatively newly 'discovered' Tahiti only two years later.[2] The *philosophes* of the Enlightenment had contested traditional religious belief and the power of the clergy, and revolutionaries in France after 1789 disestablished the church, nationalized church and monastic lands (and pillaged many churches), and attempted to 'laicize' society. The end of the revolution saw partial restoration of the Catholic Church to its position in France, and inspired the rallying of Christians. The early 1800s witnessed the establishment of new Catholic missionary societies in France, which became an important source for overseas missionaries working within and beyond the French colonial empire. Among them were the Sisters of St Joseph of Cluny, founded by Sister Anne-Marie Javouhey (1779–1851) in 1807, and the Society of Mary (the Marists), set up by Father Jean-Claude Colin (1790–1875) in Lyon in 1816. Gains in Christianity overseas, they hoped, would compensate for loss of believers in Europe and even aid in the revival of Catholicism at home.

While the French played an important role in Catholic mission activities (though by no means the only ones to do so), Protestant groups in Britain, Germany, Norway, Switzerland and the United States similarly sent out pastors to Asia and Africa – the Basel Missionary Society, active from 1815, became one of the most dynamic, revealing how the Swiss, who did not acquire colonies, nonetheless maintained a presence in the colonial world.[3] In some overseas places, missionaries represented the first continuing European presence, resident well before formal takeover of colonies; in others, they followed in the wake of annexation; in still others, as in China and Korea, they worked outside formal European empires but contributed greatly to expand Western spheres of influence.[4]

Christian missionaries enjoyed little success in the Islamic world, and some other regions proved largely impenetrable to their overtures. However, in South and Central America, Christianity has proved to be one of the longest-lasting inheritances of Spanish and Portuguese colonialism. The overwhelming majority there consider themselves Catholics, even if Christianity has overlaid or blended in with pre-Christian beliefs. The Philippines, also evangelized by Spaniards, became the most Catholic country in Asia. Catholic missionaries found a foothold in Vietnam from the 1600s. Christians faced persecution in the early 1800s, but French rule later gave them a free hand, and Vietnam, where Buddhism and Confucianism predominated, eventually counted the second largest Catholic population (though far from a majority) in Southeast Asia.[5] Christianity arrived in South Asia long before it arrived in Europe, but Catholic missionaries, led by the Portuguese in Goa in the 1500s, and later Protestants gained new converts. Sub-Saharan Africa provided further numbers of new Christians, while Christianity competed with an evangelical and spreading Islam. Christianity became the dominant religion in the Caribbean (where most descendants of the enslaved are Christian) and Oceania. On balance, in many areas, the Christians had scored considerable success, yet competition among denominations continued, pressure from other faiths remained strong and non-Christian beliefs lingered and even thrived with or without formal acceptance of Christianity. The degree to which Christianity accommodated ancestral beliefs and practices, and adapted to local populations – for example, with worship services in vernacular languages – differed greatly over time, place and church.

The role of missionaries in colonialism is complex. Missionaries' priority was to preach the Christian gospel, but they also engaged in social activities, particularly education, medical care and charitable work. In some parts of the colonized world, especially in remote areas, missionaries represented the only Europeans with whom indigenous people came into regular contact, and the only ones to provide schools, medical dispensaries and assistance to the impoverished and marginalized (such as lepers). Those of lower classes or lower castes often found Christian groups more inclusive than other communities. Missionaries engaged in commercial activities as well, setting up plantations and encouraging local people to seek waged employment. They became powerful political forces, advocating for the extension of colonial rule to places where they had established a presence, and intervening in political and social questions surrounding labour, land and 'morals' legislation.

Missionaries became implicated in the dynamics of international rivalries and the transformation of local cultures. For instance, Catholic missionaries arrived in the central Pacific archipelago of Wallis and Futuna in the 1820s and soon converted the entire population. They established a theocracy over the islands, with a religiously inspired law code and a strong clerical influence in chiefly administration. For sixty years, missionaries lobbied the French government to take over the islands, though Paris only agreed to do so in the 1880s as a preventive measure, more from fears of German designs on the islands than the priests' pleas. In Tahiti, too, missionaries became involved in power politics. The Protestant London Missionary Society enjoyed support from the British government and developed an alliance with the indigenous Polynesian government. It pressured Tahitian authorities to expel several Catholic missionaries in the 1830s, a move that provided an ostensible reason for the French to intervene and establish a protectorate in 1842. In Madagascar, the British established an early missionary presence, and the most important royal family converted to Protestantism in the mid-1800s, but the island later became a French protectorate and then a full-fledged colony, to the consternation of the Protestants; the British declined to intervene.

Critics of missionary activities claimed, with considerable evidence, that priests and pastors and their auxiliaries were deploying all strategies fair and foul to indoctrinate indigenous people, reaping monetary as well as theological profits from evangelization, and working hand in hand with colonial governments to effect cultural alienation, economic exploitation and political subjection. Defenders, including authors of countless hagiographical works about missionaries and their orders, not surprisingly, saw missionary activity not only as a theologically sound and divinely countenanced initiative but also as a humanitarian undertaking to bring 'civilization' and progress to non-Christians. Most present-day historians take a nuanced view. A persuasive study of French missionary activities by J. P. Daughton, for instance, argues that their objectives always remained the biblical directive to convert non-believers, a crusade Christians wholeheartedly believed to be beneficial to those to whom they preached. The patriotic French missionaries were willing to call on the French state for aid – funding, transport for clerics on French warships, protection of missionaries and their interests – and enthusiastically promoted the French Empire. However, the relationship remained a difficult one, especially with a strong current of anticlericalism in France and the formal separation of church and state in 1905, even if that separation was not fully imposed in the colonies.[6] Similarly, in the British case, it has been argued that seeing missionaries only as agents of political or cultural imperialism is simplistic.[7]

Missionaries had a fraught relationship with other colonial groups. One French missionary in the southwest Pacific commented that there were two populations to convert in the islands – indigenous people and Europeans. Missionaries found many European settlers, planters and traders to be godless and vice-ridden, and liable to mistreat indigenous employees. Some Christian groups (especially the Society of Friends, the Quakers, in Britain) from the late 1700s had played leading roles in efforts to end slave trading and bring about abolition; Christian ideas about the equality of God's children were marshalled in the campaign, though opponents generally considered themselves no less Christian. Even after emancipation, settlers regularly pushed back against missionaries' stances regarding the working conditions and wages of labourers. By the early twentieth century, missionaries, including a growing number of indigenous priests, pastors and members of religious orders, increasingly sought to position themselves as protectors of local people against rapacious colonizers, yet later generations and some historians often judge their actions as half-hearted or condescendingly paternalistic.

For the missionaries themselves, foreign evangelization provided a true vocation, a commitment to God and a humanitarian initiative. As well, it was a career, for work as a priest or pastor, friar or nun provided an attractive and socially validated profession. It offered the promise of salvation for a missionary and his or her converts, the sociability and solidarity of a cohesive community, training and education, a modest, but regular, salary and travel. It nevertheless entailed separation from family with only infrequent returns to home countries, the rigours of life overseas and the lack of receptiveness among potential converts. If worse came to worst, missionaries might be assured the 'martyr's crown' and, in the Catholic tradition, beatified or made saints for their sacrifice. Missionary societies undertook systematic efforts to recruit new members, set up institutes for their training, collect money from parishioners and spread news of their activities in periodicals and transcripts of letters. Overseas missionary work thereby became an important part of colonial culture at home, complete with missionary museums, missionary conferences, lectures by returned missionaries and the bringing of seminarians from overseas to Europe.

Missionaries and other religious figures were heroized at home and abroad. The relics of missionary saints, such as St Francis Xavier, martyrs from Uganda, Vietnam and other places – bones, bloodied cassocks, devices with which Christians were tortured and executed, the Bibles and missals they had used – became objects of veneration. David Livingstone (1813–73), Scottish doctor and Presbyterian evangelist in sub-Saharan Africa, was arguably the most famous of British colonial heroes in the mid-1800s. A century later, Albert Schweitzer (1875–1965), similarly a physician and a noted Protestant theologian, but in French Equatorial Africa, became an honoured figure of the late colonial world. He was awarded the Nobel Peace Prize in 1952, eight years before Gabon, where he had established a hospital, gained independence. Women missionaries, like Anne-Marie Javouhey, were central to missionary work; though women were barred from entering the Catholic priesthood (and almost never became Protestant pastors), as depicted in Figure 12.1 they played active roles in the colonial world as members of religious orders, Protestant missionaries in their own right and the spouses of ministers.[8]

Churches and other religious edifices, such as colleges, schools and hospitals, sprang up everywhere in the colonial landscape – Santo Tomas university in the Philippines traces its origins back to 1611, and French Jesuits established St Joseph University in Beirut in 1875. Christian religion became a major part of colonial life for settlers, diasporic and indigenous converts who participated in worship services, processions and fêtes. Colonial governors (except, after the 1870s, in the pointedly secularist French administration) attended religious ceremonies and, like others, invoked God in speeches

MISSIONS DES PÈRES DU SAINT-ESPRIT. — BAGAMOYO. — Le Catéchisme aux petits enfants. — LL.

Figure 12.1 Nun at the Mission des Pères du Saint-Esprit, teaching the catechism, Bagamoyo, Tanganyika (Tanzania), undated postcard. © Getty Images.

and pronouncements; prayers opened daily sittings of the parliaments in British Dominions.

By the early twentieth century, Christianity in the colonies was becoming increasingly indigenized. Religious statuary and stained-glass windows might still feature blond-haired and blue-eyed depictions of Christ, the Madonna and the saints, but there was a growing number of indigenous clergy, especially in Protestant churches. The Catholic Church had long ordained indigenous priests and more recently began consecrating African and Asian bishops; in 1960, Laurean Ruganbwa (1912–97), born in the British colony of Tanganyika, became the first modern African cardinal in the Roman Catholic Church. A number of prominent indigenous political and cultural leaders, especially in sub-Saharan Africa and the Pacific islands, as well as predictably, in settler societies, received education in church schools. Fulbert Youlou (1917–72) and Walter Lini (1944–99), the leaders of independence movements in the French Congo and the New Hebrides, respectively, were a Catholic and an Anglican priest, among other nationalist figures who were devout Christians.

In the 1950s, Christians in French West Africa and French Equatorial Africa pressed Paris for reform of colonial rule, a group of Catholic intellectuals centring their pleas on enfranchisement of Africans and greater self-government. They established contacts with the Vatican, seeking greater support for African proposals, though conservatives among Catholics in France and at the Vatican opposed the initiatives in a diehard defence of French political control of the colonies. The generally gradualist and moderate Christian reformers found themselves outflanked by more radical nationalists as colonial governments proved unresponsive to their efforts, but the issue of decolonization forced the Catholic Church, and other denominations, to re-examine their place in a changing world. Christianity in parts of the late colonial and post-independence world came to be accepted as a local and indigenized religion, and there are now far more practising Christians in the former colonies than in Europe.

Europeans and Asian religions

Religion – or, more broadly, spirituality – has historically formed a pillar of individual and collective senses of identity, though boundaries between religion, philosophy, ethical systems and cultural practices are ill-defined. The three monotheistic religions 'of the book', Judaism, Christianity and Islam, spread from cradles in the Middle East around the globe, and Christianity and Islam have both claimed to be universal religions. Hinduism is the dominant religion in India, and Buddhism widespread in Asia, but both have travelled elsewhere with diasporic communities and, especially in the case of Buddhism, new adherents. Confucianism, a code of morals and ethics that originated in China, spread in varying degrees to Japan, Korea, Vietnam and elsewhere in Asia, where it structured government and social relations. Europeans 'discovered' these spiritual systems, and other more localized ones, in their centuries of encounters around the world. They viewed non-Christian religions with a mixture of fascination and disapprobation, though occasionally with admiration and empathy, as they could not but stand in awe at the architecture and decoration of temples and mosques. Religious and spiritual beliefs and practices in Africa, Oceania and parts of Asia, especially when there were no written scriptures or places of worship that resembled churches, temples or mosques, however, were often lumped together by Westerners as 'animist', demeaned as mere 'superstition' and misunderstood as 'ancestor worship' or 'devil worship'; their leaders were 'witch doctors' and 'shamans', and their sacred objects 'idols' and 'fetishes'. While Europeans initially comprehended little about the unfamiliar beliefs and rites, deciphering religions became a major project for ethnographers, anthropologists and specialists in religious studies, art and architecture; the academic study of 'comparative religions' emerged in force in the nineteenth century, closely connected to linguistic and archaeological research, and linked in with colonialism.

Islam had long commanded particular attention because of the proximity of Muslim societies to Europe and conflicts between Christianity and Islam that reached back to the Middle Ages and the Crusades. European misunderstanding and fantasies about the Islam of North Africa, the Middle East and Muslim countries further east became an integral part of what Edward Said famously critiqued as Orientalism, in which suspicion of religion, stereotypes of cultures and political rivalries were used to justify racism and Western expansion. Other scholars, however, have disputed Said's overarching conclusion, underlining the multiple currents among and sometimes genuine interest of Western scholars in Islam and, for many, respectful portrayal of Muslim figures and Islamic customs by 'Orientalist' writers and artists (before that word acquired the negative connotation it gained with Said's pioneering work). Islam was the dominant religion in the Dutch East Indies, the British Malay states, French and Italian North Africa, the mandated territories devised from the old Ottoman Empire and the Gulf States that were British protectorates; it was widespread throughout South Asia and sub-Saharan Africa (as well as central Asia and parts of China). Colonial authorities tried to manipulate Islam to suit their objectives through collaboration with religious authorities and indigenous leaders. Coercion was used against resistance or subversion, as seen in French and Spanish wars against Muslims in North Africa, from Abd el-Kader in the nineteenth century to Abd el-Krim in the twentieth, British attacks on the Mahdi (leader of a Muslim movement in the Sudan) and the Dutch wars in Aceh (on Sumatra), as well as later independence struggles. Though some Muslims accommodated European overlordship, Islam became a powerful platform for anti-colonialists.[9]

The British, as the major colonial power in South Asia, were especially concerned with Indian religions. Muslims were numerous in India, and had ruled much of the subcontinent under the Mughal Empire. Many of the vassal princely states under the British were Muslim-dominated, and the British usually found Islam in India a less militant and rigorous tradition than in the Middle East. The majority of Indians were polytheistic rather than monotheistic, and subscribed to a very diverse set of beliefs, practices and groups that made up Hinduism – indeed, British writing and policies helped to categorize these together, rather misleadingly, into a unitary and neatly bounded religion.[10] That interest was scholarly and cultural, symbolized by the translation into English in 1785, by Charles Wilkins (with an introduction by the British governor general of India), of the *Bhagavad-Gita,* a long classic verse text in Sanskrit that forms part of a great Indian saga, the *Mahabharata.* There was much popular fantasizing about Indian gods – the dancing Shiva, the elephant-headed Ganesh – but, not surprisingly, Christian disapproval of a religion with thousands or even millions of gods for worship. There were expressions of horror at practices such as *sati* (the self-sacrifice of widows), discomfort with the practice of cremation of the dead on the banks of the holy Ganges, and obsessively voyeuristic, but negative, reactions to some penitential rites. Caste, part of Hindu social structures, evoked criticism, but survived under colonialism. As with Islam, scholarship, popular understanding or misunderstanding, political objectives and missionary perspectives combined with colonialism in complicated and ambivalent attitudes towards Indian religions.

India was home to other religions in addition to Islam and Hinduism. The practitioners of Zoroastrianism, the Parsis, formed a numerically small community, and their religion, centred on ideas about light and darkness and a veneration of fire, remained mysterious to Europeans; Westerners also had a rather morbid curiosity about the Parsi practice of leaving corpses on 'Towers of Silence' to be excarnated by birds of prey. The Parsis occupied a particular niche in colonial India, often considered as supporters of the British, though in fact there were strong Parsi supporters of Indian nationalism as well. Parsis formed a particularly prominent group in Bombay, where the Tata, Jejeebhoy and Petit families formed an elite in local and international trade and cotton manufacturing. Jamsetjee Jejeebhoy (1783–1859) amassed a huge fortune from cotton production and the opium trade with China, and became one of the very few Indians to be made both a knight and, even more unusually, a baronet by the British in recognition of commercial achievements and philanthropic contributions. Jejeebhoy financed a causeway, a hospital and a waterworks, endowed a charitable foundation, provided funding for a museum and made large donations for famine and fire relief in India, Persia, France and Ireland.

Sikhism was yet another Indian religion, particularly important in the Punjab. The Sikhs, often distinguished in appearance by the practice of men growing a beard and wearing a turban, practice a religion that emerged in the fifteenth century CE. For British colonials, the Sikhs formed a martial race of tall, physically strong and indefatigably brave men. After fighting the Punjabis, deposing their maharaja and annexing his kingdom in the 1840s, the British viewed Punjabis as perhaps the valuable recruits to the colonial army and police forces in South Asia, and Sikhs were posted overseas as well. Sikhs, like others from South Asia, also became a diasporic group with migration to British territories such as Singapore and Canada.[11]

Another religion with a complicated intersection with colonialism is Judaism (yet there were only relatively small Jewish communities in India). Jews have for millennia been an important presence in Europe, though often victims of discrimination, persecution and genocide, from their expulsion from Spain in 1492 (the year of Columbus' first voyage to the Americas) to the Holocaust of the 1940s. Substantial Jewish populations lived in or migrated to areas colonized by Europeans, notably in Palestine and other parts of the Ottoman Empire in the Middle East, and in North Africa. Jews accompanied other Europeans overseas – the first synagogue in continuous use in the Americas was founded on the Dutch Caribbean island of Curaçao in 1651, there was at least one Jew in the 'First Fleet' of migrants to Australia in 1788, and the first synagogue in Bombay was built in 1796. Colonizers' and settlers' attitudes towards Jews varied. In 1870, by the Crémieux decree, the French made the Jews of Algeria full-fledged French citizens in a move to increase the number of French nationals in a settler colony where the majority of people were Muslims. Yet, in the late 1890s, the Dreyfus crisis divided France when a Jewish army officer was accused and convicted (wrongly) of having spied for the Germans, leading to a rash of anti-Semitic propaganda and anti-Jewish violence, not only in France but also in Algeria. Four decades later, when much of France was occupied by Germany during the Second World War, the collaborationist regime of Marshal Philippe Pétain extended anti-Semitic laws to the French colonies, and the Jews of North Africa again becoming a target there and in several other colonies. However, many Jews in Algeria, Morocco and Tunisia, as well as British-dominated Egypt, became pillars of the colonial establishment, important in business, administration and cultural life.

These very brief comments on Judaism, Islam and several of the other religions of India give some idea of the history of cultural, social and political encounters between largely Christian Europeans and those of other faiths, attitudes about different creeds, and the complex connections between colonialism and spirituality in the age of empire. Though much more could be said about the dynamics of each of these relationships, Buddhism provides a case study for more detailed consideration.

A case study: Europe and Buddhism in the colonial age

Buddhism, though known in the West since Antiquity, nevertheless long remained an enigma in Europe. Through the eighteenth century, Europeans wondered if the Buddha was a god, a human or even a devil; if a man, they puzzled whether he came from South Asia, Southeast Asia or perhaps Egypt. They asked whether Buddhism was a religion or a philosophy, and mused on the significance of temples, statues, sacred texts and rites. Only in the early decades of the nineteenth century, with growing expertise in the ancient Asian languages of Sanskrit and Pali, and the arrival of Buddhist texts in Europe, did scholars begin to develop a more thorough understanding of Buddhism and the historical Gautama Buddha, who lived in northern India in the sixth to fifth (or fifth to fourth) centuries BCE.

A signal moment came in the 1830s when a young French scholar, Eugène Burnouf (1801–52), wrote to Brian Houghton Hodgson (1800–94) in Nepal, asking him to send copies of Buddhist manuscripts to Paris. Houghton, who came from an impoverished Derbyshire family, was educated at the East India Company's college, Haileybury, and went to India in its employ while still a teenager. Because of health problems, he ended up in the foothills of the Himalayas, where, like many Company employees, he managed to carry out his duties and still was able to pursue personal scholarly interests – he became an accomplished ornithologist. Furthermore, Houghton developed an interest in Buddhism and the Sanskrit texts he came upon. The works he sent to Burnouf – a Parisian with a protean knowledge of Western and Eastern languages – became the basis for the Frenchman's monumental *Introduction à l'histoire du bouddhisme indien*, published in 1844, and a translation of the key Buddhist Lotus Sutra, complete with a 647-page introduction, that appeared in the year of his death. Donald S. Lopez, Jr. states that Burnouf's work for the first time presented a largely accurate picture of Buddhist beliefs to Europeans, though his perspective, since he never journeyed to Asia, was founded on written texts rather than on vernacular and contemporary practice, and was inflected by his secularism.[12]

Through the work of Burnouf and a cohort of British, French and other European scholars, as well as nineteenth-century missionaries in India, Europeans became increasingly familiar with the basic tenets of Buddhism. To the most censorious Christian writers of the time, especially some strict Protestants, Buddhism appeared a very dangerous system of belief, especially since it did not posit the existence of a god (at least as imagined by Christians) and had no real concept of sin. To the most blinkered, it seemed atheism embroidered with tall tales about the lives of the Buddha, idolatrous and incomprehensible rites, an odd belief in reincarnation, a hidebound monastic order and puzzling differences between Theravada, Mahayana and other traditions. They might concede grudging admiration for the ethical code of Buddhism, which stresses human compassion and in principle prohibits the taking of life, and admiration for Buddhist architecture and artworks, but in their mind the creed could only be the enemy of the 'true' faith. Even when Buddhism was painted in dark colours, it continued to cast an appeal over Westerners, especially in its Tibetan form – part of European curiosity about the mysterious Himalayan realm of the Dalai Lama.

Buddhism and other 'Eastern religions' nevertheless attracted those in the West searching for an alternative spirituality to Christianity, including members of the Theosophy movement. The Russian-born mystic Helena Blavatsky (1831–91), who had been involved in spiritualism (belief in the possibility of communicating with the dead through séances), founded Theosophy in 1875 in the United States, and the movement, claiming to have discovered the secrets of ancient wisdom in an ill-defined 'East', soon spread to Europe. Blavatsky and the Theosophists liberally borrowed ideas from various systems of belief, including those of ancient Egypt, but they became more closely associated with Buddhism after setting up headquarters in India in 1880 (though Hinduism and other faiths had largely displaced Buddhism in India). She and Henry Steel Olcott (1832–1907), another Theosophist leader, also went to Ceylon, where they formally converted to Buddhism, and Olcott worked as principal of a Buddhist school. In the last decades of the century, there developed an important reform movement in Buddhism in Ceylon, where it is the dominant faith of the Sinhalese, with which the Theosophists became involved. The movement, the most notable proponent of which was Angarika Dharmapala (1864–1933), sought to purify and revivify Buddhism and to establish closer links between Ceylonese Buddhists and those in Burma and Siam.

Angarika played an important role in explaining Buddhism to foreigners through his writings and travels in Asia, North America and Europe.

Meanwhile, Buddhism established a niche as a subject of study and inspiration for literature in Europe even among non-converts. Sir Edwin Arnold's *The Light of Asia* (1879), a book-length poem about the Buddha, became an international bestseller, and Victorian novelists such as H. Rider Haggard and Rudyard Kipling wove Buddhist themes into their fiction. A Pali Text Society was set up in Oxford in 1881, with later chairs of Sanskrit and Pali in several European universities; a long list of scholarly works on Buddhism appeared in the late nineteenth century.[13]

The British had long recognized the central role of Buddhism in places such as Ceylon. There, and in Burma, and in the northernmost reaches of India, colonial officials treated the Buddhist establishment with care, despite the missionaries' disapprobation. The Theosophists continued activities, attracting converts to their esoteric blend of beliefs in the West and sparking further interest in Asia, and also became linked with a Hindu reform society. Many Theosophists became supporters of Indian freedom from British rule, religious beliefs and commitment to India manifestly not separate from their political stances.

A particularly interesting figure among them was Annie Besant (1847–1933). Born into a prosperous London family and educated at Birkbeck College, she married an Anglican clergyman, but left both him and her faith. She became drawn to radical causes, including Home Rule for Ireland, trade unionism, socialism and women's emancipation, as well as Theosophy after she read one of Blavatsky's publications. Besant represented Theosophy at a World Parliament of Religions in Chicago in 1893, and met Olcott and associated with his school in Ceylon. She was elected president of the Theosophical Society in 1907, participated in the foundation of the Home Rule League for India and set up the Central Hindu School in Benares ((Varanasi). In 1917, she was arrested by the British in India for taking part in political protests; Gandhi, Nehru and the Muslim League spoke in her favour, and she was freed from detention. Besant continued to promote 'Eastern' religion. Her protégé and adopted son, Jiddhu Krishnamurti (1895–1986), a handsome young Indian, was proclaimed a 'World Teacher' and head of the esoteric Order of the Star of the East, set up in 1911; he became an international celebrity as he travelled widely in Europe and America from the 1920s to the 1940s, though eventually disavowing the order established around him. Besant, having joined the Indian National Congress, served for a year as its president and championed the campaign for Indian independence. However, she died fourteen years before that was achieved and was cremated in India. Religious interests, social activism and politics had melded in Besant's remarkable life, work and the more than thirty books that she published.[14]

The French encountered Buddhism in Vietnam, where Buddhist, Daoist and Confucian beliefs intermingled, and in Cambodia and Laos. Engravings such as the pagoda depicted in Figure 12.2 were related to French expeditions along the Mekong in the 1860s. In Cambodia and Laos there existed especially strong links between the Buddhist monastic community (*sangha*) and local dynasties, with Buddhist kings revered as semi-divine figures. In Cambodia, in particular, the French made efforts

Figure 12.2 Buddhist temple in Luang Prabang, Laos, engraving of drawing by Louis Delaporte (1842-1925), 1867. © Getty Images.

to strengthen the monastic community and Buddhism as a buttress for their colonial authority.[15] Back in France, scholars carried on the study of Buddhism and other Asian religions pioneered by Burnouf, and in 1879, the French government commissioned a wealthy industrialist, Émile Guimet (1836–1918), to travel around Asia studying local religions. On his return, Guimet established a museum of Asian art in his hometown of Lyon. The museum moved to Paris in 1889 (where it is now the French National Museum of Asian Arts), and became a centre for exhibitions, research and lectures by visiting Buddhist clerics, yet another example of the intertwining of religious, artistic and colonial (or anti-colonial) interests in the age of empire.

Religion and decolonization

Christianity underpinned Western colonialism, and missionaries accompanied colonizers wherever they went. Not surprisingly, some nationalist and independence movements reacted against the influence of Christianity as they sought to valorize indigenous belief systems and restore local religions to the position they had enjoyed before the arrival of Christianity (though most did not seek to ban Christianity). In many colonies, the existence of multiple religions created the grounds for sectarian conflict about which should have primacy, whether future independent states ought to be secular or have established religions, and what should be the role of religious beliefs in public and private life.

European colonial authorities had made efforts to regulate non-Western religions, galvanize support among clerics and religious elites, and provide support for temples and mosques. They proclaimed freedom of religion, while remaining suspicious about religious movements, schools and publications that did not endorse colonial rule or threatened to subvert it. Colonizers sometimes played religious groups off against each other, or tried to gain the allegiance of particular faith groups. They mistakenly often saw missionaries and Christians as unwaveringly loyal auxiliaries. Their initiatives at 'managing' religion enjoyed variable success, and the cleavages and alliances between religion, on the one hand, and colonialism and anti-colonialism, on the other, are not clear-cut.

In the Islamic world, in particular, religion became a powerful basis for nationalism, whether in promotion of theocratic regimes or secularist ones. Some colonized Muslims primarily wanted greater recognition for their religion and its practices, while others promoted establishment of Islam as the official religion in an independent state and the adoption of a *shari'a* code of law. Islam served, too, as a common bond in pan-Arabic movements and in pan-Islamic movements reaching from Africa through the Middle East to Southeast Asia (and China). On the Indian subcontinent, the desire of Muslims, led by Muhammad Ali Jinnah (1876–1948), to form a separate state, in fear that their interests would be compromised in a Hindu-dominated single state that would emerge in South Asia with British withdrawal, led to the partition of the subcontinent in 1947. Mohandas Gandhi (1869–1948) was the world's most famous Hindu and most celebrated figure in the struggle for the independence of India, and his ideals were profoundly influenced by Hindu religion, a lifelong study of Indian scriptures and his practice of prayer, abstinence and simple living.[16] Religion similarly imbued the ideas of nationalists of other faiths.

Colonial Christianity produced its share of nationalists, several of whom have been mentioned, as well as those who led the British settler colonies of Canada, Australia, New Zealand and South Africa to self-government and (in the case of Canada, Australia and South Africa) federation in the late 1800s and early 1900s. Church schools and seminaries around the empires educated new elites among the colonized and, along with Christian precepts, disseminated knowledge of nationalism, parliamentarianism and sovereignty. The principles and language of biblical Christianity provided reference points for nationalists who, in some cases, compared themselves to ancient Hebrews seeking emancipation from the Egyptian pharaohs or disciples guided by the teachings of Jesus Christ.[17]

The colonial history of religion, and the encounters between spiritualities in the colonial age, thus is not a simple one. Non-Western religions such as Islam could serve as shields against colonialism and provide a spearhead for nationalism, but the Christianity brought by Western missionaries could also offer ideals, strategies and political leaders for nationalist movements. Indigenous people might hold true to ancestral religious traditions, promote reform movements within those faiths or repudiate them fully, as with those who placed their faith in Marxist 'historical materialism' or, more rarely, admitted to being agnostics or atheists. Missionaries might work as collaborators in colonialism, but could position themselves as its critics. Westerners interested in 'Eastern' regions, like Besant, promoted independence, but not all were so sympathetic or activist. Tensions between religious groups and sectarian communities festered and occasionally exploded under colonial rule and afterwards. The proliferation of syncretic religions – including Theosophy, and ones that emerged in the colonies, such as Caodaism in Vietnam (which venerates the Buddha, Jesus, Confucius, Mohammed and also Joan of Arc and Victor Hugo) – challenged orthodoxies and became bound up with politics. The ideas of secularization and the principle of the separation of religion and the state provided further challenges to both colonial and pre-colonial spiritual traditions.

As Western Christianity was taken to colonized countries, so were non-Western religions, albeit more gradually, brought to Europe through scholarship, museum collections, artistic inspiration and popular stereotypes, Western converts, movements such as Theosophy and more generalized cultural influence.[18] Migration brought those of non-Christian faiths to Europe in greater numbers than ever before, though Islam had a long history as a religion in the Balkans and as a dominant presence in southern Spain until the 1500s; some sort of institutionalized religious life for Muslims had existed in other European countries since at least the early 1800s, in the case of France partly with Muslims who arrived in the wake of Napoleon's Egyptian campaign.[19] In Britain, the first purpose-built mosque opened in Woking, in suburban London, in 1889, construction funded by the Begum of Bhopal. In the 1920s, a mosque, partly funded by the sultan of Morocco, was built in Paris in recognition of the service of Muslim soldiers in the Great War. Yet despite the Netherlands' centuries-old links with the largely Muslim East Indies, the first dedicated mosque there opened only in 1947. Since the 1950s, as immigration from outside Europe accelerated – including from the former and remaining European colonies – the presence of different religions has become more manifest. Practitioners of non-Christian religions have frequently faced antipathy and discrimination because of their faiths, yet Christianity has become ever less a religion of practising Europeans. Religious conflict, intermixed with ethnic, regional and political issues, continues to erupt around the globe, and religion remains a prime symbol of identity for many of the world's people.

CHAPTER 13
REPRESENTATIONS OF COLONIALISM

Consider three paintings by artists from colonized Southeast Asia.[1] In 1857, Raden Saleh, who came from the Netherlands East Indies, painted a depiction of the capture of the Javanese *Pangeran* (Prince) Diponegoro by the Dutch in 1830. With a mountain and luxuriantly tropical vegetation in the background, Diponegoro stands on the veranda of the residence of General H. M. De Kock at Magelang (see Figure 13.1). A carriage awaits to take the prince on the start of his journey into exile in Sulawesi, where he would spend the rest of his life. Dutch officials and soldiers look on sternly, while Diponegoro's followers (one of whom has the features of the artist) watch with consternation and distress, and a distraught woman clings to the prince's knees. Diponegoro appears tense and angry, seeming defiant, although contemporary accounts, including his own memoir, suggested that he accepted his fate with greater resignation. Indeed, when he went to Magelang, in principle invited to negotiate the end of a five-year war against the Dutch, the prince may well have felt a premonition of duplicitous Dutch intentions to capture him.[2]

Saleh's painting can be compared to one from the early 1830s, commissioned by De Kock, from the Dutch artist Nicolaas Pieneman (1809–60). Pieneman's painting is entitled 'The Submission of Diponegoro to Lieutenant-General De Kock, 28 March 1830'; Saleh, however, gave his title 'An Historical Tableau, The Arrest of Prince Diponegoro', the words suggesting a different perspective. The Dutch artist placed Diponegoro on a lower step than De Kock and shows him and his retinue looking defeated and docile as the prince is being pointed to a carriage, while the East Indian painter put them on the same level (with De Kock on the left of the prince, considered the subordinate female position), and it looks more as if De Kock is inviting him rather than commanding him to depart. In Pieneman's rendition, the Dutch flag waves in the wind above the lieutenant governor's house; in Saleh's, there is no flag.

Diponegoro (1785–1855) was the eldest son of the Sultan of Yogyakarta, the most important indigenous ruler on the populous island of Java, head of a monarchy that was kept in place, though in a vassal position, under Dutch rule.[3] When his father died, Diponegoro was passed over as successor in favour of a younger brother, whom the Dutch considered more favourable to their interests. After that sultan died, Diponegoro was again passed over as guardian of the infant prince who acceded to the throne, and he rose in rebellion. Considering himself the legitimate sultan (and using that title), he also wished to be recognized as head of the Islamic religion on Java as part of his efforts to revivify Muslim practice, which he thought had grown slack. Diponegoro amassed an army, and for some Javanese he seemed the messianic ruler that local folklore predicted

Figure 13.1 Raden Saleh, 'The Arrest of Prince Diponegoro' (1857), Istana Negara, Jakarta, Indonesia. © Wikimedia Commons (public domain).

would appear in a time of great troubles. The war he waged represented one of the most sustained and dramatic challenges to Dutch colonial rule that had begun in Java under the United East India Company in the mid-1600s. The Dutch defeated Diponegoro's forces, but the sultanate of Yogyakarta survived – in an unusual political accommodation, the hereditary sultan of Yogyakarta remains the governor of the province in today's Republic of Indonesia. Raden Saleh's painting of the capture of the man now regarded as a national hero in Indonesia was, somewhat curiously, presented to the Dutch King Willem III in 'token of thanks for his [Saleh's] education and training as an artist during (nearly) twenty-three years in Europe'. The reigning Dutch monarch returned the picture to Indonesia in 1978, and a later sovereign, King Willem-Alexander, when visiting Indonesia in 2012, returned a *kris* that had belonged to Diponegoro – in Saleh's painting, Diponegoro stands with his hand on the *kris* tucked into his belt, a highly ornamented dagger endowed with great spiritual power and cultural significance for Malays.

The second work by an indigenous artist to be considered here was painted by U Ba Nyan and shows the harbour of Rangoon (now Yangon). Founded in the eleventh century, Rangoon fell into British hands in 1852, along with the rest of what was called Lower Burma, and remained the capital of their Burmese colony until the country's independence in 1948. The major built feature in the city, clearly visible in the painting as it dominates the skyline from the hill on which it was erected in the fourteenth century or perhaps much earlier, is the magnificent Shwedagon Pagoda. A stupa over 100 metres in height with a dome and spire covered in solid gold, it is the most sacred Buddhist site in Burma (now Myanmar), still a place of pilgrimage, worship and sociability. It shimmers brightly in the misty light in the painting, but the viewer's attention is drawn to the scene in the foreground. A number of vessels bob in the water: from a tiny rowboat probably used for fishing to larger ones with sails furled, another still sailing and several moored. Crews in Burmese dress mill about as their day's labours finish, some still unloading wares. Behind these Asian seacraft there is a hulking grey steamship, its funnel billowing smoke. The contrast between older types of boats and the imposing steamship that suggests long-distance commerce, industrial power, speed and colonial investment is manifest. U Ba Nyan's painting makes the juxtaposition of different kinds of sea-going vessels and occupations, tradition and modernity, spiritual and commercial life, 'native' versus Western technology and the evolution of what was once a small river settlement into a busy colonial port. The degree to which the painter was intentionally expressing a nationalist critique of colonialism remains unclear.[4]

'Rangoon Harbour' offers a waterside view of a colonial metropolis with a population of almost 400,000 at the beginning of the 1930s, when U Ba Nyan was working. It was a city of ethnic Bamars, those from other ethnic groups in a very diverse nation, a large number of Indian migrants and the British overlords. The harbour represented an interface of the local and colonial world, from where tropical hardwood, rice, rubies and oil were exported and where foreign goods arrived. As elsewhere, around the ports stood the piers where migrants and colonial officials disembarked, and where 'natives' sought employment as dockers, carters, seamen or employees of colonial firms. Just behind the waterfront, though not visible in U Ba Nyan's painting, was the luxurious Strand Hotel (still open for business today), the imposing office-buildings of the colonial government and businesses, a grid of avenues and a large covered market. Ports, whether in Europe or other places, provided regular themes for painters trying to capture sky and water, monuments and daily life.

The third painting comes from Vietnam and was completed almost twenty-five years after the Rangoon harbour scene. Le Thanh Duc's 'Hanoi, Night of Liberation', celebrates the end of French colonial rule in 1954. In that year, the troops of the Communist-led nationalists dealt a humiliating defeat to the French at the Battle of Dien Bien Phu, bringing an end to eight years of fighting between the Vietnamese and the French, and causing the French withdrawal from Indochina after almost a century since they had gained a toehold in the Mekong delta. Perhaps not surprisingly, no French people are visible. Vietnamese vendors gather outside their shops selling food, baskets, cooking utensils and other wares. One woman in a yellow *ao dai* (tunic and trousers) sits on a bicycle, another woman pushes a food-cart, yet another rides in a *xich lo* (pedicab). A young girl races across the tidy street, and a man in a singlet balances his small son on his shoulders. A nationalist banner hangs between buildings, and the yellow-starred red flags of independent Vietnam stand out against the night sky. Eyes are drawn to a friendly-looking young soldier, still in uniform, playing with two children and chatting to a smiling elder, whose stature and goatee make him uncannily resemble the nationalist leader Ho Chi Minh. Though people go about their work, the mood is festive, the ambiance peaceful and prosperous, relations harmonious and familial: a somewhat romanticized view of Hanoi after long years of warfare, privations, French exactions and fratricidal conflict among the Vietnamese.[5]

Paintings of independence movements were another common genre of artworks. Ho Chi Minh told Vietnamese artists, 'Culture, literature and art are also a battlefront, and you are all fighters on that front,' and Vietnamese nationalists in 1950 formed a Resistance Fine Arts College in Hanoi in opposition to the French-sponsored art school. In Ho's Vietnam, a generation of 'socialist realist' painting featured gun-bearing soldiers and peasant men and women in militant and heroic style, a contrast with the impressionistic street scenes and portraits of gentle (or eroticized) women that dominated the works of French colonial artists and Vietnamese trained by them. Elsewhere as well, indigenous painters of the time and afterwards recorded struggles to end empire and to build new societies.[6]

The three works of Raden Saleh, U Ba Nyan and Le Thanh Duc come from different periods in the history of modern colonialism – the developing imperialism of the early 1800s, the apogee of European empires in the 1930s and the decolonization of the 1950s – and from countries with varying histories and artistic cultures. The painters were indigenous men who had been trained in Western artistic traditions, and their styles, at least on first sight, look more Western than Indonesian, Burmese or Vietnamese. Raden Saleh (1807–80), after studying art in the East Indies, travelled to Europe with support from the Dutch colonial government (hence the gift of his painting of Diponegoro to the Dutch sovereign) and spent twenty-three years there. He studied in Amsterdam, travelled widely and served as a court artist to one of Germany's royal houses. He won wide acclaim in Europe and at home, to which he returned in 1852, for portraits, historical paintings, landscapes, animal studies and an especially dramatic depiction of the eruption of Mount Merapi. U Ba Nyan (1897–1945), born in a small town in south-western Burma, studied at local schools, then in Rangoon, mentored by the Burma Art Club (founded in 1913) and a resident British artist. In 1921, he went to London for four years of study at the Royal College of Art, and he spent a further two years there later in the decade; back in Burma, he became head of an art school himself. His work includes village scenes and portraits, both of distinguished Burmese and 'ordinary' compatriots. Le Thanh Duc (1925–2004) was born in Hanoi and studied in the 1940s at the École des Beaux-Arts, the fine arts college established in Hanoi by the French in 1925. He later studied in Moscow and worked as a photographer, art critic and author of works on Western and Asian art, as well as painting in oil, watercolour and gouache. The three painters highlighted here show how indigenous artists who gained access to art training in the colonies and overseas adopted Western styles, techniques and media, part of the movement that John Clark calls 'the Asian modern'.[7] Yet in individualistic ways, they expressed an autonomous local viewpoint, a patriotic stance, a type of cultural resistance to European colonialism and a response to the European portrayal of the wider world in art.

The work of such painters, and their peers in fields such as literature and other creative arts, created what has been termed 'colonial modernism', new ways of painting and writing that developed from the encounters and cultural transactions in the colonial world, drawing on influences that were both traditional and local, on the one hand, and European and avant-garde on the other. Somewhat paradoxically, colonialism stimulated a vibrant cultural life among indigenous and diasporic elites as they came into contact with currents from overseas, sometimes studied in Europe and tried to make sense of twentieth-century modernity, European modernism and the colonial situation. Using time-honoured media and artistic styles, or new ones, writing in vernacular languages or European ones, they produced a large body of work encompassing varying visions of modernity, and cultural modernism, to those of Europe. Modernism can now be appreciated as a de-centred and global movement, and one whose colonial and non-European exemplars spark ever greater interest today

Visual artists who produced paintings, sculptures, posters, cartoons and photographs, alongside writers of fiction and non-fiction, architects, designers, composers of music and film-makers, in the colonial era and since, have created a boundless quantity of works that take the colonies as their theme. Though many of them were well known in their own time, and indeed had become canonical subjects of appreciation and scholarship, the 'cultural turn' in historiography in the 1980s provided new perspectives on what are generically often called 'representations' of colonialism. It is impossible here to give anywhere near a comprehensive overview of these representations, on which there now exists an enormous academic literature, and a lengthy enumeration of works and their creators would be both tedious and necessarily incomplete. The remainder of this chapter, with a limited selection of examples, seeks to make several general points about how representations of colonialism permeated European culture, how they not only reflected but also played a key role in developing European ideas about empire (and policies) and how indigenous artists, writers and other cultural figures provided their own versions of imperialism and life under the colonizers.

Colonialism in European culture

No visitor to a museum or picture gallery in Europe can be blind to the way that the non-Western world offered sustained inspiration for European visual artists. Some of these institutions dedicate particular spaces to art of the colonies, and major exhibitions are regularly held, but even in obscure works and little known collections the colonies are present if one looks closely.[8] There are naturalists' and scientists' drawings of specimens of flora and fauna, romantic landscapes of the mountains, deserts and seas that appeared so sublime to European eyes, works that celebrate battles and the heroes of conquest, portraits of colonial luminaries, depictions of 'typical' people and scenes of everyday indigenous life among many other views. Paul Gauguin's (1848–1903) *fin de siècle* paintings of Polynesia are particularly well known and easily recognizable. Although the name of Thomas Jones Barker (1815–82) is now not well known, his painting of Queen Victoria, elegantly dressed in crinolines and pearls, presenting a Bible to a kneeling African, who looks no less elegant with a leopard skin over his shoulder and a bird plume in his turban, has often been reproduced; the title of the *c.* 1863–4 painting, 'The Secret of England's Greatness', remains powerful – though no doubt read with a different sentiment in the mid-1800s and the early 2000s.

Colonial themes were immensely popular for European artists, from those who spent much time travelling around the colonial world to those who never left their studios in Paris, London or another European capital. Works range from the grandiose to the intimate, the accomplished to the amateur, but all testify to the attraction, the seduction, of foreign places, including those colonized by Europeans and those which remained independent countries. Each step made by Europeans into the wider world – early encounters with the Islamic world and the 'Far East', the 'discovery' of the Americas in the 1500s and Oceania in the 1700s, the 'opening' of Japan in the mid-1800s, advances into the interior of the Asian, African and Australian continents – opened up new horizons for artists. Even when the colonies are not the ostensible theme of a work, imperial connections can often be glimpsed: an African servant in the background, Chinese porcelain on tables and Asian fabrics as the stuff of dress and decor, the tea, coffee and tobacco being consumed, the plants in a conservatory and the animals in a menagerie, a design motif borrowed from abroad.[9] Look carefully, and the foreign appears everywhere among the familiar; think closely, and it is possible to reflect on how the dynamics of colonialism affected European visual culture and European life in general.[10]

Similarly, a reader in a library or a bookshop cannot but be overwhelmed by the volume of creative literature with colonial themes, onwards from the ancient Greek authors writing about voyages in the Mediterranean and the implantation of settlements around its shores. Many of these works hold the status of national literary treasures, such as Luís Vaz de Camões' book-length verse saga, *The Lusiads*, published in 1572, a paean to Portuguese exploration, warfare and conquests in Africa and Asia, and Shakespeare's 'The Tempest', written around 1610, which is set on a sailing ship and a remote island. Avid readers of English literature from a later age will know such works as the novels of Joseph Conrad (1857–1924), such as *Heart of Darkness*, set in Africa, and *Lord Jim*, set in Southeast Asia, Rudyard Kipling's (1865–1936) *Kim* (all published in 1899–1900), E. M. Forster's (1879–1970) *A Passage to India* (1924) and George Orwell's (1903–50) *Burmese Days* (1934) – Conrad voyaged around Asia, Forster spent time in India and Egypt, and Orwell was a British civil servant in Burma, though all became critical of colonialism, and even Kipling, who was born and grew up in India, took a much more nuanced view of British imperialism than is often conceded by commentators. Generations of young readers have enjoyed Robert Louis Stevenson's (1850–94) rip-roaring pirate story *Treasure Island* (1881–2), as well as Helen Bannerman's (1862–1946) *The Story of Little Black Sambo* (1899), yet her work is now branded racist and thought unacceptable for reading without severe caution. So, too, is *Tintin in the Congo* (1931), the work of the popular Belgian cartoonist Hergé (1907–83). The author significantly revised the first gung-ho colonialist version. Those tutored in French will know the works of such authors as André Gide (1869–1951) that evoke North Africa in the early 1900s or Marguerite Duras (1914–96), writing about the Indochina of the 1930s, both authors consecrated in the pantheon of great French literature. Many other authors with colonial interests were once best-sellers. Among them are H. Rider Haggard (1856–1925) who lived for a time in South Africa; John Buchan (1875–1940), a British colonial official and novelist who became governor general of Canada; and Pierre Loti (1850–1923), a French naval officer and prolific writer of fiction. They are now less read by a general audience because of what is considered an old-fashioned style, and they are rightly taken to task for their colonialist views.

Fictional writers thus celebrated and critiqued colonialism. Among the latter, views range from condemnation of particular types of exploitation and abuse to outright rejection of colonialism as a system. Several examples from Dutch literature provide evidence. *Max Havelaar*, published in 1860 by Eduard Douwes Dekker (1820–87), better known by his pen-name of Multatuli, provided a mordantly critical portrait of labour exploitation on the coffee plantations in the East Indies. Multatuli indeed worked in the colony until he left on being threatened with dismissal for protests at abuse of labourers. Also set in the East Indies, *Rubber* (1931) and *Coolie* (1932) by Madelon Lulofs (1899–1958) portray the poor conditions of workers on rubber plantations and satirize Dutch settlers. Hella S. Haasse's (1918–2011) *The Black Lake* (1948) laments the impossibility of real friendship between a Dutch and a Javanese boy because of the colonial situation; one of Haasse's later novels, *The Tea Lords* (1992), is a similarly critical portrayal of colonialism based on her long years of residence in the East Indies.

The world outside Europe provided inspiration for works in other fields as well as art and literature, for instance, late nineteenth- and early twentieth-century grand opera. Giacomo Puccini's 'Madama Butterfly' (1904) centres on a relationship between an American sea-captain and a Japanese woman who falls pregnant to him but is then abandoned, while Georges Bizet's 'The Pearl Fishers' (1863) is set in Ceylon, Giuseppe Verdi's 'Aïda' (1871) in Egypt, and Bizet's 'Djamileh' (1872) also in North Africa; the plots, if not the music, can be understood in the context of European fantasies and Europe's engagement with overseas places. Orchestral composers, too, borrowed from non-Western musical traditions and instrumentation to good effect, or tried to evoke Caribbean islands or North African casbahs in their music or lyrics.[11] There was, as well, a whole genre of colonialist popular music performed on vaudeville stages and broadcast on radio, songs about romantic nights in the tropics, ill-fated affairs between soldiers and their paramours, the rigours of life in the desert or at sea; many of the lyrics are shocking to present-day ears for the racist language and portrayals.[12] The 1920s and 1930s saw a vogue for music with an African inspiration, sometimes mediated through America, in particular, jazz. The Black American-born Josephine Baker (1906–75) was what would now be called a 'mega-star' in 'La Revue Nègre', her songs and dances – with Baker sometimes clad only in a belt of bananas – especially popular in France, where she settled to escape the racism of her homeland.

Designers and consumers much appreciated objects, patterns and motifs from overseas with vogues for *chinoiserie* (already popular in the 1700s), *japonisme* (a new trend in the late 1800s after the 'opening' of Japan), and Indian and Muslim styles. The early cinema featured many fanciful depictions of Arab sheiks, and indeed many cinema buildings were decorated in Middle Eastern style. Adventures and romances set in Africa, Asia and the islands – the 1918 film *Tarzan of the Apes*, often reprised afterwards, not the least of them – became mainstays of the screen. Official government film boards produced countless documentaries as publicity and propaganda, and newsreels shown in cinemas as a prelude to feature films frequently covered events in the colonies – the 'Colonial Film' website provides information on over six thousand films showing life in the British colonies.[13] The advertising industry, which came into its own in the late 1800s and early 1900s, regularly used colonial tropes, often ones blatantly racist, as with publicity for soap said to be able even to wash Black children white. Images of camels and pyramids appear in adverts for tobacco, nubile West Indian women on bottles of rum, stereotypical Africans on publicity for coffee and chocolate.[14]

In short, representations of colonialism can be found in all of the arts, from images on such quotidian objects as a packet of cigarettes or tea to masterpieces of art and literature. Images created for marketing, in particular, drew on already existing and enduring tropes that were recognizable and 'legible' to the public. Writers, artists and designers recapitulated a ready repertoire of racist figures – ferocious savages, brutal potentates, lascivious women – though there were also more noble representations of grand landscapes, beautiful buildings, the arts and crafts of everyday indigenous life. Some of those who produced representations, including ethnographic artists, film-makers and those who recorded indigenous music, had documentary intentions and claimed objective, scientific observation. Others blatantly, avidly and intentionally promoted colonialism. There were also anti-colonialists, such as photographers who documented abuses and violence (including images presented at the anti-colonial exhibition in Paris in 1931 and those published in nationalist and anti-colonial journals and newspapers). During the Franco-Algerian War, for instance, contestatory painters in France produced portraits of Algerians and anti-colonial Frenchmen arrested, tortured and sometimes killed by French authorities.[15] A painting by an international collective of activist artists (Jean-Jacques Lebel, Enrico Baj, Roberto Crippa, Gianni Dova, Antonio Recalcati and Erró) entitled 'Le Grand Tableau antifasciste' (1960) and Gillo Pontecorvo's film *The Battle of Algiers* (which premiered in 1966 four years after the end of the war, though it was long banned in France) are two signal anti-colonial representations of that conflict.

The general public – visitors to galleries, readers, purchases of consumer goods – during the age of empire were likely to come into contact with representations more favourable to colonialism, explicitly or implicitly, and these works, notwithstanding their artistic, literary or design value, often perpetuated long-standing stereotypes. Many who encountered representations of the colonies remained at least passively complicit in colonialism as they read best-sellers, watched films, enjoyed artworks or consumed products whose advertising drew on colonial imagery. A reader of *Heart of Darkness, A Passage to India* or *Burmese Days*, however, could hardly put down such a book without reflecting on the ill effects of empire – brutalities committed on local people, corrupt behaviour by colonialists, the difficulty for a European and an indigenous person fully to 'connect' in a colonial situation (as Forster put it).

Representations of the colonized world and the phenomenon of colonialism, from canonical artistic and literary works to banal consumer goods, have legitimately come under close scrutiny and negative appraisal in recent years. It must be remembered that they drew on views widely accepted in their times and milieus, not those of our own day. Opinions and portrayals varied even in the colonial age among writers, artists and consumers, and an appreciation of nuances is necessary to avoid essentializing judgements about the culture of colonialism.

Views in art and literature

Three selected fields of modern European art illustrate, in a brief overview, the ways in which painters engaged with the world that was coming, or had come, under the dominion of Western colonizers: nineteenth-century Orientalism, photography and early twentieth-century modernism. 'Oriental' in English was a malleable term, historically applied to a specific region, especially to the 'East' or just 'Far East' (as 'oriental' semantically denotes), or to the largely Muslim North Africa and the Middle East, or indeed to much of the world beyond European shores. 'Orientalism' in the nineteenth and much of the twentieth centuries was interested in or studied the cultures of the Arabo-Muslim world, South, Southeast and East Asia (as in the 'School of African and Oriental Studies' at the University of London). In more current usage – in part, because of Edward Said's landmark study of *Orientalism* (1976) – it geographically often refers more particularly to the Arabo-Muslim cultures of the Middle East and beyond, and carries the valence of perspectives on those cultures that intersected with and underpinned European expansion and rule. Orientalism, in terms of the artistic current of interest here, was a European movement in visual arts that flourished in the mid-nineteenth century, pioneered by such painters as Jean-Dominique Ingres (1780–1867) and Jean-Léon Gérôme (1824–1904), though its influence lingered long afterwards. The artistic terrain of Orientalist painters extended from Morocco across North Africa to the Arabian Peninsula and the Ottoman Empire; Ingres never left Europe, but Gérôme travelled widely in North Africa, especially in Egypt, and in the Ottoman Empire.[16]

Several reasons explain the vogue for Orientalist painting. The earlier Romantic movement in Western and Central Europe had been fascinated by classical ruins in Italy and landscapes such as high mountains and stormy oceans that conveyed a sense of the sublime, and Orientalism extended these interests across the Mediterranean and beyond. Not all Orientalist artists ventured to those places, and many only conjured works from their imagination (sometimes with major mistakes in terms of accuracy) or from images brought back by others, but for those who did, the light of southern latitudes and the vivid colours of northern Africa provided both a technical challenge and an inspiration. Since artists often search for the new and different, the landscapes, animals, vegetation, architecture and peoples of these regions were truly exotic, not previously depicted so frequently or in such detail in Europe, especially by those with on-site experience. Furthermore, for many, North Africa and the Middle East connected with two other areas of European cultural heritage. One was the legacy of Antiquity, still visible in Roman ruins in Algeria and Libya, as well as a new nineteenth-century obsession with pharaonic Egypt. The other was Christianity, as the Middle East was conflated with the biblical 'holy land', and portrayal of an idealized milieu that seemed to foreign eyes little changed since the times of Moses or Jesus; most art connoisseurs and purchasers in the 1800s were familiar with biblical narratives, and Orientalist art provided intimations of the land and lives of figures from the Old and New Testament. Negative representations of Muslim cultures furthermore suggested contrasts with Judeo-Christian traditions.

Increased intercourse between Europe and the Islamic and Jewish Middle Eastern worlds stimulated and facilitated Orientalist enthusiasm among both painters and connoisseurs. The Ottoman Empire remained one of the 'great powers', though often viewed as a declining one, and its capital, Istanbul, became a centre for travel and a network of European and local artists.[17] The European takeover of North African territories and the development of an infrastructure of steamship routes, tourist agencies, hotels and the security expected from European government and policing encouraged travel. So, too, did the establishment of art schools set up by colonial authorities (as in Algiers in the 1840s) and funding and fellowships for painters and sculptors coming from Europe (for instance, the fellowships offered at Algiers' Abd-el-Tif art centre from 1907).

Not surprisingly, therefore, Orientalist art flourished, with a plethora of painters from throughout Europe and as far away as the United States and Australia. Romanticism and realism combined in the work of such masters as Eugène Delacroix (1798–1863), who journeyed to Algeria and Morocco with a diplomatic delegation only two years after the French invasion of Algiers. Delacroix excelled at painting horses and lions, sometimes locked in combat. His 'Women of Algiers in their Apartment' (the first version painted in 1834) – three Algerian women and a Black slave woman in a lavish interior – was modelled on the people and residences of Jewish Algerians he visited. 'Sultan of Morocco and his Entourage' (1845) shows the ruler of the still independent realm as a distinguished figure, handsome with dark beard, white burnous and proud gaze; mounted on a white horse and surrounded by courtiers, he stands before an archway in the crenelated walls of the citadel in Meknès. Delacroix was one of the premier French painters of his age, now particularly known for his 'Liberty Leading the People', painted to commemorate the Revolution of 1830, and one of the first to produce widely heralded images of North Africa from personal observation. He had many followers, who interpreted 'Orientalist' landscapes and street scenes, mosques and palaces, for a European audience.

As Orientalist painters privileged the picturesque and the exotic, stereotypes proliferated, and some images are incontrovertibly derogatory or racist; others admiringly depict the beauties of Islamic architecture, provide respectful portraits of individuals ranging from scholars and imams to peasants, and render mountains and deserts with near scientific faithfulness. The choice of images, by and large, nevertheless did reinforce ideas about 'unchanging' societies, autocratic governments, dangerous environments and lands suitable for European influence and conquest. Eroticized women and fantasies of the harem and seraglio are far from uncommon in the work.

The Muslim Orient was not the only area to attract artists, though it perhaps had more than its fair share. The 'Mooi Indië' (Beautiful Indies) painters of the Dutch East Indies similarly favoured images of beautiful landscapes, picturesque local people, unfamiliar scenes and untroubled colonial life.[18] Sub-Saharan Africa and parts of Asia provided scope for artists who joined ethnographic expeditions and were eager to portray different ethnicities and their particular clothing, hairstyles and ornaments. India appealed for its diverse landscapes and cultures, and iconic buildings such as the Taj Mahal. Around the world, marketplaces, palaces and temples, and people provided ample subjects for travellers, European painters resident in the colonies and local artists adopting European styles.

Colonialist magazines and other publications, such as those of geographical societies (of which there were many in Europe in the late 1800s and early 1900s), and those issued by colonial ministries and colonial institutes, promoted particularly inflected views of European overseas possessions in image and text. Photography, from the mid-1800s, provided a powerful new medium for representations, though for decades the technology of photography – cumbersome equipment, long exposure times, difficulties of work in tropical climates, complex development of film, debates about whether photography was art or craft – limited its potential. Yet cameras appeared early on in European colonies. Felice Beato (1832–1909), for instance, was an Italian photographer who worked widely in Asia and produced images that were technically remarkable and remain important documentation. As depicted in Figure 13.2, he also provided a photographic record of the devastation left after the repression of the Great Uprising in India in 1857. However, some of the scenes were restaged or rearranged for the advantage of his camera – a reminder of

Figure 13.2 Felice Beato's photograph depicting Sikander Bagh in Lucknow, India, after repression of the 1857 'Great Uprising'. © Alamy Stock Photo.

how photographers, like painters (and also writers), carefully selected and manipulated what they wished to show. Most photographers, not surprisingly, focused on the more scenic shots, but an emphasis on 'traditional' life, men and women supposedly 'typical' of certain ethnicities, and images of ruins helped form and reinforce European perceptions. Not all representations were pro-colonialist, however, as shown with photographs, for example, of the Indian famine in the 1870s that were widely reproduced in Europe. International outrage at labour conditions in the Congo Free State from the 1890s came in part from photographic evidence of abuses, and anti-colonialists continued to marshal photographic evidence to their cause.

One particular genre of photography linked to colonialism was the erotic photograph, typically though not always of a woman. This was pornography (generally of a soft-core variety) that presented nude or semi-nude indigenous women as objects of European desire. Such voyeuristic images circulated widely, both publicly and under cover, in published works and as postcards that were becoming increasingly popular in the late 1800s. Posing for such pictures would have disgraced 'respectable' women, and thus the models came from subaltern strata of society, some working as entertainers or prostitutes; photographers posed them in ways designed to suggest their allure and availability, with apparel and accoutrements that may or may not have corresponded to their own cultures. The images comprise a troubling archive that is revealing about the European gaze, sexual exploitation and the lives of the unidentified and now largely unknown figures who were the subjects.[19]

As cameras became less expensive and easier to use, photographs of colonial scenes became increasingly common, including in innumerable photographic albums that memorialized the family life of colonials and recorded the experiences of tourists. Governments quickly recognized the propagandistic value of photographs – images of colonial railways and dams, for instance – to underline the claimed accomplishments of colonizers and reiterate perceived contrasts between old and new, primitive and modern. Favoured images of photographers working for the colonial authorities (though by no means were all doing so) by the 1940s and 1950s included pictures of neat children happily studying in pleasant-looking classrooms, and nurses and doctors busy attending to patients in immaculate hospital wards. No less than paintings of lion hunts and casbahs from a century before, these representations revealed government policies, popular perceptions and the power of visual media.

By the end of the nineteenth century Orientalism had become passé, no longer an innovative 'school' of art, yet many painters and photographers kept it flourishing for decades (and still alive today). New art movements such as Impressionism and post-Impressionism had emerged, but modernist painters with radically different styles were still drawn to the wider world; indeed, the plein-air style of painting of Impressionists, the mystical themes of Symbolists and the vibrant colours of Fauvists found new interest in the non-European world.[20] Traditionalist and modernist artists took cues from Africa and Asia, including the countries which European expansion had made more familiar and more accessible to Europeans.[21] It has been suggested, for example, that the turn-of-the-century Art Nouveau style in Belgium, with its sinuous curves in painting, architecture and furnishings recalling Africans lianas and vines, owed much to Belgian artists' discovery of African landscapes in the context of King Leopold's colonialism in the Congo.[22]

One particular new inspiration for visual artists in the early years of the twentieth century, contributing to the artistic revolution of modernism, came from the art of sub-Saharan Africa, as well as, to a lesser degree, Melanesia and the First Nations of the Pacific Northwest of North America. The expansion of colonialism in the late 1800s and the collection and display of works from these regions in such collections as the Musée Ethnographique du Trocadéro, established in Paris in the 1870s, brought what was then called 'primitive' art (and today is sometimes labelled 'primal art' or *arts premiers*) to European attention. As the word 'primitive' implies, many dismissed the arts and crafts from Africa, Oceania and native American cultures as crude in production, aesthetically unappealing and in some cases horrifying – 'heathen' deities, grotesque designs (in European eyes) and materials such as shells, bones and hair incorporated into sculpture. In conservative views, 'primitive' art appeared the polar opposite of European conventions and aesthetics handed down from Greco-Roman Antiquity through the 'old masters' of the Renaissance and taught in orthodox fine arts academies, though such orthodoxy had already been strongly challenged by new currents in the late nineteenth century.

Pablo Picasso (1881–1973), a young man destined to become the most famous artist of the twentieth century, moved from his native Catalonia (in north-eastern Spain) to Paris in the first years of the twentieth century. Paris was already well established as the artistic centre of Europe, drawing in a cosmopolitan community of painters and sculptors from around Europe and beyond, men and women reputed for their bohemian life in the cafés and *ateliers* of Montmartre where Picasso did much of his work. Picasso regularly visited the ethnographic museum and acquired his own collection of African statues and masks from the burgeoning art market in Paris for African works, many from France's colonies. The way that African and other 'primitive' artists simplified and exaggerated human features, used boldly geometric forms, and dispensed with such hallowed European conventions as perspective and 'realism' manifested very different ways of painting and sculpting, and differing conceptions of art itself. Even the incantatory features of African art – pieces such as masks often created for initiation ceremonies, worship or festivals – that shocked traditionalist Europeans suggested to avant-garde Europeans, interested in experimentation and innovation, new definitions of art, new styles and new reactions that could be evoked (or provoked) in audiences. Picasso did not investigate African art and its social context very profoundly, nor did he travel in Black Africa, but his vision of the works he saw and purchased provided one of several impetuses in the creation of Cubism by the Catalan and his peers in Belle Époque Paris. Picasso's 'Demoiselles d'Avignon', completed in 1907 and symbolically often considered the most important single work to mark a major break with customary European artistic styles and a foundational work of twentieth-century modernism, portrayed a group of prostitutes (in Avignon Street in Barcelona). However, what shocked viewers in the huge painting was the way that Picasso painted the women in angular lines and planes, their facial features jarringly unlike almost any previously known in European art. Two of the faces were indeed based on African masks in Picasso's collection. African influences can be identified in other works in Picasso's vast *oeuvre*, and in the works of many of his contemporaries.

Art historians differ concerning the role and significance of 'primitivism' and borrowings from non-Western art – and whether such borrowings constitute unjust appropriation of traditions from outside Europe. Certain it is that the African, Asian and Oceanic art put on display in European museums, at colonial exhibitions and world's fairs, and in commercial galleries, much of it brought from European colonies (and sometimes stolen or acquired in dubious circumstances), provided a major boon to modernist artists. It also led the French art critic and poet Guillaume Apollinaire (1880–1918) to argue in 1909 that 'primitive' art, such as indigenous African works, should be placed in the Louvre alongside masterpieces of European art – though a century would pass before such works systematically went on display in France's leading museum. This modernist art pioneered in Europe meanwhile would exercise a lasting influence on artists in the colonies and in independent countries around the world.

Europeanized culture in the colonies

Europeans carried their art, literature, architecture and music to the colonies, primarily for the benefit of European residents – in the settler colonies in particular, collections underscored the bond linking European settlers and their descendants to the 'mother-country'. For colonial Europeans, the construction of museums, galleries, libraries and concert halls provided proof of the rooting of 'civilization' in the colonies. Europeans proved avid producers and consumers, even if such avocations as reading and writing, painting and composing remained largely the province of the elite. Staging European plays or playing European classical music underlined the reach of European culture to distant places and affirmed the heritage acquired as a birthright by Europeans. Gradually, if slowly and only to a small cohort, it was made available to indigenous and diasporic peoples who, in European judgement, were earning access through allegiance, education and acculturation.

Spreading European culture, after all, stood as one of the self-appointed vocations of colonialists, and elite colonial schools rigorously taught Latin and Greek, modern European languages and literatures, and the natural and social sciences. European and indigenous children in these establishments, if they had access to more than elementary education (which few indigenous students did), read Shakespeare and Molière, Dante and Cervantes; they learned to play the piano or violin, and they were shown the 'great' art of Europe. Somewhat paradoxically, Europeans nevertheless continued to promote local arts and crafts, especially those that held aesthetic or commercial appeal: porcelain and ceramics, textiles, decorative objects, and even the 'primitive art' with value for tourists, merchants, collectors and gallerists.

Several of the European writers and artists mentioned in this chapter spent considerable time in the colonies as travellers, officials or residents. European men and women born and bred in the colonies – from the first colonial settlements of the 1500s onwards – produced a steady stream of novels, poems, and plays, as well as paintings and sculptures. Although a substantial number were considered modest in accomplishment back in Europe, they aptly describe local environments, recollect the adventures and misadventures of Europeans abroad and reveal political and social attitudes. Thus, for instance, a group of 'Algérianiste' poets and novelists in the early twentieth century hypothesized that the geography, climate and life of *pieds-noirs* were creating a new (white) race of hardy pioneers in the traditions of the Roman conquerors. None of the Algerian-born writers of European background, however, achieved such prominence as Albert Camus (1913–60), novelist, philosopher, essayist, winner of the Nobel Prize for Literature in 1957. In settler societies such as the Australian colonies, writers including Marcus Clarke, Henry Lawson, 'Banjo' Patterson and Miles Franklin played a leading role in developing a sense of a specifically Australian identity and sense of place and history.

Europeans also brought their styles of visual art to the colonies, including the settler societies; for instance, through the Sydney Mechanics School of Arts set up in 1833 and the Dunedin School of Art in New Zealand in 1870. A private school teaching Western art styles opened much earlier in Pune, India, in 1798, and the Calcutta Mechanics' Institute and School of Arts (an institution with a similarly edifying and moralizing intention to mechanics' institute set up in Britain and the settler colonies) opened in Calcutta in 1839. Western art schools followed in Madras (in 1850) and in Bombay, the one there a gift of Sir Jamsetjee Jejeebhoy 'for the improvement of arts and manufactures [and] the habits of industry of the middle and lower classes'. Teachers instructed students, both young Europeans and indigenous pupils, in European techniques of painting and sculpture. To local students, they introduced new media, such as oil, watercolour and gouache for painting. They had students practice the 'life drawing' (using human models) that formed an essential part of the curriculum of European art academies. Training was generally in traditional styles, 'academic art' as it was called, and the bolder experiments of modernists received short shrift from teachers and generally conservative connoisseurs.

Many indigenous students, and autodidacts, excelled in the creation of European-style works, but added in indigenous sensibilities and subjects. Raden Saleh is one such figure, and another case in point is Raja Ravi Varma (1848–1906). Born into the royal family of the princely state of Travancore, he studied in Madras. By the 1890s, his paintings were exhibited as far away as Vienna, London and Chicago. Varma painted many portraits and tableaux of Indian women, sometimes in sylvan landscapes or elegant interiors: 'Village Belle', 'Lady Lost in Thought', 'Woman Holding a Fan'. He also did paintings of Hindu gods and goddesses – the elephant-headed Ganesha and his consorts, Radha sitting in the moonlight, the many-armed Sarasvati. 'Lord Rama Conquers Varuna', 'Lord Krishna as Ambassador' and 'Victory of Indrajit' show themes taken from the Indian epics. Varma thus blended themes and styles from Asia and

Europe in an individualistic and accomplished manner whose work for some critics, as John Clark states, 'counter-appropriate[s], for Indian purposes, the techniques and many elements of the visual discourse of the colonial ruler'.[23]

The early twentieth-century modernist styles arrived relatively soon in the colonies from Europe (often to the disparagement of 'academic' artists), and younger generations experimented with the innovative styles. One notable example is the 'Group of '43' (named after the year in which they formally gathered together) in Ceylon, congregated around the photographer Lionel Wendt (1900–44), whose own works are notable; sometimes involving solarization, double-exposure and surrealistic composition, they show Buddhist temples, Kandyan dancers, modest labourers and tropical landscapes: they are local in inspiration and global in technique. George Keyt (1901–93), a key painter in the group, brought Ceylonese landscapes, figures and themes, including ones from South Asian religions and sagas, into paintings that bear the influence of Impressionism and Cubism and occasionally moved towards abstract art. Bold colours, geometrical forms, experiments with figuration mark them out from styles practised by artists of an older generation and more traditionalist bent. It is worth emphasizing that for the Ceylonese painters and photographers, unlike the Europeans, their subjects were not exotic sights envisioned by foreigners, but their compatriots and the landscapes of everyday life.[24] Similarly avant-garde painters and movements emerged in many other colonies as well.[25]

Indigenous artists in the colonies had also long portrayed European figures, representations that provide a contrast to the ways that indigenous people were depicted by Europeans.[26] From the time of the earliest Portuguese encounters in Africa, sculptors including those who carved grand metal doors characteristic of palaces in the Kingdom of Benin (in present-day Nigeria) had added in European figures wearing hats and uniforms, smoking pipes, riding horses, or sailing ships – many of these were later taken away by Europeans and, controversially, remain in European collections. Later African artists carved statues of Europeans, one of the most notable and easily recognizable a wooden figure of Queen Victoria, complete with crown, that is now in Oxford's Pitt Rivers Museum. They further developed a tradition of statues of 'typical' Europeans, such as a policeman or soldier, that became popular with tourists. In Asia, the Japanese had depicted Portuguese 'black ships', mariners and missionaries, and later Dutch merchants (sometimes with their African slaves), in 'Nanban' paintings on large screens. Indian artists produced many images of Europeans in the East India Company period (within the genre known as 'Company painting'), men in frock coats or uniforms, sometimes smoking hookahs or in various other ways blending practices from European and Indian life. There were, as well, pioneering indigenous photographers; in Asia, they included one of the early exponents of the new medium, Maharajah Ram Singh II of Jaipur (1834–80), and Kassian Cephas (1845–1912) in the East Indies. Indigenous people similarly took to the cinema, as producers as well as enthusiastic filmgoers. Dhundiraj Govind Phalke (1870–1944) directed the first Indian feature film, *Raja Harishchandra*, in 1913; by the 1930s, India was producing over 200 films a year, the genesis of today's Bollywood. In Egypt, the first short film was screened in 1896, only a year after the first brief motion picture was presented in Europe, and Egyptian film-makers did their own take on the desert adventures and other themes popular in the West. An indigenous film-maker, Albert Samama Chikly (1872–1934), was showing his work in Tunisia less than ten years later, though locally made films appeared in sub-Saharan Africa only several decades afterwards and in a limited number of places (and there were no film studios at all in the Portuguese colonies). In short, just as Europeans were looking at and portraying the people of the lands they colonized, so the gaze was returned, and so did indigenous people use European styles, media and techniques to produce representations of the wider world.

In other ways than painting and photography, local people were 'looking back' at Europeans and commenting on colonial situations. Literature was one of those ways. The world outside Europe had many types of oral and written literature, but writers beyond Europe, or of non-European background, adopted European genres, such as novels, to complement already existing styles of writing. The 1887 politically engaged novel *Noli Me Tangere* – the Latin phrase for 'touch me not' used as a title for the Spanish-language volume – was the work of José Rizal (1861–96), a young Filipino writer and nationalist (and ophthalmologist by profession) who was later executed for implication in rebellion against the Spanish colonial rulers of the archipelago. In 1921, the novel *Batouala* by René Maran (1887–1960) won France's most prestigious literary award, the Prix Goncourt. Maran, a Black man, grew up in Martinique in the West Indies, attended boarding school in Bordeaux and became a colonial official in central Africa. Depicting an African chieftain and his family life, Maran's novel is not, however, a celebration of French colonialism; indeed, its critiques of colonial abuses had the work banned in the French colonies. In the interwar period, the *négritude* movement of Francophone writers, centred in Paris, included poets, playwrights (and also political figures) such as Léopold Sedar Senghor (1906–2001) and Aimé Césaire (1913–2008), as well as others from the African diaspora. Césaire's book-length poem *Cahier d'un retour au pays natal* – translated under different titles, including *Notebook of a Return to My Native Land* – published in 1939 not only offers a searing and largely autobiographical account of the disorientation a Black man felt in France and back in his homeland of Martinique; it is also an avant-garde experiment in the use of the French language, creatively crafted in what has sometimes been labelled a surrealist or stream-of-consciousness fashion. Another notable writer from the French colonies in these years is Vu Trong Phung (1912–39), a journalist best known for *Dumb Luck* (1936), a novel that satirized the French in Vietnam and, in particular, aspirational members of the Vietnamese elite who mimicked French clothing, manners and leisure pursuits; another satirical work, *The Industry of Marrying Europeans* (1934), was a novel-reportage about Foreign Legionnaires and their concubines.

Indigenous authors writing in a Western vein appeared in almost all the colonies, even some of the smallest – *Chiquinho* (1947), by Baltasar Lopes (1907–89), for example, movingly recounted the protagonist's childhood in the Portuguese island colony of Cape Verde, punctuated by episodes of drought and famine, and chronicled his education and eventual migration to the United States. The works of many of these writers, however, have only in recent years been 'rediscovered', translated and popularized. Among the

Figure 13.3 Untitled Painting by Malangatana Ngwenya, 1967. Tate Modern, London. © Alamy Stock Photo.

best-known non-Western novelists of the late colonial period (or the years immediately afterwards) whose masterworks offer original perspectives on colonialism are the novelists Pramoedya Ananta Toer (1925–2006) from Indonesia, Mulk Raj Anand (1905–2004) and R. K. Narayan (1906–2001) from India, V. S. Naipaul (1932–2018) from Trinidad and Chinua Achebe (1930–2013) from Nigeria, as well as the St Lucian poet Derek Walcott (1930–2017), all of whom, except Pramoedya Toer, wrote largely in English; the list could be lengthened with numerous other authors writing in European and non-European languages. For all of these writers, and many more whose lives spanned the colonial and post-colonial period, colonialism has served as a theme. Present-day European as well as non-European writers – Sir Salman Rushdie (b. 1947) and Abdulrazak Gurnah (b. 1948) (the latter, winner of the Nobel Prize for Literature in 2021), to mention only two – continue to confront colonialism and its legacies in their work.

    Many present-day artists are the heirs of Raden Saleh, U Ba Nyan and Le Thanh Duc, reassessing colonialism in new styles, from painting and sculpture to installation art, costume and moving images, among the most widely known the Congolese Cheri Samba (b. 1956) and the Nigerian-British Yinka Shonibare (b. 1962).[27] A final example of colonialism and culture, to close this chapter with a visual artist, comes from Mozambique: the painter and poet Malangatana Ngwenya (1936–2011). Born in a village, a student in a mission school, he moved to Lourenço Marques (Maputo) as an adolescent and managed to combine employment with further education and a developing interest in art and politics. Malangatana joined the nationalist Front for the Liberation of Mozambique in 1962 and was occasionally placed in detention by the secret police of the Portuguese, who continued to rule the country until 1974. Malangatana nevertheless studied and also exhibited his works in Lisbon during the colonial period. His bold and vivid paintings such as the one depicted in Figure 13.3 show the influences of international modernism but develop an anti-colonial aesthetic and personal style. The often allegorical paintings, crowded with brightly coloured figures, such as depictions of a diviner and a 'witch doctor' – he used that word, *feiticeiro* in Portuguese, in the title for one work, though the witch doctor is seen not as a malevolent figure but one purifying a child – allude to African village life, but headless figures, vampire-like bloodsuckers and skeletons point to the violence of the colonial regime and the suffering of its subjects.[28]

Culture was an integral and necessary component of colonialism, producing, reflecting and challenging perceptions in Europe. The introduction and imposition of European cultures provided a vital strategy of colonial rule, yet also provided inspiration, models and techniques to be adopted and adapted by local artists and writers. Colonial-era Europeans, in their representations of non-Western lands and peoples, created documentary depictions, faithful renditions or fanciful visions and fantasies that enriched European painting and literature (as well as the other arts). Indigenous and diasporic peoples have pursued, developed and revivified their own cultural traditions, which have remained remarkably resilient despite the burdensome impact of colonialism and Westernization. They have also creatively responded to colonialism and its inheritance. They continue to re-present colonialism from vantage points that redefine and decentre global culture.

PART III
CASES

Introduction

Modern colonialism, in one form or another, covered the entire globe and stretched over many centuries. In Part III of *The Colonial World*, we zoom in to look at some colonized places at moments in their history, generally taking a particular year as a pivot for investigating a type of colonialism or decolonization.

The potential set of case studies is unlimited, and our choice is selective and somewhat eclectic; this selection is illustrative, not encyclopaedic. We have aimed to focus on different parts of the world with chapters that punctuate colonial history at more or less regular intervals since the late eighteenth century. This decision, of course, means that many places are not covered, and the pinpointing of certain years inevitably isolates one tranche in a region's or country's history at the expense of a far longer expanse. Yet that approach provides a chance for a more detailed look at the history and historiography of particular colonial situations, including some that may well be less familiar than others.

The first three chapters examine three different countries around the time of the 'imperial meridian' dividing the 'first' imperial age of the European old regimes from the imperialism of the nineteenth century: worlds in transition between old and new structures and ideas. In the Spanish Andes around 1780, indigenous people, already subjects of Spain for almost three centuries, were mobilizing a new campaign of resistance against foreign overlordship, using their ancestral heritage as a platform for armed resistance – a template for struggle to asymmetrical political and social structures to this day. On the Indian Ocean island of Mauritius in 1810, one colonial authority, France, was being replaced by another, Britain, yet with a maintenance of the institution of slavery; the agricultural and commercial economy that had been developed; international connections to Africa, Asia and Europe; and the legacy of the earlier period of colonization by the French. This shows that possessions could be and were wrested by new conquerors from earlier colonizers (and sometimes were exchanged or sold), leaving multiple layers of colonialism, with a variety of repercussions, in many places. Cuba, like Mauritius, provides another example of a plantation and slave colony, under Spanish control until the end of the nineteenth century, yet it also reveals the way that an independence movement first challenged the Spanish and then the Americans, who occupied the island after defeating the Spanish, and it highlights the long-lasting impact of colonialism on gender and race relations.

The next two chapters move to southern and south-eastern Asia, long a centre of European interest – for spices, silk, porcelain, tea, land – that were the subject of some of the most dramatic European expansion in the mid-nineteenth century (paralleled by the forced 'opening' of Japan and China). Following an insurrection in India in 1857, then called the 'Mutiny' but now often referred to as the first Indian war of independence, the British government established Crown authority over much of the subcontinent, the Raj with Queen Victoria as empress of India and Britain's most important colonial territory. Further east, in Burma and Vietnam, the British and French jousted for colonial acquisitions, by the 1880s Burma finally coming under full British control and the French consolidating rule in Vietnam, their largest Asian outpost. In both cases, one can see the overlap of political, commercial and geostrategic interests, imperial rivalries between the two leading European colonial powers, and indigenous resistance and dissent.

The years on either side of 1900, the end of one century and the beginning of another, witnessed numerous international conflicts between colonial powers – in the Caribbean and the Philippines, in South Africa and eastern Africa, in Korea and China. The British trumpeted their successes in the South African War, and a coalition of Europeans, Americans and Japanese championed actions against the 'Boxers' in China. Yet the Japanese defeat of the Russians in eastern Asia, a conflict pitting two aspiring colonizing nations against each other, provided a warning that battles did not always favour the Europeans. At a time of mounting nationalism and military tensions, the chapter shows how Europeans (and others) were fighting their wars overseas, and how conflicts on the edge of empires threatened to ignite global conflagrations.

The next three chapters examine very different colonial areas in the early years of the twentieth century, when Europeans hoped (in vain) that colonial rivalries had been settled, borders between rival empires neatly drawn and indigenous peoples 'pacified'. The South Pacific islands, with coral reefs and volcanoes, palm trees and tropical fruits, seemed a picturesque and sleepy corner of the world, yet colonialism had penetrated even the smallest and most remote archipelagos – appropriation of land, Christianization, trade – transforming what some had fantasized about as 'paradise' into what others lamented as 'paradise lost'. Ceylon, an Indian Ocean island synonymous in the foreign imaginary with 'serendipity' (from the name given by Arab traders), was famed for tea, cinnamon and gemstones, and sometimes regarded by the British as a model colony. However, demographic and commercial changes had aggravated ethnic tensions, poverty was rife, social disparities pronounced. In German Southwest Africa (present-day Namibia), a new colonial power was entrenching its rule in the face of widespread opposition to German control. The response was war and violence, culminating in a German attempt to eliminate the Herero and Nama people that today is branded a genocide. The decade before the First World War, as these chapters show, saw efforts to consolidate colonialism in old and new colonies, from islands like Ceylon that had long been colonized to Pacific outposts over which foreign flags had more recently been raised, from giant territories such as German Southwest Africa to small outposts in Oceania.

The next two chapters turn to the interwar period, and the scenario once again reveals proclamations of European triumph and benevolence against mounting underlying anti-colonial opposition, continued violence and suppression of nationalists, amidst the changing circumstances of international affairs. In 1935, Italian forces swearing loyalty to Mussolini invaded and conquered Ethiopia (a country Italians had failed to subdue in the 1890s), and established an avowedly Fascist colonial administration despite half-hearted condemnation from other colonial powers. Italian control of Ethiopia would last less than a decade, but Dutch control of the East Indies (today's Indonesia) lasted 300 years. In the 1930s, the Dutch considered their colony secure, peaceful and prosperous with its exports of spices, tobacco, rubber and coffee, yet nationalists were organizing, protesting and calling for self-government or independence – and being met with imprisonment, execution or exile. In both Africa and Asia, world war loomed, and promised major changes in colonial situations.

In the following chapters of this volume, decolonization becomes the theme. Decolonization was not simply the lowering of the flag of a foreign power and the raising of that of an independent country under the control of an indigenous population, but a complex and long-lasting set of political, social and cultural changes. Theories of anti-colonialism varied, and different ideas and strategies combined in the face of the recalcitrance or refusal of colonial powers to address demands. In some cases, decolonization was a relatively peaceful process (though seldom without some violent strife), but in others, there was sustained warfare. The examples chosen here are ones where the fight for and against independence was the most intense and violent, and where local, national, colonial and international issues most clearly intersected.

One of the most volatile parts of the world was (and is) the Middle East, the 'holy land' of the three Abrahamic religions, a theatre for intensive imperial rivalries. Britain had gained a mandate over Palestine after the eclipse of the Ottoman Empire, but unrest continued among both Jewish and Arabic populations. The British had promised a 'homeland' to the Jews, a yearning that became more ardent in the wake of the Holocaust, and in 1946, a small band of Jewish nationalists determined to pursue independence through violent means in an incident that shocked many Zionists and others alike. Israel finally gained independence two years later, but at the expense of what Arabs regarded as a new form of colonialism. Meanwhile, the French stoutly refused independence or even self-government for Algeria, its main settler colony and, constitutionally, fully a part of France; independence came only after more than seven years of war, tens of thousands of deaths, the flight of a million French settlers and the establishment of an autocratic one-party successor state. Portugal, under a dictatorship since the 1930s, even more militantly resisted decolonization of its African colonies, fighting against nationalists until the downfall of the regime in Lisbon in the mid-1970s and leaving behind socially and politically damaged countries.

The final chapters in this volume underscore connections between the colonial past and the post-colonial present. In the late 1800s, the ruler of Belgium, a small country, acquired the so-called Congo Free State in central Africa (subsequently the Belgian Congo), castigated by outsiders as one of the most notorious examples of colonial rapacity and exploitation. One chapter looks back on the history of colonization in the Congo, but also at the ways that Belgium now lives with its colonial past, as seen in particular with the renovation of the colonial-era Africa Museum in Brussels. The following chapter turns to a continuing conflict in northern Africa. When the Spanish withdrew from their African colonies, with the end of a long dictatorship in Madrid in 1975, Morocco occupied the Spanish Sahara – a territory still considered 'non-self-governing' by the United Nations; in the view of the Sahrawi people, colonialism in their homeland has not come to an end.

The concluding chapter in the volume assesses, in a more general sense, the long-lived and heavy heritage of colonialism in Europe and the wider world. It highlights current debates relating to such issues as the phenomenon of residual 'colonies', colonial legacies such as language, religion and institutions, conflicts about migrations along colonial-era pathways to European metropoles, discrimination and multiculturalism, and the memory culture of colonialism in historical narratives and public life. It shows that the colonial past is very much still present.

CHAPTER 14
THE SPANISH ANDES, 1780

'I make it known . . . that seeing the yoke so heavy that is oppressing us with so much weight, and the tyranny of those in charge, without regard to our sufferings, and given their abuses with impiety, I have determined to shake off this unbearable yoke, and to stop the bad government that we experience.' With these words José Gabriel Condorcanqui Noguera, better known today as Tupac Amaru II, an Amerindian who claimed to be 'of royal blood and the main [Inca] branch', in November 1780 addressed the Andean residents of the Peruvian Cuzco region of the Spanish South American colony of the Viceroyalty of Peru. He asserted that he was acting on behalf of the Spanish king, having received direct orders to proceed with extraordinary means against the corrupt district officers (*corregidores*) of the Spanish Empire in the territory. After a show trial, he had *corregidor* Antonio de Arriaga hanged on 10 November 1780.[1]

Tupac Amaru II was the *cacique*, an indigenous leader, of several small towns of Tinta, 50 kilometres south of Cuzco. In the second half of the eighteenth century, Cuzco, located in the Peruvian Andes at 3,300 metres above sea level, was the second largest city of Peru after the colonial capital of Lima on the Pacific coast. Before the arrival of the Spanish, Cuzco had been the imperial centre of the vast Inca Empire. Arriaga's execution was the prelude to the largest uprisings in the Andes since the days of Francisco Pizarro and the Spanish takeover of Peru in the 1530s. The rebellion outlasted its leader; Tupac Amaru II was captured in April 1781 and executed together with his wife, Micaela Bastidas Puyucahua, and their eldest son the following month. This, however, was not the end of the movement against Spanish rule. The rebellion continued under the leadership of others, such as Diego Cristóbal, Tupac Amaru's cousin, and expanded geographically from the Cuzco region towards Lake Titicaca and overlapped with the so-called Catarista Rebellion in today's Bolivia, then Upper Peru. Uprisings also haunted parts of what is now northern Argentina and southern Venezuela. This was the 'Great Rebellion in the Andes', extending over 'a larger area than the contemporaneous struggle in North America, the American Revolutionary War'.[2] The 'Great Rebellion in the Andes' escalated in a murderous frenzy, claiming about 100,000 lives among rebels, their families and loyalist troops and militias between 1780, the outbreak of the insurgency, and 1783, when Cristóbal was executed.[3]

Peru in pre-colonial times

Peru is marked by three very distinct geographical regions: the Pacific coast, the high Andes and the tropical Amazon region, usually referred to as *costa*, *sierra* and *selva* (coast, mountains and jungle). All three regions were home to a wide array of different ethnicities with rich cultures dating back before the Common Era. The inland Amazon region extends from the eastern foothills of the Andes to the Amazon River basin and was the territory of hunters and gatherers, some of whose groups have only scarce contact with the outside world today. The arid coastal area gave birth to civilizations which had adapted to desert agriculture or settled around the fertile banks of the rivers that connect the Andes with the Pacific Ocean. The third zone of Peru, the Andean region, boasts impressive mountain chains with peaks such as the Huascarán with an elevation of more than 6,700 metres. Thanks to the geographical proximity to the equator, the valleys surrounding the high mountains are characterized by fertile soil and subtropical climate with regular rainfall, allowing agricultural production.

Advanced civilizations that had developed in the highlands controlled at their zenith commerce from the Andes to the Peruvian coast. Large supra-regional religious centres in what is now Chavín de Huantar are still being explored by national and international teams of archaeologists.[4] The largest polity, the Inca Empire, emerged in the thirteenth century and expanded from its base in Cuzco. By the early 1500s, the Incas had conquered large parts of western South America, and their rule spread from what is now Ecuador and parts of Colombia throughout Peru and Bolivia to Argentina and Chile. The sun was at the centre of their world view, and the emperor was considered the Son of the Sun. The Inca Empire had a highly sophisticated culture, symbolized by the impressive dry-stone walls of the fifteenth-century citadel of Machu Picchu (located in the mountains 80 kilometres northwest of Cuzco), a major cultural signpost to this day. Complex textile work and refined road systems represented other examples of the Incas' technical prowess.

Inca expansion did not rely just on political alliances and intermarriage forging loyalty among incorporated elites. It was a violent process, leaving deep wounds in subjected societies. Inca rule was also hierarchical, with a sharp social distinction between the divine Inca ruler and his extended family, nobles and peasants, and from servants and soldiers down to slaves. Whereas the Inca imperial structure – mostly based on tribute, that is, labour – furnished the basis for the later Spanish imperial system in South America, social grievances and discontent among conquered societies brought under Inca domination provided the Spanish with the breeding ground for much-needed local alliances for their expansion. Yet the key factor for the fall of the Inca Empire was a civil war triggered by two Inca pretenders who had severely destabilized the region just at the time when the Spanish conquistador Pizarro and his soldiers arrived in the 1530s.

However, diseases such as smallpox, which had been carried from Europe to the Americas – and for which indigenous people had no immunological defence – in the late fifteenth century, travelled faster than the conquistadors. The virus quickly spread southwards from the Caribbean and Central America, severely weakening the Inca Empire and its inhabitants. The historian Nicholas A. Robins conjectures that smallpox may have killed one-half of the population of the Andes before the Spanish takeover. Estimates for the region that now covers Peru point to a population loss of about 90 per cent within the fifty years from 1530 and 1580, mostly due to the bloody wars of conquest in the name of imperial Spain and pathogens brought from the 'old' to the 'new' world.[5]

Between reform and revolution: Spain's colonial system in Latin America

Within the Spanish colonial system, countless male and female *caciques*, some of whom, like Tupac Amaru II, came from the indigenous nobility, catered on a regional and local level to the needs of the Spanish – who governed through indirect rule – and simultaneously tried to serve their own communities.[6] The *caciques*, on the one hand, were responsible for keeping their towns calm, providing tax revenues to the *corregidor*, and supplying a fixed number of workers from each territory for the mines, mainly in Potosí and Huancavelica (the forced labour scheme or *mita*). The silver mines in Potosí provided the major 'treasure' of the region for the Spanish, and mercury from Huancavelica was essential in the process of extracting the precious mineral. On the other hand, the 'colonial pact' allowed the Andean communities to maintain at least some of their cultural customs and practices, for example the use of Quechua, the main language of the former Inca Empire.

Although a *cacique* held a privileged position in colonial society, he or she was still a subordinate to the *corregidor*, often a locally born descendant of Europeans, that is, a Creole or *Criollo*, who had usually bought the office within the Spanish colonial administration. Paying a fixed sum to the Spanish Crown, the *corregidores* had free rein to exploit the populations under their jurisdiction through slave-like work in textile workshops and forced purchases of local and imported goods (*reparto mercantil* or *repartimiento*) – among them agricultural tools sold at exaggerated prices and religious books, which were useless for illiterate peasants. Extortionate taxes and many further mechanisms aimed at the colonizers' personal enrichment placed more burdens on the indigenous people. The *corregidores'* actions often went unchecked by their Spanish superiors, opening the doors for corruption and abuse. The wide margin of discretion and the relative freedom such 'men on the spot' enjoyed with regard to the empire's two centres, the Viceroyalty of Peru based in Lima and the Spanish royal court in Madrid, had characterized the Iberian model of colonial expansion in Latin America since the early sixteenth century and 'by the mid-eighteenth century the corruption of *corregidores* was a well-entrenched element of the colonial system'.[7] This system was about to change.

With the dynastic switch from Habsburg to Bourbon rule in Spain in the early eighteenth century, and the emergence in various parts of Europe of 'enlightened absolutism', a new project for reform in Iberia and in the colonies aimed to strengthen the power of the king over the territories under his rule. Inspired by the administrative system of France and its overseas empire, the Spanish Crown aimed at centralization in the long term. The goal was to regain royal authority that had been lost to the 'men on the spot' and the Catholic Church in the Americas in order to increase revenues. The church had been a pillar of the colonial enterprise in the Americas since the early 1500s, although representatives such as Bartolomé de las Casas also fervently criticized the 'destruction of the Indies' in the 1540s. Besides territorial restructuring – for example, the foundation in 1776 of the new Viceroyalty, Río de la Plata, in the south, which included large parts of today's Argentina, Bolivia, Paraguay and Uruguay as well as of Chile – a new brand of colonial officer directly responsible to the king (*visitador*) would shake up the Spanish colonies, raising sales taxes (*alcabala*) and limiting the influence of the Catholic Church and the Creoles in the colonial regime. The implementation of the reforms stretched over almost a century, and the initiative peaked after the defeat of the Spanish (and their French allies) by the British in the Seven Years' War (1756–63) that had spread through Europe, the Americas and parts of Asia. The reign of Charles III of Spain (1759–88) represented the culmination of the eighteenth-century Bourbon reform era when Spain tightened its grip over colonial Latin American societies. This administrative 'Reconquest of the Americas' with increased colonial supervision has frequently been described as a 'second conquest'.[8] The 'new imperialism',[9] with the denser administrative control and increasing taxes levied to pay for military fortifications, among other local grievances, triggered frustrations and unease among the Creole elites who had long enjoyed privileges and wealth along with a certain autonomy from distant Madrid. The reforms also impacted rural *mestizos* (those of mixed Amerindian and European ancestry) and indigenous families, for example with new taxes on coca leaves, which were both consumer goods and significant for religious practices. For many communities the colonial state became a more and more present and harassing entity.

José Gabriel Tupac Amaru was well aware of the growing resentment of both indigenous and *mestizo* peasants and of the animosity of Creoles in the Cuzco region. Thanks to his interregional trade activities as a muleteer, he was well connected from Cuzco to Puno at Lake Titicaca and from La Paz, today Bolivia's capital, to Potosí. Indeed, in the mid-seventeenth century, Cuzco, the former capital of the Inca Empire, was a significant cultural hub and an Andean trade centre connecting interregional commerce of textiles and foodstuffs, among other goods, from Upper Peru's mineral trail to both Lima and the Río de la Plata. With the Bourbon reforms and the creation of new viceroyalties, Peruvian Andean commerce was increasingly cut off, as the trading routes with Upper Peru (today's Bolivia) reoriented from Cuzco and Lima towards Buenos Aires at the Río de la Plata. Hence, administrative restructuring hampered the old trade routes, with a negative impact on rural and urban inhabitants of the Cuzco region and beyond.

As a *cacique*, Tupac Amaru II was a cultural broker. He moved easily between the different worlds of rural and urban Peru, as well as between indigenous, Creole and Spanish cultures, and as a fervent Catholic, he had close ties to the church. A member of the indigenous nobility and a son of a *cacique*, Tupac Amaru II had enjoyed an elite and religious education in Cuzco from an early age. He was fluent in Spanish as well as in Quechua, and he read religious texts in Latin. With this cultural and educational background and aged in his early forties, he was the perfect leader of an uprising, able to tailor the anti-colonial message to different audiences (see Figure 14.1).

From the very beginning of the rebellion against Spanish rule in 1780, Tupac Amaru II aimed to build a multi-ethnic movement against Spanish colonialism – particularly against the *chapetones*,[10] as Spaniards in the colony were contemptuously referred to.

Figure 14.1 Tupac Amaru II, leader of the 'Great Rebellion' in the Andes, eighteenth-century portrait. Artist unknown. © Wikimedia Commons (public domain).

His demands were comprehensive. Tupac Amaru II called for an end to unjust taxation, and he ordered the destruction of customs houses, a symbol of the Spanish reforms that hampered interregional trade. He promised the end of the much-hated forced labour practices, particularly in the Potosí mines and the textile workshops. Furthermore, Tupac Amaru called for the end of the forced purchase of goods, the *repartimiento*. He promised to improve the lot of indigenous people and *mestizos*, but also of Creoles, in order to gain the widest possible support.

In his proclamations Tupac Amaru II indeed addressed his 'beloved Creoles' and claimed that it had 'never been [his] motivation to do them any harm, but to live as brothers and congregated in one body, destroying the Europeans'. It comes as little surprise, though, that beyond his extended family – with his wife Micaela Bastidas in a particularly significant position organizing the campaign (including its finances) during her husband's absence – Creoles constituted the movement's main leadership in the early days of the uprising. In order to recruit those loyal to the Spanish Crown, Tupac Amaru claimed that his actions were taken following royal orders, yet this was not the case.

However, it is not without a certain irony that Spanish reforms implemented at the time also aimed at curbing colonial officials' corruption and abuses against the population.[11] Overall, Tupac Amaru not only deemed Creoles' wealth and access to arms critical for the success of the military campaign; he hoped to form a sort of 'united front' of indigenous people, *mestizos* and Creoles against Spanish colonialism.

Tupac Amaru addressed himself in Quechua to the people he gathered together in small towns and villages, intentionally using the language of the former Inca Empire; he also emphasized his Inca roots through his attire and performance. Furthermore, already in the years before the uprising he increasingly referred to himself as 'José Gabriel Tupac-Amaru, *Inca*'. Thereby he underlined the 'rebirth' of the Inca ruler and the Inca kingdom that had controlled large parts of South America before the Spaniards arrived. Some sort of millenarianism – the resurrection of a utopian Inca kingdom – had been deeply rooted in indigenous cultural practice and had been passed on from generation to generation since the mid-sixteenth century. Under Spanish domination Inca millenarianism merged with related Catholic beliefs. The second half of the eighteenth century provided many reasons and an ideal breeding ground for hoping that fundamental transformations of the discriminatory colonial society were pending.

The time was right and Tupac Amaru II provided the ideal leader. His claim to be a direct descendant of the last Inca king, Tupac Amaru, whom the Spaniards had executed in Cuzco in 1572, contributed to legitimizing his entitlement to leadership among indigenous communities. Furthermore, with Bastidas as an active agent of the rebellion, the movement attracted both women and men. Spanish court records, for instance, underline that 'the wife of the Cacique of Tinta [Tupac Amaru II] manifests a supermasculine will'. Indeed, of the seventy-three members of Tupac Amaru's wider family detained in Tinta on 25 March 1783, at least thirty-two were females. Women's involvement in politics, riots and rebellions had a long tradition in the Andes and the women's role in the Great Rebellion, with some engaged in armed fighting, transgressed Spanish and colonial gender paradigms.[12]

The resurgence of the Inca kingdom seemed imminent to the thousands of indigenous and *mestizo* women and men who flocked into Tupac Amaru's ranks. Moreover, the simultaneous indigenous Catarista uprising in Upper Peru (1781–3), named after the reformist Tomás Catari, sought to join with the Tupac Amaru rebellion, not least to gain additional legitimacy among local communities. Its leader, Julián Apaza, adopted the name of Tupac Catari, underlining his admiration for Tomás Catari and the close relationship with Tupac Amaru II. Close coordination between the two uprisings ultimately failed. Yet faith in Tupac Amaru and in the rebirth of the Inca kingdom did not disappear after the leader's violent death in May 1781: 'José Gabriel Tupac-Amaru, *Inca*', it was said, would rise from the dead.[13]

While Tupac Amaru II had a tremendous impact among indigenous communities, the movement struggled, despite its leader's efforts, to win large-scale support from the urban Inca nobility of Cuzco as well as from the Creoles in general. Proclamations from the early days of the uprising show how Tupac Amaru II was courting Creoles for their much-needed backing, but also threatening them if they (and others) turned their backs on the uprising. Those who would not honour Tupac Amaru II's call were to 'experience their ruin, turning my gentleness into fury and rage, reducing this province, and those opposed to my dictum, to ashes', he declared in November 1780.[14] Indeed, according to David Cahill's analysis, when Creole units and commanders abandoned the insurgents during the failed siege of Tupac Amaru's army of loyalist Cuzco between late December 1780 and early January 1781, the 'rebellion patently underwent a metamorphosis from a broad-based alliance against the colonial system and *chapetones* generally, to an insurgency that bore all the hallmarks of xenophobic caste war' – *casta* had cultural and racial connotations in the colonies, and in this sense the phrase might best be understood as meaning 'race war'.[15]

However, Tupac Amaru II and his overwhelmingly indigenous and *mestizo* armies were not the only force that contributed to the excessive use of violence. Loyalist militias and regular troops, mostly recruited in the coastal regions of Peru, as well as troops from Buenos Aires brought to the Cuzco highlands to fight the insurgents, contributed to eroding the limits of violence. The rebels' guerrilla tactics had wearisome and demoralizing effects on the units in Spanish service. Furthermore, the rugged terrain, especially with the breathtaking altitude, was difficult to master. These factors and frustrations merged with general contempt by both the Spanish and the Creoles for the Andean communities, turning the whole region – nature and population (including children) – into absolute enemies. The insurgents, for their part, persecuted and allegedly killed anyone with supposed Western features after the perceived betrayal of the Creoles during the siege of Cuzco; sometimes Western clothing and the speaking of Spanish were reasons enough for an assault.[16] There was no neutral position for civilians, as both sides demanded loyalty and waged 'total war'.

After fighting led to as many as 100,000 victims between November 1780 and July 1783, the colonial state continued the war by other means: pursuing the extirpation of indigenous culture in the Andes. Cultural repression included promoting the use of Spanish instead of Quechua, and banning books such as Garcilaso de la Vega Inca's *Royal Commentaries*, originally published in 1609 and reprinted in 1722 – it was believed that this volume on Inca traditions and politics had inspired Tupac Amaru II's uprising against Spanish rule. Furthermore, paintings of the Inca nobility, among them a portrait of Tupac Amaru and Micaela Bastidas 'dressed as an Inca royal couple', were requisitioned and either destroyed or painted over.[17] The Great Rebellion, which for four years had severely challenged Spanish colonial rule in South America, was to be wiped from collective memory as Spanish authority was rigorously restored. However, history soon took another turn.

From rebellion to independence

After the Tupac Amaru uprising had shaken the Andes in the early 1780s, Spanish rule over Peru lasted for four more decades, until the 1820s. The myriad clientelist networks centred in Lima, economic opportunities and further privileges, in particular for the coastal Creoles, not to mention the strong presence of loyal militias and regular units in the capital and the military garrison in the nearby port-fortress of Callao, all contributed to perpetuate Spanish rule.[18] Furthermore, the Spanish Cortes – the convention in Cádiz, Spain, that adopted a liberal constitution in 1812 – seemed to respond in large part to the progressive and reformist agenda of the Creoles. It was the absolutist turn in Spain, when Ferdinand VII returned to the throne in 1814, that put a sudden end to liberal hopes in the colonies. And yet, Lima's upper class of European descent, in particular, still entered the struggle for self-determination in the Americas late and rather reluctantly. In other parts of the continent committees organizing self-government (*juntas*) had gathered, for instance, in Quito, Ecuador in 1809, and Buenos Aires in 1810; American nationalists there, in Central America and elsewhere assembled armies to fight Spanish loyalists. In Peru, however, independence was literally imposed from the outside when the Argentinian general José San Martín took Lima and declared Peru's independence in 1821. But that was not the end of the Spanish Empire in Peru.

Shortly before the triumphal entry of San Martín into Lima in 1821, Peru's last viceroy, José de la Serna, had pulled back with his forces to the Andes, first to Huancayo, then Cuzco. From the old Inca capital he tried to organize the reconquest of the territory from the nationalists. Given the presence of the Spanish viceroy, the city council requested from Madrid 'the formal confirmation of Cuzco's status as viceregal capital' in April 1824. Although the viceroy seemed uncomfortable at this prospect, at least on a symbolic level Spanish rule and the Inca past seemed to be reconciled after all. The move soon became moot as the royalist forces signed their capitulation after the decisive battle of Ayacucho in the south-central Peruvian Andes in December 1824.

Interestingly enough, 'by the very end of the colonial period the civic leaders [of Cuzco] had identified royalism as a better guarantor than insurgency of their attempts to assert regional identity'.[19] Such incidents offer a reminder that the struggles for independence in Peru were a messy affair. In colonial Peru, shifting regional interests clashed with 'race' and 'class', determining loyalist, indigenist and purported national stands (among others) during more than a decade of turmoil between 1810 and 1824. The notion of civil war indeed might aptly characterize the early decades of the nineteenth century better than the idea of heroic liberators fighting a decadent colonial power.

However, in 1824, the victory of Antonio José de Sucre's nationalist army at Ayacucho sealed the end of the Spanish Viceroyalty of Peru, which had endured for almost 300 years since its foundation in 1542. Spanish loyalist attempts to reconquer parts of Latin America nevertheless dragged on until the 1830s. Peruvian self-government practically concluded the move to independence by the old Spanish colonies of South and Central America, which had been led since 1810 by General Francisco de Miranda and after 1812 by Simón Bolívar along with San Martín, the 'Protector of Peru'.

In Central America, independence came initially with less fighting than in the south in 1821, and in 1823 the United Provinces of Central America (Chiapas, Costa Rica, El Salvador, Guatemala, Honduras, Nicaragua) separated from Mexico. A process of fragmentation characterized the territories of both Central and South America. Because of different regional interests, internal struggles, distinct ideas about the form of government – in essence monarchical versus republican – and the borders among different political entities, associations and frontiers were subject to dynamic changes until the mid-nineteenth century, and, in the case of Panamá, the early twentieth century. Britain, meanwhile, held on to its Central American colony of British Honduras (Belize) from 1840 to 1981.

In South America, San Martín and his fellow Argentine military leader Manuel Belgrano, among others, had long favoured a monarchical solution. From 1815 they actually supported what has been called the 'Inca plan', a Creole-led Inca monarchy where indigenous iconography would serve as the 'guiding fiction in the emergence of the Creole nation' throughout the southern territories, particularly in what was then called the United Provinces of the Río de la Plata. Cuzco was envisioned as the political entities' capital and Tupac Amaru's half-brother, Juan Bautista, who had been banished to Ceuta (a Spanish enclave in North Africa) for more than forty years and who only returned to the continent in 1822, was promoted as a possible representative of the new Inca state. Eventually, the 'return of the Inca' did not materialize and the exclusively Creole-centred political vision gained the upper hand at the Río de la Plata. The overwhelmingly indigenous territory in the north, today's Bolivia, parted ways and became an independent nation; yet Inca symbolism (e.g. the sun on Argentina's flag) is a testimony to a (failed) project of the invention of traditions in Latin America to this day.[20]

The years from the Great Rebellion in the Andes in the 1780s until independence of Peru in the 1820s can be interpreted as a watershed in the history of empire on a global scale.[21] The revolutionary wars in the Americas – among them those in North America (1775–83) and the Haitian Revolution (1791–1804) – and in Europe were closely connected, and the Great Rebellion in the Andes should be analysed in the context of the Atlantic Revolutions, even though it ultimately failed.[22] The Napoleonic Wars (1803–15), with the French occupation of the Iberian Peninsula in 1807, had a particular impact on the Spanish and Portuguese Empires, triggering a crisis of legitimacy in the American possessions and beyond that pushed Creoles first to demand reforms and then to claim independence. One school of thought regarding the independence of Latin American colonies highlights the fact that there was not a great deal of nationalist fervour for self-determination among the Creoles in South and Central America before the crisis in Spain (and Portugal), that is, occupation by the French; Napoleon Bonaparte in fact made his brother, Joseph Bonaparte, the king of Spain. According to this interpretation, revolutionary turmoil in Europe provided the main trigger for the revolts against Spanish rule in South America. Indeed, the Napoleonic occupation of Portugal forced a transfer of the royal court from Lisbon to Rio de Janeiro in Brazil in 1807, turning imperial notions of the 'centre' and 'periphery' upside down.[23] This understanding of Latin American history has frequently been challenged by what might be called nationalist historiography, trying to foreground a national consciousness that sometimes finds its origins in the years just after the Spanish conquest, or, at the latest, with Tupac Amaru II.

In hindsight, it is indeed tempting to portray the Great Rebellion in the Andes as an expression of early nationalism (or at least of proto-nationalism), and as a harbinger of the Latin American liberation movements of the early nineteenth century – particularly given Tupac Amaru II's initial multi-ethnic aspirations. As Peter Elmore emphasizes, Tupac Amaru's 'Inca restoration was a nationalist project, rather than a nativist one'.[24] It aimed at inventing a new community, including everyone born in the Americas, not only people with an indigenous background. And yet, an indigenous-led restoration of the Inca kingdom was certainly not on the Creoles' roadmap when imagining the Republic of Peru in the 1820s. Whereas Tupac Amaru II might have inspired the Black revolutionaries in Haiti – Jean-Jacques Dessalines is said to have dubbed his troops 'the Army of the Incas' and 'Sons of the Sun' in 1802 – white Peruvian Creoles hardly drew on the *cacique*'s legacy. What is more, not only conservative Creoles from Lima were reluctant to include indigenous communities in the fight for independence. As well, their peers from Cuzco distrusted multi-ethnic rebellions, such as the Pumacahua uprising (1814–15). Led by the *cacique* Mateo García Pumacahua (who, however, had opposed Tupac Amaru), that rebellion displayed several features familiar from the Tupac insurgency, envisioning an independent Peru with Cuzco at its centre. Creoles around Cuzco still remembered with horror the bloodbath of the 1780s, and once more turned their backs on an independence movement that encompassed the territory's different ethnic groups. With the Viceroyalty in Cuzco (1822–4), the Andean city made a last stand as anti-colonial movements had prevailed elsewhere in Spanish America.

It was only after independence that Peruvian Creoles aimed at integrating indigenous communities (at least rhetorically) in the construct of the new nation. From the perspective of indigenous people and those of lower status, independence from Spain may have brought a change in the ruling classes from European Spaniards to (white) Creoles. However, it had not produced the desired equality in social, political and economic life – a social transformation. The fault lines along racialized ascriptions together with perceived differences between the three geographical and cultural regions – the coast, the Andes and Amazonia – would shape Peru for centuries to come.

The legacies of Tupac Amaru II

Official government policy in Peru in the late 1960s and early 1970s began to promote Tupac Amaru II as a precursor of the independent nation and as a key protagonist of modern Peruvian history. He joined the narrative of white Creoles such as San Martín (the 'liberator' of Argentina, Chile and Peru) and the Peruvian naval officer and martyr Miguel Grau, who died in the War of the Pacific (1879–84), in which a Peruvian and Bolivian alliance fought Chile – men who traditionally had figured largest in the nation's pantheon. To avoid misunderstandings it needs to be highlighted that Tupac Amaru II became a hero of independence, not a 'symbol of indigenous rebellion against Spanish or Criollo power'. As the anthropologist Carmen Salazar-Soler and others have pointed out, over the course of time one can distinguish an 'appropriation of the Indio by non-Indios':[25] During the early 1970s the left-leaning military government of Juan Velasco Alvarado (1968–75) felt that the rural indigenous population's support was needed for an ambitious project of agrarian reform that aimed at a transfer of ownership of large parts of the agricultural land to rural families, preferably organized in cooperatives.

At that time the top 2 per cent of Peru's population owned over 90 per cent of the agricultural land. Consequently, the reform's ultimate goal was to break up long-standing feudal systems dating back to colonial times and initiate a transformation and modernization of rural Peru through land transfers and comprehensive rural development schemes. More than 170,000 families benefited from the reform (and prior landowners often received only symbolic compensations), yet more than a million rural families still remained landless by the mid-1970s, as the *New York Times* reported in 1974. Official government figures nevertheless claimed that more than 300,000 families had been given land by 1978. Politically the cooperatives proved to be a handy tool. The Velasco government was able to set up more 'owners' without having to 'worry about people/land ratios or the viable size of the smallest farms'.[26]

Promotion of the land reform relied heavily on visual communication, conveying the emancipatory potential of agricultural reorganization for indigenous peasants (now called *campesinos* in order to avoid the offending designation *indio*) in posters and leaflets. In the 1970s, the image of the allegedly 'backward' indigene gave way to an imagined 'inclusive modernity'. Who better than the popular last Inca pretender to champion land reform and bring rural populations on board? Slogans endorsing the reform proclaimed that '190 years later, Túpac Amaru is winning the war'. Depicting a shadow of Tupac Amaru's facial features and a large hat, the tag line on one poster further asserted that 'The rapid advances of the agrarian reform and the revolution are bringing the image and the spirit of Túpac Amaru to all of Peru'.[27] The newly crafted image of the late eighteenth-century revolutionary proved to be a valuable ally for the Velasco regime. Indeed, as Walker asserts, 'The Velasco government converted the Andean insurgent into its major symbol, emblazoning his image on banners, posters, coins, bills, and publications.' Historical accuracy was of little concern, and even invented catchy phrases were directly attributed to Tupac Amaru II ('Peasant, the master will no longer feed from your hunger') in order to show that the Inca rebel was in line with a reform serving indigenous communities.[28]

In the 1970s, therefore, Tupac Amaru II was represented as a national (indigenous) hero who stood up for his kind, amalgamating a multi-ethnic movement against foreign domination. Multiracial unity and an outside enemy – in the 1970s, the United States rather than Spain – were ingredients used to construct cohesion within a nation deeply fractured along regional, socio-economic and racial lines. In Peru in the 1980s, the appropriation of Tupac Amaru took a further turn. He was no longer used as the government's poster child; now his name was claimed by a terror group of the extreme left, the Movimiento Revolucionario Túpac Amaru (MRTA, Túpac Amaru Revolutionary Movement).[29] Founded in 1982, it contributed its share to Peru's 'age of terror' from the 1980s to the late 1990s. The small number of MRTA guerrilleros predominantly attacked the Peruvian armed forces and the police, beginning 'revolutionary war' in 1984. In 1996 MRTA made it into international headlines when occupying the Japanese ambassador's residence in Lima and taking several hundred hostages among the guests gathered to celebrate the Japanese emperor Akihito's birthday. The Japanese diplomatic premises were not by mere coincidence the target of the attack: Alberto Fujimori, Peru's authoritarian leader between 1990 and 2000, was of Japanese descent. The violent and bloody 'liberation' of the premises by the Peruvian armed forces in April 1997 brought the end of MRTA's armed branch, the Ejército Popular Tupacamarista. Although MRTA never had an impact comparable to Peru's main guerrilla organization of the 1980s and 1990s, the Sendero Luminoso (Shining Path), the movement was nevertheless part and parcel of the deadly institutions that tried to impose Marxist and Maoist ideologies and projects in Peruvian society through extremely violent means.[30]

Two hundred years after the Great Rebellion in the Andes in the 1780s, during the civil war–like decades of the 1980s and 1990s, violation of basic human rights occurred on an unprecedented scale. Massacres, violations and abuse were perpetrated by both guerrilla movements and government bodies. Urban and rural guerrilla warfare targeting armed state forces and civilians, along with state terror, claimed close to 70,000 lives between 1980 and 2000. With a share of 75 per cent of all fatalities, speakers of native languages, such as the Quechua-speaking rural Andean populations, made up the largest group of victims.[31] Violence was endemic in the Viceroyalty of Peru in the eighteenth century, with Tupac Amaru's rebellion a particularly bloody incident. Towards the end of the twentieth century extreme violence again shaped life and death in rural Peru. The disenfranchised rural poor once more bore the brunt of the war.

CHAPTER 15
MAURITIUS, 1810

'From one citizen you gather the idea that Mauritius was made first, and then heaven; and that heaven was copied after Mauritius,' reads a quotation from an 1897 book by the American novelist Mark Twain, who had recently visited the Indian Ocean island. It is much beloved by tourist promoters, who generally do not add the next lines: 'Another tells you that this is an exaggeration; that the two chief villages, Port Louis and Curepipe, fall short of heavenly perfection; that nobody lives in Port Louis except under compulsion, and that Curepipe is the wettest and rainiest place in the world.'[1] A verdant tropical landscape – 'rugged clusters of crags and peaks, green to their summits', observed Twain – has beguiled visitors from the Europeans who initially landed on the unpopulated island in the 1500s to those who lounge in high-end resorts today. The first Europeans were the Portuguese, pioneers in Western ventures in the Indian Ocean, who claimed the island for their king and gave the name of an explorer, Pedro Mascarenhas, to the 'Mascarene' islands.[2] Portuguese rule, however, remained only nominal, with no real settlement. In 1638, the Dutch United East India Company (VOC) displaced the Portuguese and used the island they named after Prince Maurice of Nassau as a stopping-off point on the spice route to Asia. The Dutch only established fledgling settlements of several hundred Europeans and slaves from eastern Africa and Madagascar, and despite the island's fine ports, they abandoned the colony in 1710. Their major legacy was eradication of the indigenous dodo, a large flightless bird hunted to extinction by the Dutch and their animals.

The Ile de France

In 1715, the French moved into the island and called it the Ile de France, expanding from the neighbouring Ile Bourbon (named after France's ancien régime dynasty), a previously uninhabited island they had acquired in the mid-1600s. For almost a century, the Ile de France and the Ile Bourbon provided France with a commercial and military base in the Indian Ocean; the declaration of Port-Louis as a free port in 1769 added stimulus to import and export. French planters produced sugar (introduced into the island's ecosystem by the Dutch), indigo and cloves. However, the merchant elite earned greater wealth from privateering – wartime attacks by corsairs on British ships in the Indian Ocean – and transhipment of goods from India and elsewhere in Asia to Africa and Europe. French colonization was built on slave labour imported from Madagascar and mainland Africa, with similar horrors to the slave system practised in the West Indies, the southern United States and Brazil.[3] Officials hoped that Mauritius would play a role in French conquest of an extensive empire on the Indian subcontinent and, in wilder dreams, the ejection of the British from India.[4] Despite the failure of those designs, the 'star and key of the Indian Ocean', as the island was later branded, boasted a crucial position for geopolitical and commercial manoeuvres in the region.[5]

If possession of the island did not lead to France amassing a large Indian continental empire, it stands out in the Enlightenment of the 1700s for its role in exploration and culture as global encounters prompted new perspectives on nature and human society. Scientific interest blended with personal initiative, commercial ambitions and political considerations, as illustrated by Pierre Poivre. Born into a family of silk merchants in Lyon in 1719, and educated at Catholic schools, in 1742 he left France for China as an evangelist with Paris's venerable Société des Missions Étrangères. Though briefly imprisoned in Canton (Guangzhou), he became a protégé of the Chinese viceroy in the port city and travelled to Macau and Fai Fo (Hoi An), a cosmopolitan trading port in Vietnam where he hoped to establish a French outpost. After returning to France and abandoning plans for ordination, Poivre again set out for Asia. In the East Indies, the British captured his ship, and a bullet wound forced amputation of part of Poivre's right arm. While recovering in Batavia (Jakarta), Pierre Poivre – whose name nicely translates as 'Peter Pepper' – became familiar with the spice trade. A monopoly of the Dutch, they rigorously forbade the export of seeds or plants that could allow production of spices to compete with their lucrative commerce. Poivre successfully sneaked nutmeg and a few other plants to the Ile de France, though they died after a gardener mistakenly poured boiling water on them. Poivre, back in France in the mid-1750s, published a celebrated travelogue, *Voyages d'un philosophe*, and became a leading light in the learned societies of Lyon.

In 1765, the king appointed Poivre *intendant* of the Ile de France, effectively the senior administrator under the governor. Poivre reorganized the bureaucracy, set up the island's first printing press and created the Pamplemousses botanical garden with plants and trees from Europe, Africa and Asia. Such botanical gardens represented major centres for research and the acclimatization of non-indigenous species for commercial uses. Poivre dispatched an expedition to the Moluccas (Maluku) in the East Indies, and it managed to bring back plants for cultivation in the Ile de France and Ile Bourbon, including ginger, nutmeg, pepper, vanilla and star anise (and he sent seeds on to the Seychelles and French Guiana as well). The first French-grown nutmeg was soon harvested, though Mauritius never became the spice-growing colony that Poivre had imagined.

Poivre made the acquaintance of many navigators who stopped at the Ile de France on voyages to and from the South Pacific at a time when the British Captain James Cook and other seafarers were 'discovering' the islands of Oceania, philosophers such as Jean-Jacques Rousseau mused about 'good savages' and European scientists enthusiastically collected and studied plants and animals previously unknown to them. Louis-Antoine de Bougainville, famous for the reports of Tahiti that so excited Enlightenment *philosophes,* called at the Ile de France in 1768 during his circumnavigation of the globe. The Comte de La Pérouse used the island as the base for his naval missions around the

Indian Ocean in the late 1770s (and married a Creole woman from the Ile de France). After La Pérouse's ships disappeared on a later scientific expedition in the South Pacific in 1788, the French sent the commander of their Indian Ocean fleet, Antoine Bruni d'Entrecasteaux, in search of the lost explorer in 1791; disputes between royalists and revolutionaries soon wracked the crew, Bruni died of scurvy and La Pérouse was not found. Another major expedition, commissioned by Napoleon and headed by Nicolas Baudin, called at the Ile de France in 1801.[6] For almost seven years, the island provided a place for detention for a British explorer, Matthew Flinders, after he urgently stopped for ship repairs on his return from Australia while Britain and France were at war in 1803.

The Ile de France thus became a link for explorers and scientists on the route between Europe, Asia and the Pacific. The island also inspired much literature, including Poivre's travelogue and works by Jacques-Henri Bernardin de Saint-Pierre. An engineer by training, the eccentric Bernardin had wandered around Europe in a variety of capacities, nurturing the hope of founding a utopian colony somewhere in the world and developing a philosophy centred on the providence of nature and a cult of agriculture. In the late 1760s, he visited the Ile de France (and met Poivre). His 1773 account described the landscape and the customs, costumes and houses of its population. Bernardin damned slavery as both inhumane and an inefficient system of labour, and his volume included a long section rebutting arguments advanced by its defenders.[7] Scathing comments about French settlers put him at odds with colonial authorities. After the Revolution, Bernardin gained appointment as director of Paris's botanical garden, the Jardin des Plantes. He won plaudits for a popular novel set in Mauritius, *Paul et Virginie*. Published in 1788, the story of ill-fated love between two young Europeans denounced the treatment of slaves but was often read as an idyll of island life.

The French elite lived a life of relative comfort in the Ile de France in the late 1700s, and the island enjoyed a reputation as a refuge for nobles fleeing the Revolution of 1789. Whites, however, numbered only about 7,000, while 60,000 of the residents were slaves – about 40 per cent from Madagascar, most others from Mozambique, and some from as far away as western Africa, Ethiopia, India and the Malay islands of Southeast Asia.

The social structure, divided between a small upper class of planters, merchants and administrators, then European artisans and small farmers further down, and the mass of Black slave and ex-slave labourers, did not change after the British took over the island in 1810. During the long drawn-out revolutionary and Napoleonic Wars that pitted the two European superpowers and their allies against each other in theatres from North America to Southeast Asia, Britain wrested away its enemies' colonial outposts – the Cape Colony in South Africa, Ceylon, the Mascarene Islands, the Seychelles and the Dutch East Indies (though the East Indies were subsequently returned to the Dutch). Their aim in taking over Mauritius, as they renamed the island, initially was to make certain that the French no longer profited from possessing it. Fighting was brief, and the defeated French governor politely invited the victorious British officers to dinner before sailing away with full military honours; the British then held a ball for the Franco-Mauritian elite. Conquest completed, the British allowed the French settlers to keep their properties, the Catholic Church retained its recognized position, French law codes were left in force, French and a French-based Creole continued as the usual languages and slavery was maintained.

Mauritius under the British

The first governor of British Mauritius was Robert Townsend Farquhar. Like many Britons in the colonies, he was of Scottish ancestry, though born in London, in 1776, the year of the Declaration of Independence by thirteen British North American colonies. Farquhar's father had served as a medical doctor in the Royal Navy, but he later opened a practice in London and became physician to the Prince Regent (the future King George IV). Robert's mother came from a wealthy (white) colonial family from Barbados. He was educated at the prestigious Westminster School, but did not pursue his studies, as someone of his background might have done, at Oxford or Cambridge. Instead, at the age of seventeen, Farquhar signed on as an ordinary 'writer', or employee, of the East India Company and was sent to Madras. He rose through the ranks, and by 1798 was Commercial Resident for the Company to Amboina and Banda, two of the Spice Islands that the British had temporarily taken over because of French occupation of the Netherlands. Hard work and family connections saw his promotion in 1804 to lieutenant governor, the senior British official, of Prince of Wales Island, the British name for Penang (Pinang) Island off the west coast of what is now Malaysia. Although Farquhar held the position for only a year, he sponsored the building of Fort Cornwallis, a road network and an aqueduct in a colony that Britain had only acquired in 1786 as it pushed further eastwards in Asia. Returning to London in 1806, as debate about slavery raged (leading to prohibition of the slave trade the following year), Farquhar published a treatise suggesting that African slaves in the colonies could be replaced by Chinese labour. Farquhar was named governor of the just conquered Ile Bourbon and Mauritius when they came under British control; the Ile Bourbon was returned to the French and renamed La Réunion.[8]

As governor until 1823 Farquhar presided over Mauritius's transition from a French to a British colony; his administration faced many challenges. In 1816, a fire destroyed 700 houses in Port-Louis, then a cholera epidemic broke out and a cyclone soon wreaked more havoc. The island nevertheless underwent considerable development during Farquhar's tenure. He laid the cornerstone for a new Catholic cathedral in Port-Louis and a Royal Exchange (a kind of chamber of commerce). He secured the king's patronage for Royal College, the colony's only secondary institution at the time. He supported the rebuilding of an opera house-cum-theatre that remains a prominent edifice. In 1812, a racecourse opened in the city; horse-racing, the governor thought, would bring together the different social and ethnic groups and promote harmony. By the mid-1820s, Port-Louis, with its busy harbour and markets, was a thriving town of 26,615 residents, including 3,387 whites, 7,511 free coloureds and 15,717 slaves, according to the official census (see Figure 15.1). Non-whites remained segregated in such quarters as Malabar Town, the 'Joloff Camp' (of West Africans) and a neighbourhood of Malagasy.

Figure 15.1 View of Port-Louis, Mauritius, engraving from Armand d'Avezac, *Iles de l'Afrique*, (Paris: Firmin Didot Frères, 1839.) © Getty Images.

Prosperous whites lived in gracious manor-houses constructed on plantations in rural locations considered more salubrious than the capital. Farquhar avidly promoted the cultivation of sugar, which became Mauritius's main export and found an improved market in Britain after tariffs were lowered to equal those on West Indian sugar in 1825. During Farquhar's term other types of production similarly expanded, including silk and opium, though neither became a major activity – and the Franco-Mauritian owner of the main opium manufactory died at one of Farquhar's Christmas parties from an overdose.

Farquhar found himself on home leave in London when a financial scandal broke in Mauritius with reports of misappropriation of funds by a senior official. The slight cloud over his reputation did not deprive the governor of the applause of the Franco-Mauritian elite and the gratitude of the metropolitan government, and award of a baronetcy, for entrenching British rule in the colony. Living back in Britain, he won election to Parliament and lived until 1830.

Slavery and indentured labour in Mauritius

The majority of Mauritius's population were enslaved, and Farquhar himself owned eight slaves. The 1807 British prohibition on slave trading was roundly ignored by planters who sought to replenish supplies from clandestine shipments; the number of slaves increased to 80,000 during Farquhar's tenure, both from natural increase and from new arrivals. The governor eventually issued orders for the slave trade with Africa to cease, and he agreed a treaty with the monarch of the Merina kingdom in Madagascar, Radama I, to stop supply of slaves from that source. Yet Farquhar and his clique remained complicit, or at the very least acquiescent, in the illegal slave trading that continued. Indeed, abolitionist

MPs roundly denounced the tacit support; Farquhar and his supporters justified slavery as a necessary evil for sugar production and colonial well-being.

As in other colonies, the enslaved were subjected, in addition to denial of freedom, to hard labour, poor living conditions and violence, as shown in individual life stories and collective patterns of the 'trauma of slavery' analysed by Anthony J. Barker. After being acquired in raiding parties by Arabs or other Africans in the hinterland and sold to Europeans, the enslaved faced a 30- to 40-day journey to Mauritius, chained and packed 300–500 per ship, two-thirds adult men and one-third women or children. Air, space and food were scarce, diseases such as smallpox might infect the Africans and the crew, guns were kept trained on the captives and punishment for disobedience was swift. On landing, most of those captured were sold as plantation workers, some as house servants or artisans. A typical workday, six days a week, began at 4.30 or 5 am and lasted until 7 pm, with a short pause for breakfast and a one-and-a-half or two-hour break at midday. (More 'enlightened' planters adopted a 'task-work' regime, in which slaves could cease work after completing assigned duties.) Sunday provided a day of rest – after slaves spent two hours of *corvée* duty in public works projects. Slaves also had to prepare their food, eating repetitive staples of rice or manioc, with occasional salted meat or fish. Women's and children's work was similar to that for men, except for some lightening of women's labour after the fourth month of pregnancy. Masters did not encourage marriage, but there were many sexual liaisons between slaves, with children generally reared in single-parent female-headed families. Sexual abuse of slave women by white masters was far from uncommon, leading to the birth of *métis* (mixed-race) children. Surveillance by overseers was constant, with offences punished by shackles or the stocks, withholding of rations, floggings with rope, whips, martinets or cat-o'-nine-tails, imprisonment and torture.[9]

The view of slaves among whites revealed contemporary racist stereotypes: Black slaves were considered to be dishonest, thieving, unclean, superstitious, lubricious and promiscuous. A few slave masters claimed to be more humane; Charles Telfair, a large slave-owner (and probable illegal purchaser of slaves as well) and private secretary of Governor Farquhar, boasted that he paid small salaries to allow slaves to buy time off work, and that he had opened a school and provided religious instruction for them. There was some humanitarian attention to slaves in Mauritius, notably efforts by the Swiss missionary Jean Le Brun, who from 1813 evangelized and gave lessons to African and Indian pupils. Le Brun faced opposition from slave-owners and, as a Protestant working for the London Missionary Society, from the Catholic Church. In Britain, abolitionists bemoaned the situation in Mauritius, but focused their attention on the Caribbean islands.

Slaves had limited resources and little recourse to justice. Barker explains that possibilities for uprisings were practically precluded by the power of the white owners and the colonial state. Occasional rumours circulated about rebellion, but the only real incident that might be considered a significant revolt, led by an exiled Malagasy nobleman, Rassitatane, in 1822, involved only twenty men; judges imposed the death penalty on twelve, but commuted several sentences. Rassitatane was executed by decapitation.[10]

According to Richard B. Allen, around 5 per cent of slaves had become *marrons* (maroons) – runaways or fugitives – under the French, and the proportion rose to 11 per cent in the first decades of British rule. Runaway slaves, who hid in the countryside, risked terrible punishment if caught: amputation of ears on the first offence, execution on the third offence. Planters used other slaves to search out and capture or kill maroons in their redoubts; until Farquhar's administration ended the practice, a bounty was paid when the severed hand of a runaway was presented. *Marronage* represented a dramatic form of resistance, but Barker, expressing a difference of opinion from Allen, suggests that much *marronage* was short-lived and motivated by slaves wishing to join family, sexual partners and friends at other plantations.[11] From 1829, after passage of the Slave Protection Acts, the enslaved could appeal to a government-appointed Protector for redress of grievances, an arduous undertaking far from certain of success. On one occasion, sixty-nine slaves from a single plantation presented themselves to the Protector with complaints of ill treatment; all but two were instructed to return to the plantation. The Protector then visited the estate, but found no evidence for the complaints and ordered that the two men he had kept back be put in chains for three months.

Other forms of resistance involved personal actions. A few whites may have been poisoned by slaves. Some slaves pilfered supplies for use or sale. Feigning illness, breaking tools or going slow at work provided other strategies, even if they left slaves liable to punishment. The ability of a few slaves to maintain small gardens and keep fowl or pigs facilitated an informal economy beyond the reach of the masters. Slaves' efforts to retain pre-captivity culture and a sense of particular ethnic identities, and to develop new forms of cultural expression, such as the *séga* music typical of Mauritius, can be understood as forms of resistance as well.

In the 1820s the British government, partly in response to abolitionists' pressure, set up a Commission of Eastern Enquiry to advise on British possessions east of the Cape Colony. Commissioners who visited Mauritius in 1826 and 1827 recommended certain ameliorations of slave life in addition to appointment of a Protector. As a result, in 1828, the flogging of female slaves was prohibited, in 1830 Sunday labour was forbidden and in 1831, the slaves' workday was nominally limited to nine hours. The plantocracy in Mauritius reacted with outrage towards measures that limited their control over slaves and, they feared, would lead to eventual emancipation. When a known abolitionist, John Jeremie, was appointed the chief legal officer of Mauritius in 1832, planters reacted in muscular fashion. Led by Adrien d'Épinay, a prominent planter, lawyer, bank director, newspaper owner and member of the colonial legislative council, they set up a militia commanded by an old Bonapartist officer (with the quiet approval of the governor, Sir Charles Colville). The slave-owners organized the closure of shops, a halt to public transport and a general shutdown of Port-Louis on the day that Jeremie sailed into the harbour. He was only able to disembark two days later, accompanied by an armed escort.

Colville gave in to the planters' pressure and ordered Jeremie to leave, though this went too far for authorities in London, who recalled Colville and sent Jeremie back to Mauritius, only for him to be sent packing yet again after a couple of years because of planters' hostility. The events helped convince liberals that the complete end of slavery in the British Empire was the ultimate reform. Thus, in 1833, Parliament enacted emancipation, which was tardily implemented in Mauritius in 1835. Slave-owners received monetary compensation, which, they grumbled, did not cover their losses. As consolation, for four years, former slaves had to work, now for a wage, as 'apprentices' (in the euphemistic nomenclature) on the estates. Some managed to gain full freedom before the end of the term. Not surprisingly, former slaves and ex-apprentices disdained plantation employment, though many had little choice. The Franco-Mauritian planter elite retained much wealth and influence.[12]

Free *gens de couleur* (people of colour) constituted an increasingly numerous group in Mauritius. Some were slaves manumitted because of the regard in which they were held by masters or as an act of piety. Contrarily, owners might grant freedom as slaves aged and were unable to work and they became an economic liability Others managed to buy freedom with profits from market-gardening and other remunerative activities. Many *gens de couleur* were women – there were more women than men – who had given birth to children fathered by slave masters, who then released them from servitude. Free coloured men and women also had come to the island on their own volition, often as artisans or seamen. With a high birth rate, the population of *gens de couleur* increased rapidly from just over 7,000 in 1806 to 18,000 in 1830. Economic expansion after the mid-1820s, thanks to growing sugar production, created opportunities for free men to work as carpenters, masons, coopers, blacksmiths, wigmakers, shopkeepers or in other occupations; there were coloured farmers and even sugar planters. Half of the free women of colour in Port-Louis worked as dressmakers or seamstresses. The *gens de couleur* invested in land with capital from gifts or bequests from former masters, their earnings, loans or family finance. Some gained significant assets; free people of colour owned over 8,000 slaves in 1809, and two-thirds of *gens de couleur* households possessed at least one slave at that date. The people of colour, though a distant rung above the slaves in the hierarchy, still suffered discrimination, including restrictions on public gatherings and higher fines for offences than those imposed on whites. Their demand for the colour bar to be removed won support from the Commission of Eastern Enquiry. In 1829, discriminatory laws that banned marriage between free people of colour and whites, denied them admission to the Royal College and forbade burial in cemeteries reserved for whites were lifted.[13]

South Asians composed a burgeoning group in Mauritius, including free Indian settlers who had come as traders or artisans. The South Asian population also encompassed political exiles from Ceylon after a rebellion against the British there in 1817–18. The British transported 1,500 convicts (only six of whom were women) from India by 1836. Almost all came from the Bengal and Bombay presidencies, two-thirds of the former convicted for crimes against property, but almost half of the latter for murder and other violent crimes. Under Governor Farquhar, they were used as labourers on public works projects such as roadbuilding and construction of the Port-Louis citadel, though gradually hired out to planters as field hands and domestic workers. Though not slaves, the Indian convicts suffered similar conditions as Africans, including arbitrary corporal punishment for perceived offences.

In 1817, in a notable episode studied by Clare Anderson, forty-seven Indians fled from one plantation complaining about 'brutal treatment' and lack of sufficient food rations, though possibly in opposition to eating from the same containers and plates as slaves because of racial and caste concerns. Authorities feared that they were linking up with African maroons and planned either to mount an attack on the Bel-Ombre plantation or to escape Mauritius for Madagascar. Some were recaptured, flogged and put on trial for desertion; the court convicted thirty-two. Like slaves, convicts engaged in acts of resistance including machine-breaking, work slowdowns, going maroon, attacking planters and burgling properties and individuals – convicts indeed burgled the head of the government convict department and the colonial treasurer. One Indian, Sheik Adam, gained notoriety for repeated attempts to kill Europeans by serving them cakes laced with poison and for habitual *marronage*; he was finally deported to Van Diemen's Land (Tasmania), where he married a convict woman transported from Liverpool. For some convicts, alcohol, opium and cannabis, as well as gambling, provided solace and recreation..[14]

Convicts represented only a small cohort in a much larger current of migration from India to Mauritius, dominated by 453,000 indentured labourers who arrived before the end of the indenture system in 1910. Efforts to recruit free workers from India had occurred before the end of slavery in Mauritius, but with emancipation, the need for labour became more acute. Recruiters 'signed up' thousands – though most could only make a cross on the indenture papers since they could not read or write, and probably had only vague notions of what indenture involved: a period of assigned menial labour, generally for three years, with a portion of wages withheld until the end of the contract, though accommodation and some supplies were promised. Their lot was hard, remuneration meagre and abuse frequent, but many nevertheless re-engaged and finally stayed permanently in Mauritius, where they came, by a considerable margin, to outnumber the descendants of slaves, *gens de couleur*, whites and other migrants such as the Chinese. The large-scale arrival of indentured Indians falls largely outside this chapter's focus on the period from 1810 to the early 1830s (and the history of indentured labour is the subject of Chapter 8 of this book), but Indian migration and the way Indians transformed Mauritian society have been well documented by Marina Carter, among other scholars.[15] Indians, including Hindus and Muslims, today form the dominant group in Mauritius.

By the beginning of the twentieth century, Mauritius had become a less vital node of the British Empire than a century earlier. During the 1800s, France had proved unable to challenge Britain, which was turning the Indian Ocean into a largely British sphere of influence, but the two countries became allies in the early years of the new century. The Suez Canal, from 1869, had opened a new route for ships journeying from Europe to South Asia and beyond without the need to pass around the Cape of Good Hope and call at Mauritius en route. Trade and sugar continued to provide varying degrees of prosperity for European, Indian, African and *métis* Mauritians. The various communities cohabited, generally peacefully, though descendants of white Franco-Mauritians kept to and married among themselves. Mauritius remained a sleepy British outpost attractive to travellers like Twain. There was relatively little anti-colonialist nationalism, though the ideas of Gandhi, who visited the island for three weeks in 1901, found a receptive audience among Indians. Sentiment in favour of self-government and independence grew gradually in later decades, largely among the majority Indian population led by Sookdeo and Basdeo Bissoondoyal.

There were some suggestions of full political integration of Mauritius with Britain, and Mauritians of African and European descent worried about their position in a future state in which South Asians would form the majority. Mauritius nevertheless moved relatively smoothly towards independence in 1968, largely immune to the crises and violence experienced in other colonies. Independent Mauritius kept the British monarch as head of state until it became a republic in 1992. A French-based Creole remains the lingua franca more than two centuries after France relinquished the island; most Mauritians also speak French and English. Hindu temples, mosques and churches dot the landscape. Near the waterfront in Port-Louis, around a park set up by the East India Company, statues of an eighteenth-century French governor, Bertrand-François Mahé de la Bourdonnais, and Queen Victoria still stand near each other, joined by monuments to the Bissoondoyal brothers and other luminaries, including a humanitarian nun, Soeur Marie Barthélemy, and the much loved *séga* performer Ti Frère.

Since independence, Mauritius has distinguished itself by democratic multiparty politics, general social harmony and the development of a diversified economy in which tourism plays a major role; sugar production has declined, but manufacturing and export processing have become mainstays of the economy. Mauritius retains close links with Britain and France, Africa and South Asia forged in colonial times. The government has regularly protested at British refusal to return the Chagos archipelago, excised from Mauritius before independence (and now the British Indian Ocean Territory). The works of present-day cultural figures, such as J. M. G. Le Clézio, a Nobel Prize–winning novelist of Franco-Mauritian ancestry and dual citizenship, and Khal Torabully, poet and theorist of 'coolitude' (the identity of diasporic Indians), like the statues in the Port-Louis park, speak of the entangled histories and cultures present on the island.

Islands of empire

Mauritius illustrates many themes of colonial history: the importance of ports and plantations in European expansion, international rivalries and warfare, the creation of new colonial societies (in this case ex nihilo on an uninhabited island), the development of export-oriented economies, the institutions of slavery and indentured labour on which some of those economies rested, multiple currents of migration, the persistence of images of tropical luxuriance and the fascination of islands for explorers, scientists and travellers. It evidences the complexities of colonial societies: the diverse geographical and ethnic origins of residents, the mixtures of languages and religions, the transformations of elites and the masses, and the anomalies of colonial situations –

the phenomenon, for instance, of free people of colour who were slave-owners, and of whites who denounced slavery.

Mauritius's history in the first decade of the nineteenth century underlines the worldwide conflict between Britain and France at a pivot point in global history, and points to London's efforts to extend its *imperium* in the Indian Ocean and towards the 'Far East'. Farquhar's biography traces the itinerary of a typical senior public servant moving from colony to colony, and his work demonstrates the powers and privileges of a governor, as well as the initiatives such officials could undertake and the challenges they faced. From the French period, the life of Pierre Poivre reveals how missionary beliefs, travel and promotion of exploration, scientific curiosity, literary and scholarly endeavours, attentiveness to commercial benefits, patriotism and service in the colonial administration combined in an individual who moved between Europe, Mauritius and eastern Asia. In Mauritius, one sees the mutations and conundrums of colonial policy, for instance, with the maintenance of slavery before and after 1810, efforts to ameliorate it with reform (as mandated by the Commission of Eastern Enquiry in the 1820s) and then abolition in the 1830s. There too one notices undertakings to address changing conditions – to adapt sugar production to international demand, to use Indian indentured labour as a substitute for African slave labour. There were, of course, proposals unrealized: Poivre's hope of Mauritius becoming a commercial spice entrepôt, Bernardin's dream of a utopian community, Farquhar's suggestion of importing Chinese workers. The colonial situation formed a country of Europeans, Africans and South Asians who evolved a hybrid culture, an agricultural and trading economy, a state that retains much of its colonial French and British heritage. The history of Mauritius embodies webs of imperial connections and legacies, as well as the asymmetries of relations between colonizers and their subjects.

With the addition of larger continental possessions to imperial portfolios – the nineteenth-century consolidation of Asian empires and the 'scramble' for Africa – the tropical islands of the early stage of colonial expansion in the Atlantic, Indian Ocean and Caribbean (with some exceptions such as Cuba) somewhat receded into the background of colonial policy and colonial historiography. In contrast to the large continental territories, small insular outposts like Mauritius or La Réunion, or St Helena and Bermuda in the Atlantic, and the French, British and Dutch islands in the West Indies appear on first sight relics of an earlier imperial age and quiet corners of dynamic new empires. That, however, is not really the case.[16] Colonial powers hung on to small islands which had come under their sway, and they took over new ones – in the South Pacific, a virtual blank on the map when Mauritius was annexed by the Portuguese in the 1500s, by the end of the nineteenth century, almost every island, no matter how remote or small, had come under rule by a colonial master.

Islands continued to provide considerable benefits for colonizers through the 1800s and early 1900s, and beyond. They offered vital ports for sailing ships, and then steamships, and later hosted a chain of aerodromes across the oceans. Sugar still poured into Europe from the Caribbean colonies, and Mauritius and Fiji; rum flowed from island distilleries, marketed with advertising images of tropical charm. Exports from 'spice islands' continued to flavour European foods, and refrigerated cargo ships made possible the transport of perishable tropical fruit. The small Portuguese colony of São Tomé and Príncipe, the 'chocolate islands', off the west African coast, became a major producer of the world's most popular confectionery ingredient (with considerable criticism provoked by the use of indentured labour from mainland Africa).[17] Copra, the dried meat of coconuts, a key export of Pacific islands, provided the raw material in a growing soap-making industry by the late 1800s. Prospectors discovered valuable minerals on islands, notably phosphate on several Indian Ocean and Pacific islands; the French exploited the world's largest deposits of nickel (vital for coinage and as an alloy in steel) in New Caledonia.

Other uses for islands had presented themselves as well: the British, after all, transported convicts to Norfolk Island and Tasmania as well as the Australian mainland for over half a century from 1788, and the French sent common criminals, participants in the radical 1871 Paris Commune, and rebels from Algeria to New Caledonia from the 1860s to the 1890s. The British shipped prisoners ranging from Napoleon to defeated Boer soldiers and Zulu rebels from South Africa to St Helena, and they shifted Indian rebels to the Andaman Islands, Penang Island and Singapore. The British exiled deposed African and Asian potentates to the Seychelles and St Helena, and the French dispatched dethroned indigenous rulers and political leaders from North Africa, Vietnam and Madagascar to La Réunion. The Salazar dictatorship in twentieth-century Portugal confined many of its political prisoners in a notorious penal colony in the Cape Verde islands.

Islands remained points of political contention, disputes resolved either by warfare, as in Mauritius in 1810, or by gentlemanly agreements. In 1890, London and Berlin bargained for Britain to take control over Zanzibar, off the eastern coast of Africa, in return for cession of Heligoland – a small set of islands in the North Sea – to Germany; proximity was not necessary for imperial island-trading. In 1911, the British and the French came to an arrangement over the New Hebrides, where New Caledonian settlers and Australians both had interests. Paris and London agreed to a joint 'condominium', with neither country claiming sovereignty, and with a representative from each power resident in the archipelago. During the First World War, the Danish sold their Virgin Islands to the United States in payment for debts, and a defeated Germany's colonies in Micronesia were transferred to Japanese rule under a League of Nations mandate. Nations still deploy colonial-era maps and proclamations in disputes over island territories from the South Atlantic to the South China Sea.

There was a heavy human cost for colonialism for islands. In the West Indies, the indigenous Carib and Arawak populations were largely wiped out, and in the Pacific islands Polynesian, Melanesian and Micronesian populations declined because of warfare, disease and ill treatment; immigration in some places left survivors economically, politically and culturally marginalized. Plantation islands in the Caribbean and parts of the Indian Ocean, of course, were populated by people enslaved in Africa and by indentured labourers at times recruited by coercion or outright violence.

Conflicts occurred within islands as well as between islands and imperial powers. Most important were the slave revolts in plantation colonies. A slave uprising in Saint-

Domingue during the French Revolution led to the birth of independent Haiti in 1804. Despite valiant attempts by slaves to win freedom elsewhere, many insurrections were put down with severity. Yet emancipation occurred because of the steady resistance by the enslaved, not just the campaigns of abolitionists. Freedom, though with neither land nor compensation, left freed former slaves in dire poverty and subject to enduring racial discrimination, prompting later uprisings, most notoriously the Morant Bay Rebellion in Jamaica in 1865. The introduction of indentured labourers profoundly changed the existing societies and cultures of the island colonies. Islands proved a source for labour as well as a site of immigration, for instance, French West Indians sent to work on a canal in Panama, 'blackbird' labourers hired in the Solomon Islands and the New Hebrides for the sugar plantations of Queensland, and migrants from the Caribbean and Indian Ocean islands employed in Britain and France in increasing numbers in the 1950s and 1960s. Movements of island people around the world continue apace. In several islands – Sri Lanka, Fiji, New Caledonia, New Guinea – ethnic and social disputes in recent years have been, to varying degrees, the legacy of demographic and social transformations wrought by colonialism.

Idyllic images of tropical islands such as Mauritius mask a complex and often painful colonial history of imperial conquest, the displacement of one power by another, the violence of slavery and indentured labour, and the poverty of islanders under the power of the colonial economy and a small settler elite. There were, as well, and for better or worse, the great ecological transformations produced by introduced species of flora and fauna, and the extinction of other species (remember the dodo), as well as building programmes that forever altered landscapes. Tourists have continued to enjoy the sun and sea, but in the background fall the lingering shadows of colonial intervention.

CHAPTER 16
CUBA, 1812

In March 1812, the Spanish colonial authorities detained José Antonio Aponte, a Black Cuban carpenter and artist from the Guadalupe neighbourhood in Havana. Aponte was accused of being the ringleader of a wide-ranging conspiracy, inciting both free Blacks and African slaves to rise against their masters and Spain, the colonial power. Aponte had served in Havana's Black militias, units of free Black men in Spain's service with a rich history – Black militias defended the colonial capital of Havana against the British in 1762 during the global Seven Years' War (1756–63). As a former militia man, Aponte knew how to handle weaponry. In the eyes of the colonial authorities, this skill made him even more suspicious and potentially dangerous.

While searching Aponte's house for incriminating evidence following his arrest, a judge along with two court officials discovered 'a book with several plans and maps and figures that was hidden in a trunk'. The illustrated volume, known today as the 'book of paintings', was at the centre of Aponte's trial. The book was a homemade compilation of pictures and maps, including Havana's fortifications. In a general way, it can be described as a summary of Black history with illustrations and drawings depicting Black history from ancient Abyssinia and Egypt to recent events in Haiti. The book featured different battle scenes with Black soldiers having the upper hand over their white enemies. There were also several portraits of Black individuals, among them 'seven blacks in different attires of a General, a Monarch, an Ecclesiastic, one of them with a priest's garment and another one of a woman with Royal insignia', the court proceedings read. Interrogations of Aponte and his acquaintances brought to the fore that the volume included, among others, portraits of the Black Haitian Jean-Jacques Dessalines, leader of a revolution in the French colony of Saint-Domingue that erupted in 1791 and first ruler of the newly independent (and renamed) Haiti, as well as of Henri Christophe I, self-proclaimed emperor of northern Haiti in 1811. As the historian Aline Helg states, Aponte had created a work of art and history representing 'a military, religious, and political world in which blacks were dominant'.[1]

In the early 1800s, memories of the successful slave revolution in Haiti between 1791 and 1804 were still fresh on the neighbouring Caribbean island of Cuba. In particular, the massacre of the several thousand remaining whites on the island had sent shockwaves across the Caribbean with its large slave societies – from Spanish Cuba to British Jamaica to the disputed Lesser Antilles of Martinique, Guadeloupe and St Lucia, among others.[2] In Cuba, rumours of the successful insurrection in Haiti triggered both the slaves' hope for social change and the white planters' anxieties. For their part, colonial officials began to increase the terror directed against Afro-Cubans, and would continue to do so throughout the nineteenth century.[3]

Hence, in the early 1800s, the possession – not to mention the compilation and illustration – of a 'book of paintings' such as Aponte's was reason enough to imagine a widespread Black conspiracy against colonial rule and the white planter elite. In Cuba, the colonial order was based more and more on mass slavery in the service of a rapidly expanding plantation system with sugarcane at its heart. This new economic order was also reflected in the island's demography. The number of slaves and free Blacks rose and would soon exceed the number of those categorized as white.

While Aponte was accused of being the mastermind behind impending widespread uprisings, almost 400 people were arrested in the course of the Spanish purportedly dismantling the conspiracy, including some 30 women. These jailed women are a reminder that organized insurrection was very much a collective project of both women and men – slave rebellions should not be viewed as entirely masculine enterprises. Along with about 30 alleged co-conspirators, Aponte was sentenced to death and hanged in Havana in April 1812.[4] Yet both slavery and Spanish colonial rule endured: slavery was only abolished in 1886, and Spanish dominion ended twelve years later.

Slavery and politics

Aponte's history book did not evolve in an isolated space. Despite efforts at censorship, Cuba's Black community was aware of revolts and the revolution in Saint-Domingue. Events there fuelled hopes that a Black revolutionary army would set sail from the western tip of Hispaniola (an island that French Saint-Domingue shared with the Spanish colony of Santo Domingo) to eastern Cuba – a distance of less than 160 kilometres – and liberate Cuban slaves. Others directed their hopes for reform towards the Spanish Crown, which had granted freedom to several enslaved individuals in the past. The convening of a Cortes (parliament) at Cádiz, in metropolitan Spain, from 1810 to 1812 triggered further prospects for a better future for slaves. Representatives from Spain and across the empire – which included much of Central and South America, the Spanish Caribbean, the Philippines and outposts in Africa as well as in the western Pacific Ocean – debated the end of the Atlantic slave trade within the Spanish-speaking world and suggested gradual abolition. Among others, Peruvian, Venezuelan and Cuban representatives, all of them speaking for societies based on slave labour, strongly opposed such proposals, and the liberal constitution adopted in March 1812 did not end slavery in the Spanish colonies. Yet rumours suggesting that abolition had indeed been declared in Spain spread like a wildfire across the Spanish Caribbean. In Cuba, several slave rebellions had already been reported from Puerto Príncipe (today Camagüey) in central Cuba and from Bayamo and Holguín in the east in 1811. In early 1812, reports from Puerto Rico (another Spanish Caribbean colony, now a 'commonwealth' of the United States) and Santo Domingo (today the Dominican Republic) confirmed uprisings there as well. If there was no connection between these actions, at least a common foundation of such widespread unrest in the Spanish Caribbean seemed plausible.

In Cuba, news about the slave revolution in Saint-Domingue also spread from within the milieu of French *émigrés* who, sometimes together with their slaves, had fled Haiti. Santiago de Cuba was often their first stop and some French planters dreamed of making a new start in the Spanish colony. They arrived with capital and skills, propelling the Cuban sugar industry and the cultivation of coffee. Whereas the French colonists shared horror stories of loss and destruction with their white Cuban peers, the slaves provided vivid narratives about heroic Black generals conquering independence to the Afro-Cubans. In Cuba, however, despite supra-regional conspiracies and revolts such as the Aponte Rebellion of 1812 or the near-revolution of La Escalera (1843–4), it would be a long struggle until the cessation of the slave trade, abolition and the end of Spanish colonial rule (see Figure 16.1).

While armed struggles in the Spanish mainland colonies in Latin America finally brought independence from the southern tip of the vice-royalties of Río de la Plata (Argentina, Chile, Bolivia, Paraguay and Uruguay) to the northern borders of New Spain (encompassing Mexico, California, Florida and Central America) between 1810 and 1824, Cuba acquired the nickname of 'the ever faithful' isle. Cuba's belated independence from Spain can be explained from different angles. Cuba had held particular strategic importance for the Spanish Empire in the Americas since its early days as a colony in the late fifteenth century. The largest island of the Antilles – 1,200 kilometres from east to west and between 50 and 200 kilometres from north to south – Cuba was occupied by the Europeans in the early 1500s. At that time, the tropical island was populated

PUNISHING SLAVES IN CUBA.—[Photographed by C. D. Fredericks, Calle de Habana, 108.]

Figure 16.1 'Punishing Slaves in Cuba', engraving in *Harper's Weekly*, 28 November 1868. © Wikimedia Commons (public domain).

by around 200,000 people, mostly Taínos who had migrated from the Latin American Orinoco region to the Caribbean islands between 1000 and 1200 CE. The Ciboney, however, were the group settled in Cuba the longest, since 1000 BCE. Spanish warfare, forced labour and pathogens so far unknown to the local populations decimated the Taínos and Ciboneys throughout the sixteenth century.

Santiago de Cuba, located at the eastern tip of the island, was the first Spanish capital (1515–56). Yet it was Havana in western Cuba with its strategic position close to the Central American mainland colonies that became the most important hub within the Spanish Empire, and the Spanish governor relocated there in the 1550s. The seizure of Mexico and Peru further boosted Cuba's position within the Spanish imperial domain. In the harbour of Havana a convoy of ships, loaded with gold and silver from Spain's colonies in the Americas, gathered to cross the Atlantic. Hence, the island, particularly its new capital, was heavily fortified and militarized, as it would remain through the centuries of Spanish rule, a major obstacle facing any movements aiming at independence. Furthermore, the wars of independence on the American continent in the first two decades of the nineteenth century prompted the emigration of a significant number of Spanish loyalists, many of whom found a new home in Cuba. The influx of these conservative royalists, including those who had left the Latin American mainland after imperial Spain's last battle in Ayacucho, in the Peruvian Andes in December 1824, further contributed to Cuba's 'ever faithful' stand.

In economic terms, Cuba had vastly benefited from the revolutionary turmoil and the collapsing sugar economy in Saint-Domingue after 1791. Towards the end of the eighteenth century, Cuban planters filled the gap in sugar production and set out to conquer the world markets. At the turn of the nineteenth century Cuba also became a hotspot of the transatlantic slave trade, even though enslaved Africans had been present on the island since the sixteenth century. Agents of European empires forced more than twelve million Africans across the Atlantic to the Americas between the sixteenth and the nineteenth century, and the Spaniards were major slave traders and users of enslaved labour.

For Cuba alone, over 180,000 enslaved Africans were transported across the ocean just between 1810 and 1825. From 1821 to 1878, Cuban and Spanish *negreros* (illegal slave traders) trafficked between 700,000 and 1.3 million Africans to the Caribbean island and probably a similar number transited via Cuba to the United States until the end of slavery there in 1865. Forced migration on a massive scale transformed the structure of the Cuban society: 'by 1817, almost 40 percent of Cuba's inhabitants were slaves, and people of African descent, both free and enslaved, outnumbered whites despite heavy immigration by Spaniards and royalists fleeing the wars of independence on the [Latin American] continent.'[5] Until the 1850s, the Black and mulatto (usually a mixture between Black and white) population surpassed those categorized as 'whites' in Cuba. Meanwhile, the island's sugar production increased dramatically, with a rise of over 56 per cent in the 1830s. 'It is now beyond contradiction', a British economist contended in 1840, that Cuba is 'the wealthiest and most flourishing colony possessed by any European'.[6] Indeed, in the mid-1850s Cuba claimed about 27 per cent of the world's highly lucrative sugar market, producing 392,000 tonnes, most of it destined for export. Cuba's wealth thus depended to a large degree on the plantation economy and the forced labour of enslaved Africans.

The spectre of a possible slave revolt and a 'race war' haunted Cuban planters throughout the nineteenth century. Spain aptly exploited fears of another Haiti, reminding defiant Cuban Creole planters (*criollos*, the locally born white Spanish) that their business model depended on the Spanish government and its soldiers. Only the colonial status quo in relationship to the metropole would guarantee the continued existence of the 'successful' slave economy.

Officially, Spain had agreed to end the slave trade in 1817, yet only in 1867 was the prohibition effectively enforced. Moreover, Spain not only tolerated the illegal transatlantic slave trade on Cuban shores, but the island became a hub for the illegal trade to the United States, where enslaved Africans laboured on the cotton fields of the southern states. In fact, the years after the 'Age of Abolition' – roughly from 1808 to 1839 – saw an unprecedented surge in Spanish and Cuban involvement in the transatlantic slave trade. This was the 'Hidden Atlantic', as the historian Michael Zeuske has termed the period of the clandestine trade that lasted until the 1870s.[7]

In Cuba, the militarized environment, the influx of loyalists from South America and the dependence on a slave-based economy combined to keep the colony and its Creole elites in check, and to dissuade the upper class from seeking the sort of independence as their peers in South America had gained. At the same time, Cuba, at least in regard to the white elite, did not correspond to the cliché of an exploited and subjugated colony in the early nineteenth century. With political turbulence and war raging both in metropolitan Spain and Latin America, Cuba enjoyed a period of quasi-autonomy. Wealthy Cuban Creoles and their lobbies in Spain time and again directly influenced politics in Madrid to Cuba's favour, meaning to their own benefit. The island, with its thriving economy and vibrant cultural life, did not resemble the idea of a backward 'periphery' dominated by a culturally and economically advanced 'metropole'; Havana with its theatres and literary life as well as musical scene, in some ways, was as lively as Madrid or Barcelona. In Cuba, not in metropolitan Spain, the first Spanish railway began operations in 1837; not until 1848 was there a rail line in metropolitan Spain. In Cuba, modernization of the economy and cultural life thus advanced at a rapid pace throughout the nineteenth century.

It is not much of a surprise, therefore, that economically and culturally the 'modern' colony became dissociated from the 'backward' metropole. Profits and surplus from the Cuban tobacco, coffee and sugar industries were not invested in Spain, as Britain and later the United States became the Cubans' preferred placements for their assets. Wealthy Creoles also preferred to send their offspring to universities in the United States rather than to Spain. Towards the mid-nineteenth century, Cubans' focuses were even changing in sport, as interest in American baseball grew while the attraction of Spanish bullfighting declined.[8] Instead of offering the thriving Cuban elites further political inclusion and participation, however, Spain sought to tighten its control. It extended the authority of the captain general in Cuba,[9] granting the office power comparable to that of a viceroy in 1825. In 1837, Spain marginalized Cuban representatives from constitutional structures in the European metropole. With vague 'special laws', which however were never enacted, Spain aimed to tighten its grip over Cuba after the 1830s. Excluding Cuba from the liberal Spanish (metropolitan) constitutional politics and administration consolidated the island's colonial position in political terms throughout the remainder of the century.[10]

Against the backdrop of these and other developments, the nearby United States suited the Cuban planters more and more. The United States showcased attributes of modernity and progress, which Spain, in their view, was mostly lacking. With the US slave economy in the south, Cuban planters' business interests seemed in good hands, at least until the American Civil War (1861–5) brought abolition. The orientation towards the United States – emblematized in the Cuban flag by the lone star reminiscent of the stars on the American flag – translated into a political movement promoting possible annexation of Cuba by the United States. Although the so-called *anexionismo* was most prevalent in Cuba around the 1850s, it proved a long-lasting political current. The growing Creole disenchantment with Spain offered a clear indicator that half-hearted colonial reforms by Madrid would not suffice to maintain Cuba, 'the pearl of the Antilles', within Spain's residual empire.

War and revolution in Cuba, 1868–98

War and revolution in Cuba did not originate from a much-feared slave uprising. It was a white Creole planter from eastern Cuba, Carlos Manuel de Céspedes, who 'liberated' his slaves and rose up against Spanish domination. Céspedes and his call for war, the so-called Cry of Yara, initiated the Ten Years' War in October 1868. Along with the long-standing unease about the colonial situation, the failed attempts at reforms in Madrid and an increase in taxes might be seen as the immediate triggers for the uprising. Indeed, in its early stages, the conflict can be understood as the continuation of the reformist movement on the island, as politics by other means. Within a few months, though, the longing for self-determination and freedom made this a formidable movement for independence. What became known as the *Guerra Grande* ('Great War') only came to a negotiated end with the Pact of Zanjón in 1878.

The uprising had its origins among Creoles in eastern Cuba, where small-scale agricultural and cattle production was less dependent on slave labour than in the western part of the island with its large plantations and sugar factories. With the differences between the rather backward east (*Cuba pequeña*) and the thriving and modern west (*Cuba grande*), the conflict took on aspects of a civil war. This domestic conflict also related to the composition of the different regional populations. Besides the large slave populations of African descent, western Cuba hosted a substantial group of recent Spanish immigrants, so-called *peninsulares*. Meanwhile, the east was predominantly Creole territory with large pockets of (free) Afro-Cubans.

Throughout the Ten Years' War, armed conflict was mostly confined to the eastern part of the island. However, the reign of terror of voluntary militias in Spain's service covered the major cities across the island, including Santiago de Cuba, the second largest city. In the shadow of the 'civil war', the colonial state waged a ruthless campaign against Cuban Creoles throughout the island. Accusations of sympathizing with *Cuba libre* (Free Cuba) and the 'Republic in Arms' – founded by the insurgents in Guáimaro (Camagüey) in April 1869, with Céspedes as the first president – were reasons enough for the expropriation and sale of the goods and properties of those branded disloyal. 'Under the guise of preventing Cuban independence, socio-economic repression was consistent with peninsular attempts to radically re-Hispanize the island,' the historian Alfonso W. Quiroz argues in his socio-economic analysis of the 'Great War'.[11]

In the early days of the conflict, Afro-Cubans considered the struggle a white man's war alien to their own interests. Although Céspedes and others 'liberated' their slaves in order to fight shoulder-to-shoulder against colonial domination, the social order of the master and the slave was hardly challenged and indeed was widely reproduced within the revolutionaries' ranks. The rebels took an ambivalent stand towards the abolition of slavery. Instigating slaves to revolt would be punished, Céspedes declared in a decree in 1868. But then the rebel camp affirmed that the end of slavery would follow when the war was won. Gradual abolition seemed to be the way for the insurgents in the east to go in order not to frighten the planters in the west. However, the 1869 constitution of Guáimaro acknowledged that all inhabitants of Cuba were free even if the 'Republic in Arms' barely had the means to enforce its decision. Moreover, a restrictive decree (*Reglamento de Libertos*) for freed Blacks immediately watered down the earlier regulations, stipulating the obligation to work and masters' rights to sanction the *libertos'* alleged misdeeds. It was only in December 1870 that Céspedes as the president of the 'Republic in Arms' finally declared abolition in the name of *Cuba libre*.[12]

Imperial Spain, for its part, in July 1870 had passed the Moret Law, which guaranteed the 'freedom of wombs', ending the continuing enslavement of children from one generation to the next. Such decrees and laws are a reminder that Afro-Cubans, free and enslaved, had become an important asset for both warring parties during the Ten Years' War. It was, though, mostly within the ranks of the revolutionaries where Afro-Cubans gained recognition as fighters and won prestige as strategists. The Maceo brothers, Antonio and José, are a case in point. Enlisting in the ranks of the revolutionary army as a private, Antonio Maceo, born in Santiago de Cuba in 1845 as the son of a Venezuelan farmer and an Afro-Cuban woman, rose in the military ranks to become a major general. His military career was nevertheless hampered time and again due to racist prejudice from within the ranks of *Cuba libre*. White revolutionaries feared losing their grip over the war of independence to a supposed 'Black dictator' like Maceo. Maceo's social-revolutionary convictions also clashed with the white Creoles' rather conservative conceptions for the envisioned republic of Cuba. Many Creoles fought for political self-determination of the island, that is, the end of Spanish rule, not for the radical social change that provided an objective for some of the Afro-Cubans.[13]

Race and class were probably the most important fault lines within the rebels' camp. Regionalism, conflicts between the military and the civilian leadership and personal animosities further hampered the fight against Spanish colonialism. However, the

Pact of Zanjón at least brought freedom to all the slaves who had fought in either the revolutionaries' or empire's ranks. The protracted armed struggle with the large Afro-Cuban participation had decisively contributed to phasing out slavery by 1880, leading to formal abolition in 1886. In the Americas, only abolition of slavery in Brazil, in 1888, came later than in Cuba.

Even so, the end of slavery did not necessarily bring the change in social relations and the economic opportunities many had hoped for. Former slaves often found themselves compelled to continue working on the same sugar estates as before – now for a wage that barely guaranteed survival. Socio-economic change, particularly the industrialization of sugar production, resulted in a painful concentration of the business. Former small-scale producers became mere sugarcane suppliers or contractors. Furthermore, increasing beet sugar production in Europe after the 1860s eroded the price for cane sugar on the world market. In a nutshell, Cuba's post-war society struggled on many levels. There was widespread destruction from the war in which many had lost properties. Heavy taxes introduced by Spain – shifting the costs of the war to the Cuban population – along with a global economic recession, brought a heavy dependence on US capital and markets or pushed former producers into poverty. Spaniards controlled the administration of the island and thus the job market. As Louis A. Pérez Jr. put it: 'There seemed to be no place for Cubans in Cuba.'[14]

This challenging socio-economic situation affected Afro-Cubans in particular ways. The impact of slavery and continuing racial inequality resulted in a broad divide and imbalances, for example regarding education and property. In 1887, only 11 per cent of Afro-Cubans of any age were literate compared to 33 per cent of whites. About 14 per cent of Afro-Cubans owned or rented land in 1899, the first year that statistical data are available, while among whites, 22 per cent were either proprietors or tenants.[15]

Observing race-based inequality in Cuba from his early age, José Martí nevertheless believed that all humans were equal. Born in 1853 to Spanish parents, already as a teenager, he fervently challenged the colonial social order. Because of his precocious political writing, Martí was incarcerated in Havana at the age of seventeen and then forced into exile, first to the Isle of Pines (today Isle of Youth) south of the Cuban mainland, then to mainland Spain, where he was able to attend university in Madrid and Zaragoza. After a short sojourn in Cuba after the Ten Years' War, exile again forced Martí to Spain, then to Latin and Central American republics before he settled in the United States, in New York, where he spent the years from the 1880s to the mid-1890s. During this time, Martí became a prolific poet and writer, pioneering early Latin American modernism, as well as a tireless organizer and speaker for *Cuba libre*.[16]

'There can be no racial animosity, because there are no races,' Martí wrote in his 1891 essay 'Our America'. From the early 1880s, he was working towards Cuban unity among the exiled community in the United States, particularly among tobacco workers in southern Florida whom he frequently visited. Trying to bring the veterans of the Ten Years' War onto the same page with the young revolutionaries, his efforts resulted in the foundation of the Cuban Revolutionary Party in Florida in 1892. The party provided the fundamental political structure to prepare what was called the 'necessary war', which eventually erupted in February 1895, and culminated in a US intervention in 1898.

Explaining the political foundation of the revolution to the Cuban people, Martí and Máximo Gómez, a veteran of the Ten Years' War and general-in-chief of the Ejército Libertador Cubano (ELC, Cuban Liberation Army), insisted in the 'Manifesto of Montecristi' that the 'fear of the black race' – as they phrased it – had always been unfounded in Cuba. In an inclusive manner, they also clarified that 'this [was] not a war against the Spaniard' but rather against the colonial regime. Martí and Gómez promised an orderly and short war.[17] Yet, there was and is no such thing as a 'clean' war, and the Cuban War of Independence (1895–8) was no exception. Ruthless Spanish anti-guerrilla warfare including large-scale civilian internment, along with blockades of cities and towns by the ELC, caused massive deaths among the civilian population. Between 150,000 and 170,000 people (roughly 10 per cent of the inhabitants of the island) fell prey to a combination of hunger, disease and epidemics such as diarrhoea and smallpox. Unsanitary conditions, malnutrition and a great deal of disregard for civilians provided the breeding ground for this humanitarian disaster to unfold.[18] The 'dirty war' in Cuba was a harbinger of the wars of decolonization in Asia and Africa in the twentieth century.

Martí did not have to witness the sad spectacle of ubiquitous deaths on the island. Shortly after he had again set foot on his native Cuban soil to join the war of independence, he died in a skirmish in Dos Ríos, in eastern Cuba, in May 1895. Maceo, the prestigious Black general of the Ten Years' War, was killed in battle in December 1896. Maceo had managed to bring the war to the rich western provinces, the Spanish stronghold. Entering western Cuba felt like crossing the Pyrenees and entering Spain, a Cuban rebel noted in his diary in December 1895.[19] In January 1896, Maceo and his army of 'invasion' had reached Mantua at the western tip of the island. In contrast to the Ten Years' War, the revolution was not confined to the east. Furthermore, in August 1896, on the other side of the world, Filipino patriots led by Andrés Bonifacio took up arms against Spanish domination. 'The revolution in the Philippines is formidable', Cuban patriots excitedly commented. The 'transcendental uprising in the Philippines' would put Spain under pressure on two fronts. Cuban and Filipino nationalists were well connected, and revolutionary networks spread across the globe, from the Caribbean to Europe and south-eastern Asia.[20]

In Cuba, the 'invasion' of the western part of the island was not only a military feat, but a significant indication of the broad social basis of the war and sentiment across the island. Throughout the colony, Afro-Cubans joined the rebels' ranks in large numbers. Indeed, Afro-Cubans were highly overrepresented in the liberation army. Whereas Cubans of African descent made up less than one-third of the total population of the island in the 1890s, they accounted for almost two-thirds in the revolutionary forces. The Afro-Cuban participation in the war of 1895 was both one of resistance against Spanish overlordship and a campaign for equality within Cuban society.

Among the rebels were also women engaged in armed combat. Yet the families and partners of the insurgents mostly provided essential services in the rearguard. In cities and towns female supporters of *Cuba libre* similarly contributed their part to the revolution, furnishing the rebel forces much-needed information about Spanish military preparations. Others, such as the wealthy Marta Abreu, financially supported the insurgency from abroad. Women's contributions to the Cuban War of Independence were wide-ranging. Comments from Spanish soldiers and officials seem to confirm the significance of female participation: 'The woman has been the main factor in the increase of this war, because instead of containing [them], she has pushed the brother, the son, the boyfriend' into the revolutionaries' ranks, the Spanish governor of Santiago de Cuba stated in 1895. Other military observers assured in their memoirs that they had spotted the betrayal of the Spanish in the 'black eyes imbued with malice' of young Cuban women whom, in a paternalistic manner, they called *criollitas* (little Creole women).[21] In a war with few battles and no clear-cut front lines, the enemy was assumed to be everywhere, not least among young Cuban women.

Times of war were prone to produce extraordinarily asymmetrical power structures, which became particularly visible at the intersections of gender with race and other social markers. In the war of 1895, Spanish soldiers arriving in Cuba quickly learned that their 'whiteness' trumped their often humble social origins. In April 1896, a Catalan soldier wrote to his mother that 'there is no soldier in the company who does not have a "*negrita* [little Negress]"'. And he continued that Black women and *mulatas* were 'suffering so much misery' because of the war that 'one does what one wants with them' for only some scraps of food.[22] Imbalances of power along with old colonial stereotypes of the immoral *mulata* and the always sexually available Black woman did their part in rationalizing Spanish soldiers' actions in Cuba. Abuse and sexual exploitation of Afro-Cuban women continued beyond slavery.

From US Intervention (1898) to Martí's Unfinished Revolution (1959)

Spanish propaganda eagerly turned the 'rebels into collective and personal threats to the white population'. Revolutionaries were referred to as 'savage hordes', 'Black assassins' or simply as 'bandits' – in any case as beyond the pale of civilization. In Spanish illustrations animal-like Black creatures ambushed the captain general of the island in the jungle or a black monster just gobbled up helpless little Spain.[23] In any case, the propaganda war was just as important as actual fighting in the *manigua*, the Cuban countryside and jungle. On the propaganda front, the Cuban rebels and their revolutionary junta in the United States clearly had the upper hand. According to their narrative, brave Cuban freedom fighters rose up in arms against a decadent and backward monarchy. The Cubans' success is reflected in their countless heroic stories about fearless Cuban revolutionaries fighting bloodthirsty Spaniards published in US newspapers throughout the war. On all sides, propaganda was highly gendered. It was all metaphorically cast as saving the allegedly helpless woman or girl – whether Spanish or Cuban.[24]

Indeed, the US intervention in April 1898 and the takeover of Cuba, Puerto Rico and the Philippines has also been interpreted through the lens of gender. Virile US politicians and their armies 'fighting for American manhood' came to the rescue of the feminized neighbouring island.[25] Notwithstanding such imagery, the reasons for a military intervention and eventual annexation were manifold. There had been great US interest in Cuba since the eighteenth century and several attempts to buy the island from Spain during the nineteenth century. US capital had dominated the Cuban sugar industry since the 1880s. Together with the hawkish US consul in Havana, Fitzhugh Lee, and US presidential advisers such as Edwin F. Atkins, who was heavily entangled with Cuban businesses, this made for an explosive cocktail. When the USS *Maine*, allegedly on a friendly visit to Havana, blew up on 15 February 1898 under unclear circumstances, killing more than half its crew, this seemed reason enough to intervene. 'Remember the Maine, to hell with Spain' was the battle cry of US imperialists and the sensationalist press, both pushing for war.

Historians still do not agree if the United States intentionally left the war on Cuba to 'bleed out' before securing the supposedly easy prize; if they stole the Cubans' impending victory over Spain; or, on the contrary, if Spain had just managed a turnaround in its efforts to secure the colony before the American invasion, having granted the island autonomy only a few months earlier. Others again consider the US intervention in Cuba the first modern 'humanitarian intervention', putting an end to years of civilian suffering on the island. What is clear, though, is that the US move rhetorically turned a long and bloody struggle between Cubans, Spaniards and Filipinos into a 'splendid little war' between an old and a new colonial power, that is, the Spanish-American War fought in the Caribbean and the far western Pacific. This perspective, however, fails to grasp the Cubans' long, almost thirty-year anti-colonial struggle since 1868. It also wrongly characterizes the Filipino War of Independence (1896–8), which then continued against the new colonizers, the United States, after 1899.

With the US intervention in the Cuban War of Independence in April 1898, the perception of the brave Cuban liberator swiftly changed. What was once portrayed as a well-organized liberation army became a quarrelling crowd, incapable of self-government. After the ceasefire agreed with Spain in August 1898, US officials refused to collaborate with the overwhelmingly Black and mulatto Cuban Liberation Army. They preferred to team up with the Spanish troops they had been fighting against for guard duties in Cuban towns and hamlets (and later encouraged further white Spanish immigration). No Cuban was present when the US and Spain signed the peace treaty in Paris in December 1898, handing over Cuba, Puerto Rico, the Philippines and Guam to the United States. With the US takeover of Cuba, Martí's vision of a racial democracy seemed far away.

US occupation formally ended in Cuba in 1902, even though the island's politics would still be hampered by the large shadow cast by the neighbour in the north – first in a formal way, by the Platt Amendment to Cuba's constitution that allowed the United States to intervene in the island's political landscape whenever deemed necessary, and later informally, through the backing of corrupt Cuban politicians and dictators. It comes as no big surprise, though, that Fidel Castro and his guerrilla movement (the Movimiento 26 de Julio), which overthrew the American-supported Fulgencio Batista regime in December 1958 claimed to be fulfilling the unfinished revolution of 1895.

Castro further asserted that José Martí was the 'intellectual' author of the uprising against the Batista dictatorship.

In the years after 1959, the socialist Castro regime aptly appropriated Martí's thinking, including the idea of Cuba as a racial democracy. It is undisputed that several Afro-Cubans rose to important positions within the new government and the army. Many poor Blacks also gained access to education and healthcare. After a campaign to eliminate racial discrimination (1959–61), the regime declared that racism no longer existed in Cuba. Yet this did not solve the structural problems in society, nor did centuries-old prejudice just disappear. Colonial stereotypes are long-lasting and shape Cuba and our world to this day. The objectives of antiracism, democracy and equality are still part of the unfinished Cuban revolution.[26]

CHAPTER 17
INDIA, 1876

By the 1870s, the British felt more secure in their rule over the Indian subcontinent and its 250 million people than they had at mid-century. The 'Mutiny' of 1857 – the Great Uprising – was receding into the past, though still present in memory, with Indians seeing it as a heroic though ill-fated episode of resistance against the colonizers and the British viewing it as an equally heroic triumph over insurrection. The cities of Bombay, Calcutta and Madras were thriving entrepôts for the export of cotton, textiles, tea, the opium destined for China and a wealth of other goods. A vast network of railways, symbol of technological prowess, economic development and modernization, was rapidly covering the country. Telegraph lines sped up communication, and the opening of the Suez Canal in 1869 had shortened the voyage from Britain to India from almost three months to three weeks. The British viceroy presided over the Government of India and an Indian Civil Service in which almost all positions were held by Britons who passed competitive examinations in London (with questions on the Latin classics and horsemanship among other subjects), while the imperial Indian army, staffed largely by Indians though commanded by Britons, defended the Raj from attack from without and rebellion from within. There was, in particular, growing fear of potential Russian advances after tsarist expansion in central Asia, the 'Great Game' familiar to readers of Rudyard Kipling's novel *Kim*. Britain engaged in wars in Afghanistan and Burma to push back the frontiers of its South Asian empire, though they were far more successful in the latter case – Afghanistan, for the British and others, became the 'graveyard of empires'.[1]

The British Empire in India covered the countries that are now India, Pakistan and Bangladesh (and Burma until the 1930s was included in the viceroy of India's domains). The British ruled much of this immense territory directly ('British India'), but two-fifths of the Indian subcontinent remained under the nominal authority of almost six hundred monarchs, bearing such titles as nizam, maharaja, gaekwar and nawab, whom the British generically referred to as 'princes' (so, 'Princely India'). Their states ranged in size from Hyderabad, almost as large as the United Kingdom, to ones barely bigger than villages. When the British government assumed control over India from the East India Company in 1858, Queen Victoria promised that 'We shall respect the Rights, Dignity, and Honour of Native Princes as Our own; and We desire that they, as well as Our own Subjects, should enjoy that Prosperity and that social advancement which can only be secured by internal Peace and good Government' – that 'internal Peace and good Government' was something the British thought only they could give. The princes retained rights to mint coinage, operate railways, collect and expend revenue and enjoyed further financial, administrative and cultural prerogatives, but the presence of heavy-handed British Residents or Agents in their courts kept them on tight rein.

Meanwhile, new entrepreneurial, managerial and intellectual elites emerged in the cities of India, and were increasingly eager for a political voice. There were initially no Indian representatives on governing councils in British India, though in time Indians were elected, in limited numbers, to several municipal and legislative councils, fulfilling a notion of representative government though not responsible government: ultimate power remained with the foreigners throughout the Raj. The masses of the Indian population, the majority of whom lived in rural areas, went about their daily existence directly and indirectly affected by the workings of the colonial state, required to pay British-imposed taxes and obey colonial laws. They farmed, fished or worked at artisanal crafts, and practised Hinduism, Islam or the other religions of the subcontinent, their lives set within the contexts of caste, regional cultures and the struggle for survival against poverty, inequality, and the destructive phenomena of the natural world, such as monsoons and droughts.

India, from the peaks of the Himalayas in the far north and the fertile plains of Punjab, across the desert of Rajasthan and the delta of the Ganges in Bengal, down to the tropical landscapes of Kerala and Tamil Nadu in the south, was and is a mosaic of peoples, languages, occupations and cultures, more difficult than most countries to try to encompass in a single grasp, or to examine even with a focus on a single year or two. The years 1876 and 1877 provide one window through which to look at several developments that illustrate the paradoxes of India and the exactions of British rule. This chapter concentrates on four themes: the proclamation of Queen Victoria as 'Empress of India' in 1876 and a celebration of the event held in Delhi in early 1877; a famine that devastated the south of the subcontinent from 1876 to 1878; the first airing in 1876 of an argument by a prominent Indian intellectual, politician and businessman, Dadabhai Naoroji, that British rule was draining India of its wealth; and the establishment in the same year of the reformist Indian National Association, a precursor of the Indian National Congress, which would lead the country to independence in 1947. But first, a little travelogue by a British visitor in 1876 sets the scene and gives insight into some British perspectives on the Raj.

Isabel Burton's impressions of India, 1876

Isabel Arundell was born in 1831, in London, into a Roman Catholic family of aristocratic antecedence, and in 1860 married Richard Burton, one of Britain's leading Orientalists – a rather extraordinary man who after being expelled from Oxford University for violating regulations by attending a steeplechase, joined the British army, travelled in disguise to the holy city of Mecca (off-limits to non-Muslims), explored central Africa, served in the colonial Government of India, wrote a report on Indian brothels and a disquisition on homosexuality in what he labelled the 'Sotadic zone' of the earth, translated Persian poetry (for he spoke many languages) and was a British consul in Syria. Isabel Burton's activities were more circumscribed by gender conventions, but she was well-educated and engaged in the affairs of her day. In 1876, she journeyed to India for a brief stay with her husband and penned her impressions of the subcontinent.

Burton's words reveal the commonly held opinions of British tourists (and many others of her time). On arrival in Bombay, 'We went to see the sights of the town, and I was very much interested in all that I saw, though the populace struck me as being stupid and uninteresting.' She marvelled at near-naked children playing in the streets, and men transported in palanquins. She made an excursion to view the splendid statues in the caves of Elephanta, saw a 'Moslem miracle play' (which she attended alone since other Europeans in her party showed no interest), enjoyed British-style horse races, and visited the 'harem' of an acquaintance of her husband, 'where we women smoked a narghileh and discussed religious topics, and they tried to convert me to El Islam [sic].' Burton, like most travellers, commented with voyeuristic curiosity on the Parsi 'towers of silence' where corpses were placed to be picked clean by vultures, a custom she found 'revolting' (though she was also disconcerted by Hindu cremation practices). More cheerfully, she visited a hospital for 'sick, maimed and incurable animals' set up by the Parsi businessman and philanthropist Sir Jamsetjee Jejeebhoy.[2]

Burton remarked on the hospitality of both Indians and her British compatriots, but she found the Britons pretentious and obsessed with questions of social standing. 'The Anglo-Indian ladies of Bombay struck me for the most part as spiritless. They had a faded and washed-out look,' which she blamed on idleness and routine. The men she judged more vigorous 'because they have cricket and polo'. In Bombay, getting over her initial impression,

> I found the native populace much more interesting. The great mass consists of Konkani Moslems, with dark features and scraggly beards. They were clad in chintz turbans . . . and in long cotton coats, with shoes turned up at the toes, and short drawers or pyjamas. There were also Persians, with a totally different type of face. . . . Arabs from the Persian Gulf, sitting and lolling in the coffee-houses. . . . There were athletic Afghans, and many strange tribes. There were conjurers and snake-charmers, vendors of pipes and mangoes, and Hindu women in colours that pale those of Egypt and Syria.

Burton travelled onwards to Poona (Pune), the Portuguese colony of Goa, and Hyderabad ('ruled over by our faithful ally the Nizam', the wealthiest of the Indian princes), where a most memorable evening was spent at a fairy-tale palace, complete with a fête and dancing by nautch girls. Then on to Secunderabad, Hyderabad's twin city, which contained a British cantonment – 'a prosperous European station, with three regiments, but nothing interesting', she added dismissively, like a guidebook commentator. Afterwards came Golconda, where there were beautiful carvings, palaces and gardens, 'a romantic spot' for 'a balmy night' where 'fireflies spangled the domed tombs in the palm gardens, lit by a crescent moon'. Burton 'could not forget that [she] was in the birthplace of the famed Koh-i-noor', a huge diamond that the British had seized from the maharaja of Punjab when his realm was taken over in the 1840s, and which became part of the British crown jewels.[3] There was more travel before Isabel and Richard left for Egypt.

Burton's account is predictable in lingering on the physical features and dress of the people she encountered and describing the exotic nature of places she saw. Her comments include derogatory racially inflected generalizations – 'Bombay servants are dull and stupid' – and unsurprising complaints at the heat and difficulties of transport. Yet she perceptively grasped the vitality of Indian life, the cosmopolitanism of Bombay, the wealth of the princes compared to the subsistence life of most Indians, the prosperity and philanthropy of Parsi businessmen and the punctilious efforts of the British to keep up appearances and re-create a semblance of European life in Asia. She showed no interest in politics and commerce, nor did she make an attempt to delve past superficial appearances even if her husband had undoubtedly tutored her about Indian cultures. Her account contains an unspoken assumption, unnecessary to state to most readers of her book, that Britain's rule was firmly entrenched in India and beneficent for Britons and Indians. Such views found a new affirmation when, in the very year of Burton's tour, the British queen became empress of India.

The Delhi Durbar, 1877

In 1876, the Tory Prime Minister Benjamin Disraeli suggested to Queen Victoria that she assume the title of empress of India (with, of course, no consultation with Indians on the matter). This would affirm British paramountcy on the subcontinent and would designate the British sovereign as heir to the Mughal Empire dissolved after the Great Uprising of 1857. Disraeli hoped that the honour would encourage Victoria to emerge from the seemingly never-ending mourning and withdrawal from public life that had followed the death of her beloved husband, Prince Albert, in 1861, and would give her an imperial status on a par with the ruler of the recently unified German Empire. Not all were enthusiastic about the monarch taking on such a title – emperors and empresses were associated with autocracies in Russia and China rather than the constitutional monarchy on which Britain prided itself – but the queen, who possessed a deep and genuine interest in India, was pleased.[4] A celebration of the new title in India was deemed appropriate, and plans were laid for an 'Imperial Assemblage' in Delhi for the initial days of January 1877, though the queen would not be present. (Indeed, Queen Victoria never set foot in any of the British colonies.) This was commonly referred to as a 'durbar', a ceremonial gathering of rulers and their vassals in pre-colonial India, and the British adopted the tradition as Victoria metaphorically donned the mantle of a Mughal emperor.[5] On this occasion the viceroy, Lord (Robert) Lytton, represented the new empress, with Indian princes summoned to Delhi to pay homage. Calcutta was then the headquarters of the British government in India, but Delhi was chosen precisely because it was the capital of the old Mughal realm. The city had been the scene of battles between the British and Indians in 1857 and the capture of the last Mughal emperor, the aged Bahadur Shah Jafar, whom rebels had chosen as their nominal leader. Delhi was thus the site of a British victory over resistance to colonial rule and the centre of a historic and once great Indian empire.[6] The British would transfer the government of India there after laying out a purpose-built 'New Delhi' in the 1920s.

Lytton, the newly arrived viceroy and governor general, admitted when he was offered the appointment to 'my absolute ignorance of every fact and question concerning India'. The son of a baron (and himself later an earl), he gained a reputation as a creative writer and became one of Queen Victoria's favourite poets, though his novels and poems are now largely forgotten. Lytton served in diplomatic posts for twenty-five years, and was British minister to Portugal when chosen by the conservative Lord Salisbury, the Secretary of State for India and a family friend, for the position in India. After a brief induction into Indian affairs in London, he set sail, and on a stop in Egypt, met the Prince of Wales (the future King Edward VII), who was returning from a tour of the subcontinent. Calcutta did not immediately impress the new viceroy, who complained that his residence 'is full of cockroaches and rats as big as young elephants' and that his administrative staff 'are the most commonplace and least dignified of second and third class Englishmen and that their poor little minds are . . . almost absorbed in measuring their position and power against somebody else' – a comment about expatriates with which Burton would not have disagreed.[7]

Edwin Hirschmann's study of Lytton in India depicts a man bearing the scars of a troubled childhood (his mother was mentally ill) and prone to depression, though intelligent and charming. Lytton was, the historian says, a 'misplaced' appointment. He held markedly conservative and elitist views. He displayed limited interest in Indian culture, and his letters evidence little sympathy for Indians even in the throes of a dire famine. He shared Salisbury's opinions that Indians were unable to govern themselves and should be ruled according to 'the despotic idea', but that it was imperative for the British to secure the allegiance of the Indian princes and aristocracy. He nevertheless conducted a bitter personal quarrel with the regent of Hyderabad, who was trying to reclaim a province that the British had taken from the princely state in the 1850s. Lytton removed the already low customs duties on British exports to India, a hard blow to Indian manufacturing, particularly the textile industry. He continued to oppose promotion of Indians to middle-ranking or senior positions in the colonial service, and he had a particular disdain for the *babus*, educated Indians perceived to be partially Europeanized, who sought such appointments.[8] Another target was the 'native' press, which Lytton thought seditious; the Vernacular Press Act of 1878 forced publishers and printers of papers in Indian languages to post a bond (which some could not afford and so went out of business) to guarantee that they would circulate nothing antipathetic to the government; after one warning, the paper and printing machinery could be seized. However, Lytton did create a 'Statutory Civil Service', a lesser corps than the Indian Civil Service, to employ local men in the administration. He introduced some enlightened policies, such as limited gun control, and he took a stand against violent attacks on Indians by British individuals. Ardently Russophobe and militaristic, the viceroy favoured a pre-emptive attack on Russia, though his superiors in London did not. He pushed British forces into action against Afghanistan, where one expedition of British and Indian soldiers to Kabul was infamously slaughtered to the last man.[9]

Lytton's first order of business on arrival in India was the Imperial Assemblage, which he stated should have as much 'theatrical effect and political significance as possible'. The durbar was designed as a grand festival, a display of British power and propaganda, with the hope it would attract an audience locally and internationally. To a degree, that ambition was fulfilled. In Australia, a country over which Victoria also reigned, *The Sydney Morning Herald*, for instance, reprinted an article from *The Times of India* enthusing that 'it would be difficult for even an Oriental mind to imagine a scene of such grandeur and splendour as that witnessed from the Imperial dais . . . . It is doubtful whether any country or any age has ever known so magnificent a spectacle.'[10] Lytton was much influenced by the Gothic revivalist vogue in mid-Victorian Britain, and decided that a European medievalist style, rather than an Indian one, should be adopted for the event; the medieval reference conveniently underlined the idea that the Indian princes were feudatory vassals of a higher, paramount power, and the peasants – formally unrepresented at the durbar – voiceless subjects of their betters. John Lockwood Kipling, an artist and the father of the poet and novelist Rudyard Kipling, created uniforms and decorations, and other designers, painters and photographers were marshalled to organize and record the ceremony.

In the centre of a field just outside historic Delhi, a throne for the viceroy stood atop a huge hexagonal stone platform topped with a red, white and blue satin canopy decorated with the crown and the royal arms, the Union Flag flying. There was a large-scale portrait of Queen Victoria, present by painted proxy; the representation drew on the Indian tradition of darshan, the idea that setting eyes on a ruler or a god brought blessings on viewers, their families and communities. Saluted by trumpeters playing an excerpt from Wagner's opera *Tannhäuser*, Lytton entered the arena, 'wearing the star-bespangled sky blue mantle of a Grand Commander of the Star of India [a newly established British chivalric order], and wearing also the Imperial ermine', his train jointly carried by a midshipman from the Royal Navy and the young son of the Maharaja of Kashmir. Dozens of elephants and thousands of soldiers marched past – the Bengal Lancers and the Madras Native Infantry among the 20,000 military men at the ceremony – to the accompaniment of rousing music. Around 100,000 spectators watched the proceedings, including uniformed officials and officers, 'gaily-dressed ladies' (as the newspaper article reported) and the 'native princes' resplendent in traditional attire, colourful turbans and priceless jewels in the first ranks, as well as ordinary Indians standing in the background (see Figure 17.1).

After 'God Save the Queen', the viceroy read the proclamation announcing that Queen Victoria was henceforth Empress of India, the imperial title to be passed on to her successors. A sententious telegram from the queen-empress followed, giving assurance of

the deep interest, earnest and affectionate, with which we regard the people of our Indian Empire. . . . We trust the present occasion may tend to unite in bonds

Figure 17.1 Robert Bulwer-Lytton, Viceroy of India, reading Queen Victoria's telegram to the 1877 Delhi Imperial Asemblage at which the queen was proclaimed Empress of India. Illustration from *The Graphic*, 3 February 1877. © Getty Images.

of yet closer affection ourselves and our subjects, so that from the highest to the humblest all may feel that under our rule the great principles of liberty, equity, and fixture are secured to them, and that the promotion of their happiness, in addition to their prosperity and the advancement of their welfare, are the ever present aims and objects of our Empire.

She promised to respect local religions and enjoined Indians to pursue British-style education as a path to progress and modernization. The sixty-three maharajas present then made their obeisance to the viceroy as representative of the queen-empress. The ceremonies continued to sunset with a reception at which each prince was presented a sabre embellished with an image of the viceroy, a customized heraldic banner, honours and decorations and a portrait of the queen. A fanciful painting of the durbar commissioned from the Calcutta-born Anglo-Indian Valentine Prinsep was later presented to Queen Victoria 'by the people of India' (and remains in the Royal Collection), and a commemorative volume was published.[11]

The Imperial Assemblage used spectacle as a display of force; as Jim Masselos has remarked, the shows of homage to the British crown by the princes created an ironic performance for rulers accustomed to obeisance by their subjects at pre-colonial durbars and not to expressions of their own submission. He also points out that on the occasion of traditional durbars, the ruler would have provided generous charity and other material benefits to subjects, but the British contented themselves with handing out medals and flags. Suggestions that the show be as gaudy as manageable reflected condescending British ideas that Asians were particularly impressed by pomp and circumstance; in a memorable phrase, Lytton stated, 'The further East you go, the greater the importance of a bit of bunting.' A number of newspapers in Britain and India, including English-language and vernacular periodicals, lambasted the enormous cost of the durbar especially when India was in the midst of a famine. Most Indian intellectuals regarded the durbar as a travesty of pre-colonial traditions.[12]

The 1877 assemblage became an 'invented tradition', the first of three durbars held in Delhi; the second one took place in 1903 to mark the accession of King Edward VII to the throne, and a final and even grander one in 1911 was attended by the new King–Emperor George V and Queen–Empress Mary in person. Such events exhibited the British Empire at its most confident, ostentatious and pompous. The pageantry was intended to awe those lucky enough to witness the ceremonies or to read about them in the press and, in the case of the 1911 celebration, to see the durbar recorded in moving pictures.[13] However, even at the time of Queen Victoria's durbar, demands for reform of colonial policy were gaining momentum against a backdrop of widespread misery. Many who attended the durbars could not understand the fine words intoned in English and Urdu, and tens of millions of illiterate Indians would not have been able to read accounts even in local languages. Yet spectacles formed an integral part of imperial rule; ritual and ceremony presented vital signifiers of domination, for Indians, subjects throughout the empire, Britons at home and foreigners.

The southern Indian famine

Famines were not historically uncommon in India, with loss of life high because of the precarious situation of subsistence farmers. Millions had died after a drought in Orissa in the mid-1860s, and a particularly bad famine again occurred in the mid-1870s. Climatic conditions linked to the El Niño phenomenon wreaked devastating effects on China, Persia and India in these years. It produced a great drought in southern India, leading to high crop failure throughout the British presidencies of Bombay and Madras, and the princely states of Mysore and Hyderabad, and reached into northern India. Between 4 and 5.5 million people died from malnutrition and disease. Famine turned into starvation – 'skeletonization' of bodies suffering from hunger oedema and anaemia was horrifyingly visible in photographs – and contagious diseases such as cholera and malaria spread rapidly. There were reports of whole families starving to death, piles of corpses left in villages, dogs and wild animals feasting on human remains and isolated cases of cannibalism. The British editor of the *Madras Times*, William Digby, in reporting on 'scenes of death and disaster', 'people flocking to the towns to seek food' and 'panic and looting', added: 'Whilst the ceremonies [of the durbar] were actually in progress, 65,000 subjects of the Queen-Empress died of starvation and the diseases caused by insufficient nourishment in Madras Presidency alone.' He later published a two-volume work about the famine that did not absolve the government for lack of action. Lytton, after visiting relief camps, remarked callously that they 'were swarming with fat, idle, able-bodied paupers, who had been living for months in what is to them unusual luxury at the expense of the Government', though even he eventually became convinced of the scale of the crisis and shocked at its toll.[14]

The Government of India nevertheless continued to export grain from the subcontinent during the 'Great Famine' of 1876–8 – exports doubled between 1876 and 1877 alone; it also continued to collect land taxes from impoverished and starving peasants. Critics charged that tardy action, faulty distribution of available resources and the high price of food much exacerbated real shortages. The setting up of a famine relief commission, remarkably, sparked debate because of what some regarded as the overly generous provisions made by its head, Sir Richard Temple, in a famine in Bihar in 1873–4, when he had imported rice from Burma to alleviate hunger. Victorian policymakers held that famine and poverty relief, whether in Britain or the colonies, should not be too ample so as not to create indolence and dependency or to encourage belief that assistance would be provided on a regular basis. Some accepted Malthusian views that famine provided a natural corrector for overpopulation, and at least initially suggested a laissez-faire policy to the famine, in part to avoid burdens on the colonial budget.

In 1877, Temple tightened eligibility for relief by reducing wages for the able-bodied who had been given work to 'earn' assistance (though free relief was conceded to women, children and the indigent); this provoked strikes. Conditions, despite Lytton's comments, remained disastrous in camps to which famine-stricken people were conducted, sometimes under duress; the rations given to internees fell below caloric subsistence needs. Some of those interned fled the camps, and protests against the government broke out around southern India; the years 1876 and 1877 saw the strongest demonstrations since the 'Mutiny'. The historian Mike Davis argues that there was widespread hoarding of grain and speculation in prices by merchants. He further suggests that new technology worked to the detriment of ordinary Indians as the rail made possible the transport of grain to export markets and the telegraph allowed for the coordination of higher prices for consumers.[15]

There was, however, considerable criticism of British attitudes and policy. The celebrated nurse Florence Nightingale thought that inaction mirrored a more general lack of concern:

We do not care for the people of India. . . . Do we even care enough to know about their daily lives of lingering death from causes which we could so well remove? We have taken their lands and their rule and their rulers into our charge for State reasons of our own . . . . For their daily lives and deaths, we do *not* as a nation practically care.[16]

The famine triggered a humanitarian response in Britain and around the empire, though commentators did not generally take issue with the fundamental problem of colonial rule and its effects. The Governor of Bengal wired the Lord Mayor of London to ask for help, and the appeal spread through Britain; the Lord Mayor contacted authorities as far away as Melbourne, with the plea distributed around Australia. Newspaper reports of the famine gained added impact with harrowing photographs, many taken by a former military officer, Willoughby Wallace Hooper, who would later produce a monumental ethnographic survey, *The People of India*.

Words and images prompted sympathy couched in terms of Christian charity and, in Australia and other British outposts, a sense of empire loyalty. From Australia, Victoria's largest landowner gave £2000 to the Indian Famine Relief Committee, employees of the colony's Railway Department donated a day's wage and pupils at the Maloga Aboriginal School sent in their contribution. Such actions show the collective links felt (or instilled) between residents of widely separated British colonies, as well as the humanitarian sentiments that permeated late nineteenth-century life despite dominant notions about the racial inferiority of 'natives'. The sufferings of Indian subjects of the Crown pulled at heart-strings, but the famine also worried those concerned with labour, production, potential unrest and the security of the empire.[17] Survival of the empire for many took priority over survival of its subjects.

India recovered from the famine, and the 1880 report of a royal commission of inquiry, not surprisingly, found no fault with the government's handling of the crisis. Famine Codes adopted from the early 1880s laid out ways of predicting and avoiding future famines, and strategies for dealing with those that occurred. Famine did not disappear in India, however, and disastrous food shortages under British rule again took place, particularly in 1896–7, 1899–1900 and especially 1943, when as many as 3 million died.

Dadabhai Naoroji, 'The Poverty of India' and the Indian National Association

In April and July 1876, as the famine was taking hold, Dadabhai Naoroji read a paper to the East India Association in Bombay on 'The Poverty of India', putting forward an idea that he developed more fully in a pamphlet published two years later and in a seminal 1901 book, *Poverty and Un-British Rule in India*. Born in 1825, Naoroji was a Parsi, a follower of the Zoroastrian faith whose people had arrived in India as refugees from Persia as early as the eighth century.[18] Educated at Elphinstone College, a prestigious institution established by the British in 1834 and now part of the University of Mumbai, Naoroji later taught mathematics and natural philosophy there. He served for a time as *dewan* (senior adviser) to his patron, the Maharaja of Baroda, took part in setting up six girls' schools in 1849 – he was a strong proponent of the education of girls – and forged ties with the editor of a journal of social reform, *Anti-Caste*. In 1855, Naoroji went to London, where he took part in setting up the first Indian company in Britain – the Parsi community was notable for business acumen and included many merchants, financiers and industrialists. Four years later, he formed his own company to sell Indian cotton, a commodity much in demand by European textile factories. Over the next decades, the protean Naoroji continued to undertake various activities in Britain and in India. He played a pivotal role in the London Indian

Society, an association of South Asians set up in 1865 to advocate for political reform. He taught Gujarati at the University of London, founded the Zoroastrian Trust, published a book on the Parsi religion. Naoroji served as a member of the Legislative Council of Bombay from 1885 to 1888. Back in London, he won election as a Liberal Member of the British Parliament representing Finsbury (the first Indian in the House of Commons, though for a couple of months in the 1840s there had been a member of mixed Indian and British heritage). He held the seat from 1892 to 1895, enduring mockery and racial slurs from conservative MPs.[19] Naoroji's years in London allowed him to form close ties with British, European and American reformers, including Irish nationalists, Florence Nightingale, Josephine Butler and African Americans such as W. E. B. Du Bois; he was one of the founding members of the English Anti-Lynching Committee protesting against violence against African Americans. He helped organize a Pan-African Congress in London in 1900, and attended an international socialist conference in Amsterdam four years later; his ideas exercised considerable influence on Henry Hyndman and other British socialists. Naoroji argued that Indians should be given the full rights of citizenship and direct representation in the British Parliament along with self-government at home. Having thrice served as president of the Indian National Congress, in 1915, two years before his death, Naoroji became president of the Home Rule League.

Naoroji began his 1876 paper on 'The Poverty of India' with acknowledgement of 'the many blessings of law and order which [Britain] has conferred on India', and he characterized himself as a 'loyal subject' of the queen. However, he charged that 'under the present system of administration, India is suffering seriously in several ways, and is sinking in poverty'. He bemoaned the horrendous conditions that afflicted ordinary Indians, despite the high value of Indian production and exports. In a rather dry text replete with statistics on trade and ample quotations from British politicians and commentators, Naoroji centred his arguments on a complex explanation of how the value of Indian wages and pensions was eroded with the British change from a gold standard to a silver standard and by a balance of trade between Britain and India that always remained favourable to Britain. Britain, his analysis suggested, was pocketing the wealth of Indian workers, leading to scarcities and maldistribution of basic commodities, while the introduction of free trade had led to the flooding of the Indian market with British exports, thus ruining local production. Indians were paying for colonial administration of the country – British expenses in India, in principle, were meant to be covered by revenue raised locally – and underwriting the building of the whole British Empire more than bettering their own welfare.

Meanwhile, Britons serving in India received generous salaries and repatriated much of their earnings, further draining money from the subcontinent. Naoroji calculated as well that four-fifths of the taxes paid by Indians left the country, either for Britain or elsewhere in the empire, the monies funding new wars of expansion. He told the British: 'It is in consequence of the tremendous cost of these wars and because of the millions on millions you draw from us year by year that India is so completely exhausted and bled.' Naoroji argued his position on moral as well as economic grounds:

'The reality is that India, up to the present day, has been governed so as to bring about the impoverishment of the people. . . . If it were British rule and not un-British rule which governed us, England would be benefited ten times more than it is.' At times of famine – Naoroji made these comments in his later paper in the context of the famines in the 1890s but the points applied equally to the 1870s – he questioned, 'Is it too much to ask that when we are reduced by famine and plague you [the British] should pay for these dire calamities? You are bound in justice and in common duty to humanity to pay the cost of these dire calamities with which we are afflicted.'[20] India's poverty was, in his view, the result of 'despotic' government – he used the same word as Salisbury, though with a different inflection – exercised by the British and with the theft of India's resources and taxes. Naoroji's 'drain theory', as the argument came to be called, gained great influence, though some economists and historians disputed his exact calculations.[21]

Naoroji was a powerful orator. He pleaded for better treatment of India and its people, stating in one speech, 'We only want to be treated as a part and parcel of the Empire, and we ask you not to maintain the relationship of master over helot.' He sounded a warning about the consequences of lack of reform and the nationalism that inaction would produce: 'If India is lost to the British Empire the sun of the British Empire will be set.'[22] His speeches bear reading for the way in which he appealed to British notions of honour and democracy, cogently examined specific policies that were impoverishing India and yet acknowledged the benefits such as education that British rule had brought to a select few. The introduction to his 1901 book put the views uncompromisingly and suggested that the British had abandoned their own best principles in India: 'The present system of government is despotic and destructive to the Indians and un-British and suicidal to Britain. On the other hand, a truly British course can and will certainly be vastly beneficent both to Britain and India.'

Naoroji is considered one of the fathers of the Indian nationalist movement, standing among an increasing number of Indians demanding reform in British policy in the Raj and forming public associations to advance their claims. Jim Masselos has located the origins of organized Indian nationalism in the emergence of the public associations in which 'the educated joined with the moneyed and became involved in public affairs' from the 1850s onwards.[23] Their strategies, which included submission of petitions and memorials to British authorities, publication of pamphlets and books, personal lobbying and the holding of meetings, galvanized nineteenth-century Indian nationalism prior to the development of Gandhian tactics of boycotts of British goods and hunger strikes. The early nationalists' approach was 'designed to subvert the self-confidence of colonial elites by emphasizing their moral failure as colonial rulers'.[24]

One such group, though not the first, was the Indian Association, set up in 1876 in Calcutta, with Naoroji as a member. Masselos singles out the Bengali society for its formative influence on public opinion among both the elite and the masses, promotion of amity between Hindus and Muslims, and calls for the pursuit of common interests among all Indians. The Indian Association became a major reformist force, establishing 10 branches in its first year and 124 by 1888. Its prime mover was

Surendranath Banerjee (1848–1925), whose first name gave rise to his nickname of 'Surrender Not'. Born into a Brahmin Bengali family, the son of a doctor, Banerjee graduated from the University of Calcutta and then went to Britain, where he passed the Indian Civil Service examination and studied law. After dismissal from the Indian Civil Service for a minor breach of regulations, he became an educator and founded a college in India, working as well as a prominent journalist. Seconding him in the Indian Association was Ananda Mohan Bose (1847–1906), who likewise graduated from the University of Calcutta and took a second degree at Cambridge University, where he studied mathematics (and became 'wrangler', the top-ranking mathematics student of his year); he further qualified as a barrister. Their peers included such authors as Bankim Chandra Chatterjee (1838–94) and Rabindranath Tagore (1861–1941), who contributed to the 'Bengal Renaissance' of literature, art and science in the late nineteenth century, another component in rising nationalism. Tagore, one of India's most acclaimed poets and writers of short stories, was the first non-Westerner to win a Nobel Prize, in 1913; the first stanza of a hymn Tagore composed is India's national anthem.

The thrust of the Indian Association was politics and Indian unity, whereas Naoroji concentrated attention on economic issues, and Chatterjee and Tagore expressed their sentiments through poetry and novels. The Indian Association, a pioneer in the development of nationalism in Bengal, reached out to other groups, in particular those in Gujarat, where Poona hosted a key contemporary society, the Sarvajanik Sabha (dating from 1870), and the cultural and intellectual elites of Bombay provided a vital force in the campaign. Such analyses as those of Naoroji, and the ideas and activities of Banerjee and Bose, nurtured the seeds of a movement that, for the moment, remained reformist not revolutionary and that generally aimed at change in colonial policy and an amelioration of conditions for Indians, not outright independence. Changing times, however, would see more militant stances emerge, and by the end of the century a few radicals argued for a direct and even violent assault on British rule. The movement for independence, under the leadership of the Indian National Congress, ultimately headed by Gandhi, who returned to India from South Africa in 1915, came into its own only after the First World War, but the events and ideas of the 1870s evidenced strengthening resistance to British claims to reign supreme in India.

Less than ten years after Burton's visit to the subcontinent, the Imperial Assemblage, the famine, Naoroji's signal paper on poverty and the inaugural meetings of the Indian Association in 1876 and 1877, nationalists gathered in 1885 to form the Indian National Congress. The following year, London hosted a grand Colonial and Indian Exhibition that put on a show of art and artefacts from India and proudly boasted of British achievements in administration, law, education and commerce, but allowed no evidence of 'un-British rule', exploitation and violence, and that completely overlooked nationalist critiques.[25] In 1903 and 1911, as mentioned, further triumphal durbars were held, as nationalism, in parallel, steadily gained currency. Forty years after the events of 1876, 1.3 million Indian soldiers were fighting in the First World War to defend the British

Empire; in return for their commitment, London promised self-government, a promise that would not be honoured. More and more Indians were similarly convinced that Britain had fallen far short of bringing about the 'prosperity and . . . social advancement' of which Queen Victoria had spoken in 1858. Local and global events, and natural and man-made developments, continued to transform India and to stoke calls for full emancipation from British rule. Seven decades after 1876 – just two generations – India stood on the verge of independence.

CHAPTER 18
BURMA AND VIETNAM, 1883–5

The year 1885 was decisive in the history of colonialism in Southeast Asia, as it marked the completion of the British takeover of Burma and the French occupation of Vietnam. The subjection of the remaining parts of those two countries concluded a process of incursion and annexation by rival European powers that had begun decades earlier, considerably increasing British and particularly French territory and delineating their spheres of influence. Britain would rule in Burma (Myanmar) until 1948, and France in Vietnam until 1954.

Burma and Vietnam are large countries – Burma more than two-and-a-half times the size of today's United Kingdom, and Vietnam almost two-thirds the size of France. They spread from cool mountain ranges to hot tropical lowlands. Agriculture was traditionally based on production of rice, and river and sea ports supported wide-ranging trade long before the arrival of Europeans. Buddhism dominates the culture of Burma, the majestic gold-spired Shwedagon Pagoda in Rangoon (Yangon) symbol of the faith of the majority. The country is home to dozens of ethnic groups, including the Shan, Karen, Kachin and Muslim Rohingyas. Several million more migrants arrived during the British period, particularly from India. Buddhism is an important religion in Vietnam, and Chinese cultural influence has been very pronounced. Confucian ethics structured social relationships, and the emperor ruled from a 'forbidden city'. Administrators gained appointment through competitive examinations modelled on those of China. Vietnam, like Burma, counts numerous minority ethnic groups, especially in the highlands (the 'Montagnards', as the French collectively termed them), and many Chinese migrants, especially in the Mekong delta. Through its history, Vietnam several times resisted Chinese invaders from the north, and its southern boundary, neighbouring Cambodia, regularly fluctuated. In the late eighteenth century, Burma controlled the largest polity in Southeast Asia, stretching from the Himalayan foothills of what is now eastern India into present-day Laos and Siam (Thailand); in 1767, Burmese armies sacked the then-Siamese capital of Ayutthaya. Soon afterwards, however, the state weakened, leaving it vulnerable to the East India Company.

Europeans had manifested a keen interest in Southeast Asia since the days of the spice trade, and the Dutch entrenched themselves in the East Indies from the 1600s. In the closing decades of the 1700s, the British made a significant advance, acquiring the island of Penang (Pinang) off the west coast of peninsular Malaysia. It then temporarily occupied the Dutch possessions during the Napoleonic Wars. In 1819, Britain took Singapore, a sparsely populated island destined to become a key trading entrepôt. In the First Anglo-Burmese War of 1824–6, the East India Company gained regions claimed by

Burma on the margins of India, covering parts of Assam and Manipur, as well as Arakan and Tenasserim on the south coast. In the Second Anglo-Burmese War, in 1852–3, the British conquered yet more territory along the Irrawaddy River, and Rangoon, which became the British capital. Defeat left the Burmese king with a diminished but still large, though landlocked state centred on Mandalay.

The French, imperial competitors with the British, were meanwhile searching for a foothold in Southeast Asia, though initiatives in the southern Philippines and Cambodia had proved unsuccessful. So the French concentrated their efforts on Vietnam, where Catholic missionaries had maintained a presence since the early 1600s, and French diplomats and traders had engaged in episodic relations; a Vietnamese prince had visited the court of King Louis XVI and a French engineer designed a new citadel in Hanoi in the late 1700s. Despite amicable contacts, at the end of the 1850s, the French sent in gunboats, justifying their action by persecution of Christians – the real reason was Napoleon III's desire for Asian colonies. They forced the Vietnamese ruler, Emperor Tu Duc, to cede Saigon (Ho Chi Minh City) and a large region around the Mekong delta; the French called their new colony Cochinchina. In the early 1860s, the French established a protectorate over Cambodia to the west. Then in the 1870s, the French coerced the Vietnamese emperor into accepting a protectorate in everything but name over central Vietnam, or Annam; the agreement left the monarch on his throne in Hué, but the French increasingly consolidated power over the state. Northern Vietnam, or Tonkin, was still administered from Hanoi as a viceroyalty of the emperor of Annam. A French attempt to take Hanoi in 1873 failed, but Tonkin remained within their sights.

The 1870s similarly saw British expansion in the Malay peninsula and jousting between the British and French for influence in Siam. Colonialists in London and Paris hoped that Siam could be divided between them (if not fully taken over by one or the other), but they were unwilling to risk war between Western Europe's two colonial superpowers to achieve their aims. The Siamese king, Chulalongkorn (Rama V), who reigned from 1868 to 1910, adroitly played his cards, modernizing the country, strengthening the army, sending embassies to European capitals and employing advisers from Belgium, Denmark and Italy to counterbalance the British and French. Ultimately, Chulalongkorn was forced to cede territory to both Britain and France, but managed to keep his country independent, a notable and unique achievement in Southeast Asia.[1]

Burma and Vietnam, which presented many attractions, provided two theatres for imperialist manoeuvres that, unlike Siam, succumbed to full colonial takeover. European traders in Vietnam wanted to exploit resources such as rice and coal deposits. Vietnam also produced silk, increasingly in demand in Europe, and the silk merchants of Lyon played a key role in advocating for French expansion there. Later, although not until the twentieth century, the French would develop extensive rubber plantations. Burma possessed some of the world's largest deposits of rubies as well as jade and other gemstones. Forests of teak presented another resource as tropical hardwoods were needed for construction of boats, buildings and furniture, and Burma had oil, another commodity of increasing value. The Irrawaddy River in Burma, and the Mekong and Red rivers in Vietnam, provided arteries for commerce; the French hoped (incorrectly) that the Mekong might be navigable all the way to China. The 'celestial empire' of the Chinese loomed as a treasure-trove in European eyes, and colonizers dreamed that Southeast Asian possessions would provide access, by land, river or ocean, to its silks, porcelain, tea and other commodities, and to millions of potential consumers. Sea ports such as Rangoon, Saigon and Haiphong (near Hanoi) offered promising bases for trade and political dominion.

The contest for Upper Burma

By the 1850s, the British were in control of the entire Burmese coastline and the Irrawaddy estuary.[2] As they exploited and developed Lower Burma, they put increasing pressure on the rump kingdom in Mandalay, which they called Upper Burma. In 1871, a Burmese delegation led by the Kinwun Mingyi U Kaung (1822–1908), the king's senior minister, journeyed to Europe to defend the sovereignty of the kingdom and negotiate more favourable trading arrangements. Queen Victoria received the dignitaries, and they were shown the sights of London, as well as the might of British industry and the military on guided tours of factories and garrisons; the Kinwun Mingyi's detailed memoir offers one of the most interesting perspectives on European society written by an Asian traveller at the time.[3] While in Paris, the Burmese negotiated a trade treaty, signed in 1873, as a strategy by King Mindon (r. 1853–78) to use France as a counterweight to Britain. This fit nicely into the plans of French diplomats and colonial lobbyists in the new Third Republic for extension of the French presence in Southeast Asia.

Burma experienced a period of relative prosperity, reform and astute diplomatic manoeuvres under the popular and respected King Mindon. His son, King Thibaw, seemed unable to fill the shoes of his predecessor after he came to power in 1878. The former Buddhist monk was said to be under the sway of his ambitious wife (and half-sister), Queen Supayalat. The royal couple moved to secure Thibaw's authority with the execution, by clubbing and strangulation, of eighty of the monarch's siblings and other royals, who were feared as potential rivals. Sensationalistic reports in Britain portrayed the massacre as further evidence of the barbarity of bloodthirsty Asian potentates. Journalists added that the king was given to bouts of drunkenness and described Supayalat as scheming and evil.

Thibaw reigned within a walled citadel, a mile wide on each side, in Mandalay, the city that later inspired Kipling's famous 1890 poem 'On the Road to Mandalay' (though the British writer never visited the city) about the place where 'tinkly temple-bells' play. The court painter Saya Chone (1866–1917) in one work depicted a grand audience, with the king and queen enthroned surrounded by royal white umbrellas – the main golden 'throne' was a tall platform, elaborately decorated with mythical creatures, in the middle of which stood a door from which the royal couple emerged to seat themselves as ranks of courtiers bowed low far beneath the monarch and his consort. Saya Chone, incorporating Western pictorial techniques into traditional Burmese art, in other works portrayed the king presiding over an annual rice-planting ceremony, a sacred duty for the monarch, as well depicting the royal family sitting companionably, dressed in beautifully patterned silks. Such images contrasted with the villainous accounts in the foreign press.[4]

Most Britons (and Frenchmen) probably had little knowledge about or interest in Burma, yet Lieutenant-General Sir Arthur P. Phayre (1812–85) – commissioner for the British territory in Burma in the 1860s – published an authoritative history in 1883. Readers could inform and entertain themselves as well with *The Burman: His Life and Notions*, published the previous year by a thirty-year-old Scotsman, George Scott, curiously writing under the Burmese nom de plume of 'Shway Yoe [Golden Honest], a subject of the great queen [Victoria]'. A journalist who had just returned from several years in Burma, Scott produced a 600-page compendium about a country he clearly loved and a people he found charmingly insouciant. He discoursed on orthodox Buddhism and folk belief in *nat* spirits, ceremonies surrounding birth and death, practices such as tattooing and ear-piercing, rice cultivation, silk-weaving and the making of lacquer wares, boat races and feasting. He described the impressive royal palace and the less impressive king who had received him in an audience, explained the administrative and judicial system, and noted of the military that 'the Burmese army was not thought very much of even by the most patriotic Burman who had seen soldiers in other countries'. He remarked on the presence of Indian migrants, Chinese traders and a few Europeans in the raffish royal capital of Mandalay:

> Mandalay presented a series of violent contrasts: jewel-studded temples and gilded monasteries standing side by side with wattled hovels penetrated by every wind that blew; the haughty prince preceded by the respite murderer, his lictor; the busy Chinaman next door to the gambling scum of the low country; the astrologer, learned in his mantras, overpersuaded by the glib talk of the Western adventurer.

Though the city was becoming more modern, there remained a contrast with British-governed Rangoon, which boasted a railway, electric trams and passable roads: in the colonial capital, 'the pigs have all been eaten up, and the pariah dogs are poisoned periodically by municipal order. . . . There are no agreeable scallywags. There are Cook's tourists instead during the three cool months of the year.' Scott sounded nostalgic for a culture that was already being transformed, yet he became part of the British colonial bureaucracy pushing forward and imposing the changes when he went back to Burma in 1886; he worked there until retirement in 1910.[5]

In the years immediately following Scott's book, substantial problems beset the Burmese kingdom. Royal rule was being undermined by local authorities and ethnic groups on the periphery, especially the semi-autonomous *sawbwas* (princes) of the Shan states in the east, with some moves to replace Thibaw on the throne with his cousin. Dacoits (bandits) and millenarian prophets similarly drew support away from the monarchy. Poor rice harvests, falling prices for cotton and oil, and rising government deficits weakened the economy; an increasing current of migrants streamed into the more prosperous British-controlled Lower Burma. The Burmese ruler simultaneously faced the greatest challenge: maintaining the independence and viability of his realm in the face of political and commercial designs by the French and British.

Thibaw dispatched a delegation to France to negotiate a revised commercial treaty and to plead for political support and weapons. However, the new agreement, signed in January 1885, was limited to commercial questions, guaranteeing the right of Frenchmen to trade freely, benefit from favourable customs duties and purchase property. One article stated that 'the trading vessels of each of the two countries shall enjoy, in the waters of their respective States, all the rights, privileges, and immunities which are or shall be accorded to native vessels', though Burmese ships would unlikely make it to the waters of France – the article evidenced the unbalanced nature of most European treaties with indigenous rulers.[6] A secret protocol, said to promise French arms if Burma were involved in another war with Britain, was revealed six months later by Giuseppe Andreino. A Neapolitan adventurer, Andreino had become honorary Italian consul in Mandalay and agent of several British companies. The most important was the Bombay Burmah Trading Corporation (BBTC), which held a monopoly to fell teak, Burma's major export. The Burmese had furthermore agreed, Andreino intimated, to give Frenchmen rights to establish a bank and build a rail line. Perhaps emboldened by relations with France – notwithstanding the French foreign ministry's denial to London that the treaty represented an alliance or that they harboured territorial aspirations – the Burmese State Council on 12 August made a judgement against the BBTC, which it ruled had illicitly felled 80,000 trees on government land, and yet paid royalties for only 30,000 trees. The council ordered the BBTC to pay the full royalties and wages due to workers, and imposed a weighty fine of £250,000. The company appealed to the British government, which was sympathetic to the business, fearful that the Burmese might eventually transfer the logging concession to a French company.

That commercial conflict provided the precipitant for an invasion of Thibaw's kingdom. Other British trading companies rallied round the BBTC, and the burgeoning British merchant community in Rangoon clamoured for swift action to preserve free trade and the rights of British enterprise. They found strong support from businesses in London, where the BBTC was affiliated with the powerful finance house of Wallace Brothers; chambers of commerce in Liverpool, Glasgow and elsewhere joined the call for action. The British government, under the ardently colonialist Conservative Prime Minister, the Marquess of Salisbury, and his Secretary of State for India, Lord Randolph Churchill (father of Winston), authorized war. In addition to imperialist objectives, they hoped that a quick victory on the battlefield would ensure success for the Conservative Party at the ballot box in November elections; in the event, the conquest came just a bit too late.

Not everyone was so gung-ho about marching off to war. Officials in London had to force the hand of the Earl (later Marquess) of Dufferin, whose position as viceroy of India gave him responsibility over Burma. Dufferin privately recorded that the 'idea of a military adventure up the Irrawaddy is extremely distasteful to me', and added that 'the Burmese are a nice people and I cannot bear the thought of making war upon them'. Despite the reservations, he finally agreed that now was an 'opportune moment' for a strike since the French were preoccupied with a crisis in Vietnam (on which more below).[7]

The British on 22 October 1885 served Thibaw with their demands. A fresh enquiry into the timber case by a joint commission of British and Burmese officials should take place. The Burmese would have to accredit a British Agent in Upper Burma, who must be allowed to wear his dress sword and shoes for audiences with the king – Europeans regarded as offensive the expectation that they should remove their shoes within buildings – and who should be allowed to live in a brick-walled compound at the Irrawaddy shore with a guard of a thousand soldiers and a warship. Moreover, 'When the British Government wishes to make a road to China, the Burmese Government shall render every assistance.' Finally, and most dramatically, the British demanded that all Burmese foreign relations be conducted with the consent of the British government, which meant Burmese agreement to a protectorate. The clauses clearly showed, in addition to the British sense of superiority and willingness to enforce it, the importance of both punctilious protocol and commercial issues, and British interest in using Burma as a conduit to China.

The king reluctantly showed himself ready to accept the ultimatum except for the demand of a protectorate. His refusal on that point sparked British invasion of the kingdom on 11 November 1885. General Harry Prendergast, a veteran of the Indian 'Mutiny', led British and Indian troops, recently transferred from the subcontinent, up the Irrawaddy River, sending menacing messages to Mandalay as the force progressed. Faced with the inevitable, King Thibaw tried to arrange an armistice, but to no avail, and on 27 November, he announced that he would surrender. The following day, Prendergast arrived in Mandalay, and Edward Sladen, the political officer in charge of the takeover, informed the king that he must abdicate the throne, and gave him only a matter of hours to prepare for exile.

Saya Chone depicted the king delivering his surrender to the conquerors in the royal palace compound. The king is still sitting in an ornate pavilion, with courtiers and guards grouped on the side. Directly in front of the monarch stand the white-suited British officers, behind whom are massed ranks of pith-helmeted British soldiers. The painter also rendered the departure of Thibaw from Mandalay for exile (see Figure 18.1). The king, Queen Supayalat and their daughters are shown being driven in bullock carts, still sheltered by royal white umbrellas, alongside the moat surrounding the crenellated walls and towers of the citadel. Closely spaced British soldiers stand erectly along the route, while in the foreground Burmese subjects, some manifestly in distress, sit or kneel on the ground. The monarch and royal family, with no trial or possibility of appeal of their ouster, were transported to Ratnagiri, near Bombay, where they were lodged in relatively comfortable conditions yet kept isolated and under surveillance. The king died and was buried in a modest grave there in 1916; the British allowed Supayalat to return to Burma, where she died in 1925 and was interred near the Shwedagon Pagoda.[8]

As Thibaw and Supayalat were being taken away, British troopers were pillaging whatever the royals had not taken or that had not been spirited away by a large group of women who had entered the palace – the British kept men out – as the king prepared

Figure 18.1 The exile of King Thibaw and the Burmese royal family, Mandalay, 1885. Contemporary painting by Saya Chone (1866-1917). © Alamy Stock Photo.

for his last journey. One of Thibaw's crowns and other regalia were set aside to be sent to Queen Victoria; some of the items kept in the Royal Collection at Windsor Castle were returned to Burma eighty years later. Other objects, such as gilt mirrors, were earmarked for the viceroy's palace in Calcutta. The king's Nga Mauk ruby, perhaps the largest ruby ever mined, simply disappeared, with rumours that it was casually pocketed by Sladen; it has never been found, though descendants of the Burmese royal family in 2017 made renewed efforts to locate the jewel. The British installed a billiard table in one of the palace rooms, and turned another into an Anglican chapel; in a rogue action, drunken soldiers burned the royal library and archives.

Historians differ on the relative weight they attach to Anglo-French political rivalries and more explicitly commercial issues in the British takeover of what remained of independent Burma.[9] Certainly, the two issues intertwined, especially in the context of French expansion in Vietnam and their interest in Burma's natural resources. Concern to safeguard the frontiers of India and preclude any French colonial claim combined with protection of trading interests and domestic British political considerations to impel the British into their third military intervention in Burma.

On 1 January 1886, Burma officially became part of the British Empire, the date chosen so that the new colony could be a New Year's present for Queen Victoria. Within weeks, *The Times* reported on summary executions of Burmese prisoners by the British military; the Viceroy cabled General Prendergast in disbelief: 'Effect on public opinion in England and Europe if *Times* report is true will be most disastrous.' Violence and executions were rampant, though it is impossible to calculate the numbers in a situation not unlike other nineteenth-century conquests marked by officers' and soldiers' arbitrary and largely uncontrolled actions. An enquiry was convened, but the matter was hushed up and soon blew over in Britain.[10]

The British had formulated no plans for what to do with Burma. They were undecided about whether to place another member of the extended royal family on the throne and rule Burma as a protectorate (which Dufferin advocated) or to annex it; the latter option, favoured in London, won the day. Dufferin soon went to Mandalay to take possession of his new charge and see the city for himself; his wife Hariot noted in her diary, 'for better, for worse, Burma is annexed. It seems a rich country and Mandalay is a lovely place, and we at any rate have had a delightful visit.'[11] Over the next few months, the British fought armed rebellion around the countryside and had to increase troop numbers to 40,000, carrying out arrests, corporal punishment and executions. Deterrence through violence, as well as a famine in 1886, seemed to take the heat out of the resistance.

War and rebellion in Vietnam

Having consolidated their authority in Cochinchina, and strengthened control over Annam, the French in the early 1880s were still smarting at the reverse suffered by their expeditionary forces in Tonkin in 1873. In that year, Francis Garnier, famous for explorations of the Mekong River, led an assault on northern Vietnam, but the French were defeated by the Vietnamese, backed by a Chinese group of soldiers (or 'pirates', in the French view) known as the 'Black Flags'. Garnier was killed outside Hanoi; the decapitation (and emasculation, according to some reports) of the 34-year-old Frenchman inflamed public opinion at home. A decade later, the French made a renewed effort to seize Tonkin, which Paris saw as a promising addition to its Indochinese holdings and, via the Red River, as a gateway to southern China. In 1882, Henri Rivière, naval officer and author of a stack of now forgotten novels, led the storming of the citadel in Hanoi. The alarmed Vietnamese again called on the Chinese and the Black Flags for reinforcement. Rivière's death in battle was a reprise of that of Garnier, but confirmed French resolve, and Paris sent in 20,000 extra troops. While battling in northern Vietnam, the French determined that a strike on the capital of the emperor in Hué was necessary to secure their objectives.[12]

Seven French warships cruised up the Perfume River and bombarded Vietnamese installations on 18 August 1883, then landed soldiers. They scored a victory in the Battle of Thuan An, and marched on to the Hué citadel, pillaging and burning villages as they passed through. Reports of atrocities reached Paris, including through articles written by an eyewitness, Lieutenant Julien Viaud, better known as the up-and-coming novelist Pierre Loti (who was summoned home for casting aspersions on French forces).[13] The French on 25 August forced a formal protectorate over Annam and the viceroyalty of Tonkin on Emperor Hiep Hoa, who was soon deposed by the Vietnamese court and, probably under coercion, committed suicide. However, all would not be quiet on the Hué front.

Fighting continued in Annam and particularly Tonkin, as the French combatted regular Vietnamese troops, the Black Flags and soldiers from the Chinese Guangxi Army. France, in short, was now fighting an undeclared war with the Qing Empire. Chinese units attempting to invade the Tonkin delta were defeated in October 1884, and the French invaded and briefly occupied Keelung and Tamsui on the island of Taiwan. In early 1885, France mounted an offensive against the Chinese at Lang Son, on the Chinese–Vietnamese border. The French victory in difficult circumstances – far more French soldiers died from cholera than fighting – became the stuff of military legend, and brought the Sino-French war to a close.

The cost in money and men for the war in Asia, and what many regarded as military over-extension and acquisition of territory of uncertain value, provoked a parliamentary crisis in Paris, and led to the fall of Prime Minister Jules Ferry, derisively labelled by opponents as 'Ferry the Tonkinese'. Ferry's address to parliament in his defence, arguing that expansion was vital for commercial, political and civilizational reasons, constituted a classic statement of colonialist belief. Despite Ferry's ouster, France was now embedded in central and northern Vietnam as well as in Cochinchina (and Cambodia), and its diplomats wrangled international recognition, including the acquiescence of China, for the formal protectorate over Annam and Tonkin. The Asian ambitions of ardent colonialists did not stop there, and the French in the 1890s would add Laos to their Southeast Asian possessions.

Against the backdrop of military actions in Tonkin, dramatic events were unfolding in central Vietnam. Many Vietnamese, their country falling more fully under French control, tried to resist, and one key riposte eventually came from within the emperor's court in Hué. Emperor Tu Duc, who reigned from 1847 to 1883, had been unable to forestall French conquests in the 1860s and 1870s, but he remained an esteemed figure for the Vietnamese. When Tu Duc died childless, various candidates from the royal family came forward, and a period of chaos ensued. In 1883, Vietnam had no fewer than three emperors in succession. Tu Duc's immediate successor ruled for only three days before being toppled and either executed or left to die in captivity; the next, Hiep Hoa – who signed the protectorate treaty with France – lasted for four months; the third, an adolescent, sat on the throne for eight months before dying, rumour had it, from poison. The Vietnamese monarchy seemed, in many ways, mortally wounded. In 1884, a twelve-year-old, Ham Nghi, assumed the throne under the aegis of the French, who hoped that his youth would render him incapable of thwarting their plans.

Real power in the court lay with the regents for the adolescent emperor. One, Ton That Thuyet, the Minister of War, favoured immediate armed action against the French, while the other leading mandarin, Nguyen Van Tuong, counselled against precipitate action. Ton That Thuyet bolstered the fortification of the citadel in Hué and, for good measure, built a redoubt in the jungle, should the emperor have to leave the capital. The French became aware of a budding revolt but remained preoccupied by conflict in Tonkin, though they did move a contingent of troops to Hué under Admiral Henri de Courcy. His high-handed approach to the boy emperor exacerbated anti-French sentiment, and the hosting of a gala soirée for French residents of the capital added insult to injury. The plot against the French ignited in a midnight series of concerted attacks on 4 July 1885 by 5,000–6,000 Vietnamese soldiers against the 1,400 French troopers, targeting a French installation within the citadel and the French legation on the opposite bank of the Perfume River. The fighting, and fires that broke out, led to the death of 1,500 Vietnamese, with 60 Frenchmen killed or wounded; French repression was severe.[14]

In the midst of the chaos, Ton That Thuyet, Ham Nghi and several senior members of the royal family, including the queen grandmother and two queen mothers, fled the 'forbidden city' in the dead of night. Ham Nghi made his way to the prepared safe location and issued a proclamation rallying the Vietnamese, with a Confucian stress on the moral responsibility of the ruler for his people's well-being and the necessary obedience of subjects to the ruler. The proclamation (likely written by Thuyet) stated that 'from time immemorial, there have never been more than three alternatives when planning military strategy: to fight, to resist, and to negotiate', and now it was necessary to 'resort to expedients'. 'Our country has recently experienced much suffering . . . [and] each day, the pressure from the Western envoys becomes increasingly imperious. Recently, they even brought in additional troops and battleships.' The monarch expressed shame at the fall of the capital, and asked mandarins, ministers and literati not to abandon him:

> Those with intelligence shall contribute ideas; those with strength shall lend their force. The rich shall give money to buy military supplies. The peasants and villages shall not refuse hardship or evade danger . . . Perhaps with Heaven's assistance, we shall be able to turn chaos into order, danger into peace, and finally retrieve our entire territory. Under these circumstances, the fate of the nation must be the fate of the people.[15]

However, with no tactical leader, no coordination and no arsenal to match French weaponry, the rebellion lost ground. The royal women returned to Hué, where Nguyen Van Tuong rallied to the French; they ordered him to find Ham Nghi, and when he failed, they sent him to the prison island of Poulo Condore (Con Dao). The French replaced Ham Nghi as emperor by the 21-year-old Dong Khanh, the grandson of a previous emperor, who seemed compliant. Skirmishes between the rebel Vietnamese and the French outside Hué continued for some time, with Ham Nghi forced deeper into the jungle, accompanied by a diminishing band of supporters – indeed, Ton That Thuyet had fled to China. Ham Nghi evaded the French until November 1888, when he was betrayed by a follower, the French were able to track him down. After some debate about what to do with their captive, the French decided to exile Ham Nghi to Algeria, where he lived quietly, raising a family with the French woman he married and engaging in his avocation of painting, until his death in 1943. Though the extent of involvement of the adolescent Ham Nghi in the rebellion is debated, and there are conflicting accounts of his behaviour and statements, orthodox Vietnamese historiography hails him as one of the 'patriotic' emperors who defied the French (see Figure 18.2).[16]

The Can Vuong movement, which emerged in 1885 as part of the insurrection, continued to agitate against the French and demand the restoration of the full rights

Figure 18.2 Ham Nghi, Emperor of Annam (r. 1884-5), deposed and exiled by the French. Contemporary photograph. © Alamy Stock Photo.

of the emperor. It formed the nucleus of continuing royalist anti-colonialist resistance particularly popular among traditionalists and moderate nationalists who nourished lingering hopes that the monarchy might serve as a rallying point for the gaining of independence. Such did not prove the case, as nationalists of different ideological persuasions later led the struggle against the French, who were mistaken in claims that by the mid-1880s Vietnam had been 'pacified'.

Colonized Southeast Asia

The events of the mid-1880s illustrate the overlapping significance of commercial and geopolitical rivalries between Britain and France, their efforts to carve out new colonial territory and the importance they attached to Southeast Asia. The difficult economic and political situations in Burma and Vietnam – the inexperience of the new Burmese king and domestic challenges to his authority, and the political instability in Vietnam following the death of Tu Duc – facilitated European moves. Prior European conquests that had amputated large parts of both realms further weakened the capacity to resist additional incursions. In Europe, the pro-colonialist positions of Lord Randolph Churchill and Jules Ferry promoted armed intervention. Colonial lobby groups, such as the English and Scottish chambers of commerce and the Lyon silk industry, agitated for expansion in Southeast Asia. British merchants in Rangoon championed action against Upper Burma, and the French community in Saigon called for the takeover of Tonkin. Precipitants for war presented themselves in each case: revenge for the death of Rivière, and perceived unjust payments and fines imposed on British businessmen. Military leaders were confident of victory with troop reinforcements from overseas, including Indian soldiers for the British and men brought from New Caledonia by the French. Seasoned commanders such as General Prendergast and Admiral de Courcy led the fight, and European war matériel outclassed that available to Burmese and Vietnamese armies.

Faced with the European assault on Upper Burma and Tonkin, and then French actions in Hué, local political elites, doubtful of their wherewithal to best the Europeans in battle, were divided. The Vietnamese emperors were too young or too short-lived to take a commanding role, and in Burma, King Thibaw vacillated. One faction in Mandalay argued for a last stand against the British, though another convinced the king to surrender. When the French sent troops to Hué in 1885, similar discord separated those who sought accommodation with the French and those who sparked insurrection. The role of women in the royal families was far from insignificant. Queen Supayalat, considered by outsiders as the power behind the throne, urged resistance though she eventually gave in; the mother of Ham Nghi and the dowager empresses, who commanded respect and wielded influence in the Vietnamese court, fled the palace with the young emperor, then abandoned his doomed cause. As the French and British established control, courtly elites tried to make the best of a bad situation. The Vietnamese imperial family and mandarins threw support behind the new emperor enthroned by the French in an effort to at least save the dynasty and their own positions. In Burma, defenders of the monarchy hoped that another royal might be placed on the throne, but the lack of anyone the conquerors considered appropriate led to the abolition of the monarchy and direct British rule. However, the British did make efforts to bring members of the old elites into their orbit, none more so than the Kinwun Mingyi, the senior minister; he became a senior civil servant under the British and later member of the colonial legislative council, though he died much discontented. While abolishing the monarchy in Mandalay, the British kept in place the thirty-odd *sawbwas*, the Shan princes, and over the next years, largely maintained their allegiance through recognition of hereditary privileges, the award of honours, invitations to the Delhi durbars and the education of several of their sons in the United Kingdom.

The raising of the Union Flag over Mandalay and the French Tricolour over Hué did not end opposition. It took the French several years to track down the renegade emperor, and the principle of a restored and independent monarchy remained the platform of Vietnamese resistance for decades. Indeed the next major revolt against the French, in

1916, more directly involved the emperor, Duy Tan (who, like Ham Nghi, was deposed and exiled by the French when the insurrection failed). Despite the exile of the Burmese royal family, pretenders to the throne – though sometimes with no credible claim – as late as the 1930s mounted rebellions against the British. By that time, however, other forms of political activism had largely displaced fealty to the monarchy as a platform for anti-colonialism. For modernizing nationalists, colonial domination brought into question old hierarchies and customs that had not proved strong enough to safeguard national independence, and prompted the search for new ideologies and strategies.

The abolition of the Burmese Konbaung dynasty and the deposition of Ham Nghi, as well as severe limitations on the powers of his successors in the Nguyen dynasty, were not the only outcomes of conquest. French and British occupation of Vietnam and Burma represented an assault on those countries' basic institutions and cultures. The victors restructured law codes and taxation regimes, reoriented economic production, introduced European languages and forms of education, medicine and styles of life, brought in Western settlers and encouraged migration from India to Burma (and, to a lesser degree, from French India to Vietnam). Relatively secure for the colonizers under militarized occupation, Burma and Vietnam became prosperous outposts for European business with logging, mining, agriculture and later, in Vietnam, rubber production and, in Burma, growing export of oil. In 1887, France set up 'French Indochina', an administrative unit presided over by a governor-general that encompassed the colony of Cochinchina, the protectorates of Annam, Tonkin and Cambodia and, in the following decade, new territories in Laos. Burma remained under the authority of the viceroy of India until it became a separate jurisdiction in 1937. Cities such as Rangoon, Saigon and Hanoi grew in size and were altered in their physical form, with European-style government offices, banks and trading houses, churches and theatres, and department stores, clubs and sports facilities catering primarily to Europeans. New Westernized elites emerged, and nationalist sentiments survived and grew stronger, in part stimulated by notions of reform and radicalism adopted from the Europeans. By different routes, both Burma and Vietnam would regain independence in the years after the Second World War.

'Of course, I am a man of peace', Winston Churchill wrote in December 1899 when accompanying British Empire troops as a 25-year-old war correspondent in South Africa. 'I do not fight. But swords are not the only weapons in the world. Something may be done with a pen', he continued.[1] Indeed, towards the end of the nineteenth century war and the press had formed an intimate relationship as writers and photographers covered armed conflicts around the globe. Transoceanic cables allowed for almost instantaneous reporting from battlefields and new print technologies made possible the inclusion of photographs in newspapers of record and more popular periodicals. National and international press agencies and roving 'foreign correspondents' became ever more influential. The Cuban War of Independence (1895–8) has been labelled 'the correspondents' war' and the South African War (1899–1902) an 'imperialist media war'; the Boxer War in China (1900–1) and the Russo-Japanese War (1904–5) were also major media events.[2] The ways in which such conflicts were covered in the press could indeed change the course of events. In order to keep the upper hand, for the warring parties, it was sometimes as important to control the 'war of words', as it was to gain military superiority.

Young Churchill's experience is illustrative of the globalizing network that connected different empires and wars in new ways. Long before he began a political career that culminated in his service as Britain's prime minister during the Second World War, Churchill the newspaper reporter covered the Cuban struggle for independence from Spain for *The Daily Graphic* in 1895. Two years later, he filed dispatches from India about armed conflict on the North-West Frontier for *The Daily Telegraph*. In 1898 Churchill reported on Britain's military campaign in the Sudan, including the battle of Omdurman, before joining British troops in South Africa in 1899 as a correspondent for *The Morning Post*. At the turn of the century, the press and reporters such as Churchill were thus part and parcel of a technical, cultural and economic wave of increased interconnectedness across the (colonial) world.

In Cuba, Churchill, who had just completed his own military training in Britain, struggled to make sense of the Cuban Liberation Army's guerrilla strategy, which involved attacks on the island's economic infrastructure and ambushes of Spanish troops rather than pitched battles. On the one hand, he recognized that the Cubans' 'demand for independence [was] national and unanimous'. 'In fact, it is a war, not a rebellion', Churchill stated. On the other hand, he branded the Cuban freedom fighters 'incendiaries and brigands – burning cane fields, shooting from behind hedges, firing into sleeping camps, destroying property, wrecking trains, and throwing dynamite'. According to Churchill, these were 'not the acts upon which States are founded'. Furthermore, he called into question the stability of a prospective independent Cuban government that would include Afro-Cubans, convinced that this would 'create renewed and even more bitter conflict of a racial kind'.[3]

Racialized stereotypes of 'swarming savages' similarly popped up in Churchill's reports from the Sudan. In South Africa, however, he acknowledged the (white) Boers' courage in fighting although he added contemptuously: 'It is quite true that he [the Boer] is brave but so are many savage tribes.' Only when captured by a Boer commando and finding himself well treated did he admit in 'great surprise', 'So they were not cruel men, these enemy.' Though Churchill left South Africa in late June 1900 before the Boers resorted to all-embracing guerrilla warfare, he understood that the war had 'entered on a different phase'. Churchill was aware of the 'advantages that the Boers enjoyed among [the] mountains and kopjes [rocky hills]' in Natal, and he recognized the difficulties which an 'elusive enemy' caused to any imperial army.[4]

Churchill personally witnessed warfare that involved European colonial powers, settler populations and indigenous peoples around the globe. Although a 'world war' would erupt only in 1914, the quarter of a century before that date saw many colonial conflicts – Queen Victoria's wars of empire as well as battles in which the French, Dutch, Portuguese and other Europeans fought Africans and Asians – including overseas confrontations that threatened to provoke war among the European states.[5] Three of these conflicts, generally if reductively known as the Spanish-American War, the South African War and the Boxer Rebellion in China, provide case studies.

European and other empires: Between conflict and cooperation

It has been suggested that the end of the 1700s and early years of the 1800s marked a 'meridian' in colonial history with the changes wrought by the Atlantic revolutions and Napoleonic Wars, and the consequent redrawing of the maps of overseas empires.[6] The last years of the nineteenth century and first years of the twentieth marked another 'imperial meridian' with the 'scramble' for African colonies, the consolidation of colonial rule in Asia, and wars (or near wars) on both continents as well as in the Caribbean. The turn of the twentieth century, celebrated with a world's fair in Paris in 1900 at which colonial displays were much in evidence, saw a greater commitment than ever before in the modern world to overseas empires. These had reached an unparalleled geographical expanse, ruled by the largest ever cohort of European nations (Spain, Portugal, the Netherlands, Britain, France, Belgium, Italy, Germany, Denmark) and by ones outside Europe (notably the United States and Japan), as well as the contiguous empires of the Ottomans and the Russians.

The events of these years took place in the context of great tensions between imperial powers as they jousted for advantage and sought to parcel out the last remaining territories unclaimed by colonizers. A conflict between Britain and Portugal in southern Africa in 1890, a confrontation between Britain and France when their military faced off in the Sudan in 1898 (the Fashoda Crisis) and the Moroccan Crises of 1905-6 and 1911 involving France and Germany showed the linkage between colonial disputes and metropolitan rivalries. Colonies and would-be colonies and spheres of influence provided theatres for heightened nationalism, increased militarization, and changing international alliances and alignments from the 1880s onwards.[7]

At the same time, cooperation among imperial forces overseas and in the metropoles contrasted with, and complemented, jingoism and imperial nationalism. Indeed, the years around 1900 were characterized by a remarkable degree of cooperation between European imperial powers (and non-European ones), and their private and public representatives, at home and abroad. This is evident in the European exploration and 'opening up' of the interior of Africa for the imperial enterprise. Several of the colonial expeditions – for example, Henry Morton Stanley's search for David Livingstone in the 1870s and the quest for the source of the Nile river in the 1880s – would not have materialized without the patronage of competing European powers. Collaboration among empires included the exchange of colonial knowledge in other ways. The foundation of the Institut Colonial International in Brussels in the 1890s constituted an attempt to bundle European interests and provide a platform for the sharing of geographical, scientific, commercial and political findings to colonizers' mutual benefit.[8]

'Alliance imperialism' among otherwise competing nations characterized the British relations with the United States, at least after 1898.[9] When the British poet Rudyard Kipling memorably summoned others to take up the 'white man's burden', he directed his remarks at the Americans then embarking on overseas expansion. The Entente Cordiale signed between Britain and France in 1904 allowed the two countries, previously bitter colonial rivals, to resolve several territorial disputes, from the sea around Newfoundland in the northern Atlantic to the New Hebrides archipelago in the southern Pacific. Despite the British vetoing further Portuguese expansion in southern Africa in 1890, colonial authorities used a large number of men from Portuguese Mozambique for labour in the mines of their southern African territories. Even as tensions with Germany were building up, Britain from the northern border of South Africa assisted the Germans in warfare between 1904 and 1908 in what is today Namibia. German and British colonial pundits still maintained a lively and amicable exchange of letters in the summer of 1914, just days before the outbreak of the Great War.[10] Competition, cooperation and occasional clashes punctuated relationships among the imperial powers.

The War of 1898: 'Remember the Maine! To Hell With Spain!'

The Spanish-American War, or what might more precisely be called the Spanish-American-Cuban-Filipino War,[11] involved one of the world's oldest colonial powers, Spain – which had lost most of its South American empire in the first decades of the 1800s – and a new one, the United States, which had expanded across the American continent from the Atlantic to the Pacific during the 1800s, and had already made advances overseas. US Navy warships forced open the ports of Japan to Western trade in 1853–4. In 1867, the United States purchased Alaska from Russia. In the 1890s, Americans overthrew the royal dynasty in Honolulu and annexed the Hawaiian islands, and at the end of the century it took over islands in the archipelago of Samoa. Americans meanwhile championed an 'open door' for trade with China – free trade in which Americans, with a buoyant industrial economy, hoped to be the prime beneficiaries – enforced by unequal treaties the Chinese were coerced into signing. In the last years of the 1800s, further areas of expansion beckoned in the western Pacific, where Spain still claimed the Philippines, and closer to home in the Caribbean, where Cuba and Puerto Rico remained Spanish colonies.

Less than 150 kilometres from American shores, Cuba had long been in American sights. Politicians and geostrategists argued, from at least the early nineteenth century, that the island would necessarily gravitate towards the United States. 'There are laws of political as well as of physical gravitation', Secretary of State John Quincy Adams wrote to the US envoy in Madrid in 1823, 'and if an apple, severed by the tempest from its native tree, cannot choose but fall to the ground, Cuba, forcibly disjoined from its own unnatural connexion with Spain, and incapable of self-support, can gravitate only towards the North American Union, which by the same law of nature, cannot cast her off from its bosom'. From Washington's perspective, the 'fruit' was 'mature', and by the 1860s a US senator predicted that 'Cuba will fall, like the ripe fruit into our lap'.[12] Cuban nationalists such as José Martí – writer, poet and co-founder of the Cuban Revolutionary Party in 1892 – were well aware of the dangerous appetite of the 'Northern giant' who set out for colonial conquest 'in seven-mile-boots'.[13]

By the late nineteenth century US businesses were heavily invested in sugarcane production in Cuba and refining companies in the United States controlled the market. With nationalist agitation extending throughout the island from 1895, and cane fields set alight by the rebels, by 1897, confidence in the Spanish colonial government and its army's ability to protect foreigners' properties was waning. The insurgency wreaked havoc on the island's productive economy with the nationalists targeting large estates and Spanish troops destroying smallholders' crops and anything apt to provide shelter and subsistence for the insurgents. As a consequence, the island was plunging into a severe humanitarian crisis. War and destruction led to unhealthy living conditions for civilians in overcrowded towns and cities where diseases such as smallpox and food shortages were rampant. The years of the Cuban War of Independence from 1895 to 1898 saw the death of at least 170,000 civilians, 10 per cent of the island's population.[14]

US envoys and journalists reported on the 'horror and inhumanity' of Spanish warfare, highlighting the 'starvation tactics of these uncivilized Spanish and their shooting [of] prisoners of war'. Starving civilians were graphically described as 'a pitiful sight and a disgrace to any civilized government'. Such scenes provided a sure topic for the 'yellow press', such as Joseph Pulitzer's *New York World* and William Randolph Hearst's *Journal*. President William McKinley included in an annual message in 1897 the accusation that 'the civilized code of war [had] been disregarded . . . no less so by the Spaniards than by the Cubans'. The time seemed right for intervention under the banner of humanitarianism (see Figure 19.1).[15]

Figure 19.1 'Uncle Sam and Don Quixote Face Off on Cuba'. German cartoon, April 1898. © Getty Images.

With the explosion of the battleship USS *Maine* in the harbour of Havana, in unclear circumstances, in February 1898, the slogan 'Remember the Maine! To hell with Spain!' roused opinion even beyond the readership of tabloid newspapers. On 20 April 1898 the US Congress authorized military action, and the US Navy's first move was to establish a naval blockade; this cut off the island from much-needed supplies, which further contributed to the high death toll. Five days later, Congress voted for war against Spain, a decision that brought the Spanish colony of the Philippines into play. The war, fought in Pacific and Caribbean waters, resulted in decisive US victories in both theatres by July. After a few further clashes, Spain and the United States agreed a truce on 12 August, and on 10 December signed a peace treaty, which gave to the United States Cuba, Puerto

Rico and the Philippines; the United States also acquired smaller Spanish islands in the north-western Pacific, notably Guam.

Despite much nationalistic assurance in Spanish newspapers – the venerable 'Spanish lion' would slaughter the American 'pig' – Spain's defeat (known as the 'Disaster' to Spaniards) was to be expected. Controversy persists about why Madrid sent its armed forces into battle against the United States, knowing they stood little chance against a better equipped adversary. For Spanish politicians, an unsuccessful war would nevertheless make a retreat from Cuba easier to accept at home. Were the island given up without a fight against the United States, they feared that the Spanish political system would collapse. Although the regime survived, the end of empire in the Caribbean and the Pacific triggered an intellectual crisis in the Iberian country; internationally, Spain was perceived as one of the 'dying nations' of the colonial world.[16]

From a US perspective, however, the experience had been a 'splendid little war', as John Hay, US representative in Britain and future Secretary of State, phrased it. Within a few months the United States managed to gain greater control of its Caribbean 'backyard' – where there were still British, French Dutch and Danish colonies – and get hold of territories in the western Pacific. However, imperial expansion was not unanimously welcomed at home. Fears about a 'black' Cuban republic on America's shores and general anxiety about 'degeneration' as the United States joined in the international colonial enterprise went beyond the small circles of the American Anti-Imperialist League, founded during the war. On the flipside, the war helped to amalgamate a deeply divided nation (the scars of the Civil War of 1861–5 were still painful) against a common, outside enemy.

Cuban revolutionaries opted for 'patriotic' cooperation with the United States, choosing to work with the American authorities on the island for a supposedly limited time to the benefit of a future independent nation. By contrast, Filipinos, who had fought for independence from Spain between 1896 and 1898, once more resorted to guerrilla warfare – this time challenging the American colonizers who replaced the Spanish. In the Philippines, the United States embarked on a protracted counter-insurgency campaign, trying to fend off Filipino self-determination, resorting at times to extremely violent means, but ultimately entrenching US authority; the Philippines would remain a US colony until 1946.[17] Puerto Rico and Guam are still American territories today.

The South African War, 1899–1902

The South African War was long referred to as the Boer War, a battle between Britain and British colonists (and empire troops), on the one hand, and the Boers, the descendants of Dutch colonists who first arrived in South Africa in the 1600s, on the other. Since the 1980s historians have increasingly challenged the 'myth of a white man's war' and paid close attention to the indigenous Khoi, San and other Africans groups, as well as those of mixed ethnic background and Indian migrants who were drawn into the affray and whose fates were determined by the peace settlement and subsequent conflicts. Over the course of the almost three-year confrontation, the South

African War affected more than four million Black people in the region, of whom 100,000 'became directly involved in the struggle as scouts, spies, guards, servants and messengers, and in a wide range of other occupations with the white armies', according to Peter Warwick.[18]

The Boers had been challenged with the British takeover of the Cape Colony from the Dutch in the 1790s. Old and new colonizers and settlers cohabited uneasily. After 1834, many Boers, the 'Voortrekkers', migrated eastwards, established new settlements, and, ultimately, set up and gained British recognition of the South African Republic (Transvaal) in 1852 and the Orange Free State in 1854. Meanwhile, the British had moved into the south-eastern corner of the continent, in 1843 establishing the colony of Natal, which threatened to encroach on the Boer outposts.

The two main British cities, Cape Town (in the Cape Colony) and Durban (in Natal), were important ports on the route from Europe to the Indian Ocean, and through them funnelled diamonds and gold, two of South Africa's most precious mining exports. Gold, first discovered in 1886 in Witwatersrand, particularly excited prospectors, traders and colonizers, chief among them Cecil Rhodes (1853–1902), businessman, mining magnate and from 1890 to 1896 prime minister of the Cape Colony, one of the most celebrated and most vilified of British imperialists. With eyes set on the rich mines located in the Boer republics, Rhodes avidly promoted colonial expansion; he wielded considerable political influence in London, where calls for takeover of the Boer states were also being heard.

Considering offence as the best defence, the Boer republics eventually went to war against the British, aiming to preserve their independence and control over the bustling mining industry. In October 1899 Boer troops invaded the British colony of Natal and besieged Ladysmith, Kimberley and Mafeking. This first phase of the war was characterized by regular battles, as at Colenso in December, which resulted in a stunning Boer victory (see Figure 19.2). Both the world's assembled war correspondents, such as Churchill, and military leaders were impressed by the Boer army's intelligent use of the difficult South African terrain and innovative trench warfare, and by their daring commanders, among them Louis Botha. Born in 1862, Botha quickly rose through the ranks and eventually commanded the Boers' Transvaal army against the British and empire troops. After the early setbacks, the British by March 1900 had mobilized the might of the empire, dispatching to South Africa 200,000 soldiers, among them 30,000 men from the colonies, including volunteers from Canada, Australia and New Zealand. The Boers counted 45,000 fighters, along with 'the hired scum from Europe' – as Churchill phrased it – most of them Germans and Dutch.[19]

By June 1900, the British had taken Pretoria, the major Boer city. 'The first British flag was hoisted', Churchill reported, 'Time 8.47, 5 June'. Paul Kruger, president of the Transvaal Republic, had escaped before the British troops occupied the city and travelled to Europe in October. There he had little success in lobbying for the Boers' cause. Despite the British having gained the momentum, Churchill concluded at the time that 'it were premature and foolish to imagine that because the Republics have vanished [with their takeover by the British,] the war is at, or even near, its end'.[20] Indeed, the Boers with Botha retreated, and their commandos resorted to fully

"INTO THE BOER'S JAWS."

[From the "Evening World," New York.

Figure 19.2 'Into the Boer's jaws'. Cartoon showing the British 18th Hussars charging into the mouth of a large boar - a play on the word 'Boer'. *The Evening World*, New York, reprinted in the (London) *Daily Mail*, 23 November 1899. © Alamy Stock Photo.

fledged guerrilla warfare, the relentless hit-and-run tactics demoralizing the British imperial forces.

In November 1900, Horatio H. Kitchener had replaced Lord (Frederick) Roberts as British commander in South Africa. In fighting the Boer guerrillas, Kitchener turned to similar methods known from Spain's campaign in Cuba and widely condemned as 'uncivilized' warfare: clearing the countryside of civilians and destroying farms and crops that could provide shelter and subsistence to the Boers. Thousands of blockhouses and countless kilometres of barbed wire were meant to secure control over large areas. With nothing left in the *veld* to live on, the enemy would be forced to battle or surrender, the military brass concluded. In Cuba, Captain General Valeriano Weyler had ordered the 'concentration' of 400,000 peoples in fortified towns and villages throughout the island – with disastrous consequences reflected in soaring deaths. In South Africa, the British military nevertheless similarly herded displaced persons and surrendered Boer soldiers into hastily improvised tented camps. (Prisoners of war caught in action were mostly sent to Ceylon and St Helena.) The high mortality in what was called concentration camps was vividly described in Emily Hobhouse's *The Brunt of the War and Where it Fell* (1902), based on her visit late in 1900. It revealed the hypocrisy of a proclaimed humanitarian objective of providing shelter to women and children displaced by the war while in around forty 'white' camps (mostly in the Transvaal and the Orange Free State), at least 25,000 of 150,000 inmates died. For sixty 'black' camps, figures are difficult to reconstruct, though British sources conservatively recorded 14,000 fatalities; the true number is probably nearer to 20,000.[21]

In London, the liberal opposition did not hesitate to speak of 'methods of barbarism' applied in the South African War, likening Kitchener's policies to those of Weyler. Similar criticism sounded elsewhere – the American Transvaal League echoed the charge that Kitchener was pursuing a strategy 'similar in character and equal in atrocity to the measures of reconcentration . . . adopted by General Weyler'.[22] There was much support for the Boers in France and Germany, though sentiment there was strongly inflected by international and imperial rivalries between Paris, Berlin and London. The public outcry, among other reasons, caused the British to replace military with civilian authority over the camps, much of it handed to administrators from India with experience in managing large populations in hunger relief and plague camps. The British system of 'white' camps, according to one scholar, was transformed into an instrument of social engineering, 'a tool for modernisation' of supposedly backward Boers meant to become useful partners in British South Africa.[23] Concentration camps in South Africa were (and remain) a very controversial and often emotional subject, and memory of the Boer experience shaped Afrikaner identity through the twentieth century.

The Treaty of Vereeniging brokered an understanding between the British and the Boers in May 1902. Self-rule for the white minority within the British realm was soon granted. 'Having won the war, they [the British] lost the peace to a mobilised Afrikaner nationalist movement which swept into power as soon as elections were held. The Union of South Africa, which came into being in 1910, was Boer-led and Boer-dominated and skilfully achieved under the leadership of Botha and [Jan Christiaan] Smuts'.[24] Botha and Smuts made political careers in the Union as well as in the British army, with Smuts holding senior posts and gaining a heroic reputation in both world wars. An Afrikaner-dominated nationalist movement formally adopted a policy of apartheid in the 1940s, and a white elite of Afrikaners and descendants of British settlers ruled over the Black majority until the 1990s.

China and the Boxer War, 1900–1

China to an almost unparalleled degree had obsessed Europeans for centuries with dreams about its exotic culture and desire for its porcelain, silk and other prized goods. Despite multiple diplomatic initiatives from the West, China had remained resistant to European incursions, with the ports of Portuguese Macau and Chinese-controlled Canton (now Guangzhou) two of the few points allowed for international trade until the mid-1800s. The Chinese displayed limited interest in Western products, or in cultural interaction with outsiders, although the northern border region had long seen cultural and economic exchange with the adjacent Russian Empire.[25]

Europeans searched for articles that might be exchanged in China – among the few trade goods that attracted Chinese buyers were sandalwood (used for making incense) and *bêche-de-mer* (a sea slug appreciated in Chinese cuisine). Opium, however, was the most promising trade commodity, and the British found that they could grow opium easily in India and use it to buy coveted goods from China. The Chinese, worried about the terms of trade and the spreading use of the addictive drug, tried to curb sales, and the result was war in the 1840s and 1850s. While generally known as the 'Opium Wars' (and, in the case of the 1850s war, the 'Arrow War', from the name of a ship), the Anglo-Chinese wars were in fact broad-ranging conflicts in which the British and their allies, primarily the French and the Spanish, sought to force China to engage in trade. The Westerners got the upper hand; one of the key results of the first Anglo-Chinese war was cession of Hong Kong island to the British in 1842. Though rather an inauspicious site, Hong Kong grew to become one of the busiest and most profitable colonies in the world, and with territory on the Kowloon peninsula remained in British hands until 1997.

The French, in 1849, acquired a substantial grant of land in Shanghai, the 'French Concession', and an 'International Settlement' was opened from combined British and American concessions there in 1863. By the 1890s, Western impositions on China were becoming ever greater. In 1898, the British secured a ninety-nine-year lease on the 'New Territories' adjacent to the Kowloon peninsula, and Germany obtained a lease to territory in Qingdao and Hankou. Missionaries from Europe, and especially the United States, eagerly undertook proselytism among the Chinese, winning a considerable number of converts. Colonial powers made no secret of hopes eventually to divide China among themselves. Within China, dissidents were meanwhile undermining a dynasty that seemed incapable of defending China's sovereignty and status in the world, or to modernize the economy and society. The powerful Empress Dowager Cixi (1835–1908), the power behind the throne, undercut reform efforts, and the European presence – particularly that of the Christian missionaries – fuelled conflicts in both rural and urban China. Natural disasters particularly affecting northern China added to the crisis of the late 1890s.[26]

The situation provided a breeding ground for the Yihetuan Movement, known in the West as the Boxers, because many of their adherents practised martial arts (then known as 'Chinese boxing'). The Boxers began to mount assaults on the foreigners and Chinese Christians they blamed for the ills of the country. In 1898, Boxers' attacks on a Christian community, Liyuantun village, significantly heightened tensions. The decentralized organization of the Boxer movement, grouped around local leaders, made it difficult for the Chinese state forces to bring the violent outbursts under control. Western powers read the inaction as a lack of commitment to protect their expatriate citizens and diplomatic representatives.

In response, the British led an unsuccessful international military delegation, the Seymour expedition, to Peking (Beijing) from their base in Tientsin (Tianjin) in April 1900. The murder of the German representative to China two months later (although

Figure 19.3 'Partition of China at the time of the Boxer Rebellion, 1900'. © Alamy Stock Photo.

not by a Boxer) provided justification for a joint intervention by a cohort of international powers interested in China, including Austria-Hungary, Britain, France, Germany, Italy, Japan, the United States and Russia (see Figure 19.3). The 90,000 troops under the command of a German field marshal, Alfred von Waldersee, claimed to represent 'the whole civilised world'.[27] Confronted with the threat, Beijing's regular troops joined forces with the Boxer movement against the Western and Christian presence. Neither side issued a formal declaration of war, a feature not uncommon in colonial conflicts, but the foreign soldiers first relieved the Boxer siege of Beijing's diplomatic district in August 1900, then moved on to carry out 'punitive expeditions' in the Zhili province around Beijing and neighbouring Shanxi. The war only came to a formal end with the Boxer Protocol signed in September 1901.

Just as were the Cuban and the South African wars, the Boxer War was a media event. A large group of reporters closely followed the course of events and paid particular attention to the complicated cooperation (and the frictions) among imperial nations engaged against the Chinese. The Japanese troops and their commanders received particular attention from Western observers, with the Japanese – who in 1895 had won a war against China, taking the island of Taiwan as colonial booty – perceived both as an 'invaluable ally' in China as well as a potentially 'dangerous rival'.[28]

Eugen Binder-Krieglstein, an Austrian who had earlier reported on the Spanish-American War, in 1902 provided a detailed analysis of German engagement in China and an assessment of the allied forces. Deeply rooted in colonial stereotypes, he dwelt on a racially different and uncivilized Chinese foe, the distinct Chinese climate and the country's unknown topography. Interestingly enough, he considered the Boxer War as a 'classical' colonial military engagement, since difficult mountainous terrain in the

Shanxi province provided an ideal environment for guerrilla warfare, complicating the international army's task. Binder-Krieglstein contended that the Boxer War was 'not a regular but a guerrilla war' which came 'close to an insurgency'. Moreover, he noted a 'certain similarity' with the South African War. Overall, after having compared the German performance to that of other imperial nations in China, the correspondent was convinced that 'German virility and German bravery' would soon make up for the troops' lack of experience in colonial conflict – perhaps a prediction of German actions in Africa a few years later.[29]

The suppression of the Boxers brought benefits for the Westerners, including the expansion of the 'concessions'. These were parcels of territory, generally relatively small, conceded to foreign nations in numerous cities along the coast and occasionally in the hinterland. In the first five years of the new century, the Chinese granted such concessions to the Russians, Italians, Austro-Hungarians, Belgians and Japanese. This gave their nationals rights of residence, allowed foreign firms to do business, and permitted cultural and religious activities, including evangelization. Most humiliatingly to the Chinese, the concessions wrested from them provided extraterritoriality – that is, foreign law prevailed (and foreigners usually could not be tried by Chinese courts); foreign police forces patrolled the concessions and maintained law and order. China, in essence, no longer exercised real sovereignty over these territories.

The concessions were some of the most curious foreign outposts of the colonial era, technically not colonies even if effectively administered as such by resident consuls. In Tientsin, for instance, concessions were held by the British and the French (from 1860), the Americans (1869), Japanese (1898), Germans (1899), Russians (1900), Austro-Hungarians and Italians (1901) and Belgians (1902). Though most covered only several square kilometres and had correspondingly small populations, buildings were erected in national styles lining streets bearing European names, such as the Piazza Regina Margarita (named after the Italian queen). They boasted Protestant, Catholic and Orthodox churches, imposing bank buildings and warehouses, gentlemen's clubs and sports facilities, among other institutions of European life. The French Concession in Shanghai was the best known with leafy streets, grand French-style houses and sports clubs. Shanghai, with the French quarter, the International Settlement and Japanese zone, became one of the most cosmopolitan of all cities during the early decades of the twentieth century, famous for the Art Deco architecture along the riverside Bund and equally notorious for a vibrant nightlife, underworld crime and political conspiracies. The Chinese Communist Party was founded in the French Concession in 1921.

The Qing government did not survive a republican revolution in 1911, though colonizers were never able to divide China, other than for Macau, Hong Kong, the tiny French enclave of Guangzhouwan and the concessions. Yet the impositions on the Chinese government amounted to informal colonialism, and foreign powers were beneficiaries of unequal terms of trade and the political sway they exercised. Western ideas had great influence on such republican leaders as Sun Yat-sen and other reformers. Long-standing opposition to asymmetrical treaties, extraterritoriality and Western intervention, plus a Marxist ideology imported from Europe, would provide an important plank in the Communist movement led by Mao Zedong, which came to power in 1949.

Colonial, European and world conflicts

Despite episodic clashes, Europe did not plunge into a general war until 1914, but overseas conflicts had changed colonial alignments. Britain and France, nearly at war in the Sudan in 1898, collaborated in China and by the early twentieth century were de facto allies. In the year of the Fashoda conflict, the United States became a colonial power in Asia. In the Russo-Japanese War of 1904–5, Japan, which had signed an alliance with Britain, dealt a signal and ignominious defeat to a European power, and in 1905 Tokyo established a protectorate over Korea. France soon came to loggerheads with Germany over Morocco, with Berlin chastened by the establishment of a French protectorate (and a smaller Spanish one) over the sultan's realm.

A world war was neither imminent nor inevitable, but heightened nationalism, militarization and imperial ambitions did not bode well. The conflicts that occurred on either side of the year 1900 had evidenced an escalation of violence and the implementation of new military tactics used by Europeans and, resorting to still effective age-old guerrilla war, by indigenous and local forces. These years saw a paroxysm of colonial expansion that left only rare pockets of South and Southeast Asia, Africa, the Caribbean and Oceania free from foreign overlordship. As evident to roving reporters and the readers of the press, they demonstrated, too, the simultaneous and interconnected ways in which the powers manoeuvred, and they showed the ways in which subject peoples – from Black South Africans to Afro-Cubans, from Filipinos to Chinese – continued resistance to outside incursions.

CHAPTER 20
THE SOUTH PACIFIC, 1903

In 1903, Paul Gauguin, the French post-Impressionist painter, died at the age of fifty-four in the village of Atuona in the Marquesas Islands, today part of French Polynesia. Although Gauguin had travelled the world and drawn inspiration from many cultures, his paintings are today virtually synonymous with a certain Western vision of Polynesia. Posed against luxuriant vegetation, alluring coppery-coloured and often semi-nude women and men incarnate the exoticism and eroticism associated with the Polynesian islands – and still perpetually reprised in tourist brochures. Yet the paintings also reveal changes that had taken place since Europeans arrived in eastern Oceania. Some of the women wear flowing 'mission dresses' introduced by Christian evangelists for the sake of modesty. In one haunting image, a woman is smoking a cigarette, another Western export. Among Gauguin's most beautiful and famous works is 'Where Do We Come From? What Are We? Where Are We Going?' It depicts Polynesians of different ages – an infant, adolescents, an elderly woman – in an Edenic setting, a taut young man in the foreground plucking a fruit from a tree, a spooky grey statue of a pagan deity standing in the background, a duck and dogs and cats wandering around. The figures in the painting bear expressions of melancholy and anomie, and the picture and title intimate the notion of a paradise lost. Polynesia, for Gauguin, had been spoiled by a hundred years of Western intervention, its residents losing the compass points to their ancestral culture and their twentieth-century future.[1]

Gauguin, however, contributed to the very phenomenon he decried. After all, he was a Frenchman, a representative of a European country that had taken over Tahiti and the Marquesas islands in 1842 and subsequently expanded further in what were then called the 'French Settlements in Oceania'. Gauguin had fled urban, industrialized France (leaving behind his wife) to seek adventure, pleasure and *dépaysement*. Yet he bickered with other Frenchmen in Tahiti and sailed to the outer archipelagos to escape Europeans, while nevertheless earning his living selling pictures of Polynesia on the Parisian art market, where 'primitive' cultures were in vogue. Gauguin's morals, by present-day light, seemed typical of masculine privilege and sexual exploitation, as he bedded nubile women, some of them adolescents – critical observers today castigate Gauguin's paintings as South Pacific voyeurism (and his personal conduct as possible sexual abuse), though they remain some of the most popular, and indeed most innovatively significant, artworks of the turn of the century.

The Pacific Islands in the Western imaginary

Old stereotypes died hard, washing around the world like the waters of the Pacific. Oceania was seen as the land and the sea of 'savages', children of nature – the idea inherited from Jean-Jacques Rousseau's Enlightenment version of the 'good savage' suggested by the voyages of the first Europeans in the South Seas (see Figure 20.1). To Westerners, the region was also the home of ignoble 'savages', the heathens, cannibals and head-hunters damned by missionaries that regularly appeared in sensationalist novels and memoirs, paintings, photographs and later in film. An island in the Pacific provided the legendary destination of the Englishman Daniel Defoe's early eighteenth-century novel *Robinson Crusoe*, about literature's most famous castaway, and the sea provided the site for epic struggles between men and whales in the American Herman Melville's mid-nineteenth-century saga *Moby Dick*. Oceania was associated with the search for *Treasure Island*; though that buccaneering late nineteenth-century story was set in the Caribbean, its Scottish author, Robert Louis Stevenson, settled in Samoa. Not to be outdone, the French novelist Pierre Loti, an officer in the French Navy, depicted an idyllic Tahiti of the lost loves of a Westerner in *Le Mariage de Loti* in 1880, while Victor Segalen, a French Navy doctor, offered a pessimistic portrayal of the decline of Polynesian civilization in *Les Immémoriaux*, published four years after the death of Gauguin.

The myths lived on, but the islands of Oceania were firmly set cogs in the colonial machine of geopolitical rivalries, trade and migration well before the start of the twentieth century. Just as there occurred a 'scramble for Africa', there was a 'scramble for Oceania', which began back in the days of Iberian seafarers from the 1500s, and continued with

Figure 20.1 Photograph of Polynesian islanders plaiting flowers into a garland. © Getty Images.

Captains Cook and the Comte de Bougainville, who 'discovered' places as yet unknown to Europeans in the mid-1700s. 'Discovery' led to *prises de possession*, with the profound political, cultural and economic changes that they engendered. The colonial competition for stakes in the Pacific persisted through the mid-twentieth century; in some ways, the islands still provide a terrain of big-power commercial and military manoeuvres for influence and profit.

The Pacific islands vary widely in natural endowments and culture, some relatively large landmasses, others only minuscule parcels of land; some volcanic islands, others coral atolls. Europeans traditionally divided the islands into three groups: Polynesia (meaning 'many islands') in the south-eastern and central Pacific, Melanesia ('dark islands') in the southwest, and Micronesia in the northwest, though in reality the arbitrary mappings belie significant differences within each zone, overlook 'outlier' islands that do not fit neatly into the cartography and minimize common cultural features. For Europeans, Polynesia – including the Hawaiian islands, Samoa, Tonga and indigenous New Zealand (or Aotearoa) – was the most attractive region, peopled by noble chiefs, handsome warriors and lissom maidens whom Westerners fancifully compared to the ancient Greeks, even if the 'natives' were stalled in a primitive stage of civilizational development.

Melanesia, by contrast, was considered a region of dark-skinned people and dark morals, inaccessible in dense jungles, and sometimes unfriendly to foreign contact (though images of Fiji and other Melanesian islands later changed thanks to tourist promotion). Micronesia, whose islands were small and less prominent in travelogues and commentaries, elicited fewer strong images. Customs such as tattooing and taboos (incidentally, giving two Polynesian words to English) fascinated Europeans, who nevertheless misunderstood and disparaged customs they regarded as 'savage'. The absence of most mammals and the lack of metal utensils reinforced notions about backwardness.

Europeans too quickly assumed that social structures such as chieftainships paralleled ones familiar from the Americas and Africa, and they dismissed indigenous spiritualities as superstition. 'First contact' – a term now used for the initial encounters – thus produced much incomprehension that endured. In many respects it was mutual, as European customs appeared as puzzling to islanders as were their own practices and beliefs to the foreigners. Early encounters, as evidenced by a congenial reception for Captain Cook on his first visit to Hawai'i and his murder on a subsequent landing, sent mixed messages.[2] The remoteness of islands scattered over a vast zone, and their extraordinary diversity, especially in Melanesia – 800 indigenous languages are spoken in Papua New Guinea alone – made both access and understanding difficult, but in a sense shielded some islanders from more immediate Western incursion.[3]

The 'scramble' for Oceania

In 1840, the British claimed New Zealand, narrowly beating a private French initiative to establish a settlement there. They signed a treaty with the Maori chiefs, the Waitangi

Treaty, through which sovereignty was (in the British view) ceded to the Crown, but rights to chieftainship and land, and full rights as British subjects, were in principle accorded to the Maori. The treaty, unusual in colonial history for its broad acknowledgement of indigenous people, remains a cornerstone of the New Zealand political system. From the 1840s, tit-for-tat acquisitions divided up the island Pacific. The French established a protectorate over the Society Islands (centred on Tahiti) and annexed the Marquesas Islands in 1842, then in 1853 took over New Caledonia, one of the largest islands of Melanesia. The British established a colony in Fiji in 1874, and in the next decades the islands of Samoa were divided among the British, Germans and Americans (the latter two new entrants in the colonizing game), and France picked up Wallis and Futuna.[4]

In the south-western Pacific, the large island of New Guinea was shared out among the Dutch (nominally present in the western part of the island, at the extremity of their East Indian possessions, for several centuries), the Germans in the northeast and the British in the southeast. The British took the Solomon Islands, and the Gilbert and Ellice Islands, and established a protectorate over Tonga. In 1888, Chile annexed Easter Island off the coast of South America. A decade later, the United States gained control of the Hawaiian islands from its indigenous royal dynasty. In 1898, the United States bought Guam from Spain. By the end of the century, almost every island between Australia and the Americas, even uninhabited specks of land, had come under the dominion of a colonial master.

One of the oddest arrangements would soon be adopted for the still unclaimed New Hebrides archipelago, coveted both by French settlers in nearby New Caledonia and Australians still subjects of the British but finding their own footing in the Pacific. In the early years of the twentieth century, Britain and France established a 'condominium' over the New Hebrides: neither country held legal sovereignty, but each had a small settler community presided over by an official appointed in London and Paris. With careful protocol, the flags of their two residences flew at exactly the same height. The French franc and the British pound sterling circulated as currency, Protestants and Catholics vied for islanders' souls and foreign landowners who acquired properties by all means fair and foul set up coconut plantations – the largest landholder, John Higginson, was an Anglophobic Irishman who favoured French interests. Settlers had to opt to be governed under French or British law. As for the indigenous people, they remained stateless; disputes between them were resolved by a joint court with three judges, one French, one British and the third, initially, a Spaniard, chosen, with impeccable but curious logic, because a Spanish ship had been the first European vessel to visit the islands. This 'pandemonium', as it was branded, lasted until 1980, when the islands gained independence (the last country in the South Pacific to do so) as Vanuatu.

Colonialism in the Islands

Foreign occupation undermined pre-existing political, social and religious structures in the South Seas. Paradoxically, however, it also strengthened some pre-colonial institutions and created solid new ones. Thus, although the French abolished the Tahitian monarchy in 1880, one of the senior chiefs in Samoa outbid his rivals, with British assistance, to become the king of (Western) Samoa, and the monarchy survived until 2007; the still surviving dynasty of Tonga consolidated power and remodelled itself on the British monarchy, complete with a European-style crown, throne and royal robes. Some of the old elites such as noblemen in French Polynesia transitioned into a new elite as pastors and deacons in Protestant churches and administrative officers. Missionaries scored great success in the islands; priests transformed Wallis and Futuna into a Catholic theocracy in the 1820s, more than five decades before France annexed the territory, and most islanders elsewhere, except in the more remote hinterlands of New Guinea, were converted by Catholic, Anglican, Presbyterian and later Mormon missionaries during the 1800s and early 1900s. Ardent Christian observance became and remains one of the main cultural traits in the island Pacific, but with pre-Christian traditions incorporated into spiritual life.[5]

Missionaries proved less successful in efforts to stamp out sexual practices, forms of music and dancing, and traditions such as the drinking of kava (a mildly intoxicating libation made from a plant root drunk on ceremonial and social occasions) that they condemned as immoral. European-introduced alcohol and prostitution also aroused the ire of priests and pastors, though to little avail. In French Polynesia, intermarriage or informal sexual liaisons between Europeans and Polynesians was common, and many of the country's residents today are *demis* ('halves', as they are locally called), though *métissage* is rare elsewhere in the Pacific islands except for Hawai'i. More Westernized elites appeared primarily in small port towns and among the Christian clergy. Islanders in peripheral archipelagos and the New Guinea highlands experienced less impact from European colonization except for conversion to Christianity, though the labour trade in Tokelau and Melanesia, and the establishment of coffee plantations in the New Guinea highlands, among other developments, showed that they were hardly exempt from the effects of colonialism.

For Europeans, even small islands in the Pacific presented attractions beyond beaches and palm trees, tropical languor and the fantasy of romance. They lay along shipping routes between the Americas and Asia for whaling ships and merchant vessels in search of tea, silk and porcelain in China. The sandalwood grown on such islands as New Caledonia provided a good commodity for trade in China, where the fragrant wood was turned into joss sticks; the Chinese also had a taste for sea cucumber (*bêche-de-mer*, a marine animal) that Europeans traded. At a time when sailing ships needed a chain of ports and sources of fresh water and food, islands offered vital harbours and supplies. As telegraphic cables began to be laid across the ocean, there was a need for cable stations for maintenance of the lines. Later, steamships required stockpiles of the coal used as fuel; later still, the first generations of airplanes, which could manage only short flights, needed landing strips as they hopped their way across the Pacific.

From the early 1800s, engineers mooted plans to build a canal across the Central American isthmus, with hopes buoyed by the wealth of mid-century gold rushes in California and Australia, growing trade across the Pacific and the technological prowess proved with the completion of the Suez Canal in 1869. Lobbyists argued that a Central American canal would contribute to a revolution in the world's economy, moving the centre of gravity from the Atlantic to the Pacific. Indeed, in the late 1800s, businessmen, politicians, geographers and scientists with a passion for expansion were claiming that the twentieth century would be the century of the Pacific, and that island holdings would provide key commercial and geostrategic nodes in that new world.[6] The rise of Japan as a military, industrial and colonial power, and Western designs on a weakening Chinese empire, focused attention on the Asian shore of the Pacific. In the event, the Panama Canal, begun by the French, who had constructed the Suez Canal with an international labour force but were defeated in Central America by climate, disease, financial problems and scandal, was finally completed under American authority and opened in 1914. The date was inauspicious, but the First World War, and even more dramatically the Second World War, with the Japanese attack on Pearl Harbor in the American colony of Hawai'i and intense fighting throughout the Pacific theatre, showed that not all of the nineteenth-century prognostications about the future of the Pacific islands were invalid.

In the first decade of the twentieth century, those wars lay in the future, though expansion by Germany into the islands, and near paranoid Western fears about the 'yellow peril' thought to be represented by Asian countries such as Japan and China, dramatically illustrated the rising tensions in international affairs. The islands in Gauguin's time, though tiny by comparison with giant colonial holdings in Asia and Africa, were far from insignificant for colonial overlords. They produced commodities of commercial value, notable among them copra, or the dried meat of coconuts. Copra provided the key ingredient in industrially manufactured soap, and the making of soap was a rapidly growing business; the Lever Brothers company in Britain became a world leader, and *savon de Marseille* was marketed as a signature product of the French Mediterranean port that imported raw materials from tropical colonies. For Hawai'i, the staple export was pineapple, and the Dole Pineapple Company was a major landholder in the islands and the fulcrum for American takeover and abolition of Hawaiian sovereignty in the 1890s. The ever-rising Western addiction to sugar created a huge demand, with supplies from the Caribbean and Indian Ocean, where sugarcane had long been grown, supplemented from new plantations, such as those in Fiji, where it became the leading export under the British. Colonials experimented with other cash crops as well. Cotton planted in Tahiti found a niche during the American Civil War of the 1860s, when world markets registered a dearth, and there were efforts, with modest success in other islands in the late 1800s and early 1900s, to grow coffee, indigo and tobacco for export.

Minerals offered another important resource, none more so that the nickel of New Caledonia, which has one of the world's largest supplies. Nickel served for coinage, but even more profitably, provided a crucial alloy in steel; with steel-clad steamships and new sorts of armaments and military hardware in the last decades of the nineteenth century, nickel gained immense value. It became (as it remains) the territory's leading export and through companies such as the Rothschild concern, New Caledonia was brought into international circuits of capital. Elsewhere in the Pacific – particularly in Nauru, Banaba and the French Polynesian island of Makatea – phosphate became a lucrative resource for colonial miners, important as an ingredient in the synthetic fertilizers that, like steel, were a product of the late nineteenth-century 'second industrial revolution'. Gold was discovered in New Guinea in 1852, though large-scale mining of the precious metal (and copper, which is also plentiful there) did not develop until more than a century later.

To handle business, expansive trading companies sprang up in the Pacific, such as the German Godeffroy Company (a major trader in eastern Oceania), the German Handels-und Plantagen-Gesellschaft in Samoa and the Australian Burns Philp Company; shippers such as the British P&O lines and the French Messageries Maritimes similarly won shares of the business. Island ports – Honolulu in Hawai'i, Noumea in New Caledonia, Suva in Fiji and Apia in Samoa – became bustling, if small-scale, entrepôts with banks and warehouses, European-style lodging for the foreigners and churches of various denominations. These places nevertheless retained a rough-and-ready feel through the early twentieth century mirroring the roving life of traders, sailors, stevedores and adventurers. Images of bumboats lying at anchor framed by palm trees, and ramshackle bars and tumbledown houses on the shore, provided further stereotypes of the South Pacific in the imaginary of outsiders. As elsewhere, European conquest brought new residents, and offered opportunities for local people to leave, though unwillingly for some going in both directions. There was the usual assortment of planters and traders, fortune-seekers and beachcombers, government officials, soldiers and sailors, though European numbers remained relatively small in most archipelagos. An eccentric French marquis tried to implant a settlement in New Guinea, yet it came to nought, and a French utopian socialist movement attempted to set up a communitarian phalanstery in New Caledonia, but it proved short-lived.

France annexed New Caledonia not just to counter the imperial rivals whom they feared would turn the South Pacific into a 'British lake' but with the twin objectives of obtaining a base in the south-western ocean for France's military and mercantile fleets and of acquiring territory for a penal colony. Following the British example on the Australian mainland, Tasmania and Norfolk Island (even if transportation there almost entirely ceased several decades before the French began to remove prisoners to the South Pacific), the French hoped to 'better' that British precedent. Their intention was to use transported convicts to create an 'austral France', a process in which the prisoners exiled from metropolitan France would, in theory, become honest yeoman farmers and pastoralists for the new colony.

From the mid-nineteenth century until 1897, common criminals were transported to New Caledonia, with those sentenced to more than seven years required to spend the remainder of their lives there. Most came from urban areas, possessed little aptitude for a new rural life as pioneers and felt no rapport with the indigenous people. Some nevertheless made their way to modest prosperity in the *brousse* (the countryside) or the growing city of Noumea, and a few became mining magnates, though others succumbed to alcohol and 'vice', finally convincing the government to turn off the 'dirty tap water' (as one minister put it) of transportation. Common criminals were not the only unwilling migrants to New Caledonia, as France sent rebels from an insurrection in Algeria in 1870 and revolutionaries who had participated in the Paris Commune uprising in 1871.

Political and common prisoners transported to New Caledonia numbered around 22,000; most Communards, following an amnesty, returned home in the early 1880s. Convicts and Communards initially gave colonial New Caledonia a less than salutary reputation, but the government tried to attract free settlers from France and brought in indentured labourers from Asia.

Indentured labour was a feature of several South Pacific island groups. (Indenture is a thorny topic and is discussed in more detail in Chapters 8 and 15 of this book.) Descendants of indentured labourers today often speak of the 'slavery' to which their ancestors were subjected, though historians point out the differences between indentured labour and slavery as practised in the Americas. Certain it is that their conditions were often miserable and exploitation common, but it seems that some at least of those who accepted contracts viewed indenture as a chance to better their lot. The French recruited labourers for New Caledonia from Tonkin (northern Vietnam), Dutch Java and Japan, and they contracted Chinese to work the cotton plantations of Tahiti. The Japanese were expelled at the start of the Second World War, but other Asians stayed on, becoming market gardeners or shopkeepers and, particularly in Tahiti, rising into the higher echelons of society. Between 1879 and 1916, the British brought 60,000 Indians to Fiji for work on sugar plantations; most took root in the colony, where they came to outnumber indigenous Fijians, not without friction in the post-colonial period.[7] Meanwhile, Chinese migrants fanned out across the Pacific, often working as traders; 'overseas Chinese' now represent a population of around 80,000 in Oceania, with particularly large numbers in Fiji and Papua New Guinea. These groups carried with them their languages and traditions, though the passage of time and intermarriage hybridized cultures.

Islanders also moved away from home. The recruitment of workers, primarily from the New Hebrides and the Solomon Islands, for the sugarcane fields of Queensland, on the Australian continent, opened a major conduit in the labour trade, with 50,000–60,000 Melanesians arriving in north-eastern Australia between 1863 and 1908. Critics condemned 'blackbirding' (as it was called) because of the poor conditions of engagement and work, but they were as much or more preoccupied with keeping the newly unified Australian colonies 'white' as they were concerned with the islanders' welfare. Many returned home, though frequently with outstanding wages left unpaid. Other sorts of population movements occurred, as with the men who found jobs as seamen and provided crucial navigation skills and manpower in the Pacific and beyond. Some Maori from New Zealand moved to Australia, Loyalty Islanders to the New Caledonian mainland and those from outlying islands to larger centres elsewhere; given the relatively small size of island populations, even limited movements in or out could produce demographic and social disruption.

Resistance and transformation in the 1900s

Inevitably, clashes erupted between colonial rulers and their island subjects. The New Zealand Wars (formerly called the Maori Wars, though Maoris ranged themselves in both pro- and anti-British camps) raged episodically, from 1845 to 1872, despite the Treaty of Waitangi. On the New Caledonian mainland, the dispossession of Kanaks, the indigenous Melanesians – whose lands were reduced to one-tenth of the total area as the French moved them into reservations – and depredations by settlers' cattle on remaining fields led to a major revolt in 1878. The settlers (and even most of the radical Communards) joined the French army and police in putting down the rebellion. The Melanesian leader Atai was killed, and his head shipped to an anthropological laboratory in Paris; he became the symbolic forebear of a later pro-independence movement. New Caledonia experienced another revolt in 1917, this one touched off, in part, by French efforts to recruit soldiers during the Great War.

In many islands, episodic or more systematic violence accompanied colonialism. Racial discrimination of the sort common throughout the colonial world remained ever-present. In New Caledonia, for instance, the *code de l'indigénat* (indigenous code) of regulations permitted even subaltern administrators rather than judges and warders to mete out corporal punishment, fines and incarceration for a variety of minor offences. In Papua New Guinea, the 1926 White Women's Protection Ordinance, adopted by the Australian administration then in control of the territory, forbade a 'native' man to be alone with a white woman and instituted the death penalty for (attempted) rape of a European woman – an illustration of racist perceptions about unbridled indigenous sexuality.

In the early years of the twentieth century, few questioned racial hierarchies, yet some voices were raised against the treatment of indigenous peoples, such as that of the ethnographer and Protestant missionary Maurice Leenhardt in New Caledonia. Islander populations (and Australian Aborigines), it was widely predicted, were fated, in a literal sense, to die out. Those who survived had to be trained to European ways, though their ability to 'assimilate' into modern society was often questioned. In the early 1930s, an Australian gold prospector, Mick Leahy, travelled to the Western Highlands of New Guinea, and encountered populations without previous contact with foreigners. The tardy 'discovery' of new terrains and 'tribes' reanimated the excitement and stereotypes created by eighteenth-century voyagers and their successors, and were brought to life in Leahy's film footage of the expedition.

The Pacific during these decades, therefore, remained a field for exploration and theorizing for outsiders. Bronislaw Malinowski, a Europe-based ethnographer, found in the islands evidence for his pioneering theories, for example, concerning gift-giving and systems of reciprocity in human society, though the titles of his books reveal the spirit of the age: *Myth in Primitive Psychology* (1926), *Crime and Custom in Savage Society* (also 1926) and *The Sexual Life of Savages in North-Western Melanesia* (1929). The 1928 book *Coming of Age in Samoa*, based on fieldwork by a young and soon to be famous American anthropologist, Margaret Mead, became a bestseller with its depiction of an easy sexual maturation so different, she opined, from the conflicted adolescence and constrained morals of her compatriots; later anthropologists would discredit her views.

The islands continued to inspire theorists, whose ideas ranged from the persuasive to the outright bizarre. In 1947, the Norwegian adventurer Thor Heyerdahl sailed a raft, the *Kon-Tiki*, 8,000 kilometres across the Pacific trying to prove that eastern Oceania was originally settled from South America; though the hypothesis has been debunked, it enjoyed considerable currency at the time. In 1966, Alan Moorehad's *The Fatal Impact* posited the wholesale destruction of indigenous cultures in the island Pacific with the onslaught in Westernization – a generalization that the resilience of Oceanic cultures has disproved. The enigmatic carved stone statues of Easter Island (Rapa Nui) have provoked much serious and fanciful (and wrong) speculation about their origin and supposed connection with lost civilizations, including Erich von Däniken's 1969 suggestion that they were built by extra-terrestrials, 'gods from outer space'.

More academically, Oskar Spate's magisterial three-volume *The Pacific since Magellan*, published from 1978 to 1988, recast the *longue durée* of the colonial history of the islands in the wider context of European expansion from the time of the Spanish and Portuguese in the 1500s. A school of 'Pacific history' emerged in Australia in the 1940s, some of its first practitioners having had personal experience of colonialism in the islands as administrators or missionaries. Spate's 'oceanic' view of the islands contrasted with an alternative 'island-oriented' approach that privileged investigation and presentation of island history from local and indigenous viewpoints, and that incorporated oral histories and ethnohistory. Other scholars wrote the history of non-Western migrants in the islands. Meanwhile, anthropologists from around the world showed themselves so eager to study Pacific island societies that it was quipped that a typical Polynesian family included parents, children and the resident foreign social scientist. Scientists today use the Pacific islands as exemplars of climate change in the Anthropocene.

Islanders themselves have played a central role as keepers of their region's history, through the passing down of genealogies, creation myths, oral histories and forms of art, music and storytelling. Though few islanders had access to Western-style university studies until the late twentieth century, academics such as Epeli Hau'ofa, Tracey Banivanua-Mar and Damon Salesa have provided new viewpoints on Oceanic history from islander perspectives. Creative works, such as the novels of the Samoan Albert Wendt, the best-known fiction writer from the South Pacific, have reflected on themes ranging from the Homeric-style voyages of the ancient Polynesians to the place of diasporic Polynesians in today's world. Museums in the islands, and outside Oceania, contain collections of old and contemporary island artwork, weaving and carving (with some of the works housed overseas now the object of demands for restitution). Collections such as those of the Jean-Marie Tjibaou Cultural Centre in New Caledonia (named for the leader of the unsuccessful independence movement in the French territory in the 1980s) illustrate the ways that islanders innovatively engage with ancestral traditions, colonialism and its legacies and present-day life.

At the time of Gauguin's death, and for long afterwards, Westerners gazing on the Pacific islands saw paradise and paradise lost (and sometimes inferno), visions or mirages that say as much about the outsiders as about the local life. Islanders paid a large price for encounters with the foreigners, and for the occupation and rule of their countries by colonial powers. They suffered the effects of disease and depopulation. In some islands, foreigners seized much of the indigenous people's land, and Western rule conceded few if any political or legal rights. Yet chiefly structures and the strength of 'custom' – ancestral beliefs, traditions, social relationships, taboos – remained strong. Daily life changed with wage employment, new forms of trade and transport, European law and Christian religion, and the presence of Europeans, diasporic populations and *métis*. For better or worse, the islands and their peoples were integrated into global systems of commerce, governance and cultural exchange, though not without sustained, and often successful, efforts to safeguard inherited cultures or to hybridize them with foreign influences.

During of Gauguin's sojourn in the eastern Polynesian islands, more than a century after 'first contact' and after half a century of French rule there, the impact of Western colonialism had already greatly altered life. More political changes were in store in the Pacific islands; after the First World War, Germany lost its colonies in Oceania – Papua taken over by Australia, German Samoa by New Zealand, Germany's Micronesian islands by Japan. The end of the Second World War saw the eviction of Japan, with its islands placed as 'trust territories' under US administration. Not until the 1970s did most of the Pacific islands gain independence, decades after Asian colonies and at a significant remove from the round of independence in Africa around 1960.

From the standpoint of the colonizers, the Pacific territories were simply too small and too remote, their populations too 'backward' and some too resource poor, to sustain independence. But they still presented some interest for the colonizers, for instance, with British and French (and American) nuclear testing in islands that continued, in the French case, until 1996. (Indeed, French Polynesia, New Caledonia and Wallis and Futuna remain overseas territories of the French Republic, and American Samoa and Guam, alongside several island groups in the northern Pacific, are territories of United States.) China, offering aid and striving for influence, has most recently been making inroads in the island Pacific. Hopes for exploiting the geostrategic potential and resources of the islands, not just ethnocentric cultural notions, have provided an imperative for continued dominion. However, in several cases, as in the British Solomon Islands and the Gilbert and Ellice Islands (Kiribati and Tuvalu) at the end of the 1970s, when independence occurred, it ironically could represent less a response to nationalist pressure than a desire by colonizing countries to divest themselves of holdings that seemed to have lost value.[8]

CHAPTER 21
CEYLON, 1907

Ceylon, the Indian Ocean island country now known as Sri Lanka, was 'the Happy Island' and the 'Pearl of the Imperial Crown', 'steadily advancing in material prosperity, the progress of education . . . and the peace and security which British rule had given the people'. The author added: 'There is no other portion of the Empire which stands to-day in such a desirable position as regards the well-being of the inhabitants or in which there is a brighter promise of sustained prosperity in the future.' Such at least was the opinion of the Ceylonese barrister and scholar Edward W. Perrera in a historical overview published in *Twentieth-Century Impressions of Ceylon* in 1907. The summation no doubt brought a rousing 'Hear! Hear!' from British colonialists and probably more critical comments from some others.[1]

Twentieth-Century Impressions, edited by Arnold Wright, is an artefact of the imperial age, a monumental, elegantly printed and expensive volume of no fewer than 916 pages and hundreds of illustrations. Encompassing chapters on the island's 'history, people, commerce, industries, and resources', as the subtitle announces, it was an encyclopaedic presentation of Ceylon. It represented a panoptical survey, though not surprisingly, with areas on which authors did not turn their gaze. It was meant, as the preface suggests, to promote 'the tightening of bonds which unite the component parts of the King's dominions'. The book opened with a map and a full-page portrait of 'His Excellency The Governor and Commander-in-Chief of Ceylon, Vice-Admiral Sir Henry Arthur Blake, G.C.M.G. [Knight Grand Cross of the Most Distinguished Order of St Michael and St George] FRCI [Fellow of the Royal Colonial Institute]', looking as resplendent in ceremonial dress as his title sounds; also pictured, wearing a tiara and an evening gown, is his wife. Lengthy sections provided countless biographical profiles, often graced by photographs, of leading local and expatriate worthies. The authors of chapters included British officials and scholars resident in Ceylon and Ceylonese intellectuals. The name of the publisher, Lloyd's Greater Britain Publishing Company – established in Western Australia and headquartered in South Africa – echoed imperial pride.

To the historian, *Twentieth-Century Impressions* offers a variegated if propagandistic portrait of one of Britain's major colonies at what was perhaps the high point of the British Empire. Only between the lines and in passing references are less glorious sides of the imperial epic revealed – poverty, exploitation, disenfranchisement, ethnic tensions – for they jarred with a triumphalist perspective meant to be scientific and factual, but intended at the same time to vaunt the beneficence of British rule and the unstoppable progress it brought. The book, what it says and left unstated, provides the pivot for this chapter. Though much in Wright's sprawling volume is tedious and repetitive, it is a rich mosaic of the British presence in Ceylon, some aspects of local cultures, and cross-cultural encounters and social change. For a better understanding of Ceylon around 1907, it is first useful to consider the longer history of the island and the passage of a procession of colonizers across its shores.

From Taprobane to Ceylon

The arrival of different waves of migrants from the Indian subcontinent through the millennia overwhelmed the small aboriginal Veddah population, who by the early 1900s numbered only about a thousand mostly forest-dwellers. The largest groups in the island were, and are, the mostly Buddhist Sinhalese and, concentrated in the north and east, the usually Hindu Tamils; both groups migrated to Ceylon many centuries before Europeans set foot there. A smaller population of Muslims, locally known as 'Moors', also settled. Tamils and Sinhalese established kingdoms in Ceylon, and the island was almost never politically unified in pre-colonial times. The longest-lived kingdom centred on the inland town of Kandy, whose dynasties constructed Buddhist temples, royal palaces and crucial water reservoirs. The ensemble of temples in Anuradhapura and Polonnaruwa, and a dramatic fortress atop a rocky outcrop in Sigiriya, remain architectural masterworks, and the archaeological sites (and World Heritage Sites) still attract pilgrims, scholars and tourists. In Kandy, the ornate Temple of the Tooth, said to enshrine a relic of the Lord Buddha, is a sacred site for Buddhists from the island and overseas. A complex society developed in the Kandyan kingdom, with a monarch and court, land-holding nobility, Buddhist monks and a majority of peasants.[2]

Ceylon was known for gemstones such as sapphires and rubies, and another export, cinnamon – the bark of the cinnamon tree, peeled and curled into quills – was almost as coveted by spice traders and foreign consumers as the precious stones. Europeans had known of Ceylon since Antiquity, when the Greeks called the island Taprobane, and the Chinese and Arabs traded there as well. Arabs were so impressed with verdant landscapes and rich resources that they gave the island the name Serendip, whence the word 'serendipity'. They were content to do business and move on, but the Portuguese who arrived in the early 1500s were intent on conquest. In the Tamil kingdom of Jaffna, they forced the monarch to convert to Christianity before exiling him to Goa in Portuguese India; they then put the monarch to death and sent his wife and daughter into a convent. The Portuguese, who devised the name *Ceilão* that gave the English Ceylon, gained control of part of the coast and hinterland, built fortresses and sent missionaries, such as the Jesuit St Francis Xavier, who converted a number of local people to Catholicism. In the mid-1600s, the Dutch displaced the Portuguese, extended European holdings, introduced Protestantism and established links with the East Indies, from which the Dutch brought Malay slaves and political exiles. Under the Portuguese and Dutch, yet another social group emerged, the 'Burghers' of mixed European and local parentage. Intermarriage among the Ceylonese population and new arrivals, as evidenced by many Portuguese and Dutch surnames today, left intertwined genealogies and cultures.

Dominant for a century and a half, the Dutch gave way to the British as the Royal Navy occupied Dutch possessions that had nominally fallen into the hands of the French during the revolutionary wars. In 1796, the British took over the Dutch possessions, which included all of the coast, though the landlocked kingdom of Kandy remained independent. Ceylon gave the British an attractive, well-situated and resource-laden possession, with the harbours of Colombo, Jaffna and Trincomalee providing valuable strategic bases in the Indian Ocean. The survival of the Kandy state, however, rankled empire-builders eager to dominate the entire island. An attempt to conquer Kandy in 1804 was repelled by King Vickrama Rajasinha's troops and the arduous conditions of the jungle environment. In 1815, the British tried again, this time successfully, in league with a dissident nobleman who galvanized opposition to a king whose legitimacy and power were contested by some in the Kandy elite. The British occupied Kandy, captured the king and sent the royal family into exile in India, and abolished a dynasty that claimed to have reigned for more than two thousand years. They signed a convention with the Kandyan nobles, promising to honour their rights (which included income from properties and taxation) and, very importantly, to respect Buddhism. The accord made fine promises that were not fully honoured; within several years, a major rebellion erupted, and resistance continued for decades. The British meanwhile put in place a colonial administration, though leaving a network of Ceylonese administrators, many from the nobility, charged with collecting tax, apprehending criminals, preserving public order and overseeing economic projects.[3]

Ceylon under the British

The British continued to exploit Ceylon for gemstones and cinnamon, but in the 1820s, they introduced a new crop, coffee. Forests were cleared, shrubs planted and within a few years coffee became Ceylon's major export. Cultivation of coffee grew ever more important, until in 1871, a fungoid pest invaded the plantations and destroyed the coffee plants; within a decade, all commercial coffee-growing had ceased.

Fortunately, there was another crop, the one that made Ceylon world famous. The first significant planting of tea in Ceylon, the work of James Taylor, dated to the mid-1860s, and an unquenchable thirst for tea in Britain and its empire, the United States and Russia meant there was a ready market.[4] Tea grew particularly well on the hillsides in central Ceylon, and land the British Crown had taken with the conquest was sold to tea planters, a number of them, like Taylor, migrants from Scotland. Tea plantations spread like wildfire; in 1867, 10 acres were planted in tea, 10 years later 2,720 acres, and in another 10 years, 170,000; by 1897, 350,000 acres were covered in tea bushes. Production demanded machinery for drying, rolling and packaging tea leaves, and road and rail transport to get exports from the highlands to ports. Most importantly, plantations needed labour (see Figure 21.1). Sinhalese, most of whom worked as small farmers or artisans, showed little affinity for the hard labour of plucking tea leaves, day after day in the hot sun, so the British recruited workers from the Tamil regions of south-eastern

Figure 21.1 'Sorting and rolling tea leaves in factory in Ceylon (23 March 1923)'. © Alamy Stock Photo.

India. Around 400,000 Tamils, including a substantial number of women, were brought to Ceylon. They swelled the number of indigenous Tamils (and Hindus), though cultural and occupational divides separated local Tamils and the new arrivals; over time, local Tamils, and some of the former indentured workers, became increasingly important in trade, the professions and the administration. Tea continued to be Ceylon's main export and remains so, and planters such as Sir Thomas Lipton became synonymous with the beverage they marketed. Throughout the world, Ceylon *was* tea, the product advertised with picturesque images of island landscapes, seemingly contented tea-pickers and prosperous planters.

To serve the tea industry and an increasingly dynamic colonial economy, the British developed a dense infrastructure, as detailed in *Twentieth-Century Impressions*. Colombo, from the old market and port area to expanding residential zones, became a bustling centre of administration and trade. A telegraph line had linked Colombo and Galle, on the south coast, in 1858, and the island was soon joined to international cable networks. By the end of the century there was the telephone as well (though with only 150 subscribers in 1907). A 120-kilometre rail line from Colombo to Kandy opened in 1867, followed by rail connections to Galle in 1894 and Jaffna in 1901. A breakwater was erected in the Colombo port in the early 1880s, along with a graving dock, coaling jetties and shipways. From 1899, the city boasted an electric tramway. Grand buildings rose in the capital: a General Post Office completed in 1895, a Public Hall, Anglican and Catholic cathedrals, Wesleyan and Baptist houses of worship and a YMCA and YWCA, joining the Buddhist and Hindu temples and Muslim mosques. A statue of Queen Victoria was erected for her Diamond Jubilee in 1897. Galle Face Green and Victoria Park provided green space, and gas street lighting brightened the night, but in the early 1900s the lake in the centre of Colombo was still a noxious tip for sewage. The local working class lived in poverty with meagre wages, limited access to education and lack of facilities for hygiene; the killing of 42,000 rats in Colombo in 1905 testified both to unsanitary conditions and to efforts by municipal authorities to address the problem.

Mansions in Colombo's prestigious Cinnamon Gardens neighbourhood, by contrast, gave evidence of the wealth of the Sinhalese, Tamil, Muslim, Burgher and British elite, and those with the means and interest had access to active social institutions. Elite schools, such as Royal College (established in 1835) and St Thomas School in Colombo, and Trinity College in Kandy, provided a British-style education for young men, and there were Buddhist, Hindu and Islamic schools, and schools for girls. (Aspirational young ladies, for instance, might attend such establishments as Miss Violet Muthukrishna's Shorthand and Typewriting Institute – with, *Twentieth-Century Impressions* suggested, 'handsome prospects offered by this line of business, at once light and lucrative'.) An impressive museum opened in Colombo in 1877 with collections of archaeological relics, religious and artisanal objects and art. The Colombo Society of Arts formed in 1890 to encourage European-style painting and sculpture. Gentlemen's clubs opened for the leisure of Europeans (though generally off-limits to local people and non-white migrants), such as the Colombo Club in 1871 – 'for the promotion of social intercourse among gentlemen residing in Ceylon' – and the Hill Club established in Nuwara Eliya, near the tea plantations, in 1876. There was a range of English-language newspapers, led by the *Ceylon Observer* founded in 1834, four Sinhalese-language newspapers, the first dating from 1862, and a Tamil newspaper started in 1841. The still majestic Galle Face Hotel opened in 1864 to accommodate business and political travellers and an increasing number of well-heeled tourists.

Ceylon in 1907

Twentieth-Century Impressions appeared at a moment when Ceylon seemed a model colony for the British. There was little open anti-colonial dissent. The administration prided itself on efficient management, tea planters earned generous profits and a burgeoning group of local Ceylonese entrepreneurs, traders and professional people looked to have gained advantage from British imperial rule. The labour force had grown from migration and provided a ready and inexpensive supply for plantations and other businesses. Technology gave proof of modernization, from the telegraph and rail lines, and electric machines used to process tea, to the typewriters increasingly common in offices and the Singer sewing machines becoming prized features in even many modest homes.[5] The chants of Buddhist and Hindu monks and Muslim muezzins blended with the peals of church bells and the sounds of steamships, motorcars and bullock carts. A careful examination of the *Twentieth-Century Impressions*, however, provides deeper insight into the fabric of society, glimmers of the lives of those less fortunate within the colonial order, and examples of the paradoxes of the British reign.

Statistics were always important to colonial rule; counting people and tabulating production, like mapping landscapes, was vital to colonial knowledge and domination. In 1904, Ceylon counted 3,767,826 residents: 2,476,349 (or roughly two-thirds) Sinhalese, 1,000,173 Tamils, 235,595 Moors, 24,088 Burghers and 12,002 Malays. There were 13,198 'others' as well, but only 6,421 Europeans – a tiny number relative to the power the colonizers wielded. Immigration topped emigration, largely because of Tamils coming from India: 21,056 in 1904, 91,567 the following year. Over 88 per cent of Ceylonese lived in rural areas with 12 per cent in cities. That figure underlines the centrality of agriculture and village life, and the disparities between cities and the countryside; for most Ceylonese, modernized urban life was distant, unfamiliar and largely inaccessible. Colombo was the primate city, with 200,000 residents (according to the 1901 census), followed by Galle (37,000), Jaffna (34,000) and Kandy (26,000). Ethnic groups were not equally spread around the provinces, and as an appendix on 'vital statistics' to *Twentieth-Century Impressions* further revealed, there existed profound differences in standards of living among various groups. Infant mortality figures, in general, compared favourably with European countries, one author claimed without specifying which countries served as benchmarks, but rose dramatically among Tamils. Deaths in childbirth, however, were 2.1 per cent, compared to 0.7 per cent in Britain. Death rates, the appendix added, were particularly high among Tamil plantation 'coolies', victims of chronic dysentery because of contaminated food and bad sanitation – a rare statement in the volume about poor conditions endured by large parts of the island's population.

Government departments proliferated, each described in detail, from the Traffic and Forest Departments to the Archaeological Commission. There was a Department of Prisons, a Harbour Department, a Medical Department, a Customs Department, an Education Department, among others staffed by the Ceylon Civil Service and local employees, though Britons monopolized the top positions. The authors expressed pride that the colony had 65 government hospitals, 404 government dispensaries and a further 142 clinics located on plantations, 140 medical officers, 247 apothecaries, 152 nurses and 114 vaccinators. Ceylon had a 'lunatic asylum', a leper hospital, a women's hospital, an ophthalmic hospital, a bacteriological institute and a medical college opened in 1870. Progress in public health was considered one of the signal achievements of colonialism; the statistics are impressive, but less so when one considers the size of the population – 140 medical officers for almost 3.5 million people was creditable in the colonial world, but still hardly sufficient. Government schools, only 64 in 1869, had grown to 554 35 years later; progress indeed, but with education left out of the reach of many children.

The variety of sports and sporting teams – another marker of British civilization in colonizers' eyes – is telling: cricket arrived in the 1860s and a dozen teams are profiled in the 1907 book, a Boxing Club organized in 1865, and the Colombo Football Club in 1880. A tennis club existed in Colombo from 1879, and the 300 members enjoyed 16 courts (and 4 croquet courts), a clubhouse with ballroom, a 'withdrawing-room for ladies' and catering facilities. Hockey was introduced in 1896; the 'Rugger season' was in full swing every year, there was a rowing club, and anglers might join a fishing club set up in 1896. Horse-racing, capped by the Governor's Cup, offered a popular spectator sport for Britishers and local people. Many of the sports clubs were European-only, but 'native' and mixed clubs did exist, such as the Sinhalese Sports Club set up in Colombo in 1899, which the book rather patronizingly notes was intended 'to introduce some diversions into the lives of the people and keep them from pernicious amusements' and to provide a place where all communities could meet 'with an ultimate view of facilitating a removal of distinctions'. Race was an ever-present signifier of social status and entitlement, the superiority of Europeans too evident to need stating, yet every section of *Twentieth-Century Impressions* bears testimony to the way that race (and religion) divided groups, established hierarchies and, for the colonizers, justified discrimination and allowed abuse.

Wright's edited volume occasionally engaged in lyric descriptions of the beauties of Ceylon and vaunted the quality of transport that facilitated visits. A short section on 'information for travellers' alerted tourists to hotels and rest-houses of good standard. It spent far more space discussing natural scenery than archaeological sites and indigenous culture, no doubt a reflection of the perceived interests of tourists. The beaches, which today attract crowds of holiday-makers, garnered little attention in a period not yet keen on sea-bathing, though the Botanic Gardens in Peradeniya rightly merited mention.

The 1907 book shows how internationally connected Ceylon was. Prominent expatriates included not only Britons but enough Germans for a German Club to be opened by a visiting German prince in 1903. There were a few French residents such as the Catholic bishop of Jaffna and other Continental Europeans, as well as people from around Asia, and pearl-divers and merchants from the Persian Gulf. Among the honorary consuls in Ceylon, most of them businessmen, were representatives of Austria-Hungary and Italy (the same person), Belgium, France, Germany, Denmark, Norway, Spain and Portugal (again, the same person), Sweden, Russia, Turkey, Persia, Japan, Siam and the United States – the American consul, born in Ceylon, had studied engineering at the University of Maine and headed a bridge and iron company in Virginia before his return.

Ships connected Ceylon to foreign ports in increasingly rapid time. Steamers from Colombo reached Bombay in three days, Singapore in five, Cape Town in seventeen and London in twenty-four. Ships from British, French, German, Austro-Hungarian and Japanese lines regularly called at Ceylon's ports, bringing passengers and cargoes from around the world and exporting Ceylon's own products – indeed, Ceylon tea was exported to China, among many other markets. Imported goods were available at Colombo's block-sized Cargill's emporium, opened in 1906; Cargill's had started business in Kandy in 1844, and more than half a century later, employed 42 Europeans and 400 locals (and the company is still in operation). Other department stores and specialty shops competed for customers. And if locals or visitors wanted to have their picture taken, and clearly many Ceylonese did so judging by the photographs in the 1907 volume, numerous photographic studios offered their services. The most famous was the still existing Plâté and Company, set up in 1890, which also printed half a million picture postcards of Ceylon every year – postcards were at the time a very popular type of communication and souvenir, conveying alluring images of colonial landscapes and people, if often perpetuating stereotypes.

Alongside facts and figures and biographies of luminaries, *Twentieth-Century Impressions* provides extensive information on tea, fishing, plumbago (graphite) mining, rubber, cacao, spices and other economic activities. There are also chapters on culture and two historical surveys, including one on Kandyans and Kandy culture by Frank Modder (the Ceylon-born son of a British justice, and later a professor in the United States). Several of these sections figure among the most interesting, not least because of their authors. The chapter on population was written by Ponnambalam Arunachalam (1853–1924), a member of the Legislative Council. From a prominent Tamil family, Arunachalam had studied at Cambridge University, where he became a friend of the writer and social reformer Edward Carpenter, with whom he exchanged letters on such topics as religion and sexuality. Arunachalam qualified as a barrister while in Britain, and in Ceylon progressed from being a police magistrate to a district judge and then Registrar-General of the colony, in which capacity he was responsible for its first census in 1901. He promoted the establishment of a university (founded only after his death), was one of the founders of the Ceylon Congress Party, the leading reformist political organization of the early twentieth century, and wrote widely on Hinduism. He was given a knighthood for his service, as was his equally distinguished brother, Ponnambalam Ramanathan.[6] Arunachalam's contribution to *Twentieth-Century Impressions* drew on the remarkable census that he organized and his broad historical and cultural knowledge. His chapter discussed the background and traditions of different groups in Ceylon, carefully explained the idea of caste (always a mysterious and often misunderstood subject for Europeans) and decoded customs and ceremonies.

Two other chapters were written by another internationally reputed Ceylonese intellectual of Tamil background, Ananda K. Coomaraswamy (1877–1947), who was linked to the Arunachalam family by marriage. Born in Colombo, the son of a lawyer – yet another Ceylonese knighted by the British – and an English mother, Coomaraswamy moved to Britain, after his father's death, when he was two years old. He studied geology and botany at the University of London, and earned a doctorate for research on theodolite and Ceylonese mineralogy. That scientific background provided qualifications for his chapter on geology and mineralogy. Coomaraswamy's other contribution to the volume was on 'Native Arts and Handicrafts', which foreshadowed the book for which he is best known, *Mediaeval Sinhalese Art*, published in 1908 (illustrated with photographs taken by his then wife, Ethel Mary Coomaraswamy). He went on to publish almost forty books on South Asian art, Western and Eastern religion and metaphysics, Indian music and architecture. Coomaraswamy spent much of his life in the United States, where he was Keeper of Indian Art at the Boston Museum of Fine Arts from 1917 until his death, though he made regular return visits to Ceylon. Perhaps more than any other figure of his time, Coomaraswamy interpreted South Asian material culture for Westerners.

Coomaraswamy's piece on 'Native Arts and Handicrafts' – the wording seems anachronistic in today's language – introduced readers to the wealth of Ceylonese art, sculpture, metalwork, ivory-carving, pottery and textiles. The author began with a quotation from John Ruskin about the importance of artisanship and noted the changes in European and non-European styles over the ages. However, he bemoaned the decadence into which Ceylonese traditional arts and crafts had fallen, which he intimated resulted from foreign influences and new European techniques. (In his *Mediaeval Sinhalese Art*, Coomaraswamy blamed that decline in part on the British abolition of the Kandyan royal court, which had been a patron of the arts and home of artisans.) He lamented that many contemporary works were 'degraded examples' of earlier craftsmanship – Coomaraswamy belonged to an international group of philosophers and art historians who espoused traditionalism, or 'perennialism' as they termed it. His views underscored the paradoxes and contradictions of the modernization of Ceylon heralded elsewhere in Wright's volume, but the resilience of local arts and crafts as well.

Some echoes of Coomaraswamy's views on art, and a certain critique of Westernization, appear in *Twentieth-Century Impressions*' chapter on Buddhism, written by Anagarika Dharmapala (1864–1933), a contemporary of Coomaraswamy and Arunachalam. Born into a prosperous merchant family, Dharmapala was a devout Sinhalese Buddhist. He argued that Buddhism, like local arts, had fallen into decay from slack observance, doctrinal impurity and foreign occupation of Ceylon dating back to the days of the Portuguese. The 'glorious period of Buddhism in Ceylon in the days when the foreigner was not in the land' had given way to the nefarious influence of the outsider 'with his licenced opium dens, arrack taverns, whisky saloons and butcher stalls for slaughtering animals', said Dharmapala (whose religious practices disapproved of alcohol and meat-eating). Pointedly, he added: 'The British have built roads, extended railways, and generally introduced the blessings of their materialistic civilisation into the land; and in this inception of the modern era the Aryan Sinhalese has lost his true identity and become a hybrid.' The Sinhalese, 'once the lord of the land, is but a stranger in his land'. Dharmapala was a leading figure in the 'Buddhist revivalist movement' in the late 1800s and early 1900s. In Ceylon, it established Buddhist newspapers and opened 400 Buddhist schools, including the renowned Ananda College in Colombo, as Dharmapala enjoined monks and lay people to greater study of Buddhist scriptures and more devout practice. The movement strengthened Sinhalese links with Buddhist communities in Burma and Thailand. Dharmapala travelled widely overseas, wrote books on Buddhism and was a leading global Buddhist spokesman of his time, yet in the late twentieth century, some of his views were marshalled by extremist Buddhists.[7]

Dharmapala, Coomaraswamy and Arunachalam were not the only Sinhalese and Tamil contributors to Wright's compendium; the chapter on the constitution and law, for instance, was the work of a Sinhalese barrister. Their participation, even as a minority of the authors, evidenced the dynamism of cultural life in Ceylon and the international significance of Asian scholars and thinkers in the early twentieth century. Many other local figures appear prominently elsewhere in *Twentieth-Century Impressions*, several hundred pages of which are devoted to short biographies of the 'great and good'. The book comprises a veritable 'Who's Who' of worthies, both local and British: planters, merchants and government agents, a large cohort of lawyers and doctors, all men of wealth, accomplishment and power – however, not a single woman is deemed worthy of a dedicated profile, even if many are mentioned and are present in photographs, largely in the role of spouses. Reading through the biographies, an unabashed elitism is evident. The 'gentlemen' (a frequently used word) are often described as scions of ancient and prominent Sinhalese, Tamil or Muslim families; the British appear more *arriviste*, colonial civil servants risen up the ladder or settlers who made good. The adoption of British norms of status is manifest, as biographies point out the posh schools and sometimes overseas universities where men were educated, note the grandeur of urban residences and country estates, list the clubs to which they belonged, the sports they practised and the philanthropies they supported. Important, too, is the high degree of intermarriage among the 'top' families, even if it did not extend to marriages across religious communities.[8]

A single example, from many, proves the point. S.C. Obeyesekere (1848–1927), from 'one of the oldest and proudest of the Southern Province families', was born in 1848, son of a *mudaliyar*, an official in the pre-colonial elite and the British administration. Educated at the Royal College, St Thomas College and the University of Calcutta, he scored at the top of examinations to enter the law profession in Ceylon, yet decided not to practice. He engaged in cattle-raising and agriculture with estates 'all over the island', but often lived in a city mansion, 'Hill Castle'. Though Sinhalese, he belonged to the Church of England; he was a member of the Irrigation Board, the Royal Colonial Institute and the Royal Asiatic Society, and was well known for philanthropy. Obeyesekere was appointed a member of the colony's Legislative Council and represented Ceylon in London at the coronation of King Edward VII. His wife was the daughter of a former member of the Legislative Council, and his family was related to the prominent Alwis and Dias Bandaranaike dynasties. His daughter married Solomon Dias Bandaranaike, the senior *mudaliyar* in Ceylon, aide-de-camp to the governor, and a wealthy rubber- and coconut-planter; their son, S.W.R.D. Bandaranaike became the prime minister of Ceylon after it gained independence, and their granddaughter became in turn prime minister and president of the country.

Such men as Obeyesekere stood at the apex of Ceylonese society while it was under the overlordship of British colonizers. Not surprisingly, *Twentieth-Century Impressions* included no profiles of peasant cultivators, fishers, cinnamon-peelers, tea-pickers or dockers. These men and women appear nameless – though not always faceless, as they do stare out from some of the images – yet they provided the labour that produced the wealth of the elite. The 'lower orders', despite their travails, are presented as beneficiaries of British rule, economic development and progress in such statements as an observation about Tamil indentured labourers: 'They are good workers, and are well looked after, medical assistance being rendered free. Their conditions of living and their power to earn money are far superior to those prevailing in their native villages [of India].'

Objectively, the last statement may be true, but the realities of plantation life were extremely hard.

Wright's book has other lacunas. There was a short essay on opium, its use not widely practised, the author said, and one on toddy and arrack (an alcoholic beverage generally made from coconut flowers), which inspired adverse comments about widespread consumption and alcoholism, but little else in the volume on social problems. There was nothing on the large number of domestic workers in Ceylon, the cooks, gardeners, nannies, drivers and cleaners who served their 'betters'. There was not a word on prostitution. The book avoided any discussion of crime, except for a warning to prospective buyers to be aware of forged antiquities. No comment revealed abuse of workers by employers and administrators or the effects of racism. There was no reference to a strike by carters in 1906, perhaps the first such industrial action in Ceylon. A smallpox epidemic in 1905 was mentioned only briefly. Information about tensions between ethnic groups, which on occasion erupted into violence, was missing. Any criticism of the British government was muted. Edward Perrera's historical section did mention rampant land speculation by British settlers and planters, and failure to live up to the promises to protect Buddhism contained in the 1815 Kandyan Convention, but with the implication that these were problems of the past, not the present. Environmental degradation attracted little attention; one author predicted that 'the progressive development of Ceylon will in time gradually dispossess the elephant, bear, leopard, and other denizens of the jungle', though he immediately added that 'the virgin lands of these parts will be brought within the sphere of civilised effort'.[9] There was no criticism of the butchery of animals through the British 'sport' of hunting. Other, rare negative views of colonialism were generally expressed as hope for further improvement. Ceylon remained the 'happy island'.

Twentieth-Century Impressions of Ceylon does not make for the most riveting reading, but it offers a rich source of information about the colony in 1907, the structures under which it was governed, and the social, economic and cultural life there. The capsule biographies provide insight into lived experiences among the elite and the way in which some Sinhalese, Tamils, Muslims and Burghers accommodated a colonial overlordship still constructed around notions of racial superiority and the inherent rights of Europeans.

Critical British perspectives

Other views of Ceylon in the first decade of the twentieth century are available, including critical perspectives in the works of European authors. One of the most insightful was Leonard Woolf (1880–1969).[10] The Cambridge-educated Woolf, later a significant London publisher, husband of the novelist Virginia Woolf and a central figure in the modernist Bloomsbury group in London, began his working life as a cadet in the Ceylon Colonial Service. He arrived in his first posting, in Jaffna, in 1905, and remained on the island, moving to postings in Kandy and Hambantota (on the south coast), until 1911, when he returned to Britain and, disenchanted with British imperialism, resigned from the colonial service. Woolf wrote about Ceylon in various genres. A novel, *A Village in the*

Jungle, published in 1913, paints a portrait of village life under the British, and is notable because all of the characters are Ceylonese. *Stories from the East*, in 1921, exposed the foibles and brutalities of the colonizers. In 1961, a volume of Woolf's autobiography, *Growing*, explored his years in Ceylon, and two years later, Woolf's diaries of his Ceylon years were published.

A foreshadowing of Woolf's first experiences in Ceylon came on the ship that carried him to the colony, with shock at the philistinism of Britons returning to Ceylon after home leave. Though Woolf developed empathy with some compatriots and admiration for a few fellow administrators, he did not spare those he accused of racism, anti-intellectualism, cruelty to local people and alcohol-fuelled bad behaviour. The British in Ceylon, said Woolf, were a fractious lot marked by 'class war and hatred' – government agents trumped planters in the social hierarchy, who for their part viewed businessmen with condescension. Social relations were marked by 'snobbery, pretentiousness, and false pretensions', as well as 'the complete social exclusion from our social suburbia of all Sinhalese and Tamils'. The Britishers liked playing great lords and masters: 'We were grand because we were a ruling caste in a strange Asiatic country' at a time when 'the British Empire was at its zenith of both glory and girth'. For many Europeans, the tropical colony offered an attractive alternative to London, 'grey, grim, grimy, dripping with rain and fog'. In the outstations Woolf served among only a handful of Britons – in the Jaffna station, 'a white population of ten or twelve government officers, perhaps ten missionaries, a retired civil servant with a daughter and two granddaughters, an appalling ex-army officer with an appalling wife and an appalling son', the lot gathering for evening tennis ('a serious business, a ritual, almost a sacrament'), copious drinks and conversation that 'as we sipped our whisky and sodas, consisted almost entirely of platitudes, chaff, or gossip'.

Such quotations, taken just from the first pages of *Growing*, illustrate Woolf's mordant judgements on colonial society. Woolf nevertheless evoked the demanding work and sometimes humorously varied duties and misadventures of a colonial agent: devising budgets, seeing to public works, settling court cases, issuing hunting permits to descendants of visiting French royalty, arranging a tour of the Temple of the Tooth for former French Empress Eugénie, getting lost in the jungle, keeping a pet leopard and seeing Halley's comet soar over the ocean. He recalled his efforts to staunch an epidemic of rinderpest, defuse a violent confrontation between Buddhists and Muslims and promote new agricultural techniques. He presided over a pearl fishery in the north and oversaw a pilgrimage of 4,000 people to the shrine of Kataragama in the south. He affirmed deep interest in the local people and his resolve to improve their condition. Read against Wright's triumphalist compendium, Woolf's works provide a personalized rather than an encyclopaedic approach, and with rather different narratives about colonized Ceylon.

Ceylon continued to change, of course, after *Twentieth-Century Impressions* was published and Woolf returned home. A forty-minute film documentary, 'Song of Ceylon', produced for the Ceylon Tea Propaganda Board in 1936, provides an interesting view of the colony thirty years later, with images of 'traditional' culture and busy modern life set to a script taken from a late seventeenth-century traveller's account. It was narrated by Lionel Wendt, a Burgher trained as a lawyer and concert pianist in London, a brilliant photographer who became the animating force in a modernist group of painters and other cultural figures active for several decades from the 1930s.

In 1948, Ceylon became independent as a Dominion, retaining the British monarch as head of state and adopting a Westminster system of government. The first prime minister, D.S. Senanayake, came from one of the prominent families of planters and graphite-miners profiled in *Twentieth-Century Impressions*; though a Buddhist, he was educated in Anglican schools, and he was an avid cricketer. By the 1970s, politics took a leftist turn and a Sinhalese nationalist inflection under the radical Oxford-educated S.W.R.D. Bandaranaike, who made Sinhala the sole official language, nationalized tea plantations and turned Ceylon into the Democratic Socialist Republic of Sri Lanka. Communal tensions between Sinhalese and Tamils, always simmering, began to reach boiling point. The conflict turned into a bloody civil war – a Tamil independence movement marked by a guerrilla campaign, terrorism and assassination answered by violent repression by state forces – that began in 1983 and did not conclude until 2009: the image of Sri Lanka turned from a 'happy island' to a blood-stained battlefield. Between 80,000 and 100,000 people were killed, and a further 30,000 people tragically died in a tsunami in 2004.

The wounds have not fully healed, and the country is far from immune to political problems, social discord and economic challenges. Some of the families whose biographies fill the pages of *Twentieth-Century Impression of Ceylon* – Obeyesekere, Seneviratne, Gooneratne, De Saram, De Alvis, Senanayake, Kotelawala, Rajapaksa, Dias, Bandaranaike – still play leading political and cultural roles, Cargill's operates supermarkets, tourists sip 'sundowners' at the Galle Face Hotel, members of the Hill Club (now Sri Lankans) dine on roast lamb and mint jelly, the statue of Queen Victoria is still standing in Colombo. Tea remains the island country's largest export, the archaeological, religious and natural sites awe visitors and pilgrims, and local people have an abiding passion for cricket.

CHAPTER 22
GERMAN SOUTHWEST AFRICA, 1908

'On 16 November 1883 we left Hamburg on board the "Professor Woermann". It should take eight full weeks until we reach Luanda, the first destination of our journey,' the German military officer and adventurer Hermann Wissmann began his account of *The Interior of Africa*, published in 1888. It was the kick-off of the so-called Wissmann expedition heading towards the Kasai River in the years between 1883 and 1885, that is, in the midst of the late nineteenth-century 'scramble for Africa'. The Kasai River, which originates in Angola and is part of the large Congo River system, had not yet been charted in detail by the Europeans who had been surveying the Congo basin since the 1850s (among them the Scottish missionary David Livingstone and the Welsh-born journalist Henry Morton Stanley).

In 1883 Wissmann and his German comrades – a physician and ethnologist, a geographer, a meteorologist, a zoologist and botanist, and two gunsmiths, all of whom had a military background – had set out on behalf of Leopold II, King of the Belgians, to 'solve the Kasai problem', that is, to chart the river system in detail. When, in July 1885, the Germans along with their African crew had successfully made their way downstream to Léopoldville, today's Kinshasa in the Democratic Republic of Congo, they considered their mission accomplished. 'The problem of the Kasai river course was solved', they proudly noted in their chronicle.[1]

Wissmann's expedition to the 'heart of the dark continent', exploring 'virgin territories', as he put it, was sponsored by the Belgian king who earlier had financed Stanley's explorations that led to the establishment of the Congo Free State in 1885. This was the monarch's privately ruled colony from 1885 until 1908, when international criticism of the gruesome exploitation of the territory and its people forced its transfer to the Belgian state; the Belgian Congo remained a colony until independence in 1960.

Although in Belgian service, Wissmann's expedition was permitted to travel under the flag of Germany, which had been unified only in 1871. They were allowed to gather scientific and anthropological data as well as to collect cultural artefacts for museums in Berlin. Throughout their journey, they measured temperature, humidity, wind speeds, altitude and the width, depth and speed of rivers. Lieutenant Hans Mueller, a meteorologist and photographer, recorded an inventory of insects and plants 'collected and so far identified'. The reports on the expedition's 'activities and events' listed encounters with venomous snakes and described the deadly impact of tropical fevers as well as arduous treks across the jungle terrain. One member of the team compiled rudimentary vocabulary lists of the different linguistic communities they met. Wissmann and his companions, like many adventurers of the time, also conducted 'anthropological measurements', including calibrating the length of skulls and distance between the eyes of the African people they encountered. Racialized stereotypes about 'natives' with 'erratic and treacherous' physiognomy paralleled a romantic fascination for the exotic, both people and nature.[2]

Such expeditions, following the example of the Prussian naturalist Alexander von Humboldt, who had travelled throughout the Americas in the late 1790s and early 1800s, claimed a scholarly motivation not a desire for conquest. Yet Wissmann seemed to be obeying the injunction of Richard Wagner, the composer and promoter of a romantic vision of Germany's history, who called on his compatriots to take part in the global colonial enterprise. They should neither focus only on trade, as did the British in their colonies, according to Wagner, nor transform the territories they reconnoitred into a Catholic 'butcher's house' as he said the Spanish had done in Latin America.[3] However, indiscriminate use of force against Africans nevertheless became a feature of Wissmann's expedition, as did economic exploitation. The Germans' accounts of 'the exploration of the Kasai River' and the Congo basin concluded with a short discussion of the region's potential and 'significance for world trade and culture'. Development of the territory, including its populations, they argued, would turn central Africa into a market for German exports and a source for imports of rubber and ivory, among other raw materials – a view of Africa gaining increased currency during a long recession in the global economy from the 1870s to the 1890s.[4]

In the years following the expedition, several of its members occupied key positions in the German colonial empire that formally took shape when the European powers met at an international conference on Africa held in Berlin in 1884 and 1885. The knowledge they had gathered easily abetted political domination and economic profit-making. Wissmann himself became commander of a predominantly African militia, the Wissmann Truppe (which in 1891 became the *Schutztruppe*) in German East Africa, roughly today's Tanzania. The chartered company entrusted with the commercial exploitation of the colony, the Deutsch-Ostafrikanische Gesellschaft founded in 1885, had collapsed due to local African resistance, which Wissmann quelled on the orders of the German chancellor Otto von Bismarck. Given the fading power of the chartered company, Germany set up a formal colonial state.

Wissmann had joined the Prussian army at the age of seventeen and only four years later was promoted to the rank of lieutenant. However, he was a troubled character who had spent several months in prison after taking part in a duel. The colonial expedition, distant from social constraints in Germany as well as far from his military superiors, was Wissmann's ideal outlet. Later as an administrator and commander in German East Africa, Wissmann continued to pursue his goals of conquest far beyond the brief he received from the German chancellor even though asthma, rheumatism, alcohol abuse and morphine addiction necessitated extended periods of leave.

After burning villages in the coastal areas and hinterland of German East Africa in extending German colonial possessions in 1889 and 1890, Wissmann on returning to Berlin was greeted as 'Germany's greatest African' and a street was named after him in Berlin – Wissmannstraße kept its name well into the twenty-first century. Wissmann's indifference towards orders from his superiors and nonchalance regarding budgetary restrictions probably cost him appointment as the commander-in-chief of German East Africa in the early 1890s. The position was filled by Lothar von Trotha, later to gain notoriety as military commander of German Southwest Africa, today's Namibia.[5] The 'men on the spot' who had spearheaded German expansion, such as Wissmann, were difficult to control remotely from Berlin. Hence, side-lining the experienced Wissmann in the military command pointed to the increasing 'metropolization' of German colonial rule in the late nineteenth century. Still, Wissmann managed to serve for a year as civil governor in German East Africa before returning to Germany in 1896; still troubled, he committed suicide in 1905.[6]

Wissmann's trajectory in Africa is telling in several respects. Though short, it produced a long-lasting impact – just as did German rule in Africa, which was limited to the relatively brief period between 1884 and 1918. After the defeat of Germany in the First World War, its colonies were transferred by the victors to Britain and France as protectorates under a League of Nations mandate, though German settlers and much of the imprint of the German presence remained. Moreover, the Wissmann expedition is a reminder of the Germans' imperial entanglements in scientific, cultural and economic terms even before the nation formally became a colonial power.[7]

The Berlin Africa Conference, 1884–5

Wissmann's expedition took place in a period that witnessed a close linkage of science, particularly anthropology, with colonial domination in the European carving up of the African continent. Indeed, while Wissmann was touring central Africa between 1883 and 1885, the colonial landscape of Africa was about to change, at least on paper. From November 1884 to February 1885 Bismarck presided over the Berlin Conference (or Congo Conference), in which the European powers, the United States, Russia and the Ottoman Empire took part. The objective was both to harmonize foreign policy and discuss widened economic access to Africa, which in large areas was dominated by British trade. The participants agreed on free trade in the vast Congo region of central Africa, and on the right of passage for all traders on major bodies of water, including the Niger and Congo Rivers and Lake Malawi. However, the liberal promise of free trade was not honoured, and the conference's self-proclaimed mission of abolishing the slave trade in Africa 'in the name of Almighty God', according to its communiqué, was more of a humanitarian posture to enable further conquest than a real commitment.[8]

The Berlin Conference is often seen as a launching pad for the 'scramble for Africa', ushering in the age of 'high imperialism', although the partition of sub-Saharan Africa among European powers had started long before, beginning with the first European incursions and acquisition of trading posts in the 1500s. Moreover, what were seen as the most rewarding parts of the wider world, from the Americas to India, had already been exploited for centuries. Ronald Robinson and John Gallagher have argued that scholars who seek to understand late nineteenth-century imperialism should not only focus on the partition of Africa but pay closer attention to 'informal empire' – the establishment of lucrative trade links and political influence – in other areas of the globe through the 1800s: 'The best finds and prizes had already been made; in tropical Africa the imperialists were merely scraping the bottom of the barrel', according to the British scholars.[9] From an economic perspective, they make a persuasive point. Yet from a cultural vantage point, Africa provided the canvas for many a colonial dream and for an unparalleled bout of takeovers and aggrandisement (or in the case of some European countries, the creation) of overseas empires in the short period from the 1880s to 1900.

This is particularly true for Germany, where new colonial visions tied into the ambitions of the newly unified country for great power status. Bismarck also consolidated his position by appeasing the aggressive colonial lobby composed of businessmen, an important part of the military and much of the German bourgeoisie, as well as of scientists and adventurers of diverse backgrounds.[10] The conference provided the opportunity to claim what became German East Africa, which included Tanganyika (now part of Tanzania), the island of Zanzibar (traded to Britain for Heligoland in the North Sea in 1890), Burundi and Rwanda in central Africa, as well as parts of what is today Mozambique. Germany also took over Cameroon and Togo on the west African coast, and German Southwest Africa (now Namibia) in 1884 and 1885. With the lease of Kiautschou (around today's Jiaozhou Bay) on the Shandong peninsula in northeast China in 1897, and the acquisition in the Pacific Ocean of the north-eastern quadrant of the island of New Guinea in Melanesia, German Samoa, and the Marshall, Caroline, Mariana and Palau islands in Micronesia in 1899, the German Empire went global.

At the turn of the twentieth century, the German possessions made up one of the largest European Empires, fulfilling the dreams of Wissmann and fellow German colonizers. In their chronicles they reflected upon the significance of the colonial arena for national self-assurance. For instance, as the expedition passed through Portuguese Angola on the way towards the Kasai, its members celebrated Kaiser Wilhelm I's birthday on 22 March 1884 with patriotic exultation:

> While in the fatherland the individual is a small part of the whole among his countless comrades, in a foreign land he is the whole itself. He is the representative of his nation. National pride and national consciousness are more alive in his soul. . . . Today . . . the Germans everywhere rejoiced, today we too rejoiced in the dark continent.[11]

The statement evidences the way in which the colonial ventures – or hopes – contributed to the development of European nationalism in an era of increased commercial and military rivalries. Colonies furnished the stage on which to perform the nation's supposed virtues. Stereotyping, segregation and exclusion of the racialized 'other', especially an African, Asian or Pacific islander, furnished for all colonizers a facile contrast to concepts of one's 'own' nation and people, and in this regard, Germany was no exception.

Nevertheless, the realities of the tropics sometimes swiftly overwhelmed colonial nationalism, as was the case with the Wissmann expedition. Just a few days after celebrating the emperor's birthday, one of Wissmann's companions died of a 'malignant fever' at the age of only twenty-six. Although the tools of empire, including tropical medicine, had advanced significantly in the second half of the nineteenth century, the interior of Africa, as well as other parts of the world, could still become a 'white man's grave'. Still, when in July 1885 Wissmann and his fellow travellers, who had just reached the confluence of the Kasai with the Congo and 'finally found peace and quiet . . . to inquire about the political events of the last year', they were full of joy: 'We heard about the formation of the Congo [Free] State [by the Belgian King Leopold II], about the acquisition of Usagara [in present-day Tanzania] and Cameroon for Germany and were delighted that our fatherland now belonged among the colonial powers.'[12] Sketches of what was to become the German colonial empire had already emerged before the Berlin Conference in 1884 and 1885. And in the German imagination and cultural life, the empire persisted well beyond its formal end in 1918. Advertising drawing on colonial images, novels and motion pictures set in the colonies remained common currency in the interwar period. Artefacts and street names, referring to colonial 'heroes' in some cases, persist to this day.

War and genocide, 1904–8

It was hoped that the colonies, particularly German Southwest Africa, would provide a home for the emigrants leaving Germany in their hundreds of thousands during the second half of the nineteenth century. German Southwest Africa, covering over 800,000 square kilometres (one-and-a-half times larger than Germany itself), was sparsely populated. The territory was home to some 200,000 people, with Herero and the (Oorlam-) Nama the largest groups.[13] Despite an arid climate, Southwest Africa was envisioned as a settler colony with the central plateau, where altitudes reached over 2,000 metres, providing a new home for settlers. In Southwest Africa, 'typical' German settlers, recruited from around the country, came from the lower-middle class. Although Germans claimed large areas for cattle farms, fuelling conflicts about land between the migrants and indigenous people, many settlers worked for merchants and lived in urban areas such as the capital of Windhoek. Around 1900 Windhoek was still a small town with barely more than 1,500 inhabitants, but Germans could enjoy familiar hobbies such as bowling, and gather at their shooting association's clubhouse. By the eve of the First World War, 14,000 European settlers, overwhelmingly Germans, had moved to the colony.

An agreement with one of the Herero leaders favoured by the German administration in the north of the colony, Samuel Maherero, was meant to consolidate colonial rule in the 1890s. Backing Maherero and, in the south, courting Hendrik Witbooi, who established himself as the main Nama and Oorlam leader, formed part of the divide-and-rule approach of Governor Theodor von Leutwein in the early days of the colony. However, the Christian missions' assistance might well have been just as decisive for expanding colonial control over the territory.[14] As was frequently the case in colonial situations, 'exploitation, brute force and forms of cooperation often occurred simultaneously', as one study on the mechanisms of colonial rule puts it.[15] Accords with Herero and Nama leaders did not prevent 'punitive' expeditions when the colonial government deemed them necessary to set an example. Yet resistance was triggered when disasters such as a cattle plague in 1897 coincided with the German authorities' confiscation of large tracts of land for settlers, particularly given the settlers' continuous resort to violence and abuse of indigenous people. In retrospect Abraham Kaffer, a man identifying as part of the Bondelswarts tribe on Namibia's southern border, described the colonial situation in the following terms:

> We have never been able to understand the German Government. It was so different to our ideas of a Government; because every German officer, sergeant, and soldier, every German policeman and every German farmer seemed to be the 'Government'. By this we mean that every German farmer seemed to be able to do towards us just what he pleased, and to make his own laws, and he never got punished. The police and the soldiers might flog us and ill-treat us, the farmers might do as they pleased towards us and our wives, the soldiers might molest and even rape our women and young girls, and no one was punished.[16]

Open warfare eventually broke out in January 1904 when Herero troops attacked German farms and killed more than a hundred whites. The German military forces, including militias and volunteers, outnumbered by a factor of four, faced a formidable Herero army of 8,000 fighters armed with rifles. The Herero insurgents caused severe losses to the Germans in battles throughout March and April; Nama people joined the armed rebellion in October. Witnessing Germany's relentless warfare against the Herero provided a key trigger for the Nama insurgency. In contrast to the Herero, the Nama resorted to guerrilla tactics, which contributed to the war dragging on until 1908.

By the end of May 1904, however, additional forces had arrived from Germany, and Herero warriors had retreated with their families and livestock to the Waterberg Plateau, in the central region of Southwest Africa, probably in order to initiate negotiations with the German commander. The German military culture, though, allowed no room for compromise in colonial warfare. Lieutenant-General Lothar von Trotha, who had succeeded Leutwein as commander-in-chief, envisaged 'absolute destruction' of the enemy followed by their total surrender and submission. Trotha, born in 1848, was a battle-hardened officer who had served in German East Africa in the 1890s, his tour of duty overlapping with Wissmann's term as a civil governor; he had also fought in the Boxer War, the international intervention in northern China (1900–1). On 11 August 1904, Trotha led German troops in an attack at Waterberg but failed to bring the Herero to battle and did not score the decisive victory he intended.[17]

A substantial contingent of the Herero fighters had managed to break the German encirclement at its weakest point, covering access to the Omaheke desert. With no water and limited provisions, the Herero, including women and children escaping German troops, were facing almost certain death in the rough barren land. After the failure of what was meant to be the decisive battle against the rebels, in early September 1904, Trotha issued an infamous proclamation, the *Vernichtungsbefehl*, or 'extermination proclamation'. Trotha stipulated that 'within the German border, every Herero, armed or unarmed, with or without cattle, will be shot. I will no longer give shelter to women and children, but will drive them back to their people or have them shot. These are my words to the Herero people.' Although military and civil superiors in Berlin revoked Trotha's order in December, the killing and the destruction of the Herero in the desert had already begun and it continued; in April 1905 the German military command issued a similar order targeting the Nama people.[18]

German colonial warfare in Southwest Africa from 1904 to 1908 was characterized by a shifting 'strategic horizon'. This notion provides an understanding of the transformation from Leutwein's concept of limited warfare to the 'political extermination' envisioned by the general staff in Berlin, and finally to Trotha's notorious scheme of total domination. Phrases such as 'wars of extermination' and 'battles of annihilation' would take on a more horrific connotation in the mid-twentieth century, but at the time of the confrontation in Southwest Africa, they held strategic and tactical meaning within the German military tradition and did not necessarily mean physical annihilation. And yet, as in other colonial arenas in the late nineteenth and early twentieth century, in German Southwest Africa, the boundaries between strategic perceptions and physical extermination of the enemy were often blurred. The asymmetries usually inherent in colonial warfare contributed to brutalization in combat and beyond. Analysis of German soldiers' and junior officers' journals, as well as private letters, has shown how enemies were dehumanized as 'black devils': the African was a 'predator-like opponent' operating in an unfamiliar and hostile environment to German soldiers. In a climate of constant fear, cruelty became the new norm among German troops. Debates about the actual meaning of the 'extermination proclamation', which has preoccupied many historians, are rather sterile, as there was no need for direct orders to rationalize the killing of Herero and Nama women and children. In fact, settler militias and soldiers had become an 'independent engine of annihilation', as Matthias Häussler explains.[19]

What from a German perspective had begun as a 'small war' in a remote colony soon turned in a large military undertaking with close to 20,000 German soldiers deployed in Southwest Africa (of whom 2,000 died, mostly due to disease and not in battle); it was also a costly war that strained the German coffers with expenses of almost 600 million *Reichsmark*. For the Herero and Nama people the war was an absolute disaster. Although numbers are only estimates, research suggests that the Herero population had been reduced from between 35,000 and 100,000 before the war to only 14,000–16,000 people in its aftermath, and the Nama from 20,000 to between 9,000 and 13,000 people.[20] Of those who survived the fighting, many died in camps set up from 1905 and closed down in 1908. Forced labour, insufficient rations and unhealthy living conditions contributed to the death of 40–50 per cent of Herero and Nama confined in the camps (see Figure 22.1).[21] The war and its aftermath were thus of genocidal dimensions. The cultures of the Herero and Nama had been virtually destroyed.

Figure 22.1 'Herero prisoners' (1904-5). Contemporary photograph. © Getty Images.

Only a few years after the war in German Southwest Africa, war broke out in Europe and reached global proportions. The First World War was also fought in the colonies. South African troops occupied German Southwest Africa in September 1914. In German East Africa, the Germans, led by General Paul von Lettow-Vorbeck, and the British imperial army even continued fighting beyond the ceasefire in November 1918, news of which only reached them weeks after the official date. With the peace treaty of Versailles in 1919, all of Germany's colonies were taken away and assigned to the victors, with Southwest Africa handed over to South Africa. In the 1960s the Namibian independence movement, the South West African People's Organisation (SWAPO), resorted to guerrilla warfare, pushing the United Nations to declare the continuing South African occupation illegal. SWAPO's fight continued until a truce was brokered in 1989. A new constitution was adopted and the country achieved formal independence in March 1990.

War, violence, genocide: Interpretations and legacies

In the mid-1960s, a historian from the German Democratic Republic (East Germany), Horst Drechsler, launched a debate about war and genocide in German Southwest Africa. Drechsler argued that the war against the Herero and Nama peoples between 1904 and 1908 'can only be described as genocide'. 'German imperialism,' he added, 'resorted to methods of genocide, thus earning unenviable notoriety in later years.'[22]

His use of the word 'genocide' was intentionally striking, as that word and concept had become associated with Hitler's war on the Jews and the Holocaust. The concept itself, coined by Raphael Lemkin in the wake of the Second World War, was adopted (and adapted) by the United Nations in the 'Convention on the Prevention and Punishment of the Crime of Genocide' in 1948. Ever since Drechsler published his work, controversies about alleged paths and (dis)continuities from German colonialism to Nazi terror in Europe have resonated beyond the German historiographical debate. *From Windhoek to Auschwitz?* – a provocative book title used by Jürgen Zimmerer – has become the slogan for the controversy. Linking Windhoek, the capital of German Southwest Africa, to Auschwitz, site of one of the most notorious Nazi extermination camps, points to the extremes of a debate about the relationship of war and genocide in Namibia and Nazi-occupied Europe.[23]

The connection between colonialism and Hitler's 'Third Reich' had indeed been suggested much earlier. The philosopher Hannah Arendt reminded readers in *The Origins of Totalitarianism* (1948) that 'many things that nowadays have become the speciality of totalitarian governments are only too well known from the study of history', in which she included the history of colonialism. 'Not even concentration camps are an invention of totalitarian movements', she stated. Anti-colonial figures such as the Martinican poet and politician Aimé Césaire picked up on Arendt's remarks and argued in the 1950s that Nazism had 'applied to Europe colonialist procedures which until then had been reserved for' colonized peoples. His countryman, the psychiatrist and philosopher Frantz Fanon, went further, and stated in the early 1960s that Nazi violence had 'transformed the whole of Europe into a veritable colony'.[24] In the early 2000s, as the centenary of the war in Namibia was approaching, German colonialism moved to the centre of debate.

Research on the short-lived German Empire in Africa and the Asia-Pacific has become an innovative, diverse and fertile field of international enquiry.[25] Older scholarship focused on military and political decision-making and individual biographies as well as on race relations in Southwest Africa and Nazi Germany. Recent research highlights the dynamics of violence unleashed from 'below'. It emphasizes the role of the German settler community and their volunteer militias in the genocidal actions, and analyses what has been called the 'violence as usual' that continued after the war until the end of German rule. The settler community in Southwest Africa was characterized by a 'double antagonism', competing on the one hand with indigenous societies for land and other resources, and confronting, on the other hand, the colonial state in order to push their own agenda and further their prestige as 'white masters'. The German settlers, many with racist beliefs, pressed time and again for the escalation of violence and a radical restructuring of the colony through war. In fact, as was the case in other colonial settings, mainly young male settlers constituted an 'independent engine of expansion'.[26]

In contrast to other settler societies (for instance, in the Americas), the white colonists in Southwest Africa had little autonomy on the frontier. From the early days of the settlement process, and increasingly after war broke out in 1904, German colonists – consisting mainly of traders, urban craftsmen, and farmers – faced a colonial state that perceived itself as an extension of the metropole, reproducing social hierarchies from Europe in Africa, which led to conflicts with the settlers' self-perception. In Southwest Africa, the German settlers had little in common with the notion of the 'white colonist' as the 'ideal prefabricated collaborator' of the colonial state. Analyses of violence from 'below' – including the weight of emotions – have significantly contributed to discussions about the history and theory of colonial rule in Namibia.[27]

Whereas scholarly discussion on German Southwest Africa has arrived at greater consensus on the question of genocide, political and legal debate about reparations is ongoing. While German payments to the Jewish community after the Second World War have shaped the approach of 'compensation for injustice' demanded by the Pan-African Conference on Reparations for African Enslavement, Colonization and Neo-Colonization, held in Abuja, Nigeria, in 1993, Germany has long blocked calls for redress with regard to its colonial past.[28] German officials have argued that the country had assumed its historical and political responsibility since Namibia's independence by donating a billion Euros in foreign aid and technical assistance to its former colony. However, development projects hardly touched the centre and the south of the country, the region most severely affected by war and genocide between 1904 and 1908. Furthermore, in the interest of nation-building, the Namibian government that emerged from the nationalist SWAPO independence movement held back its claims against Germany after 1990. Imagined national unity ran counter to reparations for minority ethnic groups, that is, the Herero and Nama, in a country dominated by the Ovambo majority. Therefore the Namibian government's position favoured a regional approach for reparations, not one centring exclusively on descendants of Herero and Nama victims. Competing positions among Ovambo officials and Herero and Nama leaders persist, and the latter two groups claim a role in negotiations with Germany.[29]

On a symbolic level Namibian and German activists, historians, diplomats and politicians have maintained a regular dialogue for more than twenty years. In 2004 Heidemarie Wieczorek-Zeul, then German Minister for Economic Cooperation, on a visit to Namibia to commemorate the battle at Waterberg, apologized for 'violence, discrimination, racism and annihilation' perpetrated under German rule. Her words met with harsh reactions at home: 'What will be the cost of the minister's tears?', the German tabloid *Bild* pondered.[30] Over the years, several symbolic gestures have been made, such as the return to Namibia of African human remains taken to Germany in colonial times. In 2014 Namibia and Germany pledged to work jointly on efforts to come to terms with the colonial past. As for reparations, however, German courts have declined to engage with legal claims filed by descendants of Herero and Nama victims in Germany. Related class action suits against Germany have also been declined by US courts.[31] It seems that after nearly all legal avenues have been explored, a political solution points the way forward with an official apology and recognition of the genocide carried out in Namibia by Germans between 1904 and 1908, and, eventually, could lead to financial compensation.

CHAPTER 23
ETHIOPIA, 1936

On 30 June 1936, a slightly built, bearded African man, clad in a white tunic and trousers, and the black silk cloak traditionally worn by his country's noblemen, came to the rostrum of the General Council of the League of Nations in Geneva, a forum established after the First World War to resolve international disputes and promote global development (see Figure 23.1). 'I, Haile Selassie, Emperor of Ethiopia', he said in Amharic, 'am here today to claim that justice which is due to my people, and the assistance promised to it eight months ago, when fifty nations asserted that aggression had been committed in violation of international treaties.' The emperor was referring to the Italian invasion of Ethiopia (or Abyssinia, as it was also called), a country of almost 15 million people, in October 1935; the League had formally condemned Italy's move and imposed sanctions on Italy, but to no avail. When Italian troops had completed what Rome called the 'seven months' campaign' to conquer Ethiopia – an independent state four times the size of Italy – and occupied its capital of Addis Ababa and driven Haile Selassie into exile, the Fascist leader Benito Mussolini had joyfully proclaimed the King of Italy, Victor Emmanuel III, to be 'Emperor of Abyssinia'.

A speech to the League by a head of state was without precedent, Haile Selassie noted:

> But there is also no precedent for a people being victim of such injustice and being at present threatened by abandonment to its aggressor. Also, there has never before been an example of any Government proceeding to the systematic extermination of a nation by barbarous means, in violation of the most solemn promises made by the nations of the earth that there should not be used against innocent human beings the terrible poison of harmful gases.

He charged, to the jeers of Italian journalists present in the League's chamber, that the Italians had attacked Ethiopian civilians 'in order to terrorise and exterminate them', and he detailed the strategy of using aircraft to drop poison gas, 'a fine, death-dealing rain', over vast areas 'in order to kill off systematically all living creatures, in order to more surely poison waters and pastures'. The use of poison gas, the Ethiopian emperor pointed out, violated an international ban on chemical warfare that Italy had signed in 1925. The invasion also violated a 1928 Treaty of Friendship between Rome and Addis Ababa in which the two countries had agreed to submit any dispute to arbitration by the League of Nations. Haile Selassie warned that international security and the 'very existence of the League of Nations' were threatened. He concluded the impassioned speech with a question. 'Representatives of the World, I have come to Geneva to discharge in your

Figure 23.1 'Ethiopian Leader Haile Selassie Speaking at League of Nations' on 30 June 1936. © Getty Images.

midst the most painful of the duties of the head of a state. What reply shall I have to take back to my people?'[1]

The Ethiopian Empire

Ethiopia had remained (along with the small country of Liberia), by the 1930s, the only part of the African continent not taken over by Europeans at some point during centuries of colonial incursions and the late nineteenth- and early twentieth-century 'scramble for Africa'. Foreigners certainly had displayed interest in the country, and sometimes intervened. Britain sent troops to Ethiopia in 1868 in a 'punitive expedition' waged to redress perceived slights to British citizens. Emperor Tewodros II (r. 1855–68) committed suicide rather than be taken captive by the victorious British, though they abducted his seven-year-old son and heir, Prince Alemayehu, and removed him to Britain. The British also raided the emperor's treasure, spiriting regalia and jewels back to Europe. They did not establish a colony in Ethiopia, however, despite its large land area and strategic location. The region would soon gain greater importance with the opening of the Suez Canal in 1869, and with new British, German and subsequent French expansion. In the late 1880s, seeking a place in the colonial sun, Italy made a push into the Horn of Africa, conquering Eritrea (a territory claimed by the Ethiopian Empire) and part of Somalia, which they named Italian Somaliland.[2] A few years later the Italians mounted an assault on Ethiopia but suffered an ignominious defeat at the Battle of Adwa in 1896, a signal victory of African forces over European armies.[3] Meanwhile, Britain and France had taken their share of Somali lands – British and French Somaliland – leaving Ethiopia landlocked and territorially and commercially further endangered.

Ethiopia held a unique position in Africa since the majority of its population was Christian. It is uncertain when Christianity first arrived, but it became the state religion of the Axum kingdom in 330 CE. Ethiopian Orthodoxy, which evolved elaborate rites and vestments and worshipped in imposing churches sometimes hewn from solid rock and decorated with murals of biblical figures, angels and saints, was thus not a religion brought by colonizers to Africa. Christianity was not the sole religion, as about a third of Ethiopians were Muslim, and there were black Jews and followers of 'animist' faiths. Christianity was nevertheless the religion of the Ethiopian dynasty, which traced its lineage back to the biblical King Solomon and the Queen of Sheba, and the religion of the Amhara, the largest of eighty ethnic groups. Politics was based on a feudal system, with noblemen – bearing titles equivalent to king, prince and duke, referred to by the honorific *Ras* – controlling provinces with considerable autonomy and their own armies, under the paramountcy of the Negus Neghesti, the 'King of Kings' or Emperor. The reign of Emperor Menelik II (r. 1889–1913) brought increased unity and stability, but Emperor Iyasu (r. 1913–16) provoked opposition because his ties with Muslims, and rumours of conversion to Islam, threatened Christian dominance. Nobles overthrew Iyasu in 1916, a development viewed favourably in the midst of the First World War in London and Paris, where he was feared to harbour pro-German sympathies. After a brief civil war, Menelik's daughter Zewditu (r. 1916–30) succeeded to the throne, with her cousin Ras Tafari appointed as regent since the sovereign was now a woman, and as heir because she was childless. In his new position, Ras Tafari, the future Emperor Haile Selassie, undertook limited administrative and social reforms, though any change disconcerted the traditionalist aristocracy.

Ras Tafari, born in 1892, was the son of Ras Makonnen, a cousin of Emperor Menelik II who had commanded Ethiopian forces in the war against the Italians in the 1890s and served as governor of Harar. Tafari spent several years in a school run by French Catholic missionaries in Harar (and throughout his life generally spoke with foreigners in French), then continued his education in Addis Ababa. Iyasu appointed Ras Tafari as governor, at the age of only fifteen, of a small province, then promoted him to his father's old post as governor of Harar. Tafari's subsequent dismissal exacerbated the two men's rivalry. After the fall of Iyasu, Tafari became the power behind the empress' throne. Grouping around himself a cohort of often foreign-educated young Ethiopians, he sought to strengthen ties with European countries in order to give Ethiopia greater international status and preclude colonial designs. In 1923, though only after Ras Tafari had agreed to ban the slave trade that persisted in Ethiopia (where several million were enslaved), he successfully applied for membership in the League of Nations, unprecedented recognition for a Black African state.

The following year, the 31-year-old regent toured Europe – Paris, London, Rome, Brussels, Stockholm and other cities. The welcome the African ruler was accorded varied; the British king and government, in particular, received the royal frostily, yet Cambridge

University awarded him an honorary doctorate. In addition to bolstering Ethiopia's and his own prestige, Tafari's aim was to negotiate access for Ethiopia to the Red Sea; only a rail line, built by the French in the early years of the century, linked Addis Ababa to a port, Djibouti, in French Somaliland. He achieved no real success in talks with French, British or Italian ministers. The European public and press gave a more enthusiastic reception to the emperor and his entourage. He was also coming to the attention of those further afield; in the United States, a Black Jamaican-born activist, Marcus Garvey (1887–1940), had founded a Pan-African movement which hoped for unification of the continent under an African king, and his supporters saw Tafari as such a figure. In the African diaspora, the Ethiopian royal stood proudly as a symbol of African history and culture, and of the sovereignty and modernization of an independent African country.

Ethiopians congratulated the returning Tafari on his mission, despite failure to win a concession for a port. He proceeded with further administrative reforms, development of an electricity and telephone network, a roadbuilding programme, the creation of a central bank and an effort to free the Ethiopian church from control by the Orthodox patriarch of Alexandria. Tafari meanwhile strengthened his personal position, and the empress gave him the title of King of Gondar in 1928. On her death two years later, Tafari was proclaimed emperor, 'Conquering Lion of the Kingdom of Judah, King of Kings of Ethiopia and Elect of God'; he took the regnal name of Haile Selassie, meaning 'The Power of the Trinity', an allusion to the Christian doctrine. After an all-night vigil in Addis Ababa's cathedral, Haile Selassie pronounced the oath of office, and was anointed with holy oil, clothed in embroidered robes and presented with a gold crown, orb, sceptre, ring, daggers and spears. His wife Menen was crowned empress and his son Asfa-Wossen installed as crown prince. The royal family was then driven away from the ceremony, in a carriage that had once belonged to the German Kaiser, to a banquet for 24,000 dignitaries and soldiers. The countries with which Ethiopia maintained diplomatic relations were well represented – Britain by the royal Duke of Gloucester, France by a marshal of the army, with emissaries from Belgium, the Netherlands, Sweden, Egypt, Japan and the United States. The diplomatic visitors vied with each other to present appropriate gifts – Italy and France gave airplanes to the new emperor (though the French aircraft crashed during the celebrations). The grand coronation was widely reported by European eyewitnesses and journalists, including the novelist Evelyn Waugh (who wrote a disobliging account of the pomp) and Wilfred Thesiger, son of the British consul-general in Addis Ababa, who was to become a well-known travel-writer, photographer and long-time supporter of the emperor.[4]

A correspondent for *The Times* of London, however, described the country's poverty, lack of development, rudimentary finances, endemic diseases and enduring slavery, and concluded acidly: 'It is absurd to pretend that Ethiopia is a civilized nation in any Western sense of the word.'[5] Western politicians looked with some consternation and condescension on the pageantry in Addis Ababa and the power it suggested. According to Asfa-Wossen Asserate, a historian and biographer of Haile Selassie, who is an Ethiopian prince with close ties to Haile Selassie's dynasty: 'No European nation – irrespective of whether it (still) had its own colonies – would countenance the idea of a self-assured

African state decisively pursuing its own political, economic and security interests, actions which might begin to instil the populations of neighbouring European colonies with thoughts of independence.'[6] A reigning monarch of an independent African nation was an anomaly in the interwar political order, and any claim by a Black African to be a peer of a European monarch sat uneasily with colonialist foreigners.

Duly enthroned, Haile Selassie and his ministers pressed on with remodelling his kingdom, while Ethiopia's economy boomed with traders, including an increasing number of European businesses, exporting coffee, spices, livestock and oilseed, and importing manufactured goods and other commodities. The year following his coronation, Haile Selassie issued Ethiopia's first constitution, with the objective of centralizing power in an autocratic monarchy – at the expense of provincial princes and nobles – rather than democracy. He also inaugurated the country's first parliament, whose members were all appointed by the emperor. He strengthened the army (with Swedish officers providing training) and the tiny air force (with French pilots). If his approach appeared despotic to critics, they were hardly out of step with developments either in European countries in the interwar years or with colonial regimes.

Italian colonialism

Italy was one of the European powers where politics had taken a dramatic turn in the early decades of the twentieth century. The First World War left Italy facing grave economic, social and political problems, which liberal governments seemed unable to resolve. A far right-wing movement, the Fascists, steadily gained ground with an ideology of national regeneration based on authoritarian and charismatic leadership, corporatist organization of society, expansive militarism and programmes of economic and social modernization. Through parliamentary channels and violence, the Fascists and their 'blackshirts' positioned themselves as would-be saviours of Italy, and in 1922 the king appointed their leader, Benito Mussolini (1883–1945), as prime minister. Among the objectives of the Fascists was overseas expansion, including extension of Italian territory in the Mediterranean and Aegean. Neither the acquisition of Eritrea and Italian Somaliland, nor the conquest of the Ottoman provinces of Cyrenaica, Tripolitania and Fezzan in northern Africa (now Libya) in 1911, had satisfied colonialists' appetite. As in other countries, the colonial lobby, an informal group of political, commercial, missionary and academic interests, in both liberal and Fascist Italy championed colonies as a vital source of international prestige, profit and, particularly in the case of Italy, as sites for settlement by the migrants leaving the country in droves for the Americas. The humiliating defeat at Adwa rankled, especially for right-wing activists who placed great store on military prowess. Mussolini knew that, in 1906, a secret pact signed by Italy, Britain and France had acknowledged an Italian sphere of influence in the area from the border of Eritrea and Addis Ababa. This foreshadowed a probable lack of opposition to further Italian expansion if the Ethiopian state fell apart, as many expected would occur. He also shared the feelings of resentment that Italy had not received its just bounty as a victor in the First World War, when many hoped that the British and French might relinquish their Somali colonies to the Italians. London was not totally opposed, but the French refused, and Rome was left with no gains. Mussolini nonetheless moved slowly with his plans, as seen with the congenial reception of Ras Tafari in 1924 and the pact with Ethiopia four years later. Meanwhile, in Libya, the Fascists used conventional military means, aerial bombardment, chemical warfare and civilian concentration to 'pacify' resistance, a campaign that some have not hesitated to brand genocide.[7]

The mid-1930s looked to be an increasingly propitious moment for an Italian move on Ethiopia. Mussolini had consolidated power in Italy, and boasted of having subdued Libya and begun a programme of settlement and intensified economic activity in the North African colony. The effects of the Depression underlined the perceived importance of colonies as reservoirs of raw materials and preferential markets. Hitler's appointment as German chancellor in early 1933 placed an ideological comrade-in-arms of Mussolini in power there. Though Mussolini and Hitler were wary of each other, they shared ideas about national revitalization, the cult of the political leader, the staunching of dissent and revision of the First World War settlement. While more worried about Hitler than Mussolini, Britain and France, still traumatized by the horrors of the First World War, in the 1930s, favoured 'appeasement' of both Germans and Italians. In particular, they hoped to preclude an alliance between Rome and Berlin; although Mussolini's policies were anathema to many, they attracted some conservative support, and Fascist Italy appeared a bulwark against Communism and the Soviet Union. Heightened tensions in Spain between republicans, supported to varying degrees by socialists and Communists, versus archconservative parties and the Falangists led by Francisco Franco, further unsettled the political situation in Europe. Franco's ideological sympathies lay with Hitler and Mussolini, and he would benefit from their support during the civil war that began in Spain in 1936 and was won by Franco's armies three years later.

The Italian War on Ethiopia

The mid-1930s thus provided an opportunity for the Italians to make a move on Ethiopia, with Mussolini expecting that a short and victorious war would strengthen his regime and increase Italy's European and colonial clout.[8] The Fascists predicted that international conditions would mute, at least to an extent, foreign condemnation for Italy's expansion. Indeed, the Colonial Minister, Emilio De Bono, had already formulated plans in 1932 for the eventual conquest of Ethiopia, and from 1934, Italy moved ever-increasing numbers of troops – eventually totalling around 400,000 – into Eritrea and Somaliland; it used the seven Italian consulates in Ethiopia as bases for intelligence-gathering and infiltration. In December 1934 a conflict over a disputed border region between Ethiopia and Italian Somaliland, the Wal-Wal incident, erupted into violence, provoked by the Italians, which led to the deaths of 107 Ethiopians and 30 Italian Somali troops. In Italian eyes, this provided a casus belli for an attack on Ethiopia, yet they waited for several months in order to gather their forces. Haile Selassie was aware of

Italy's designs and sought weaponry, though only Germany would provide armaments; Hitler did not wish Mussolini to grow too strong and presumptuous.

On 3 October 1935, 100,000 Italian soldiers advanced into Ethiopia from Eritrea in the north, an invasion soon paralleled by invasion from Italian Somaliland in the south. Ethiopia managed to mount an army of 250,000 troops but they proved no match in training or armaments for the Europeans. A contemporary observer stated that 'this isn't a war – it isn't even slaughter – it's the torture of tens of thousands of defenceless men, women and children, with bombs and poison gas'.[9] Italians forced the Ethiopians to retreat, and Haile Selassie, after intense debate with advisers and faced with inevitable defeat, decided on 4 May 1936 to flee into exile, leaving via Djibouti for Europe. The following day, the Italian commander, Marshal Pietro Badoglio, occupied Ethiopia's capital. Mussolini proudly proclaimed from his famous balcony in Rome: 'Italy finally has its empire, a Fascist empire' and, connecting Fascist Italy with classical Rome, he saluted 'after fifteen centuries, the reappearance of the empire on the fabled hills of Rome'.[10]

Both before and after claiming victory for Italy and the Fascists, the propaganda machine whipped up support for the war and applause at its success. The government-controlled press and newsreels heralded the bravery and heroism of Italian soldiers and the sagacity of military strategists. Not surprisingly, authorities drew on racist tropes about Africans branded savage and barbarous, and an African country dismissed as no more than a collection of warring and misruled tribes. Newspapers and the radio closely followed the campaign with enthusiastic reports and evocative imagery. The government requested that citizens donate jewellery and other gold for the war effort, and even the Italian queen was shown giving up her wedding ring, though in practice a certain amount of coercion prompted 'voluntary' offerings. Interest in the colonies, never particularly strong in Italy, now rose to new heights with publications, propaganda posters and even the odd song composed in honour of the war. War booty further manifested the Italian conquest. An Ethiopian statue of a lion, symbol of Haile Selassie's dynasty, was re-erected outside Rome's rail station near the monument to soldiers who fought in the 1890s colonial wars. In 1937, the Italians took from the sacred city of Axum a 24-metre tall, 160 tonne stele dating from the fourth century; transported to Rome, it was raised next to the new Ministry of Italian Africa. The lion was repatriated in the 1960s, the stele not until 2008.

Italian rule and Ethiopian resistance

The Italian war was supposedly won within a matter of months, but Ethiopia, like many other colonies, was never fully 'pacified'. Acts of resistance continued and included, in 1937, an attempt to assassinate the Italian viceroy, Marshal Rodolfo Graziani, at a ceremony celebrating the birth of the Italian crown prince. Among the people, mostly indigents awaiting a handout of alms, who had gathered in front of the palace serving as the viceroy's headquarters, were nationalist activists, one of whom threw a grenade. The federal secretary of the Fascist party shot off his pistol, and Italian soldiers opened fire with machine-guns, killing a large number in the crowd of three thousand. A seriously injured Graziani was rushed to hospital (and survived), and the Fascist party official within hours of the incident gave carte blanche to Fascist militia, soldiers and police to engage in reprisals. In an orgy of indiscriminate violence, they killed Ethiopian men, women and children by gunshot, hanging, attaching them to vehicles and dragging them around until they died, or even running over them with lorries. The heads of some victims were cut off and mounted on pikes. Widespread pillaging of Ethiopian properties took place, and many African houses in Addis Ababa were burned; there were widespread assaults elsewhere as well. Ian Campbell, in a meticulous examination of contemporary sources and accounts by survivors, estimates that in addition to the Ethiopians who died outside the vice-regal palace, as many as 1,500 were slaughtered within a cordon demarcated for repression by officials in nearby areas, and 6,000–9,000 perished over the three days of violence on 19, 20 and 21 February. Campbell puts the Ethiopian death toll at 19,000 people. Mussolini's secret message to Graziani on 8 July 1936 – 'I repeat my authorisation to Your Excellency to initiate and systematically conduct a policy of terror and extermination' – had been followed. The Italians moved quickly to hush up the atrocities; Ethiopian sympathizers overseas spread word of the massacre. No Italians were brought to justice, and the rallying of Italy to the Allied side in the Second World War after the ouster of Mussolini meant that, unlike the Germans, Italians were never subsequently put on trial for war crimes. 'Yeketi 12' (the date in the Ethiopian calendar) has remained the most heinous of Italian actions for Ethiopians.[11]

At the time of the Addis Ababa massacre, Haile Selassie was in Britain, where he lived in straitened circumstances in Bath. The British did not particularly welcome the exile; despite London's condemnation of Italian aggression, the government still wanted to keep Mussolini away from an alliance with Hitler. Both King Edward VIII, during his brief reign, and the prime minister refused to receive the Ethiopian ruler; the British government counselled him to avoid public appearances and refused to extend any financial aid. However, the British and international public showed much support for the beleaguered Ethiopians. Demonstrations took place outside Italian embassies throughout Europe, and as far away as China and the United States, and left-wing organizations, such as the socialist and Communist parties, lambasted the Italian invasion. Sympathizers organized meetings and published journals, one of them, *New Times and Ethiopian News*, founded in London by the suffragette and political activist Sylvia Pankhurst (who later wrote a cultural history of Ethiopia and whose son Richard became a leading scholar of Ethiopian history).

The Italian invasion of Ethiopia, as Neelam Sri Vastava suggests, 'acted as a catalyst for anti-fascist and anti-colonial resistance movements on the eve of World War II'. It had particular resonance in the African diaspora: 'By triggering a shared solidarity among diasporic Africans the Ethiopian war offered the occasion for articulating a transnational discourse of black liberation.' The International African Friends of Abyssinia formed in London to protest Italian aggression. The chairman was the Trinidadian-born historian C. L. R. James, most famous for a study of *The Black Jacobins* and other accounts of

Toussaint Louverture's Haitian revolution and a promoter of independence for the West Indian islands. Other members included Amy Ashwood Garvey, a journalist and Pan-Africanist (and former wife of Marcus Garvey), and Jomo Kenyatta, who became the first president of independent Kenya. Kwame Nkrumah, later the first president of Ghana, who learned of the invasion while in London, saw in it a significant influence on the formation of his political opinions. Two prominent members of the 'Harlem Renaissance' in the United States, where enormous sympathy existed for the Ethiopians, Claude McKay and George Schuyler, wrote fictional works about the war. The Jamaican-born McKay's *Amiable with Big Teeth* (only published many decades later) centred on efforts of African American intellectuals in New York to organize support for the Ethiopians.[12]

The Ethiopian war was brought before the League of Nations, which on 7 October 1935, declared Italy the aggressor, and from November 1935 until July 1936 imposed limited sanctions on Italian trade. The British voted with a majority of members on 15 July 1936 for a removal of the sanctions, and London became the first foreign government formally to recognize Italian rule over Ethiopia. The French similarly proved willing to appease the Italians; government crises and an unsettled political landscape in Paris diverted French attention from eastern Africa. The plight of Ethiopians might tug at the heart-strings, but in the minds of European policymakers, the Italian victory was a fait accompli that, they hoped, would not produce major repercussions in Europe or Africa. In any case, both countries, and other colonial powers, could hardly mount a full-scale action against Italian colonialism because of discomfort at the idea of Black African countries throwing off colonial overlordship and winning independence.

Nicola Labanca, an authoritative scholar of Italian colonial history, emphasizes that the Ethiopian campaign was not just a colonial war but a Fascist war with a radical and totalitarian character. Mussolini's prime intention was more to score a victory for his regime, and reverse Italy's 1896 military defeat in Africa, than to gain a new colony. He and the Fascists had limited interest in Ethiopia as such, and did not even mouth the usual platitudes about a European 'civilising mission'. Rather than a military expedition in the style of the traditional 'little wars' of colonial conquest by European powers – generally with limited *matériel* and manpower – Mussolini learned from tactics of the First World War to undertake 'total war' in the Ethiopian invasion. He dispatched a huge military force to the battlefront, employed the most modern military technology, used propaganda to rouse the home front and ignored international condemnation (in part, by withdrawing Italy from the League of Nations in late 1937 when new sanctions were imposed).

The Italian war in Ethiopia was brutal, yet Ethiopians occasionally practised grim tactics as well, including emasculation of Italian corpses. In violation of international law, the Italians bombed twelve Red Cross camps. Most insidiously, and on direct orders from Mussolini, they used poison gas, though that, too, was illegal according to an international convention to which Italy was a signatory. During the war and occupation, Italians dropped 2,100 poison gas bombs containing 500 tonnes of gas, and also fired gas from mortars. The yperite gas, the infamous 'mustard' gas used in the First World

War, caused lethal suffocation, and arsine gas produced severe burns, blisters and ulcers. There were documented cases of rape, pillage and other abuses as well. Ethiopian deaths in the war and in Italian massacres and executions during the occupation are estimated to have cost Ethiopia 400,000 lives, with the Italians and their Somali and Eritrean troops counting 25,000 killed.[13]

The new colony of Ethiopia was joined with Eritrea and Italian Somaliland to form *Africa Orientale Italiana* (AOF, Italian East Africa) under a viceroy given extensive powers. From 1936, he was Prince Amedeo d'Aosta, a cousin of King Victor Emmanuel III. Unusually for an Italian royal, he had studied at Eton and Oxford; he served in the Italian army in the First World War and lived for brief periods in Somaliland, the Congo and Libya, where he had taken part in the colonial war in the late 1920s. As viceroy, Amedeo implemented a less aggressive and militaristic approach, in relative terms, than his military predecessor, and he personally tried to keep some distance from the Fascists. Nevertheless, Fascist institutions were brought into Ethiopia, as was the personality cult surrounding Mussolini. The gist of Italian colonization remained full domination of the indigenous population and development of the colony solely for Italian profit; a few visiting foreign observers were impressed by Amedeo and his regime.[14] Despite the grand claims made in Rome for the glorious future of Italian East Africa, however, neither Mussolini nor the Italian 'Emperor of Abyssinia' visited Ethiopia, though they had toured Libya in the late 1930s, and Victor Emmanuel III had earlier travelled to Libya, Eritrea and Somalia.[15]

The Italians determined that there would be no power-sharing in the government of Ethiopia with local nobles, who were considered enemies rather than potential collaborators. In 1937, 400 noblemen were nevertheless taken to Italy to show them the might of Fascist Italy. After their Eritrean interpreter publicly made remarks in favour of Haile Selassie, the authorities quickly sent the noblemen and their families home, and Mussolini let it be known that he wanted to see no more Blacks on Rome's streets. The Italians did appoint a few lower-level officials from among the Ethiopians, rewarding them with salaries and honours, in an attempt to win some indigenous support. They followed the rule of 'divide and conquer', trying to foment discord between the Amhara, who had been favoured by the pre-colonial regime, and other ethnic groups. The Italians also catered to Muslims, another disenfranchised group, by declaring freedom of worship and providing funding for mosques and Koranic schools.

The Italians roundly suppressed dissent; many intellectuals, including notable members of the Orthodox clergy, were killed, imprisoned or driven into exile. A form of apartheid kept Ethiopians and Italians separate, yet full segregation was never entirely possible or successful. Inter-racial sex and marriage were nominally prohibited. Married Italians posted to the colony were required to take their families, and bachelors were not allowed to employ female servants. However, *madamismo*, as Italians termed concubinage, was widespread, with as many as 35,000 mixed-race children born in Ethiopia under Italian rule; they were denied Italian citizenship and kept out of schools for Italian pupils. Under such legislation as the 'Penal sanctions for the defence of the prestige of the race before the natives of Italian Africa', Europeans in the colony could be fined for any behaviour, such as public drunkenness, considered detrimental to the reputation of the white race. Italians were not allowed to take what were thought demeaning jobs, for instance, working as porters or shoe-shiners. At the same time Rome proclaimed that Italian settlement was a kind of 'proletarian' colonization by ordinary Italians. Authorities planned large-scale migration, with wildly optimistic projections of over six million settlers, but lack of land concessions, mismanagement of migration schemes and the limited appeal of Africa by comparison with other destinations meant that few actually came. In 1939, around 130,000 Italians lived in Italian East Africa, half of them in Ethiopia. Ten times that number of Italians lived in New York.[16]

Rome announced grand goals for economic development of Ethiopia, but cultivation of cotton largely failed, and hoped for large deposits of platinum and gold were never found. Wheat farming and pastoralism did somewhat better, and Ethiopia's fine coffee constituted a major export. The colonial government promoted Italian business, with 4000 industrial firms and nearly 5000 commercial ones, though many of them very small-scale operations, engaged in Ethiopia by the early 1940s. The state invested in the building or upgrading of 900 kilometres of railway and construction of port facilities, schools and hospitals, but few Ethiopians had access to the educational and medical institutions. Ethiopians did find increased employment opportunities, but solely in subaltern positions.[17]

In June 1940, Italy entered the Second World War on the side of the Axis, which sparked a more positive attitude towards the Ethiopian cause in Britain. The new prime minister, Winston Churchill, approved a British and Commonwealth invasion of Italian East Africa two months later and arranged for Haile Selassie to be flown to Khartoum in British-controlled Sudan in July in the hopes that he could rally resistance. Along with as many as 100,000 Ethiopian fighters, the Allies defeated the Italian army, and five years to the day after the Italians had occupied Addis Ababa, the capital was liberated. The British moved Viceroy Amedeo to a prison camp in Kenya (where he died of tuberculosis and malaria), and distributed Italian soldiers around prisoner of war camps in Britain and Commonwealth countries; most of the Italian settlers were eventually repatriated. In the years from 1935 to 1940, the Italian army command's soldiers and workers, many of them Africans, suffered around 200,000 dead and wounded in Ethiopia.[18] Allied military victory in the Second World War saw Rome lose Libya as well as Italian East Africa.

The fate of Ethiopia lay in the balance, as British civilian and military officials did not really relish either the return of Haile Selassie to the throne or the independence of Ethiopia. Somewhat reluctantly, however, they transported the emperor back to his homeland from across the border in Sudan, and to the cheers of his subjects, Haile Selassie made his way to Addis Ababa to take up his position as emperor once again. The British acknowledged Ethiopian sovereignty, but the British 'Occupied Enemy Territory Administration' and an Anglo-Ethiopian agreement in January 1942 made Ethiopia into a virtual British protectorate. The emperor was required to consult the British on foreign policy, Britons occupied key positions in the public service, and telecommunications and the railways were placed under British control.[19]

Over the next several years, Haile Selassie moved away from British domination and towards an alliance with the United States, as President Franklin D. Roosevelt had formed a good impression of the African ruler when they met in early 1945. The emperor sent a token contingent of soldiers to join the Americans in the Korean War in the early 1950s, and he made a celebrated tour of Washington and European capitals in 1954. Haile Selassie won applause as a heroic defender of his country, sage monarch and valued ally. He also became a figure of veneration for the Rastafarian movement (the name coming from the emperor's early name and title), which had emerged in Jamaica in 1933. Its leader, Leonard Howell, a member of Garvey's Pan-African association, proclaimed Haile Selassie a divine figure and leader for Africans and the diaspora; associated with black activism, reggae music and the use of cannabis (regarded as having a sacramental quality), Rastafarianism spread around the Caribbean and beyond.

In Ethiopia, the emperor weathered several coup attempts, though by the early 1970s, discontent was rising with his strong-armed regime, increasing prices and poor social conditions. In 1974, a military coup overthrew Haile Selassie and placed him under arrest; he died in suspicious circumstances the following year, at the age of eighty-three. There followed decades of civil strife, dictatorial governments and misguided economic and social programmes. In 1991, the old Italian colony of Eritrea, which had been re-incorporated into Ethiopia following the Second World War, broke away after a war of independence, and at the early 2020s the government of Addis Ababa was engaged in bitter fighting against a secessionist movement in Tigray.

Ethiopia and colonialism

In some ways, Italian colonialism in Ethiopia is a singular case. The Italian war on Ethiopia marked the last attempt by a European power to conquer a new colony in Africa. Along with the Japanese invasion of China, it represented the only significant bout of colonial expansion in the 1930s. Furthermore, the new Italian colony was the only one established, from its inception, on the explicit basis of Fascist ideology and institutions. It was one of the shortest-lived colonies, since the Italians ruled for less than six years. The last African country to be colonized, Ethiopia was the first to be decolonized. Ethiopia provided a very rare case in which a pre-colonial ruler returned to his throne after the eviction of the colonizer, though to be overthrown for a second time three decades later.

Yet in other ways, Ethiopia seems to illustrate, indeed to condense in time and space, many themes of European colonialism in Black Africa. It showed the pattern of expansion based on a claim of European entitlement to take over 'unclaimed' and 'backward' countries, perceived geopolitical imperatives, and the necessity of colonies for metropolitan commercial benefits. It manifested the racial and racist underpinnings of colonial domination in perceptions of the superiority of white Europeans over Africans, and the adoption of policies aimed at keeping indigenous people in a state of subjection, exploitation and disenfranchisement. It revealed how, despite European rivalries, the great powers in practice appeased each other's colonial ambitions so long as their own interests were not threatened. It showed how the dissymmetry in power between modern European military forces and those of a technologically less developed country – the 450 aircraft Italy used in Ethiopia, compared with that country's eight functional airplanes, for instance – contributed to the outcome of confrontations. Italy, like colonial powers of earlier years and elsewhere, used violence to gain and maintain authority, and it deployed the most modern weaponry and military tactics, even in contravention of international accords. It mobilized mass support in the metropole through finely honed techniques of propaganda. It sought, though with only limited and temporary success, to establish a new colonial society affording benefits to European settlers and businesses.

Italian actions made Emperor Haile Selassie into a victim and a hero, an enduring symbol of African culture around the continent and in the African diaspora. It left a mixed legacy in Ethiopia, if less of an imprint than in colonies Europeans ruled for longer periods. In Italy, the end of empire instigated an effort to avoid the colonial memory, and to efface the colonial record, with a long-living myth about Italians as 'brava gente', benign colonizers – a myth not strongly challenged before a wave of historical research, activism and public debate in the last decades of the twentieth century,. This reassessment of the colonial past is ongoing.[20]

In 1938, the Dutch celebrated the fortieth anniversary of the swearing-in – the equivalent of a coronation in the Netherlands – of Queen Wilhelmina, who had inherited the throne in 1890 but only assumed her functions when, eight years later, she reached the age of eighteen. She would rule for another ten years after 1938, until abdicating in favour of her daughter, Juliana, to whom the birth of a daughter and heir (the future Queen Beatrix) was another cause for celebration in 1938. Wilhelmina reigned over six islands in the Caribbean and Dutch Guiana (now Suriname) on the South American continent, but the Netherlands' most important colony by far was the Dutch East Indies. Encompassing five major islands and thousands of smaller ones over an area of almost two million square kilometres, and with a population of 70 million people in 1940, the Netherlands East Indies was geographically and demographically far larger than the Netherlands (an area of 52,500 square kilometres and 8.3 million people).

The Dutch engagement in Southeast Asia dated back to the foundation of the outposts of the Vereenigde Oost Indische Compagnie (VOC, United East India Company), where the Dutch traded for precious spices and other commodities from the early 1600s. At the beginning of the nineteenth century, the Dutch Crown took control of the possessions from the disestablished VOC, but only gradually were claims of dominion extended over all of what is today Indonesia. In the early years of Wilhelmina's reign, the Dutch undertook brutal military campaigns to consolidate conquest in Aceh (on the island of Sumatra) and Bali. Little changed even though the queen, in 1901, announced a new *ethische politiek* ('ethical policy') promising to indigenous people a more humanitarian sort of colonialism with economic and social development.[1]

Queen's Day, the annual commemoration of the monarch's birth, marked a major holiday in the East Indies in 1938 just as in the Netherlands. In Batavia (today called Jakarta), a two-week fair and market were held on the capital's central square with *krongcong* music – a genre that traced its origins to the days of the Portuguese presence in Southeast Asia – and the popular *stambul* theatre for the 300,000 who attended, as well as football matches and shows of prize doves (the keeping of which was a local hobby).[2] Festivities took place in locations far from Batavia as well. The Indo (i.e. Eurasian) novelist Beb Vuyk (1905–91) provided a description from Namlea, a village on Buru, in the Moluccas (Maluku) islands, where she and her husband owned a plantation:

The festivities for the queen's birthday have started by sunrise, otherwise the overloaded program could not be taken care of in twenty-four hours. It's barely six when the schoolchildren file past in a long row. Each school has its own banner, but the children also wave small flags and play their bamboo flutes. Most of them wear blue shorts and new white shirts. The Muslims wear black *sonkos*, a kind of fez, and the Chinese boys wear white suits and big caps. . . . All the children stop in front of the district officer's house, they serenade him with the national anthem and the smartest child quickly rattles off a speech in High Malay. . . . They get cookies and pink syrup drinks before they march off to the jetty where the *praos* [fishing boats] are now lining up for the race.

There followed a church service and reception (for the elite) with performances by different ethnic groups at the district officer's residence. There were games for the children, an open-air feast – 'Once a year Namlea can boast of a restaurant', Vuyk quipped – and a soccer game between the local *Oranje* and Dutch military teams, and in the evening, a dance, with plenty of beer to keep the party going. Perhaps the queen was pleased that her faraway settler compatriots and Asian subjects enjoyed a good time on her birthday.[3] The event, of course, also affirmed Dutch colonial overlordship, and the dispossession and disenfranchisement of East Indians, even if Dutch accounts intimated that colonizers had won the hearts and minds of the indigenous populations.

Visions of the Indies: Photographs and films

Queen Wilhelmina never set foot in the Indies, nor any of the other Dutch colonies. The queen nevertheless had been familiar with her eastern realm since, as a child, she had played with a set of three hundred dolls, representing different 'types' of people from the very diverse Indies sent to her by the colonial government. She kept abreast of Indies affairs through briefings by ministers, receptions for visitors, and visits to the Colonial Museum (now the Tropenmuseum) in Amsterdam. Taking advantage of the new technology of radio transmission, East Indian music had been beamed directly to the Netherlands during Princess Juliana's engagement party in 1937. The monarch was represented in the East Indies by a governor general, in the late 1930s, a grandly named nobleman, *Jonkheer* Alidius Tjarda van Starkenborgh Stachouwer. A photograph from 1938 shows him sitting beside one of the sultans in the Indies, the *Susuhunan* Pakubuwono X of Surakarta, each wearing a uniform heavy with medals and sashes (the Indonesian also wears a traditional head-cloth), accompanied by their daughters, the Dutch woman in an evening gown, the Indonesian in a *kebaya* (white blouse) and sarong printed with a pattern specific to royals of the sultanate. They pose on a European sofa in front of a gigantic portrait of Queen Wilhelmina.

Such images were vital to Dutch colonialism in the East Indies.[4] Pictures of the queen provided a visual presence of the absent sovereign. Photographs of the dozens of hereditary aristocrats who had ruled over territories before Dutch colonization and were co-opted into the Dutch administrative system of indirect rule as 'regents' were compiled into elegantly bound albums and offered to the queen. As images and gifts, they spoke of princes' and sultans' own royal status, the maintenance of ancestral political, social and spiritual positions in their realms even under Dutch domination, and their role as auxiliaries in government. The images depicted adoptions and adaptations in personal style: sultans sporting the medals of honorific orders, dressed for formal portraits in European-style jackets matched with sarongs of *batik* (wax-resist printed textiles), their wives fully in local dress, often in settings with European furniture.[5]

Photographs, like the radio and the electric illumination of public buildings for events such as the queen's birthday, testify to technologies introduced into the Indies. Another vision of the Dutch colony, employing yet another innovation, came with moving pictures, such as a documentary created by Deane H. Dickason, an American producer and director of travelogues. 'The East Indies in Color, 1938-1939' opens in Batavia with scenes of bargemen, women washing clothes and a policeman directing traffic.[6] There are the imposing buildings, in neo-classical or modernist design, of the Netherlands Trading Society, the City Hall, the *Volksraad* (colonial council) and Societeit de Harmonie (a social club). A sequence on Menteng, a recently laid-out and fashionable neighbourhood for prosperous Dutch residents, pictures comfortable bungalows and pretty gardens, and the camera focuses on Governor General Tjarda and his family, elegantly attired and sitting around the viceroy's palace reading magazines, playing tennis, swimming and walking around the grounds: an idyllic portrait of happy family life in the tropics and the benign paternalism of Dutch officialdom. Perhaps not surprising in the context of the late 1930s, the film shows numerous scenes of military life: armoured tanks and airplanes, soldiers from the East Indies Home Guard, volunteers from the Air Defence Service (some with gas masks), young women practising first-aid, children drilling to take shelter in an underground bunker. But to indicate that life goes on as normal, there are markets, women selling *batik*, roving vendors plying their wares, a speeding train and a Mickey Mouse sign.

The documentary moves on from Batavia to the city of Bandung, once again juxtaposing footage of the airplanes of ML-KNIL (the colonial Air Force) and lively streets where signs advertise Kodak film and Java beer. Yogyakarta provides another site for the cinematographer: a rice field, the extraordinary ninth-century temple of Borobudur and the sultan's grand *kraton* (palace compound). Workers busily harvest sugar cane, the stalks transported to factories on a small train or in bullock carts. From Sumatra, there are pictures of mining operations and of the houses of the Batak people with characteristic soaring upturned roofs, a mosque and minaret, harbours crowded with ships and boats, roadways traversed by automobiles, bicycles and *becak* (pedicabs) and peaceful villages. The film closes with a pointed shot of the Dutch flag flying against a bright sky.

Dickason's documentary presents a roseate portrait of Dutch rule in the Indies, a colony where tradition is preserved and modernity welcomed, one of orderliness, industriousness and prosperity in which the Dutch are at home. Indigenous people productively labour on plantations and in mines, print *batik* and trade, or take their leisure, eating, feeding deer, relaxing and playing with children. Almost without exception, each woman, man and child smiles broadly, if shyly (perhaps an understandable reaction in the encounter with the voyeuristic film-making apparatus), composing a gallery of happy 'native' people content with their modest lot. Left unshown are less picturesque sights.

The Colonial World

One or two of the local people are dressed in rags, but the overall impression is of relative comfort, not the poverty that was the lot of many in the countryside and city, especially during the Depression years of the 1930s when the film was shot. Batavia's canals look charming, though in fact, they served as dumping-grounds for rubbish and sewerage. The great divide between bourgeois areas like Menteng and the dusty *kampongs* (villages or 'native quarters') where indigenous people lived is evident only as a happenstance not an outcome of colonialism. It goes without saying that the corporal punishment still inflicted on plantation workers for misdemeanours is not shown, and a viewer gets little sense of the back-breaking labour involved in harvesting coffee, planting rice or mining ore. There is no recollection of the bloody campaign waged from 1873 to 1903 to 'pacify' Aceh in which 37,000 soldiers in the Dutch colonial army (most of them Asian recruits) and as many as 70,000 Acehnese died. Nor is there a hint of the Dutch wars in Bali in 1906 and 1908, at the conclusion of which 1,300 of the island's ruling class ritually committed suicide by marching directly into a barrage of Dutch bullets rather than surrender. These and many other shadows over East Indian life are invisible in a travelogue that provides a shining panorama. The scenes of military men and *matériel*, however, are a reminder that the skies were not so clear in the late 1930s as the closing shot suggests.

The Indies in a colonial novel

Yet another vision of the Indies in the 1930s comes from *Country of Origin*, by Edgar Du Perron, one of a whole shelf of novels published by Dutch writers.[7] The author had a prosperous background; his mother's family was linked to the military, and that of his father, proud of distant French ancestry, was part of the planter elite and judiciary. Du Perron wrote his fictional, but autobiographical, work in retrospect twelve years after the narrator (and the author himself) had left the Indies and was living in Paris, making a living as a journalist, and wrangling with the settlement of his recently deceased mother's estate. The long book presents vivid memories of a charmed childhood in Batavia and the Javanese hinterland where the narrator's father possessed a rice plantation and factory. The writer nevertheless warns himself: 'I must also be careful not to lapse into that disgusting European exoticism, that false romanticism that is fashioned from a few resonant names, some brown skins and velvet eyes. For some people this never fails to have the desired effect, this and some mention of the docile oriental soul.' He speaks with fondness of Eurasian nannies (and alludes to the awkward position of Indo-Europeans in colonial society), childhood games with Javanese boys, and long chats – in Malay, Sundanese and Dutch – with local storytellers, such as a learned lady who 'knew the Koran better than most, wrote poetry herself, and told me the adventures of two great Arab heroes'. He recalls visits to shops such as 'a typical Chinese *warung* where you could buy everything: candy, matches, canned goods, candles, cigars, macaroni, and spices – all this piled up and mixed together to form towers of boxes and jars'. He describes his wanderings about the *kampong* across the river from his family's mansion, a house where bronze sculptures of Christopher Columbus, the Portuguese seafarer Vasco Da Gama, and the sixteenth-century poets Camões and Ariosto lined a marble hall. He remembers the sounds of the *gamelan* (percussion orchestra), and the spectacle of *wayang* (shadow puppet plays), as well as the first showings of moving pictures and the family's acquisition of a gramophone.

Du Perron covers in less detail the poor conditions endured by indigenous people, though using the word 'starvation' to refer to the hunger common among peasants. He makes a reference to the slaughter of the Aceh war and evokes the casually racist attitudes of many colonists. Anecdotes sketch various questionable aspects of colonial life, such as the narrator losing his virginity with a local prostitute. Life in European circles was also not always carefree: Arthur has a fraught relationship with his neurasthenic, violent and autocratic father, who beats his Indonesian employees (and occasionally his wife and son), once spends a month in a debtor's prison and eventually commits suicide. Arthur's mother, fluent in Sundanese, is portrayed more positively, encouraging her son in his pursuits and kindly ministering to the Malays in her household.[8]

Early in the novel, the expatriate Arthur converses with an acquaintance, with whom he has sought out an Indonesian restaurant in Paris. The friend expresses relief that the food, perhaps modified for European tastes, is not especially spicy. Arthur replies with a very pithy, if facile, long-term overview of Dutch colonialism in the East Indies:

'Don't denigrate Indonesian spices', I tell him. 'Remember that they turned hordes of [Dutch] Calvinists into determined bandits. It's unbelievable what those shopkeepers did in their search for new wares. They became seafarers and then found out that they could also change into robber barons. . . . They politely asked permission from their dark-skinned brothers to open a grocery store in their territory, almost as if asking for their protection. Afterwards it turned out to be a fortress, which allowed them to plunder the surroundings quite easily. Running these predatory expeditions provided the education for our first great governors. With his Calvinistic hand in the cookie jar the greatest of them wrote to the home office that they could easily continue to rely on the God of robbery. . . . They had brought their own magic formulas with them: their own Bible, which proved quite clearly that they were completely justified in attacking their fellow human beings who had never even heard of it'.[9]

Du Perron's novel is, in part, a story of Arthur's disillusionment with colonialism, general world-weariness and, at the end, as he witnesses confrontations between the police and extreme right-wing rioters in Paris, worry about the current political climate. The narrator recounts how planters tried to subvert the new 'Ethical Policy', and how they demeaned and punished East Indians, for instance, by shutting down shops when shopkeepers could not pay rent. Discriminatory practices, in his view, were indeed inherent in the colonial situation: 'my father . . . was irrevocably one of the landowners. He was born in the Indies and had always known the Javanese as subservient beings.'

The novel illustrates the ambivalence of colonials, including those born and bred in the East Indies, through the character of Arthur: bittersweet but genuine attachment to the 'country of origin' in Asia, European pretensions or aspirations of grandeur in the tropics, yearning for an idealized European homeland, but nostalgia for a lost colonial world after they depart.[10] It evidences the disquiet that at least some felt at the excesses and evils of colonialism. Du Perron himself returned to the East Indies in 1936, at the age of thirty-seven, and remained until 1939, becoming an acquaintance of some of the emerging nationalist leaders; he died in the Netherlands, in 1940, before the independence of Indonesia.

Anti-colonial nationalism

Among Du Perron's friends was Sutan Sjahrir (1909–66), a prominent Indies nationalist and the prime minister of Indonesia from 1945 to 1947. He later fell out with the leader of the independence movement, President Sukarno, who had him imprisoned in 1962. Released in 1965 to seek medical treatment overseas, Sjahrir died in Zurich a year later. In the 1930s, Sjahrir, along with Mohammed Hatta (later the first vice-president of Indonesia), had been sent into internal exile by the Dutch for anti-colonialist activities, first to western Java, then to Dutch New Guinea and finally to Banda island in the Maluku archipelago. Sjahrir's writings from exile in the years from 1934 to 1939, largely in the form of letters collected by his French-born wife, Maria Duchâteau-Sjahrir, provide much insight into conditions of the time. Though guarded in tone because of censorship, they reveal his lively personality, deep learning and insightful perspectives on contemporary politics.[11]

Sjahrir's forced sojourn on Banda was relatively comfortable, as he and Hatta were lodged in a large house and given freedom of movement; they opened a school for Arab children. While Hatta was personally reserved and rather strict, Sjahrir was fun-loving. He enjoyed playing tennis and football – though he refused to take part in a game on Queen's Day and characterized the celebration in Banda as a 'barren demonstration' – and he taught some of the islanders the fox trot, tango and other dances he had learned while a law student at the University of Leiden in the Netherlands.[12]

Though firmly grounded in Sumatran and Islamic culture, Sjahrir manifested a deep appreciation of European culture, and his letters refer to Plato, Goethe, Kant, John Stuart Mill, Tolstoy, the historians Johan Huizinga and Benedetto Croce and a host of other European authors, conceding his 'Western inclinations and Hollandophile sentiments'. 'What we in the East admire most in the West is its indestructible vitality, its love for life and for the fulfilment of life', Sjahrir states: 'Every vital young man and young woman in the East ought to look toward the West, for he or she can learn only from the West to regard himself or herself as a center of vitality capable of changing and bettering the world.' Furthermore, 'the East is being westernized. It can be deplored or applauded, but the process goes forward inexorably and rapidly. It is a fact that must be accepted and considered.' He thus disagreed with Indonesians who rejected European institutions and practices in large measure or wholesale. At the same time, he gently mocked romantic Europeans who 'long for the East, which signifies to them tranquillity and reflection'.

He evoked the beauty of the Moluccas, the 'Spice Islands', but cautioned: 'And here on these beautiful islands one of the blackest pages in the history of the East India Company was written: a page of brutality, greed, and inhumanity – the extirpation not only of flowering gardens but also, through plunder and murder, of large numbers of peaceful and industrious people.'[13] The reference was to a massacre ordered by VOC governor general Jan Pieterszoon Coen in 1621 because of alleged violations of a treaty the Dutch had forced Banda rulers to sign to facilitate the spice trade. Villagers were tortured and forty beheaded by the Dutch and Japanese mercenaries, and several villages were razed.

Sjahrir said that period lay in the distant past, but he similarly rebelled against contemporary colonial rule, placing the nationalist movement in a psychological and ethical context (as did Gandhi in India). 'At present', he argued, 'the whole political struggle has a very strong moral element for us in the East. For most of the people, politics is not planning and premeditation, but ethical and moral eminence and actions'. He spoke about the immorality of colonialism, 'this colonial life with its senseless relationships and its psychopathic participants: on the one hand the sadists and the megalomaniacs, and on the other hand the souls that are warped by inferiority complexes': the Dutch colonizers and their subjects, respectively. Decolonization was a personal as well as national struggle for both colonizers and colonized:

> One can go so far as to emancipate oneself – to a certain extent; that is to say, one can arrive at a point where neither sadism and megalomania nor an inferiority complex disrupts one's equilibrium . . . . One can also keep oneself free from senseless, impotent hate. I think I am able to do this. But one can absolutely never forget that he is still living among these sufferers and sadists. One must even exert all his will so that he *never* forgets this vital fact, because forgetting it would signify such an egregious adaptability that it would amount to living lunatically in a society of lunatics.

That state of affairs impelled his compatriots to anti-colonial militancy and sometimes extremism: 'The source and lifeblood of all nationalist extremism is the socially and intellectually inferior station in which the Indonesians are forced to live. Extremism springs from the resentment that they, the oppressed millions, feel at being looked down upon as an inferior race. This fact cannot be eliminated by any welfare or ethical colonial policy', he wrote in March 1938. The regime of Governor General Tjarda

> has inherited from the previous administration the faith that if it is not possible to stop these currents [of nationalism], it is still possible to propel them in a desirable direction; and that by the use of force . . . . That, of course, is not new, and every dictatorial regime has this same faith. The apparent success that such methods have achieved in Germany and Italy must certainly have an encouraging effect on other dictatorial regimes, including those in the colonial countries. What it amounts to is the belief that a positive, loyal mentality can be formed through intimidation.

For those arrested and exiled like Sjahrir, 'the government is related to us as a conqueror to prisoners of war'. Therefore, for the nationalists, there could be no acceptable remodelling of the colonial order but only its abolition.[14]

Sjahrir was very attentive to the deteriorating political situation in the late 1930s. His letters, for instance, mention the Spanish Civil War waged between republicans and followers of the authoritarian General Francisco Franco, a conflict that attracted much attention around the colonial world. If 'reactionaries in Spain win out, then the triumphal march of fascism throughout the world will gain further momentum, and the defeat of the French, Belgian, and Dutch democracies will be at hand', he warned in mid-1936. He wrote, as well, of the violent conflict between Chiang Kai-shek and Mao Zedong in China, and of the rule of Hitler in Germany – and of the popularity of Nazi ideas among some Dutch colonizers, including the wife of the doctor in Banda who greeted others with 'Heil Hitler!'. Sjahrir's letters dwelt on Japan, a country that enjoyed immense popularity amongst Indonesians for its strong government, resistance to Western colonialism and proclamations about an Asia for Asians:

The Japanese have a great advantage over the whites, despite all propaganda that may be attempted to offset it . . . . It is simply due to the fact that the Japanese habits and general manner have won the people's hearts . . . . Now Indonesians regard the Japanese as 'fine people', 'civilized', they say; and they regard the Chinese and the whites as *kasar* or coarse. This disaffection with the whites derives, naturally, from the three hundred years of white rule.

He nonetheless expressed concern about Japan's own colonialism (which would be apparent anew in the Japanese invasion of China in 1937) and its potential economic and political designs in the Indies. Dutch authorities, he lamented in 1937, were blind to the dangers presented by tumultuous world affairs: 'The colonial rulers here regard all this as such a distant danger that they do not see the necessity for bringing about a basic alteration in the old, time-worn method of ruling over this country. Instead, they continue at the same old stand.' Nevertheless, in the menacing situation developing in the late 1930s in Europe and Asia, Sjahrir held out a hand to the Dutch because, as he presciently stated and literally underlined, '*the existence of the Netherlands Indies and the existence of the Netherlands itself are both now threatened*'.[15]

Sjahrir's views represented a moderate strand among the ideologies that competed for Indonesian support by the 1930s.[16] Nationalist and reformist movements had emerged in the Indies from the early years of the twentieth century. In 1912, a group of students set up an association calling for reform at STOVIA, a school for indigenous medical practitioners and a rare institution of tertiary education in the colony. The same year saw the establishment of the Muhammadiya, which aimed to purge Islam in the East Indies of unorthodox beliefs and practices, and affirmed its centrality to ethnic Malay identity; another Muslim organization, the Nahdlatul Ulama, which sought to preserve local traditions within Islam, was founded in 1926. (Both still exist in Indonesia.) In 1920, the Indonesian Communist Party was formed; brief Communist uprisings in 1926 and 1927 were fiercely put down by the Dutch. In 1927 the Indonesian National Party was founded, with a prime mover the future President Sukarno.

Participants in a nationalist youth conference in 1928 adopted a flag and anthem for Indonesia and took a pledge: 'Firstly, we the sons and daughters of Indonesia acknowledge one motherland, Indonesia. Secondly, we . . . are one people, the nation of Indonesia. Thirdly, we . . . respect one language, Indonesian.' The words, which now appear straightforward, at the time sounded a clarion call to solidarity and anti-colonial action. The Dutch had always rejected the word 'Indonesia', with its suggestion of unity among diverse peoples – divide and conquer served as a tactic of the Dutch no less than for other colonizers. By acknowledging 'one nation', those who took the pledge not only expressed belief in a commonality of interests among the colonized and commitment to a unified, independent country, but they abjured allegiance to another state, the Netherlands. By choosing Bahasa Indonesia, the Indonesian version of Malay, as a *lingua franca*, they pointed to a strategy of nation- and state-building through which the ethnic and linguistic differences in an archipelago of two hundred languages could be surmounted.

In the 1930s, more political parties emerged, with fission and fusion of earlier groups. The colonial *Volksraad*, a colony-wide council set up in 1918 (but given no legislative powers until 1926) and local councils provided limited forums for parliamentary-style political participation. A petition was presented in 1936 calling for Indonesian independence within a Dutch Commonwealth. Such nationalist ructions alarmed the Dutch, especially with the global spread of Communism as theory and political organization, the prominence and charisma of nationalist leaders in the Indies, the disastrous effects of the Depression on the colonial economy and labour, and the changing political circumstances in Europe and Asia. One response was widespread arrest and detention of dissidents, often without trial. By the late 1930s, the Dutch had arrested and sent into internal exile most of the leading nationalist figures, including men who would play signal roles in the independence movement during and after the Second World War, such as Sjahrir, Hatta and Sukarno.

The Surabaya-born son of an aristocratic Javanese father and a Balinese mother, Sukarno (1901–70) was educated in Dutch schools, took an engineering degree in Bandung and worked for an architectural firm before becoming involved in politics as a founder of the Indonesian Nationalist Party. Arrested by the Dutch in 1931, he was released the following year but his continued nationalist activism and writing led in 1933 to his re-arrest and exile, first on the island of Flores, then in February 1938 to Benkoelen (Bengkulu) on Sumatra. Hatta (1902–80), who came from a wealthy Minangkabau family, graduated in 1932 from the Rotterdam School of Commerce. Like his two comrades, he joined the Indonesian Nationalist Party, was arrested and exiled, in his case, first to Dutch New Guinea and in 1936 to Maluku. All three men remained in internal exile and under strict Dutch surveillance until after the Japanese invasion of the Indies in 1942.

The Colonial World

From the 'Island of Love' to an archipelago at war

The Indies, as was true for most colonies, was full of fault lines in the 1930s. The sultans stood as guardians of tradition with their palaces, gamelans and retinues, the royal *batiks* and sacred *kris* daggers; most continued to accommodate and even support the Dutch. A growing group of young people, often educated in Dutch schools and sometimes in the Netherlands, such as Sjahrir, Hatta and Sukarno, meanwhile turned against the colonial order and joined movements that sought independence for Indonesia though they remained divided about the ways to obtain it or what sort of future government should be established. Some Muslim leaders advocated for a country with strict adherence to the principles of Islam, others tended to a more secular outlook. Though Muslims accounted for an overwhelming majority of the population, there were significant Christian communities (especially in the Maluku islands), the Balinese were predominantly Hindu, and the majority of those on the Dutch part of the islands of Borneo and New Guinea followed beliefs foreigners characterized as 'animist'. Javanese and Sumatrans, on the two largest islands, have very different cultures and languages, and there are many others as well. The Chinese numbered about 1.2 million in 1940, often occupying positions as merchants, shopkeepers and moneylenders, and were viewed with suspicion by both Malays and the Dutch. Arabs from the Middle East, Japanese and non-Dutch Europeans counted in the cosmopolitan population as well. Around 240,000 people in the Indies were Europeans or Eurasians, but they hardly constituted a homogenous cohort. The Dutch population was divided between the old 'stayers' whose families had lived in the Indies since the days of the VOC, and the more recent arrivals; the 'pures' took pride in living apart from 'natives' and maintaining 'white' bloodlines. Eurasians, or Indos as they were generally called, occupied the interstices between colonizers and colonized, mixing and mingling with the Europeans when possible, though marginalized by their heredity. The aggravated racial politics infecting the world in the 1930s created heightened tensions, with ethnic and cultural groups retreating to their own spheres. Yet the East Indies continued to be heralded by colonialists as a place of beauty, harmony and growing prosperity, and tourist promoters draw on traditional images to attract visitors (see Figure 24.1).

Developments on the island of Bali in the late 1930s illustrate the paradoxes of a society that bore the deep scars of colonial conquest, enchanted the wider world with its landscapes and culture and yet was far from immune to contemporary problems. The Dutch secured control over Bali, as mentioned earlier, by war in the first years of the twentieth century that culminated in *puputan*, ritual mass suicide by some in the royal dynasties on the island. Despite that dark stain, in the following decades Bali was touted as a paradise for inhabitants and tourists – Bali, became one of the first major tourist spots in Asia. It was the 'island of love', with beautiful beaches and luxuriant jungles, picturesque temples and bare-chested young women and men who danced to the haunting rhythms of the metallophone *gamelan* and reverently offered flowers and incense to Hindu gods. Visitors included the Austrian writer Vicki Baum, who published a searing novel about the *puputan*, and the Mexican painter and ethnographer Miguel Covarrubias and his wife Rosa Rolanda, an artist, choreographer and dancer, who jointly

Figure 24.1 Although Bali was proclaimed the tourist paradise of the East Indies, colonial officials also promoted tourism to Java and the archipelago's other islands. 'Visit Java. Only 36 hours from Singapore', Vintage travel poster, *c*. 1920s–40s. © Getty Images.

wrote and illustrated *Island of Bali* in 1937. Other visitors and authors included the American anthropological photographer Jane Belo and her then husband, the Canadian Colin McPhee. Belo published a study of *Trance in Bali*, and McPhee wrote a memoir about life on the island (which glosses over his homosexuality) and a notable Balinese-inspired musical composition, *Tabu-Tabuhan*. The American anthropologist Margaret Mead and her husband Gregory Bateson toured as well, and made a film on 'Trance and Dance in Bali'. Another widely distributed film about Bali, from 1935, was 'Legong, Dance of the Virgins', directed by a Frenchman, Henry de La Falaise.[17]

At the centre of the expatriate cultural elite so captivated by Bali was Walter Spies. The son of a wealthy German family living in Russia, he was born in 1895 in Moscow and grew up in the tsarist empire. In the early 1920s, he trained as a painter and musician in Dresden, and in Berlin collaborated with the director Friedrich Murnau on the expressionist film 'Nosferatu'. In 1923, Spies went to Java to work as conductor of the Western orchestra of the Sultan of Yogyakarta; four years later, he moved to Bali, where he spent the rest of his life. Spies became a renowned painter, developing a bold style both primitivist and modernist in which he depicted Bali – water buffalos in rice paddies, peasants returning home from work, deer on mountain slopes, a hermit deep in the jungle. Spies hosted and entertained passing celebrities at his finely landscaped mansion compound, including Charlie Chaplin, Noël Coward and the German sexologist and homosexual emancipationist Magnus Hirschfeld, and he was close to the Covarrubias, McPhee and Mead couples. Spies planned the Bali display for the 1931 international colonial exhibition in Paris, and he became curator of the museum in Denpasar, Bali's capital. He collaborated on Baron Victor von Plessen's 1933 ethnographic film 'The Island of Demons', and with the English dancer Beryl de Zoete, wrote *Dance and Drama in Bali*. He was also an avid and accomplished photographer. Spies gathered around himself aspiring Balinese artists, for whom he provided an introduction to Western styles of painting. Some of the young men in his entourage became his lovers, though the relationships, it seems, posed little problem for most of the Balinese.[18]

The Dutch proved less tolerant – homosexual acts were illegal in the Netherlands and its empire – even if for a while they turned a blind eye. However, by the mid-1930s, a moralizing and archconservative Christian political movement in the Netherlands, and its supporters in the Indies, had gained sway and set out to eradicate 'vice', a reflection of a wider reactionary European current that, for instance, had seen the Nazis burn the library of Hirschfeld's sexological research institute in Berlin. A witch-hunt against homosexuals began in the Indies and inevitably arrived in Bali. On the last day of 1938, Dutch police arrested Spies and charged him with having sex with a 'minor' (as defined by Dutch law). The judges convicted Spies, and he was held in prison until 1 September 1939, coincidentally the date of the German invasion of Poland and the beginning of the Second World War. After Germany invaded the Netherlands, Spies, still a German citizen, was interned with other enemy nationals. In January 1942, he was boarded onto a ship bound for the Netherlands; a Japanese aeroplane bombed the ship between the Indies and Ceylon, and all of the passengers perished. Spies left a legacy in Bali; his paintings hang in local museums, and a 'school' of Balinese modernist art flourished in his wake, one example of a fertile cultural encounter between Europe and Asia.[19]

The German defeat of the Netherlands in 1940 raised questions about the future of the Dutch overseas empire, especially since the Indies, according to the American journal *Foreign Affairs* in that year, 'constitutes the richest colonial plum in the world' – it accounted for 17 per cent of the Netherlands' national income, and produced 35 per cent of the world's rubber, 17 per cent of its tin, 90 per cent of its quinine and large quantities of sugar, coffee, tobacco, copra and palm oil. The Indies was also the world's fifth largest producer of petroleum, already the new fuel of industry. With its huge territory – spreading from west to east over as large an expanse as the continental United States – and prime location, the colony occupied a key strategic site between the Indian and Pacific Oceans and between Asia and Australasia. It was hardly a secret that the Japanese, as Sjahir noted in his letters, were eyeing off the Indies' resources and potential use as a base in Southeast Asia, and that some anti-colonialist Indonesians held sympathies for the Japanese. *Foreign Affairs* remarked that 'the nationalist movement is strong and no great love is lost for the Dutch rulers', and it wondered 'whether the East Indies will be able to survive as a Dutch possession'.[20] Indeed, the Second World War unleashed a process that led to Indonesia's independence.

The visions of the Netherlands East Indies presented in this chapter – images of the queen and an Indo's account of the Queen's Day celebrations, an American's filmed travelogue, an autobiographical novel written by the son of a Dutch planter, the letters of an Indonesian nationalist, and a brief account of a German's social circle in Bali – cannot begin to cover the complexity of the Indies in the late 1930s or canvas the spectrum of contemporary opinions and historical interpretations. Every one of the seventy million residents spread over around six thousand occupied islands in the East Indies, indeed, had his or her own experiences of colonialism and perspectives on Dutch rule. Each person in the Netherlands no doubt also had a view about the Indies, as did foreigners ranging from tourists and ethnographers to businessmen and military strategists.

In 1938, the Dutch seemed confident that their *imperium* in Southeast Asia would endure, with rising nationalism suppressed by propaganda, censorship and the imprisonment or internal exile of the movement's leaders. Two years later, the world war inevitably distended ties between the Netherlands and its colony, and the Japanese invasion in 1942 opened another chapter, one featuring a different colonizer. Wartime would see Japan's appropriation of the Indies' resources, the suppression of dissent, the violence of the occupation army and police forces, and the coercion of local women into prostitution as 'comfort women'.[21] However, Japanese rule also provided an opening for the nationalists released from prison, even if some refused cooperation with the Japanese. On 17 August 1945, two days after the Japanese surrender to the Allies, Sukarno proclaimed the independence of Indonesia. For four years, the Dutch sought to reimpose their authority by military and political means, but in vain.[22] Only eleven years after the triumphal celebrations of Queen Wilhelmina in 1938, though almost three and a half centuries after the Dutch VOC first gained a foothold in Southeast Asia, her successor Queen Juliana signed the act that formally transferred sovereignty of the Netherlands East Indies to the new republican government of Indonesia.

CHAPTER 25
PALESTINE AND THE MIDDLE EAST, 1946

'Suddenly the whole town seemed to shudder . . . . The force of the explosion was greater than had been expected . . . the entire wing of a huge building was cut off as with a knife.'[1] This is how Menachem Begin (1913–92), a future prime minister of Israel, described the bombing of the King David Hotel in Jerusalem on 22 July 1946 in his memoirs, *The Revolt*. The attack destroyed the south wing of Jerusalem's premier luxury hotel, which housed the headquarters of the British mandate government of Palestine, including its military and intelligence divisions (see Figure 25.1). Over ninety people died, including forty-one Palestinian Arabs, twenty-eight Britons, seventeen Jews, two Armenians, a Russian, an Egyptian and a Greek, and another forty-six were injured. Begin, who as a youngish militant had taken control of the Zionist paramilitary Irgun Zvai Le'umi (National Military Organization) in 1943, was involved in the planning, though not in the execution, of the hit. The attack took place under the auspices of the Hebrew Resistance Movement, a broad coalition including diverse militant and violent Zionist armed groups, such as Irgun, that were all part of the Jewish Agency for Palestine, the operative branch of the global Zionist Organization founded in 1897.[2]

The British Labour prime minister, Clement Attlee, immediately denounced the bombing as an 'insane act of terrorism' and a 'dastardly outrage'.[3] The Conservative politician Viscount Cranborne took up Attlee's statement and commented in the House of Lords that 'Terrorism is a futile and wicked weapon; it solves nothing and can only recoil on the heads of those who use it'. For his part, the Liberal Earl of Perth condemned what he labelled 'the terrible outrage' in Jerusalem. He was worried, however, about an 'increase of anti-Semitism' in Britain because of the attack, which 'would almost lead to a triumph of the ideas of Hitler', whose armies had been defeated only the previous year.[4] As memories of the horrors of the Second World War and the industrialized mass-killing of European Jews were still fresh in Britain, the notion of a terrorist Zionist group bearing responsibility for the attack for many seemed unthinkable. Yet, at the time, various Zionist and Jewish civil and military organizations active in Palestine were closing ranks, a development about which British politicians (and British intelligence in Palestine) were not aware.[5]

The umbrella organization of the Hebrew Resistance Movement, too, was quick to denounce its allies publically and to condemn 'the heavy toll of lives caused in the dissidents' operation at the King David Hotel'. However, its allies in the Haganah (Defence), the main Jewish paramilitary organization in Palestine, had seen the King David Hotel with the British administrative centre as a legitimate target; an attack against the occupying British, who administered Palestine under a mandate

Figure 25.1 Troops inspect the wreckage of the King David Hotel in Jerusalem, headquarters of the British Mandate of Palestine, 22 July 1946. © Getty Images.

from the League of Nations, was therefore part of a political strategy aiming at the establishment of a Jewish state. A few weeks before the attack, British police forces had seized documentation disclosing the Jewish Agency's cooperation with the Hebrew Resistance Movement. The widely respected Jewish Agency considered British knowledge about the collaboration with terrorist groups detrimental to the Zionist cause. Therefore the compromising documents that were probably kept in the King David Hotel should be destroyed before the British had time to thoroughly analyse them. Hence, beyond the symbolic dimension of attacking the heart of the British administration in Palestine, the strike also had a specific objective, at least according to Begin's memoirs. Furthermore, he wrote, Irgun had informed the hotel and tenants of neighbouring buildings, such as the French embassy, about the upcoming attack, pressing for an evacuation of the premises; he argued that no casualties had been intended.[6]

There are several hypotheses about why the King David Hotel was not cleared despite the alert, including that doubts existed about the credibility of the warning because of recurring and often false threats, and that the notice of an impending blast gave no time to vacate the premises. Whatever the case, the explosion was so strong that even if the building had been emptied, anyone who remained in the immediate vicinity could well have died. The bombing remained the deadliest terrorist assault in the region until Hezbollah, a Shia Islamist group based in Lebanon, claimed that ignoble record in the 1980s.[7]

Violent campaigns by some Zionists in the 1940s, though disavowed by many supporters of a Jewish state, contributed to the eventual formation of the independent state of Israel in 1948.[8] However, Begin's brand of militancy represented only a small part of the wider campaign for a Jewish state. Whereas Begin's memoirs appeared under the title *The Revolt*, the diaries of David Ben-Gurion (1886–1973), Israel's first prime minister, were published as *The War of Independence*, the differences in wording symbolic of varying perceptions.[9] Both phrases illustrate the colonial dimension of the Jewish struggle against imperial Britain. Ben-Gurion, however, argued that 'colonialism' did not do justice to the Israeli settlement process; there was no colonial exploitation of a people in Israel, he stated. Where there once had been vacant land, endemic malaria and a stagnant economy, there was now development and modernity to the benefit of Arabs as well as Jews. He emphasized that there had been no acts of violence.[10] As interesting as it is to identify a set of centuries-old colonial tropes – *terra nullius*, a civilizing and modernizing mission to the benefit of local people – to prove the non-colonial nature of Israel's state-building project, it is Ben-Gurion's short memory of the Jewish terror campaigns directed against British forces (and Palestinians) that is most striking. At the time of his writing in the late 1960s, Israel was strongly condemning the terror tactics used by the Palestinians against Israel, which they considered the new colonial power in the region. Hence, Palestinian-Arab strategies can be seen to have parallels with Zionist attacks against the British in the 1940s and perhaps with some later episodes.[11]

Questions about coloniality and particularly settler colonialism in Palestine increased after the founding of Israel in 1948 and still characterize discussions about conflicts in the Middle East. Though Israel's founding fathers, including Ben-Gurion, as well as later leaders, have rejected the idea that Zionism was a colonial ideology,[12] using 'empire' and 'colonialism' – British imperialism and what has been labelled Jewish settler colonialism – as an analytical lens allows greater understanding of the many layers of conflict in the Middle East. As the Palestinian-American historian Rashid Khalidi argues, the 'modern history of Palestine can best be understood . . . as a colonial war waged against the indigenous population, by a variety of parties, to force them to relinquish their homeland to another people against their will'.[13] This chapter does not pretend to give a comprehensive overview of events in the Middle East – a term that has been used to encompass lands from north-eastern Africa across the Arabian Peninsula to Iran and Iraq – and the complex scholarly debate about that region. It seeks to provide, however, a glimpse into key historical processes there from the end of Ottoman rule to the foundation of Israel.

Between empires: From Ottoman rule to the British and French mandates

The region that included the British mandate of Palestine had been part of the Ottoman Empire since 1516. Moving from central Asia, the Ottomans in 1453 conquered Constantinople, the capital of the Byzantine empire, the surviving part of the Christian Roman empire. They renamed the city Istanbul, set up a new state under a sultan, introduced Islam and expanded further around the Aegean and Mediterranean. The Ottoman Empire constituted a vast contiguous entity, extending from the Balkans in south-eastern Europe (including Greece), across the far western Asian continent – covering what is now Israel, Palestine, Jordan, Syria and Lebanon, as well as much of the Arabian Peninsula – and northern Africa from Egypt through Algeria. The sultan's dominion covered provinces with varying degrees of suzerainty as well as quasi-independent and vassal states, with in 1800 a population of over 32 million people. As a multi-ethnic, multi-religious and multilingual polity, the long-lived Ottoman Empire showcased a capacity to accommodate many cultures.

The Ottomans practised both direct and indirect rule, secured the collaboration of local elites and provided for representation of the minority Jewish, Christian and other religious groups, but also resorted to violence and suppression of dissent, resettlement of populations and coerced modernization of what the rulers considered backward peoples. In the eyes of many Europeans, the sultan was the very model of an authoritarian potentate, though they courted his favour, contracted alliances with the 'Sublime Porte' (as diplomats referred to the empire) and fantasized about the exotic Levant of palaces, markets, mosques and harems. Istanbul, sited on both sides of the Bosporus Strait and located in both Europe and Asia, was a metropolis of 600,000 people (in 1800) that for centuries had been a cultural and commercial crossroads between East and West.

At its apogee in the late sixteenth and seventeenth century, the Ottoman Empire was a wealthy and powerful state, reputed for its rich culture and a major force in international politics. In the eighteenth century, the Ottoman 'Enlightenment' introduced modest reforms into the conservative Muslim polity, though it remained an absolute monarchy. Ottoman authorities in the nineteenth century undertook more wide-ranging social, administrative, political and military renovation aimed at modernizing the empire and safeguarding the international status of a state coming to be known in the West as the 'sick man of Europe'. As Ussama Makdisi has argued, research on the Ottoman Empire has long underestimated its efforts to incorporate the different religious and ethnic groups as citizens in its polity, particularly during the reformist *Tanzimat* era between 1839 and 1876.[14] This included attempts to buttress control over Istanbul's disparate territories, though regions distant from the capital, such as Egypt under the khedive and Tunisia under a bey – nominally, vice-regal representatives of the sultan – exercised effective autonomy. The Ottomans faced a successful revolt that led to independence in Greece in 1830 and continuing irredentist efforts to bring further territory into the new Greek kingdom. Several other Balkan states broke away from the Ottoman Empire later in the nineteenth century. Meanwhile, France conquered Algeria over the period from 1830 to 1870, and eleven years later, established a protectorate over Tunisia; the following year, the British bombarded Alexandria and gained a de facto protectorate over Egypt.

Effective Ottoman rule over the Arabian Peninsula, extending from today's Iraq southwards to the Red Sea and eastwards to the Persian Gulf, had waxed and waned over the centuries, and Istanbul maintained only nominal claims, if that, to peripheral regions. Much of the centre and east of the peninsula was covered by desert and inhabited by largely nomadic populations, although port cities, such as Muscat in Oman, had long been thriving centres for trade, especially with South Asia and eastern Africa; indeed, the sultan of Oman reigned over Zanzibar far to the south. On the extreme southwest coast of the peninsula, at the entry to the Red Sea, the British East India Company had established a base in 1839 at Aden (in present-day Yemen). The opening of the Suez Canal in 1869, which made the Red Sea the key route to Asia – and, pertinently for the British, to India – enhanced the importance of Aden, which became one of the world's busiest ports and one of Britain's most strategic outposts. Further north, European powers tried to gain influence in the Ottoman lands. The French, for instance, sent six thousand soldiers to Lebanon during anti-Christian disturbances in 1860, and French culture took root among the country's elite. The Germans, in the years before the First World War, also made overtures, with a visit by the kaiser to the 'Holy Land' in 1898, the start in 1910 of construction of a railway linking Berlin to Baghdad, and dreams by some of acquiring a German colony in the Middle East.[15] British, French, German and also Russian designs – notably Russia's hope to obtain access to the Mediterranean – encouraged the Ottomans to reassert their authority. The construction of the Hejaz railway from Damascus (in today's Syria) to Medina (Saudi Arabia), and plans for extension of the line to the Muslim holy site of Mecca, was one initiative to tighten the empire's control over its territory. The Ottoman lands thus provided a terrain for rivalries among European empires as well as for resistance by local people to imperial rule.

From the late nineteenth century, the Ottoman Empire was further weakened by wars, including a war with Russia in the 1870s and the Balkan Wars of 1912–13. Western European powers, while still paying respect to the 'Sublime Porte', waited eagerly to parcel out the remains of what they considered a moribund empire. In 1914, the Ottomans sided with Germany and Austria-Hungary, and four years later emerged on the losing side of the First World War. While the Ottomans, notwithstanding heavy losses, withstood the Allied troops, many of whom came from Australia and New Zealand, at Gallipoli in 1915, rebellion instigated by the Allies within Ottoman lands shook the empire to its core. From 1916 to 1918, the allies supported an 'Arab revolt' led by Sharif Hussein bin Ali (1853–1931) and other notables aligned with the British, and memorably associated with the archaeologist, military officer and writer T.E. Lawrence (1888–1935), or 'Lawrence of Arabia', and Gertrude Bell (1868–1926), another well-known archaeologist and author. The revolt blazed its way through the Arabian Peninsula with the aim of establishing independent Arab states. With Ottoman defeat in 1918, the empire was on the road to its demise, though it struggled on until the abolition of the sultanate in 1922 and the establishment of a rump Turkish Republic under Kemal Atatürk (1881–1938). An independent monarchy, in the meantime, had been set up by the Al-Saud family in what is now Saudi Arabia, and the British sponsored the establishment of an indigenous monarchy in Iraq in 1922.

With the end of the First World War, people from Lebanon to Palestine 'looked forward to the fulfillment of our grand dream: the rise of a great Arab state from the Atlantic Ocean to the Gulf', as the Lebanese feminist and author Anbara Salam Khalidi (1897–1986) put it in her memoirs.[16] However, France and the United Kingdom had come to a secret agreement regarding post-war spheres of influence in the Middle East with the 1916 Sykes-Picot Agreement that foreshadowed the dismantlement of the Ottoman Empire; a unified Arab state was not part of the plan, but rather partition of territories between the two Western European powers. The modus vivendi brokered by the victors of the First World War was formalized at the San Remo Conference in 1920, and confirmed through 'mandates' from the newly established League of Nations.

Under the mandate system, the old Ottoman territories were not formally colonies, but London and Paris were given near full rights of administration and development 'until such time as they [were] able to stand alone'. In practice, the Europeans ruled as colonial masters. For many in Beirut and elsewhere who had cheered 'the glad news that Turkish rule had ended and that Arab rule was to take its place', the British and French takeover in December 1918 felt like an occupation. The French received mandates over Syria and Lebanon, and in its early days, one young Lebanese commented that 'the French [had] arrived in our country with the mentality of an absolute ruler as though they intended to remain with us forever'.[17] The French, in the event, continued to administer the two territories until 1946. The British were granted mandates over Iraq, which lasted until 1932, and Palestine – including present-day Israel, the areas now under the Palestinian authority, and Jordan (then known as Transjordan) – that were maintained until the 1940s.

Britain and France thus acquired, as booty of the First World War, large and strategically important territories that offered promising natural resources – in particular, petroleum, the new fuel of the twentieth century, as well as mineral salts (potash and bromine) used for fertilizers and insecticides, among other products. Opportunities for trade, investment and the extension of cultural influence presented themselves as well. For the British, a mandate over Palestine and domination of Egypt, on either side of the Suez Canal, secured effective control over the vital waterway linking Europe to Asia. The dividing up of the Ottoman Empire, in progress since the early 1800s, now seemed complete, to the satisfaction of British and French expansionist designs. However, the European powers were immediately confronted with regional, religious and ethnic tensions in their mandated territories. These were evidenced, in particular, by the 'Druze Rebellion' or the 'Great Syrian Revolt' of 1925–7. The objective – intertwined with fratricidal and sectarian local disputes – was to oust France from Syria and Lebanon, though French military forces defeated and punished the rebels, consolidated their authority and pursued their political, economic and social plans for the territory.[18] Meanwhile, conflict was festering in Palestine.[19]

Of settlers and colonies

With Jerusalem, Mecca and Medina, the Middle East is home to the sanctuaries of three world religions: Judaism, Christianity and Islam. For centuries, their followers had lived together in the region, Jews and Christians as minorities since the rise of Islam in the seventh century. Towards the end of the nineteenth century, Jewish migration towards what was considered Eretz Israel, the biblical land of Israel between the Jordan river and the Mediterranean Sea, had increased. Widespread anti-Semitism in Western Europe – sparked by rising nationalism, pseudo-scientific notions of race, the Dreyfus affair in France and the emergence of explicitly anti-Jewish political movements in Germany and elsewhere – and violent pogroms in Poland and Russia (which continued in the later Soviet Union) triggered waves of Jewish relocation. At the same time, especially with the work of the Hungarian-born theorist and journalist Theodor Herzl (1860–1904), the idea of Jewish settlement in the ancient land of the Hebrews gained currency. Inspired by European nationalism, Herzl and other Zionists, as supporters called themselves, put forward modern nationalist concepts of a Jewish 'homeland' in Palestine as an alternative to assimilation in Europe (though a potential Jewish state in Argentina also figured among Herzl's proposals to resolve the 'Jewish question' in 1896).[20] Between the early 1880s and the late 1930s about 380,000 Jews arrived in Palestine, joining the 15,000 Jews who already lived there among 450,000 mostly Muslim Arabs, though there was a significant community of Christian Arabs as well. Although both local Jews and Arabs could claim to be indigenous people, the new arrivals were settlers within the Ottoman domains. Their growing presence inevitably became an issue with the post-war plans for the British takeover of Palestine after the fragmentation of the Ottoman Empire.

Conflicting promises made by the British during the First World War set the stage for future struggles. In 1915, the British High Commissioner in Egypt, Sir Henry McMahon, made a commitment to the Arab leader Sharif Hussein, the senior religious figure of the Hejaz (which covers Mecca and Medina), for an independent state encompassing the whole Arabian Peninsula in exchange for Arab support in the war against the Ottomans. This was a promise honoured only in breach, as the 1916 Sykes-Picot Agreement emphasizes. Furthermore, the United Kingdom's Foreign Secretary, Arthur Balfour, in part in order to secure financial assistance in the Allied war effort, assured Lord Rothschild, a banker, politician and key figure of the Jewish community in Britain, of London's support for 'the establishment in Palestine of a national home for the Jewish people'. The pledge made in November 1917 in the name of 'His Majesty's Government', known as the Balfour Declaration, clashed with an Anglo-French Declaration in November of the following year, which envisaged 'the complete and final liberation of the peoples who have for so long been oppressed by the Turks, and the setting up of national governments and administrations deriving their authority from the free exercise of the initiative and choice of the indigenous populations'. The rhetoric of liberation and support for the establishment of largely Muslim Arabic and Jewish polities, therefore, went hand in hand with claims to imperial domination.[21]

In the late Ottoman Empire, the province of Syria (including today's Israel/Palestine) had enjoyed varying degrees of autonomy. After several constitutional reforms, the different regions also acquired limited parliamentary representation in Istanbul. Yet religion provided a stronger base for allegiance and sense of belonging than did the sultan or the Ottoman state. After the establishment of the post-war mandates, the British (and French) authorities aimed at curbing local participation in politics. In mandatory Palestine, the British saw Jewish migrants and settlers as crucial partners in spearheading British imperial modernity in the region. Overall, the French and the British colonial presence in the Middle East after the First World War made for a continuing tense sociopolitical landscape through the first half of the twentieth century.[22]

New settlers competed with established residents for scarce resources, such as fertile lands and fresh water, in Palestine. Consequently, many Arabs perceived the Jewish settlements both as a land grab and part of a British colonial enterprise. In Jerusalem, Arab women protested in the streets leading to the residence of the High Commissioner, as one militant recalled, 'expressing their fears about the increase in Jewish immigration, the Mandate's obvious partiality for Zionism [and] the neglect of Arab rights in their own homeland'.[23] Growing tensions with the migrants as well as with the British mandate authorities fuelled Arab unrest, and inter-communal violence escalated in Jerusalem in April 1920 during the Nebi Musa riots. Against the backdrop of such violence, the first British High Commissioner for Palestine, Sir (later Viscount) Herbert Samuel, made clear in his inaugural address in July 1920 that 'disturbances will be suppressed with all the resources at my command'. Samuel and his successors delivered on that promise, particularly during the Arab revolts between 1936 and 1939.[24]

The international context of the 1930s, with great impact on Palestine, was the rise of an explicitly and violently anti-Semitic movement in Germany. Although the 'Final Solution' programming the extermination of Europe's Jews was not decided until around 1942, soon after coming to power in 1933, Hitler and his followers put into practice the campaign against Jews that had been one of the promises on which they had recruited support. Accused of being foreigners (though most German Jews were well integrated into German society), people whose 'racial' characteristics made them inferior to 'Aryans', and who were condemned as both capitalist exploiters and Bolsheviks, Jews became the victims of increasing discrimination, and were barred from many professions, subjected to virulent propaganda and physically assaulted. *Kristallnacht* ('Crystal Night') in 1938, when 7,000 Jewish businesses and synagogues were attacked – the word refers to the broken glass windows – and 30,000 Jews were arrested and sent to concentration camps marked a more intense escalation of anti-Jewish policy. Western leaders did relatively little to aid the Jews, including the many thousands fleeing Hitler's Germany. Indeed, British authorities curbed Jewish migration to Palestine. 'Fear of indefinite Jewish immigration is widespread amongst the Arab population', a British White Paper of 1939 recognized, and this resulted in regular violent 'disturbances' (in British colonial parlance) that hampered London's plans for socio-economic development of the territory. In order to calm the situation, the White Paper fixed the number of Jewish immigrants at 10,000 a year for a period of five years; together with 25,000 resettled refugees, this imposed a quota of '75,000 immigrants over the next five years', meaning until March 1944. After this 'period . . . no further Jewish immigration will be permitted unless the Arabs of Palestine are prepared to acquiesce in it', the White Paper stated. The empire project thus remained Britain's first concern; the fate of European Jewry came second.[25]

The Second World War and the unfolding of the Holocaust, the industrial destruction of Jews (and of the Sinti, Roma and other minority groups in Europe), led to further Jewish flight to Palestine. Whereas in 1932 Jewish people made up 18 per cent of the population in Palestine, in 1946 the proportion was around 30 per cent. 'In 1935 alone, more than sixty thousand Jewish immigrants came to Palestine, a number greater than the entire Jewish population of the country in 1917'.[26] Then in the war years between 1939 and 1945 about 80,000 Jews looked for refuge in the Middle East, though Britain sought to curb what was considered illegal migration. While the Nazis were in the process of murdering six million Jews on the European continent, Jewish refugees intercepted by the British at sea were deported to Mauritius and Trinidad, though Jews also managed to escape to Britain and other British Dominions and colonies. The defeat of the Nazis nevertheless left many surviving Jews still fearful for their future in Europe. Jewish emigration continued after the end of the war, as numerous 'wretched people sailed illegally in leaky and unserviceable boats, crowded like cockroaches' towards the promised land, as the last British High Commissioner for Palestine, Sir Alan Cunningham, put it.[27] By 1947, over 600,000 Jews were living in Palestine (alongside 1.2 million Palestinian-Arabs). Since the 1880s, when Jews comprised 3 per cent of the total population in Palestine, the ratio had increased more than tenfold, making Jews close to a third of the inhabitants of the territory. Several international fact-finding missions were tasked to address what was increasingly framed as the 'Palestine problem'. For many international observers, partition of the territory into separate Palestinian and Jewish states seemed an answer to the question of its future.

Empire in the shadows of the Second World War

During the Second World War mixed units of Jewish and Arab soldiers provided the British in Palestine with much-needed manpower as they prepared for a possible German invasion. The Nazi-aligned Vichy regime in France meanwhile kept control of the French mandates of Syria and Lebanon, and held the upper hand in Algeria, Morocco and Tunisia in 1940. The Germans and Italians sought support from Arabs through radio broadcasts and other propaganda. While the Muslim leader Amin-al Husseini (Grand Mufti of Jerusalem from 1921 until 1948) collaborated with the Axis powers, Fascist Italy tried to cling on to its North African colony of Libya, and Eritrea and Ethiopia on the Horn of Africa (and Mussolini made claims on French Djibouti). Mussolini's air force repeatedly bombed cities in Palestine such as Tel-Aviv and Haifa in 1940 and 1941, as the German Afrika-Korps led by General Erwin Rommel was advancing towards Egypt and the Suez Canal. The risk to the British of losing access to the eastern Mediterranean and the Arabian Sea seemed imminent.[28]

In May 1941 British Empire troops along with Charles de Gaulle's Free French forces, and units of the Jewish Haganah militias, seized control of Syria and Lebanon, and Allied armies mounted an offensive against the Germans in North Africa in November. The Axis threat to Palestine was deflected, yet it took until 1943 for the Germans to capitulate in northern Africa. While Jewish volunteers and military units such as the Jewish Brigade fought shoulder to shoulder with the British against the Nazis and their allies all over Europe, in Palestine Menachem Begin and the Irgun (among others) turned again to acts of sabotage against the British, which – on a small scale – had been a recurrent feature since the early days of the mandate. With the outbreak of the Second World War, they had put their actions on hold, but in 1943, in view of Britain's limiting Jewish immigration to Palestine, they resumed attacks on police stations, blew up bridges and pressed for Palestine to become a refuge for Jews escaping the Holocaust.

Somehow counterintuitively, for Palestine as a whole, the 1940s had been a rather prosperous period, both for Arabs and Jews. The hundreds of thousands of British Empire troops stationed in the mandate had to be provisioned, boosting local economies in agriculture and other sectors. The military presence and war in Europe directly and indirectly generated jobs, while expansion of the military infrastructure advanced regional commerce. From 1943, however, the British had to deal with renewed Zionist sabotage and attacks, some of which took place beyond the borders of mandatory Palestine, such as the 1944 assassination in Cairo of the British minister-resident for the Middle East, Walter Guinness (Baron Moyne), by the Fighters for the Freedom of Israel. For their part, Palestinian-Arabs' opposition to Britain's colonial overlordship was still hampered from the blow received during the Arab rebellion in the late 1930s – many of its leaders had been killed or deported, and others forced into exile.[29]

When in October 1945 several competing Jewish paramilitary groups joined forces to form the Hebrew Resistance Movement, the British were not caught 'between two hotly contesting sides', as Cunningham later stated. (In fact, since the late 1930s, Palestinian-Arabs had contributed little to the explosive situation.) Shocking news about Nazi concentration and extermination camps reached a wider public, yet the Hebrew Resistance Movement considered British forces in Palestine as unwelcome colonial overlords and an obstacle to the establishment of a Zionist state. When news of the bombing of the King David Hotel reached the United Kingdom, Attlee's government, which 'seemed entirely committed to the Zionist project', struggled to make sense of the fact that Jewish militants were responsible for the attack. Referring the 'Palestine question' to the recently founded United Nations for conflict resolution seemed an appropriate way out.[30]

In 1947, the United Nations tasked a Special Committee on Palestine (UNSCOP) with elaborating solutions for the future government of Palestine. Members interviewed Zionist representatives and convened Jewish organizations in Palestine and the United States, but the Arab Higher Committee, the Palestinians' political institution in mandatory Palestine, declined to meet with the UN envoys, whom they considered biased. The leaders of five Arab countries (Egypt, Iraq, Syria, Jordan and Lebanon) had already declared in 1944 that they were second to none in regretting the woes that have been inflicted upon the Jews of Europe by European dictatorial states. But the question of these Jews should not be confused with Zionism, for there can be no greater injustice and aggression than solving the problem of the Jews of Europe by another injustice, that is, by inflicting injustice on the Palestine Arabs of various religions and denominations.[31]

Arab dignitaries and intellectuals such as Hussein Fakhri al-Khalidi (1895–1962) – Anbara Salam Khalidi's brother-in-law and the former mayor of Jerusalem (and, later briefly prime minister of Jordan in 1957) – nevertheless met informally with UNSCOP emissaries and took a stand in favour of a single Arab-majority state. Al-Khalidi, a physician, had been co-founder in 1935 of the Palestinian-Arab Reform Party, one of the six major political Arab parties. He became a member of the Arab Higher Committee, which spearheaded the Arab Revolt (1936–9), for which the British deported him to the Seychelles Islands in 1937; allowed to return to Palestine in 1943, al-Khalidi became Secretary of the Arab Higher Commission. In 1947, his recommendation for the creation of a unitary Arab state in Palestine went unheeded.[32]

A majority of the UN special committee expressed support for an end to the British mandate and partition of the mandate territory into separate Jewish and Arab states, with Jerusalem under international administration. The General Assembly of the United Nations – at that time a forum of fewer than sixty nations – accepted the proposal, notwithstanding the negative votes of the Arab states, in November 1947. In the background, the United States, which had emerged as a global power in the Second World War, also backed partition and pressed for a Jewish state. Palestinian-Arabs rejected the resolution, while the Zionists formally accepted it. Armed conflict between Arabs and Jews began in December 1947, even before Ben-Gurion's proclamation of an independent state of Israel in May 1948.

Disorderly decolonization

'And so we left', as High Commissioner Cunningham soberly summed up British retreat from Palestine in 1948. It was a 'melancholy business presiding over such an occasion', he reminisced in an address to the Royal Institute of International Affairs in London. Colonizers often perceived the lowering of a flag over a territory in terms of losing a limb, as the amputation of a part of the body.[33] For Cunningham, however, melancholy had its limits, as the months between the UN vote in November 1947 and 15 May 1948 had been tense for the British. International pressure, particularly from the United States and also from the Soviet Union (which had supported establishment of the state of Israel), further contributed to Cunningham's 'unhappy experience' in Palestine. The High Commissioner was indeed relieved when British troops and civil servants began to leave. Now, 'there can no longer be any doubt in the eyes of the world as to the true nature of the problem' in Palestine, he was convinced. According to his perspective, this was a bitter contest between Jews and Arabs, each fearing domination by the other, in which the Mandatory Power, standing between, has been continually denounced, first by one community and then by the other, as showing favour to the other side. The true problem is now clear and so history will judge it. I am sure all of us who have had to work in Palestine during the term of the Mandate are well content to accept that judgement.

Cunningham was convinced that the British 'left with dignity, using all our efforts to the last for the good of Palestine'.[34] And yet, 'disorderly decolonisation'[35] might be a more adequate way to describe Britain's flight. As Gudrun Krämer states in her *History of Palestine*, the British had made 'no formal arrangement . . . as to how power would be handed on or to whom. While the Jews had functioning institutions of self-government, the Arabs did not.'[36]

For many Arab Palestinians, the months between the eruption of fighting in 1947 and Israeli independence in 1948 represented an existential threat. 'We could barely believe the horrors that the Jews inflicted on Arab villages with the slaughter of innocents and the destruction of peaceful homes', Anbara Salam Khalidi described those years in her memoirs.[37] More than 300,000 Arab Palestinians, mostly Muslims, were forced to flee to neighbouring countries before the end of 1948. By 1950, between 600,000 and 760,000 Palestinian-Arabs were either internally displaced or had fled to Jordan, Syria or Lebanon. Today the UN counts about five million Palestinian refugees. This massive exodus – Al-Nakba, the 'catastrophe', in the Palestinian culture of remembrance – is one of the main reasons why many Palestinian-Arabs perceive Israel's post-independence policy, with its continuing settler projects, as a colonial enterprise.[38] In recent years parts of international scholarship have also moved towards an understanding of the foundation of Israel as a 'settler colonial logic of conquest through displacement, dispossession, and elimination of the native Palestinians from their land'.[39] The 'settler colonial' lens nevertheless remains a subject of heated debate, and in the official Israeli narrative the Palestinian-Arabs' displacement was a 'voluntary' process, not a policy.

For the Zionists who had pioneered late nineteenth- and early twentieth-century Jewish migration and settlement in Palestine, and those who fled Nazi persecution, as well as a large number of Jews who migrated in the wake of the independence of Morocco, Tunisia and especially Algeria, and those who escaped the Soviet Union, Israel provided a homeland, just as the Americas and Australasia had been. Economic development and a largely democratic government provided prosperity and pride, though the rule of difference and the continuing exclusion of Arabs from the nation has contributed to their living with fear in a permanently militarized state. Arabs in Israel, and in the territories occupied in Israel's wars with Arab countries in 1967 and 1973, suffered hostility, discrimination and abuse. Jerusalem, divided by the UN in 1947, was captured and annexed by the Israelis in the 'Six-Day War' of 1967. Some, though not all of the other territory taken in that conflict, was returned; the remaining territory, illegally occupied according to international law, has been the object of moves for annexation by the Jewish state. Palestinian groups have used tactics from negotiation to terrorism to try to obtain their objective of an independent homeland for their people, and to secure their rights and regain their lands. For the Zionists, the creation of Israel as an independent Jewish state had brought British colonialism to an end; for Palestinian-Arabs, decolonization is still pending.

Events moved quickly in Algeria in early 1962, as an almost eight-year war between the nationalist Front de Libération Nationale (FLN, National Liberation Front) fighting for independence, and French forces defending *Algérie française* was drawing to a close. On 5 February, at a news conference, the French president, Charles de Gaulle, foreshadowed that a solution to the intractable conflict was in sight, an allusion to continuing negotiations between the FLN and Paris. Violence nevertheless continued, carried out by the FLN, the French army and the Organisation Armée Secrète (OAS), a diehard militia of supporters of continued European rule in Algeria. The FLN for years had engaged in guerrilla warfare, including indiscriminate attacks on the *Français d'Algérie*, or the *pieds-noirs*,[1] and their properties, as well as on Muslim Algerians who refused to back the campaign for independence. The OAS, ratcheting up violence against Algerians by the French, similarly undertook arbitrary attacks, in Algeria and in France, and lambasted de Gaulle's government for its willingness to 'abandon' the territory.

Three days after de Gaulle's press conference, a large and peaceful demonstration, organized by a Communist Party-aligned trades union, took place in Paris in opposition to the OAS and continuation of the war. A protest the previous year had turned dramatic when police attacked demonstrators. The tragic situation repeated itself, as a mêlée erupted not far from the iconic Place de la Bastille, near the Charonne Métro station, the entrance to which had been locked. In the crush of people trying to escape as police advanced, nine people were killed or later died from wounds.

On 7 March, the French government opened another round of negotiations with the FLN in the spa town of Évian-les-Bains, and eleven days later, the two parties signed the Évian Accords. The agreement on 18 March – often taken as the symbolic date for the end of the war – provided for an immediate ceasefire, the release of some prisoners, and a timetable for a vote on self-determination in Algeria. Nationalists promised to respect the lives and property of non-Muslims. *Pieds-noirs* remained unconvinced, and on 26 March, the French army fired on Europeans in Algiers protesting the agreement, killing forty-six. In a referendum in France on 8 April, however, 91 per cent of voters supported the Accords.

On 1 July, Algerians went to the polls, though most *Français d'Algérie* boycotted the ballot: 5,975,581 voted for independence, and 16,534 against. On 3 July, de Gaulle officially proclaimed the independence of Algeria, and the FLN Provisional Government moved to Algiers from its headquarters in Tunisia. The major celebrations in Algeria took place on 5 July, the anniversary of the day 132 years earlier, in 1830, when the French had invaded and occupied Algiers. World leaders, particularly from Arabic and

Muslim states, sent congratulations. Meanwhile tens of thousands of panicked *Français d'Algérie* were fleeing Algeria for France, a place where many had never set foot. On 22 August, a renegade member of the OAS attempted to assassinate President de Gaulle in a Paris suburb. The FLN meanwhile began murderous exactions against the *harkis*, those Algerian Muslims who had fought with the French.

The war of independence claimed up to 30,000 victims among French soldiers and *pieds-noirs* between 1954 and 1962, and between 300,000 and 500,000 Algerians (or 1.5 million, according to the FLN), including civilians. Two million had been displaced within the country, and most of the one million Europeans (and many indigenous Jews) left Algeria. Thus ended the long war of decolonization waged over Africa's largest country – four times the size of France. Algeria was France's largest settler colony, home to a million European settlers and their descendants, outnumbered seven to one by Muslim Algerians. *Algérie Française*, in constitutional terms, was fully part of the French Republic, not a colony. However, the currents of nationalism and anti-colonialism that swept the world inevitably reached Algerian shores, and neither the French state nor *pieds-noirs* could push back the tide.

The year 1962 is momentous in the history of decolonization, seeming to mark the end of a wave that had brought independence to most colonized countries of Asia and Africa (though the Portuguese and Spanish colonies remained notable exceptions). Algeria became a beacon for activists around the world, from Black Panthers in the United States to opponents of apartheid in South Africa.[2] The 'Algerian Revolution' proclaimed by the victors promised a democratic and socialist republic with justice, peace and prosperity. The newly independent state, however, faced poverty, the loss of capital and entrepreneurial skills with the Europeans' departure, tempestuous relations with the old colonizing power, and intense rivalries within the FLN and between it and other groups. Within three years, an authoritarian leader came to power and ruled the country with an iron hand as a one-party state until 1976. Unrest and poverty endured, and growing numbers of Algerians migrated to France in search of jobs and security. Algeria eventually plunged into a civil war that lasted from 1991 to 2002 and cost the lives of as many as 200,000 people.[3]

Algérie Française

In the early twentieth century, the French believed that Algeria would be permanently part of France – France, some said, was one country divided by the Mediterranean, just as Paris was one city divided by the Seine river. Algeria had been fully incorporated into France since 1848. Residents elected representatives to the French parliament, though with two unequal electoral colleges, one for citizens, the other for non-citizens. The citizens were mostly of European ancestry, including descendants of large numbers of Spanish, Italian and Maltese migrants naturalized en masse in 1889, and indigenous Jews given citizenship in 1870. Muslim Algerians could only become citizens, until the late 1950s, if they met stringent criteria (including that they lived in a 'European' manner) and renounced the *statut personnel*, which allowed them to be judged on such matters as land-holding, marriage and inheritance according to Islamic law; few qualified or chose to take that step.[4]

Though there was poverty among the *pieds-noirs*, many enjoyed prosperity derived from agriculture and viticulture (wine provided Algeria's major export), positions in the urban economy or employment in the administration. So-called *Algérianiste* writers lauded the pioneer spirit of settlers and took pride in the new Latinate culture they claimed had emerged among the disparate European people. Modern architecture had turned the capital, Algiers, into a French-style metropolis with a busy port, boulevards, cafés, a museum, university and other amenities such as cinemas (see Figure 26.1). While well-to-do *pieds-noirs* lived in airy seaside neighbourhoods, Muslims clustered in the warren-like streets of the old casbah. Most Muslim Algerians, however, lived in rural areas, working as subsistence farmers and pastoralists, or subaltern employees of the French; possibilities for social advancement were limited. The average *pied-noir* income in the 1950s was seven times the earnings of a Muslim. A limited number of Muslim Algerians became lawyers, doctors, pharmacists and teachers, and others occupied positions as French-appointed 'tribal' officials, but most occupied the lower ranks of the labour force. About 100,000 Algerians lived in the *métropole*, mainland France, by the 1950s, providing cheap labour for industry, public works and agriculture. Disparities in wealth, political rights and status between *pieds-noirs* and Muslims were marked, and endemic racial profiling and discrimination common.

Pieds-noirs had continually resisted reforms that might give a significantly greater share of power or wealth to Muslim Algerians. Though professing indefectible allegiance

Figure 26.1 Street scene in Algiers during the Algerian war of independence, 1960. © Getty Images.

to France, they nevertheless rankled at intervention by Paris in local affairs. In the metropole, politicians on the ideological left campaigned for greater equality for Muslims (and a few called for independence for Algeria), but the dominant view – as expressed in 1954 by François Mitterrand, then a socialist minister and several decades later president of France – was that 'Algérie, c'est la France'.

The development of Algerian nationalism

Politically, the lines between Muslim Algerians and Europeans were increasingly impassable. The *Français d'Algérie* were determined to remain in the country that they considered a homeland and which they claimed to have developed and modernized. Most French politicians argued for the legitimacy of *pied-noir* views, championed the benefits of French rule and believed Algeria vital to France's political, strategic and economic welfare. Muslim grievances were long-lasting: colonial conquest, dispossession of Algerians from their land in favour of the *pieds-noirs*, economic exploitation, the imposition of a foreign culture, the domination of French interests in policymaking, and violence. According to the historian Martin Evans, 'the long hatreds produced by the original French invasion in 1830' and its aftermath meant that 'two societies existed uneasily in conditions of mistrust, segregation, and mutual incomprehension'.[5]

Algerian resistance had been manifest since the initial French invasion even though after the 1870s the French declared that they had 'pacified' the country. Early twentieth-century Algerian political groups, such as the generally middle-class and French-educated 'Young Algerians' founded in 1907, were 'assimilationists', calling for the economic and political amelioration of Muslims' situation within the French Republic. A federation of elected Muslim officials, set up in 1926, which similarly put forward plans for gradual reform, was headed by Mohammed Saleh Bendjelloul (1893–1985), a medical doctor and member of the French parliament, and Ferhat Abbas (1899–1985), the son of a *caid* – *caids* were pre-colonial tax collectors and judges incorporated into the French system – and a pharmacist by training. The author of an article in 1936 titled 'I am France', like others he became more radical as reforms failed to eventuate.

More stridently anti-colonial, the Étoile Nord-Africaine (North African Star) was established in 1926 by Algerians in Paris. Its leader, Messali Hadj (1898–1974), counted among around 170,000 Muslim Algerians who had served in the French army in the First World War. With his trademark patriarchal beard and a flowing cloak worn over a Western suit, Messali remained, alongside Abbas, one of the most prominent and charismatic Algerian political figures over the next decades. The programme of the Étoile Nord-Africaine, published in 1933, was wide-ranging and non-compromising. It called for immediate abolition of the 'native code' that permitted arbitrary individual and collective punishments of Algerians outside judicial channels, release of political prisoners, freedom of the press and association, opening of all public service positions to all Algerians, free education, teaching in Arabic and recognition of Arabic as an official language, universal suffrage, nationalized banks, mines and transport, and the confiscation of large settler properties. The manifesto signalled three longer-term objectives: total independence for Algeria, withdrawal of 'occupation troops' and the setting up of a 'revolutionary national government'.[6]

Another plea for change issued from the religious milieu, exemplified by Abelhamid Ben Badis (1889–1940), a Muslim scholar who in 1931 launched an association of *ulema* (groups of Islamic scholars). This effort formed part of an Islamic revivalism throughout the Muslim world following creation of the influential Muslim Brotherhood in Egypt in 1928. Ben Badis became famous for the declaration 'Islam is my religion, Arabic is my language and Algeria is my fatherland', a succinct affirmation of cultural and political identity.

The election in France in 1936 of a coalition government of radicals and socialists supported by Communists boosted hopes of reform among Algerian nationalists. The Popular Front aimed to create a 'third force' between conservative *pieds-noirs* and increasingly militant anti-colonialists, but even proposals for limited reforms foundered on bitter opposition from *pieds-noirs*. Meanwhile, a general conference of nationalist organizations largely adopted the principles of the Étoile Nord-Africaine, provoking a French crackdown. The French banned several nationalist groups, including in 1937 Messali's Parti du Peuple Algérien, and sent Messali to prison. By the end of the 1930s, Evans judges that chances for satisfaction of Muslim grievances within a reformed colonial state were effectively dead.[7]

The Second World War raised new questions about French rule. The Algiers government sided with the collaborationist Vichy regime and further strengthened political repression – in 1941, Abbas was arrested for alleged complicity in a mutiny. The government also implemented Pétain's 'national revolution', including anti-Semitic measures, with much support from *pieds-noirs*. Allied military forces retook Algeria at the end of 1942, Free France established a provisional headquarters in Algiers, and North African soldiers took part in the Liberation of mainland France – a contribution that only gained recognition decades later. After his release in 1943, Abbas issued a 'Manifesto of the Algerian People', which called for self-determination for Algeria. When the French predictably rejected the demand, Abbas joined Messali to reiterate the goal of a self-governing Algerian republic, though one formally affiliated with France. The French banned their new organization, and re-arrested the two men. General de Gaulle, leader of the Free French, ruled out independence for any of the French overseas territories, and many *Français d'Algérie* hoped for a return to the pre-war status quo.

Algerian frustrations exploded on 'V-E Day', Victory in Europe day. On 8 May 1945, as the French celebrated the end of the war with Germany, protesters in Sétif, in eastern Algeria, demanded the release of Messali and Abbas. The demonstration degenerated into a riot, with the killing of 102 Europeans, and attacks on European shops and Catholic churches. Reports of the violence, including the rape of women and the mutilation of corpses of French victims, led to an immediate French response of frenzied violence. The official French figure at the time was 1,020 deaths at the hand of the army or settler militias; later historians' estimates range from 3,000 to 30,000. The French followed up with the arrest of several thousand Algerians; almost a hundred were sentenced to execution. Violence also broke out in Guelma; after the killing of 12 French people, settler militias killed around 1,500 Muslims. Although the French in 1946 declared an amnesty for those involved in the violence, and political prisoners such as Abbas and Messali were released, what became known as the Sétif and Guelma massacres further inflamed both anti-colonial sentiments and defence of Algérie Française. Views polarized amidst a climate of heightened fear and suspicion. The French abolished the 'native code' in 1946, and a new statute for Algeria established an Algerian Assembly (still with separate and unequal Muslim and European electoral colleges), granted the vote to women, and provided greater recognition for Arabic. The changes sparked ire from *Français d'Algérie* but failed to reconcile nationalists. From 1948, nationalist paramilitary units began to stockpile weapons and train recruits in guerrilla warfare.

As time passed, Algerian nationalist demands became in French eyes ever more intractable, and token reforms no longer offered enough when India and Indonesia, and the French territories of Lebanon and Syria, gained independence in the 1940s. The Vietnamese, from 1946, were fighting a war of independence, providing inspiration and suggesting tactics for the Algerians. Overthrow of the monarchy in Egypt in 1952 and promotion of Algerian decolonization and pan-Arabic cooperation by that country's new leader, Gamal Abdel Nasser, further emboldened activists. A meeting of newly decolonized countries and non-aligned states at Bandung in Indonesia in 1955 underlined the growing strength of global anti-colonialism. Though some Algerian nationalists did not demand full and immediate independence, and pursued largely peaceful strategies of parliamentary campaigns, demonstrations and lobbying, a more aggressive nationalism spread through religious schools, reconstituted political movements, international networks, recruitment drives and clandestine training camps. Despite French suppression of dissent through censorship, imprisonment and harassment, and sharp internal divisions, the movement against the French was gaining force.

Nine years after Sétif, unparalleled violent incidents surprised the French and touched off a war lasting for years. After paramilitary nationalist cells had mounted one attack a week on the French and 'loyalist' Muslims in early 1954, seventy synchronized attacks occurred during the night between 31 October and the 1 November public holiday. A further 178 attacks followed in November and 201 in December. Nationalists also set up a new organization, the FLN, announcing a goal of 'national independence through restoration of the Algerian state, sovereign, democratic, and social, within the framework of the principles of Islam'. Struggle would be 'by every means', including armed actions and the use of violence, though the FLN's manifesto held out an offer for 'discussion with the French authorities'. If demands were met, 'French cultural and economic interests will be respected, as well as persons and families'; the *Français d'Algérie* could opt for citizenship in an independent state (or otherwise remain there as foreigners).[8] The FLN benefited from grassroots organization, trained cadres, a newly formed Armée de Libération Nationale (ALN), international support (especially from Arab countries) and donations raised, sometimes by coercion, in Algeria and the diaspora.

Algeria now descended into a cycle of violence and counter-violence, punctuated by periods of relative calm. 'Violence was central to FLN culture', according to Evans,[9] and the FLN intentionally carried out random attacks on the French, sparing no one. Their targets extended to Muslims either considered loyal to the French or who refused to support the independence struggle; increasingly, victims included members of rival political groups. In the catalogue of violence, the 'Philippeville Massacre' in August 1955 marked a particularly deadly attack, in which 123 French people – from a five-day-old infant to a 73-year-old – were murdered; the French responded with reprisals that took the lives of more than 1,200 people, and by some accounts ten times that number.

Gendering resistance

Many FLN and ALN operatives were young men trained in the Front's camps and told that they were *moudjahidin* fighting a holy war. Women participated, though in relatively small numbers (about 1,700 in the *maquis,* the underground) and most commonly as nurses, cooks or messengers.[10] Some male commanders were unhappy with non-traditional gender roles and the mingling of men and women in guerrilla camps; one FLN commander in 1960 promised that 'in independent Algeria, the freedom of Muslim women stops at the step of the door. A woman will never be the equal of a man.' Yet women's support roles proved extremely valuable, and women such as Djamila Bouhired (b. 1935) and Zohra Drif (b. 1934) assumed front-line positions.

Drif's memoir provides a fascinating perspective on the war from inside. She comments of the history of colonial Algeria: 'We Algerians had our truth while the French had their own'. From a middle-class family, she attended a French secondary school where she enjoyed studies of French literature, and was exposed to radical ideas by a Communist history and geography teacher. As an adolescent, she understood that 'I was forbidden to be "Algerian" and expected to be "French" – yes, "French Muslim", but French nonetheless'. The news of the French military defeat by nationalists in Vietnam in 1954, the year of her graduation, showed that 'France was not invincible'. Drif then began studying law, her parents supportive but aware that 'the racist and discriminatory colonial system . . . offered nothing to their daughter, and made nothing easy for her'. 'Sadly, the university taught us nothing about our country or our people', but while there she began attending political meetings. In 1955, Drif was visiting a spa town in France at the time of the Philippeville massacre and 'wondered if these peaceful inhabitants [even] knew where Algeria was'.

Back in Algeria, Drif's first contacts with the FLN came soon afterwards, and she started covertly passing messages for the militants. In doing so, she began to discover unfamiliar parts of Algiers such as the casbah, which she had earlier considered a place of 'dangerous gambling dens and houses of ill repute'; 'the casbah introduced me to the generosity of the humblest of the humble'. Drif remarked in particular that it was women who kept alive Algerian identity and history, resisted the French through the years of colonization and now provided refuge for the independence fighters pursued by the police:

> I will never stop paying homage to these women: they not only maintained the fire in the hearth of our hearts so that our flame would never be extinguished even

in the worst of storms . . . . We were nothing without them – without them being the first to confront the noise and fury of the French soldiers, their police, and the *harki* traitors who collaborated with them.

Her political positions gradually hardened, as reflected in language she used in response to the killing of Muslims by a militia that also alludes to France's own revolutionaries: 'the descendants of Robespierre and Danton were acting as worthy heirs of Hitler.' Inducted into an armed FLN group, she proclaimed: 'We had always considered it better to die with honour in the armed struggle for dignity and liberty than to survive in the disgrace of tolerating colonialism.' Drif personally became involved in violent assaults on the French. On 30 September 1956, along with two other female militants, she placed a bomb in the popular Milk Bar in Algiers, a site she chose as it 'symbolized colonial modernity in the service of the Europeans, their offensive carefree attitude, their shameful indifference to our woes, and the arrogance of the colonial regime'. The explosion killed three people and wounded dozens. In her memoir, Drif responded to an inevitable question:

> Perhaps the reader of today expects me to regret having placed bombs in public places frequented by European civilians. I do not. To do so would be to obscure the central problem of settler colonialism by trying to pass off the European civilians of the day for (at best) mere tourists visiting Algeria or (at worst) the 'natural' inheritors of our land in place of its legitimate children.

Describing her arrest and detention, the memoir closes in 1957, a thoughtful, articulate, sometimes chilling book by a self-described 'frail girl whose crime was wanting the independence of her country'.[11]

Not all supporters of the FLN, male or female, however, engaged in or condoned such violence. A few Algerian Muslim women, like some male counterparts, indeed backed the French; Nafissa Sid Cara (1910-2002), for instance, in 1959 was elected to parliament and became the first woman minister in a French government. French authorities proclaimed that female suffrage, social programmes aimed at women and new legislation on marriage and divorce emancipated women, and it invested considerable funds in attempts to win support from rural women. The French also encouraged Muslim women to cast off face coverings and headscarves, sometimes forcing them to do so; such actions and bodily searches of women suspected of carrying weapons or nationalist communications added to resentment.[12]

Continuing the war

The French government underlined its determination to retain control over Algeria, though offering a few concessions to nationalists. It responded to FLN offensives by reprisals, arrests, intelligence-gathering and an increase in troops in Algeria – soldiers eventually numbered over 400,000 (and 2.3 million Frenchmen, most of them conscripts to national military service, served in Algeria during the war). The army devised strategies of *quadrillage*, the establishment of a dense network of small garrisons, and *regroupement*, forcible resettlement of rural Algerians into supposedly 'safe' areas outside FNL infiltration. Both policies failed and provoked further hostility.

In 1956 and 1957, attention focused on the 'Battle of Algiers' (made famous in a fictionalized 1966 film by Gillo Pontecorvo that was long banned in France) This was not a battle in the conventional sense, but a series of actions over a number of months, beginning with the 30 September 1956 Milk Bar bombing. Images of the carnage at the ice-cream parlour, and other FLN attacks, proudly claimed as victories by the nationalists, infuriated the *Français d'Algérie* and shocked those in the metropole. Soldiers and police tried to root out militants in the casbah, filtering entry and exit, carrying out random searches, and engaging in other counter-insurgence activities. They located dozens of bombs, detonators and explosives and made hundreds of arrests, among them Larbi Ben M'hidi (1923–57), who questionably was reported to have committed suicide in French custody; another key militant, known as Ali la Pointe (1930–57), died when the French blew up a building in which he was hiding. Yet another victim was a young French mathematician, Maurice Audin (1932–57), a Communist supporter of the nationalists who died after torture by the French. Frequent reports had already circulated of French torture of Muslim suspects by waterboarding (submerging prisoners' heads in buckets of water to the point of suffocation), electric shocks on sensitive parts of the body including the genitals, the hanging of prisoners upside down then letting them fall rapidly (sometimes dislocating limbs), beatings, and sleep and food deprivation, as well as summary execution. Torture, it has been documented, was widely practised and systematic, and French administrators, officers and judges generally fostered a climate where such abuse was possible and condoned.[13] The nationalists also engaged in wanton violence and threats; when 300 villagers in the town of Mélouze refused to support the FLN, for instance, the ALN killed all of them and mutilated the corpses. Whenever elections were held, the FLN warned that it would kill any Muslim who dared to vote.

Any middle ground between militant nationalists and defenders of Algérie Française had disappeared, and extreme violence on both sides instigated visceral reactions and barricaded positions. After the Battle of Algiers, the French army managed to regain some lost ground, but the long-term French position was undermined as Algerian opinion rallied behind a resilient FLN; *pieds-noirs* harboured growing suspicion about government overtures to the nationalists. Already early in 1956, Europeans in Algiers pelted the visiting prime minister, Guy Mollet, with rotten tomatoes because of rumours that he favoured a negotiated political solution to the Algerian affair. International opinion was meanwhile moving against France. Paris in 1956 reluctantly conceded independence to the protectorates of Morocco and Tunisia, where there existed much sympathy for the Algerian nationalists. In the same year, Egypt's President Nasser nationalized the Suez Canal, an action regarded as a sign of his radicalism, distancing from the West and threats to Israel at a time when the Cold War divided the world into hostile camps. A joint French, British and Israeli military attack on Egypt in October proved a humiliation as coalition forces were forced to retreat under UN and US pressure and seriously tarnished

France's reputation, but strengthened Nasser's position as a patron for the Algerian nationalists and bolstered the FLN. In the *métropole*, opposition to the war had become open and strong, spreading beyond supporters of the FLN. Use of conscripted soldiers, the cost of the operations, lack of success at 'pacification' and the issue of torture made the war increasingly unpopular. Politics in the Fourth Republic, furthermore, were unstable, with rapid changes of prime ministers and cabinets because of the difficulty of any party gaining a parliamentary majority under the constitution of the Fourth Republic.

The nomination of a new government, under Pierre Pflimlin, was approved by the National Assembly on 13 May 1958; at least to the *Français d'Algérie*, it seemed that the new prime minister was ready to make major concessions to the FLN. The same day large demonstrations in Algiers protested against any negotiations with the nationalists. Army officers, led by General Jacques Massu (who was credited with 'winning' the Battle of Algiers), occupied public buildings and formed a 'Committee of Public Safety', effectively taking over the local government. Rebel army units from Algeria were dispatched to Corsica, and threatened to move on to the mainland and attempt a coup. The aim of the putsch was to force the replacement of Pflimlin. The leading candidate was Charles de Gaulle; the hero of the French Resistance and the nation's most honoured soldier, now at the age of sixty-eight and largely outside politics for twelve years, remained a staunch defender of French *grandeur*. De Gaulle agreed to return to power and indeed may have manoeuvred to do so, and three days after being appointed prime minister on 1 June 1958, he flew to Algiers. From the balcony of the city hall, he intoned to cheering European crowds, 'Je vous ai compris' ('I have understood you'). The sibylline utterance appeared to them a commitment to preserve *Algérie française*.

As a condition for taking up government, de Gaulle had demanded a new constitution to replace the weak parliamentary system with a strong executive presidency, and he duly won election as first president of the new Fifth French Republic. De Gaulle then organized balloting in which each French overseas territory (as colonies were now called) – though not Algeria – chose between remaining part of a new French *Communauté* and retaining French rule, or gaining independence; the latter option, he warned, meant termination of French aid and support. For Algeria, de Gaulle announced a programme of public works and government investment, the Constantine Plan, with promises of 400,000 jobs and 200,000 new houses. All Muslims were finally made French citizens. The president nonetheless ruled out negotiations with the FLN, which did not budge in its demands.

It is unclear when de Gaulle decided that independence for Algeria served France's interest. By 1959, the army had recovered greater control over Algeria, but de Gaulle, it seems, considered the war a diversion from his projects for French economic and social modernization, plans for the European Economic Community (established in 1957, and now the European Union), and Paris's relations with the Third World. He nevertheless pursued the war, despite ever louder calls within France for its termination and such statements as a 'Manifesto of 121', in which leading intellectuals in 1960 called on conscripts to refuse to fight in Algeria.

Quietly de Gaulle was sending out feelers to the FLN. In September 1959, he first publicly uttered the words 'self-determination' as a possibility for Algeria, and in

November 1960, he used the phrase '*Algérie algérienne*'. This seemed to defenders of *Algérie française* to foreshadow French withdrawal – treason, in their view. In January 1961, de Gaulle put to the electorate a referendum on self-determination for Algeria; three-quarters overall, and more than two-thirds in Algeria, approved. This further alarmed *pieds-noirs* and led to the formation of the OAS, which stood ready to disobey the government and mount terrorist attacks to forestall Algerian independence. Its supporters included several senior retired French military officers, Generals Raoul Salan, Maurice Challe and Edmond Jouhaud, and a former governor general of Algeria, Jacques Soustelle. In April 1961, the military cohort staged a putsch in Algiers, occupying key government offices. De Gaulle took to radio and television to demand submission; the putsch collapsed and the officers involved were arrested or fled into hiding.

Against a backdrop of chaos in Algeria, Prime Minister Georges Pompidou was holding formal meetings with the FLN. A key sticking point was the future of the Sahara – over which the French hoped to retain sovereignty because of gas and oil reserves, and sites for testing nuclear weapons in the desert – though Paris finally agreed to full withdrawal.

Dilemmas of the colonizing and the colonized

For *pieds-noirs*, Algerian Muslims and Algerian Jews, the war and the approach of independence presented a soul-wrenching situation. Decades of political pronouncements and propaganda had maintained that Algeria was truly part of France, and the *Français d'Algérie* considered themselves not a transient population but a people rooted in a land they had made their own. Among them was Albert Camus, French Algeria's most famous intellectual of European background. His mother was of Spanish ancestry; his father, an agricultural worker, died in the First World War, the year after Camus's birth in 1913. Camus grew up in very poor circumstances in Algiers, where his mother worked as a cleaner, a childhood movingly depicted in his posthumously published autobiographical novel *Le Premier Homme*. Camus evoked the torrid summer heat, the cramped apartment where he lived with his brother, mother, grandmother and an uncle, the colours and sounds of streets and markets, the many privations and rare treats, but also the pleasures of school-boy friendships, football (soccer) and study. For Camus, education opened a wider world – neither his mother nor his grandmother could read or write – yet without the encouragement of a dearly beloved teacher, he would have been unlikely to go past primary school. Camus won a scholarship to the *lycée*, graduated with a degree in philosophy from the University of Algiers, and became a journalist and writer in France. During the Second World War, he took an active part in the Resistance and edited its newspaper.

Camus was linked to the *Algérianiste* movement, though without sharing their more fanciful views about restoring ancient European civilization to North Africa. Deeply imbued with the culture of the Mediterranean, Camus wrote lyrically about the 'nationalism of the sun'. Yet he gained fame primarily as an existentialist novelist with *L'Étranger* (1942), *La Peste* (1947) and *La Chute* (1956), for which he won the

Nobel Prize in Literature in 1957. Camus's empathy with the Muslim Algerians was manifest, and he declared their grievances well founded. He deplored the violence in Algeria and promoted reconciliation between Europeans and Muslims. When that proved impossible, he revealed where his primal loyalty lay: 'I have always condemned terror. I must condemn also a terrorism that operates blindly, in the streets of Algiers for example, and which one day can strike my mother or my family. I believe in justice, but I will defend my mother before justice.' The statement was understood as a sign of support for *Algérie Française* and led to a break with fellow intellectuals who supported the independence movement. Camus, in vain, continued to seek compromise; he died in an automobile accident in 1960, before the end of the war.

A few *pieds-noirs*, however, rallied to the nationalists. Jean Sénac (1926–73) was born to an impoverished mother of Catalan origin and an unknown French father. After completing school and recovering from tuberculosis, Sénac became a promising poet mentored by Camus, and published his first book in 1954, just as the Algerian War began. Sénac remained in France during the war, writing articles and poems identifying with both the culture of French Algeria and the nationalist cause. Immediately after independence, he flew back to Algiers – one of just a handful who journeyed in that direction as most *pieds-noirs* rushed the opposite way. He worked for the new Algerian broadcasting company, started a literary journal and published poems praising the Algerian revolution and its martyrs, yet he remained – partly because of his open homosexuality – a somewhat marginal figure. He was eventually murdered, though it seems not from political motives.[14]

Some other French people, including those without personal connections to Algeria, strongly backed decolonization. Jean-Paul Sartre and Simone de Beauvoir – novelists, philosophers, political activists and two of the best-known French cultural figures of the 1950s and 1960s – counted among them. Like other Marxists, Sartre argued in the journal *Les Temps modernes* that decolonization was a necessary part of an international revolutionary movement. Some writers of a very different political and philosophical orientation similarly pleaded for an end to the war and acceptance of Algerian self-determination, including contributors to the Catholic periodicals *Esprit* and *Témoignage chrétien*. Anti-war sentiment indeed brought together such intellectual rivals as the leftist Sartre and the conservative philosopher Raymond Aron. Some French FLN backers joined Francis Jeanson's network of '*porteurs de valise*' ('suitcase-carriers') who clandestinely carried money and papers for the independence movement out of France.[15]

For Muslim Algerians, the relationship with France was perhaps less complicated. Though there were pro-French Muslim Algerians such as Said Boualem (1906–82), colonel in the French army, member of the French parliament and founder of the Front Algérie Française, most supported the nationalist cause. Intellectuals' backing for independence can be seen in such figures as Kateb Yacine (1929–89), arguably the outstanding Algerian Muslim novelist of his time, born into a Berber family in Constantine. The son of a lawyer, Yacine was educated in religious and secular schools. Participation in demonstrations in 1945, at the time of the Sétif and Guelma massacres, led to his expulsion from school and imprisonment. Yacine then worked as a longshoreman, and joined the Communist Party in 1947. He lived abroad from 1950 to 1959, travelling widely because of harassment by French security services, and earned plaudits for his French-language surrealistic novel *Nedjma* (1956). Yacine returned to Algeria after independence, became involved in theatre, and for a time ceased publishing in French. The views of men such as Camus and Sénac, Boualem and Yacine illustrate how cultures intertwined under colonialism, and the difficult personal choices individuals faced in the midst of wars of decolonization.

The rapatriés *and the memory of the Algerian War*

Europeans left Algeria in large numbers over the months before the ceasefire in March 1962, and the exodus then accelerated, with 300,000 fleeing in July 1962 alone. Some *pieds-noirs* burned their houses or set their cars alight rather than abandoning them to fall into Algerian hands, and the OAS destroyed such facilities as the university library). They struggled for passage on crowded ships or airplanes, carrying belongings packed into the two suitcases allowed. The *rapatriés* ('repatriated', as they were termed) arrived in France as angry and traumatized refugees, though with full rights of citizenship. They sought shelter with family and friends, but more often lodged in rudimentary government barracks. Some continued their journeys, settling in Spain, France's remaining overseas territories or elsewhere. French compatriots did not offer a warm welcome to those sometimes castigated as unrepentant colonialists and racists, and demeaned as rustic and vulgar. They were considered a drain on French state finances and competitors for jobs and housing. Even less cordially received were the *harkis*, Muslims who had fought alongside the French (and Muslim civilians who had backed the French). De Gaulle decided that France would not 'repatriate' the *harkis*, though private networks spirited many into France, where the French reluctantly took them in charge. They languished for years in camps, sometimes the facilities built by the German occupiers for French prisoners during the Second World War. Even afterwards they continued to suffer racial discrimination. In Algeria, meanwhile, *harkis* and French sympathizers were branded traitors, and some who remained after the war were killed.

For decades after the war, *rapatriés* expressed resentment at 'abandonment' by the French state, loss of assets despite compensation eventually provided by the French government, and the failure of compatriots to recognize what they considered the achievements of the *Française d'Algérie*. The *pieds-noirs*, in fact, often did well in France, contributing skills and labour to the economic boom that continued through the 1960s. A number of Algerian-born French men and women, including ones who did not oppose independence, became prominent – the literary critic Jacques Derrida, the feminist theorist Hélène Cixous, the philosophers Louis Althusser and Bernard-Henri Levy, and the fashion designer Yves Saint Laurent. Not all of the *rapatriés* made efforts to nurture a *pied-noir* culture – food, music, a particular accent – though many joined *pied-noir* associations, wrote memoirs and eventually visited Algeria as tourists. Some *pieds-noirs*, and soldiers who served in the war, however, became active in extreme right-wing organizations such as the anti-immigrant and anti-Muslim Front National (now called the Rassemblement National); its founder, Jean-Marie Le Pen, had been an army officer in Algeria accused of mistreatment of Arab prisoners.[16]

In Algeria, the war of independence occupies a central position in the national narrative, with the FLN playing the leading role. The orthodox view stresses a unified anti-colonialist movement and the righteousness of resistance. Monuments celebrating the French were often taken down (and occasionally brought back to France), and colonialist street names have been changed; old churches and particularly synagogues have been transformed into mosques. Demands have been made for restitution of art and artefacts in French collections and for apologies – which to date have not been forthcoming – for colonial misdeeds.

The war inspired a vast outpouring of scholarly literature, memoirs, novels, films, television documentaries, artwork and exhibitions; one bibliography of publications just from 1954 to 1995 runs to four hundred pages. Historians still heatedly debate the record of colonialism and the war, with particularly politicized discussion centring on torture and other acts of extreme violence, the exact number of people killed, whether the French military was defeated or could have held on to Algeria and whether the *Français d'Algérie* were 'abandoned'. Even the notion of 'war' was a matter of contention; since Algeria was officially part of France, military intervention involved operations for the 'maintenance of law and order'. Not until 1999 did the French parliament officially recognize the conflict as a 'war'.[17] Dates, too, have been subject to dispute; some veterans' organizations campaigned for streets to be named '18 March 1962' in commemoration of the war's end, while others retorted that Algerian attacks on *pieds-noirs* after the ceasefire made the name inappropriate. Meanwhile, the heritage of the Algerian War has become linked to domestic issues. The presence of large numbers of North Africans and their descendants in France, including migrants who arrived in increasing numbers after the war, became a subject manipulated by opponents of migration from the 1970s onwards. Anti-Muslim and anti-migrant feelings surged, leading to retorts that French policies towards people of non-European background remained racist and still colonial. Debates around multiculturalism and the role of religion and *laïcité* (secularism) in French society focused in the 1980s on the wearing of headscarves and face coverings by some Muslim women. Such issues have spread into wider discussions about the nature of French identity and the history of French colonialism.

The way in which the war was remembered or forgotten is a subject for competing views.[18] The Algerian-born French historian Benjamin Stora, an authoritative and prolific scholar who has done more than any other to unravel the history of colonial Algeria, in 1991 published *La Gangrène et l'oubli* ('Gangrene and forgetfulness'). In essence, Stora argued that the French after 1962 tried to move beyond the trauma of the war, but this involved an intentional occlusion in public memory of its horrors. Stora said that the French must ultimately come to terms with violence, the record of colonization and the repercussions of the war. His study inspired an intensification of research and debate. New confessions about torture that surfaced in France in 2000, especially when the retired General Paul Aussaresses stated that he had personally taken part in torture of prisoners (and refused to apologize for doing so), and the FLN militant Louisette

Ighilahriz spoke about how she had been abused and tortured. The revelations opened old wounds and again brought the war to French attention. They called into question French behaviour and pointed to the side-lining of the war in national narrative and memory. That provoked new defences, especially among *pieds-noirs* and former soldiers, about tactics said to have been necessary to save the lives of people menaced by terrorism; they said such accusatory views represented attempts to besmirch the honour of the military. In 2005, the French parliament passed a law recognizing the 'positive' aspects of French colonialism, and requiring instruction in schools about French achievements in North Africa; the clause concerned with education caused an outcry, and was suspended on a technicality. The war thus remains an enduring theme in historical study and in public life.

The Franco-Algerian War was a signpost event in French history and the history of decolonization. It provided a major French preoccupation for years, and became entangled in global issues such as the Cold War, and the rise of the 'new left' and social protest movements. With elements of a civil war, it pitted Algerians against Algerians, and French against French, as well as against each other. The conflict brought down the government of the Fourth Republic, structured the institutions of the Fifth Republic and influenced the evolution of French society. On the other side of the Mediterranean, it led to an 'Algerian revolution' whose promises of remaking society to secure peace and prosperity turned into disappointment and recrimination under an authoritarian regime and in civil war. The heritage of the war indelibly marked the lives of many French and Algerian people, with the imprint visible in the two countries more than half a century afterwards.

CHAPTER 27
THE PORTUGUESE EMPIRE IN AFRICA, 1971

Portugal 1961-1971: A Decade of Progress was the title of an anonymously authored illustrated booklet 'presented by the Overseas Companies of Portugal' in the early 1970s. Published in English, the brochure addressed an international audience, particularly in the United States, where the businesses were represented by a 'public relations counsel' based in Washington. The Overseas Companies of Portugal described themselves as 'an organization of companies that have business interests in Portugal and [the] Portuguese Overseas provinces' – the authoritarian Portuguese state presided over by António de Oliveira Salazar had rebranded the colonies as 'provinces' in 1951.[1] In fact, the companies and their representatives in the United States were 'an intermediary through which the Salazar government could operate with anonymity' and 'publicize Portugal's policies and achievements in Angola and other Overseas territories', as critical observers had already pointed out in the 1960s.[2]

A Decade of Progress tried to convey – with colour photographs of development projects, and tables of economic and social data – Portugal's 'major achievements' in the 'political, social and economic' realms in recent years. A free trade agreement with the European Common Market (later integrated into the European Union) was seen as a further asset when promoting 'modern' Portugal and its colonies as reliable destinations for foreign investment. Portugal was 'catch[ing] up with the rest of Europe' and the world: 'a small country, with a great history but with scant natural resources and at the bottom of Europe's economic' tables was now moving 'into a new dimension'; with regard to the colonies, assumptions of '"a great leap forward" . . . would not be misplaced'. The claims were underlined with images of large university buildings, modern operating theatres in hospitals, and huge multinational dam projects for electricity and irrigation under construction in Angola and Mozambique. Photographs of international airports, port facilities and railways symbolized the arteries of modern trade, while shots of sunny beaches pointed to the rapidly expanding tourist industry.[3]

A Decade of Progress exemplifies how political elites' notions of the evolution of the colonies and metropolitan Portugal intertwined through the 1960s and 1970s, both in official rhetoric and in popular imagination. Furthermore, jumping on the bandwagon of 'modernization theory', with its promises of 'modernity' and 'progress' through economic and social development, offers a reminder that the Portuguese Empire at least in its policies was pursuing a path shared with other European countries. The difference was that by 1971 Britain, France, the Netherlands and Belgium had largely withdrawn from their colonies, yet Portugal had not. The themes presented in *A Decade of Progress* provide a common thread for a discussion of the last decades of what has been termed the 'third Portuguese empire' in its two largest colonies, Angola and Mozambique, before they gained independence in 1975. In large part, this is a history of aspirations and delusions, given Portugal's financial and political constraints, as well as the repressive nature of the *Estado Novo* (New State).

Portugal's new state: Nation and empire, 1930s–70s

The quest for 'modernity' pervades the twentieth century. In Portugal, among the major landmarks labelled as modern was the 'magnificent Salazar suspension bridge', today called the 25 de Abril bridge, in honour of the 1974 revolution that overthrew the authoritarian government in power since the 1930s. The bridge stretches over 2 kilometres and connects Lisbon, Portugal's capital, with the municipality of Almada, on the south bank of the Tagus river. Construction began in 1962 and the inauguration came in August 1966, months ahead of schedule, 'provid[ing] a great stimulus to the burgeoning economy of the South of Portugal', as the bridge and its impact was heralded in *A Decade of Progress*. The original name of the bridge honoured Portugal's long-term leader, António de Oliveira Salazar. A trained economist, Salazar became minister of finance in 1928, and served as prime minister from 1932 until 1968, ceding government to Marcello Caetano only after he suffered a stroke. Portugal's 1933 constitution founded the *Estado Novo*, a one-party system under which the secret police, the Polícia Internacional e de Defesa do Estado (PIDE, International and State Defense Police), suppressed dissent, and elections became mere window-dressing. The regime's slogan, 'God, Fatherland, Family', symbolized its conservative and traditionalist orientation.[4] In retrospect, observers quipped that the state championed 'fado, Fátima *e futebol*' to keep the population in check – an allusion to Portugal's melancholic folk music, the supposed apparition of the Virgin Mary to a group of young shepherds in 1916 (an important event in a strongly Catholic country) and the national sport of soccer.

Technocratic management from the centre and PIDE's long and heavy arm guaranteed the survival of the regime long after the other dictatorships of the 1930s had disappeared. In fact, it was the protracted anti-colonial guerrilla wars in the African colonies, ongoing since 1961, that finally brought down the undemocratic government in Lisbon during the 'Carnation Revolution' of 1974 that was spearheaded by disenchanted military officers, many of whom had served in Africa.[5]

Geopolitical factors, as well as the tight rein of the Salazar government, had contributed to the long life of the *Estado Novo*. Portugal's strategic location near the Strait of Gibraltar provided access to the Mediterranean, and military bases on the Azores, a group of volcanic Portuguese islands in the North Atlantic Ocean, were key in the security strategy of the North Atlantic Treaty Organisation (NATO); Portugal was a founding member of the Western alliance against Communism in 1949. Lisbon's strategic assets and anti-Communist stance prompted Western acquiescence for continuing Portuguese colonialism well into the 1960s and 1970s.

After the loss of Brazil in the 1820s, the Portuguese overseas empire encompassed two very large colonies, Angola in western Africa and Mozambique in eastern Africa.

Portugal also claimed the smaller Guinea-Bissau in western Africa, and Cape Verde, and São Tomé and Príncipe off the African coast, the enclave of Goa (and the tiny nearby territories of Diu and Daman) on the western Indian coast, Portuguese Timor in the East Indies and Macau on the South China Sea. These were the remains, although substantial ones, of a once much more extensive Portuguese Empire acquired in the 1500s when Portuguese ships pioneered new routes from Europe to the Americas, Africa and Asia.

In the mid-twentieth century, the regime in Lisbon promoted Portugal as a 'pluri-continental' and 'multi-racial' nation stretching around the globe. Ever since the days of early Portuguese colonialism, official rhetoric built on what the Brazilian anthropologist and sociologist Gilberto Freyre termed *Lusotropicalismo*: the supposedly unique Portuguese skills of cultural adaptation and fusion in the tropics. What the Portuguese called a 'pluri-continental nation', in which colonial 'provinces' were considered fully integrated regions of Portugal, and the myth of the multiracial nation, provided legal and ideological constructs that shielded Portugal from growing international criticism of colonialism. After Portugal joined the United Nations in 1955, countering anti-colonial resolutions supported by the dozens of newly independent countries from Asia and Africa that had joined the international organization became even more difficult. In the 1970s, designating the colonies as 'provinces' and the trope of the egalitarian and good-hearted Portuguese could no longer suffice to legitimize domination.[6]

For the ruling elite in Portugal, however, the empire remained one of the ideological pillars of the regime. Salazar and Caetano drew on the country's long history of sailors and explorers – celebrated in Luís Vaz de Camões' *The Lusiads* (1572), Portugal's national epic – and the Portuguese, in general, equated nation and empire. As an oft-repeated phrase put it, 'Portugal is not a small country' precisely because of its colonies. In this imperial world view, Portugal included not only cities such as Lisbon and Porto but Luanda (in Angola), Lourenço Marques (today's Maputo, Mozambique) and Bissau (Guinea-Bissau), as well as Macau and Dili (East Timor). Famously superimposed over Europe, a map of Portugal and its overseas territories stretched across a large portion of the continent (see Figure 27.1). While Portugal accounted for 8.5 million inhabitants around 1970, in Salazar's propaganda 'Greater Portugal' – in the Portuguese imagination citizens of the colonies but also Brazilians and Portuguese emigrants around the globe – comprised over 100 million Portuguese speakers.[7]

Given the historical and ideological entanglements between empire and nation, Portugal's elite and government feared that the disintegration of the empire would necessarily bring about the end of the regime in Lisbon as well. Cultural and ideological issues, rather than the economics of empire, thus explain Portugal's last stand as a colonial power and the protracted wars it waged in Africa against armed anti-colonial resistance in Angola from 1961, Guinea-Bissau from 1963 and Mozambique from 1964. Nationalist movements had indeed been gaining traction from the 1950s, since Lisbon made few concessions to power-sharing with the majority African populations. Moreover, forced labour practices and the maintenance of separate juridical categories of *indígenas*, *assimilados* (those considered to have assimilated into Western culture

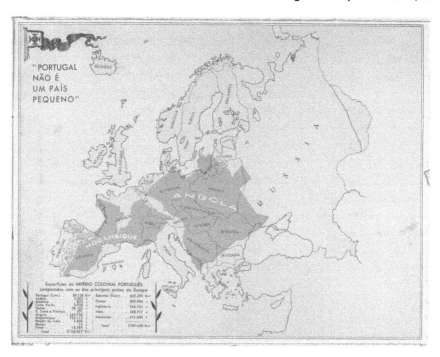

Figure 27.1 'Portugal Is Not a Small Country'. Propaganda map, 1934. © Cornell University – PJ Mode Collection of Persuasive Cartography.

through language, education or employment) and Europeans until 1961 heightened resentment against Portuguese domination.

As in other cases of anti-colonial nationalism, competing parties and movements with varying ideologies and strategies emerged. The Movimento Popular de Libertação de Angola (MPLA, People's Movement for the Liberation of Angola) was an urban and socialist-leaning group founded in 1956 under the leadership of António Agostinho Neto (1922–79), mostly supported by the Mbundu people. While the MPLA was able to open a front against the Portuguese in rural eastern Angola in the mid-1960s, clashes with rival anti-colonial movements in the colony, such as the Frente Nacional de Libertação de Angola (FNLA, National Liberation Front of Angola) of Holden Roberto (1923–2007), supported predominantly by the Bakongo people, and the União Nacional para a Independência Total de Angola (UNITA, National Union for the Total Independence of Angola) founded in 1966 by Jonas Savimbi (1934–2002), were not uncommon. In Mozambique the Frente de Libertação de Moçambique (FRELIMO, Mozambican Liberation Front) formed a multi-ethnic umbrella organization of several nationalist movements founded in 1962 and led by Eduardo Mondlane (1920–69). After Mondlane's death, revolutionaries such as Samora Machel (1933–86) pushed FRELIMO and then independent Mozambique towards Marxist-Leninism. The Partido Africano para a Independência da Guiné e Cabo Verde (PAIGC, African Party for the Independence of Guinea and Cape Verde) found a charismatic leader in the intellectual and poet Amílcar Cabral (1924–73). Even though Cabral was killed in a putsch by fellow nationalists, Guinea-Bissau was the first of the Portuguese colonies in Africa to declare independence in 1973, though Portugal recognized its independence only after the Carnation Revolution. The different parties in both countries show the regional, ethnic, ideological and personal fractures that marked independence movements, in the Portuguese colonies as in many others.

The anti-colonial movements connected with each other through an organization set up in Morocco in 1961. International support was widespread but changed over the course of the wars. While the United States initially sponsored FRELIMO, Scandinavian countries and their non-governmental organizations along with nations such as East Germany, Cuba, the Soviet Union and China provided funding, military matériel and medical training. Western European countries such as Italy similarly sponsored the education of medical personnel from the African liberation movements. Pope Paul VI received the leaders of the three major anti-colonial parties in Rome in 1970, a major shift from the Catholic Church's earlier attitudes towards the anti-colonial movements in the Portuguese territories.

When Salazar left power in 1968, many in the colonies and Portugal hoped in vain that Caetano, his successor, would bring peace and reform. The political thaw did not materialize and the costly wars in Africa dragged on until the revolution in Lisbon brought the fighting to an end in 1974. Conflicts among the anti-colonial movements and the differing interests of the West and the East during the global Cold War, however, dragged the newly independent countries into long-lasting civil wars.

Over thirteen years of colonial warfare, close to a million conscripts, about 20 per cent of Portugal's male population, had been sent to the theatres of war in Angola, Guinea-Bissau and Mozambique. Many officials and soldiers manifested scant commitment to the struggle against guerrilla forces in the harsh African environment far away from their homeland. One soldier, identified only as Luís in a study of soldiers' letters home, was an officer from Braga in northern Portugal; born in 1945, he served two terms in Africa, in Angola in the mid-1960s and Mozambique in the early 1970s. Luís's letters to his girlfriend and later wife Teresa expressed growing scepticism and doubts about the war:

> I will tell you honestly what I think of this war.. . . Today, as a man and as an officer in an army fighting for a cause that is not his own, I wonder if this is the right way to preserve the interests of our community. We are fighting on three fronts, against peoples whom we have been subjugating for centuries and who remain in utmost poverty, in a struggle without glory and with dubious results. I saw men falling at my side and I could not keep silent about this pressing question that was always on my lips: who benefits from these deaths, what is the use of another life lost? How many times have I clenched my teeth in anger. I have carried on, yet without conviction.[8]

In addition to increasing individual concerns, junior officers as a group feared becoming the regime's villains, held responsible for the eventual loss of the empire, as had been the case (although on a smaller scale) when India invaded and occupied the enclaves of Goa and Diu in 1961. Loosely organized into the Movimento das Forças Armadas (MFA, Armed Forces Movement) in Portugal and the colonies from the early 1970s, it was such disheartened and dissident army captains who staged the almost bloodless insurrection in Lisbon in 1974. Putting an end to both the dictatorial government and the colonial wars had been joint goals of the MFA, yet the establishment of democracy in Portugal was a work in progress, and the political orientation of the new government and the path towards decolonization remained uncertain.

Colonial and metropolitan tropes of modernization and development

'Change' had acquired many meanings and was occurring on various levels in Portugal and the colonies before the 1974 revolution. 'A new lower middle class, working families with motor cars, better fed and better dressed people' counted among the social and economic transformations of Portugal in the 1960s, as depicted in the 1972 booklet introduced earlier. Portugal 'has seen the rise of a working-class life-style from conditions of relative poverty to standards approaching those enjoyed elsewhere in Western Europe'. For the colonies the picture was even 'much more dramatic, despite the handicap of nagging guerrilla wars'. 'In ten years the Budget for Mozambique has doubled. In Angola the Budget is three times what it was in 1961': proof of investment and economic vitality. Exports of petroleum and mineral resources such as diamonds had increased 400 per cent between 1961 and 1971, and attendance at primary schools in Angola had skyrocketed by 500 per cent. The 1960s saw growing numbers of automobiles on new highway systems, an increasing 'amount of electricity used per head of the population' and a rise in per capita meat consumption – statistics proudly cited as indices of development and progress.[9] Yet the Portuguese government, through the Overseas Companies' publication, painted too rosy a picture. In the 1960s and 1970s, Portugal remained one of Europe's poorest countries and illiteracy rates topped 30 per cent. Highlighting economic growth and social progress in relative terms in the colonies allowed the regime's defenders to boast about spectacular increases while concealing the low point of departure.

Portugal, in fact, was rather late in adopting the transnational idioms of development. In Portuguese Africa the vocabulary of 'progress' and 'modernization' only gained the upper hand in the 1950s and 1960s over classic phrases about the European 'civilizing mission'.[10] Around the globe 'science', particularly applied social sciences, became the new religion and development was raised to the rank of a god. Belief in 'modernization' – more efficient farming, industrialization, greater access to education – was shared by dictatorships such as the Portuguese and the Spanish regimes, Western democracies and Communist states, and most newly independent countries. This was the 'Age of Development', as the historian Joseph M. Hodge has characterized the years between the 1930s and the 1970s. From an ideological perspective, the question seemed to be simply about the best form of modernity.[11]

Theorists and policymakers expected that development and modernization would help to stabilize societies in transition. 'Development is the new name for peace,' Pope Paul VI declared in an encyclical in 1967. Interestingly enough, in the Portuguese colonies, much of what fell under that rubric overwhelmingly benefited the Portuguese armed forces in the wars against the nationalist movements: the building of roads and communication systems, and of such infrastructure as airports and port facilities, rural development and education. Furthermore, the state channelled its investments towards the white settler communities. Mozambique counted no more than 200,000 white settlers in a population of just under eight million in 1970, and in Angola, 350,000 Europeans lived in a total population of 5.5 million. Many of the Europeans had arrived only in the 1950s and 1960s in migration organized through state-sponsored settlement schemes intended to strengthen Portuguese rule. While the authorities of other powers were dealing with receding colonial rule, the Portuguese were 'settling against the tide'.[12]

European settlement in the African colonies, moreover, was meant to shield the possessions against anti-colonial movements and provide a stimulus for modernization. Hence, the Portuguese government presented 'pacification', and defeat of the rebel forces, as 'synonymous with progress'.[13] Ideology at times trumped the logic of science, as was the case with the Portuguese colonatos, the state-run settlement schemes, in Angola and Mozambique. Efforts to portray Angola as a 'new Brazil' for cultivators – a discourse dating back to the nineteenth century – were based on assumptions that dark and therefore supposedly fertile soil was sufficient enough to produce profits for hardworking Portuguese farmers. That did not prove the case. The 'uncritical imitation of Portuguese rural reality [was] transplanted to Africa for geo-strategic, political, demographic, social and propaganda purposes', as Cláudia Castelo has suggested. The ideology of reproducing a peasant Portugal abroad, along with racist concepts about backward African agricultural practices, proved to be stronger than analysis of the quality of the soil.[14]

If Portugal shared international attitudes about the benefits of modernization, Lisbon's counter-insurgency measures were in tune with the tactics used by the British in Kenya and French in Algeria in the 1950s and 1960s against armed anti-colonial movements. Since the turn of the twentieth century, and more explicitly after 1945, military strategists had argued that pure military force would not quell insurgency. The 'hearts and minds' of the local populations had to be conquered with a promise of a better life, and an offer of development – access to potable water, medical care, education, higher wages and, in general, a better standard of living. In model villages sited at strategic locations, and purportedly safe from attacks by insurgents, the African populations were to experience a new Europeanized life. The setting up of such villages was further intended to integrate rural areas into a market-oriented economy. In essence, the whole African lifestyle, colonial planners argued, had to be transformed within a few years in order to ensure greater prosperity and thereby loyalty to the empire.

To implement this line of thought, Portuguese authorities deployed troops, alongside civilian planners, agronomists and technicians, to Africa to bring 'economic, social, and cultural progress', as colonial hardliners still insisted in 1970. The army, imperial propaganda also proclaimed, was fighting for 'social justice'. The government masked expenditures allocated for colonial wars as development aid, the accounting a sleight-of-hand making Portugal, on paper, one of the largest donor countries in the Organisation for Economic Co-operation and Development. Euphemistic statistics fictitiously suggested that the Iberian country, itself considered a developing nation at the time, largely outspent France and the United States as 'partners in development' in terms of relative gross domestic products.[15]

In Angola and Mozambique more than a million people, in each case, had been forced to resettle into new villages (*aldeamentos*) during the wars of the 1960s and 1970s, and another 150,000 in Guinea-Bissau (amounting to 30 per cent of the total population of that colony). Strategic resettlement has a long colonial history, from the *reconcentrado* centres in Spanish Cuba in the 1890s and Britain's concentration camps for Boers and Africans in South Africa around 1900 to France's *camps de regroupement* in Algeria in the 1950s and 1960s. However, malnutrition, overcrowding, disease, the choice of barren land unfit for subsistence farming and administrators' general contempt for local populations contributed to high death tolls among civilians in resettlement schemes. The military mind nevertheless conceived population control and regroupment as key elements in what they claimed was the humane conduct of warfare, where civilians were separated from insurgents and presumably protected from guerrilla fighters. Military strategists around the globe regularly used fish and water metaphors: as anti-colonial guerrillas would move among people like fish in water, so the counter-revolutionary approach was to 'drain the swamp' and 'suffocate the fish'.[16]

Prejudice and lack of resources characterized much of the Portuguese army's 'development' efforts, though rhetoric promoted social action to benefit the entire population, including women and children. Children, the argument went, would gain in particular from education and protection, and gratitude and enthusiasm would engender a feeling of belonging to the Portuguese 'pluri-continental' nation. Social action, in short, would show the 'native populations' the benefits of 'the integration . . . in the PORTUGUESE NATION', the upper-case letters emphasizing the point.[17] Efforts in furthering their welfare through literacy classes, medical treatment and training in mechanics for men, and cooking and sewing for women, were regularly listed in official reports about the army's activities. Instilling trust and confidence among Africans was endorsed as a significant aspect of the military mission.[18]

Portuguese soldiers' and officials' private letters provide a reality check on imperial rhetoric and government pronouncements. Luís, the Portuguese army officer quoted earlier, described how his unit, which had actually seldom encountered the enemy in Angola, was accustomed to 'retaliate against the population that has fed them (the *turras*[19]) and given them shelter'. From Mozambique he later reported that 'with regard to the advancement of the population (*promoção das populações*) some achievements have already been made'. Among them was the foundation of an agricultural cooperative and, thanks to a tractor, the first steps towards mechanization of farming. 'The aim is to encourage the people to create a certain standard of living, i.e. to work and earn income and then spend it buying goods that will raise their "standard of living"', Luís explained in one letter. And yet, what was seen as uplifting local populations, that is, 'winning the hearts and minds' as part of the war effort, too often resulted in failure. It was again Luís who described to his wife the deplorable conditions of people, mostly the elderly and children, who lived close to the military garrison at Nangade, in the far northeast of Mozambique's Cabo Delgado district, near the Tanzanian border. Instead of providing much-needed food items, the army commander ordered large amounts of 'women's underwear', including bras and tights. For a population that lived barefoot, and went hungry, with 'children having swollen bellies' from malnutrition, the commander provided 'baby dolls!!!! . . . only to suggest that the population of Nangade has reached a social level that allows them to enter a market economy where such products are sold'. Luís underlined his indignation with multiple exclamation marks and highlighted the most disturbing aspects in capital letters.[20]

In the early phase of the wars, Portuguese strategists were convinced that whole villages could be won over by offering a piece of 'chorizo and some chocolates'. Such small gestures, planners were convinced, would mark the beginning for more 'magnificent and complex' efforts leading to the 'conquest of the people'. Despite minor and major measures, Luís asserted, in Cabo Delgado 'the population continues to flee towards the bush'. According to his reasoning, Portuguese counter-insurgency was stuck in an 'atmosphere of fantasy and lies'. Time and again, modern counter-insurgency, including forced resettlement and further 'schemes to improve the human condition', resulted in humanitarian catastrophes.[21] Ultimately, such schemes failed to win the support of the Africans that the Portuguese so confidently expected.

Gendering war, development and progress

Forced removals and regroupment of populations usually went beyond the merely military strategy of separating insurgents from civilians. Ideas of resettlement were intrinsically entangled with attitudes about modernization and development.[22] In the Portuguese case, as elsewhere, resettlement schemes can be tracked back at least to the interwar period.[23] The village, the home and particularly the family were the units where socio-economic change, engineered by the state, was supposed to take place. What was labelled development – also comprising modern counter-insurgency – became more and more gendered from the 1950s onwards. In particular, the advancement of women, including through education, was perceived within a broader social and economic framework. In this vein, participants at an international conference in Brussels in 1958 focused on 'Women's Roles in the Development of Tropical and Sub-Tropical Countries'. One of the opening addresses stated that 'to neglect the education of one half of the human race', that is, women, was 'an astonishing waste of human resources'. The United Nations extended such utilitarian arguments in the 1960s by recognizing women's essential role in development, 'both as beneficiaries and as agents of change'. One of the UN's declared goals in the following decade was 'the full integration of women in the total development effort', and the 'campaign for women's advancement' gained further traction with the UN's International Women's Year in 1975. 'Equality, development and peace' became the UN's slogan for gendered development, which echoed throughout the Portuguese Empire and elsewhere in what was pointedly called the 'developing world'.[24]

The Portuguese propaganda booklet *A Decade of Progress* reflected the rhetoric of gender, development and progress. It highlighted that women in the Portuguese world were still banned from only a few professions, among them 'distilling alcoholic liquids'. Furthermore, 'the Portuguese educational statistics show[ed] a strikingly large proportion of female students', with women totalling 40 per cent of those enrolled at university in Portugal in 1971; faculties of medicine fared well in the male-to-female ratio in international comparisons. In the African colonies, however, tertiary education was introduced only in the 1960s and courses were limited. Angolans and Mozambicans were mainly channelled towards professions perceived as useful, mainly 'engineering, medicine, agronomy, forestry and veterinary science. . . . This emphasis is due to the demand for skilled technicians in the overseas provinces', as the booklet had it.

Beyond the major cities that might well be described as islands of modernity, the overall picture was different. In the vast and 'remote rural areas', the church and the armed forces provided the bulk of teaching, often limited to rudimentary instruction in basic skills such as reading and writing in Portuguese and arithmetic. Portuguese propaganda nevertheless boasted that 'many of the Army teachers . . . are university graduates from Portugal, doing their military service in Africa'. Moreover, it advertised 'the complete lack of racial discrimination' as 'one of the salient features of education in the Portuguese overseas provinces', part of the myth of a multiracial society that had become a pillar of late Portuguese colonialism. Recapitulating notions of Lusotropicalism, the work suggested that benign Portuguese colonialism went hand in hand with the belief that 'the Portuguese always and anywhere knew how to create [a] bond that truly connects people'. For good measure, Portuguese colonial benevolence was contrasted with exploitative British or French colonialism.[25]

As part of the envisaged expansion of education in the 1960s, the official Portuguese female youth organization, the Mocidade Portuguesa Feminina (MPF), extended its actions towards the empire. The MPF's conservative Catholic programme aimed to reproduce the *Estado Novo*'s gender ideology in the colonies; the slogan 'each one according to their place' pointed explicitly to labour divisions according to sex. In Africa, the Portuguese task was supposedly to uplift and empower women and girls in order to have them 'fulfil [their] mission' as genuine and preferably Catholic wives and mothers. African girls were to acquire skills in areas such as hygiene, nursing, nutrition and childcare. A sense for femininity, that is, style and a taste for decoration and tidiness, should not be missing in the modern African woman either. The MPF's branch in Mozambique stated with great self-confidence in its 1964 annual report: 'It is the woman who produces and transforms the environment in the family and it is the family which transforms and uplifts society.' Rhetoric aside, throughout the period of its activities in the colonies from 1960 to 1974, the MPF nonetheless struggled to bring its message to rural areas. The organization's records draw a picture of a rather white and urban organization that failed to include African girls and women, particularly beyond the big cities and their suburbs, though reports often blamed a lack of funds and leaders for limited influence.[26]

Indeed, the conservative youth organization with its uniforms and marches – members still practising the Roman salute – was already considered outdated at home. However, the outbreak of warfare in the colonies provided the MPF with a new mission and placed their agenda at centre stage. Advancing African youth, and winning hearts and minds, should help to ensure the preservation of the empire, an assignment in line with the military effort. Courses on counter-subversive warfare reminded the Portuguese soldiers that 'nothing in life is done without a direct or indirect intervention of women. . . . Women's influence is . . . capital and decisive for our future in the whole Overseas (*Ultramar*)', read one military instruction manual. From the upper echelon to district commanders, 'the social development of women' throughout the colonies was considered one of 'the most important' concerns.

Following the French example in Algeria, socio-medical brigades toured rural areas, ideally with an African female nurse who would provide access to local populations. However, prejudice, stereotypes and gender hierarchies were mirrored within the mobile brigades themselves. In Mozambique, an inspector warned that the units' 'good reputation' was in danger because of sexual relationships among members; all staff were advised to display 'the most exemplary behaviour in all acts of their life'. It was usually the brigade's female enlistee, and never a male, who was dismissed due to 'indecent and discrediting behaviour'. Although reports from the field highlighted the key role of women within the teams and promoted multi-ethnic brigades as an illustration of 'multiracial' Portugal, the units often reproduced the unequal and gendered power structures that characterized the general colonial situation in the Portuguese Empire.[27]

The other modernizers

Aiming to win over the female African population, and gendering progress and development, was not limited to the Portuguese. The African liberation movements were following a parallel path. The Organisation of Angolan Women, a branch of the MPLA, and the Organisation of Mozambican Women, the women's section of FRELIMO, both campaigned for modernizing their societies. Polygamy, bride prices, child marriages and initiation rites were perceived as characteristic of 'traditional' societies, which had to be transformed, in principle, for the better. Although from opposite ideological standpoints, official anti-colonial rhetoric instrumentalizing African women for nationalist and revolutionary purposes resembled Portuguese propaganda and goals. Samora Machel, FRELIMO leader and later the first president of independent Mozambique, stated in his opening address to the nationalists' first conference on Mozambican women in March 1973: 'The liberation of women is a fundamental necessity of the revolution, a guarantee of its continuity, a condition of its triumph.' Mozambican women were expected to contribute to the revolution, he explained, by fulfilling the specific functions assigned to them: giving birth, caring for and rearing the next generation of revolutionaries, and guaranteeing that socialist ideals would spread and endure. 'Women bear the responsibility for educating new generations, free from tribalism, regionalism and racism, free from the archaic mentality of oppressing women or passively accepting oppression, free from superstition, imbued with our class spirit with an international feeling.' African women were thus once again called on to transmit cultural values, and belief in development and progress, to the next generation.[28]

Similarity and continuity in the modernizing endeavour – albeit from opposing ideological viewpoints – continued after independence. This can be seen in late colonial Portuguese mega-projects, such as the Cabora Bassa dam in Mozambique and the Cunene river project in Angola, as well as the resettlement schemes. In Mozambique, the Portuguese 'new villages' were neatly integrated into FRELIMO's development plans as 'communal villages' after 1975. Again in Mozambique, the Cabora Bassa dam 'for harnessing the Zambesi river' in the northern Tete province was lauded in *A Decade of Progress* as one 'of the greatest development undertakings in the whole of the African continent'. The Portuguese promised that the dam would 'bring thousands of African families out of subsistence farming and into the market economy'. However, when completed in 1974, cheap electricity mostly benefited industries in South Africa (to which it was sold), while local residents were left to confront the dam's negative environmental impacts. During the struggle against Portuguese colonialism, FRELIMO had identified the multinational dam scheme, built with South African, British, German, and Portuguese capital, as a symbol of the 'colonial-imperialist war', and as one of 'the most criminal strategic plans'. With Mozambican independence in 1975, the name changed to Cahora Bassa, and the corresponding framework also needed a spin, but the project remained: 'We must domesticate the white elephant Cahora Bassa,' Machel declared, and state planners envisaged developing the Zambesi Valley in view of the 'socialization of the countryside': a new socialist mega-project was born, and a new 'decade of progress' was promised.[29]

CHAPTER 28
WESTERN SAHARA, 1975

'I went to the Sahara in 1974 with the express mandate from the Spanish government to prepare the Sahrawi people for independence. They [the government of Spain] deceived me by handing [the territory] over to Morocco,' Luis Rodríguez de Viguri, the last secretary-general of Spanish Sahara (today Western Sahara) between 1974 and 1976, explained in retrospect.[1] He shared the notion of betrayal with many Spanish soldiers who had been serving in Western Sahara, as well as with a large number of Sahrawis who have now been living in Moroccan-controlled Western Sahara or as refugees in southern Algeria for more than forty-five years.

The government's betrayal to which Rodríguez de Viguri referred is embodied in the Madrid Agreement that Spain signed on 14 November 1975 with Morocco and Mauritania, handing over the Spanish Sahara to the two neighbouring countries. In times of mounting Sahrawi resistance, international pressure to decolonize, and a domestic crisis with Spain's long-term dictator Francisco Franco (who had stifled dissent, limiting anti-colonial perspectives in Spain) on his deathbed, the eclipse of the once global Spanish empire was sealed with a secretive deal. Only a few months after the Madrid Agreement, and the invasion of Western Sahara by 300,000 Moroccan civilians (with the military in their wake) – called the 'Green March', as green is the colour of Islam – Spain's colonial last will and testament also engendered the birth of a refugee nation, the Sahrawi Arab Democratic Republic (SADR), founded on 27 February 1976 in Bir Lehlou, an oasis town in the north-eastern part of Western Sahara.

Spain, as the colonial power, had earlier agreed to organize a referendum on independence in the territory and, indeed, taking a census in order to identify the electorate was one of Rodríguez de Viguri's main tasks when he was appointed in 1974. However, the vote on self-determination has never materialized, and large parts of Western Sahara remain under Moroccan control. The United Nations has not acknowledged the Moroccan kingdom as the administering power, and the territory remains on the UN's list of non-self-governing territories where it was initially placed in 1963. Measured against the standards set by the UN, which requires a democratic expression of consent for independence, full assimilation into another state or an agreed form of free association, Spain's exit represented incomplete decolonization (Figure 28.1).

Spanish colonialism in Western Sahara

Spain had formalized its claims over much of Western Sahara at the Berlin Conference (1884–5), when large parts of Africa were carved up among the European powers. The

Figure 28.1 Demonstration supporting independence for Western Sahara in Madrid, 11 November 2006. © Wikimedia Commons (public domain).

Spanish presence in Western Sahara, however, had long been limited to a few coastal enclaves, such as the trading post on the Villa Cisneros peninsula, today called Dakhla. This situation changed little after the arrival of the first military governor, Francisco Bens, in 1904, and Spain's projection of imperial power remained virtually non-existent for decades. The people of the nominal possession considered the weak Spanish colonizers not as alien overlords but as mere trading partners.

In 1898, after being defeated in a war with the United States, Spain lost its colonies of Cuba and Puerto Rico in the Caribbean, the Philippines in Southeast Asia and several small Pacific archipelagos. Pressure groups and so-called Africanists (*africanistas*) in Spain had long complained about the lack of attention given to Madrid's African outposts, including those of the Sahara, and they now argued that it was time to recover what they perceived as Spain's African destiny. Spain's African empire at that time was confined to Western Sahara and Ifni, Equatorial Guinea in sub-Saharan Africa and the Mediterranean enclaves of Ceuta and Melilla. Between 1904 and 1912, treaties between France and Spain gave Madrid a stronger position in North Africa through a protectorate over a strip of land along the Mediterranean coastline of Morocco, the remainder of that country becoming a French protectorate. Spanish colonization in the areas of Tarfaya in southern Morocco and Río de Oro (Wad ad-Dahab Peninsula, Western Sahara) still existed only on paper. Yet it was the Saharan protectorate on the Atlantic, about the same size as Italy, that *africanistas* hoped to turn into a new *El Dorado*, a source

421

of wealth for the 'motherland'. Although the mostly flat landscape largely comprised a hot, dry and rocky desert where rain was rare and sand-laden sirocco winds a common feature, the rich fishing grounds off the coast were already known while further natural resources such as phosphate, petroleum and subterranean freshwater deposits were to be discovered in later decades. There was also the strategic position of the territory because of proximity to the Canary Islands, which Spain had settled in the early 1400s. Last but not least, after losing its Latin American colonies in the 1820s, then its other major colonies by the end of the century, Africa seemed to offer a last chance to Spanish colonialists to escape the fate of their country becoming an insignificant regional power on the European periphery.

The shift of focus from the Americas (and the Philippines) to Africa is reflected in the career of Spain's first military governor in Western Sahara. Born in Havana in 1867, Francisco Bens began his military service in the Cuban capital when the Caribbean island was still under Spanish rule. He then moved to various posts around the empire and in Spain, and in the 1890s, fought in the Spanish army against Cubans waging a war of independence. Leaving Cuba after the Spanish defeat by the United States, Bens became administrator of a hitherto neglected corner of the remaining empire: Río de Oro. In contrast to the centuries of Spanish colonialism in the Americas, occupation of the Saharan territory had hardly begun when Bens took up the position in 1904. Spanish historiography credits Bens with virtually single-handedly extending the colonial presence from a few coastal footholds towards the interior, though when he was replaced as governor in 1925, colonial commerce, development and settlement remained limited.[2]

After Francisco Franco's troops and the Falange political movement had defeated the republicans in the Spanish Civil War (1936–9) and established an authoritarian regime in Madrid, the new government's daydreams explicitly built on the purported continuity of the 'glorious' days of Spanish conquest in the Americas in the 1500s and present-day imperial expansion in Africa. In one Falangist publication, *Reivindicaciones de España*, which can be roughly translated as 'Spain's Demands', published in 1941, José María de Areilza and Fernando María Castiella indeed laid claims to a Spanish sphere of influence and dominion that extended from Morocco through Algeria, southwards over Mauritania (all then under French rule) and beyond, and even advanced further territorial demands in the Gulf of Guinea. It envisioned Hitler's Germany, which Franco supported, as the sponsor of Spain's new African empire. As might be expected, these fantasies were never realized. The 'Empire towards God' (*imperio hacia Dios*), as the strongly Catholic Falangist ideology had it, was mostly reduced to symbolic gestures and propaganda.

However, in the 1940s discovery of large reserves of high-quality phosphate in Western Sahara appeared to fulfil the promise of Spain's future in Africa. Phosphate was to become a key staple for artificial fertilizers during the global Cold War, though mining in Western Sahara proved difficult and became possible on a large scale only in the 1960s. As mentioned earlier, further incentives for Spain to hold on to its territory were the rich coastal fishing grounds, as well as expected oil deposits on- and offshore. The potential to exploit Western Sahara's natural resources, along with ideological and geopolitical constraints, provided good reasons for the Franco regime's reluctance to decolonize when most colonies in Asia and Africa had achieved independence between the 1940s and the 1960s.

Moreover, Spanish rhetoric stressed 'absolute respect for the preferences of the people', in this case, the indigenous Sahrawi, and the supposedly 'altruistic action of Spain benefitting in particular the inhabitants of the territory'. In contrast to other colonial powers, Franco and his ideologues argued, Spain did not aim to plunder its colonies but to pursue the 'task of civilizing' (*tarea civilizadora*) the territories, especially in a cultural sense. The myth of benevolence usually included Christianization; in the case of the Sahara, however, the almost entirely Muslim population was not to be converted. Lack of proselytism should help to guarantee continuing diplomatic support from the Arab countries. Even if differing in faith, their backing was not to be jeopardized, as the politically and diplomatically isolated Franco government reckoned. The hoary gospel of modernization of 'backward' societies was thus applied in Western Sahara. Time and again such exculpatory narratives had been revived and adapted to new circumstances, serving to disguise or rationalize exploitation and abuse; the language of altruism repeated during Franco's regime was no exception.

Franco himself declared that Spain had 'never practiced *coloniaje*', which should not be mixed up with *colonialismo*. *Coloniaje* was synonymous with exploitation, while colonialism in its pure (and Spanish) sense was, purportedly, the 'most civilizing assignment' and even an 'unavoidable duty' for a nation such as Spain. In the face of mounting pressure from the UN to decolonize, Franco and his ideologues reinforced the narrative: the designation of Spanish Guinea, Spanish Sahara and Ifni – a separate Spanish enclave also located on the Moroccan Atlantic coast – as Spanish 'provinces' at the end of the 1950s was meant to further conceal the enduring colonial situation.[3]

Western Sahara and Ifni were made provinces in the midst of an anti-colonial war that had begun with guerrilla-style actions by Moroccan irredentists and Sahrawi anti-colonial fighters in the mid-1950s. The intensity of armed resistance in the Ifni and Tarfaya regions, as well as in parts of Western Sahara, had increased since 1955 and became particularly virulent after Morocco's independence from France and Spain in 1956. Moroccan nationalists now claimed a 'greater Morocco' extending beyond the Spanish Sahara, although the sultan's dynasty had never possessed formal control over those areas. The conflict evolved into a formidable guerrilla war, reaching a peak between November 1957 and March 1958, the Ifni-Sahara War, with the Moroccan-sponsored so-called Liberation Army's coordinated attacks on Spanish and also French garrisons and towns in the border regions of Algeria and Mauritania. Joint Spanish and French military actions brutally suppressed the uprising and targeted the civilian population by destroying camels and wells on which the nomads depended for survival in the desert. The Spanish military, in collaboration with the French air force, also carried out area bombardment. In the wake of the short-lived conflict, Spain in 1958 returned to Morocco the southern protectorate of Tarfaya, which was now of little use. As a friendly gesture and due to international pressure, Spain subsequently ceded the Ifni enclave in 1969, while it clung on to Western Sahara.[4]

After wreaking destruction during the Ifni-Sahara War, Spanish authorities extended the colonial presence over the interior of Western Sahara by winning over Sahrawi (male) notables to work closely with the Spanish administration. Leading figures received Spanish monetary compensation, foodstuffs and material goods as redress for the losses their people suffered during the war. Distribution of goods and funds among their community was at the notables' discretion. Hence, cooperating solely with notables, Spanish colonialism contributed to strengthening male leaders' positions, augmenting the power they were able to exert over their communities. The Spanish also pursued economic and social transformation of the territory through forced sedentarization of its inhabitants and development of its natural resources. Projects included phosphate mining at Bou Craa and an urbanization scheme. Construction thus followed on the heels of destruction.[5]

The Spanish 'Plan for the Advancement of the Sahara' with a certain time-lag undertook similar strategies to those that the French and British had implemented for their African colonies from the 1940s onwards. At least in rhetoric, though with some particularities, Spain increasingly appropriated contemporary guidelines for modernization put forward by 'experts' from international bodies such as the World Bank and United Nations. Colonial theory indeed smoothly translated into development projects and aid in the 1960s and 1970s as most former colonies gained independence.[6]

In a colonial and paternalistic sense, the Spanish aspired to radically change the social reality and thereby advance into the 'twentieth century' a Western Saharan society that in their view lagged 'centuries behind'.[7] They aimed to transform a nomadic people into a sedentary population that was 'more Europeanized and dynamic'. Spain's development plans declared that 'one of the objectives of these social changes [was] to break up the tribal structure and the substitution of ethnic links by territorial ones; in short, the substitution of the tribe by the municipality'. Enforcing 'modernization', theorists and those who put theory into practice undermined local social structures, 'seeking the creation of a feeling of solidarity that could serve as a basis for the formation of a broader, national idea' in a Sahrawi nation under Spanish rule. Yet the cultural effort to 'Hispanicize' the Sahara through Spanish-style education, and in order to create allegiance, proved a double-edged sword.[8]

Young and educated Sahrawis opposing Spanish colonialism gathered around Mohammed Bassiri towards the late 1960s. Born in the 1940s, Bassiri (formally, Bassir Mohamed uld hach Brahim uld Lebser), studied in Morocco, Egypt and Syria, where he was influenced by pan-Arab socialism as well as by the writings of Frantz Fanon and Mehdi Ben Barka, a left-wing Moroccan politician and anti-colonial critic. In the late 1960s he addressed petitions to the Spanish colonial authorities calling for further inclusion of Sahrawis in political processes, not for an armed struggle. Bassiri's movement for home rule, Harakat Tahrir, indeed took inspiration from Gandhi's nonviolent actions in India decades earlier. After Bassiri's forced disappearance – he was probably killed in a Spanish prison – in the wake of a peaceful protest in the Zemla district in Western Sahara's capital, El Aaiún (Laayoune), in 1970, a new nationalist movement among young Sahrawis emerged. It was formally constituted as the Frente Popular por la Liberación de Saguia el Hamra y Río de Oro (POLISARIO) in 1973, with El-Ouali Mustapha Sayed as first secretary-general. POLISARIO, a clandestinely organized movement inside Western Sahara, immediately took up arms against Spanish overlordship. In its early days, POLISARIO was a Marxist-leaning anti-colonial movement that later as a political party established a Sahrawi government-in-exile. After the Spanish withdrawal of what became known as the 'Western Sahara' in 1975, POLISARIO then challenged Mauritanian and Moroccan colonialism.

New faces of colonialism: Mauritania and Morocco in Western Sahara

Francisco Franco died on 20 November 1975, after more than thirty-five years of dictatorial rule, and Spain entered into a period of political turmoil in the transition to democracy. Spain hurriedly withdrew from the Western Sahara, moving out its citizens and their belongings in a military undertaking named 'Operation Swallow'. The hastily concluded Madrid Agreements in November left the Western Sahara to the new occupying powers Morocco and Mauritania, though the last Spanish soldiers only departed early the following year. Meanwhile, POLISARIO, supported by Algeria (which had gained independence from France in 1962), pushed the occupying Mauritanian armed forces south and twice raided Nouakchott, the capital of Mauritania, in 1976 and 1977. Subsequently Mauritania evacuated the southern part of Western Sahara and signed a peace agreement with POLISARIO in 1979. However, after Mauritania pulled out, Moroccan troops swiftly occupied the vacated region, which in the Madrid Agreement had been adjudicated to Nouakchott. POLISARIO's armed actions against Moroccan troops and the economic infrastructure in Western Sahara continued. In particular, attacks on the profitable phosphate mining facilities now operated by Morocco were intended to make occupation financially unviable for the Moroccans. Yet, with US military and Saudi Arabian financial assistance, the Moroccan army, starting in the early 1980s, pushed POLISARIO eastward towards the desert and erected a series of fortified barriers. By the end of the decade, these walls extended over 2,700 kilometres, and separated Moroccan-controlled Western Sahara (which includes most of the territory's natural resources) from a thin, landlocked and inhospitable eastern strip under POLISARIO control. Their construction helped to transform POLISARIO's guerrilla war into a war of attrition.

As negotiations between the SADR and Morocco, under the auspices of the Organisation of African Unity (now the African Union), had produced no settlement, the UN took over discussions and, in September 1991, brokered a ceasefire. Subsequently, a UN Mission for the Referendum in Western Sahara (MINURSO) arrived in the territory, with peacekeepers deployed to strategic locations, though with no mandate to intervene. Recurrent diplomatic efforts by UN envoys aimed to end the conflict and bring about a peace settlement. Among other initiatives, the Baker Plans stand out; during his tenure as UN special envoy for Western Sahara (1997–2004), James Baker, formerly US secretary of state under George H. W. Bush, sought to secure autonomy for Sahrawis within the Moroccan kingdom. In 1997 Baker brought together all the interested parties, but negotiations dragged on for years without tangible outcomes. A proposed agreement that Baker put forward in 2001 did not clearly address Sahrawis' claim for self-determination and was rejected by both the SADR and Algeria, its main supporter. Baker's second proposal foresaw a five-year period of autonomy for Western Sahara within a Moroccan-controlled political framework, followed by a referendum in which Moroccan settlers residing in the territory since 1999 would be allowed to vote.[9] The SADR surprisingly accepted their inclusion, having previously insisted that only those registered in the final Spanish census of 1974 (then about 80,000 people) and their descendants as well as inhabitants of refugee camps in the Algerian Tindouf region (some 150,000) should be eligible. Morocco, however, has refused any referendum including an option for Sahrawi independence. The Moroccan settler population in Western Sahara, benefiting from higher wages than Sahrawis in the public sector, tax cuts and further advantages, by the 1990s had risen to between 150,000 and 450,000. (The large discrepancy is due to the opaque declarations in the Moroccan census regarding military personnel.) It seems clear that after almost thirty years of settlement and administration in Western Sahara, the Moroccan royal dynasty began to doubt the loyalty of the settlers, preferring no vote at all.[10] With its allies in the UN Security Council, notably France and the United States, Morocco felt little international pressure to move away from the status quo, other than perhaps to consider some limited autonomy for Western Sahara.

Spain, in its hasty withdrawal from the Saharan colony, had failed to make adequate provisions for the transfer of power, and the UN has not succeeded in resolving the conflict. Morocco exercises greater international influence than the Sahrawi government-in-exile, its position as a strategic ally for Western countries reinforced after the Islamist terrorist attacks in the United States in September 2001. Morocco has also become a pivotal gatekeeper in supporting Europe's efforts to control African immigration. The relationship between Spain and Morocco is delicate because of the two enclaves under Spanish sovereignty on the Moroccan Mediterranean coast, the cities of Ceuta and Melilla, which Morocco claims. Spain is thus unwilling to force the Sahrawi issue. Meanwhile, in December 2020, the United States under President Donald Trump recognized Morocco's claim to Western Sahara or what Morocco calls the 'southern provinces'. Morocco, in turn, agreed to normalize relations with the state of Israel, becoming one of the few Arab countries to have done so. In March 2022 the Spanish government under Prime Minister Pedro Sánchez also declared its support for Morocco's 'autonomy' plans for Western Sahara. Shortly after the announcement, Morocco and Spain signed a security pact. After decades of multilateral negotiations, bilateral agreements were thereby establishing new diplomatic situations.

Since the 1990s, Sahrawi activists have turned from guerrilla action to peaceful protest, though with several waves of organized and sometimes violent mass protests, referred to as the intifadas, in 1999, 2005 and 2010, all relentlessly suppressed by Moroccan security forces.[11] Sahrawis have drawn on various strategies to promote their struggle, most recently, including international concern about environmental issues. Since a large protest camp, Gdeim Izik, was set up in the desert close to El Aaiún in 2010, questions about the access to Western Sahara's natural resources have come to the fore. As the UN considers Western Sahara a non-self-governing territory, Morocco, in principle, is not allowed to mine or extract oil without the consent of and benefit for the local population.

With growing global opposition to unsustainable extraction of fossil resources, Sahrawi activists have found a new way to mobilize the international community for their cause.[12]

Gendered resistance: From Spanish to Moroccan occupation

The role of women in the Western Sahara, under the Spanish and since Spain's withdrawal, is a subject of importance. Resistance in Western Sahara has been gendered since colonial times. Many Sahrawi women repeat the catchphrase 'we have always been very free' when describing their social position to Western interlocutors.[13] The trope of the energetic 'free' woman with equal rights both within the family and within the political realm of the SADR in exile has been cultivated by scholars and activists.[14] SADR and POLISARIO discourse has aptly and strategically promoted to Western donors the image of empowered Muslim women. Portraying modern Sahrawi women as standing out from a sea of veiled and supposedly oppressed women in the Muslim world acts as a strong incentive for Western state-sponsored aid agencies and the activities of non-governmental organizations (NGOs).

Yet 'the official prioritization and centralization of idealized and homogenized "Sahrawi women" has been detrimental to those Sahrawi refugees who are marginalized, silenced, and displaced' in exile, as the refugee and development scholar Elena Fiddian-Qasmiye explains. In fact, age, social and family origin, marital status and education, along with further cultural, social, and ethnic traits, have long determined a woman's standing in Saharawi society. In the refugee camps in Algeria, the characteristics of 'ideal women' were (and are) largely defined by a male-dominated political agenda and shaped by the concept and expectations of Western NGO representatives,[15] though this is not to diminish Sahrawi women's crucial contributions in the struggle against colonialism.

Under the Spanish, Sahrawi women and teenagers contributed in different ways to anti-colonial resistance. Among Sahrawi militants, young women took over significant tasks, visibly shaping the opposition movement from the early 1970s. A case in point was the organization of the Zemla protests with Bassiri's Harakat Tahrir in June 1970, which were suppressed by Spanish security forces.[16] Ironically, several of the young female activists had been trained and educated by Spain's official women's organization, the Sección Femenina (SF, Women's Section). While Spain aimed to benefit from 'the new generations of [educated] women' who would 'serve as a trigger for social change' in the territory, the young Sahrawis constituted an important nucleus in the organization of resistance and anti-colonial protest. This came much to the surprise of SF teachers and instructors, as well as to the 'official mind' in Spain. Spanish colonial theorists had agreed that the 'necessary nationalism' of the younger generations was to be 'conveniently channelled' in Western Sahara. However, in the 1970s, attempts to guide Sahrawi nationalism in controlled orbits were in vain. Colonial social engineering paradoxically contributed to producing anti-colonial nationalism.[17]

Only in hindsight did the SF leadership in Western Sahara become aware of their protégées increasingly leaning towards the independence cause. In 1974, a report analysing the previous ten years of Spanish rule in Western Sahara concluded that 'the woman of this territory not only has influence, she is in command'. Supposedly passive Muslim women were now seen as completely transformed; they had become an independent and confident part of an emerging Sahrawi society, the report conceded. Private letters from Spanish SF personnel in El Aaiún during the imperial endgame supported this view. When describing anti-colonial 'public demonstrations, sabotage' and insecurity in the colonial capital, the additional comment that one could find 'our women' in the middle of all these 'troubles' comes as little surprise. Although the SF took some pride in having purportedly provided the stimulus for the now politically active women, this was certainly not the kind of empowerment authorities had envisaged. Adequately educated women were meant to bring Spanish customs and 'culture' to the remotest parts of the empire, but SF-trained women stood at the forefront of demands for Sahrawi self-determination.[18]

After Spain's withdrawal from Western Sahara, Sahrawi women became key organizers and administrators in the refugee camps in Algeria. As about half of Western Sahara's population had fled the advancing Moroccan troops towards the desert and into Algerian exile, schooling of children in the camps posed a great challenge. Since the late 1970s, thousands of young Sahrawis have been trained in Cuba, which formally recognized the SADR in 1980. After as long as a decade of studying and living in Cuba, young women and men returned to the camps as trained teachers, nurses and doctors. Trying to re-adapt to Sahrawi lifestyle and culture was a formidable task for many. Cultural idiosyncrasies characterizing the Sahrawis educated in Cuba make them stand out as a new 'tribe' of 'Cubarawis'. Given the different gender roles in Cuba and among Sahrawis, returning women were often denounced as 'bad girls'. Since the late 1980s, Sahrawi families have thus preferred to send their daughters for education to Algeria, Libya and Syria rather than to Cuba. Notwithstanding this change, Cuban-educated Sahrawi women are still strategically brought forward as guides for mostly Spanish visitors to the camps, showcasing women's supposed freedom of movement within the camp society and reproducing the notion of liberated, 'ideal' Sahrawi women.[19]

In the Moroccan-controlled territory, Sahrawis' gendered resistance, as a deliberate strategy to expose Moroccan discrimination and physical abuse, has been discernible at least since 2010. Given the fragile economic situation of many activist families, salaried men – often the sole breadwinners – agitate behind the scenes, fearful of losing their employment. Hence, it has often been militant women, such as Aminatou Haidar, a Sahrawi human rights activist from El Aaiún, who have spearheaded nonviolent protests and borne the brunt of repression, enduring prison sentences, forced disappearances and sometimes torture.[20]

In recent years, pressure on Morocco from international human rights organizations has resulted in what Joanna Allan described as 'genderwashing'; that is, publicizing to an international audience efforts to take gender into account in policymaking both in Morocco and in Western Sahara. Apparently 'the "victimized" and "oppressed" Muslim woman is still a legitimate "rescue project" for the West, just as she was in colonial times'. However, Sahrawi activists such as Haidar provide a reminder that Sahrawi women are in no need for a 'saviour'.[21]

Western Sahara: One of Africa's last colonies?

Framing the prolonged conflict in Western Sahara solely in colonial terms, a conflict in 'the last colony' does not do justice to the different layers of a struggle ongoing for more than four decades. Given the dynamics and the 'inward shift' of the confrontations between Sahrawi nationalists and Moroccan loyalists, among other factors, it is also useful to examine the conflict through the lens of 'identity' and 'secessionism'.[22] Yet the colonial aspects of the situation, from the days of Spanish rule to the present, remain pertinent. There is, on the one hand, the legal situation that, in the view of the UN, still defines Western Sahara as a territory pending decolonization. Spain, however, declines any continuing responsibility. On the other, the high degree of militarization by Morocco, the different legal status of Sahrawis and Moroccan settlers within the territory, a pattern of settler colonialism through migration and exploitation of the territory's natural resources to the benefit of a small ruling class are all reminders of the 'colonial situation' that continues to characterize Western Sahara. Therefore, colonial history and (post-)colonial theory provide valuable tools to address Spain's failed decolonization of its Saharan 'province'.

When Rodríguez de Viguri left the Spanish colony in 1976, he was particularly worried about loss of the 'influence of the Spanish culture that so many efforts, so much money, so much affection and even blood of our soldiers have cost'. He was afraid that Sahrawis, within a few years after Spain's exit, would 'speak and think in French,' the major European language of Morocco and Algeria.[23] Rodríguez de Viguri's anxiety was in vain. Spanish has become Sahrawi activists' language of choice, used to explain to a Western public what the Sahrawis regard as Moroccan colonial oppression.

CHAPTER 29
BELGIUM AND THE CONGO, 1897 AND 2018

In 1897, Brussels, the capital of Belgium, hosted an international exposition, the sort of grand fair that had become a regular event in Europe since the 1850s and that was designed to show off a nation's economic, technical and cultural achievements. Belgium had only become an independent state in 1830, and was a small country of 30,000 square kilometres and 7 million people in the 1890s. The population was divided between often antagonistic French-speaking Walloons and the Dutch speakers of the Flanders region, alongside a small German community. With large deposits of coal and iron, busy ports such as Antwerp and a good infrastructure, Belgium had become during the middle of the nineteenth century the second most industrialized country in the world. The home of a lively artistic and literary culture, *fin de siècle* Brussels had much to show off in the exhibition. Fourteen kilometres to the east of the central city, in the parklands of a royal estate in Tervuren, the fair also boasted a colonial section.[1]

King Leopold's Congo Free State

The Tervuren exposition celebrated the Congo Free State (CFS), a personal colony of the Belgian king, Leopold II which was not yet the 'Belgian Congo'. Born in 1835, from his twenties, Prince Leopold travelled widely around the Mediterranean, and visited India and China. His global experiences convinced him that – as he famously put it – 'Il faut à la Belgique une colonie' (Belgium must have a colony). Colonies, he had observed, formed important assets of great powers such as Britain and France. The would-be colonizer's eyes fixed on sites from China and Japan to the Nile, from Eritrea to the Philippines, though he had no success in realizing his imperial dream even when he assumed the throne in 1865. The next decades, however, provided new opportunities with the 'opening' of sub-Saharan Africa by adventurers and explorers like Henry Morton Stanley. In the midst of Stanley's much publicized expeditions, Leopold organized a conference in Brussels, in 1876, at which he set up the International African Association to promote scientific discoveries in the 'dark continent' and, he claimed, to combat the slave trade widely practiced by Arab, Zanzibari and indigenous African merchants. Stanley himself received a warm reception from the king in 1878. The following year, Leopold commissioned and funded a five-year expedition during which Stanley, setting out from the estuary of the mighty Congo river, crossed central Africa from west to east.

Leopold's aim, subcontracted to Stanley, was to carve out a colony, and to do so as soon as possible, since the French – whom the Belgian king considered rivals –

were exploring the northern bank of the Congo river. On Leopold's behalf, Stanley convinced or coerced African rulers to 'sign' treaties conceding certain rights to the International African Association. Leopold in 1885 grandly declared the creation of the Congo Free State, and he sought its recognition at a conference, convened by the German chancellor Otto von Bismarck, where the great powers discussed African issues. The Berlin conference did not create the CFS, but simply took 'note' of Leopold's claim, considering the territory a useful buffer between French, Portuguese and British possessions in central Africa. Delegates also adopted resolutions in favour of free trade in sub-Saharan Africa. Leopold persuaded a rather reluctant Belgian parliament to acknowledge him as 'sovereign king' over the CFS, and secured recognition from several foreign countries.

In one of the anomalies that marked Belgian colonialism, Leopold II was thus head of state of two countries, Belgium and the nominally independent CFS. His new domain – seventy-seven times the size of Belgium (and equivalent in size to all of Western Europe) – was, in legal terms, administratively and financially separate from Belgium. The CFS was, effectively, a privately founded, funded and operated state under the absolute rule of Leopold. Needless to say, none of its over 200 ethnic groups was either consulted about the arrangements or given any role in the administration. Most of the European subjects of the king of the Belgians were dubious about his distant and costly ventures, and only gradually did the monarch convince businessmen, missionaries and the political elite of the potential for trade and conversion of 'heathens'. Ivory and other resources offered valuable commodities, but the invention of the inflatable rubber tyre in 1888 held out most promise because of the virtually unlimited supplies of wild rubber growing in the Congo jungle. By the time of the Tervuren exposition, significant political, business and missionary interests had become rooted in Leopold's colony, and, along with the king himself, were reaping the benefits. Some Belgians and other Europeans were nevertheless becoming outraged at the king's 'pillaging' of the Congo's resources (a word used at the time and by later historians) and especially at the treatment of African labour.

Leopold was determined that the Tervuren exhibition would show off the CFS to good advantage. A new tram line was constructed to take fair-goers from central Brussels to a purpose-built neo-classical 'Palais des Colonies'. In the *salon d'honneur*, they gazed on Hélène De Rudder's murals that left no doubt about the beneficent changes Leopold thought his rule had already wrought: the titles, unsubtly referring to periods before and after European takeover, were 'Barbarism' and 'Civilisation', 'Idolatry' and 'Religion', and 'Slavery' and 'Liberty'. There were statues and figures carved in ivory, generally representing mythological or allegorical figures rather than Africans, though it has been suggested that Belgium's 'Art Nouveau', with its sinuous curves and floral motifs, owes much to the jungle landscapes of central Africa.[2] One sculpture, by Charles Samuel, represented 'Vuakusu Batetela defending a woman against an Arab' – a subject hardly devoid of ideological preconceptions about Black Africans, Arabs and, implicitly, about Belgians as protectors of Africans and saviours of women. Paintings of a Congolese village, a caravan of porters crossing a river, a wrestling match, dances, a market, artisans and a burial decorated a large ethnographic gallery. The display contained samples of textiles, baskets and other crafts, as well as models of African houses. There were vitrines of the flora and fauna that excited European curiosity, alongside more mundane displays of imports and exports. In short, the Palais des Colonies offered a panorama of the Congo Free State and Leopold's purported achievements there.

Outside the main exhibition building stood four Congolese 'villages'. They housed 267 Congolese, primarily Bangala, Mayombe and Basoko people (but also a 'pygmy' and an 'Arab'), expressly brought to Tervuren for the fair. Three of the 'villages' showed 'typical' – and, thus, in the European view, primitive – African life. The fourth was for Africans 'civilized' by Christianity and Western ways; a group of musicians entertained spectators with the Belgian national anthem and other European compositions. The African men, women and children stayed in Belgium for two months, occasionally exploring other areas of Brussels while kept under close supervision. When they returned home, they carried trunks packed with clothing and other European goods. Seven of the Congolese, however, died during their sojourn and were buried in Tervuren.

Debates over the Congo

Some newspaper reports were critical of the exhibition of Africans, and other aspects of the Congo displays, but Belgians and other Europeans considered the fair generally as a public success. It did not stanch concern about the abusive policies and appalling working conditions for Africans in the CFS. Leopold had confided the commercial exploitation of the colony to private companies, whose 'concessions' – one of which, given to an Antwerp business, covered an area twice the size of Ireland – accorded the right to hire and manage labour and harvest wild rubber, as well as to develop other commercial activities. The companies gained notoriety for the brutality of their methods: forced recruitment of labourers and porters, working conditions that differed little from slavery, corporal punishment of any who disobeyed or failed to fulfil production quotas, sexual abuse, the killing of workers who were apprehended after escape. Words and images in the press brought the horrors to a European audience, the most gruesome photographs showing African men holding severed hands – those of workers who had escaped, and whose hands were brought back by those tasked with killing them to claim rewards, though the hands of other Africans were cut off simply for failing to collect their quota of rubber. Pictures and reports recounted in graphic detail the flogging of Africans and other physical punishments. Such evidence clearly contradicted the 'civilizing' impulses championed by colonialists and the anti-slavery campaign that Leopold used to legitimize his endeavours. They also made Leopold and his countrymen the target for more 'humane', if self-serving, colonial officials, as well as reformers and humanitarians, from other countries, particularly Britain and the United States. Condemnation of the treatment of Africans and the concessionary system, voiced from the early 1890s, became stronger after the turn of the century as E. D. Morel (1873–1924), a French-born British journalist, and his Congo Reform Association, founded in 1904, revealed the systematic abuses. A report in that year by the Irish-born Roger Casement (1864–1916), a British consul (later executed by the British during the First World War for activities in connection with his support for Irish independence), provided further documentation about slave-like conditions, torture and mutilation, kidnapping and the holding of hostages.

Adam Hochschild's bestselling *King Leopold's Ghost*, published in 1998, focused attention anew on the historical situation in the Congo and the campaign mounted by Morel, Casement and others.[3] For the wider public, the volume represented a signal reassessment of colonialism a hundred years after the Tervuren exhibition had presented a triumphalist and whitewashed portrayal of Belgian actions. It nevertheless provoked hostility in some quarters in Belgium as a sensationalistic and unbalanced account. Debate still takes place about Leopold's motives and policies, and how they differed or not from those of other colonizers, though the evidence of widespread and systematic abuse of Africans is incontrovertible. Calculating the precise number of Africans who died from poor labour conditions, overwork, epidemics or killing by Europeans is impossible since there were no censuses of the Congo until the 1920s. Whether the number is in the tens of thousands, hundreds of thousands or millions – even ten million has been suggested – the abuse took place on a 'staggering scale', to use the historian David Van Reybrouck's characterization. Though Belgium is by no means the only colonial power guilty of such mistreatment, this has led some such as Hochschild to refer to the 'genocidal proportions' (though not, for him, a 'genocide') and 'Holocaust dimensions' of the situation.[4] Van Reybrouck, while deploring the huge death toll, nevertheless cautions that it is 'absurd in this context to speak of an act of "genocide" or "holocaust"', which 'implies the conscious, planned annihilation of a specific population, and that was never intended here'.[5]

King Leopold II never visited his African colony, but the carte blanche he gave to the concessionary companies and administrators, and the general views of Africa that he espoused, clearly implicated him; although aware of widespread mistreatment, he did almost nothing to stop the abuse. Present-day historians use such words as 'megalomaniacal' and 'rapacious' to describe the king, and it is clear that the primary motives in his African ventures were personal aggrandisement and financial returns. In the words of the Belgian historian Guy Vanthemsche, 'the creation of the Congo was not inspired by diplomatic, religious or humanitarian motives'; Leopold II 'wanted to make money and amass a fortune'.[6] However, Leopold also hoped that his initiatives would benefit Belgian industry and trade, provide opportunities for evangelization and gain status for his dynasty and the European country over which he ruled. As Van Reybrouck puts it, 'to limit one's view of his enterprise to a case of unbridled self-enrichment would be to do injustice to the national and social motives for his imperialism'.[7] Leopold participated in a movement of territorial acquisition that in fact engaged many European rulers (and private adventurers), and he sought a colony to bolster a small and diplomatically neutral country surrounded by larger powers and beset by domestic disputes. Leopold sought to 'develop' the Congo, though that development – including the building of rail lines and port facilities, and creation of an export economy – primarily served European interests, and did so at great human cost. In the slow construction of the 366-kilometre rail line from Matadi to Stanley Pool, from 1890 to 1898, for instance, 900 Africans and 42 Europeans died, and another 300 Europeans were repatriated because of disease or accidents. Leopold's supporters, meanwhile boasted that by 1908, 16,000 Congolese children were enrolled in schools and 200,000 had received Christian baptism.

Turn-of-the-century exposés of the Congo abuses severely tarnished the king's reputation and, by extension, that of the Belgians. Though the Congo was separate from Belgium, Leopold had borrowed money from the Belgian government, Belgians were the largest cohort of Europeans in the Congo, Belgians provided the bureaucrats for colonial administration, and Belgian companies were the key commercial actors. Faced with the campaign about colonial horrors, Leopold agreed to transfer the CFS to the Belgian government, and in 1908, the Congo Free State became the Belgian Congo; it remained a colony until 1960.

Leopold died in 1909, and his successor, King Albert I, opened a permanent Royal Museum for Central Africa in Tervuren the following year. The museum was housed in a palatial building that incorporated many of the murals and sculptures, including a bust of Leopold, displayed in 1897. The grandiose rotunda featured heroic statues of Belgians, including a missionary bringing Christianity to central Africa. The ethnographic displays reprised earlier ones with masks and sculptures, jewellery, weaponry, musical instruments and other objects, all appropriately catalogued and described in ways common at the time. Labels and displays thus underlined the perceived exoticism of African cultures, neatly divided into the 'typical' beliefs and practices of various 'tribes'. They conceded the skilled craftsmanship but with predictable perspectives about 'primitive' art. The museum also maintained the natural history displays of the earlier exposition; the 'crocodile room', not surprisingly, counted among the highlights for visitors. Museum-goers could enjoy displays of other beasts great and small, minerals, prehistoric African artefacts and 'Orientalist' Belgian art. The Memorial Hall chronicled the history of Belgian exploration and colonial service, contained an honour roll of Belgians who had died in the CFS and highlighted military actions against the Africanized Arab chiefs Tippo Tip and Msiri in the eastern Congo, the service of the Force Publique (gendarmerie and military force) and the anti-slavery movement. Mention was not made of the abuses revealed by Morel and Casement nor of debates about Leopold's policies. The poster for the opening depicted a peaceful idyll of an African woman – adorned with a jewelled headband and ear-rings, and modestly clothed in a fabric wrap – playing a 'native' stringed instrument as she looked over her shoulder at the new colonial museum. The displays at the Tervuren institution did not alter substantially over the next half-century, and even after the independence of the Belgian Congo.

The Belgian Congo

With its African outpost from 1908, Belgium as a country officially entered the rank of European colonial powers. The Belgians established a Ministry of the Colonies, an aspirational plural as they possessed only one colony (though they would gain administration over parts of former German East Africa, the countries of Rwanda and Burundi, after the First World War). The Belgian trading and financial concerns established in the CFS, notably the banking giant Société Générale de Belgique, continued to do business and indeed expanded. The economic focus, however, moved from rubber to minerals, for the Congo was (and is) a treasure-trove of sub-soil resources. The Union Minière du Katanga, set up early in the twentieth century and operating in the mineral-rich eastern Katanga province, became the leading mining company. Meanwhile, colonial organizations proliferated in Belgium: institutes of tropical health and scientific research, the royal colonial institute and an academy to train civil servants for the Congo (called the Colonial University from 1923). As Matthew Stanard has shown, public and private interests undertook a concerted effort to promote the Congo, championing the benefits colonialism brought to Belgium. Central Africa began to appear more frequently in daily life in the form of products from the Congo, news reports and advertising.[8] Unlike some other colonial powers, however, Belgium did not encourage large-scale migration, and particularly not by foreigners – it aimed to ensure that the colony's European residents and businesses were primarily Belgian.

Studies by authors such as Guy Vanthemsche, David Van Reybrouck, Jean-Luc Vellut and Jean Stengers detail and analyse the history of the Belgian Congo in a way that cannot be done in the present chapter. In his forensic work on the Congo in Belgium's political and economic life, Vanthemsche says that the colony did not spark enthusiasm among the working classes (either in the Leopoldian period or afterwards), though the socialist party supported Belgian takeover of the CFS on humanitarian grounds. Vanthemsche argues that 'the colonial enterprise was not supported by a great wave of popular fervour, except in very specific and somewhat limited segments of the population': 'former or actual colonial civil servants, businessmen, soldiers, scientists and missionaries'. The colony was closely tied to the monarchy, a particularly strong and unifying institution in Belgium. Colonialism was more popular among the Walloons than the Flemish, yet the Flemish city of Antwerp was, in terms of business, shipping and general engagement, Belgium's colonial 'capital'. After 1908, the Congo 'rapidly began to occupy a prime position in official patriotic discourse' and was 'promoted as a source of enrichment for Belgium'. Even though not all were convinced, the Congo was vaunted as Belgium's 'tenth province', a territory which created 'Greater Belgium' – an echo of the 'Greater Britain', 'Greater France' and 'Greater Portugal' of other colonialists. Vanthemsche adds that there was little anti-colonialism in Belgium, unlike in other European countries, in part because the colony was not a burden on the Belgian state budget.[9]

Despite military support for colonialism, the Belgian army had limited involvement in the Congo; the Force Publique was formed of European volunteers (who monopolized the officer ranks) and African troops. African soldiers did not serve in the metropolitan army. The Belgian state was necessarily involved as administrator – providing a governor-general and other bureaucrats and appointing indigenous men as local chiefs – and as an economic actor. But even in the 1950s, the colonial ministry employed only 500 civil servants in Brussels; the portfolio was not considered especially prestigious, and the average term of a minister barely exceeded two years. The Catholic Church, a supporter of Leopold's undertakings, maintained a great stake in the Congo as the major provider of education and healthcare, and it converted a substantial number of Congolese (three-quarters of whom are now Christian, though not all Catholic).[10] By the end of the 1950s, 89,000 non-Africans lived in the Congo, only 0.6 per cent of the total population, many of them recent migrants; only 400–500 Congolese lived in Belgium. Economically, and despite its extensive resources and the unremitting propaganda about the wealth the Congo would produce, the colony accounted, as Vanthemsche has shown, for only between 1 and 2 per cent of Belgium's imports and exports in the early decades of the twentieth century, and almost never more than 7 per cent afterwards. That modest level of trade does not mean that the Congo was unimportant for certain sectors and companies; it provided the raison d'être for several mining companies, and the Société Générale and its subsidiaries and affiliates were heavily involved in Africa. The giant colony's exports encompassed minerals – copper, tin, gold, cobalt, zinc, diamonds and (from 1921) uranium – and such agricultural products as cotton, palm oil, palm nuts and coffee, though copper comprised around 40 per cent of total exports by the 1950s. There was much local industry, and the Congo became the second most industrialized African country after South Africa.

The colony was drawn into the First World War, with military campaigns waged from the Congo against the Germans in their African outposts; unlike in Britain and France – African troops were not deployed to Europe. After the war, policymakers devised further development plans, but the Congo, like other colonies, suffered economically with the plummeting of prices for primary products during the Depression. Government remained firmly with administrators from the metropole, with little participation even by Belgian settlers. During the Second World War, when Germany occupied Belgium, the Congo was left largely in the hands of its governor-general, Pierre Ryckmans, who rallied the colony to the Allies. Further planning initiatives eventuated after the war, in particular a wide-ranging ten-year plan adopted in 1949. The predominant opinion among Belgian authorities was that the Congo would remain a colony for decades to come, despite the emergence of anti-colonial movements elsewhere in Africa and nationalist stirrings in the Congo itself. At yet another great international exhibition, held in Brussels in 1958, the impression conveyed to visitors in the colonial pavilions was of secure and benevolent Belgian governance of a colony marked by progress, modernization and increasing prosperity.

The reality, of course, was somewhat different. The Belgians had made little effort to promote African participation in public life; those who worked in the Force Publique, the administration and private companies almost all held subaltern positions. Despite increased building of schools (and the opening of a university in 1954), only a very few Congolese continued their studies past primary education. At the time of independence, the Congo counted only twenty graduates (all of them men) from the local Louvanium University, and there were no indigenous physicians, engineers, lawyers or economists. There were, however, Congolese clerics – the first ordination of a Congolese Catholic priest dated from 1917.

The number of Western-style intellectuals and political activists was very limited in the early twentieth century, with Paul Panda Farnana (1888–1930) a notable exception. The son of a government-appointed chief, he attracted the attention of a colonial official who sent him to Belgium for education. Farnana spent his adolescence in a bourgeois host family, completed secondary school and studied agronomy in Brussels and Paris, becoming the first Congolese to gain tertiary qualifications in Europe. He enlisted in the Belgian army in the First World War, but was soon captured and spent almost four years as a German prisoner of war. After his release, and working as an agronomist in Belgium, Farnana in 1919 formed the Union Congolaise (with an initial membership of thirty-three), which called for gradualistic reform. Farnana took a public role as the only Congolese to address a National Colonial Congress in 1920; he participated in international Pan-African Congresses in 1919 and 1921. In 1929, he returned to the Congo, when he was appointed manager of an oil mill, but died from illness only a few months later, bringing to an end what might have been the long political career of the leading reformist.

By the mid-1950s, Léopoldville, the capital of the Belgian Congo, had grown into a city of 300,000 with a vibrant cohort of young Africans and *évolués* – those considered Westernized, and given a government document to indicate their status. The privileged young people were renowned for their taste for fashionable clothes, jazz music and nightlife. Photographs (many used for propagandistic purposes) show smart young Congolese dancing to Western orchestras, living in tidy houses with the 'modern comforts' that became the rage in the 1950s, and working in offices, scientific laboratories and other white-collar workplaces. Women were signed up for sewing circles, choirs and home economics classes. There was also an Association of Middle-Class Africans. Football (soccer) became wildly popular among all groups of Africans and Europeans, with thirty-nine teams in Léopoldville alone in 1939; teams of Europeans and Africans rarely competed against each other because of European sensitivities about white players losing to Blacks.

A growing Congolese intelligentsia included teachers, civil servants, journalists and 'assistant' doctors (given lesser qualifications than European practitioners). One of those prominent medical practitioners was Paul Bolya (1924–2002), who received his diploma locally in 1948 and then studied in Belgium. He later published articles on the future of the Congo, became the president of the Parti National du Progrès and served as spokesmen for African participants in a 1959 Brussels round-table meeting of Belgians and Congolese. There were also creative writers such as Antoine-Roger Bolamba (1913– 2002), an acclaimed French-language poet and editor of the government-aligned *La Voix du Congolais*. A more critical voice was Paul Lomami-Tshibamba (1914–85), a Catholic who in 1945 wrote a pioneering article about the *évolués*, 'What Will Be Our Place in the World of Tomorrow?' and who became an early promoter of Congolese independence. Three years later, he published the first Congolese novel, *Ngando* (Crocodile), which won a prize in Brussels despite earlier censorship.

The *évolués* and intellectuals comprised a very small group, and the majority of Congolese lived in shanty towns in the big cities, eked out a subsistence life in the countryside, laboured in harsh conditions in mines or worked as service personnel in

Belgian employ. Overt resistance episodically erupted, as in a revolt among the Pende people in 1931 and a strike by railwaymen and dockers in 1941, both rapidly suppressed. The involvement of Congolese in certain hybrid religious movements can also be interpreted as a type of resistance, though the largest, Kimbanguism – the Church of Jesus Christ on Earth, founded by a self-proclaimed prophet, Simon Kimbangu (1887–1951) – was not especially anti-colonialist.

The growth of the population of Belgians in the Congo from 36,000 in 1945 to 89,000 in 1952 suggested proof of economic growth in the post-war period as well as confidence in the colony's future and, presumably, faith in continued Belgian control. Europeans counted for a tiny minority in a total population of 16.6 million, but they monopolized political and Western-style economic life. They were honoured by a visit from King Baudouin in 1955, the first by a Belgian monarch. That same year, the Congolese intellectual Joseph Kasavubu (c. 1915–69) published in a Belgian journal a 'Thirty-Year Plan for Political Emancipation of Belgian Africa'. Other militant nationalists were emerging, among them Patrice Lumumba (1925–61). Born into a farming family and educated in Catholic and Protestant schools, Lumumba first worked as a postal clerk and beer salesman. He spent much of his free time reading European literature, and he visited Belgium, where he joined a liberal political party. After returning to the Congo, however, he lost his position in the colonial postal department, and spent a term in gaol, on conviction for embezzlement. Subsequent to his release, he joined in founding and became leader of the Mouvement National Congolais in 1958. The movement explicitly espoused independence, and Lumumba established contacts with other African political figures, such as Kwame Nkrumah, who had led the British Gold Coast (Ghana) to independence in 1957. The independence of French Guinea the following year, and moves towards independence in other African colonies, showed the gathering momentum of anti-colonialism and nationalism.

It came as something of a surprise to Belgians when riots broke out in Léopoldville on 4 January 1959 after the prohibition of a political rally planned by Kasavubu's Bakongo Alliance (ABAKO). Protesters nevertheless gathered and were joined by a crowd leaving a football match, with 35,000 people finally massing in the streets. Random attacks on European-owned shops and Christian missions occurred before the police regained control; the incident left 47 dead and 241 wounded according to official figures, though the toll may have been higher. Nationalists, such as Kasavubu, were arrested, and later in the year, Lumumba was also arrested for allegedly inciting a riot in Stanleyville. The demonstrations and arrests both spread the influence of the nationalists and prompted the government into consideration of political change.

In January 1960, Kasavubu (who had been released), Moïse Tshombé (1916–69) from Katanga, and other leaders of eight political groups were brought to Brussels for round-table discussions; Lumumba was soon freed and joined the meeting. Opinion was divided among the Belgians about the exact course of reform, but most of the Congolese pressed for independence rather than the status quo or a 'Belgo-Congolese Community'. After some wrangling, the conference decided, and the government accepted the recommendation, that after elections in May, the Congo would gain independence at the

Figure 29.1 Patrice Lumumba, soon-to-be prime minister of the independent Democratic Republic of the Congo, Brussels, January 1960. © Wikimedia Commons (public domain).

end of June. Given the way that the British and French had spent years in discussions about their African colonies, and the persistence with which the French had tried to retain their holdings as part of a Union Française and then Communauté, the speed and relative consensus with which Belgians agreed to withdraw are remarkable, an acknowledgement that the colonial situation had become untenable. The elections resulted in a victory for the nationalists, with Kasavubu chosen as president and Lumumba appointed as prime minister (Figure 29.1).

The independent Congo

Just days before the independence of the Congo, the Belgian government – which despite acquiescence to independence had continued repressive actions against dissidents and was charged by some with trying to thwart or postpone the emancipation of the Congo – deported from the Congolese capital a political activist named Andrée Blouin (1921–86). When a colonial customs official in Léopoldville asked if she planned to return, she reportedly asked him if he planned to leave. Blouin was a remarkable figure whose life and political activities traversed several frontiers. Born in the French colony of Oubanghi-Chari (now the Central African Republic) to an African mother and a French father, she was soon placed in a home for mixed-race 'orphans'. After fourteen years, she was able to leave and worked as a seamstress before establishing a relationship (which turned out to be short-lived) with a Belgian nobleman who was head of the Kasai mining company. She later returned home, and married and divorced a Frenchman, and then married another Frenchman, whose surname of Blouin she took. Her politicization, she recalled, came when her son was denied medical treatment for malaria at a French hospital because of his race and died from the disease. Blouin, with her husband, went to Guinea in support of nationalists there, but was expelled by the French government. She then went to the Belgian Congo where, in 1960, she founded the Feminine Movement for African Solidarity, which promoted enfranchisement, health and education for women. She also became personally and politically close to Patrice Lumumba; journalists sometimes tried to discredit her as a Communist, but she referred to herself as an African nationalist and pan-Africanist.[11]

In due order, and in the presence of King Baudouin, who was visiting once again, the Congo was declared independent on 30 June 1960. The monarch's speech began with the words: 'The independence of the Congo constitutes the outcome of the work conceived with the genius of King Leopold II, undertaken with tenacity by him and continued with perseverance by Belgium.' Baudouin's royal ancestor who founded the CFS 'did not present himself to you as a conqueror but as a civiliser', and he and Belgium brought the blessings of international trade, national unity, modern infrastructure and medical care – words with which nationalists and many historians might well take issue. Baudouin paid only nominal tribute to those who campaigned for independence, and warned about the challenges and dangers that lay ahead as he welcomed 'with joy and emotion' the independence of the Congo 'in full accord and friendship with Belgium'. President Kasavubu then delivered a conciliatory oration in which he commented on the personal 'solicitude' of Baudouin and expressed 'gratitude for the benefits that you and your illustrious predecessors provided'. Prime Minister Lumumba, who gave the third speech in a very different vein, did not mince words. Independence had been won by a long struggle to end 'the humiliating bondage forced upon us'. Lumumba continued:

We have experienced forced labour in exchange for pay that did not allow us to satisfy our hunger, to clothe ourselves, to have decent lodgings or to bring up our children as dearly loved ones. Morning, noon and night we were subjected to jeers, insults and blows because we were 'Negroes'. Who will ever forget that the black was addressed as '*tu*' [the informal second-person French singular pronoun used for close friends, family members, and also children and animals], not because he was a friend, but because the polite '*vous*' was reserved for the white man? We have seen our lands seized in the name of ostensibly just laws, which gave recognition only to the right of might. We have not forgotten that the law was never the same for the white and the black, that it was lenient to the ones, and cruel and inhuman to the others. We have experienced atrocious sufferings, been persecuted for political convictions and religious beliefs, and exiled from our native land: our lot was worse than death itself. We have not forgotten that in the cities the mansions were for the whites and the tumbledown huts for the blacks; that a black was not admitted to the cinemas, restaurants and shops set aside for 'Europeans'; that a black travelled in the holds [of ships], under the feet of the whites in their luxury cabins. Who will ever forget the shootings which killed so many of our brothers, or the cells into which were mercilessly thrown those who no longer wished to submit to the regime of injustice, oppression and exploitation used by the colonialists as a tool of their domination? All that, my brothers, brought us untold suffering.

The speech – the sentiments expressed and the breach of protocol it represented – angered Baudouin, but Lumumba's words won rounds of applause in Africa, and his speech is remembered as one of the most dynamic from the period of African decolonization.[12]

Belgium weathered decolonization without great difficulty. Belgians began to leave the Congo as the date of independence neared and afterwards; in July 1960 alone, Sabena airlines evacuated 25,000 people. Many Belgian mining and financial companies nevertheless continued to operate without hindrance at least until the mid-1960s, when nationalization of foreign businesses began, and missionaries similarly continued their work. However, the Congo did not fare well. Ethnic tensions erupted as independence broke, with secessionist movements in the Katanga and Kasai provinces. Lumumba's radicalism sparked fears in Belgium and elsewhere in the West in the context of the Cold War. Opposition also came from within the Congolese political elite, leading to a political stalemate. Joseph-Désiré Mobutu (1930–97), later known as Mobutu Sese Seko, a journalist and veteran of the Force Publique, took charge of the anti-Lumumba forces, and drove the prime minister from office. He was taken into custody and killed in unclear circumstances; evidence now shows complicity by the Belgian government in Lumumba's ouster and assassination. The United Nations sent in peace-keeping forces to quell the secessionist movement in Katanga, and that province and Kasai were incorporated into the Congo. The country emerged under the rule of Mobutu, who from 1965 to 1997 was the dictatorial president of the country that he renamed Zaire; in the wake of his removal, a civil war wracked the Congo from 1998 until 2003.

Meanwhile, the Belgians – like many in other countries with a colonial past – tried to move on, and indeed forget a colonial period that seemed 'history'. By the 1970s, Belgium maintained only limited political and business links with the Congo, though Brussels continued to provide aid. The population of Congolese in Belgium (including opponents of the Mobutu regime) grew larger, and Brussels became a centre for a lively migrant culture. Sub-Saharan Africans now make up 2 per cent of the Belgian population with 40 per cent of those of Congolese origin, far below the proportion of Africans in countries such as France.

Colonialism and Belgium's African museum

Through and after the last decades of colonialism, the Royal Museum of Central Africa in Tervuren enshrined a little changed and increasingly anachronistic vision of Africa and empire. The museum remained popular largely because of exhibits of natural history, but it seemed old-fashioned in *mise en scène* and questionable in its interpretations of history and culture by the late 1900s. In 2005, the museum held a major exhibition on 'The Memory of the Congo – the Colonial Period', with an impressive collection of maps, paintings, photographs and documents curated by the historian Jean-Luc Vellut, and a catalogue with essays on a variety of topics, including Congolese figures such as Fanana. The museum and Vellut, however, were taken to task, in particular by Hochschild, for what he charged was a largely uncritical and un-decolonized version of history. Discussions revived about the colonial record and the future of the Tervuren institution.[13]

Plans were already in train for an overhaul, and in 2013, the Tervuren museum closed for five years. During that time debate about the colonial past and its legacies gained in intensity, with demands from groups ranging from governments of former colonies to diasporic associations for official apologies for colonialism, the 'decolonizing' of museums, restitution of art and artefacts taken from overseas, and payment of compensation for slavery and colonial rule. Forums in Belgium and a popular television series refocused attention on colonialism in the lead-up to the museum's re-opening in 2018. Just beforehand, President Laurent Kabila of the Democratic Republic of the Congo (as the former Zaire since 1997 styles itself) repeated a plea for the restitution of Congolese art and documents, and a group of academics (and others) signed an open letter under the title 'What Are 300 Congolese Skulls Doing in Belgium?' King Philippe did not attend the official re-opening of the Africa Museum (as the Tervuren museum was renamed), the palace explaining that the monarch does not take part in events that do not enjoy consensual support. On the occasion of the Democratic Republic of Congo's sixtieth anniversary of independence in 2020, King Philippe in a letter to President Félix Tshisekedi expressed his 'deepest regrets' for Belgium's colonial record, a statement he repeated while visiting the Congo in 2022. He added that the colonial regime 'was one of unequal relations, unjustifiable in itself, marked by paternalism, discrimination and racism'.[14]

In 2019, Guido Gryseels, the long-serving director of the Tervuren museum who guided its renovation, straightforwardly conceded that, historically, 'We carry the responsibility for giving generations of Belgians a colonialist, almost racism-inspired message – that white civilisation is superior to black civilisation'. The new incarnation of the museum, he added, showed that 'We're certainly moving toward the direction of a decolonised museum'.[15] The present-day exhibition in Tervuren has indeed come a long way from the colonial exhibitions of 1897 and 1910 (and the world's fair of 1958). An introductory panel acknowledges that the museum's origin lay in the 'World's Fair of 1897, an initiative of King Leopold II. He saw it as a propaganda tool for presenting his colonial project in a positive light'; today's museum 'works closely with African institutions and the African diaspora'. The museum building itself is a classified monument, so much of the old ornamentation, such as wall maps of Africa and colonial-era murals, remain in place, as do colonialist-era statues in the rotunda. However, the rotunda now also contains a large sculptural profile of an African head, entitled 'New Breath, or Burgeoning Congo', by the Congolese Aimé Mpané that according to a display panel 'is an explicit response to the colonial statues in this space'. Visitors arrive inside the museum not via the rotunda, as in the past, but through an underground corridor that features a long African canoe, suggesting a connection between Belgium and Africa, and between the European world outside and the African collections inside. A wall inscription in various languages, 'Everything passes, except the past', provides an injunction to consider the museum in an historical but also present-day perspective. A side gallery near the entrance contains many sculptures from 1897 (and later) that most explicitly embody stereotypes of Africa, including a famous (or notorious) statue of an African man in a leopard cape and headdress standing over a supine figure; signposts warn that the room contains works now considered offensive.

Colonial history features elsewhere as well. There are, for instance, relics of Stanley's exhibition donated by his son-in-law in 1954 and documents from his archive, which the museum later acquired. The names of the 1508 Belgians who died in Leopold's CFS are still inscribed on a historic commemorative wall plaque, but a panel notes that 'the memorial does not refer in any way to the hundreds of thousands, perhaps even millions, of Congolese who died in the same period as direct or indirect victims of the Congo Free State, or to the population deficit that this violence caused'. The Congolese artist Freddy Tsimba has etched the names of the seven Congolese who died in the 'African village' at the 1897 exposition onto glass windows in counterpoint to the list of Belgians. A group of nude figures, standing outside the museum, holding their hands aloft in the pose of stripped captives, is another work by Tsimba. A historical gallery encompassing documents and objects, including a whip for corporal punishment and a painting of a flogging, provides a critical perspective on the CFS and the Belgian Congo. The concessionary companies are presented in a dark light: 'All means were used to exploit new areas. . . . Violence, hostage-taking, looting, and torture were the order of the day in many places.' Efforts have been made to balance ethnocentric concepts; a vitrine on education – championed as a colonial achievement in earlier iterations – points out, for example, that 'for centuries, African societies have organised schools for boys and girls. These supplemented the upbringing that children got from their parents. . . . The transfer of knowledge, skills, and values was part of the curriculum.' There are several displays on the independence movement. One on Patrice Lumumba speaks of the 'struggle against (neo)colonialism and for pan-Africanism' that 'makes him an icon, nationally and internationally'; the panel adds that 'in 2001, a Belgian parliamentary inquiry commission acknowledge[d] that the then Belgian government bore a moral responsibility for [his] murder'.

The old natural history displays remain largely in place, complete with taxidermied elephants, zebras and gorillas, and the 'Crocodile Room' is a popular hold-over – 'the museum has deliberately chosen to keep this room frozen in time. It shows how Congolese nature was collected, preserved, depicted and exhibited in the 1920s'. Ethnographic galleries include masks, sculptures, textiles, weaponry, utensils, photographs and documents, though the way they are explained follows present-day rather than colonialist museographical and anthropological perspectives. In screened interviews, Africans (many from the diaspora) discuss the artefacts and cultural practices. Visitors can see excerpts from colonial-era films, but also watch AfricaTube, 'a virtual library on contemporary digital Africa with blogs, audiovisual material, platforms and music'. There are allusions throughout the museum to debates about former colonial museums and contemporary collections of non-European art. An imaginative 2002 painting, commissioned from the Congolese artist Chéri Samba, 'Réorganisation', depicts Africans and Europeans engaged in a tug-of-war over the 'Leopard Man' statue while the museum director looks on, a nod to conflicts about the Tervuren institution.[16]

The Africa Museum contains an excellent collection of old art and artefacts, as well as historical documents, more recent acquisitions and commissioned works. Similar to the former colonial museums of Amsterdam and Paris – now the Musée National de l'Histoire de l'Immigration and the Tropenmuseum, respectively – the Tervuren building is a relic of a colonial age erected to celebrate empire. These and other museums, such as the Victoria and Albert Museum in London and the old ethnographic museum in Berlin (now part of the Humboldt Forum), have been forced to rethink their objectives, the provenance of their collections and the forms of their displays as part of a process of coming to terms with the colonial past. Intense debates and actions concerning that past continue – in Belgium, the marking of several statues of King Leopold II with graffiti by protesters. There is now close scrutiny of statues, monuments, museums and other public reminders of the Europeans' colonial ventures.[17]

Exhibitions, such as those organized in the Brussels area in 1897, and 1958, and museums that emerged, like the 'permanent' African museum created in 1910, presented the history of colonialism and the countries conquered in ways largely accepted in Europe at the time. They are part of that history; the architecture, decorative motifs and collections are testimony to particular periods and views, and to certain styles of collecting and museographical practice. They remain important parts of the national and international patrimony. Curators in the former colonial capitals have made efforts to reframe the ideas, and the works, that are exposed, though constrained by budgets, spaces within which displays are held, and competing pressures from diverse sectors of the public and political elite. Not everyone is or can be satisfied. The refurbished Tervuren museum remains a monument of colonialism (though now not a monument *to* colonialism) and an evolving institution, an object for debate on the colonial past and an active participant in that conversation.

CHAPTER 30
EPILOGUE
THE LEGACIES OF EMPIRES

In 1997, the Union Flag was lowered over Hong Kong, the British colony not gaining independence but, after 155 years, being retroceded to China, with assurances from Beijing that some of its laws and traditions would be preserved as it became a 'special administrative region' of the People's Republic. Two years later, the Portuguese flag came down in Macau, just a few years short of that colony's 500th anniversary as a Portuguese possession, the longest-lived European outpost in eastern Asia. The events in Hong Kong and Macau seemed postscripts to a process that had taken most European colonies in Asia to independence in the 1940s and 1950s, most of the African possessions in the late 1950s and early 1960s (with the exception of the late independence of Portuguese and Spanish colonies), and many of the remaining colonies in the Caribbean, Indian Ocean and Pacific by the end of the 1970s. However, colonialism in its long and complex history has left an indelible imprint on societies everywhere, including the European countries that expanded around the globe. This chapter will consider some aspects of that heritage.

'Leftover' colonies?

While European and other colonizers left most of their overseas territories, they did not quit all of them. What actually constitutes a 'colony' is a subject for legal, historical and perhaps moral debate, and charges of 'colonialism' can become potent political statements even in Europe. Nationalist Corsicans, whose island became part of France in 1769, have argued that they have been politically, economically and culturally colonized by the mainland French. Promoters of independence in Scotland have used similar arguments about the English, though in 2014, Scottish voters rejected independence in a formal referendum. Catalan campaigners for independence have advanced colonialist accusations against the Castilians in Spain. In 2017, most of the Catalans who turned out at the polls – yet a majority chose not to participate in a referendum that Madrid had declared illegal – voted in favour of separation from Spain. The fracturing of the Soviet Union and Yugoslavia in the 1990s and the formation of more than twenty new states in the wake represented for many people emancipation from colonial hegemony exercised by Moscow and Belgrade, and the break-up has sparked further nationalist and 'anti-colonialist' campaigns in the Balkans and central Asia.

European states (and several others) still administer forty-odd territories that were once colonies. Britain has Gibraltar, Bermuda, a host of Caribbean islands, St Helena and other islands in the eastern Atlantic, the British Indian Ocean Territory and the minuscule Pitcairn islands in the South Pacific – as well as the Falkland Islands, which Britain went to war to defend against Argentinian invasion in 1982. Overseas France extends from Saint-Pierre et Miquelon off the coast of eastern Canada to Martinique, Guadeloupe and smaller islands in the Caribbean and French Guiana in South America, La Réunion and Mayotte in the Indian Ocean, and New Caledonia, French Polynesia, and Wallis and Futuna in the Pacific. Greenland and the Faroes Islands form part of the Kingdom of Denmark. The Spanish monarch rules over Ceuta and Melilla, enclaves on the Moroccan coast. The kingdom of the Netherlands reaches to six islands in the Caribbean.[1]

These overseas territories do not form colonies in the classical sense, even if the ancestry and cultures of their population – indigenous peoples in some and many descendants of enslaved Africans in others, particularly in the West Indies – differ markedly from those of the metropoles. Their legal residents enjoy full citizenship in the nation states of which they are a part, rights of abode in the metropole and, in a number of cases, representation in national parliaments as well as elected local assemblies. They generally enjoy higher standards of living, and better access to education and medical care, than small neighbouring independent states. They boast democratic political systems, a free press, high levels of security and multiple political parties, but with public life occasionally tarnished by corruption, money-laundering, smuggling and marked ethnic disparities in income. Many residents consider, however, that they remain second-class citizens by comparison with compatriots in the metropoles, lacking parity in wages and government services.

In the 1970s, motivated by the tide of independence elsewhere and inspired by the militant ideas of the 'New Left', movements in a number of these territories agitated for independence, with a few fringe groups resorting to violence. In the 1980s a virtual civil war in New Caledonia, set indigenous Kanaks demanding independence against descendants of French settlers who opposed severing links with France. Images of violent demonstrations, hostage-taking, assassination and strong-armed police and army actions recalled the bad old days of the war in Algeria. The pro-independence Front de Libération Nationale Kanak et Socialiste, its name adapted from the Algerian nationalists, claimed independence as a right for indigenous people – by the 1980s, over a century of immigration had reduced the Kanaks' (Melanesians) to a minority. Opponents countered with arguments about majority rule and benefits of continued incorporation into the French Republic. Politicians in France insisted on the geostrategic and commercial value of the territory and the need to honour France's constitution. Negotiators finally worked out a *modus vivendi*, yet a disaffected Kanak assassinated the leader of the pro-independence movement, Jean-Marie Tjibaou (1936–89). Referenda in 2018, 2020 and 2021 produced a majority against independence, with voting divided along ethnic lines, and with a boycott by pro-independence voters of the 2021 referendum.

Other than in New Caledonia, no significant independence movement remains active in the remaining European overseas territories; the Western Sahara constitutes a special case because of Spain's full withdrawal. Indeed, voters in most places where the question has been put to a referendum have rejected independence. There nevertheless exist international conflicts about sovereignty: in addition to Argentina's claims on the Falklands, Spain claims Gibraltar, Morocco claims Ceuta and Melilla, and the independent Comoros Islands claims French-ruled Mayotte. It remains unlikely that any of these territories will be ceded or gain independence soon.

Colonialism, for unsatisfied present-day nationalist groups around the world, has been perpetuated by 'Third World' or 'Southern' states – many of whose borders were drawn by colonizers – since they gained independence. Attempts at secession by the Moluccas islands in the former Dutch East Indies, the Kantanga region in ex-Belgian Congo and Biafra in Britain's old colony of Nigeria proved unsuccessful. Bangladesh, however, broke away from Pakistan, Eritrea from Ethiopia and South Sudan from Sudan. East Timor was a Portuguese colony from the early 1500s until 1974, then had a very brief period of independence before invasion and occupation by Indonesia; it secured independence, after a bloody war against the Indonesian army and militias, in 2002. An independence movement has gained strength in the Indonesian province of West Papua, which has a Melanesian population; the territory had remained a Dutch colony after Indonesia's independence in the 1940s until a referendum, widely considered fraudulent, allowed its transfer to Indonesia in the mid-1960s. Elsewhere in the former colonial world, regional or ethnic groups have occasionally attempted secession though none with the level of blood-letting through guerrilla actions and bloody state suppression that occurred during a failed twenty-five-year violent campaign by Tamil Tigers in Sri Lanka, brought to an end in 2009.

These examples, as well as Western Sahara, reveal unresolved disputes on boundaries and sovereignty, and the grievances of particular peoples against rulers sometimes branded colonial. At the same time, there have occurred what may be considered efforts to 'recolonize' parts of the world, not necessarily by Europeans. Several nations, for instance, maintain extensive bases in Antarctica, yet international treaties do not recognize any claims to legal sovereignty; that presence is reinforced by scientific and military activities, prospecting for minerals, tourism and even the building of a church (on a Russian base) or the flying in of pregnant women to give birth to an Antarctic-born citizen (in the case of Argentina). Outer space may yet provide a further frontier for 'colonization' – human settlement on the moon, long a subject for science fiction, seems increasingly less so. Meanwhile back on earth, the Chinese have built permanent installations, including military facilities, on disputed islands in the South China Sea, reclaiming land by constructing platforms to turn partly submerged atolls into permanent bases. Claiming suzerainty over the whole South China Sea, in spite of other claims and international law, Beijing has harassed ships and airplanes travelling through the waters and skies. Beijing since 2010 has meanwhile extended its power through 'unequal treaties' with African nations, burdensome loans, a 'Belt and Road' arrangement with Asian countries and aggressive exploitation of natural resources in

Africa and South America. Chinese repression in Tibet since the 1950s, then in Xinjiang and most recently Hong Kong – in contravention of 1997 agreements with Britain – appears colonialist in strategy and objective. Russia, for its part, invaded Georgia in 2008 to back up two renegade would-be secessionist 'republics'. In 2014, Russia annexed the Crimea, then legally part of independent Ukraine but which had earlier formed part of the tsarist and Soviet empires. In 2022, Moscow launched a brutal invasion of Ukraine, the Russian president claiming that Ukraine was historically part of Russia; subsequent Russian atrocities have been widely considered war crimes. Colonialism, in various forms, endures.

The cultural legacies of colonialism

The long-lasting changes brought about around the world by colonialism can be discerned in countless ways, with language being one example. Although Amerindian languages are still spoken and officially recognized in parts of Central and South America, the languages of administration are Portuguese in Brazil, English in Guyana and Belize, Dutch in Suriname, French in French Guiana and Spanish elsewhere. English and French are European colonial languages brought into North America, with widespread Spanish an indirect legacy of colonialism. English is the national language of Canada (alongside French), Australia, New Zealand (with Maori), South Africa (with Afrikaans and several indigenous African languages), Singapore and the former British colonies in the Caribbean. It is widely used in Malaysia, South Asia and the Pacific islands. Portuguese remains the official language in Lisbon's former colonies, although sometimes spoken primarily by an urban minority; of the 220 million Portuguese speakers in the world, only ten million live in Portugal. The languages have all evolved in vocabulary, structure and pronunciation from European roots, often with introduction of words from indigenous languages, but they continue to provide links across continents and cultures institutionalized in the Commonwealth of Nations and organizations of Spanish- and Portuguese-speaking countries. European literature remains a patrimony of people far removed from the birthplaces of Shakespeare, Molière, Cervantes or Camões. A European language provides a lingua franca in countries with a multiplicity of languages and a vehicle for international transactions and cultural exchange.[2]

Hybrid languages survive from colonial days, including ones derived from English, such as the widely used Tok Pisin in Papua New Guinea (which has over 600 indigenous languages), and Bislama, the official language of Vanuatu (with 300 languages). French-based Creoles are spoken in independent Haiti, Dominica and St Lucia in the Caribbean, and Mauritius and the Seychelles in the Indian Ocean, which have not been French colonies since the Napoleonic Wars. Portuguese Creole is the vernacular of the Cape Verde Islands and São Tomé and Príncipe, and a Portuguese-influenced Creole, Papiamentu, is dominant in the Dutch Caribbean islands of Aruba, Bonaire and Curaçao; another Portuguese Creole, Kristang, barely survives in Malacca 400 years after the Portuguese were ejected from that Malaysian city. Migrants also took their languages around the colonized world

– the Indian languages now widely used in Fiji, Mauritius, Trinidad, Malaysia and South Africa, for instance, and the Chinese spoken throughout Southeast Asia.

Religion, particularly Christianity, represents another lasting legacy of colonial-era evangelization; migrants similarly carried Buddhism, Hinduism and Islam around the world. The Philippines and Brazil are two of the most Catholic countries in the world, and one of the largest Catholic basilicas is located in the former French colony of the Ivory Coast. Pacific islanders are devout Christians, and there and elsewhere Christianity has effectively been 'indigenized'. Christian practice indeed is more assiduous in former colonies than in a Europe progressively secularized and de-Christianized. Nominally Christian festivals, Christmas above all, are widely celebrated even in non-Christian societies, complete in tropical countries with images of reindeer and sleighs in the snow.

Daily life is increasingly globalized, and a process accelerated in the colonial period. Western-style coats and ties for men, and skirts, dresses and trousers for women replaced local apparel in many places. Foods introduced by colonizers continue to be consumed, including French-style baguettes and pâté, and strong coffee, in Vietnam. (Non-European foods, many of colonial origin or adapted from foreign cuisines – the curries beloved in Britain – have travelled along opposite foodways.) European sports represent another successful colonial export; football, rugby and cricket accompanied the British wherever they went. Cricket, the British imperial game, remains a link between sporting teams and audiences in South Asia, the West Indies, Australia and southern Africa. Soccer, imported from Britain to continental Europe in the late nineteenth century, followed the French, Dutch, Germans, Portuguese, Spanish and Italians, as well as the British, around the globe to become the 'world sport'.

The colonial legacy is visible in institutions modelled on European antecedents, for instance, universities, financial institutions such as national banks, systems of taxation and business organization (such as the limited liability company) and the written codification of laws. Many former British colonies have a Westminster system of government with a unicameral or bicameral parliament, prime minister and cabinet, and a tradition of debate and law-making borrowed from the British Houses of Parliament (though without hereditary members of an upper house). Indeed, the British monarch remains the nominal head of state, represented by a governor-general, in fourteen independent countries beyond the UK, from Australia and New Zealand to the Solomon Islands and Jamaica. Legal systems in former British colonies generally draw on English law and court systems; elsewhere, forms of law and governance bear the distinct imprint of the French, Dutch, Spanish or Portuguese. It is no surprise that European or Western countries have been characterized as long-lived hegemonic powers within the 'world system'.

Neo-colonialism and reactions

The prominence of European norms, and continued ties between European countries and their ex-colonies, provoked considerable criticism after independence. Kwame

Nkrumah, the president of Ghana, in *Neo-Colonialism, the Last Stage of Imperialism*, published in 1965, persuasively argued that the former colonial powers, through the capitalist economic system which they dominated, continued to exploit the resources and labour of the former colonies for their own profit and to the detriment of independent countries. Trade continued to perpetuate the exchange of primary products for manufactured goods with terms determined in metropolitan centres, while peripheral areas, including ex-colonies, were reliant on outside capital, technology and markets. Even widely touted development projects (sometimes reformulated on colonial models) for the Third World or the 'South' often were designed, critics said, for the benefit of metropolitan investors, businesses and consumers, leaving producers in Africa or Asia structurally handicapped by asymmetric relations of aid, finance and commerce.[3]

At the same time as Nkrumah's ideas were gaining currency, other critical commentators articulated 'dependency theory', mostly from Latin American perspectives. In this view, it was to the advantage of the more industrialized world to keep poor countries dependent in order to assure ready supplies of cheap fuel, minerals, agricultural products and labour. Dependency, they alleged, was an inevitable part of a capitalist system heavily weighted towards developed European countries and the United States. Marxism strongly influenced such views, and some theorists and activists suggested that countries such as the Soviet Union, Communist China and Fidel Castro's Cuba offered alternatives and promised more equitable economic, political and social systems.

Governments of a number of newly independent former colonies did try a radical restructuring away from Western models, most intentional and evident in avowedly Communist or Marxist countries, such as (North) Vietnam. In India, Prime Minister Jawaharlal Nehru propounded a more moderate socialist system that aimed at industrialization and a 'green revolution' in agriculture. In Tanzania, President Julius Nyerere promoted a brand of 'African socialism' that, he conjectured, would draw on indigenous African communitarianism along with Chinese models. Radical governments from Algeria to Madagascar sought dramatic breaks with Western schemes in the 1960s and 1970s through widespread nationalization of key industries and expropriation of private property, takeover of foreign companies, central economic planning and occasional collectivization. Often violent attacks on non-indigenous ethnic groups (and sometimes their expulsion) targeted diasporic Indians or Chinese, thought to control an unfair share of business and profit.

The more radical measures rarely produced great success, and countries that adopted them often suffered loss of overseas investment capital, technology and skills, as well as local strife. Corruption, mismanagement and authoritarianism were widespread. Gradually the pendulum swung back in the 1980s, though not without opposition, towards freer markets, greater receptivity to overseas direct investment, more business-friendly legal and taxation systems, and greater encouragement for private enterprise. Such was the case, for instance, with the *doi moi* or economic reform policy announced in Vietnam in 1986 which produced greater prosperity but retained one-party rule. The great economic growth of such countries as Japan and the 'Four Tigers' of the Asian economy in the 1990s – Singapore, Hong Kong (still a British colony at the time), Taiwan and South Korea – suggested new models of directed development. Singapore's heavy-handed state-led capitalist development achieved high standards of living compared to other former colonies in Asia under the long-term prime minister Lee Kuan Yew. Such economies as those of eastern and south-eastern Asia represented, for promoters, a different sort of capitalism than that of the West, in part because of the strong, even overweening, role of the state, intimate links between the state and private enterprise, and a focus on export-oriented production, as well as a tightly supervised political system.

Not only in economics did ex-colonies sometimes reject Western templates and influences. Though Iran had not been formally colonized by Europeans, Western economic interests had become prominent there in the mid-twentieth century. The attempt by the Iranian prime minister to nationalize the petroleum industry provoked a coup in the 1950s. Increasing American influence, matched by political repression under the Pahlavi dynasty of shahs, grew stronger. An 'Islamic revolution' inspired by an exiled cleric in 1979, dramatically marked by the holding hostage of American embassy staff, led to the establishment of a theocratic state based on shari'a law. Islamist groups elsewhere took inspiration from Teheran with the formation of new religious-based political parties and attacks on secularism and Western ways. These included the murderous terrorist attacks in New York and Washington in September 2001, and subsequently in London, Madrid, Paris and other cities inside and outside of Europe, as well as the establishment of the Taliban regime in Afghanistan (in both its first and current incarnations) and efforts to set up an Islamic 'caliphate' by an armed movement in western Africa. Such actions may be interpreted, in part, as a rejection of the Westernization that some Muslims closely identified with colonialism and neo-colonialism, though in the case of the Taliban also a fight against the Soviets, then the Americans. Fundamentalist movements in other religions, such as the Hindutva in India, have similarly campaigned against Westernization, globalization, cultural imperialism and neo-colonialism, phenomena frequently conjoined in rhetoric.

In different and non-violent ways, independent countries also pushed back against legacies of colonialism, while retaining others. The founders of independent Indonesia in the 1940s articulated a national ideology called Pancasila, based on the five principles of belief in one God, a just humanity, a unified country, democracy and a sense of social justice; commitment to democracy was brought into question, however, when a coup d'état in 1965 brought to power a military government that ruled for thirty-one years. Malaysia's prime minister Mahathir Mohammed, architect of that country's economic and social modernization in the 1990s, proclaimed the importance of 'Asian values' – a vague conceptualization of the perceived sense of the family, the land, collective action and religion. In Oceania, the Fijian prime minister Ratu Sir Kamisese Mara promoted a 'Pacific way' based on social consensus, island community and fidelity to Christianity. Latin American countries such as Ecuador and Bolivia have included notions of *buen vivir*, a good life, in their constitutions, building on pre-colonial values as alternatives to Western-dominated paths of development and economic growth. Bhutan developed a principle of 'gross national happiness', which leaders of the small Buddhist kingdom in the Himalayas proposed would provide a better gauge and goal of well-being than 'gross national product'.

Few independent countries, however, have wanted (or been able to) purge their societies of the manifold legacies of colonialism, nor foresworn Western imports and capital. In most cases, a combination of the local and global, indigenous and Western precepts, practices and institutions have ultimately won out. Even countries that once tried to pursue radically independent paths, such as Mao Zedong's China at the time of the 'Great Leap Forward' and the 'Cultural Revolution' or Cambodia under the genocidal Khmers Rouges of Pol Pot, eventually retreated (though in the case of China without abandoning Maoist ideology and political institutions).

Migration

One of the most significant colonial legacies has been the conduits of international migration created in the age of empires.[4] Colonialism forced, allowed and promoted migration in many directions – settlers (and convicts) moving from metropoles to colonies, slaves and indentured labourers shifted around the world, free migration from one colony to another, and one country to another. However, people from the colonies also moved to Europe, from the colonial-born of European ancestry who returned 'home' to indigenous and diasporic people who went to Europe to work, study, serve in military forces or for other reasons. There had been a Black presence in cities such as London, Paris and Lisbon for centuries, and that increased substantially in the 1800s and 1900s – Black people in Britain at the beginning of the twentieth century numbered as many as 30,000, and in Lisbon, a group of young African students in 1911 established a journal, *O Negro* (though it managed to publish only three issues). Black people were far from uncommon in Paris, especially by the mid-twentieth century, from factory workers to dockers, politicians, jazz singers and dancers, and the poets and novelists of the *négritude* movement.

Decolonization provided further opportunities or a compunction to move to the metropole. A million *rapatriés* fled Algeria for France in 1962, and some 800,000 *retornados* left the Portuguese African colonies in the mid-1970s, a staggering volume of people who fled countries on the verge of independence for 'homelands' that many had never known. Europeans and a large proportion of Eurasians similarly left South Asia and the Dutch East Indies for Britain and the Netherlands, or moved to other countries like Australia. Many of the remaining Portuguese in the former African colonies moved to Brazil in the 1970s. Jews in French North Africa migrated in large numbers to Israel in the 1950s and 1960s. However, Europeans also continued migrating to the former colonies. Of the more than four million migrants to Australia between 1945 and 1985, 40 per cent came from Britain and Ireland, and many others arrived from former British colonies such as Malta, Cyprus and, in particular, New Zealand. Towards the end of the twentieth century, more French men and women lived in the Ivory Coast than before independence, and after the socio-economic crisis in 2008, a stream of Portuguese and Spaniards set off for growing Brazil and oil-rich Angola; Portuguese nationals numbered 200,000 in Angola in 2013. Burgeoning economies and job opportunities attracted businessmen to booming countries, and tropical beaches and the low cost of living lured retirees to holiday islands in the Caribbean, and more recently the possibilities of remote working, thanks to computers and the internet, attracts others to places with pleasant climates.

Men and women from former colonies moved to Europe after independence in much larger numbers than ever before. The growth of European economies during the decades immediately following the Second World War created a huge demand for labour. Men and women from former colonies (and places such as Turkey, in the case of Germany) fled dire economic problems, and sometimes social and political strife, at home to seek work in Europe, though most found only jobs in subaltern positions for low wages and in poor conditions. Ironically, some of the workers moving from Africa to countries such as Portugal were replacing southern Europeans who had headed north to Germany, France or Switzerland. The French had long brought in North Africans and Black Africans as workers, and the government allowed citizens of its former colonies relatively open access to France – mostly because their labour was needed in the bustling economies. However, migrants often received a cold welcome, finding themselves socially segregated and culturally excluded from the rest of the nation, victims of widespread racism and discrimination. Migrants once thought temporary nevertheless settled permanently, and brought in family members from overseas. Some neighbourhoods of European cities began to be associated with particular migrant groups – Brick Lane in East London with South Asians, the Goutte d'Or in Paris with Black Africans, the Chinatowns in many cities home to migrants from East and Southeast Asia. Cities such as Marseille in France and Bradford in Britain became closely identified with large populations from the former colonies.

Algerians and Black Africans arrived in greater numbers in France in the 1950s and 1960s to fill jobs in factories, construction and domestic service; Tunisians made a speciality in operating corner groceries. Many South Asians migrated to Britain; Bangladeshis became a prominent group of restaurateurs. Both the British and French looked to their West Indian colonies as sources of labour for the lower echelons of the public service (especially the post office) and for hospital work. Meanwhile, swelling cohorts of students came to European universities and other educational institutions, sometimes on scholarships. Wealthy Africans and Asians invested in property in London or Paris, or placed their money in bank accounts in Switzerland, sometimes under barely legal circumstances.

Migrants from the former colonies (and other parts of the world who arrived or stayed without authorisation) were more and more often referred to as 'clandestine', 'irregular' or 'illegal' migrants – words with a marked political valence. They fled poverty, lack of job opportunities, social tensions and, in certain cases, civil war, ethnic conflict and political repression. In attempting to reach Europe, they risked their lives on hazardous journeys crossing borders or crossing the ocean, and they faced arrest and deportation without appropriate 'papers' and rights to remain. Many arrived in desperate straits, with no funds and few, if any, possessions. The policies among European governments towards such migrants differed greatly, as did public opinion.

Migration provoked populist political reaction. In 1968, one extremist British politician, Enoch Powell, declared that 'rivers of blood' would flow in conflicts between

The Colonial World

'real' English people and increasing 'coloured' migrants from the former empire. In 1972, in France, Jean-Marie Le Pen formed the National Front, a political movement centred on opposition to Muslim immigration (particularly migrants from France's former territories in North Africa). The movement waxed and waned, as did similar ones elsewhere, but immigration – and the economic and cultural repercussions it produced – had been placed squarely on the European political agenda. In the early twenty-first century, racially inflected anti-immigrant sentiment and political parties mobilizing such sentiment have heightened and spread to most European countries, accompanied by episodes of violence directed at new migrants and those from Africa and Asia whose families arrived in Europe many decades, or even centuries, earlier.

Though there are heart-rending images of refugees and other desperate migrants arriving in Europe, and sobering reports of poverty and discrimination as the lot of many Arabs, Africans and Asians already there, it is important to remember that many migrants from the former colonies have succeeded in overcoming the obstacles put in their way by the host societies and made remarkable contributions to the European countries to which they came. European countries are more multi-ethnic than even colonialists imagined, not because of the maintenance of a 'Greater Britain', 'Greater France' or 'Greater Portugal', but because of the arrival and integration of overseas migrants and their cultures into post-colonial metropoles.[5]

Post-colonial Europe

Both European and non-European countries have become far more cosmopolitan in recent decades, in part because of the links maintained between former colonizing countries and the ex-colonies. Cities such as London, Paris and Brussels provide centres for the musical, artistic, literary and academic creativity of diasporic populations. Europeans dance to the beat of Jamaican reggae and listen to North African *raï*. They eat Indian curries, Algerian couscous and Vietnamese spring rolls. They read novels, watch films and attend art exhibitions by African and Asian creators, and they practice yoga and 'easterrn' religions. Clothing designers and interior designers incorporate motifs from non-European traditions. Travellers book trips to the former colonies – and it is no surprise that places such as Cape Verde are popular with the Portuguese, Barbados with the British and La Réunion with the French, or indeed Greenland with the Danish. In a myriad of ways, the colonial era has left multiple connections between Europe and other parts of the world, at times still reflecting the asymmetrical power structures and stereotypes of colonial times.[6]

As the years of the colonial epoch receded, Europeans harboured disparate visions of empire. Many celebrated the independence of former colonies, and honoured and drew inspiration from such anti-colonial leaders as Mahatma Gandhi (Figure 30.1). Growing consensus emerged about the misdeeds of imperial conquerors and rulers, and horror at slavery, violence and colonial exactions Some saw the old days through rose-coloured lenses that mixed exoticism with a romanticization of imperial days. Stimulated

Figure 30.1 Statue of Mahatma Gandhi by Fredda Brilliant erected in 1968 in Tavistock Square, London. © Alamy Stock Photo.

by exhibitions, novels, films, television serials and tourism, such views could easily shade into 'Raj nostalgia', *Indochic* (chic Indochina) or a recollection of the *mooi Indië*, the beautiful Indies. Yet those perspectives also had a harder edge. Extremist political organizations in France bemoaned the 'loss' of *Algérie Française*, and lambasted the arrival of migrants from countries French colonizers once proudly claimed. Regretting the end of empire, and not just in France, for some meant mourning the decline of national greatness. Colonialism inflected new debates and conflicts in Europe, such as in France, concerning the wearing of headscarves or facial coverings by a minority of Muslim women, and – prompted by newspaper testimonies around 2000 – about the torture practiced by the colonial military and police force in Algeria (and, earlier, in Indochina). In Britain, there were impassioned debates about repression of the Mau Mau rebellion in Kenya in the 1950s, as well as the 'Windrush affair' concerning the detention and deportation of British subjects, particularly from Caribbean countries, who had come to Britain from the 1940s to the early 1970s. In Germany, discussion focused on whether massacres of the Herero and Nama peoples in Southwest Africa between 1904 and 1908 provided a template for Nazi-era genocide and Nazi 'colonization' of eastern Europe. In Italy, exposés about aerial bombing and the use of poison gas in Libya and Ethiopia contradicted still widely held ideas about Italian colonizers as benign *brava gente*. The 500th anniversaries of the voyages of Columbus in Spain and Vasco Da Gama in Portugal provided occasions for debates about the 'discoverers' (but 'invaders' for others) and the papering over of the violence and exploitation, and a continuing triumphalist portrayal of empire. The horrors of the Congo Free State set off acrimonious debate in Belgium towards the end of the twentieth century. Throughout Europe, the United States and beyond, discussion about slave trading, slavery and the long-lasting effects of the slave system remains timely and potent.

Debate rocked settler societies as well. In Australia, the bicentenary of the arrival of the 'First Fleet' in 1788 provoked conflict about whether that event was the beginning of British 'settlement' or represented a British 'invasion'. During the so-called 'history wars' of the 1980s, the opposing stances were caricatured as 'white blindfold' versus a 'black armband' version of history. Canada, New Zealand and South Africa, as well, have experienced their debates on the colonial past and about the record of post-independence governments in the treatment of First Nations people.

Many issues that were raised remain unresolved, and new ones appear. There are calls for 'decolonizing' school curricula and museums said to present a one-sided and whitewashed view of colonialism. There have been demands for apologies for colonialism – and indeed some have been issued, from Dutch apologies for violence in the East Indies to Canadian apologies for the treatment of First Nations people in that country. There have been calls for restitution of indigenous works collected during the colonial area – often as the booty of conquest or through shady purchases – from European museums; a report commissioned by French president Emmanuel Macron, authored by a Senegalese and a French expert, Selwine Sarr and Bénédicte Savoy, in 2018, recommended large-scale return of African objects in French museums.[7] Yet other calls have been for payment of compensation to descendants of slaves and the countries from which slaves were taken. And there has been the question, too, of the pulling down of monuments and statues of figures whose reputations are tarnished because of colonial actions deemed heinous (see Figure 30.2). In 2020 protesters in Bristol toppled a statue

Figure 30.2 Students protest calling for removal of the statue of Cecil Rhodes at Oriel College, Oxford University, 2021. © Getty Images.

of Edward Colston, a British merchant, philanthropist and member of Parliament in the late 1600s and early 1700s, because of his involvement in the Atlantic slave trade. This was an emblematic attempt to address – or in the views of some, to rewrite – the past as commemorated in European landscape and memory. The issues of the colonial past, and coming to terms with the colonial past, have thus been vented in schools and universities, in publications, films and television documentaries, in parliaments and museums, through the activities of individuals and groups and in public demonstrations.

Europeans and those outside Europe are increasingly taking account of the huge role that colonialism played in their history. The legacy of colonialism for some is individual – an ancestor who served in a colonial army or public administration, a missionary society or trading house, or an ancestor who was a slave, an indentured labourer, an employee of European colonizers, a soldier in a colonial army, or perhaps a visitor or migrant to Europe from Asia or Africa – or a fighter for independence of his or her homeland.

The heritage is also collective, the way in which European and non-European societies were implicated in colonial expansion, how they were reshaped by colonialism and how attitudes and institutions, and cultural, commercial and international connections developed during the colonial era endure today.

NOTES

Chapter 1

1   For recent overviews on colonialism and empire, see Jane Burbank and Frederick Cooper, *Empires in World History: Power and the Politics of Difference* (Princeton, NJ: Princeton University Press, 2010), and Norrie MacQueen, *Colonialism* (Harlow: Pearson Longman, 2007).

2   John Atkinson Hobson, *Imperialism: A Study* (London: James Nisbet & Co., 1902).

3   Vladimir I. Lenin, *Imperialism: The Highest Stage of Capitalism* (London: Pluto Press, 1996 [1917]).

4   Wolfgang J. Mommsen *Theories of Imperialism* (Chicago, IL: University of Chicago Press, 1982) is still a concise and readable overview of these early developments.

5   John Gallagher and Ronald Robinson, 'The Imperialism of Free Trade', *The Economic History Review* 6, no. 1 (August 1953): 1–15.

6   Peter J. Cain and Antony G. Hopkins, 'Gentlemanly Capitalism and British Expansion Overseas. I. The Old Colonial System, 1688–1850', *Economic History Review* 39, no. 4 (November 1986): 501–25, and 'II. New Imperialism, 1850–1945', *Economic History Review* 40, no. 1 (February 1987): 1–26. For the debate, see Raymond E. Dumett, ed., *Gentlemanly Capitalism and British Imperialism: The New Debate on Empire* (London: Routledge, 1999).

7   Jacques Marseille, *Empire colonial et capitalisme français: Histoire d'un divorce* (Paris: Albin Michel, 1984).

8   Henri Brunschwig, *French Colonialism, 1871–1914: Myths and Realities* (London: Pall Mall Press, 1966), first published in French in 1960.

9   Kwame Nkrumah, *Neo-Colonialism: The Last Stage of Imperialism* (London: Nelson, 1965); Fernando Henrique Cardoso, *Dependency and Development in Latin America* (Berkeley, CA: University of California Press, 1979).

10 Ranajit Guha and Gayatri Chakravorty Spivak, eds, *Selected Subaltern Studies* (Oxford: Oxford University Press, 1989).

11 See the review essay by Malia B. Formes, 'Beyond Complicity versus Resistance: Recent Work on Gender and European Imperialism', *Journal of Social History* 28, no. 3 (1995): 629–41. For overviews, see Philippa Levine, ed., *Gender and Empire* (Oxford: Oxford University Press, 2004), and Angela Woollacott, *Gender and Empire* (Houndmills: Palgrave Macmillan, 2006).

12 Edward Said, *Orientalism* (New York: Pantheon, 1978).

13 Edward Said, *Culture and Imperialism* (New York: Knopf, 1993).

14 John M. MacKenzie, *Orientalism: History, Theory and the Arts* (Manchester: Manchester University Press, 1995).

15   Sebastian Conrad, *What is Global History?* (Princeton, NJ: Princeton University Press, 2017).

16   Ann Laura Stoler, *Race and the Education of Desire: Foucault's History of Sexuality and the Colonial Order of Things* (Durham, NC: Duke University Press, 1995).

17   Robert Marks, *The Origins of the Modern World: A Global and Environmental Narrative from the Fifteenth to the Twenty-First Century* (Lanham, MD: Rowman & Littlefield, 2020).

18   See Andrew Thompson, ed., *Writing Imperial History* (Manchester: Manchester University Press, 2013), and Robin Winks, Wm. Roger Louis, and Alaine Low, eds, *The Oxford History of the British Empire*, vol. V: *Historiography* (Oxford: Oxford University Press, 1999).

19   Walter D. Mignolo and Catherine E. Walsh, *On Decoloniality: Concepts, Analytics, Praxis* (Durham, NC: Duke University Press, 2018).

Chapter 6

1   Fedor Jagor, *Reisen in den Philippinen: Mit zahlreichen Abbildungen und einer Karte* (Berlin: Weidmannsche Buchhandlung, 1873), v.

2   María Dolores Elizalde, 'The Philippines in the Context of the Nineteenth-Century Spanish Empire', in *The Routledge Hispanic Studies Companion to Nineteenth-Century Spain*, ed. Elisa Martí López (London: Routledge, 2020), 108.

3   See Bernhard C. Schär, '"The Swiss of All People!": Politics of Embarrassment and Dutch Imperialism around 1900', in *Anxieties, Fear and Panic in Colonial Settings: Empires on the Verge of a Nervous Breakdown*, ed. Harald Fischer-Tiné (Cham: Palgrave Macmillan, 2016), 279–303.

4   Fedor Jagor, *Viajes por Filipinas*, trans. S. Vidal y Soler (Madrid: Aribau, 1875).

5   For Mexico, see Vera S. Candiani, 'Social and Ecological Impacts of Conquest and Colonization in New Spain', in *The Oxford Handbook of Mexican History*, ed. William Beezly (Oxford: Oxford University Press, 2021), 1–37.

6   Patricia Prutscher, *Kolonialität und Geschlecht: Eine Geschichte der weißen Schweiz* (Bielefeld: Transcript, 2019).

7   Alfred W. Crosby, *Ecological Imperialism: The Biological Expansion of Europe, 900–1900* (Cambridge: Cambridge University Press, 2013); Richard H. Grove, *Green Imperialism: Colonial Expansion, Tropical Island Edens and the Origins of Environmentalism, 1600–1860* (Cambridge: Cambridge University Press, 1995). See also Corey Ross, *Ecology and Power in the Age of Empire: Europe and the Transformation of the Tropical World* (Oxford: Oxford University Press, 2017). There are a number of regional histories of the environment, such as Michael H. Fisher, *An Environmental History of India: From Earliest Times to the Twenty-First Century* (Cambridge: Cambridge University Press, 2018), and Tom Griffiths and Libby Robin, eds, *Ecology and Empire: Environmental History of Settler Societies* (Melbourne: Melbourne University Press, 1997).

8   Shawn W. Miller, *An Environmental History of Latin America* (Cambridge: Cambridge University Press, 2007), 60–3.

9   Ann Moyal, *Platypus: The Extraordinary Story of How a Curious Creature Baffled the World* (Crows Nest NSW: Allen & Unwin, 2010).

10   For colonial expansion, for example, in South Africa, see Sandra Swart, 'Riding High: Horses, Power and Settler Society, *c.* 1654–1840', *Kronos* 29 (November 2003): 47–63.

11 Olivier Lebleu, *In the Footsteps of Zarafa, First Giraffe in France: A Chronicle of Giraffomania, 1826–1845* (Lanham, MD: Rowman & Littlefield, 2020).

12 Joseph Sramek, '"Face Him Like a Briton": Tiger Hunting, Imperialism, and British Masculinity in Colonial India, 1800–1875', *Victorian Studies* 48, no. 4 (Summer 2006): 659–80.

13 Peter Hobbins, *Venomous Encounters: Snakes, Vivisection and Scientific Medicine in Colonial Australia* (Manchester: Manchester University Press, 2017).

14 On Java, a European planter boasted in the mid-nineteenth century of having killed over 144 tigers, sometimes shooting up to four on a single day. Fedor Jagor, *Singapore – Malacca – Java: Reiseskizzen* (Berlin: Verlag von Julius Springer, 1866), 163.

15 Sujit Sivasundaram, 'Trading Knowledge: The East India Company's Elephants in India and Britain', *The Historical Journal* 48, no. 1 (March 2005): 27–63.

16 Tim Bonyhady, *The Colonial Earth* (Melbourne: Melbourne University Press, 2000).

17 Valeska Huber, *Channelling Mobilities: Migration and Globalisation in the Suez Canal Region and Beyond, 1869–1914* (Cambridge: Cambridge University Press, 2013).

18 On rubber and palm trees, see Jonathan E. Robins, *Oil Palm: A Global History* (Chapel Hill, NC: University of North Carolina Press, 2021) and William G. Clarence-Smith, 'Rubber Cultivation in Indonesia and the Congo from the 1910s to the 1950s: Divergent Paths', in *Colonial Exploitation and Economic Development: the Belgian Congo and the Netherlands Indies compared*, ed. Ewout Frankema and Frans Buelens (London: Routledge, 2013), 193–210.

19 Grove, *Green Imperialism*; Zaheer Baber, 'The Plants of Empire: Botanic Gardens, Colonial Power and Botanical Knowledge', *Journal of Contemporary Asia* 46, no. 4 (2016): 659–79; Michael A. Osborne, 'Acclimatizing the World: A History of the Paradigmatic Colonial Science', *Osiris* 15, no. 1 (2000): 135–51.

20 John L. Tone, *War and Genocide in Cuba, 1895–1898* (Chapel Hill, NC: University of North Carolina Press, 2006), 97; Andreas Stucki, *Las Guerras de Cuba: Violencia y campos de concentración, 1868–1898* (Madrid: Esfera de los Libros, 2017), 159.

21 Mariola Espinosa, *Epidemic Invasions: Yellow Fever and the Limits of Cuban Independence, 1878–1930* (Chicago, IL: University of Chicago Press, 2009).

22 Fasil Demissie, ed., *Colonial Architecture and Urbanism in Africa* (London: Routledge, 2016), Robert Home, *Planning and Planting: The Making of British Colonial Cities* (London: Routledge, 2013), and Gwendolyn Wright, *The Politics of Design in French Colonial Urbanism* (Chicago, IL: University of Chicago Press, 1991) are three studies, among many others.

23 Graeme Davison, *The Rise and Fall of Marvellous Melbourne* (Melbourne: Melbourne University Press, 2014).

24 William S. Logan, *Hanoi: Biography of a City* (Sydney: University of New South Wales Press, 2000).

25 Sean Anderson, *Modern Architecture and its Representation in Colonial Eritrea: An In-visible Colony, 1890–1941* (London: Routledge, 2016).

26 Maurizio Peleggi, 'The Social and Material Life of Colonial Hotels: Comfort Zones as Contact Zones in British Colombo and Singapore, *c.* 1870–1930', *Journal of Social History* 46, no. 1 (Fall 2012): 124–53.

27 Benjamin B. Cohen, *In the Club: Associational Life in Colonial South Asia* (Manchester: Manchester University Press, 2015).

Notes

28 Ashley Jackson, *Buildings of Empire* (Oxford: Oxford University Press, 2013).

29 Elizabeth A. Foster, 'An Ambiguous Monument: Dakar's Colonial Cathedral of the Souvenir Africain', *French Historical Studies* 32, no. 1 (2009): 85–119.

30 Prashant Kidambi, Manjiri Kamat and Rachel Dwyers, eds, *Bombay Before Mumbai: Essays in Honour of Jim Masselos* (Oxford: Oxford University Press, 2019); Sumanta Bannerjee, *Memoirs of Roads: Calcutta from Colonial Urbanization to Global Modernization* (Oxford: Oxford University Press, 2016); Zeynep Çelik, *Urban Forms and Colonial Confrontations: Algiers under French Rule* (Berkeley, CA: University of California Press, 1997); Liora Bigon and Xavier Ricou, *French Colonial Dakar: The Morphogenesis of an African Regional Capital* (Manchester: Manchester University Press, 2016).

31 Andrew Barber, *Colonial Penang, 1786–1957* (Kuala Lumpur: Karamoja Press, 2017).

32 Miller, *An Environmental History*, 4–5.

Chapter 7

1 Miguel Barnet, *Biografía de un cimarrón* (Barcelona: Ariel, 1968), 41. English translation in Esteban Montejo, 'Life in the Woods', *Diogenes* 45, no. 179 (September 1997): 209.

2 Miguel Barnet, 'The Documentary Novel', *Cuban Studies/Estudios Cubanos* 11, no. 1 (January 1981): 19–32.

3 See Barnet's 'Introducción', in his *Biografía*, 1–10.

4 William Luis, 'Introduction: Memory and Politics in Writing *Biography of a Runaway Slave*', in Miguel Barnet, *Biography of a Runaway Slave: Fiftieth Anniversary Edition* (Evanston: Northwestern University Press, 2016), xiii–xiv, xxv, xxxiii, xxix–xli.

5 Barnet, *Biografía*, 60.

6 Luis, 'Introduction', xii and xxix.

7 Upahat Ba Phoi, *The History of Kham Thong Luang*, translation and study by Peter Koret with the assistance of Maha Kaew Sirivongsa (np: Broken Hand Press, 2018); quotations are taken from the first volume or Koret's introduction, as the second volume of the translation had not been published at the time of writing. The numbers refer to lines of his poem (which has been translated to prose by Koret).

8 Emmanuel Kwaku Akyeampong and Henry Louis Gates, Jr., eds, *Dictionary of African Biography* (Oxford: Oxford University Press, 2012). Recent full-scale studies include Anaïs Angelo, *Power and the Presidency: The Jomo Kenyatta Years* (Cambridge: Cambridge University Press, 2020); Paul Bjerk, *Julius Nyerere* (Athens, OH: Ohio University Press, 2017); Susan Williams, *Colour Bar: The Triumph of Seretse Khama and His Nation* (London: Penguin, 2007); there is no recent biography of Kaunda or Banda. Comparisons could also be made with the first presidents of other former British African colonies, e.g., Nnamdi Azikiwe (1904–96) of Nigeria, Sir Dawda Jawara (1924–2019) of the Gambia; Kwame Nkrumah (1909–72) of Ghana, and from Uganda, Mutesa II (1924–69), who was the Kabaka (king) of Buganda.

9 On the evolving discussions about women in the colonies, see Formes, 'Beyond Complicity versus Resistance', 629–41, and Durba Gosh, 'Gender and Colonialism: Expansion or Marginalization?' *The Historical Journal* 47, no. 3 (September 2004): 737–55.

10 See the essays in Nuno Domingos, Miguel Bandeira Jerónimo, and Ricardo Roque, eds, *Resistance and Colonialism: Insurgent Peoples in World History* (Cham: Palgrave Macmillan,

2019) and Tanja Bührer et al., eds, *Cooperation and Empire: Local Realities of Global Processes* (New York: Berghahn, 2017).

11 The phrase is borrowed from Ann Laura Stoler, 'Making Empire Respectable: The Politics of Race and Sexual Morality in 20th-Century Colonial Cultures', *American Ethnologist* 16, no. 4 (November 1989): 634–60.

12 This refers to the Escolas Rita Norton de Matos in Angola, founded 1912–13. See José Norton de Matos, *A nação una: Organização política e administrativa dos territórios do ultramar português* (Lisbon: Paulino Ferreira, 1953), 93–5.

13 For the African context, see the introduction in Benjamin N. Lawrance, Emily Lynn Osborn, and Richard L. Roberts, eds, *Intermediaries, Interpreters, and Clerks: African Employees in the Making of Colonial Africa* (Madison, WI: University of Wisconsin Press, 2006), 4, 27. For a recent contribution, Philip J. Havik, 'Gendering Public Health: Shifting Health Workforce Policies and Priorities in Portugal's African Colonies, 1945–1975', in *Gendering the Portuguese-Speaking World: From the Middle Ages to the Present*, ed. Francisco Bethencourt (Leiden: Brill, 2021), 199–228.

14 Spain also claimed the enclave of Ifni on Morocco's Western Atlantic coast until 1969. The enclaves of Ceuta and Melilla on Morocco's Mediterranean coast remain under Spanish control. See John Connell and Robert Aldrich, *The Ends of Empire: The Last Colonies Revisited* (Cham: Palgrave Macmillan, 2020), 96–7.

15 The phrase was an allusion to the uniforms of the Women's Section – a skirt and the blue blouse, dating back to the founding days of Spanish fascism. The term is borrowed from Inbal Ofer, *Señoritas in Blue: The Making of a Female Political Elite in Franco's Spain* (Brighton: Sussex Academic Press, 2009).

16 This and the following sections draw on Andreas Stucki, *Violence and Gender in Africa's Iberian Colonies: Feminizing the Portuguese and Spanish Empire, 1950s–1970s* (Cham: Palgrave Macmillan, 2019).

17 Elisa Rizo, 'Entrevista a Trinidad Morgades', *Revista Iberoamericana* 80, no. 248–49 (July–December 2014): 1141–4.

18 Secretaría Técnica, Soledad de Santiago, to Auxiliar Central de Juventudes, Madrid 27 May 1967, Archivo General de la Administración (Alcalá de Henares, Spain) (3)51.19, caja 249, carpeta nº 5/476.

19 For Morgades' literary work, see Elisa G. Rizo, 'Glocalizing Democracy through a Reception of the Classics in Equatorial Guinean Theatre: The Case of Morgades' Antígona', in *Receptions of the Classics in the African Diaspora of the Hispanophone and Lusophone Worlds*, ed. Elisa G. Rizo and Madeleine Henry (Lanham, MD: Lexington Books, 2016), 91–109.

20 See the special issue of *Culture and History* 9, no. 2 (2020), 'Local Versions and the Global Impacts of Euro-African Memories: A Revision Through Spanish Colonial Imprints', ed. Yolanda Aixelà-Cabré.

21 M'bare N'gom, 'Teatro y escritura femenina en Guinea Ecuatorial: entrevista a Trinidad Morgades Besari', *Afro-Hispanic Review* 19, no. 1 (Spring 2000): 104.

22 Rizo, 'Glocalizing Democracy', 91.

23 See, for example, Amadou Hampâté Bâ, *Mémoires* (Paris: Actes Sud, 2012); Zohra Drif-Bitat, *Inside the Battle of Algiers: Memoir of a Woman Freedom Fighter* (Charlottesville: Just World Books, 2017); Tran Bu Binh, *The Red Earth: A Vietnamese Memoir of Life on a Colonial Rubber Plantation* (Athens, OH: Ohio University Center for International Studies, 1985).

Notes

Chapter 8

1   Brij V. Lal, 'Kunti's Cry: Indentured Women on Fiji Plantations', *The Indian Economic and Social History Review* 22, no. 1 (March 1985): 55, 57. There are valuable accounts of other individuals' experiences, for instance, Munshi Rahman Khan, *Autobiography of an Indian Indentured Labourer* (New Delhi: Shipra Publications, 2005) and Gaiutra Bahadur, *Coolie Woman: The Odyssey of Indenture* (Chicago, IL: University of Chicago Press, 2013), about an Indian man in Dutch Guyana and an Indian woman in British Guyana.

2   The quota was about 40 women for every 100 men. Karen A. Ray, 'Kunti, Lakshmibhai and the "Ladies": Women's Labour and the Abolition of Indentured Emigration from India', *Labour, Capital, Society* 29, no. 1–2 (April/November 1996): 129–30.

3   Lal, 'Kunti's Cry', 58.

4   Lal, 'Kunti's Cry', 56.

5   Charles F. Andrews and W. W. Pearson, 'Report on Indentured Labour in Fiji: An Independent Enquiry', Calcutta 1916, available online: https://nla.gov.au/nla.obj-506079796/view?partId=nla.obj-506080298.

6   Andrews and Pearson, 'Report on Indentured Labour', 11.

7   There is a burgeoning literature on the history of migration in the colonial age. See, e.g., Robin Cohen, *Global Diasporas: An Introduction* (London: Routledge, 2008), and Marjory Harper and Stephen Constantine, eds, *Migration and Empire* (Oxford: Oxford Univerisity Press, 2010).

8   For an overview, see Gad Heuman and Trevor Burnard, eds, *The Routledge History of Slavery* (Abingdon: Routledge, 2011).

9   For Chinese contract labourers in nineteenth-century Cuba, see e.g., Lisa Yun, *The Coolie Speaks: Chinese Indentured Laborers and African Slaves in Cuba* (Philadelphia, PA: Temple University Press, 2008).

10   Natasha Pairaudeau, *Mobile Citizens: French Indians in Indochina, 1858–1954* (Copenhagen: NIAS Press, 2016).

11   Brij V. Lal, Peter Reeves, and Rajesh Rai, eds, *The Encyclopedia of the Indian Diaspora* (Singapore: Editions Didier Millet, 2006), which provides a good general overview and material on specific countries and has been used for many of the statistics in this section. Among other studies, in addition to works by Lal on Fiji, are Maurits S. Hassankhan, Brij V. Lal and Doug Munro, eds, *Resistance and Indian Indenture Experience: Comparative Perspectives* (New Delhi: Manohar, 2014), Reshaad Durgahee, *The Indentured Archipelago: Experiences of Indian Labour in Mauritius and Fiji, 1871–1916* (Cambridge: Cambridge University Press, 2021) and Arunima Datta, *Fleeting Agencies: A Social History of Indian Coolie Women in British Malaya* (Cambridge: Cambridge University Press, 2021). Samia Khatun, *Australianama: The South Asian Odyssey in Australia* (London: Hurst, 2018), provides good insight on Indian (non-indentured) migration and its legacy in Australia.

12   Lal, 'Kunti's Cry', 71; Andrews and Pearson, 'Report on Indentured Labour', 18, 14.

13   Sunil S. Amrith, 'Tamil Diasporas across the Bay of Bengal', *The American Historical Review* 114, no. 3 (June 2009): 556, 549.

14   Amrith, 'Tamil Diasporas'; see also his 'Indians Overseas? Governing Tamil Migration to Malaya 1870–1941', *Past and Present* 208, no. 1 (August 2010): 231–61.

15   Ritesh Kumar Jaiswal, 'Mediated (Im)mobility: Indian Labour Migration to Ceylon under the Kangany System (*c.* 1850–1940)', in *The Palgrave Handbook of Bondage and Human*

Rights in Africa and Asia, ed. Gwyn Campbell and Alessandro Stanziani (London: Palgrave Macmillan, 2019), 157–88; the volume includes chapters on bonded labour migration in other regions.

16 Edward A. Alpers, 'Recollecting Africa: Diasporic Memory in the Indian Ocean World', *African Studies Review* 43, no. 1 (April 2000): 85; Sugata Bose, *A Hundred Horizons: The Indian Ocean in the Age of Global Empire* (Cambridge, MA: Harvard University Press, 2006), 3.

17 Susana Trovão and Sandra Araújo, 'Ambivalent Relationships: The Portuguese State and the Indian Nationals in Mozambique in the Aftermath of the Goa Crisis, 1961–1971', *Itinerario* 44, no. 1 (April 2020): 106–39.

Chapter 9

1 Quoted in Peter McArthur, *Sir Wilfred Laurier* (London: J.M. Dent, 1919), 42.

2 See Lorenzo Veracini, '"Settler Colonialism": Career of a Concept', *Journal of Imperial and Commonwealth History* 41, no. 2 (2013): 313–33, Eva Bischoff, ed., *Dimensions of Settler Colonialism in a Transnational Perspective: Experiences, Actors, Spaces* (New York: Routledge, 2018), Caroline Elkins and Susan Pederson, eds, *Settler Colonialism in the Twentieth Century* (New York: Routledge, 2005), and Edward Cavanagh and Lorenzo Veracini, eds, *The Routledge Handbook of the History of Settler Colonialism* (London: Routledge, 2017).

3 For a discussion of the historiography, see Saul Dubow and Richard Drayton, eds, *Commonwealth History in the Twenty-First Century* (Cham: Palgrave Macmillan, 2020). It is impossible to reference here more than a very small number of books on the four Dominions. Good starting points for further reading are Margaret Conrad, *A Concise History of Canada* (Cambridge: Cambridge University Press, 2012), Mark Peel and Christina Twomey, *A History of Australia* (London: Macmillan, 2017), Nigel Worden, *The Making of Modern South Africa: Conquest, Apartheid, Democracy* (Oxford: Wiley-Blackwell, 2011), and Philippa Mein Smith, *A Concise History of New Zealand* (Cambridge: Cambridge University Press, 2011).

4 Jeffrey J. Rossman, 'Genocide and Empire', in *The Encyclopedia of Empire*, ed. John M. MacKenzie (Chichester: John Wiley, 2016), 1–2; Patrick Wolfe, 'Settler Imperialism and the Elimination of the Native', *Journal of Genocide Research* 8, no. 4 (2006): 387–409.

5 Anna Clark, *Making Australian History* (Sydney: Penguin Books, 2022).

6 An Exemplary Australian works are Grace Karskens, *The Colony: A History of Early Sydney* (Sydney: Allen & Unwin, 2010), and *People of the River: Lost Worlds of Early Australia* (Sydney: Allen & Unwin, 2020).

7 *Great Exhibition of the Works of Industry of all Nations, 1851, Official and Descriptive Catalogue* (London: Great Britain Royal Commission for the Exhibition of 1851, 1851).

8 See Zoë Laidlaw and Alan Lester, eds, *Indigenous Communities and Settler Colonialism: Land Holding, Loss and Survival in an Interconnected World* (London: Palgrave Macmillan, 2015).

9 See https://c21ch.newcastle.edu.au/colonialmassacres/map.php.

10 James Heartfield, *The Aborigines' Protection Society: Humanitarian Imperialism in Australia, New Zealand, Fiji, Canada, South Africa and the Congo, 1836–1909* (London: Hurst, 2011), 47.

Notes

11 James Belich, *Replenishing the Earth: The Settler Revolution and the Rise of the Anglo-World, 1783–1939* (Oxford: Oxford University Press, 2009).

12 See Kirsten McKenzie, *Scandal in the Colonies: Sydney & Cape Town, 1820–1850* (Melbourne: Melbourne University Press, 2004), and *A Swindler's Progress: Nobles and Convicts in the Age of Liberty* (Sydney: UNSW Press, 2009).

13 Alexis Bergantz, *French Connection: The Culture of Frenchness in Australia* (Sydney: NewSouth, 2021).

Chapter 10

1 E. M. Collingham, *Imperial Bodies: The Physical Experience of the Raj, c. 1800–1947* (Cambridge: Polity Press, 2001).

2 Aro Velmet, 'The Making of a Pastorian Empire: Tuberculosis and Bacteriological Technopolitics in French Colonialism and International Science, 1890–1940', *Journal of Global History* 14, no. 2 (July 2019): 199–217. See also his *Pasteur's Empire: Bacteriology and Politics in France, its Colonies and the World* (New York: Oxford University Press, 2020).

3 Jeffrey A. Auerbach, *Imperial Boredom: Monotony and the British Empire* (Oxford: Oxford University Press, 2018); Jane Lydon, *Imperial Emotions: The Politics of Empathy across the British Empire* (Cambridge: Cambridge University Press, 2019).

4 Mrinalini Sinha, *Colonial Masculinity: The 'Manly Englishman' and the 'Effeminate Bengali' in the Late Nineteenth Century* (Manchester: Manchester University Press, 1995).

5 Gilberto Freyre, *Portuguese Integration in the Tropics* (Lisbon: Junta de Investigações do Ultramar, 1958), 82, 113 119–20, 128.

6 Francis A. de Caro and Rosan A. Jordan, 'The Wrong Topi: Personal Narratives, Ritual, and the Sun Helmet as a Symbol', *Western Folklore* 43, no. 4 (October 1984): 233–48.

7 Collingham, *Imperial Bodies*, chapter 2.

8 For the French campaign of 'unveiling' Algerian women, see Neil MacMaster, *Burning the Veil: The Algerian War and the 'Emancipation' of Muslim Women, 1954–1962* (Manchester: Manchester University Press, 2009).

9 For case studies of clothing, see, for example, Nira Wickramasinghe, *Dressing the Colonised Body: Politics, Clothing and Identity in Colonial Sri Lanka* (London: Orient Longman, 2004); Steve O. Buckridge, *The Language of Dress: Resistance and Accommodation in Jamaica, 1750–1890* (Kingston: University of the West Indies Press, 2004); Susanne Küchler and Graeme Were, eds, *The Art of Clothing: A Pacific Experience* (London: Routledge, 2014); Hildi Hendrickson, ed., *Clothing and Difference: Embodied Identities in Colonial and Post Colonial Africa* (Durham, NC: Duke University Press, 1996).

10 Nira Wickramasinghe, *Metallic Modern: Everyday Machines in Colonial Sri Lanka* (London: Berghahn Books, 2014); Jean Gelman Taylor, 'The Sewing-Machine in Colonial-Era Photographs: A Record from Dutch Indonesia', *Modern Asian Studies* 46, no. 1 (January 2012): 71–95.

11 Daniel J. Walther, *Sex and Control: Venereal Disease, Colonial Physicians, and Indigenous Agency in German Colonialism, 1884–1914* (New York: Berghahn Books, 2015).

12 Ronald Hyam, *Empire and Sexuality: The British Experience* (Manchester: Manchester University Press, 1990).

13 Two general studies are Julie Peakman, *Licentious Worlds: Sex and Exploitation in Global Empires* (London: Reaktion Books, 2019), and Richard Phillips, *Sex, Politics and Empire: A Postcolonial Geography* (Manchester: Manchester University Press, 2006). See also Chelsea Schields and Dagmar Herzog, eds, *The Routledge Companion to Sexuality and Colonialism* (New York: Routledge, 2021).

14 Stucki, *Violence and Gender in Africa's Iberian Colonies*, 147–9.

15 Jan Severin, 'Male Same-Sex Conduct and Masculinity in German Southwest Africa', in *New Perspectives on the History of Gender and Empire: Comparative and Global Approaches*, ed. Ulrike Lindner and Dörte Lerp (London: Bloomsbury, 2020), 149–76.

16 Robert Aldrich, *Colonialism and Homosexuality* (London: Routledge, 2003).

17 Philippa Levine, *Prostitution, Race and Politics: Policing Venereal Disease in the British Empire* (London: Routledge, 2003). On prostitution, see also Luise White, *The Comforts of Home: Prostitution in Colonial Nairobi* (Chicago, IL: University of Chicago Press, 1990); Saheed Aderinto, *When Sex Threatened the State: Illicit Sexuality, Nationalism, and Politics in Colonial Nigeria, 1900–1958* (Champaign-Urbana: University of Illinois Press, 2014); Liat Kozma, *Global Women, Colonial Ports: Prostitution in the Interwar Middle East* (Albany, NY: State University of New York Press, 2017); Ashwini Tambe, *Codes of Misconduct: Regulating Prostitution in Late Colonial Bombay* (Minneapolis, MN: University of Minnesota Press, 2009); Christelle Taraud, *Prostitution coloniale: Algérie, Tunisie, Maroc (1830–1962)* (Paris: Payot, 2003).

18 Julia Clancy-Smith and Frances Gouda, eds, *Domesticating the Empire: Race, Gender, and Family Life in French and Dutch Colonialism* (Charlottesville, VA: University of Virginia Press, 1998); Penny Russell, *Savage or Civilised? Manners in Colonial Australia* (Sydney: UNSW Press, 2010).

19 Among other works are Megan Vaughan, *Curing their Ills: Colonial Power and African Illness* (Cambridge: Polity, 1991); Biswamoy Pati and Mark Harrison, eds, *The Social History of Health and Medicine in Colonial India* (London: Routledge, 2011), Kalala Ngalamulume, *Colonial Pathologies, Environment, and Western Medicine in Saint-Louis-du-Sénégal, 1860–1920* (Bern: Peter Lang, 2012); Laurence Monnais, *Médicine et colonisation: l'aventure indochinoise, 1869–1939* (Paris: CNRS Éditions, 1999); William Gallois, *The Administration of Sickness: Medicine and Ethics in Nineteenth-Century Algeria* (London: Palgrave Macmillan, 2008), and Warwick Anderson, *Colonial Pathologies: American Tropical Medicine, Race, and Hygiene in the Philippines* (Durham, NC: Duke University Press, 2006).

20 Eric Jennings, *Curing the Colonisers: Hydrotherapy, Climatology, and French Colonial Spas* (Durham, NC: Duke University Press, 2006), and *Imperial Heights: Dalat and the Making and Undoing of French Indochina* (Berkeley, CA: University of California Press, 2011).

21 Alison Bashford, *Imperial Hygiene: A Critical History of Colonialism, Nationalism and Public Health* (London: Palgrave Macmillan, 2004).

22 Philip Curtin, *Disease and Empire: The Health of European Troops in the Conquest of Africa* (Cambridge: Cambridge University Press, 1998).

23 Erica Wald, *Vice in the Barracks: Medicine, the Military and the Making of Colonial India, 1780–1868* (London: Palgrave Macmillan, 2014).

24 Sujata Mukherjee, *Gender, Medicine, and Society in Colonial India: Women's Health Care in Nineteenth- and Early Twentieth-Century Bengal* (New Delhi: Oxford University Press, 2016) and Narin Hassan, *Diagnosing Empire: Women, Medical Knowledge, and Colonial Medicine* (London: Routledge, 2011).

Notes

25 Dane Kennedy, 'Minds in Crisis: Medico-moral Theories of Disorder in the Late Colonial World', in *Anxieties, Fear and Panic in Colonial Settings: Empires on the Verge of a Nervous Breakdown*, ed. Harald Fischer-Tiné (Cham: Palgrave Macmillan, 2016), 31–2.

26 Anna Crozier, 'What Was Tropical about Tropical Neurasthenia? The Utility of the Diagnosis in the Management of British East Africa', *Journal of the History of Medicine and Allied Sciences* 64, no. 4 (October 2009): 518–48.

27 Terence Ranger, 'The Invention of Tradition in Colonial Africa', in *The Invention of Tradition*, ed. Eric Hobsbawm and Terence Ranger (Cambridge: Cambridge University Press, 2005), 238–9.

28 See Anna Crozier, *Practicing Colonial Medicine: The Colonial Medical Service in British East Africa* (London: I.B. Tauris, 2007), and Anna Greenwood, ed., *Beyond the State: The Colonial Medical Service in British Africa* (Manchester: Manchester University Press, 2016).

29 Hans Pols, *Nurturing Indonesia: Medicine and Decolonisation in the Dutch East Indies* (Cambridge: Cambridge University Press, 2018).

30 See Markku Hokkanen and Kalle Kananoja, eds, *Healers and Empires in Global History: Healing as Hybrid and Contested Knowledge* (Cham: Palgrave Macmillan, 2019); Ellen J. Amster, *Medicine and the Saints: Science, Islam, and the Colonial Encounter in Morocco, 1877–1956* (Austin, TX: University of Texas Press, 2013).

31 Richard C. Keller, *Colonial Madness: Psychiatry in French North Africa* (Chicago, IL: University of Chicago Press, 2008); Waltraud Ernst, *Mad Tales from the Raj: Colonial Psychiatry in South Asia, 1800–58* (London: Anthem Press, 2010); Lynette A. Jackson, *Surfacing Up: Psychiatry and Social Order in Colonial Zimbabwe, 1908–1968* (Ithaca, NY: Cornell University Press, 2005).

32 See Aro Velmet, *Pasteur's Empire: Bacteriology and Politics in France, its Colonies, and the World* (New York: Oxford University Press, 2020).

33 Sokhieng Au, *Mixed Medicines: Health and Culture in French Colonial Cambodia* (Chicago, IL: University of Chicago Press, 2011).

34 Au, *Mixed Medicines*, chapter 5.

35 Alison Bashford, *Imperial Hygiene*, and Bashford, ed., *Quarantine: Local and Global Histories* (Basingstoke: Palgrave Macmillan, 2016).

36 Frank Proschan, '"Syphilis, Opiomania, and Pederasty": Colonial Constructions of Vietnamese (and French) Social Diseases', *Journal of the History of Sexuality* 11, no. 4 (October 2002): 610–36.

37 Tony Ballantyne and Antoinette Burton, 'Postscript: Bodies, Genders, Empires: Reimagining World History'. In *Bodies in Contact. Rethinking Colonial Encounters in World History*, ed. Ballantyne and Burton (Durham, NC: Duke University Press, 2005), 406–7.

Chapter 11

1 William Marsden, *The History of Sumatra* (Cambridge: Cambridge University Press, 2012 [1783]).

2 Tim Barringer and Tom Flynn, eds, *Colonialism and the Object: Empire, Material Culture and the Museum* (London: Routledge, 2012), provides a good introduction.

Notes

3 *Journal of the Royal Asiatic Society of Great Britain and Ireland* 1, no. 1 (1834), available online: https://archive.org/details/bub_gb_MwABAAAAYAAJ/mode/2up.

4 Pierre Singaravélou, *L'École française d'Extrême-Orient, ou l'institution des marges, 1898–1956: essai d'histoire sociale et politique de la science coloniale* (Paris: L'Harmattan, 1999).

5 Luis Calvo Calvo, 'África y la Antropología española: La aportación del Instituto de Estudios Africanos', *Revista de Dialectología y Tradiciones Populares* 52 no. 2 (1997): 169–85.

6 Arnauld Le Brusq, 'Les Musées de l'Indochine dans le processus colonial', *Outre-mers* 94, no. 356–7 (2007): 97–110.

7 The following paragraphs are based on Anne Gaugue, 'Musées et colonisation en Afrique tropicale', *Cahiers d'études africaines* 39, no. 155–156 (1999): 727–45.

8 Quoted in Gaugue, 'Musées et colonisation en Afrique tropicale', 731.

9 For the discussion in Germany, see Götz Aly, *Das Prachtboot: Wie Deutsche die Kunstschätze der Südsee raubten* (Frankfurt Main: Fischer, 2021).

10 See, for example, Dan Hicks, *The British Museum: The Benin Bronzes, Colonial Violence, and Cultural Restitution* (London: Pluto Press, 2020).

11 Nancy C. Wilkie, 'Colonization and Its Effect on the Cultural Property of Libya', in *Cultural Heritage Issues: The Legacy of Conquest, Colonization and Commerce*, ed. James A. R. Nafziger and Ann M. Nicgorski (Leiden: Brill, 2010), 169–83.

12 Margarita Diaz-Andrew, *A World History of Nineteenth-Century Archaeology: Nationalism, Colonialism and the Past* (Oxford: Oxford University Press, 2008) offers an overview.

13 Robert Aldrich, 'France and the *Patrimoine* of Empire: Heritage Policy under Colonial Rule', *French History and Civilisation* 4 (2011): 200–9, published online by H-France at https://h-france.net/rude/vol4/aldrich4/

14 Stephen L. Keck, '"It Has Now Passed For Ever Into Our Hands": Lord Curzon and the Construction of Imperial Heritage in Colonial Burma', *Journal of Burma Studies* 11 (2007): 49–83.

15 Sarah Tiffin, *Southeast Asia in Ruins: Art and Ruins in the Early 19th Century* (Singapore: NUS Press, 2016).

16 Michael Palser, *Angkor Wat* (Berlin: De Gruyter, 2018).

17 Penny Edwards, *Cambodge: The Cultivation of a Nation, 1860–1945* (Honolulu, HI: University of Hawai'i Press, 2008).

18 Creighton Gabel, 'Archaeology in Sub-Saharan Africa, 1800–1960', *The International Journal of African Historical Studies* 18, no. 2 (1985): 241–64.

19 Webber Ndoro, 'Great Zimbabwe', *Scientific American* 277, no. 5 (November 1997): 94–9.

20 Clémentine Gutron, 'Une archéologie coloniale pour la Tunisie? Cadres et usages d'un savoir au temps du Protectorat', in *Cultures d'empires: Échanges et affrontements culturels en situation coloniale*, ed. Romain Bertrand, Hélène Blais, and Emmanuelle Sibeud (Paris: Karthala, 2015), 79–96.

Chapter 12

1 Dauril Alden, *The Making of an Enterprise: The Society of Jesus in Portugal, Its Empire, and Beyond, 1540–1750* (Stanford, CA: Stanford University Press, 1996).

Notes

2 Anna Johnston, *Missionary Writing and Empire* (Cambridge: Cambridge University Press, 2003).

3 Jon Miller, *Missionary Zeal and Institutional Control: Organizational Contradictions in the Basel Mission on the Gold Coast 1828–1917* (London: Routledge, 2003).

4 Liam M. Brockey, *Journey to the East: The Jesuit Mission to China, 1579–1724* (Cambridge, MA: Belknap Press of Harvard University Press, 2007).

5 See Peter C. Phan, ed., *Christianities in Asia* (Chichester: Wiley-Blackwell, 2011).

6 James P. Daughton, *An Empire Divided: Religion, Republicanism and the Making of French Colonialism, 1880–1914* (Oxford: Oxford University Press, 2006). See also Owen White and James P. Daughton, eds, *In God's Empire: French Missionaries and the Modern World* (Oxford: Oxford University Press, 2012).

7 Andrew Porter, *Religion versus Empire? British Protestant Missionaries and Overseas Expansion* (Manchester: Manchester University Press, 2004); Norman Etherington, ed., *Missions and Empire* (Oxford: Oxford University Press, 2008).

8 On women and religious orders in the French colonies, see Sarah A. Curtis, *Civilizing Habits: Women Missionaries and the Revival of French Empire* (New York: Oxford University Press, 2010). For the Spanish in Peru, see Kathryn Burns, *Colonial Habits: Convents and the Spiritual Economy of Cuzco, Peru* (Durham, NC: Duke University Press, 1999).

9 David Motadel, ed., *Islam and the European Empires* (Oxford: Oxford University Press, 2014).

10 Geoffrey A. Oddie, *Imagined Hinduism: British Protestant Missionary Constructions of Hinduism, 1793–1900* (New Delhi: Sage Publications, 2006).

11 See Yin Cao, *From Policemen to Revolutionaries: A Sikh Diaspora in Global Shanghai, 1885–1945* (Leiden: Brill, 2017).

12 Donald S. Lopez Jr., *From Stone to Flesh: A Short History of the Buddha* (Chicago, IL: University of Chicago Press, 2013).

13 J. Jeffrey Franklin, *The Lotus and the Lion: Buddhism and the British Empire* (Ithaca, NY: Cornell University Press, 2008). On Sri Lanka, Elizabeth J. Harris, *Theravada Buddhism and the British Encounter: Religious, Missionary and Colonial Experience in Nineteenth-Century Sri Lanka* (London: Routledge, 2006); Anne M. Blackburn, *Locations of Buddhism: Colonialism and Modernity in Sri Lanka* (Chicago, IL: University of Chicago Press, 2010); and Stephen Kemper, *Rescued from the Nation: Angarika Dharmapala and the Buddhist World* (Chicago, IL: University of Chicago Press, 2014).

14 On Besant and other Britons who supported Indian independence, see Ramachandra Guha, *Rebels against the Raj: Western Fighters for India's Freedom* (London: William Collins, 2022).

15 For one case study, see Anne Ruth Hansen, *How to Behave: Buddhism and Modernity in Colonial Cambodia, 1860–1930* (Honolulu, HI: University of Hawai'i Press, 2007).

16 The spiritual side of Gandhi's life and ideas is a focus of the biography by Jad Adams, *Gandhi: Naked Ambition* (London: Quercus Books, 2011).

17 See Elizabeth A. Foster, *African Catholic: Decolonization and the Transformation of the Church* (Cambridge, MA: Harvard University Press, 2019).

18 For some examples of those influenced by Indian spirituality, see Jeffrey Paine, *Father India: Westerners under the Spell of an Ancient Culture* (London: Penguin, 1999), and Antony Copley, *Gay Writers in Search of the Divine: Hinduism and Homosexuality in the Lives and Writings of Edward Carpenter, E.M. Forster, and Christopher Isherwood* (New Delhi: Yoda Press, 2006).

19 Leonard P. Harvey, *Islamic Spain 1250–1500* (Chicago, IL: University of Chicago Press, 1990); Ian Coller, *Arab France: Islam and the Making of Modern Europe, 1798–1831* (Berkeley, CA: University of California Press, 2011).

Chapter 13

1   Colour reproductions of these paintings can be found on various internet websites.

2   Peter B. R. Carey, 'Dipanagara [*sic*] and the Painting of the Capture of Dipanagara at Magelang (28 March 1830)', *Journal of the Malaysian Branch of the Royal Asiatic Society* 55, no. 1 (1982): 1–25, and W. Kraus, 'Raden Saleh's Interpretation of the Arrest of Diponegoro: An Example of Indonesian "Proto-Nationalist" Modernism', *Archipel* 69 (2005): 259–94.

3   Peter Carey, *Destiny: The Life of Prince Diponegoro of Yogyakarta, 1785–1855* (Oxford: Peter Lang, 2014).

4   Andrew Rainald, *Burmese Painting: A Linear and Lateral History* (Chiang Mai: Silkworm Books, 2009).

5   See Catherine Noppe and Jean-François Hubert, *Art of Vietnam* (New York: Parkstone Press, 2003).

6   Some examples can be seen in the exhibition catalogue *Between Declarations and Dreams* (Singapore: National Gallery Singapore, 2015), and Alison Carroll, *The Revolutionary Century: Art in Asia, 1900–2000* (South Yarra, VIC: Macmillan Australia, 2010).

7   John Clark, *The Asian Modern* (Singapore: National Gallery Singapore, 2021), an astute theoretical study with essays on a number of artists, including Raden Saleh (47–58).

8   See Alison Smith, David Blayney Brown, and Carol Jacobi, *Artist and Empire: Facing Britain's Imperial Past* (London: Tate Publishing, 2013), from an exhibition at Tate Britain; Yves Le Fur, ed., *D'un regard l'autre: histoire des regards européens sur l'Afrique, l'Amérique et l'Océanie* (Paris: Musée du Quai Branly / Réunion des Musées nationaux, 2006); *Peintures des lointains: La collection du Musée du Quai Branly Jacques Chirac* (Paris: Musée du Quai Branly Jacques Chirac / Skira, 2018); and Jacqueline Guisset, ed., *Le Congo et l'art belge, 1880–1960* (Paris: La Renaissance du livre, 2003). There are catalogues of many other exhibitions, as well as works on individual artists too numerous to reference here.

9   Tim Barringer, Geoff Quilley, and Douglas Fordham, eds, *Art and the British Empire* (Manchester: Manchester University Press, 2007), provides an excellent introduction.

10 See, for example, John M. MacKenzie, *European Empires and the People: Popular Responses to Imperialism in France, Britain, the Netherlands, Belgium, Germany and Italy* (Manchester: Manchester University Press, 2011); Pascal Blanchard et al., eds, *Colonial Culture in France since the Revolution* (Bloomington, IN: Indiana University Press, 2013), Patrizio Palumbo et al., eds, *A Place in the Sun: Africa in Italian Colonial Culture from Post-Unification to the Present* (Berkeley, CA: University of California Press, 2003).

11 See, for example, Martin Clayton and Bennett Zon, *Music and Orientalism in the British Empire, 1780s–1940s* (London: Routledge, 2007).

12 A two-CD compilation, *Chansons coloniales et exotiques* produced by EPM provides a good selection of period pieces in French.

13 The website is http://www.colonialfilm.org.uk. See Tom Rice, *Films for the Colonies: Cinema and the Preservation of the British Empire* (Berkeley, CA: University of California Press, 2019); David Henry Slavin, *Colonial Cinema and Imperial France, 1919–1939: White Blind Spots, Male*

Fantasies, Settler Myths (Baltimore, MD: Johns Hopkins University Press, 2001), and Roberta Di Carmine, *Italy Meets Africa: Colonial Discourses in Italian Cinema* (Oxford: Peter Lang, 2011).

14 Anandi Ramamurthy, *Imperial Persuaders: Images of Africa and Asia in British Advertising* (Manchester: Manchester University Press, 2003).

15 'Les artistes face à la guerre d'Algérie', an exhibition at the Centre culturel algérien in Paris: https://histoirecoloniale.net/Les-artistes-face-a-la-guerre-d-Algerie.html.

16 There is a large scholarly literature on Orientalism. Good overviews are Roger Benjamin, *Orientalist Aesthetics: Art, Colonialism, and French North Africa, 1880–1930* (Berkeley, CA: University of California Press, 2003); and Nicholas Tromans, ed., *The Lure of the East: British Orientalist Painting* (New Haven, CT: Yale University Press, 2008).

17 Mary Roberts, *Istanbul Exchanges: Ottomans, Orientalists, and Nineteenth-Century Visual Culture* (Berkeley, CA: University of California Press, 2015).

18 Susie Protschky, *Images of the Tropics: Environment and Visual Culture in Colonial Indonesia* (Leiden: Brill, 2011).

19 On colonial photography – another subject that has inspired many academic works – see, for example, Susie Protschky, ed., *Photography, Modernity and the Governed in Late-Colonial Indonesia* (Amsterdam: Amsterdam University Press, 2014); Ali Behdad and Luke Gartlan, *Photography's Orientalism: New Essays on Colonial Representation* (Los Angeles: Getty Research Institute, 2013); and Simon Dell, *The Portrait and the Colonial Imaginary: Photography between France and Africa, 1900–1939* (Leuven: Leuven University Press, 2020). On Beato, see Anne Lacoste, *Felice Beato: A Photographer on the Eastern Road* (Los Angeles: J. Paul Getty Museum, 2010).

20 See Roger Benjamin, *Renoir and Algeria* (New Haven, CT: Yale University Press, 2003), *Kandinsky and Klee in Tunisia* (Berkeley, CA: University of California Press, 2015) and *Biskra: Sortilèges d'une oasis* (Paris: Institut du Monde Arabe, 2016) on three notable modern artists – Pierre-Auguste Renoir, Wassily Kandinsky and Paul Klee, and one site in Algeria where many artists congregated.

21 William Rubin, *'Primitivism' in 20th Century Art*, 2 vols (New York: Museum of Modern Art, 1984), provided a pioneering survey though some of its conclusions have subsequently been contested by other art historians.

22 Deborah Silverman, 'Art Nouveau, Art of Darkness: African Lineages of Belgian Modernism', *West 86th: A Journal of Decorative Arts, Design History, and Material Culture* 18, no. 2 (2011): 139–81, and two articles in subsequent issues of the same journal.

23 Rupika Chawla, *Raja Ravi Varma: Painter of Colonial India* (Ahmedabad: Mapin Books, 2010), and the essay on Varma in Clark, 79–87 (quotation, 87).

24 Senake Bandaranayake and Albert Dharmasiri, *Sri Lankan Painting in the 20th Century* (Colombo: The National Trust of Sri Lanka, 2009).

25 See, for example, Adrian Vickers, *Balinese Art: Paintings and Drawings of Bali, 1800–2010* (Tokyo: Tuttle Publishing, 2012).

26 C. A. Burland, *The Exotic White Man* (London: Weidenfeld and Nicolson, 1968) provides an introduction, and there are many later works on different artistic traditions, for example, William Dalrymple, *Forgotten Masters: Indian Painting for the East India Company* (London: Philip Wilson Publishers, 2019).

27 See Ch. 11 of Clark's *The Asian Modern* for examples from that region.

28 'Malangatana: Mozambique Modern', *Art Institute of Chicago Website*, https://www.artic.edu/exhibitions/9169/malangatana-mozambique-modern.

Chapter 14

1　See José Gabriel Tupac Amaru's proclamation to the residents of the Lampa province, 25 November 1780 and his edict signed in Tungasuca, 15 November 1780, in *Documentos para la historia de la sublevación de José Gabriel de Tupac-Amaru: Cacique de la provincia de Tinta, en el Perú* (Buenos Aires: Imprenta del Estado, 1835), 17–8, esp. 12–3.

2　Charles F. Walker, *The Tupac Amaru Rebellion* (Cambridge, MA: Harvard University Press, 2014), 16.

3　Numbers of victims are disputed matter. See David Cahill, 'Genocide from Below: The Great Rebellion of 1780–82 in the Southern Andes', in *Empire, Colony, Genocide: Conquest, Occupation, and Subaltern Resistance in World History*, ed. A. Dirk Moses (New York: Berghahn Books, 2008), 408–9.

4　See for example John W. Rick, 'The Nature of Ritual Space at Chavín de Huántar', in *Rituals of the Past: Prehispanic and Colonial Case Studies in Andean Archaeology*, ed. Silvana A. Rosenfeld and Stefanie L. Bautista (Boulder, CO: University Press of Colorado, 2017), 21–49.

5　See a brief discussion of the loss of population due to the impact of the colonisation of Latin America in Nicholas A. Robins, 'Colonial Latin America', in *The Oxford Handbook of Genocide Studies*, ed. Donald Bloxham and A. Dirk Moses (Oxford: Oxford University Press, 2010), 304–21, particularly 308 (quotation).

6　On 'Caciques and the Indian Nobility', see David T. Garrett, *Shadows of Empire: The Indian Nobility of Cusco, 1750–1825* (Cambridge: Cambridge University Press, 2005), 34–44.

7　Alfonso W. Quiroz, *Corrupt Circles: A History of Unbound Graft in Peru* (Washington, DC: Woodrow Wilson Center Press, 2008), 30.

8　David A. Brading, 'Bourbon Spain and Its American Empire', in *The Cambridge History of Latin America, vol. I: Colonial Latin America*, ed. Leslie Bethell (Cambridge: Cambridge University Press, 1997), 400; John Lynch, *The Spanish American Revolutions, 1808–1826* (New York: Norton, 1986), 7.

9　Linch, *The Spanish American Revolutions*, 2.

10　*Chapetón* literally refers to the reddish cheeks of Europeans. With regard to recent arrivals from Spain it was a mockery, pointing to their inexperience in the Americas.

11　Peter Elmore, 'The Tupac Amaru Rebellion: Anticolonialism and Protonationalism in Late Colonial Peru', in *A Companion to Latin American Literature and Culture*, ed. Sara Castro-Klaren (Malden: Blackwell, 2008), 216.

12　Leon G. Campbell, 'Women and the Great Rebellion in Peru, 1780–1783', *The Americas* 42, no. 2 (October 1985): 163, 168, 191.

13　For a comparative analysis, see Sergio Serulnikov, *Revolution in the Andes: The Age of Túpac Amaru* (Durham, NC: Duke University Press, 2013).

14　Proclamation to the residents of the Lampa province, 25 November 1780, *Documentos para la historia*, 17.

15　Cahill, 'Genocide from Below', 418.

16　Walker, *Tupac Amaru*, 11–15.

17　Elmore, 'The Tupac Amaru Rebellion', 223; Walker, *Tupac Amaru*, 171.

18　For clientelist networks and corruption, see Quiroz, *Corrupt Circles*, 58–71.

19　John R. Fisher, *Bourbon Peru 1750–1824* (Liverpool: Liverpool University Press, 2003), 123, 139.

Notes

20 Jesús Díaz Caballero, 'Incaísmo as the First Guiding Fiction in the Emergence of the Creole Nation in the United Provinces of Río de la Plata', *Journal of Latin American Cultural Studies* 17 no. 1 (2008): 1–22; Sinclair Thomson, 'El reencabezamiento: Impactos, lecciones y memorias de la insurrección amarista/katarista en la independencia andina', in *De Juntas, Guerrillas, Héroes y Conmemoraciones*, ed. Rossana Barragán (La Paz: Gobierno Municipal de la Paz, 2009), 11–46.

21 For a comparative perspective, see Josep M. Fradera, *The Imperial Nation: Citizens and Subjects in the British, French, Spanish, and American Empires* (Princeton, NJ: Princeton University Press, 2018).

22 Sinclair Thomson, 'Sovereignty Disavowed: The Tupac Amaru Revolution in the Atlantic World', *Atlantic Studies* 13, no. 3 (2016): 407–31.

23 Jeremy Adelman, *Sovereignty and Revolution in the Iberian Atlantic* (Princeton, NJ: Princeton University Press, 2006).

24 Elmore, 'The Tupac Amaru Rebellion', 223.

25 Carmen Salazar-Soler, '¿El despertar indio en el Perú andino?', in *De la política indígena: Perú y Bolivia*, ed. Georges Lominé (Lima: Instituto de Estudios Peruanos, 2014), 74.

26 Jonathan Kandell, 'Peru's Land Reform an Uneven Success', *The New York Times*, 6 November 1974, 2. Enrique Mayer, *Ugly Stories of the Peruvian Agrarian Reform* (Durham, NC: Duke University Press, 2009), 22–3.

27 Anna Cant, '"Land for Those Who Work It": A Visual Analysis of Agrarian Reform Posters in Velasco's Peru', *Journal of Latin American Studies* 44, no. 1 (2012): 19, 22, the poster is reproduced on page 21.

28 Fisher, *Bourbon Peru*, 108; Mayer, *Ugly Stories*, 43; Walker, *Tupac Amaru*, 276 (quotation).

29 For further uses and abuses of Tupac Amaru's legacy, see Raúl Asensio, 'Un héroe para el bicentenario: Tupac Amaru y las transformaciones del imaginario político peruano', in *La promesa incumplida: Ensayos críticos sobre 200 años de vida republicana*, ed. Natalia González and Raúl Asensio (Lima: Instituto de Estudios Peruanos, 2021), 339–417.

30 *Hatun Willakuy: Versión abreviada del Informe Final de la Comisión de la Verdad y Reconciliación*, ed. Félix Reátegui Carrillo (Lima: Comisión de la Verdad y Reconciliación, 2004), 191, 193, 206.

31 *Hatun Willakuy*, 433–4.

Chapter 15

1 Mark Twain, *Following the Equator: A Journey Around the World* (Hartford: The American Publishing Company, 1897).

2 The political geography of the Mascarene islands is complicated. The Ile de France (Mauritius) and the Ile Bourbon (La Réunion) are sister islands. La Réunion remains a French *département d'outre-mer*. Mauritius, which also encompasses Rodrigues Island and several smaller islands and reefs, gained independence from Britain in 1968. The Chagos archipelago, which was part of Mauritius, was detached to become the British Indian Ocean Territory and its population deported; the territory, centred on Diego Garcia, is currently leased to the United States as a military base. The Seychelles archipelago, about 1,750 kilometres from Mauritius and technically not part of the Mascarenes, was also a French possession peopled by African slaves from the mid-1700s, but was taken over by Britain in 1794; at first administered from Mauritius, it became a separate crown colony in 1903, and gained independence in 1976.

3   Meaghan Vaughan, *Creating the Creole Island: Slavery in Eighteenth-Century Mauritius* (Durham, NC: Duke University Press, 2005).

4   Denis Piat, *Mauritius on the Spice Route, 1598–1810* (Singapore: Éditions Didier Millet, 2010), provides a general overview, though one largely devoid of discussion of slavery.

5   Michael Pearson, *The Indian Ocean* (London: Routledge, 2003); Bose, *A Hundred Horizons*.

6   Tony Ballantyne, ed., *Science, Empire and the European Exploration of the Pacific* (Aldershot: Ashgate, 2004).

7   Robin Howells, 'Bernardin de Saint-Pierre's Founding Work: The *Voyages à l'Île de France*', *Modern Language Review* 107, no. 3 (July 2012): 756–71.

8   Michael and Mary Allan, *The Man and the Island: Sir Robert Townsend Farquhar Bt., First British Governor of Mauritius, 1810–1823* (Cambridge: Michael & Mary Allan, 2010).

9   Anthony J. Barker, *Slavery and Anti-Slavery in Mauritius, 1810–33: The Conflict between Economic Expansion and Humanitarian Reform under British Rule* (London: Macmillan, 1996), Ch. 7.

10   Richard B. Allen, *European Slave Trading in the Indian Ocean, 1500–1850* (Athens, OH: Ohio University Press, 2014); Barker, *Slavery and Anti-Slavery in Mauritius*, 113.

11   Barker, *Slavery and Anti-Slavery in Mauritius*, 124.

12   Peter Burroughs, 'The Mauritius Rebellion of 1832 and the Abolition of British Colonial Slavery', *Journal of Imperial and Commonwealth History* 4, no. 3 (1976): 243–65.

13   Richard B. Allen, *Slaves, Freedmen and Indentured Laborers in Colonial Mauritius* (Cambridge: Cambridge University Press, 1998), Ch. 4.

14   Clare Anderson, *Convicts in the Indian Ocean: Transportation from South Asia to Mauritius, 1815–53* (London: Macmillan, 2000), and 'The Bel-Ombre Rebellion: Indian Convicts in Mauritius, 1815–53', in *Abolition and its Aftermath in the Indian Ocean, Africa and Asia*, ed. Gwyn Campbell (London, 2005), 50–65.

15   Marina Carter, *Servants, Sirdars and Settlers: Indians in Mauritius, 1834–1874* (Delhi: Oxford University Press, 1995).

16   Robert Aldrich and Miranda Johnson, 'History and Colonisation', in *The Routledge International Handbook of Island Studies*, ed. Godfrey Baldacchino (London: Routledge, 2018), 153–72.

17   Catherine Higgs, *Chocolate Islands: Cocoa, Slavery, and Colonial Africa* (Athens, OH: Ohio University Press, 2012).

Chapter 16

1   Aline Helg, *Slave No More: Self-Liberation before Abolitionism in the Americas* (Chapel Hill, NC: University of North Carolina Press, 2019), 216. A transcript, with commentary, of the court records by Jorge Pavez Ojeda is available at Digital Aponte, http://aponte.hosting.nyu .edu/wp-content/uploads/2017/10/Aponte-Trial-Transcript-Jorge-Pavez-Ojeda.pdf.

2   See Flavio Eichmann, *Krieg und Revolution in der Karibik: Die Kleinen Antillen, 1789–1815* (Berlin: De Gruyter, 2019); Philippe R. Girard, 'Caribbean Genocide: Racial War in Haiti, 1802–4', *Patterns of Prejudice* 39, no. 2 (2005): 138–61.

3   Ada Ferrer, *Freedom's Mirror: Cuba and Haiti in the Age of Revolution* (New York: Cambridge University Press, 2014).

Notes

4   For a comprehensive account, see Matt D. Childs, *The 1812 Aponte Rebellion in Cuba and the Struggle Against Atlantic Slavery* (Chapel Hill, NC: University of North Carolina Press, 2006).

5   Helg, *Slave no More*, 215.

6   Herman Merivale, *Lectures on Colonization and Colonies*, vol. I (Cambridge: Cambridge University Press 2010 [1841]), Lecture II: 'Spanish Colonies in the West Indies', 33–4 (quotation).

7   Dorothea Fischer-Hornung, 'The Hidden Atlantic: Michael Zeuske Reflects on his Recent Research', *Atlantic Studies* 15, no. 1 (2018): 136–47. For Spain and the slave trade, see the essays in Josep M. Fradera and Christopher Schmidt-Nowara, eds, *Slavery and Antislavery in Spain's Atlantic Empire* (New York: Berghahn, 2013).

8   Louis A. Pérez Jr., 'Between Baseball and Bullfighting: The Quest for Nationality in Cuba, 1868–1898', *Journal of American History* 81, no. 2 (September 1994): 493–517.

9   The dual position of captain general combined the highest civil and military office on the island.

10 For a comparative perspective, see Fradera, *The Imperial Nation*.

11 Alfonso W. Quiroz, 'Loyalist Overkill: The Socioeconomic Costs of "Repressing" the Separatist Insurrection in Cuba, 1868–1878', *Hispanic American Historical Review* 78, no. 2 (May 1998): 304.

12 See Rebecca C. Scott, *Slave Emancipation in Cuba: The Transition to Free Labor, 1860–1899* (Princeton, NJ: Princeton University Press, 1985).

13 Philip S. Foner, *Antonio Maceo: The 'Bronze Titan' of Cuba's Struggle for Independence* (New York: Monthly Review Press, 1977).

14 Louis A. Pérez Jr., *Cuba: Between Reform and Revolution* (New York: Oxford University Press, 1988), 135.

15 Aline Helg, *Our Rightful Share: The Afro-Cuban Struggle for Equality, 1886–1912* (Chapel Hill, NC: University of North Carolina Press, 1995), 25–6.

16 Paul Estrade, *José Martí: Los fundamentos de la democracia en Latinoamérica* (Aranjuez: Doce Calles, 2000).

17 For 'Nuestra América' and the 'Manifiesto de Montecristi', see José Martí, *Obras Completas*, vols. 4 and 6 (Havana: Editorial de Ciencias Sociales, 1991).

18 Tone, *War and Genocide in Cuba, 1895–1898*, chapter 14.

19 Bernabé Boza Sánchez, *Mi diario de la guerra: Desde Baire hasta la intervención americana*, Vol. I (Havana: Editorial de Ciencias Sociales, 1974), 58.

20 See the letter from New York, 26 September 1896, and Carlos María de Rojas to José Lacret Morlot, 22 September 1896, Archivo General Militar de Madrid, Capitanía General de Cuba, nº 3444, resp. nº 3446. On the revolutionary networks, see Benedict Anderson, *Under Three Flags: Anarchism and the Anti-Colonial Imagination* (London: Verso, 2005).

21 Federico Ordax Avecilla, *Cuba: antecedentes, reformas y estado actual* (Madrid: Imprenta de Diego Pacheco Latorre, 1895), 24–5; Ricardo Burguete, *¡La Guerra! Cuba: Diario de un testigo* (Barcelona: Maucci, 1902), 152–3.

22 For an analysis, see Albert Garcia Balañà, '"No hay ningún soldado que no tenga una negrita": Raza, género, sexualidad y nación en la experiencia metropolitana de la Guerra colonial (Cuba, 1895–1898)', in *Vivir la nación: Nuevos debates sobre nacionalismo español*, ed. Xavier Andreu Miralles (Granada: Comares, 2019), 173 (quotation).

23 Helg, *Our Rightful Share*, 81; Andreas Stucki, '¿Guerra entre hermanos en la Gran Antilla? La imagen del rebelde Cubano (1868–98)', in *Los enemigos de España: Imagen del otro, conflictos bélicos y disputas nacionales (siglos XVI–XX)*, ed. Xosé M. Núñez Seixas and Francisco Sevillano Calero (Madrid: Centro de Estudios Políticos y Constitucionales, 2010), 269–91.

24 Louis A. Pérez Jr., *Cuba in the American Imagination: Metaphor and the Imperial Ethos* (Chapel Hill, NC: University of North Carolina Press, 2008), 65–94.

25 Kristin L. Hoganson, *Fighting for American Manhood: How Gender Politics Provoked the Spanish-American and Philippine-American Wars* (New Haven, CT: Yale University Press, 1998).

26 Katrin Hansing and Bert Hoffmann, 'Cuba's New Social Structure: Assessing the Re-Stratification of Cuban Society 60 Years After Revolution', *GIGA Working Papers* 315 (2019): 11, 14–5; Devyn Spence Benson, *Antiracism in Cuba: The Unfinished Revolution* (Chapel Hill, NC: University of North Carolina Press, 2016).

Chapter 17

1   See William Dalrymple, *Return of a King: The Battle for Afghanistan* (London: Bloomsbury, 2013).

2   Lady Isabel Burton, *The Romance of Isabel Lady Burton, vol. II: The Story of Her Life*, ed. W. H. Wilkins (London: Hutchinson, 1897), chapter 22. For a joint biography of the couple, see Mary S. Lovell, *A Rage to Live: A Biography of Richard and Isabel Burton* (London: Little, Brown, 1998).

3   See William Dalrymple and Anita Anand, *Koh-i-Noor: The History of the World's Most Infamous Diamond* (London: Bloomsbury, 2017).

4   Miles Taylor, *Empress: Queen Victoria and India* (New Haven, CT: Yale University Press, 2018).

5   Julie F. Codell, ed., *Power and Resistance: The Delhi Coronation Durbars, 1877, 1903, 1911* (New Delhi: Mapin Publishing Company, 2012).

6   On Delhi, see Amar Farooqui, *Zafar and the Raj: Anglo-Muslim Delhi, c. 1800–1850* (Delhi: Primus Books, 2013), and on the end of the Mughal Empire, William Dalrymple, *The Last Mughal: The Fall of a Dynasty, Delhi, 1857* (London: Bloomsbury, 2006).

7   Lytton is quoted in Edwin Hirschmann, *The Accidental Viceroy: Robert Lytton in India* (Lanham, MD: Lexington Books, 2020), 33 and 32.

8   Salisbury is quoted in Hirschmann, *The Accidental Viceroy*, 17.

9   See Hirschmann, *The Accidental Viceroy*.

10 *The Sydney Morning Herald*, 6 February 1877.

11 *The Sydney Morning Herald*, 7 February 1877.

12 Jim Masselos, 'The Great Durbar Crowds: The Participant Audience', in *Power and Resistance*, ed. Codell, esp. 192–7.

13 See 'Our King Emperor and Queen Empress Hold a Durbar in Delhi', https://www.youtube.com/watch?v=5_kKAfRxPPs.

14 Quoted in Hirschmann, *The Accidental Viceroy*, 50 (Digby) and 53 (Lytton).

15 On Indian famine camps, see Aidan Forth, *Barbed-Wire Imperialism: Britain's Empire of Camps, 1876–1903* (Oakland, CA: University of California Press, 2017), chapter 2. Davis's

characterization of the Great Indian Famine as 'colonial genocide' may be debated. See Mike Davis, *Late Victorian Holocausts: El Niño Famines and the Making of the Third World* (London: Verso, 2001), chapter 2.

16   Quoted in Hirschmann, *The Accidental Viceroy*, 54–5.

17   Christina Twomey and Andrew J. May, 'Australian Responses to the Indian Famine, 1876–78: Sympathy, Photography and the British Empire', *Australian Historical Studies* 43, no. 2 (2012): 233–52.

18   Dinyar Patel, *Naoroji: Pioneer of Indian Nationalism* (Cambridge, MA: Harvard University Press, 2020). See also Christopher A. Bayly, *Recovering Liberties: Indian Thought in the Age of Liberalism and Empire* (Cambridge: Cambridge University Press, 2011).

19   David Ochterlony Dyce Sombre briefly served as an MP in 1841 and 1842. See Antoinette Burton, 'Tongues Untied: Lord Salisbury's "Black Man" and the Boundaries of Imperial Democracy', *Comparative Study of Society and History* 42, no. 3 (July 2000): 632–61.

20   Quotations, respectively, from a speech on 'Indian Famine Relief' in Walthamstow, 1 July 1900, in A. Moin Zaidi, ed., *The Grand Little Man of India – Dadabhai Naoroji: Speeches & Writings*, vol. 1 (New Delhi: Indian Institute of Applied Political Research, 1985), 220, 222, 223.

21   It remains prominent in the historiography, notably in such works as Shashi Tharoor, *Inglorious Empire: What the British Did to India* (London: C. Hurst, 2017), which argues that the British, from the early days of colonialism onwards, systematically 'underdeveloped' India.

22   'The Condition of India', speech of 31 January 1901, in Zaidi, ed., *The Grand Little Man of India*, 224.

23   Jim Masselos, *Indian Nationalism: A History* (New Delhi: Sterling Publishers, revised ed., 2010).

24   Teresa Segura-Garica, 'Dadabhai Naoroji: Indian Member of Parliament in Westminster, 1892–5', in *Unexpected Voices in Imperial Parliaments*, ed. Josep M. Fradera, José María Portillo, and Teresa Segura-Garcia (London: Bloomsbury, 2021), 154.

25   Saloni Mathur, *India by Design: Colonial History and Cultural Display* (Berkeley, CA: University of California Press, 2007).

Chapter 18

1   Nigel J. Brailey, *Imperial Amnesia: Britain, France and 'The Question of Siam'* (Dordrecht: Republic of Letters Publishing, 2009).

2   The most comprehensive account of Burma immediately before and after the takeover of the Mandalay kingdom is Thant Myint-U, *The Making of Modern Burma* (Cambridge: Cambridge University Press, 2001). For a general overview, see Michael Aung-Thwin and Maitrii Aung-Thwin, *A History of Myanmar since Ancient Times* (London: Reaktion Books, 2012).

3   L. E. Bagshawe, ed., *The Kinwun Min-Gyi's London Diary: The First Mission of a Burmese Minister in Britain* (Bangkok: Orchid Press, 2006).

4   Andrew Rainald, *Burmese Art: A Linear and Lateral History* (Chiang Mai: Silkworm Books, 2009).

5   Shway Yoe [Sir George Scott], *The Burman: His Life and Notions* (New York: The Norton Library, 1963 [first published in 1882]).

6   The treaty is reprinted in Hla Thein, *Myanmar and the Europeans (1878–1885)* (Yangon: Tun Foundation Bank Literary Committee, 2010), 236 (quotation).

7   Dufferin is quoted in Andrew Gailey, *The Lost Imperialist: Lord Dufferin, Memory and Mythmaking in an Age of Celebrity* (London: John Murray, 2015), 228, 229.

8   Sudha Shah, *The King in Exile: The Fall of the Royal Family of Burma* (New York: Harper Collins, 2012). See also the excellent novel by Amitav Ghosh, *The Glass Palace* (New Delhi: Ravi Dayal Publisher 2000).

9   Anthony Webster, 'Business and Empire: A Reassessment of the British Conquest of Burma in 1885', *The Historical Journal* 43, no. 4 (December 2000): 1003–25, provides a historiographical overview and makes a case for the primacy of commercial considerations and the role of 'gentlemanly capitalism' spearheaded by London and regional financiers.

10 Terence R. Blackburn, *Executions by the Half-Dozen: The Pacification of Burma* (New Delhi: APH Publishing Corporation, 2008), 31–8.

11 Quoted in Gailey, *The Lost Imperialist*, 238.

12 The French conquest of Vietnam is well documented in Christopher Goscha, *Vietnam: A New History* (New York: Basic Books, 2016), and Ben Kiernan, *Việt Nam: A History from Earliest Times to the Present* (New York: Oxford University Press, 2017).

13 Sylvain Venayre, *Une Guerre au loin: Annam, 1883* (Paris: Les Belles Lettres, 2016).

14 Le Général X, *L'Annam du 5 juillet 1885 au 4 avril 1886* (Paris: R. Chapelot, 1901) – the officer did not reveal his identity.

15 'Royal Edict on Resistance (1885)', in *Sources of Vietnamese Tradition*, ed. George E. Dutton, Jayne S. Werner, and John K. Whitmore (New York: Columbia University Press, 2012), 339–42.

16 Robert Aldrich, *Banished Potentates: Dethroning and Exiling Indigenous Monarchs under British and French Colonial Rule, 1815–1955* (Manchester: Manchester University Press, 2018), chapter 4, which contains references to contemporary accounts.

Chapter 19

1   See *Winston S. Churchill: War Correspondent, 1895–1900*, ed. Frederick Woods (London: Brassey's, 1992), 196 (quotation). If not otherwise indicated, all Churchill quotations are taken from this volume.

2   Charles Henry Brown, *The Correspondents' War: Journalists in the Spanish-American War* (New York: Scribner, 1967); Andreas Steinsieck, 'Ein imperialistischer Medienkrieg: Kriegsberichterstatter im Südafrikanischen Krieg (1899–1902)', in *Augenzeugen: Kriegsberichterstattung vom 18. zum 21. Jahrhundert*, ed. Ute Daniel (Göttingen: Vandenhoeck & Ruprecht, 2006), 87–112; Donal Lowry, 'Introduction: Not Just a "Teatime War"', in *The South African War Reappraised*, ed. Donal Lowry (Manchester: Manchester University Press, 2000), 5.

3   Churchill's dispatches from Sancti Spíritus, 23 November 1895 (quotations on page 9); from Arroyo Blanco, 27 November 1895; and from Tampa, Florida, 14 December 1895 (quotation on page 21). On Churchill and the prospect of race war in Cuba, see William Manchester,

Notes

Winston Spencer Churchill: Visions of Glory, 1874–1932 (Boston: Little, Brown & Company, 1983), part two.

4   Churchill's dispatches from Khartoum, 5 September 1898 (quotation on page 120); from East London, 5 November 1899 (quotation on page 176); from Pretoria, 20 November 1899 (quotation on page 192); from Durban, 10 March 1900 (quotation on page 297); from Pretoria, 8 and 14 June 1900 (quotations on pages 323 and 331).

5   The phrase comes from Bryan Falwell, *Queen Victoria's Little Wars* (New York: Harper & Row, 1972).

6   Christopher A. Bayley, *Imperial Meridian: The British Empire and the World, 1780–1830* (London: Longman, 1993).

7   For conflicts among empires, see Josep M. Fradera, '1780–1880: A Century of Imperial Transformation', in *Atlantic Transformations: Empire, Politics, and Slavery During the Nineteenth Century*, ed. Dale W. Tomich (Albany, NY: State University of New York Press, 2020), 1–2, 9–11.

8   Ulrike Lindner, 'New Forms of Knowledge Exchange Between Imperial Powers: The Development of the Institut Colonial International (ICI) Since the End of the Nineteenth Century', in *Imperial Cooperation and Transfer, 1870–1930*, ed. Volker Barth and Roland Cvetkowski (London: Bloomsbury, 2015), 57–78.

9   Courtney Johnson, '"Alliance Imperialism" and Anglo-American Power after 1898', in *Endless Empire: Spain's Retreat, Europe's Eclipse, America's Decline*, ed. Alfred W. McCoy, Josep M. Fradera, and Stephen Jacobson (Madison, WI: University of Wisconsin Press, 2012), 123.

10 See Ulrike Lindner, *Koloniale Begegnungen: Deutschland und Großbritannien als Imperialmächte in Afrika, 1880–1914* (Frankfurt: Campus, 2011), 18, 459–61, and 'Colonialism as a European Project in Africa Before 1914? British and German Concepts of Colonial Rule in Sub-Saharan Africa', *Comparativ* 19, no. 1 (2009): 88–106.

11 See Thomas G. Paterson, 'U.S. Intervention in Cuba, 1898: Interpreting the Spanish-American-Cuban-Filipino War', *OAH Magazine of History* 12, no. 3 (Spring 1998): 5–10.

12 Adams and Senator Trusten Polk are quoted in Louis A. Pérez Jr., *Cuba in the American Imagination*, 30.

13 See 'Nuestra América' (1891) and letter to Manuel Mercado, 18 May 1895, in José Martí, *Obras Completas, vol. 6: Nuestra América* (Havana: Editorial de Ciencias Sociales, 1991), 15, resp. vol. 20: *Epistolario*, 161.

14 See Tone, *War and Genocide in Cuba, 1895–1898*, chapter 14.

15 See Donnell Rockwell to Clemencia Arango, 6, 17 and 27 July 1897, Biblioteca Nacional 'José Martí', Colección Manuscritos 'Arango' n° 57, 60, resp. 58; *Papers Relating to the Foreign Relations of the United States, With the Annual Message of the President Transmitted to Congress, December 6, 1897* (Washington, DC: United States Government Printing Office,1898), XII.

16 'Living and Dying Nations: From Lord Salisbury's Speech to The Primrose League, May 4', *The New York Times*, 18 May 1898.

17 Louis A. Pérez Jr., 'Cuba Between Empires, 1898–1899', *Pacific Historical Review* 48, no. 4 (November 1979): 498; Paul A. Kramer, *The Blood of Government: Race, Empire, the United States & the Philippines* (Chapel Hill, NC: University of North Carolina Press, 2006); Frank Schumacher, 'The American Way of Empire: The United States and the Search for Colonial Order in the Philippines', *Comparativ* 19, no. 1 (2009): 53–70.

18 Peter Warwick, *Black People and the South African War, 1899–1902* (Cambridge: Cambridge University Press, 2004), 4, 6, 91–2.

19 Churchill from Pretoria, 8 June 1900 (quotation on page 323).

20 Churchill from Pretoria, 8 June 1900 (quotation on pages 322 and 323).

21 See Iain R. Smith and Andreas Stucki, 'The Colonial Development of Concentration Camps (1868–1902)', *Journal of Imperial and Commonwealth History* 39, no. 3 (2011): 427.

22 See for the 'methods of barbarism' Henry Campbell-Bannerman's speech, 14 July 1901, reproduced in John Wilson, *CB: A Life of Sir Henry Campbell-Bannerman* (London: Constable, 1973), 349.

23 See on the imperial connection with India Forth, *Barbed-Wire Imperialism*; Elizabeth van Heyningen, 'A Tool for Modernisation? The Boer Concentration Camps of the South African War, 1900–1902', *South African Journal of Science* 106, no. 5–6 (2010): 1–10.

24 Smith and Stucki, 'Colonial Development', 430–1.

25 Gregory Afinogenov, *Spies and Scholars: Chinese Secrets and Imperial Russia's Quest for World Power* (Cambridge, MA: Harvard University Press, 2020).

26 The description of the course of events follows Thoralf Klein, 'Straffeldzug im Namen der Zivilisation: Der 'Boxerkrieg' in China (1900–1901)', in *Kolonialkriege: Militärische Gewalt im Zeichen des Imperialismus*, ed. Thoralf Klein and Ralf Schumacher (Hamburg: Hamburger Edition, 2006), 147–52.

27 Eugen Baron Binder-Krieglstein, *Die Kämpfe des Deutschen Expeditionskorps in China und ihre militärische Lehren* (Berlin: Mittler, 1902), III (quotation).

28 Binder-Krieglstein, *Die Kämpfe*, 222 and 271 (quotation).

29 Binder-Krieglstein referred to 'Rasseneigenthümlichkeiten der Bewohner, ungewohnte klimatische Verhältnisse und ein unbekanntes Gelände'. See Binder-Krieglstein, *Die Kämpfe*, III–IV, 221, 223–4.

Chapter 20

1 Flemming Friborg, *Gauguin: The Master, the Monster, and the Myth* (Copenhagen: Strandberg Publishing, 2023); Bernard Smith, *European Vision and the South Pacific*, ed. Sheridan Palmer, 3rd edn. (Melbourne: Melbourne University Press, 2018 [1960]) is a classic overview of European perspectives in art.

2 On 'first encounters', see Anne Salmond, *Two Worlds: First Meetings between Maori and Europeans 1642–1772* (Honolulu, HI: University of Hawaii Press, 1991), Greg Dening, *Islands and Beaches, Discourse on a Silent Land: Marquesas 1774–1880* (Honolulu, HI: University of Hawaii Press, 1980); and Margaret Jolly, Serge Tcherkézoff and Darrell Tryon, eds, *Oceanic Encounters: Exchange, Desire, Violence* (Canberra: ANU E-press, 2009). For differing interpretations of Cook in Hawaii, Gananath Obeyesekere, *The Apotheosis of Captain Cook: European Mythmaking in the Pacific* (Princeton, NJ: Princeton University Press, 1992), and Marshall Sahlins, *How 'Natives' Think: About Captain Cook, For Example* (Chicago, IL: University of Chicago Press, 1995).

3 For general histories, see Steven Roger Fischer, *A History of the Pacific Islands* (London: Palgrave Macmillan, 2013), Alison Bashford and David Armitage, eds, *Pacific Histories: Ocean, Land, People* (London: Palgrave Macmillan, 2014), and

Ian C. Campbell, *Worlds Apart: A History of the Pacific Islands* (Christchurch: Canterbury University Press, 2011). Histories of particular island groups include Ian C. Campbell, *Island Kingdom: Tonga Ancient and Modern* (Christchurch: Canterbury University Press, 2016); Holger Droessler, *Coconut Colonialism: Workers and the Globalization of Samoa* (Cambridge, MA: Harvard University Press, 2022), Robert Nicole, *Disturbing History: Resistance in Early Colonial Fiji, 1874–1914* (Honolulu, HI: University of Hawai'i Press, 2009); Clive Moore, *New Guinea: Crossing Boundaries and History* (Honolulu, HI: University of Hawai'i Press, 2003).

4   Hermann J. Hiery and John M. MacKenzie, eds, *European Impact and Pacific Influence: British and German Colonial Policy in the Pacific Islands and the Indigenous Response* (London: Bloomsbury, 2021), Jane Samson, ed., *British Imperial Strategies in the Pacific, 1750–1900* (London: Routledge, 2003); Peter J. Hempenstall, *Pacific Islanders under German Rule: A Study in the Meaning of Colonial Resistance* (Canberra: Australian National University Press, 1978), and Robert Aldrich, *The French Presence in the South Pacific, 1842–1940* (London: Macmillan, 1990).

5   See Jane Samson, *Race and Redemption: British Missionaries Encounter Pacific Peoples, 1797–1920* (Grand Rapids, MI: Eerdman, 2017).

6   Robert Aldrich, 'Le Lobby colonial de l'Océanie française', *Revue Française d'Histoire d'Outre-Mer* 76, no. 284–5 (1989): 411–24.

7   Epeli Hau'ofa, *We Are the Ocean: Selected Works* (Honolulu, HI: University of Hawai'i Press, 2008); Brij V. Lal and Vicki Luker, eds, *Telling Pacific Lives: Prisms of Process* (Canberra: ANU Press, 2008); Damon Ieremia Salesa, *Racial Crossings: Race, Intermarriage and the Victorian British Empire* (Oxford: Oxford University Press, 2011).

8   On decolonization, Tracey Banivanua-Mar, *Decolonisation and the Pacific: Indigenous Globalisation and the Ends of Empire* (Cambridge: Cambridge University Press, 2019), and W. David McIntyre, *Winding up the British Empire in the Pacific Islands* (Oxford: Oxford University Press, 2011).

Chapter 21

1   Arnold Wright, ed., *Twentieth-Century Impressions of Ceylon* (London: Greater Britain Publishing Company, 1907).

2   K. M. de Silva, *A History of Sri Lanka* (Colombo: Vijitha Yapa Publications, 2005) and Nira Wickramasinghe, *Sri Lanka in the Modern Age: A History of Contested Identities* (London: Hurst and Company, 2006) provide good introductions.

3   Sujit Sivasundaram, *Islanded: Britain, Sri Lanka & the Bounds of an Indian Ocean Colony* (Chicago, IL: University of Chicago Press, 2013) offers a wide-ranging account of the early period of British rule and treats topics such as science, trade and medicine.

4   Angela McCarthy and T. M. Devine, *Tea & Empire: James Taylor in Victorian Ceylon* (Manchester: Manchester University Press, 2017).

5   Wickramasinghe, *Metallic Modern*.

6   Harshan Kumarsingham, ed., *Speeches and Writings of Sir Ponnambalam Arunachalam* (Colombo: Centre for Policy Alternatives, 2019).

7   Stephen Kemper, *Rescued from the Nation: Anagarika Dharmapala and the Buddhist World* (Chicago, IL: University of Chicago Press, 2015).

8   See Kumari Jayawardena, *Nobodies to Somebodies: The Rise of the Colonial Bourgeoisie in Sri Lanka* (Colombo: Social Scientists' Association and Sanjiva Books, 2012).

9   For a study of the environment, see James L. A. Webb, Jr., *Tropical Pioneers: Human Agency and Ecological Change in the Highlands of Sri Lanka, 1800–1900* (Athens, OH: Ohio University Press, 2012).

10   See Victoria Glendenning, *Leonard Woolf: A Life* (New York: Simon and Schuster, 2006), and Christopher Ondaatje, *Woolf in Ceylon: An Imperial Journey in the Shadow of Leonard Woolf – 1904–1911* (n.p.: Long Riders Guild Press, 2005).

Chapter 22

1   Quotations from Hermann von Wissmann, *Im Innern Afrikas: Die Erforschung des Flusses Kasai, 1883–1885*, ed. Tanja Bührer (Wiesbaden: Erdmann, 2013), 25, 31, 484.

2   Wissmann, *Im Innern Afrikas*, 26, 247, 252, 432, 488. See Appendices I–III for the collected data.

3   Wagner's speech at the Dresdner Vaterlandsverein, 15 June 1848, is quoted in Birthe Kundrus, *Moderne Imperialisten: Das Kaiserreich im Spiegel seiner Kolonien* (Köln: Böhlau, 2003), 43.

4   Wissmann, *Im Innern Afrikas*, 435–8; 490.

5   See Tanja Bührer, 'Einleitung', in Wissmann, *Im Innern Afrikas*, 13–4, 19–20, 22; Claudia Prinz, 'Hermann von Wissmann als "Kolonialpionier"', *Peripherie* 118–19, no. 30 (2010): 321, 330–1; Tanja Bührer, 'Chartergesellschaft, privatrechtliche Wissmann-Truppe, Kaiserliche Schutztruppe: Deutsch-Ostafrika, 1885–1918', in *Rückkehr der Condottieri? Krieg und Militär zwischen staatlichem Monopol und Privatisierung, von der Antike bis zur Gegenwart*, ed. Stig Förster, Christian Jansen, and Günther Kronenbitter (Paderborn: Schöningh, 2009, 237–50).

6   Tanja Bührer, *Die Kaiserliche Schutztruppe für Deutsch-Ostafrika: Koloniale Sicherheitspolitik und transkulturelle Kriegführung, 1885–1918* (München: Oldenbourg, 2011), 172; Matthias Häussler, *War, Emotion, and Extreme Violence in Colonial Namibia* (New York: Berghahn, 2021).

7   On Latin America in the German (colonial) imagination, see Hinnerk Onken, *Ambivalente Bilder: Fotografien und Bildpostkarten aus Südamerika im Deutschen Reich, 1880–1930* (Bielefeld: Transcript, 2019).

8   For the quotations, see 'Aktenstücke betreffend die Kongo-Frage. Dem Bundesrath und dem Reichstag vorgelegt im April 1885', in *Stenographische Berichte: Verhandlungen des Reichstages, 6. Legislaturperiode. I. Session 1884/85, Siebenter Band* (Berlin: Julius Sittenfeld, 1885), 1664, 1666, and for the conference, see Stig Förster, Wolfgang J. Mommsen, and Ronald Robinson, eds, *Bismarck, Europe, and Africa: The Berlin Africa Conference 1884–1885 and the Onset of Partition* (Oxford: Oxford University Press, 1988).

9   Gallagher and Robinson, 'The Imperialism of Free Trade', 15.

10   See Birthe Kundrus, ed., *Phantasiereiche: Zur Kulturgeschichte des deutschen Kolonialismus* (Frankfurt am Main: Campus, 2003), and Tanja Bührer, 'Bismarck und der *Scramble for Africa*: Von einer "hybriden Art der Verantwortung"', in *Realpolitik für Europa: Bismarcks Weg*, ed. Ulrich Lappenküper und Karina Urbach (Paderborn: Ferdinand Schöningh, 2016), 237–65.

11   Wissmann, *Im Innern Afrikas*, 52.

Notes

12 Wissmann, *Im Innern Afrikas*, 52–3, 471. With Usagara they referred to the Erste Usagara-Expedition led by Carl Peters between October and December 1884, which provided the foundation for German colonialism in eastern Africa.

13 In fact, the Ovambo people constituted the largest socio- and ethnopolitical group of the region; their territory was, however, not colonized by the Germans.

14 Matthias Häussler, 'Why OvaHerero Accommodated the Germans? On the "Pacification" of an Acephalous Society: Co-operation and Violence', in *Nuanced Considerations: Recent Voices in Namibian-German Colonial History*, ed. Wolfram Hartmann (Windhoek: Orumbonde Press, 2019), 41–60.

15 Tanja Bührer et al., 'Introduction: Cooperation and Empire, Local Realities of Global Processes', in *Cooperation and Empire: Local Realities of Global Processes*, ed. Tanja Bührer et al. (New York: Berghahn, 2017), 6.

16 Abraham Kaffer, 'A Venerable Old Man of Over Seventy, Who Was for Many Years "Chief Magistrate" of the Bondelswartz Tribe and One of the Councillors', is quoted in Jeremy Silvester and Jan-Bart Gewald, *Words Cannot Be Found: German Colonial Rule in Namibia. An Annotated Reprint of the 1918 Blue Book* (Leiden: Brill, 2003), 159.

17 Susanne Kuss, *German Colonial Wars and the Context of Military Violence* (Cambridge, MA: Harvard University Press, 2017), 37, 40–2; Isabel V. Hull, *Absolute Destruction: Military Culture and the Practices of War in Imperial Germany* (Ithaca, NY: Cornell University Press, 2005).

18 Kuss, *German Colonial Wars*, 50–1.

19 Häussler, *The Herero Genocide*.

20 Kuss, *German Colonial Wars*, 44–5; Hull, *Absolute Destruction*, 88–90.

21 Claudia Siebrecht, 'Formen von Unfreiheit und Extreme der Gewalt: Die Konzentrationslager in Deutsch-Südwestafrika, 1904–1908', in *Welt der Lager: Zur "Erfolgsgeschichte" einer Institution*, ed. Bettina Greiner and Alan Kramer (Hamburg: Hamburger Edition, 2013), 98; Jonas Kreienbaum, *A Sad Fiasco: Colonial Concentration Camps in Southern Africa, 1900–1908* (New York: Berghahn, 2019).

22 Horst Drechsler, *'Let Us Die Fighting': The Struggle of the Herero and Nama against German Imperialism (1884–1915)* (Berlin: Akademie-Verlag, 1980 [1966]), 155.

23 Jürgen Zimmerer, *Von Windhuk nach Auschwitz? Beiträge zum Verhältnis von Kolonialismus und Holocaust* (Münster: LIT, 2011). See also Birthe Kundrus, 'Colonialism, Imperialism, National Socialism: How Imperial Was the Third Reich?', in *German Colonialism in a Global Age*, ed. Bradley Naranch and Geoff Eley (Durham, NC: Duke University Press, 2014), 330–46, esp. 338–41.

24 Hannah Arendt, *The Origins of Totalitarianism* (New York: Schocken Brooks, 2004 [1951]), 568. Aimé Césaire, *Discourse on Colonialism* [1950], ed. Robin D. G. Kelly (New York: New York University Press, 2000 [1950]), 36; Frantz Fanon, *The Wretched of the Earth* (New York: Grove Press, 1963 [1961]), 101.

25 For an overview, see Bradley Naranch, 'Introduction: German Colonialism Made Simple', in *German Colonialism*, 1–18.

26 The argument here follows Häussler, *The Herero Genocide*. For policing and everyday violence, see Marie Muschalek, *Violence as Usual: Policing and the Colonial State in German Southwest Africa* (Ithaca, NY: Cornell University Press, 2019).

27 Ronald Robinson, 'Non-European Foundations of European Imperialism: Sketch for a Theory of Collaboration', in *Studies in the Theory of Imperialism*, ed. Roger Owen and Bob

Sutcliffe (London: Longman, 1972), 124. For new research on settlers' conflicting loyalties, see the essays in Bührer et al., eds, *Cooperation and Empire*.

28 See Robert Aldrich, 'Apologies, Restitutions and Compensation: Making Reparations for Colonialism', in *The Oxford Handbook of the Ends of Empire*, ed. Martin Thomas and Andrew Thompson (Oxford: Oxford University Press, 2018), 714–32.

29 Reinhard Kößler, 'Postcolonial Asymmetry: Coping With the Consequences of Genocide Between Namibia and Germany', in *Postcolonialism Cross-Examined: Multidirectional Perspectives on Imperial and Colonial Pasts and the Neocolonial Present*, ed. Monika Albrecht (London: Routledge, 2020), 118, 129; Henning Melber, 'The Genocide in "German South-West Africa" and the Politics of Commemoration: How (Not) to Come to Terms with the Past', in *German Colonialism and National Identity*, ed. Michael Perraudin and Jürgen Zimmerer (New York: Routledge, 2011), 254.

30 Quoted in Michael Perraudin and Jürgen Zimmerer, 'Introduction: German Colonialism and National Identity', in *German Colonialism*, 1.

31 Jeremiah J. Garsha, 'Expanding *Vergangenheitsbewältigung*? Repatriation of Colonial Artefacts and Human Remains', *Journal of Genocide Research* 22, no. 1 (2020): 46–61.

Chapter 23

1 'Speech by His Majesty Haile Selassie I, Emperor of Ethiopia, at the Assembly of the League of Nations of June-July 1936', accessible at https://dl.wdl.org/11602/service/11602 .pdf.

2 See Giuseppe Finaldi, *A History of Italian Colonialism, 1860–1907: Europe's Last Empire* (London: Routledge, 2016), Ruth Ben-Ghiat and Mia Fuller, eds, *Italian Colonialism* (London: Palgrave Macmillan, 2005), and Nicola Labanca, *Oltremare: Storia dell'espansione coloniale italiana* (Bologna: Il Mulino, 2002).

3 Raymond Jonas, *The Battle of Adwa: African Victory in the Age of Empire* (Cambridge, MA: Harvard University Press, 2011); Paulos Milkias and Getachew Metaferia, eds, *The Battle of Adwa: Reflections on Ethiopia's Historic Victory against European Colonialism* (New York: Algora Publishing, 2005).

4 Evelyn Waugh, *Remote People* (London: Duckworth, 1931); Wilfred Thesiger, *The Life of My Choice* (London: HarperCollins, 1987) – the volume is dedicated to Haile Selassie – and *The Danakil Diaries: Journeys through Abyssinia, 1930–1934* (London: Hammersmith, 1996).

5 Quoted in Asfa-Wossen Asserate, *King of Kings: The Triumph and Tragedy of Emperor Haile Selassie I of Ethiopia* (London: Haus Publishing, 2015), 90.

6 Asserate, *King of Kings*, 91–2.

7 Eric Salerno, *Genocidio in Libia: le atrocità nascoste dell'avventura coloniale italiana (1911–1931)* (Rome: Manifestolibri, 2005).

8 This account draws largely on Nicola Labanca, *La Guerra d'Etiopia, 1935–1941* (Bologna: Il Mulino, 2015), as well as Alberto Sbacchi, *Ethiopia under Mussolini: Fascism and the Colonial Experience* (London: Zed Books, 1985) and *Legacy of Bitterness: Ethiopia and Fascist Italy, 1935–1941* (Lawrenceville: The Red Sea Press, 1997).

9 John Melly to K.N., 12 April 1936, in *John Melly of Ethiopia*, ed. Kathleen Nelson and Alan Sullivan (London: Faber and Faber, 1937), 240. See also Aram Mattioli, 'Ein vergessenes Schlüsselereignis der Weltkriegsepoche', in *Der erste faschistische Vernichtungskrieg: Die*

italienische Aggression gegen Äthiopien 1935–1941, ed. Asfa-Wossen Asserate and Aram Mattioli (Cologne: SH-Verlag, 2006), 10.

10 Labanca, *La Guerra d'Etiopia, 1935–1941*, 23–4.

11 Ian Campbell, *The Addis Ababa Massacre: Italy's National Shame* (London: C. Hurst, 2017).

12 Neelam Srivastava, *Italian Colonialism and Resistances to Empire, 1930–1970* (London: Palgrave Macmillan, 2018), 15 and 65 (quotations).

13 Sbacchi, *Legacy of Bitterness*, Ch. 3 (poison gas and atrocities) and Ch. 4 (the number of casualties), which also provides a good discussion of Italian colonization projects in Ethiopia.

14 Alessandro Pes, 'An Empire for a Kingdom: Monarchy and Fascism in the Italian Colonies', in *Crowns and Colonies: European Monarchies and Overseas Empires*, ed. Robert Aldrich and Cindy McCreery (Manchester: Manchester University Press, 2016), 245–61.

15 Mark Seymour, 'The Throne Behind the Power? Royal Tours of "Africa Italiana" under Fascism', in *Royals on Tour: Politics, Pageantry and Colonialism*, ed. Robert Aldrich and Cindy McCreery (Manchester: Manchester University Press, 2018), 211–32.

16 On the settlers, Emanuele Ertola, *In terra d'Africa: Gli italiani che colonizzarono l'impero* (Bari: Editoria Laterza, 2017); on Italian migration more generally, Mark D. Choate, *Emigrant Nation: The Making of Italy Abroad* (Cambridge, MA: Harvard University Press, 2008).

17 Haile Laribo, 'Empire Building and Its Limitations: Ethiopia (1935–1941)', in *Italian Colonialism*, ed. Ben-Ghiat and Fuller, 83–94, and Sbacchi, *Legacy of Bitterness*, Ch. 5.

18 Sbacchi, *Legacy of Bitterness*, 94.

19 Asserate, *King of Kings*, 163.

20 The notion of *brava gente* has been debunked by Angelo Del Boca, *Italiani, brava gente? Un mito duro a morire* (Vicenza: Neri Pozza Editore, 2006). See also Daniela Baratieri, *Memories and Silences Haunted by Fascism: Italian Colonialism* (Bern: Peter Lang, 2010).

Chapter 24

1 For general overviews, see Jean Gelman Taylor, *Indonesia: Peoples and Histories* (New Haven, CT: Yale University Press, 2003) and Adrian Vickers, *A History of Modern Indonesia*, 2nd edn. (Cambridge: Cambridge University Press, 2013). On Dutch colonialism more generally, Gert Oostindie, ed., *Dutch Colonialism, Migration and Cultural Heritage* (Leiden: KITLV Press, 2008).

2 Susan Abeyasekere, *Jakarta: A History* (Singapore: Oxford University Press, 1987), 93.

3 Beb Vuyk, 'The Last House in the World', in *Two Tales of the East Indies*, ed. E. M. Beekman (Dartmouth, MA: University of Massachusetts Press, 1972); Vuyk's novel was first published in Dutch in 1935.

4 On Dutch perceptions of the Indies and the way they were projected in Europe, see Ayu L. Saraswaty, *Seeing Beauty, Sensing Race in Transnational Indonesia* (Honolulu, HI: University of Hawai'i Press, 2013) and Marieke Bloembergen, *Colonial Spectacles: The Netherlands and the Dutch East Indies at the World Exhibitions, 1880–1931* (Singapore: Singapore University Press, 2006).

5 Susie Protschky, *Photographic Subjects: Monarchy and Visual Culture in Colonial Indonesia* (Manchester: Manchester University Press, 2019). Her *Images of the Tropics:*

Environment and Visual Culture in Colonial Indonesia (Leiden: KITLV Press, 2011) offers a complementary study of Dutch views of nature in the East Indies

6 The entire film can be seen at https://www.youtube.com/watch?v=3vtOdImMfLA&t=520s.

7 E. Du Perron, *Country of Origin* (Singapore: Periplus, 1999, first published in Dutch in 1935). Other important Dutch novelists include Multatuli, Maria Demoût, Madelon Szekely-Lulofs and Helle Haasse; Indonesian perspectives can be found in the novels of Ananta Pramoedya Toer and Umar Kayam.

8 Du Perron, *Country of Origin*, 129, 19, 138, 75, 168.

9 Du Perron, *Country of Origin*, 10–11, 52.

10 For a historical study of the Dutch and Eurasians, see Jean Gelman Taylor, *The Social World of Batavia: Europeans and Eurasians in Colonial Indonesia*, 2nd edn. (New Haven, CT: Yale University Press, 2003).

11 Soetan Sjahrir, *Out of Exile* (New York: Greenwood Press, 1949); the old Dutch spelling of 'Soetan' is used on the cover rather than the now preferred 'Sutan'.

12 Des Alwi, *Friends and Exiles: A Memoir of the Nutmeg Islands and the Indian Nationalist Movement* (Ithaca, NY: Cornell University Press, 2019), Ch. 3, 'Political Exiles in Banda'.

13 Sjahrir, *Out of Exile*, 190, 85, 146–7, 178, 159, 48.

14 Sjahrir, *Out of Exile*, 86, 189, 207, 200–1.

15 Sjahrir, *Out of Exile*, 115, 187, 212.

16 See Kris Alexanderson, *Subversive Seas: Anticolonial Networks across the Twentieth-Century Dutch Empire* (Cambridge: Cambridge University Press, 2019).

17 Adrian Vickers, *Bali – A Paradise Created* (Berkeley, CA: Periplus Books, 1989); see also his *Balinese Art: Paintings and Drawings, 1800–2010* (Jakarta: Periplus Editions, 2012).

18 John Stowell, *Walter Spies: A Life in Art* (Jakarta: Afterhours Books, 2011).

19 Aldrich, *Colonialism and Homosexuality*, 161–5.

20 Rupert Emerson, 'The Dutch East Indies Adrift', *Foreign Affairs* 18, no. 4 (July 1940): 735–41.

21 See, among other works, Theodore Friend, *The Blue-Eyed Enemy: Japan against the West in Java and Luzón, 1942–1945* (Princeton, NJ: Princeton University Press, 2014).

22 Rémy Limpach, 'Business as Usual: Dutch Mass Violence in the Indonesian War of Independence 1945–1949', in *Colonial Counterinsurgency and Mass Violence: The Dutch Empire in Indonesia*, ed. Bart Luttikhuis and Dirk Moses (New York: Routledge, 2014), 64–90.

Chapter 25

1 Menachem Begin, *The Revolt: The Warrior Years of Israel's Brilliant Architect of Peace* (New York: Dell, 1978), 294–5.

2 The Jewish Agency for Palestine emerged in 1929 from the Zionist Palestine Office (founded in 1908) and was eventually renamed as the Jewish Agency for Israel in 1948. It continues to operate as a nonprofit organization around the world. The Agency's self-declared mission is that it 'provides the global framework for Aliyah [immigration of Jews to Israel], ensures global Jewish safety, strengthens Jewish identity and connects Jews to Israel and one another, and conveys the voice of the Jewish People to the State of Israel to help shape its society'. See https://www.jewishagency.org/who-we-are/.

Notes

3   Attlee is quoted by Viscount Addison, secretary of State for Dominion Affairs, in 'The Bomb Outrage in Jerusalem', Parliamentary Debates (Official Report of the House of Lords), *Hansard*, 23 July 1946, vol. 142, accessible at https://api.parliament.uk/historic-hansard/lords/1946/jul/23/the-bomb-outrage-in-jerusalem.

4   For the remarks, see 'The Bomb Outrage in Jerusalem'.

5   Steven Wagner, 'British Intelligence and the Jewish Resistance Movement in the Palestine Mandate, 1945–46', *Intelligence and National Security* 23, no. 5 (2008): 629–57.

6   Quoted in Begin, *The Revolt*, 299, for Begin's account, see 285–307.

7   Bruce Hoffman states that it was 'surpassed only in 1983 with the suicide bomb attack on the U.S. Marine barracks in Beirut', when more than 200 Marines died by a Hezbollah suicide bomber conducting a truck full of explosives. See Bruce Hoffman, 'The Bombing of The King David Hotel, July 1946', *Small Wars and Insurgencies* 31, no. 3 (2020): 600, and 599 for the victims.

8   Hoffman, 'The Bombing', 606.

9   David Ben-Gurion, *The War of Independence: Ben-Gurion's Diary*, 3 vols., ed. Gershon Rivlin and Elhanan Orren (Tel-Aviv: Ministry of Defence, 1982) [text in Hebrew].

10 David Ben-Gurion, *Erinnerung und Vermächtnis*, ed. Thomas R. Bransten (Frankfurt am Main: Fischer, 1971), 74–5.

11 Hoffman, 'The Bombing', 606.

12 See among others, Lorenzo Veracini, 'Israel-Palestine Through a Settler-Colonial Studies Lens', *Interventions* 21, no. 4 (2019): 568–81; Ben-Gurion, *Erinnerung*, 75.

13 Rashid Khalidi, *The Hundred Years' War on Palestine: A History of Settler Colonialism and Resistance, 1917–2017* (New York: Metropolitan Books, 2020), 9.

14 Ussama Makdisi, *Age of Coexistence: The Ecumenical Frame and the Making of the Modern Arab World* (Oakland, CA: University of California Press, 2019).

15 Matthew P. Fitzpatrick, 'Performing Monarchy: The Kaiser and Kaiserin's Voyage to the Levant, 1898', in *Royals on Tour: Politics, Pageantry and Colonialism*, ed. Robert Aldrich and Cindy McCreery (Manchester: Manchester University Press, 2018), 110–24.

16 Anabara Salam Khalidi, *Memoirs of an Early Arab Feminist: The Life and Activism of Anbara Salam Khalidi* (London: Pluto Press, 2013), 91.

17 Khalidi, *Memoirs*, 91, 93.

18 Philip Shukry Khoury, *Syria and the French Mandate: The Politics of Arab Nationalism, 1920–1945* (Princeton, NJ: Princeton University Press, 1987), Daniel Neep, *Occupying Syria under the French Mandate: Insurgency, Space and State Formation* (Cambridge: Cambridge University Press, 2014), and Idir Ouahes, *Syria and Lebanon under the French Mandate* (New York: I.B. Tauris, 2018).

19 On the British Empire's ideas of 'development', Jacob Norris, 'Colonialism in Palestine: Science, Religion and the Western Appropriation of the Dead Sea in the Long Nineteenth Century', in *The Routledge History of Western Empires*, ed. Robert Aldrich and Kirsten McKenzie (London: Routledge, 2014), 165–77.

20 Theodor Herzl, *The Jewish State* (New York: American Zionist Emergency Council, 1946), chapter 2: 'The Jewish Question'. The original German version, *Der Judenstaat: Versuch einer modernen Lösung der Judenfrage*, was published in Leipzig in 1896.

21 See the Anglo-French Declaration at https://balfourproject.org/anglo-french-declaration/.

22 Jacob Norris, *Land of Progress: Palestine in the Age of Colonial Development, 1905–1948* (Oxford: Oxford University Press, 2013).

23   Khalidi, *Memoirs*, 135.

24   Samuel is quoted in Cyrus Schayegh and Andrew Arsan's 'Introduction', in *The Routledge Handbook of the History of the Middle East Mandates* (London: Routledge, 2015), 5.

25   The British White Paper on Palestine is accessible at https://avalon.law.yale.edu/20th _century/brwh1939.asp.

26   Khalidi, *Hundred Years' War*, 8, 41.

27   Alan Cunningham, 'Palestine: The Last Days of the Mandate', *International Affairs* 24, no. 4 (1948): 484.

28   Gudrun Krämer, *A History of Palestine: From the Ottoman Conquest to the Founding of the State of Israel* (Princeton, NJ: Princeton University Press, 2008), 297–8.

29   Krämer, *A History of Palestine*, 298–9, 301; Lorenz M. Lüthi, *Cold Wars: Asia, the Middle East, Europe* (Cambridge: Cambridge University Press, 2020), 240–1.

30   Cunningham, 'Palestine', 487; Tom Segev, *David Ben-Gurion: Ein Staat um jeden Preis* (München: Siedler, 2018), 393–6; Krämer, *A History of Palestine*, 304 (second quotation).

31   The 'Alexandria Protocol' of October 1944, which led to the formation of the League of Arab States, is accessible at https://avalon.law.yale.edu/20th_century/alex.asp#1.

32   See *Exiled from Jerusalem: The Diaries of Hussein Fakhri al-Khalidi*, ed. Rafiq Husseini (London: I.B. Tauris, 2020), esp. viii–ix.

33   Cunningham, 'Palestine', 490; Elizabeth Buettner, 'Extended Families or Bodily Decomposition? Biological Metaphors in the Age of European Decolonization', in *Rhetorics of Empire: Languages of Colonial Conflict After 1900*, ed. Martin Thomas and Richard Toye (Manchester: Manchester University Press, 2017), 208–27.

34   Cunningham, 'Palestine', 490.

35   The term is borrowed from Lauren Elise Apter, 'Disorderly Decolonization: The White Paper of 1939 and the End of British Rule in Palestine' (PhD diss., University of Texas at Austin, 2008).

36   Krämer, *A History of Palestine*, 306.

37   Khalidi, *Memoirs*, 140–1.

38   Benny Morris, *The Birth of the Palestinian Refugee Problem Revisited* (Cambridge: Cambridge University Press, 2003); for the UN, see https://www.unrwa.org/palestine-refugees.

39   See the Introduction by Francesco Amoruso, Ilan Pappé and Sophie Richter-Devroe, 'Knowledge, Power, and the "Settler Colonial Turn" in Palestine Studies', to the special issue of *Interventions* 21, no. 4 (2019): 453.

Chapter 26

1   The origin of *pieds-noirs* ('black feet') is obscure. It may have been a description for the Europeans who wore black leather shoes rather than the sandals preferred by Arabs, or it may have been adopted from a popular American film of the early 1950s about the 'Blackfeet' tribe of Amerindians. The term was not widely used until the 1950s and was considered derogatory at the time, though it was later adopted – and an image of a black foot often used with pride – by the French who left Algeria.

2   Elaine Mokhtefi, *Algiers, Third World Capital: Freedom Fighters, Revolutionaries, Black Panthers* (London: Verso, 2018).

Notes

3   Of the many works on the war, the best study is Martin Evans, *Algeria: France's Undeclared War* (Oxford: Oxford University Press, 2012), on which this chapter draws heavily. Alistair Horne, *A Savage War of Peace* (New York: New York Review of Books, 2015), originally published in 1977, is another readable and detailed study in English. On the military side, see Martin S. Alexander and J. F. V. Keiger, *France and the Algerian War, 1952–1962: Strategy, Operations and Diplomacy* (London: Routledge, 2013), and Martin S. Alexander, Martin Evans and J. F. V. Keiger, eds, *The Algerian War and the French Army, 1954–62: Experiences, Images, Testimonies* (London: Palgrave Macmillan, 2002). The French literature is huge; a good starting point are the numerous works by Benjamin Stora and the essays in Mohammed Harbi and Benjamin Stora, eds, *La Guerre d'Algérie, 1954–2004, la fin de l'amnésie* (Paris: Robert Laffont, 2004).

4   See Todd Shepard, *The Invention of Decolonization: The Algerian War and the Remaking of France* (Ithaca, NY: Cornell University Press, 2008).

5   Evans, *Algeria*, xi.

6   Reprinted in *L'Histoire* 140 (January 1991), special issue on 'Le temps de l'Algérie française', 92.

7   Evans, *Algeria*, 75.

8   Quoted in Evans, *Algeria*, 116.

9   Evans, *Algeria*, 120.

10   Ryme Seferdjeli, 'Rethinking the History of the Mujahidat During the Algerian War: Competing Voices, Reconstructed Memories and Contrasting Historiographies', *Interventions* 14, no. 2 (2012): 238–55.

11   Drif-Bitat, *Inside the Battle of Algiers* (originally published in French in 2013).

12   Evans, *Algeria*, 127, 173, 175, 249–50. Neil MacMaster, *Burning the Veil: The Algerian War and the 'Emancipation' of Muslim Women, 1954–62* (Manchester: Manchester University Press, 2012).

13   Raphaëlle Branche, *La torture et l'armée pendant la Guerre d'Algérie, 1954–1962* (Paris: Gallimard 2001). See Neil MacMaster, 'The Torture Controversy (1998–2002): Towards a "New History" of the Algerian War?' *Modern & Contemporary France* 10, no. 4 (2002): 449–59.

14   Robert Aldrich, 'A Poet's Politics: Jean Sénac's Writings during the Algerian War', in *Transnational Spaces and Identities in the Francophone World*, ed. Hafid Gafaïti, Patricia M. E. Lorcin and David G. Troyansky (Lincoln, NE: University of Nebraska Press, 2009), 149–81. More generally, see Martin Evans, *The Memory of Resistance: French Opposition to the Algerian War* (London: Bloomsbury, 1997).

15   Marie-Pierre Ulloa, *Francis Jeanson: A Dissident Intellectual from the French Resistance to the Algerian War* (Stanford, CA: Stanford University Press, 2008).

16   Clare Eldridge, *From Empire to Exile: History and Memory within the Pied-Noir and Harki Communities, 1962–2012* (Manchester: Manchester University Press, 2012).

17   William B. Cohen, 'The Algerian War, the French State and Official Memory', *Historical Reflections* 28, no. 2 (Summer 2002): 219–39.

18   Amy L. Hubbell, *Hoarding Memory* (London: Bloomsbury, 2020).

Chapter 27

1   *Portugal 1961–1971: A Decade of Progress*, ed. The Overseas Companies of Portugal (Lisbon: Anuário Comercial, [1972]).

2   Daniel M. Friedenberg, 'The Public Relations of Colonialism: Salazar's Mouthpiece in the U.S.', *Africa Today* 9, no. 3 (April 1962): 4.

3   *Portugal 1961–1971*, 2, 3, 19.

4   *Portugal 1961–1971*, 13 (quotation); Filipe Ribeiro de Meneses, *Salazar: A Political Biography* (New York: Enigma, 2010).

5   Norrie MacQueen, *The Decolonization of Portuguese Africa: Metropolitan Revolution and the Dissolution of the Empire* (London: Longman, 1997); Duncan Simpson, 'Approaching the PIDE "From Below": Petitions, Spontaneous Applications and Denunciation Letters to Salazar's Secret Police in 1964', *Contemporary European History* 30, no. 3 (August 2021): 398–413.

6   On Lusotropicalism, see Warwick Anderson, Ricardo Roque and Ricardo Ventura Santos, eds, *Luso-Tropicalism and its Discontents: The Making and Unmaking of Racial Exceptionalism* (New York: Berghahn, 2019); and on Portuguese colonialism and the UN, Bruno Cardoso Reis, 'As primeiras décadas de Portugal nas Nações Unidas: Um *Estado Pária* contra a norma da descolonização', in *Portugal e o fim do colonialismo: dimensões internacionais*, ed. Miguel Bandeira Jerónimo and António Costa Pinto (Lisbon: Edições 70, 2014), 179–215, esp. 189.

7   For population figures and the notion of the Portuguese-speaking world, see *Portugal 1961–1971*, 22; 'Semana do Ultramar', *Boletim Geral do Ultramar* 44, no. 513 (1968): 91.

8   Luís to Teresa, quoted in Joana Pontes, *Sinais de Vida: Cartas da Guerra, 1961–1974* (Lisbon: Tinta da China, 2019), 269, on Luís and his background, see 42–3.

9   *Portugal 1961–1971*, 3, 16–7, 19, 22, 27.

10 Victor Pereira, 'A economia do império e os planos de Fomento', in *O império colonial em questão (sécs. XIX–XX): Poderes, saberes e instituições*, ed. Miguel Bandeira Jerónimo (Lisbon: Edições 70), 251–2; Cláudia Castelo, '"Novos Brasis" em África: Desenvolvimento e colonialismo português tardio', *Varia Historia* 30, no. 53 (2014): 507–32; Sara Lorenzini, *Global Development: A Cold War History* (Princeton, NJ: Princeton University Press, 2019), 17.

11 *Portugal 1961–1971*, 24; Stucki, *Violence and Gender in Africa's Iberian Colonies*, 98, 267, 281; Joseph M. Hodge, 'Beyond Dependency: North-South Relationships in the Age of Development', in *The Oxford Handbook of the Ends of Empire*, ed. Martin Thomas and Andrew Thompson (Oxford: Oxford University Press, 2018), 621–38.

12 Jeanne Marie Penvenne, 'Settling Against the Tide: The Layered Contradictions of Twentieth-Century Portuguese Settlement in Mozambique', in *Settler Colonialism in the Twentieth Century: Projects, Practices, Legacies*, ed. Caroline Elkins and Susan Pedersen (New York: Routledge, 2005), 79–94; Cláudia Castelo, 'Colonial Migration to Angola and Mozambique: Constraints and Illusions', in *Imperial Migrations: Colonial Communities and Diaspora in the Portuguese World*, ed. Eric Morier-Genoud and Michel Cahen (London: Palgrave Macmillan, 2013), 107–28.

13 Stucki, *Violence and Gender in Africa's Iberian Colonies*, 92.

14 Cláudia Castelo, 'Reproducing Portuguese Villages in Africa: Agricultural Science, Ideology and Empire', *Journal of Southern African Studies* 42, no. 2 (2016): abstract and 281.

15 Manuel Barão Cunha, 'A pacificação de Angola é sinónimo de "promoção"', *Permanência* 6 (1970): 10–11; Stucki, *Violence and Gender in Africa's Iberian Colonies*, 92; Patricia Honlger, *Den Süden erzählen: Berichte aus dem kolonialen Archiv der OECD (1948–1975)* (Chronos: Zurich, 2019), 119–25, 210–12.

16 Andreas Stucki, '"Frequent Deaths": The Development of Colonial Concentration Camps Reconsidered, 1868–1974', *Journal of Genocide Research* 20, no. 3 (2018): 305–26. The 'fish'

Notes

and 'water' metaphor (often associated with Mao Zedong's guerrilla warfare in China) was pervasive in Portuguese sources of the time.

17 Hermes de Araújo Oliveira, *Guerra Revolucionária* (Rio de Janeiro: Biblioteca do Exército, 1965), 274; Romeu Ivens Ferraz de Freitas, *Conquista da adesão das populações* (Lourenço Marques: Serviços de Centralização e Coordenação de Informações, 1965), 14.

18 Illiteracy among Portuguese soldiers was an additional challenge. See Pontes, *Sinais de Vida*, 227, 254. All subsequent quotations from soldiers' letters are extracts from this book.

19 *Turras* was a pejorative term derived from a mix of 'terrorists' and troublemakers, widely used by the Portuguese to refer to the independence fighters in the Portuguese colonies in Africa.

20 See Luís to Teresa, 264, 320–2.

21 Centro de Instrução de Operações Especiais, 'Curso de guerra subversiva e Curso de acção psico-social e política', n.d., 63–5, Arquivo Histórico Ultramarino (AHU)/Ministério do Ultramar (MU)/Gabinete do Ministro/Gabinete dos Negócios Políticos/60/Pt. 1; Luís to Teresa, 324, 327; James C. Scott, *Seeing Like a State: How Certain Schemes to Improve the Human Condition Have Failed* (New Haven, CT: Yale University Press, 1998).

22 See a sophisticated analysis for rural Angola in Cláudia Castelo, 'O projecto-piloto de extensão rural do Andulo (Angola): conhecimento, desenvolvimento e contra-subversão', *Ler História* 76 (2020): 153–78.

23 Miguel Bandeira Jerónimo, 'A Robust Operation: Resettling, Security, and Development in Late Colonial Angola (1960s–1970s)', *Itinerario* 44, no. 1 (2020): 58.

24 See the contribution by Pierre Wigny, Belgium's Minister for Foreign Affairs, in International Institute of Differing Civilizations, ed., *Women's Rôle in the Development of Tropical and Sub-tropical Countries* (Brussels: INCIDI, 1959); United Nations, *The United Nations and The Advancement of Women, 1945–1996* (New York: Department of Public Information, United Nations, 1996), 5, 26, 78, 183, 187–211.

25 *Portugal 1961–1971*, 24, 28, 30; 'Política de Povoamento, ano de 1970', AHU/MU/Direcção-Geral de Economia/Repartição do Povoamento e dos Assuntos Demográficos, cx. 84.

26 Maria José Salema, 'Provinces portugaises d'Afrique', in *Women's Rôle*, ed. INCIDI, 120, 122.

27 This and the following paragraphs stem from Andreas Stucki, 'Gendering Development and Social Control in the Iberian Empires in Africa, 1950s–1970s', in *The Oxford Handbook on Late Colonial Insurgencies and Counter-Insurgencies*, ed. Martin Thomas and Gareth Curless (Oxford: Oxford University Press, 2022).

28 Samora Moisés Machel, 'Discurso de abertura: 1ª conferência da mulher moçambicana', 4 March 1973, quoted and translated in Stucki, *Violence and Gender in Africa's Iberian Colonies*, 259.

29 *Portugal 1961–1971*, 2, 3, 32; 'A State Born of our People's Struggle: The President's Message to the Nation on Independence Day', *Mozambique Revolution* 61 (25 June 1975): 20; Allen Isaacman, 'Displaced People, Displaced Energy, and Displaced Memories: The Case of Cahora Bassa, 1970–2004', *International Journal of African Historical Studies* 38, no. 2 (2005): 204.

Chapter 28

1 Quoted in Ana Camacho, 'Rodríguez de Viguri: "Me engañaron entregando el Sáhara a Marruecos"', *El País*, 13 September 1988.

2   José Ramón Diego Aguirre, 'La obra colonizadora del General Bens', *Revista de Historia Militar* 60 (1986): 105–28; José Luis Rodríguez Jiménez, *Agonía, traición, huida: El final del Sahara español* (Barcelona: Crítica, 2015), 21–2, 25, 28.

3   Andreas Stucki, 'The Hard Side of Soft Power: Spanish Rhetorics of Empire from the 1950s to the 1970s', in *Rhetorics of Empire: Languages of Colonial Conflict after 1900*, ed. Martin Thomas and Richard Toye (Manchester: Manchester University Press, 2017), 144.

4   On the war, see José Ramón Diego Aguirre, *La última Guerra colonial de España: Ifni-Sáhara (1957–1958)* (Málaga: Algazara, 1993); and on its historiography, see Francesco Correale, 'Le Sahara espagnol: histoire et mémoire du rapport colonial. Un essai d'interprétation', in *La question du pouvoir en Afrique du Nord et de l'Ouest: Du rapport colonial au rapport de développement*, ed. Sophie Caratini (Paris: L'Harmattan, 2009), 103–52.

5   Enrique Bengochea Tirado and Francesco Correale, 'Modernising Violence and Social Change in the Spanish Sahara (1957–1975)', *Itinerario* 44, no. 1 (2020): 33–54.

6   See 'Plan de promoción de Sáhara', Fundación Sur (Madrid), Fondo Documental Luis Rodríguez de Viguri (DLRV), nº 1881.

7   'Charla sobre la labor de la Sección Femenina en las provincias Africanas de España', 25 January 1966, Real Academia de la Historia (RAH), Madrid, Archivo Documental de 'Nueva Andadura' (NA), 3ª etapa, carpeta nº 166, 1-A.

8   Andreas Stucki, '1975: El fin del Sáhara español', in *Historia Mundial de España*, ed. Xosé M. Núñez Seixas (Barcelona: Ediciones Destino, 2018), 869–70 (quotations).

9   The intended voting options were (1) inclusion into Morocco; (2) autonomy within the Moroccan kingdom; (3) full Sahrawi independence.

10 Jacob Mundy and Stephen Zunes, 'Moroccan Settlers in Western Sahara: Colonists or Fifth Column?' in *Settlers in Contested Lands: Territorial Disputes and Ethnic Conflicts*, ed. Oded Haklai and Neophytos Loizides (Stanford, CA: Stanford University Press, 2015), 58–68.

11 Joanna Allan, *Silenced Resistance: Women, Dictatorships, and Genderwashing in Western Sahara and Equatorial Guinea* (Madison, WI: The University of Wisconsin Press, 2019), 170–8; Stephen Zunes and Jacob Mundy, *Western Sahara: War, Nationalism, and Conflict Irresolution* (Syracuse, NY: Syracuse University Press, 2010), 151–6.

12 See Joanna Allan, 'Natural Resources and Intifada: Oil, Phosphates and Resistance to Colonialism in Western Sahara', *Journal of North African Studies* 21, no. 4 (2016): 645–66.

13 Dolores Juliano, *La causa saharaui y las mujeres: 'siempre hemos sido muy libres'* (Barcelona: Icaria, 1998), 54.

14 For an example of promoting the trope in the early 1990s, see Anne Lippert, 'Sahrawi Women in the Liberation Struggle of the Sahrawi People', *Signs* 17, no. 3 (Spring 1992): 636–51.

15 Elena Fiddian-Qasmiyeh, *The Ideal Refugees: Gender, Islam, and the Sahrawi Politics of Survival* (Syracuse, NY: Syracuse University Press, 2014), 221 (quotation); Elena Fiddian-Qasmiyeh, 'Ideal Women, Invisible Girls? The Challenges of/to Feminist Solidarity in the Sahrawi Refugee Camps', in *Feminism and the Politics of Childhood: Friends or Foes?*, ed. Rachel Rosen and Katherine Twamley (London: UCL Press, 2018), 91–108.

16 Allan, *Silenced Resistance*, 53–64.

17 'Plan de promoción de Sáhara' (quotations). For an overview, see Andreas Stucki, 'Beyond Resistance and Collaboration: The 'Bargains' of Cooperation in the Spanish Sahara, 1950s–1970s', in *Resistance and Colonialism: Insurgent Peoples in World History*, 251–70.

Notes

18 María Concepción Mateo Merino, 'La situación y actitud política de la mujer sahraui', October 1974, 4–6, RAH, NA, 3ª etapa, carpeta 166, 3-9; letter to María Dolores Trías, Delegada Provincial de la S. Femenina Pamplona, Aaiún, 26 November 1974, Archivo General de la Administración, (15)24 caja S-2802.

19 Elena Fiddian-Qasmiyeh, 'Representing Sahrawi Refugees' "Educational Displacement" to Cuba: Self-Sufficient Agents and/or Manipulated Victims in Conflict?', *Journal of Refugee Studies* 22, no. 3 (September 2009): 17–19; see also Pablo San Martín', "'¡Estos locos cubarauis!": The Hispanisation of Sahrawi Society (… after Spain)', *Journal of Transatlantic Studies* 7, no. 3 (2009): 249–63.

20 Allan, *Silenced Resistance*, 176.

21 Allan, *Silenced Resistance*, 174; see for Haidar's comments https://rightlivelihood.org/speech/acceptance-speech-aminatou-haidar/.

22 See Irene Fernández Molina, 'Introduction: Towards a Multilevel Analysis of the Western Sahara Conflict and the Effects of its Protractedness', in *Global, Regional and Local Dimensions of Western Sahara's Protracted Decolonization: When a Conflict Gets Old*, ed. Raquel Ojeda García, Fernández Molina, and Victoria Veguilla (New York: Palgrave Macmillan, 2017), 12.

23 See Gobierno General de Sahara. Secretaría General, 'Constitución de la Administración de Gobierno en el momento de Evacuación del Ejército Español', El Aaiún, 20 November 1975, Fundación Sur, DLRV, nº 1418.

Chapter 29

1 Maurits Wynants, *Des Ducs de Brabant aux villages congolais: Tervuren et l'Exposition coloniale 1897* (Tervuren: Musée Royal de l'Afrique Centrale, 1997). See also Matthew G. Stanard, *Selling the Congo: A History of European Pro-Empire Propaganda and the Making of Belgian Imperialism* (Lincoln, NE: University of Nebraska Press, 2011), Chs 2–3.

2 Debora A. Silverman, 'Art Nouveau, Art of Darkness: African Lineages of Belgium Modernism, part 1', *West 86th: A Journal of Decorative Arts, Design History, and Material Culture* 18, no. 2 (Fall/Winter 2011): 139–81; part 2: 19, no. 2 (Fall/Winter 2012): 175–95.

3 Adam Hochschild, *King Leopold's Ghost: A Story of Greed, Terror, and Heroism in Colonial Africa* (Boston, MA: Houghton Mifflin, 1998). See also Martin Ewans, *European Atrocity, African Catastrophe: Leopold II, the Congo Free State and its Aftermath* (London: Routledge, 2002), and Nancy Rose Hunt, *A Nervous State: Violence, Remedies, and Reverie in Colonial Congo* (Durham, NC: Duke University Press, 2016).

4 Hochschild, *King Leopold's Ghost*, 4, 225.

5 David Van Reybrouck, *Congo: The Epic History of a People* (London: HarperCollins, 2014), 94 (quotation).

6 Guy Vanthemsche, *Belgium and the Congo, 1885–1980* (Cambridge: Cambridge University Press, 2012), 197.

7 Van Rebybrouck, *Congo*, 60.

8 Stanard, *Selling the Congo*.

9 Vanthemsche, *Belgium and the Congo*, 80, 47 (quotations).

10 See Vincent Viaene, Bram Cleys and Jan de Maeyer, eds, *Religion, Colonization and Decolonization in Congo, 1885–1960* (Leuven: Leuven University Press, 2020).

11 Andrée Blouin in collaboration with Jean MacKellar, *My Country, Africa: Autobiography of a Black Pasionaria* (New York: Praeger, 1983); Annette Joseph-Gabriel, *Reimagining Liberation: How Black Women Transformed Citizenship in the French Empire* (Champaign-Urbana, IL: University of Illinois Press, 2019).

12 Lumumba's speech is accessible at http://www.salo.org.za/wp-content/uploads/2013/05/Patrice-Lumumba-Speech.pdf.

13 *La Mémoire du Congo: le temps colonial* (Ghent: Éditions Snoeck / Musée royal de l'Afrique centrale, 2005). A selection of the exhibition texts in English is accessible at https://www.ugent.be/ea/architectuur/en/research/research-projects/all-research-projects/the-memory-of-congo-the-colonial-era/the-memory-of-congo-brochure-en.pdf.

14 *BBC News*, 8 June 2022 https://www.bbc.com/news/world-africa-61730651.

15 Quoted in *Flanders Today*, 8 August 2019.

16 *The Making of: The Renovation of the Royal Museum of Central Africa* (Tervuren: BAI / Africa Museum, 2018) provides detail of the project and interviews with curators and artists, and the new *Guidebook* (Tervuren: Africa Museum, 2018), which provides an introduction to the collections, can be profitably compared with earlier guidebooks. The discussion here draws on Robert Aldrich's visit to the museum.

17 Matthew G. Stanard, *The Leopard, the Lion, and the Cock: Colonial Memories and Monuments in Belgium* (Leuven: Leuven University Press, 2019).

Chapter 30

1 This section is based on John Connell and Robert Aldrich, *The Ends of Empire: The Last Colonies Revisited* (London: Palgrave Macmillan, 2020).

2 For a critical assessment of the British case, see Kwasi Kwarteng, *Ghosts of Empire: Britain's Legacies in the Modern World* (London: Bloomsbury, 2012).

3 For an assessment of Nkrumah's concept and its applicability today, see Mark Langan, *Neo-Colonialism and the Poverty of 'Development' in Africa* (London: Palgrave Macmillan, 2018).

4 Peter Gatrell, *The Unsettling of Europe: The Great Migration, 1945 to the Present* (London: Penguin, 2021), provides a good introduction.

5 Among numerous works on contemporary migration, see Asfa-Woosen Asserate, *African Exodus: Migration and the Future of Europe* (London: Haus Publishing, 2018).

6 Among other works, see Andrew Thompson, *The Empire Strikes Back?: The Impact of Imperialism on Britain from the Mid-Nineteenth Century* (Harlow: Pearson, Longman, 2005), Herman Lebovics, *Bringing the Empire Back Home: France in the Global Age* (Durham, NC: Duke University Press, 2004), Jacqueline Andall and Derek Duncan, eds, *Italian Colonialism: Legacy and Memory* (Bern: Peter Lang, 2005), Sara Friedrichsmeyer, Sara Lennox and Susanne Zantop, eds, *The Imperialist Imagination: German Colonialism and its Legacy* (Ann Arbor, MI: University of Michigan Press, 1998), and Paul M. M. Doolan, *Collective Memory and the Dutch East Indies: Unremembering Decolonization* (Amsterdam: Amsterdam University Press, 2021).

7 Felwine Sarr and Bénédicte Savoy, 'The Restitution of African Cultural Heritage: Toward a New Relational Ethics', report to the French government, 2018, accessible at http://restitutionreport2018.com/sarr_savoy_en.pdf.

FURTHER READING

Abeyasekere, Susan. *Jakarta: A History.* Singapore: Oxford University Press, 1987.

Adelman, Jeremy. *Sovereignty and Revolution in the Iberian Atlantic.* Princeton, NJ: Princeton University Press, 2006.

Aïssaoui, Rabah, and Claire Eldrige, eds. *Algeria Revisited: History, Culture and Identity.* London, Bloomsbury, 2017.

Alden, Dauril. *The Making of an Enterprise: The Society of Jesus in Portugal, Its Empire, and Beyond, 1540–1750.* Stanford, CA: Stanford University Press, 1996.

Aldrich, Robert. *Banished Potentates: Dethroning and Exiling Indigenous Monarchs under British and French Colonial Rule, 1815–1955.* Manchester: Manchester University Press, 2018.

Aldrich, Robert. *Colonialism and Homosexuality.* London: Routledge, 2003.

Aldrich, Robert. *Cultural Encounters and Homoeroticism in Sri Lanka.* London: Routledge, 2014.

Aldrich, Robert, ed. *The Age of Empires.* London: Thames & Hudson, 2007.

Aldrich, Robert. *The French Presence in the South Pacific, 1842–1940.* London: Palgrave Macmillan, 1990.

Aldrich, Robert, and Cindy McCreery, eds. *Crowns and Colonies: European Monarchies and Overseas Empires.* Manchester: Manchester University Press, 2016.

Aldrich, Robert, and Kirsten McKenzie, eds. *The Routledge History of Western Empires.* London: Routledge, 2013.

Alexander, Martin S., Martin Evans, and J. F. V. Keiger, eds. *The Algerian War and the French Army, 1954–62: Experiences, Images, Testimonies.* London: Palgrave Macmillan, 2002.

Alexander, Martin S., and J. F. V. Keiger. *France and the Algerian War, 1952–1962: Strategy, Operations and Diplomacy.* London: Routledge, 2013.

Alexanderson, Kris. *Subversive Seas: Anticolonial Networks across the Twentieth-Century Dutch Empire.* Cambridge: Cambridge University Press, 2019.

Allan, Joanna. *Silenced Resistance: Women, Dictatorships, and Genderwashing in Western Sahara and Equatorial Guinea.* Madison, WI: University of Wisconsin Press, 2019.

Allen, Richard B. *European Slave Trading in the Indian Ocean, 1500–1850.* Athens, OH: Ohio University Press, 2014.

Allina, Eric. *Slavery by Any Other Name? African Life under Company Rule in Colonial Mozambique.* Charlottesville, VA: University of Virginia Press, 2012.

Andall, Jacqueline and Derek, Duncan, eds. *Italian Colonialism: Legacy and Memory.* Bern: Peter Lang, 2005.

Anderson, Clare. *Convicts in the Indian Ocean: Transportation from South Asia to Mauritius, 1815–53.* London: Macmillan, 2000.

Anderson, Warwick, Ricardo Roque, and Ricardo Ventura Santos, eds. *Luso-Tropicalism and its Discontents: The Making and Unmaking of Racial Exceptionalism.* New York: Berghahn, 2019.

Armitage, David, and Alison Bashford, eds. *Pacific Histories: Ocean, Land, People.* London: Palgrave Macmillan, 2013.

Asserate, Asfa-Wossen. *African Exodus: Migration and the Future of Europe.* London: Haus Publishing, 2018.

Asserate, Asfa-Wossen. *King of Kings: The Triumph and Tragedy of Emperor Haile Selassie I of Ethiopia.* London: Haus Publishing, 2015.

Aung-Thwin, Michael, and Maitrii Aung-Thwin. *A History of Myanmar since Ancient Times*. London: Reaktion Books, 2012.

Ballantyne, Tony, ed. *Science, Empire and the European Exploration of the Pacific*. Aldershot: Ashgate, 2004.

Ballantyne, Tony, and Antoinette Burton, eds. *Bodies in Contact: Rethinking Colonial Encounters in World History*. Durham, NC: Duke University Press, 2005.

Baratieri, Daniela. *Memories and Silences Haunted By Fascism: Italian Colonialism*. Bern: Peter Lang, 2010.

Barker, Anthony J. *Slavery and Anti-Slavery in Mauritius, 1810–33: The Conflict between Economic Expansion and Humanitarian Reform under British Rule*. London: Macmillan, 1996.

Barkey, Karen. *Empire of Difference: The Ottomans in Comparative Perspective*. Cambridge: Cambridge University Press.

Barringer, Tim, and Tom Flynn, eds. *Colonialism and the Object: Empire, Material Culture and the Museum*. London: Routledge, 2012.

Barringer, Tim, Geoff Quilley, and Douglas Fordham, eds. *Art and the British Empire*. Manchester: Manchester University Press, 2007.

Bashford, Alison. *Imperial Hygiene: A Critical History of Colonialism, Nationalism and Public Health*. London: Palgrave Macmillan, 2004.

Bayly, Christopher A. *Imperial Meridian: The British Empire and the World 1780–1830*. London: Longman, 1993.

Bayly, Christopher A. *Recovering Liberties: Indian Thought in the Age of Liberalism and Empire*. Cambridge: Cambridge University Press, 2011.

Belich, James. *Making Peoples: A History of the New Zealanders*. London: Penguin, 2007.

Belich, James. *Replenishing the Earth: The Settler Revolution and the Rise of the Angloworld*. Oxford: Oxford University Press, 2009.

Ben-Ghiat, Ruth, and Mia Fuller, eds. *Italian Colonialism*. London: Palgrave Macmillan, 2005.

Bethencourt, Francisco, ed. *Gendering the Portuguese-Speaking World: From the Middle Ages to the Present*. Leiden: Brill, 2021.

Bethencourt, Francisco. *Racisms: From the Crusades to the Twentieth Century*. Princeton, NJ: Princeton University Press, 2013.

Bickers, Robert. *The Scramble for China: Foreign Devils in the Qing Empire, 1832–1914*. London: Allen Lane, 2011.

Bischoff, Eva, ed. *Dimensions of Settler Colonialism in a Transnational Perspective: Experiences, Actors, Spaces*. New York: Routledge, 2019.

Blackburn, Terence R. *Executions by the Half-Dozen: The Pacification of Burma*. New Delhi: APH Publishing Corporation, 2008.

Blanchard, Pascal, Sandrine Lemaire, Nicolas Bancel, and Dominic Thomas, eds. *Colonial Culture in France since the Revolution*. Bloomington, IN: Indiana University Press, 2013.

Blanchard, Pascal, Sandrine Lemaire, Nicolas Bancel, and Dominic Thomas. *Human Zoos: Science and Spectacle in the Age of Empire*. Liverpool: Liverpool University Press, 2008.

Bleichmar, Daniel, Paula de Vos, Kristin Huffine, and Kevin Sheehan, eds. *Science in the Spanish and Portuguese Empires, 1500–1800*. Stanford, CA: Stanford University Press, 2019.

Bloembergen, Marieke, *Colonial Spectacles: The Netherlands and the Dutch East Indies at the World Exhibitions*. Singapore: National University of Singapore Press, 2006.

Bongiorno, Frank. *The Sex Lives of Australians*. Sydney: Black Inc, 2015.

Bose, Sugata. *A Hundred Horizons: The Indian Ocean in the Age of Global Empire*. Cambridge, MA: Harvard University Press, 2006.

Brailey, Nigel J. *Imperial Amnesia: Britain, France and "The Question of Siam"*. Dordrecht: Republic of Letters Publishing, 2009.

Buckner, Philip, ed. *Canada and the British Empire*. Oxford: Oxford University Press, 2008.

Further Reading

Buettner, Elizabeth. *Europe after Empire: Decolonization, Society, and Culture*. Cambridge: Cambridge University Press, 2016.

Burbank, Jane, and Frederick Cooper. *Empires in World History: Power and the Politics of Difference*. Princeton, NJ: Princeton University Press, 2011.

Burton, Antoinette, ed. *A Cultural History of Empire*, 6 vols. London: Bloomsbury, 2018.

Burton, Antoinette. *The Trouble with Empire: Challenges to Modern British Imperialism*. New York: Oxford University Press, 2015.

Butler, Larry, and Sarah Stockwell, eds. *The Wind of Change: Harold Macmillan and British Decolonization*. Basingstoke: Palgrave Macmillan, 2013.

Campbell, Ian. *The Addis Ababa Massacre: Italy's National Shame*. London: C. Hurst, 2017.

Cann, John P. *Counterinsurgency in Africa: The Portuguese Way of War, 1961–1974*. Westport, CT: Greenwood Press, 1997.

Carter, Marina. *Servants, Sirdars and Settlers: Indians in Mauritius, 1834–1874*. Delhi: Oxford University Press, 1995.

Cavanagh, Edward, and Lorenzo Veracini, eds. *The Routledge Handbook of the History of Settler Colonialism*. London: Routledge, 2017.

Chabal, Patrick. *Amílcar Cabral: Revolutionary Leadership and People's War*. Trenton: Africa World Press, 2003.

Chafer, Tony. *The End of Empire in French West Africa*. London: Berg, 2002.

Chatterjee, Arup K. *Indians in London: From the Birth of the East India Company to Independent India*. London: Bloomsbury, 2021.

Chaudhuri, Kirti N. *Asia before Europe: Economy and the Civilisation of the Indian Ocean from the Rise of Islam to 1750*. Cambridge: Cambridge University Press, 1991.

Childs, Matt D. *The 1812 Aponte Rebellion in Cuba and the Struggle Against Atlantic Slavery*. Chapel Hill, NC: University of North Carolina Press, 2006.

Choate, Mark D. *Emigrant Nation: The Making of Italy Abroad*. Cambridge, MA: Harvard University Press, 2008.

Clancy-Smith, Julia, and Frances Gouda, eds. *Domesticating the Empire: Race, Gender, and Family Life in French and Dutch Colonialism*. Charlottesville, VA: University of Virginia Press, 1998.

Clarence-Smith, William G. *The Third Portuguese Empire 1825–1975: A Study in Economic Imperialism*. Manchester: Manchester University Press, 1985.

Clark, Anna. *Making Australian History*. Sydney: Penguin Books, 2022.

Clark, John. *The Asian Modern*. Singapore: National Gallery Singapore, 2021.

Codell, Julie F., ed. *Power and Resistance: The Delhi Coronation Durbars, 1877, 1903, 1911*. New Delhi: Mapin Publishing Company, 2012.

Collingham, E. M. *Imperial Bodies: The Physical Experience of the Raj, c. 1800–1947*. Cambridge: Polity Press, 2001.

Conklin, Alice. *In the Museum of Man: Race, Anthropology, and Empire in France, 1850–1950*. Ithaca, NY: Cornell University Press, 2013.

Connell, John, and Robert Aldrich. *The Ends of Empire: The Last Colonies Revisited*. Singapore: Palgrave Macmillan, 2020.

Conrad, Margaret. *A Concise History of Canada*. Cambridge: Cambridge University Press, 2012.

Conrad, Sebastian. *German Colonialism: A Short History*. Cambridge: Cambridge University Press, 2011.

Coombs, Annie E. *Rethinking Settler Colonialism: History and Memory in Australia, Canada, New Zealand and South Africa*. Manchester: Manchester University Press, 2006.

Cooper, Frederick. *Citizenship between Empire and Nation: Remaking France and French Africa, 1945–1960*. Princeton, NJ: Princeton University Press, 2014.

Cooper, Frederick, and Ann Laura Stoler, eds. *Tensions of Empire: Colonial Cultures in a Bourgeois World*. Berkeley, CA: University of California Press, 1997.

Crosby, Alfred W. *Ecological Imperialism: The Biological Expansion of Europe, 900–1900*. Cambridge: Cambridge University Press, 2013.

Crozier, Anna. *Practicing Colonial Medicine: The Colonial Medical Service in British East Africa*. London: I.B. Tauris, 2007.

Curtis, Sarah A. *Civilizing Habits: Women Missionaries and the Revival of French Empire*. New York: Oxford University Press, 2010.

Dalrymple, William. *The Anarchy: The Relentless Rise of the East India Company*. London: Bloomsbury, 2019.

Dalrymple, William. *The Last Mughal: The Fall of a Dynasty, Delhi, 1857*. London: Bloomsbury, 2006.

Damousi, Joy. *Depraved and Disorderly: Female Convicts, Sexuality and Gender in Colonial Australia*. Cambridge: Cambridge University Press, 2008.

Darwin, John. *The Empire Project: The Rise and Fall of the British World-System, 1830–1970*. Cambridge: Cambridge University Press, 2009.

Das, Santanu, ed. *Race, Empire and First World War Writing*. Cambridge: Cambridge University Press, 2011.

Datta, Arunima. *Fleeting Agencies: A Social History of Indian Coolie Women in British Malaya*. Cambridge: Cambridge University Press, 2021.

Daughton, James P. *An Empire Divided: Religion, Republicanism and the Making of French Colonialism, 1880–1914*. Oxford: Oxford University Press, 2006.

Demissie, Fasil, ed. *Colonial Architecture and Urbanism in Africa*. London: Routledge, 2016.

Diaz-Andrew, Margarita. *A World History of Nineteenth-Century Archaeology: Nationalism, Colonialism, and the Past*. Oxford: Oxford University Press, 2008.

Doolan, Paul M.M.. *Collective Memory and the Dutch East Indies: Unremembering Decolonization*. Amsterdam: Amsterdam University Press, 2021.

Dubois, Laurent. *Avengers of the New World: The Story of the Haitian Revolution*. Cambridge, MA: Harvard University Press, 2005.

Dubow, Saul, and Richard Drayton, eds. *Commonwealth History in the Twenty-First Century*. Cham: Palgrave Macmillan, 2020.

Durgahee, Reshaad. *The Indentured Archipelago: Experiences of Indian Labour in Mauritius and Fiji, 1871–1916*. Cambridge: Cambridge University Press, 2021.

Edwards, Penny. *Cambodge: The Cultivation of a Nation, 1860–1945*. Honolulu, HI: University of Hawai'i Press, 2008.

Eldridge, Clare. *From Empire to Exile: History and Memory within the Pied-Noir and Harki Communities, 1962–2012*. Manchester: Manchester University Press, 2012.

Elkins, Caroline, and Susan Pederson, eds. *Settler Colonialism in the Twentieth Century: Projects, Practices, Legacies*. New York: Routledge, 2005.

Elliott, John H. *Spain, Europe & the Wider World, 1500–1800*. New Haven, CT: Yale University Press, 2009.

Emmer, Pieter C., and Jos J. L. Gommans. *The Dutch Overseas Empire, 1600–1800*. Cambridge: Cambridge University Press, 2020.

Eslava, Luis, Michael Fakhri, and Vasuki Nesiah, eds. *Bandung, Global History, and International Law: Critical Pasts and Pending Futures*. Cambridge: Cambridge University Press, 2017.

Etherington, Norman, ed. *Missions and Empire*. Oxford: Oxford University Press, 2005.

Evans, Martin. *Algeria: France's Undeclared War*. Oxford: Oxford University Press, 2012.

Evans, Martin. *The Memory of Resistance: French Opposition to the Algerian War*. Oxford: Berg, 1997.

Further Reading

Ewans, Martin. *European Atrocity, African Catastrophe: Leopold II, the Congo Free State and its Aftermath.* London: Routledge, 2002.

Farooqui, Amar. *Zafar and the Raj: Anglo-Muslim Delhi, c. 1800–1850.* Delhi: Primus Books, 2013.

Fawaz, Leila. *A Land of Aching Hearts: The Middle East in the Great War.* Cambridge, MA: Harvard University Press, 2014.

Ferrer, Ada. *Freedom's Mirror: Cuba and Haiti in the Age of Revolution.* New York: Cambridge University Press, 2014.

Fibiger Bang, Peter, Christopher A. Bayly, and Walter Scheidel, eds. *The Oxford World History of Empire.* Oxford: Oxford University Press, 2021.

Finaldi, Giuseppe. *The History of Italian Colonialism, 1860–1907: Europe's Last Empire.* London: Routledge, 2016.

Fisher, John R. *Bourbon Peru 1750–1824.* Liverpool: Liverpool University Press, 2003.

Fisher, Michael H. *An Environmental History of India: From Earliest Times to the Twenty-First Century.* Cambridge: Cambridge University Press, 2018.

Fitzpatrick, Matthew P. *The Kaiser and the Colonies: Monarchy in the Age of Empire.* Oxford: Oxford University Press, 2022.

Fitzpatrick, Matthew P., and Peter Monteath, eds. *Savage Worlds: German Encounters Abroad, 1798–1914.* Manchester: Manchester University Press, 2018.

Fradera, Josep. *The Imperial Nation: Citizens and Subjects in the British, French, Spanish, and American Empires.* Princeton, NJ: Princeton University Press, 2018.

Fradera, Josep M., and Christopher Schmidt-Nowara, eds. *Slavery and Antislavery in Spain's Atlantic Empire.* New York: Berghahn, 2013.

Franklin, J. Jeffrey. *The Lotus and the Lion: Buddhism and the British Empire.* Ithaca, NY: Cornell University Press, 2008.

French, Howard W. *Born in Blackness: Africa, Africans, and the Making of the Modern World, 1471 to the Second World War.* New York: Liveright, 2021.

Friedrichsmeyer, Sara. Sara Lennox and Susanne Zantop, eds, *The Imperialist Imagination: German Colonism and its Legacy.* Ann Arbor: University of Michigan Press, 1998.

Fryer, Peter. *Black People in the British Empire.* London: Pluto Press, 2021.

Gardner, Leigh, and Tirthankar Roy. *The Economic History of Colonialism.* Bristol: Bristol University Press, 2020.

Gattrell, Peter. *The Unsettling of Europe: The Great Migration, 1945 to the Present.* London: Penguin, 2021.

Geggus, David P., and Norman Fiering, eds. *The World of the Haitian Revolution.* Bloomington, IN: Indiana University Press, 2009.

Gerwarth, Robert, and Erez Manela, eds. *Empires at War, 1911–1923.* Oxford: Oxford University Press, 2014.

Gilmour, David. *The British In India: Three Centuries of Ambition and Experience.* London: Allen Lane, 2018.

Goebel, Michael. *Anti-Imperial Metropolis: Interwar Paris and the Seeds of Third World Nationalism.* Cambridge: Cambridge University Press, 2015.

Goscha, Christopher. *The Road to Dien Bien Phu: A History of the First War for Vietnam.* Princeton, NJ: Princeton University Press, 2022.

Goscha, Christopher. *Vietnam: A New History.* New York: Basic Books, 2016.

Grant, Kevin. *A Civilised Savagery: Britain and the New Slaveries in Africa, 1884–1926.* New York: Routledge, 2005.

Griffiths, Tom, and Libby Robin, eds. *Ecology and Empire: Environmental History of Settler Societies.* Melbourne: Melbourne University Press, 1997.

Grove, Richard H. *Green Imperialism: Colonial Expansion, Tropical Island Edens and the Origins of Environmentalism, 1600–1860*. Cambridge: Cambridge University Press, 1996.

Guha, Ranajit. *Subaltern Studies Reader, 1986–1995*. Minneapolis, MN: University of Minnesota Press, 1997.

Ha, Marie-Paule. *French Women in the Empire: The Case of Indochina*. Oxford: Oxford University Press, 2014.

Hack, Karl. *Defence and Decolonization in Southeast Asia: Britain, Malaya and Singapore 1941–1968*. London: Routledge, 2013.

Hall, Catherine. *Cultures of Empire, A Reader: Colonizers in Britain and the Empire in the Nineteenth and Twentieth Centuries*. Manchester: Manchester University Press, 2000.

Hall, Catherine, and Keith McClelland. *Race, Nation and Empire: Making Histories, 1750 to the Present*. Manchester: Manchester University Press, 2010.

Hargreaves, Alec. *Memory, Empire, and Postcolonialism: Legacies of French Colonialism*. New York: Lexington Books, 2005.

Harper, Marjory, and Stephen Constantine, eds. *Migration and Empire*. Oxford: Oxford University Press, 2010.

Harper, Tim. *Underground Asia: Global Revolutionaries and the Assault on Empire*. London: Allen Lane, 2020.

Harris, Cole. *A Bounded Land: Reflections on Settler Colonialism in Canada*. Vancouver: UBC Press, 2020.

Hassankhan, Maurits S., Brij V. Lal and Doug Munro, eds. *Resistance and Indian Indenture Experience: Comparative Perspectives*. New Delhi: Manohar, 2014.

Häussler, Matthias. *The Herero Genocide: War, Emotion, and Extreme Violence in Colonial Namibia*. New York: Berghahn, 2021.

Hazareesingh, Sudhir. *Black Spartacus: The Epic Life of Toussaint Louverture*. London: Penguin, 2021.

Headrick, Daniel R. *Power over Peoples: Technology, Environments, and Western Imperialism, 1400 to the Present*. Princeton, NJ: Princeton University Press, 2010.

Helg, Aline. *Slave no More: Self-Liberation before Abolitionism in the Americas*. Chapel Hill, NC: University of North Carolina Press, 2019.

Hempenstall, Peter J. *Pacific Islanders under German Rule: A Study in the Meaning of Colonial Resistance*. Canberra: Australian National University Press, 1978.

Heyningen, Elizabeth van. *The Concentration Camps of the Anglo-Boer War: A Social History*. Auckland Park, South Africa: Jacana, 2014.

Hicks, Dan. *The British Museum: The Benin Bronzes, Colonial Violence, and Cultural Restitution*. London: Pluto Press, 2020.

Hirschmann, Edwin. *The Accidental Viceroy: Robert Lytton in India*. Lanham, MD: Lexington Books, 2020.

Hochschild, Adam. *King Leopold's Ghost: A Story of Greed, Terror, and Heroism in Colonial Africa*. Boston: Houghton Mifflin, 1998.

Home, Robert. *Of Planting and Planning: The Making of British Colonial Cities*. London: Routledge, 2013.

Horne, Alistair. *A Savage War of Peace*. New York: New York Review of Books, 2015.

Howard, Douglas. *A History of the Ottoman Empire*. Cambridge: Cambridge University Press, 2017.

Howe, Stephen, ed. *The New Imperial Histories Reader*. London: Routledge, 2010.

Hull, Isabel V. *Absolute Destruction: Military Culture and the Practices of War in Imperial Germany*. Ithaca, NY: Cornell University Press, 2005.

Hunt, Nancy Rose. *A Nervous State: Violence, Remedies, and Reverie in Colonial Congo*. Durham, NC: Duke University Press, 2016.

Further Reading

Isaacman, Allen F., and Barbara S. Isaacman. *Dams, Displacement, and the Delusion of Development: Cahora Bassa and its Legacies in Mozambique, 1965–2007.* Athens: Ohio University Press, 2013.

Isidoros, Konstantina. *Nomads and Nation-Building in the Western Sahara: Gender, Politics, and the Saharawi.* London: Bloomsbury 2018.

Jackson, Ashley. *The British Empire and the Second World War.* London: Hambledon Continuum, 2006.

Jacobson, Abigail. *From Empire to Empire: Jerusalem between Ottoman and British Rule.* New York: Syracuse University Press, 2011.

Jasanoff, Maya. *Edge of Empire: Lives, Culture, and Conquest in the East, 1750–1850.* New York: Knopf, 2005.

Jay, Martin, and Sumathi Ramaswamy, eds. *Empires of Vision: A Reader.* Durham, NC: Duke University Press, 2014.

Jayawardena, Kumari. *Nobodies to Somebodies: The Rise of the Colonial Bourgeoisie in Sri Lanka.* Colombo: Social Scientists' Association and Sanjiva Books, 2012.

Jennings, Eric. *Vichy in the Tropics: Pétain's National Revolution in Madagascar, Guadeloupe, and Indochina, 1940–44.* Stanford, CA: Stanford University Press, 2002.

Jennings, Eric T. *Curing the Colonizers: Hydrotherapy, Climatology, and French Colonial Spas.* Durham, NC: Duke University Press, 2006.

Jennings, Eric T. *French Africa in World War II: The African Resistance.* Cambridge: Cambridge University Press, 2015.

Jensen, Erik. *The Struggle for Western Sahara: The UN and the Challenge to Diplomacy.* London: I.B. Tauris, 2021.

Jerónimo, Miguel Bandeira. *The "Civilising Mission" of Portuguese Colonialism, 1870–1930.* London: Palgrave Macmillan, 2015.

Jonas, Raymond. *The Battle of Adwa: African Victory in the Age of Empire.* Cambridge, MA: Harvard University Press, 2011.

Joseph-Gabriel, Annette J. *Reimagining Liberation: How Black Women Transformed Citizenship in the French Empire.* Champaign-Urbana, IL: University of Illinois Press, 2019.

Karskens, Grace. *People of the River: Lost Worlds of Early Australia.* Sydney: Allen & Unwin, 2020.

Kennedy, Dane. *The Imperial History Wars: Debating the British Empire.* London: Bloomsbury, 2018.

Khalidi, Rashid. *The Hundred Years' War on Palestine: A History of Settler Colonialism and Resistance, 1917–2017.* New York: Metropolitan Books, 2020.

Klein, Thoralf, ed. *The Boxer War: Media and Memory of an Imperialist Intervention.* Kiel: Solivagus Praeteritum, 2020.

Klose, Fabian. *Human Rights in the Shadow of Colonial Violence: The Wars of Independence in Kenya and Algeria.* Philadelphia, PA: University of Pennsylvania Press, 2013.

Knudsen, Britta Timm, John Oldfield, Elizabeth Buettner, and Elvan Zabunyan, eds. *Decolonizing Colonial Heritage: New Agendas, Actors and Practices in and Beyond Europe.* London: Routledge, 2021.

Krämer, Gudrun. *A History of Palestine: From the Ottoman Conquest to the Founding of the State of Israel.* Princeton, NJ: Princeton University Press, 2008.

Kuss, Susanne. *German Colonial Wars and the Context of Military Violence.* Cambridge, MA: Harvard University Press, 2017.

Kwarteng, Kwasi. *Ghosts of Empire: Britain's Legacies in the Modern World.* London: Bloomsbury, 2012.

Laidlaw, Zoë, and Alan Lester, eds. *Indigenous Communities and Settler Colonialism: Land Holding, Loss and Survival in an Interconnected World.* London: Palgrave Macmillan, 2015.

Lake, Marilyn, and Henry Reynolds. *Drawing the Colour Line: White Men's Countries and the International Challenge of Racial Equality.* Cambridge: Cambridge University Press, 2008.

Lal, Brij V., Peter Reeves, and Rajesh Rai, eds. *The Encyclopedia of the Indian Diaspora.* Singapore: Editions Didier Millet, 2006.

Lambert, David, and Alan Lester, eds. *Colonial Lives Across the British Empire: Imperial Careering in the Long Nineteenth Century.* Cambridge: Cambridge University Press, 2006.

Langan, Mark. *Neo-Colonialism and the Poverty of 'Development' in Africa.* London: Palgrave Macmillan, 2018.

Lebovics, Herman. *Bringing the Empire Back Home: France in the Global Age.* Durham, NC: Duke University Press, 2004.

Lebovics, Herman. *Imperialism and the Corruption of Democracies.* Durham, NC: Duke University Press, 2006.

Lemaires, Gérard-Georges. *The Orient in Western Art.* Cologne: Könemann, 2000.

Levine, Philippa, and John Marriott, eds. *The Ashgate Research Companion to Modern Imperial Histories.* London: Routledge, 2017.

Levine, Philippa. *Prostitution, Race and Politics: Policing Venereal Disease in the British Empire.* London: Routledge, 2003.

Levine, Philippa, ed. *The Rise and Fall of Modern Empires,* 4 vols. Farnham: Ashgate, 2013.

Lloyd-Jones, Stewart, and António Costa Pinto, eds. *The Last Empire: Thirty Years of Portuguese Decolonization.* Bristol: Intellect, 2003.

Lotem, Itay. *The Memory of Colonialism in Britain and France: The Sins of Silence.* Cambridge: Cambridge University Press, 2021.

Lowry, Donal, ed. *The South African War Reappraised.* Manchester: Manchester University Press, 2000.

Luttikhuis, Bart, and A. Dirk Moses, eds. *Colonial Counterinsurgency and Mass Violence: The Dutch Empire in Indonesia.* New York: Routledge, 2014.

MacKenzie, John M. *European Empires and the People: Popular Responses to Imperialism in France, Britain, the Netherlands, Belgium, Germany and Italy.* Manchester: Manchester University Press, 2011.

MacKenzie, John M. *Orientalism: History, Theory and the Arts.* Manchester: Manchester University Press, 2004.

MacKenzie, John M. *The British Empire through Buildings: Structure, Function and Meaning.* Manchester: Manchester University Press, 2020.

MacMaster, Neil. *Burning the Veil: The Algerian War and the 'Emancipation' of Muslim Women, 1954–62.* Manchester: Manchester University Press, 2012.

Macmillan, Margaret. *Women of the Raj: The Mothers, Wives and Daughters of the British Empire in India.* London: Thames and Hudson, 2018.

MacQueen, Norrie. *The Decolonization of Portuguese Africa: Metropolitan Revolution and the Dissolution of Empire.* London: Longman, 1997.

Majumdar, Rochona. *Writing Postcolonial History.* London: Bloomsbury Academic, 2010.

Manela, Erez. *Wilsonian Moment: Self-Determination and the International Origins of Anticolonial Nationalism.* Oxford: Oxford University Press, 2007.

Mar, Tracey Banivanua. *Decolonisation and the Pacific: Indigenous Globalisation and the Ends of Empire.* Cambridge: Cambridge University Press, 2019.

Masselos, Jim. *Indian Nationalism: A History.* New Delhi: Sterling Publishers, revised edn. 2010.

Masselos, Jim, ed. *The Great Empires of Asia.* London: Thames and Hudson, 2010.

Mathur, Saloni. *India by Design: Colonial History and Cultural Display.* Berkeley, CA: University of California Press, 2007.

McCarthy, Angela, and T. M. Devine. *Tea & Empire: James Taylor in Victorian Ceylon.* Manchester: Manchester University Press, 2017.

Further Reading

McCarthy, Angela, and John M. MacKenzie, *Global Migration and the Scottish Diaspora since 1600*. Edinburgh: Edinburgh University Press, 2016.

McIntyre, David, ed. *Winding Up the British Empire in the Pacific Islands*. Oxford: Oxford University Press, 2016.

McKenna, Mark. *From the Edge: Australia's Lost Histories*. Melbourne: Melbourne University Press, 2016.

McKenzie, Kirsten. *A Swindler's Progress: Nobles and Convicts in the Age of Liberty*. Cambridge, MA: Harvard University Press, 2010.

Meneses, Filipe Ribeiro de. *Salazar: A Political Biography*. New York: Enigma, 2010.

Meneses, Filipe Ribeiro de, and McNamara, Robert. *The White Redoubt, the Great Powers and the Struggle for Southern Africa, 1960–1980*. London: Palgrave Macmillan, 2018.

Miller, Shawn W. *An Environmental History of Latin America*. Cambridge: Cambridge University Press, 2007.

Mishra, Pankaj. *From the Ruins of Empire: The Revolt against the West and the Remaking of Asia*. London: Allen Lane, 2012.

Mokhtefi, Elaine. *Algiers, Third World Capital: Freedom Fighters, Revolutionaries, Black Panthers*. London: Verso, 2018.

Morris, Benny. *The Birth of the Palestinian Refugee Problem Revisited*. Cambridge: Cambridge University Press, 2003.

Moses, A. Dirk, ed. *Empire, Colony, Genocide: Conquest, Occupation, and Subaltern Resistance in World History*. New York: Berghahn Books, 2008.

Motadel, David, ed. *Islam and the European Empires*. Oxford: Oxford University Press, 2014.

Moyá, José C., ed. *The Oxford Handbook of Latin American History*. Oxford: Oxford University Press, 2010.

Muschalek, Marie. *Violence as Usual: Policing and the Colonial State in German Southwest Africa*. Ithaca, NY: Cornell University Press, 2019.

Myint-U, Thant. *The Making of Modern Burma*. Cambridge University Press, 2001.

Nafziger, James A. R., and Ann M. Nicgorski, eds. *Cultural Heritage Issues: The Legacy of Conquest, Colonization and Commerce*. Leiden: Brill, 2010.

Naranch, Bradley, and Geoff Eley, ed. *German Colonialism in a Global Age*. Durham, NC: Duke University Press, 2014.

Nicolaïdis, Kalypso, Berny Sèbe, and Gabrielle Maas, eds. *Echoes of Empire: Memory, Identity and Colonial Legacies*. London: I.B. Tauris, 2015.

Norris, Jacob. *Land of Progress: Palestine in the Age of Colonial Development, 1905–1948*. Oxford: Oxford University Press, 2013.

Ojeda García, Raquel, Irene Fernández Molina, and Victoria Veguilla, eds. *Global, Regional and Local Dimensions of Western Sahara's Protracted Decolonization: When a Conflict Gets Old*. New York: Palgrave Macmillan, 2017.

Omissi, David, and Andrew S. Thompson, ed. *The Impact of the South African War*. Basingstoke: Palgrave, 2002.

Oostindie, Gert, ed. *Dutch Colonialism, Migration and Cultural Heritage*. Leiden: KITLV Press, 2008.

Osterhammel, Jürgen. *Colonialism: A Theoretical Overview*. Princeton, NJ: Markus Wiener, 2005.

Osterhammel, Jürgen. *The Transformation of the World: A Global History of the Nineteenth Century*. Princeton, NJ: Princeton University Press, 2014.

Oxford History of the British Empire. Oxford: Oxford University Press, 1998– (five general volumes and a series of thematic companion volumes).

Palmié, Stephan, and Francisco A. Scarano, eds. *The Caribbean: A History of the Region and Its Peoples*. Chicago, IL: The University of Chicago Press, 2011.

Palser, Michael. *Angkor Wat*, 2 vols. Berlin: De Gruyter, 2018.

Paquette, Gabriel. *The European Seaborne Empires: From the Thirty Years' War to the Age of Revolutions*. New Haven, CT: Yale University Press, 2019.

Patel, Dinyar. *Naoroji: Pioneer of Indian Nationalism*. Cambridge, MA: Harvard University Press, 2020.

Pearson, Michael. *The Indian Ocean*. London: Routledge, 2003.

Pederson, Susan. *The Guardians: The League of Nations and the Crisis of Empire*. Oxford: Oxford University Press, 2015.

Peel, Mark, and Christina Twomey. *A History of Australia*. London: Palgrave Macmillan, 2017.

Penslar, Derek J. *Israel in History: The Jewish State in Comparative Perspective*. London: Routledge, 2007.

Pérez Jr., Louis A. *Cuba in the American Imagination: Metaphor and the Imperial Ethos*. Chapel Hill, NC: University of North Carolina Press, 2008.

Pérez Jr., Louis A. *The War of 1898: The United States and Cuba in History and Historiography*. Chapel Hill, NC: University of North Carolina Press, 2007.

Phan, Peter C., ed. *Christianities in Asia*. Chichester: Wiley-Blackwell, 2011.

Phillips, Andrew, and J. C. Sharman. *Outsourcing Empire: How Company-States Made the Modern World*. Princeton, NJ: Princeton University Press, 2020.

Piat, Denis. *Mauritius on the Spice Route, 1598–1810*. Singapore: Éditions Didier Millet, 2010.

Pols, Hans. *Nurturing Indonesia: Medicine and Decolonisation in the Dutch East Indies*. Cambridge: Cambridge University Press, 2018.

Porter, Andrew. *Religion versus Empire? British Protestant Missionaries and Overseas Expansion*. Manchester: Manchester University Press, 2004.

Protschky, Susie. *Images of the Tropics: Environment and Visual Culture in Colonial Indonesia*. Leiden: KITLV Press, 2011.

Protschky, Susie. *Photographic Subjects: Monarchy and Visual Culture in Colonial Indonesia*. Manchester: Manchester University Press, 2019.

Reid, Anthony. *A History of Southeast Asia: Critical Crossroads*. New York: Wiley-Blackwell, 2015.

Reynolds, Henry. *The Other Side of the Frontier: Aboriginal Resistance to European Invasion of Australia*. Kensington, NSW: University of New South Wales Press, 2006.

Røge, Pernille. *Economistes and the Reinvention of Empire: France in the Americas and Africa, c. 1750–1802*. Cambridge: Cambridge University Press, 2019.

Ross, Corey. *Ecology and Power in the Age of Empire: Europe and the Transformation of the Tropical World*. Oxford: Oxford University Press, 2017.

Rothermund, Dietmar. *The Global Impact of the Great Depression 1929–1939*. London: Routledge, 1996.

Rud, Søren. *Colonialism in Greenland: Tradition, Governance and Legacy*. London: Palgrave Macmillan, 2017.

Russell, Penny. *Savage or Civilised? Manners in Colonial Australia*. Sydney: UNSW Press, 2010.

Russell-Wood, A. J. R. *The Portuguese Empire, 1415–1808: A World on the Move*. Baltimore, MD: Johns Hopkins University Press, 1998.

Said, Edward. *Culture and Imperialism*. London: Chatto & Windus, 1993.

Said, Edward. *Orientalism*. New York: Pantheon, 1978.

Salesa, Damon Ieremia. *Racial Crossings: Race, Intermarriage and the Victorian British Empire*. Oxford: Oxford University Press, 2011.

Salmond, Ann. *Two Worlds: First Meetings between Maori and Europeans, 1642–1772*. Honolulu, HI: University of Hawai'i Press, 1991.

Samson, Jane. *British Imperial Strategies in the Pacific, 1750–1900*. London: Routledge, 2003.

Sanghera, Sathnam. *Empireland: How Imperialism Has Shaped Modern Britain*. London: Viking, 2021.

Saraswaty, Ayu L. *Seeing Beauty, Sensing Race in Transnational Indonesia*. Honolulu, HI: University of Hawai'i Press, 2013.

Further Reading

Sarr, Savoy. 'The Restitution of African Cultural Heritage: Toward a New Relational Ethics', report to the French government, 2018, accessible at http://restitutionreport2018.com/sarr_savoy_en.pdf.

Sartorius, David. *Ever Faithful: Race, Loyalty, and the Ends of Empire in Spanish Cuba*. Durham, NC: Duke University Press, 2013.

Sbacchi, Alberto. *Legacy of Bitterness: Ethiopia and Fascist Italy, 1935–1941*. Lawrenceville: The Red Sea Press, 1997.

Schayegh, Cyrus, and Andrew Arsan, eds. *The Routledge Handbook of the History of the Middle East Mandates*. London: Routledge, 2015.

Schields, Chelsea, and Dagmar Herzog, eds. *The Routledge Companion to Sexuality and Colonialism*. New York: Routledge, 2021.

Schmid-Nowara, Christopher, ed. *The Conquest of History: Spanish Colonialism and National Histories in the Nineteenth Century*. Pittsburgh, PA: University of Pittsburgh Press, 2008.

Schmidt-Nowara, Christopher. *Empire and Antislavery: Spain, Cuba, and Puerto Rico, 1833–1874*. Pittsburgh, PA: University of Pittsburgh Press, 1999.

Schultz, Kirsten. *Tropical Versailles: Empire, Monarchy, and the Portuguese Royal Court in Rio de Janeiro, 1808–1821*. London: Routledge, 2001.

Serulnikov, Sergio. *Revolution in the Andes: The Age of Túpac Amaru*. Durham, NC: Duke University Press, 2013.

Shah, Sudha. *The King in Exile: The Fall of the Royal Family of Burma*. New York: Harper Collins, 2012.

Shepard, Todd. *The Invention of Decolonization: The Algerian War and the Remaking of France*. Ithaca, NY: Cornell University Press, 2008.

Silbey, David. *The Boxer Rebellion and the Great Game in China*. New York: Hill and Wang, 2012.

Silva, K. M. de. *A History of Sri Lanka*. Colombo: Vijitha Yapa Publications, 2005.

Singha, Radhika. *The Coolie's Great War: Indian Labour in a Global Conflict, 1914–1921*. London: Hurst, 2020.

Sinha, Mrinalini. *Colonial Masculinity: The 'Manly Englishman' and the 'Effeminate Bengali' in the Late Nineteenth Century*. Manchester: Manchester University Press, 1995.

Sivasundaram, Sujit. *Islanded: Britain, Sri Lanka & the Bounds of an Indian Ocean Colony*. Chicago, IL: University of Chicago Press, 2013.

Sivasundaram, Sujit. *Waves Across the South: A New History of Revolution and Empire* London: William Collins, 2020.

Smith, Alison, David Blayney Brown, and Carol Jacobi. *Artists and Empire: Facing Britain's Imperial Past*. London: Tate Publishing, 2013.

Smith, Bernard. *European Vision and the South Pacific*, edited by Sheridan Palmer. Melbourne: Melbourne University Press, third ed., 2018 [1960].

Smith, Philippa Mein. *A Concise History of New Zealand*. Cambridge: Cambridge University Press, 2011.

Spies, S. B. *Methods of Barbarism? Roberts and Kitchener and Civilians in the Boer Republics, January 1900-May 1902*. Johannesburg: Jonathan Ball Publishers, 2001.

Srivastava, Neelam. *Italian Colonialism and Resistances to Empire, 1930–1970*. London: Palgrave Macmillan, 2018.

Stanard, Matthew G. *Selling the Congo: A History of European Pro-Empire Propaganda and the Making of Belgian Imperialism*. Lincoln: University of Nebraska Press, 2011.

Stanard, Matthew G. *The Leopard, the Lion, and the Cock: Colonial Memories and Monuments in Belgium*. Leuven: Leuven University Press, 2019.

Steinmetz, George. *The Devil's Handwriting: Precoloniality and the German Colonial State in Qingdao, Samoa, and Southwest Africa*. Chicago, IL: University of Chicago Press, 2007.

Stenner, David. *Globalizing Morocco: Transnational Activism and the Postcolonial State*. Stanford, CA: Stanford University Press, 2019.

Stucki, Andreas. *Violence and Gender in Africa's Iberian Colonies: Feminizing the Portuguese and Spanish Empire*. Cham: Palgrave Macmillan, 2019.

Subrahmanyam, Sanjay. *The Career and Legend of Vasco da Gama*. Cambridge: Cambridge University Press, 1997.

Taylor, Miles. *Empress: Queen Victoria and India*. New Haven, CT: Yale University Press, 2018.

Tharoor, Shashi. *Inglorious Empire: What the British Did to India*. London: C. Hurst, 2017.

Thein, Hla. *Myanmar and the Europeans (1878–1885)*. Yangon: Tun Foundation Bank Literary Committee, 2010.

Thomas, Martin. *Fight or Flight: Britain, France, and their Roads from Empire*. Oxford: Oxford University Press, 2014.

Thomas, Martin, ed. *The French Colonial Mind*, 2 vols. Lincoln, NE: University of Nebraska Press, 2012.

Thomas, Martin. *The French Empire at War, 1940–1945*. Manchester: Manchester University Press, 1998.

Thomas, Martin and Andrew S. Thompson. *The Oxford Handbook of the Ends of Empire*. Oxford: Oxford University Press, 2018.

Thompson, Andrew S. *The Empire Strikes Back?: The Impact of Imperialism on Britain from the Mid-Nineteenth Century*. London: Routledge, 2014.

Thornton, John. *Africa and Africans in the Making of the Atlantic World, 1400–1800*. Cambridge: Cambridge University Press, 2005.

Tiffin, Sarah. *Southeast Asia in Ruins: Art and Ruins in the Early 19th Century*. Singapore: NUS Press, 2016.

Todd, David. *A Velvet Empire: French Informal Imperialism in the Nineteenth Century*. Princeton, NJ: Princeton University Press, 2021.

Tomich, Dale W., and Paul E. Lovejoy, eds. *The Atlantic and Africa: The Second Slavery and Beyond*. New York: State University of New York Press, 2021.

Tone, John L. *War and Genocide in Cuba, 1895–1898*. Chapel Hill, NC: University of North Carolina Press, 2006.

Trindade, Luís, ed. *The Making of Modern Portugal*. Newcastle upon Tyne: Cambridge Scholars, 2013.

Van Der Cruysse, Dirk. *Siam and the West 1500–1700*. Chiang Mai: Silkworm Books, 2002.

Van Reybrouck, David. *Congo: The Epic History of a People*. London: HarperCollins, 2014.

Vanthemsche, Guy. *Belgium and the Congo, 1885–1980*. Cambridge: Cambridge University Press, 2012.

Vaughan, Meaghan. *Creating the Creole Island: Slavery in Eighteenth-Century Mauritius*. Durham, NC: Duke University Press, 2005.

Velmet, Aro. *Pasteur's Empire: Bacteriology and Politics in France, Its Colonies, and the World*. New York: Oxford University Press, 2020.

Viaene, Vincent, Bram Cleys, and Jan de Maeyer, eds. *Religion, Colonization and Decolonization in Congo, 1885–1960*. Leuven: Leuven University Press, 2020.

Vickers, Adrian. *A History of Modern Indonesia*. Cambridge: Cambridge University Press, 2nd edn., 2013.

Vickers, Adrian. *Balinese Art: Paintings and Drawings, 1800–2010*. Jakarta: Periplus Editions, 2012.

Wagner, Kim. *Amritsar 1919: An Empire of Fear and the Making of a Massacre*. New Haven: Yale University Press, 2019.

Walker, Charles F. *The Tupac Amaru Rebellion*. Cambridge, MA: Harvard University Press, 2014.

Walvin, James. *A Short History of Slavery*. London: Penguin, 2007.

Ward, Stuart, and Astrid Rasch, eds. *Embers of Empire in Brexit Britain*. London: Bloomsbury, 2019.

Further Reading

Webb Jr., James L. A. *Tropical Pioneers: Human Agency and Ecological Change in the Highlands of Sri Lanka, 1800–1900*. Athens, OH: Ohio University Press, 2012.

Wesseling, Hendrik L. *Divide and Rule: The Partition of Africa, 1880–1914*. Westport, CT: Praeger, 1996.

Wesseling, Hendrik L. *The European Colonial Empires: 1815–1919*. London: Routledge, 2015.

Westad, Odd Arne. *The Global Cold War: Third World Interventions and the Making of Our Times*. Cambridge: Cambridge University Press, 2007.

Wickramasinghe, Nira. *Sri Lanka in the Modern Age: A History of Contested Identities*. London: Hurst and Company, 2006.

Winter, Bronwyn. *Hijab and the Republic: Uncovering the French Headscarf Debate*. Syracuse, NY: Syracuse University Press, 2008.

Woollacott, Angela. *Gender and Empire*. Houndmills: Palgrave Macmillan, 2006.

Worden, Nigel. *The Making of Modern South Africa: Conquest, Apartheid, Democracy*. Oxford: Wiley-Blackwell, 2011.

Wright, Gwendolyn. *The Politics of Design in French Colonial Urbanism*. Chicago, IL: University of Chicago Press, 1991.

Yadav, Surya Narayan, and Indu Baghel. *Nationalism in Portuguese Africa*. New Delhi: Jnanada Prakashan, 2010.

Yao, Souchou. *The Malayan Emergency: Essays on a Small, Distant War*. Copenhagen: NIAS Press, 2016.

Zeuske, Michael. *Amistad: A Hidden Network of Slavers and Merchants*. Princeton, NJ: Markus Wiener, 2014.

INDEX

Note: Page numbers followed by 'n' refer notes.

Index

Index

Index

Index

Index

Index

Index

Index

Index

Index

Index

Index